MAKING SENSE OF SUICIDE MISSIONS

Making Sense of
SUICIDE MISSIONS

Edited by

DIEGO GAMBETTA

OXFORD
UNIVERSITY PRESS

OXFORD

UNIVERSITY PRESS

Great Clarendon Street, Oxford OX2 6DP

Oxford University Press is a department of the University of Oxford.
It furthers the University's objective of excellence in research, scholarship,
and education by publishing worldwide in

Oxford New York

Auckland Cape Town Dar es Salaam Hong Kong Karachi
Kuala Lumpur Madrid Melbourne Mexico City Nairobi New Delhi
Shanghai Taipei Toronto

With offices in

Argentina Austria Brazil Chile Czech Republic France Greece
Guatemala Hungary Italy Japan South Korea Poland Portugal
Singapore Switzerland Thailand Turkey Ukraine Vietnam

Published in the United States
by Oxford University Press Inc., New York

British Library Cataloguing in Publication Data

Data available

Library of Congress Cataloging in Publication Data

Making sense of suicide missions / edited by Diego Gambetta.
p.cm.
Summary: "Suicide attacks are a defining act of political violence and an extraordinary social
phenomenon. This book investigates the organizers of suicide missions and the perpetrators alike"–
Provided by publisher

Includes bibliographical references.
ISBN 0–19–927699–4 (alk paper)

1. Suicide–Political aspects. 2. Suicide bombings. 3. Kamikaze airplanes. I. Gambetta, Diego, 1952–
HV6545.M252 2005
303.6'25–dc22

2004025887

ISBN 0–19–927699–4

1 3 5 7 9 10 8 6 4 2

Typeset by Kolam Information Services Pvt. Ltd, Pondicherry, India
Printed in Great Britain
on acid-free paper by
Biddles Ltd., King's Lynn

FOREWORD

The aim of this volume is to provide the reader with as full and systematic an account of suicide missions (SMs) as possible. Working closely together for nearly three years, we delved into the phenomenon, which has become the defining act of political violence of our age, without any preconception, motivated by an intense and dispassionate interest in the explanatory challenges that it poses to social scientists, but also by our dissatisfaction with the simplistic or ideological interpretations of it that were being proposed.

In order to make sense of SMs, we need to rely on solid, wide-ranging, empirical evidence and to identify the theoretical questions that we should meaningfully ask about them. Both tasks are vigorously pursued by this book through a wealth of factual details, comparative analyses, and carefully reasoned arguments. We endeavour to uncover the general conditions under which SMs emerge and the patterns they follow as well as the motivations of both the perpetrators and those who send them.

The volume is not, however, an encyclopaedia of suicide attacks—the Russian anarchists who introduced SMs in their modern form in the early twentieth century, and the recent cases of the insurgents in Chechnya, Kashmir, and Turkey receive attention in the book but are not the object of our original research. We concentrate on four main instances: Peter Hill provides a concise description of all that is known about the Kamikaze (chapter 1); Stephen Hopgood tries to discover the logic of the missions carried out by the Tamil Tigers in the civil war in Sri Lanka (chapter 2); Luca Ricolfi, on the basis of the most comprehensive databse hitherto put together, deals with the Lebanese and Palestinian groups in the Middle East (chapter 3); and Stephen Holmes provides a challenging new interpretation of the al-Qaeda 9/11 attack on the World Trade Center and the Pentagon (chapter 4). The authors take particular care in presenting and filtering all the available evidence, restraining their speculative arguments as much as possible, but struggling with obstacles of varying difficulty. The knowledge of the Kamikaze case is well-established now, but in both Sri Lanka and the Middle East, where the issue is painfully alive, the warring parties impose their selective and manipulative pressures on the facts, making it hard to discover all one would ideally like to discover and sometimes to feel fully confident in the quality of the data. The hardest task is perhaps to make sense of the organizers and perpetrators of

9/11, who, despite much being now known about them, remain enigmatic figures.

While the careful and detailed examinations of the individual cases form the backbone of the book, its overall explanatory force is, however, realised by the comparative framework we adopted, which is directly in evidence in the following four chapters. In Chapter 5, Michael Biggs investigates why, since 1963, when the Buddhist monk Thich Quang Duc set himself alight in Saigon to protest against the oppression of Buddhism, no less than a thousand protesters worldwide chose to die for a cause without killing others. Biggs examines whether the conditions under which peaceful self-immolations occur are akin to those of SMs. In Chapter 6, Stathis Kalyvas and Ignacio Sanchez-Cuenca address the question of why most fighting organizations eschew SMs and choose to kill while trying not to die. Finally, in Chapters 7 and 8, Jon Elster and I reflect on the evidence comparatively, trying to make sense of SMs with respect to both the micro behaviours and the macro patterns of the phenomenon. Some of the answers we come to are robust and rely on clear generalizations, while others are tentative and raise new challenges for research.

We do not wish to anticipate our results or prime the reader. The richness of the information found in each chapter makes it possible for the readers to develop their views, independently of our interpretations. It may nonetheless be useful to say a few words about the definition of SM and the guiding questions of our inquiry.

The standard case of an SM that we consider consists of a violent attack designed in such a way as to make the death of the perpetrators strictly essential for its success. Even though an SM can fail and the perpetrators still die in it, the reverse is not the case: if they survive the SM certainly fails.

SMs have been employed largely for killing enemies—soldiers, authorities, and civilians—but also against symbolic targets and, less often, against military installations and equipment. Although the use of other lethal devices is conceivable—for example, an infected individual could be dispatched to spread a deadly virus by contagion—all SMs carried out thus far have used explosive devices. They did so in two ways: in one case, so-called 'suicide bombers' carry the explosive on their body and detonate it without escaping. In the other, the perpetrators crash a vehicle—car, truck, boat, airplane— into a target; the vehicle can be loaded with explosive that is detonated on impact or itself, loaded with fuel, turn into an explosive device when colliding against the target, as the hijacked airplanes did on 9/11.

Two further conditions are required to characterize the standard case we investigate: those who take part in an SM must be neither deceived about their prospect of survival nor blackmailed into carrying it out. Even if there may be a cost for those who defect, such as ostracism by peers, agents should be free not to volunteer. If the agents are deceived or coerced, the puzzle of why they engage in an SM disappears. Our interest is in understanding the motivations of those who carry out SMs willingly and knowingly.

This definition does not encompass, high-risk missions, as death is not necessary for their success; nor does it include other forms of extreme self-sacrifice, such as the self-immolations in which no one else is killed. The definition of the standard case can, however, be relaxed to include two types of attacks that result in the death of the perpetrators, without this being strictly essential.

One is the case of a no-escape attack, in which the perpetrator's death is certain but is not self-inflicted. In cases of this kind, which have been practised since well before the discovery of high explosives, the agents attack a target with some weapon—daggers, hand grenades, or firearms—knowing that the enemy will respond by killing them. Conceptually, the difference between this type of attack and the standard case of SM is that the agents' death is not technically essential to the success of the mission. Whether, however, this difference is significant in other ways—psychological, oper-ational, or in terms of legitimacy—is controversial, and addressed in detail by several chapters in the book. This difference is particularly relevant when we try to discover whether SMs in the standard sense are a new type of action or have ancestors, since all attacks to the death before the age of modern explosives are of the no-escape kind.

The next case is counterfactual, thus harder to establish empirically, yet theoretically important. It refers to an SM in which the same destructive results could have been achieved without sacrificing the perpetrators. It raises a substantive question concerning the exact purpose of dying in an SM. This question has to do with whether the agents' death is deemed to be strictly instrumental—a cost—to achieving the destructive effects hard to achieve otherwise, or is itself an intermediate goal of the perpetrators, who for some reason believe it is important not just to kill but to die at the same time. Once again, this issue is taken up and discussed in the book.

Adopting the term 'suicide mission' is bound to be controversial. Those involved in SMs universally reject the idea that what they are doing amounts to a suicide. However, our choice of vocabulary, dictated by the lack of a better alternative and a wish to keep the label clear and short, does not imply a moral judgement. We have no difficulty accepting the possibility that the perpetrators do not want to die for personal reasons or because they are mentally unbalanced, but that they choose to sacrifice their lives for the cause they believe in. We consider this matter without prejudice, comparing the SM perpetrators not only to peaceful self-immolators but also to war heroes.

With respect to motivations, all chapters distinguish systematically between those of the organizers and those of the perpetrators, for it is one thing to have an interest in an SM to be carried out and quite another to be prepared to bear the extreme cost of carrying it out oneself. To believe that SMs are of value in achieving the goals of an organization is not a sufficient reason for an individual to carry one out. One may agree that SMs are a rational option, but still prefer if someone else carries them out.

In fact, most fighting organizations either lack the volunteers or refrain from resorting to SMs for some other reason. Luca Ricolfi calculates in his chapter that, from 1981 to December 2003, more than twenty organizations carried out (if failed and foiled attempts are excluded) no fewer than 535 SMs.[1] Before that period there were at least a dozen anarchist SMs in Russia in the early part of the twentieth century (see Chapter 8), and over 3,000 Japanese Kamikaze sorties from October 1944 to August 1945—still the highest number of SMs organized by any one source (Peter Hill, Chapter 1). Since 2003 there have been many attacks in the bloody aftermath of the US-led invasion of Iraq. According to the Brooking Institution,[2] from May 2003 to October 2004 there were 131 mass-casualty bombing episodes in Iraq, at least 85 of which were SMs.[3] In total, therefore, our estimate is that there have been over 3,600 SMs. However, SMs are no more than a tiny fraction of the overall number of non-suicidal attacks that have occurred in the same period, regardless of how one quantifies the latter. Despite their impact on political agendas and public perceptions, SMs are a rare phenomenon when one considers the universe of armed conflicts. Their rarity raises the question, addressed in the volume, of why there are not more SMs.

For those organizers who can count on volunteers, SMs can be seen as a tactic to choose from among others. The goals that might be achieved by SMs are not restricted to military results. By considering the array of targets and conditions under which SMs are undertaken, we explore to what extent other aims, such as spreading terror, wrecking peace prospects, or proselytizing through martyrdom, are part of an organization's motivations.

Contrary to a widespread belief, the majority of SMs have been carried out by secular rather than religious organizations. This suggests that if special and exalted motivations to self-sacrifice are involved, religious beliefs and

---

[1] This is the most complete estimate to date. Pape (2003) counted 188 from 1980 to 2001; Berman and Laitin (2004) have counted 236 up to 2002.

[2] Iraq Index Tracking Variables of Reconstruction & Security in Post-Saddam Iraq, p. 8, www.brookings.edu/iraqindex, updated to 4 October 2004. Ricolfi already includes twenty of those missions in his calculation, which extends only to the end of 2003.

[3] Ricolfi's estimate, which ends seven months earlier, includes only twenty SMs in Iraq.

preaching are not the only way to induce or to exploit them. Still, the relevance of religion—particularly of Islam—is not to be denied. Several chapters deal with it, exploring whether there is anything in religious beliefs that is specifically motivating groups to resort to SMs or whether they serve as a language in which to clothe political grievances effectively.

Questions that concern the perpetrators' motivations are partially different from those that concern the organizers' motivations. While one may see the rationale of SMs for an organization—in war the ends justify any means—one is more hard put, at least from the comfort of one's armchair, to see why anyone should sacrifice one's life in that way. SM perpetrators violate common expectations about people's behaviour, perhaps more than any one can think of. Like all intentional suicides, they violate a widely held preference for preserving one's life over losing it; more weakly, they violate the desire even of those taking risky actions to have at least a sporting chance to make it back safely. That violation becomes all the more puzzling since some SMs seem to breach the dictates of instrumental rationality: agents should seek to employ means that do not involve their death if the same or similar results can otherwise be achieved. Why do Palestinians, for instance, not just leave all their bombs on buses and in cafés and run off before they explode? While some missions may be the best means to an end, others make one wonder whether all alternative options have been taken into account.

Furthermore, SMs also violate the notion, popular in modern Darwinian thinking, that extreme altruism is to be expected only towards one's kin; some suicide bombers do say that they do it to save or revenge family or friends, but most say that they do it for their group and its cause. Finally, they violate the expectation that acts of extreme altruism and heroism are hot, that is, occurring on the spur of the moment, prompted by a special urgency, and not calculated in cold blood. SMs are calculated in cold blood.

These violations of standard behavioural expectations pose a major challenge for social science. Altruism, even in its most extreme manifestations, is not *ipso facto* irrational. Rationality has to do with means not with preferences. If one considers all the options that could satisfy one's preferences, and decides that an SM is the best possible means, then why not. Yet, this is a shallow conclusion. *Ex post*, one can find a rationale for just about anything. Before one can conclude that embarking on an SM is individually rational, one has first to meet the challenges that SMs pose.

Even whether SM agents are really altruistically motivated is an open question. Some agents' accounts are cast in a selfish, albeit extreme rhetoric, which makes us wonder. Some say that they want to achieve worldly immortality, guaranteed by the respect and status bestowed on them and their families by their communities. But can posthumous glory really motivate? And some say that they do it to acquire the status of martyr and reap the heavenly benefits that come with that. But can the Islamic attackers be truly motivated by the belief that they will enjoy paradise and the company of seventy-two black-eyed virgins?

I wish to thank All Souls College, Oxford, and the Juan March Institute, Madrid, for hosting our two workshops. I also gratefully acknowledge a British Academy Research Readership, which gave me the time to start this project. My gratitude goes to Alison Bateman for assisting me with patience and kindness in the preparation of the manuscript.

Diego Gambetta
Nuffield College, Oxford

August 2004

CONTENTS

Foreword	v
List of Tables	xii
List of Figures	xiii
List of Contributors	xiv
1. Kamikaze, 1943–5 PETER HILL	1
2. Tamil Tigers, 1987–2002 STEPHEN HOPGOOD	43
3. Palestinians, 1981–2003 LUCA RICOLFI	77
4. Al-Qaeda, September 11, 2001 STEPHEN HOLMES	131
5. Dying Without Killing: Self-Immolations, 1963–2002 MICHAEL BIGGS	173
6. Killing Without Dying: The Absence of Suicide Missions STATHIS KALYVAS AND IGNACIO SÁNCHEZ-CUENCA	209
7. Motivations and Beliefs in Suicide Missions JON ELSTER	233
8. Can We Make Sense of Suicide Missions? DIEGO GAMBETTA	259
Notes	301
References	337
Index	357

LIST OF TABLES

1.1. Impact of Kamikaze attacks in the Philippines, October
1944–January 1945   10

1.2. Impact of Kamikaze attacks in the Okinawa campaign,
March–August 1945   10

2.1. Breakdown of Tamil and Black Tigers killed, 27
November 1982–30 September 2002   68

2.2. Breakdown of Tamil and Black Tigers killed, 27
November 1982–30 November 1996   68

3.1. Technology of suicide missions   98

3.2. Correlations between internecine violence and
attacks (weekly data)   101

3.3. Some recent studies of terrorists   106

A3.1. Organizations in the Israeli–Palestinian conflict resorting
to suicide missions   120

A3.2. Suicide missions by result and technology   124

A3.3. Main correlations between variables   127

A3.4. Relative weight of nationalists and Islamists in two
samples: leaders   129

A3.5. Relative weight of nationalist and Islamist parties in
the two samples: parties   129

5.1. Self-immolation by country, 1963–2002   185

5.2. Waves involving more than three acts of
self-immolation, 1963–2002   189

8.1. Suicide missions by main Islamic and secular
organizations, 1981–September 2003   262

8.2. Varying and uniform features of suicide missions   265

8.3. Year of first suicide mission by different organizations   288

8.4. Main suicide mission waves by religious affiliation or
religious background of the opponents   290

LIST OF FIGURES

1.1.	Kamikaze sorties, October 1944–August 1945	11
1.2.	Results claimed for Kamikaze missions, October 1944–August 1945	11
3.1.	Suicide missions worldwide: rough estimates, 1 January 1981–31 December 2003	82
3.2.	Number of suicide missions in the Middle East area, 1981–2003 (three-year moving average)	84
3.3.	Frequency index of total attacks in Middle East area	85
3.4.	Total attacks and propensity to suicide missions	86
3.5.	The al-Aqsa wave	95
3.6.	The turn of the 1970s: from air hijackings to suicide missions	102
A3.1.	Relative coverage of main sources (1981–2003)	123
5.1.	Self-immolation, 1963–2002	183
6.1.	Organizational choices given individual choices	226
8.1.	Types of suicide mission by organizational goals and relevance of agents' death	264
8.2.	Frequency of civil wars and of suicide missions by religion divide and balance of military force between factions	291

LIST OF CONTRIBUTORS

MICHAEL BIGGS
Assistant Professor of Sociology
University of Illinois at Urbana-Champaign

JON ELSTER
Robert K. Merton Professor of Social and Political Science
Columbia University

DIEGO GAMBETTA
Professor of Sociology and Official Fellow
Nuffield College, Oxford

PETER HILL
British Academy Post-doctoral Fellow
Department of Sociology, University of Oxford

STEPHEN HOLMES
Professor of Law and Political Science
New York University

STEPHEN HOPGOOD
Lecturer in International Politics
School of Oriental and African Studies
University of London

STATHIS KALYVAS
Arnold Wolfers Professor of Political Science
Yale University

LUCA RICOLFI
Professor of Sociology
University of Turin

IGNACIO SANCHEZ-CUENCA
Associate Professor of Political Science
Centre for Advanced Studies in the Social Sciences
Juan March Institute, Madrid

1

Kamikaze, 1943–5

PETER HILL

From October 1944 to August 1945, over 3,000 Japanese army and navy pilots died attempting to crash their planes into Allied ships. Smaller numbers died manning weapons that were specifically designed for missions which offered no hope of survival for their operators. At the time of Japan's surrender, thousands of such weapons, along with their crews, were stationed in readiness for the defence of the homeland.

Although formally the term 'Kamikaze' refers only to the *Shinpū* ('divine wind') Special Attack Corps formed at the instigation of Admiral Ōnishi in October 1944, in this chapter it is used to refer to all premeditated suicide missions (SMs) conducted by the Japanese military during this period. The human-wave assaults by Japanese soldiers that characterized the defence of islands in the latter stage of the war are, however, excluded even though they resulted in almost certain death (the only soldiers to be captured were those too weak to blow themselves up). This exclusion is justified on the grounds that they were conducted by men already in battle and, given their refusal to surrender, facing imminent destruction. Although far less numerous, SMs were also conducted by other countries during the same conflict (see Appendix to Chapter 3).

Kamikaze Precedents

Throughout the Pacific War, aircraft crashed into enemy ships. Such attacks increased from the battle for Guadalcanal in the latter half of 1942. In many cases these planes or their pilots had suffered from enemy fire and were unlikely to make the journey back home. Some, however, were deliberate attacks by undamaged planes. Although the vast majority of these acts were committed by Japanese pilots, there are at least two incidents of deliberate suicidal attacks by US airmen on Japanese ships, one during the battle of Coral Sea in May 1942, the other at Midway the following month. In both cases witnesses claimed the pilots need not have died.

In addition to this plane-to-ship crashing, there are numerous examples of plane-to-plane ramming. These were individual acts conducted in the heat of battle and without official sanction.[1] They are therefore conceptually different from the Kamikaze missions that followed. As Japan's military situation deteriorated, there was increasing discussion among Japanese pilots about the efficacy of this tactic vis-à-vis conventional attacks. Several middle-ranking officers even sent proposals to their superiors in Tokyo that suicide attacks be formally employed—a severe breach of military protocol that in earlier times would have been punished.

Higher-ranking officers also suggested the use of 'special attack'[2] methods. General Ushiroku, senior deputy chief at Army General Staff, proposed the use of backpack bombs by infantry in New Guinea and Bougainville. This suggestion was accepted by the general staff but was strongly resisted by other senior officers and was consequently shelved. Senior naval officers also unsuccessfully proposed SMs.

The reasons why special attacks were rejected by most senior officers were not based purely on a distaste for sending men to certain death. Rather, as Vice-Admiral Yokoi later pointed out, there were three significant flaws with Kamikaze missions. First, it was a highly expensive tactic as a trained pilot and his aircraft are used up in a single attack. This conflicted with a basic military principle of achieving goals with the minimum loss to one's own resources (though the suicidal infantry counter-attacks by the defenders on islands in the Aleutians, Philippines, and elsewhere suggest that a time comes when such calculations break down). Second, plane-crash attacks lacked sufficient penetrative power to strike a mortal blow to aircraft carriers. To cause significant damage they had to take place when the decks were fully laden with aircraft. Third, Yokoi argued, it was enormously difficult to evaluate the success of such missions as the protagonists themselves would be dead. At the same time, their commanders would be inclined to overestimate the gains achieved by the death of their men (Yokoi 1986: 455). Naitō (1989: 22) further suggested that professional military pride was another factor: the officers of the high command believed they could win by conventional means.

Some of the literature (for example, Naitō 1989: 22) suggests that it was comparatively junior officers that provided the main impetus for the adoption of special attack methods and that their superiors opposed them on moral grounds. Yet as early as mid-1943 Captain (later Rear Admiral) Kuroshima, head of the Naval General Staff's second section (responsible for developing new weapons) had proposed the use of ramming warships with motor boats filled with explosives. On 11 August, at a meeting attended by navy minister Yonai and other senior naval personnel, Kuroshima stressed the need for 'certain death: certain kill' tactics. Rear Admiral Nakazawa, the head of the Naval General Staff's first section (in charge of strategy and tactics), was receptive to this line of argument and, on 9 April 1944, they secured Yonai's approval for budgetary allocations for the development of several types of special attack weapons (Mita 1998: 28–34). By this time Prime Minister Tōjō had also instructed Army Air Corps to get ready to conduct special attack missions (Naitō 1989: 22). These developments were considerably ahead of at least some of the events usually portrayed as seminal in the development of the various suicide weapons and strategies discussed below. It is thus at least plausible that accrediting this tactic to front-line junior officers rather than rear-echelon staff officers was a device to provide it with greater public acceptance, and, as Naitō (1989: 206) suggests, to reduce the latter's culpability.

Military Context

At the beginning of the war, Japan's air combat capability was superior to that of its opponents in terms of both pilot training and aircraft design. From the Battle of Midway (June 1942) onwards Japanese air superiority was lost as trained pilots killed in combat were replaced with progressively poorer aviators. Such was the rate of attrition of naval pilots (in the first three-quarters of 1944, the Japanese Imperial Navy lost 42 per cent of its aircrew) that training courses had to be radically shortened in order to provide the necessary number of pilots. Hashiuchi a former naval Kamikaze pilot interviewed in Tokyo on 16 January 2002) recalls that, by the time he joined the navy late in the war, flight-training time had been reduced from 500 to 130 hours.

Training was further curtailed by dire shortages of aviation fuel arising from successful submarine warfare against ships supplying Japan from its empire. Much training was conducted using a mixture of regular fuel and alcohol, which caused planes to stall in mid-air with fatal results.

At the same time, the advances in US aircraft design, especially the Hellcat fighter, outclassed the Japanese Zero. Fighter ace Sakai reminisces that at the beginning of the war in China, Japanese pilots had enjoyed picking off their opponents; by the end of the war it was the other way round (Sakai 2000: 138). In the air war over the Marianas, the US navy pilots referred to it as the 'Marianas turkey-shoot'.

Following Midway, the allied forces in the Pacific whittled away Japan's Pacific empire. Southern New Guinea was held by Australian troops in 1942 and, in February 1943, the Americans took Guadalcanal in the Solomon Islands. The Marshall Islands, and then the Mariana Islands, were taken, with Guam in US hands by August 1944. The loss of the Marianas was especially significant, for two reasons. First, under the Versailles treaty Japan had been granted a mandate over these islands, so they were part of the 'old'

Japanese empire. Second, airfields on Saipan in the Marianas put Tokyo within range of US heavy bombers.

Frequently, the Japanese defenders of these islands fought to the last man with suicidal human-wave attacks (often including Japanese civilians). In the case of Saipan, the defenders were ordered to fight to the last man by their commanding officers who then committed suicide themselves. The poetic euphemism for these mass-suicidal last stands was *gyokusai* ('shattering jewel'). Although these actions were not premeditated Kamikaze operations, they are important to our study in that they informed the decision-making processes of other servicemen, and allusions to shattering jewels can be found in the last writings of Kamikaze. In July 1944, Japanese newspapers actually carried a translated article from *Time* magazine describing the mass suicide of civilians on Saipan, the subtext being that their example would bolster the courage of all Japanese.

By this stage of the war, the Japanese high command had begun to pin all its hope on one decisive battle that would destroy the Allies and hold them at the outskirts of Japan's pre-1930s imperial boundaries. This would put them in a position from which they could honourably conclude the war. Japan's only major offensive assets in the Pacific theatre were her land-based air forces and big battleships (though these were vulnerable because they now lacked carrier-based air support). In order for Japan's battleships to successfully engage the main Allied fleet, then at Leyte Gulf in the Philippines, it would first be necessary to put the enemy aircraft carriers out of action, if only temporarily.

Admiral Ōnishi, the man newly appointed to command the first Air Fleet in the Philippines, was tasked to carry out this mission. Although he had initially been opposed to the idea of SMs, Ōnishi reluctantly realized that, with the forces at his disposal, he had little option but to destroy the carriers' wooden flight decks by bomb-laden Zero fighters crashing into them. The 201st Air Corps was selected for this mission.

The pilots of the 201st had been in constant combat for over eight months, their losses had been enormous, and all of the remaining pilots had already experienced a close shave with death; none of them could realistically expect to survive the war. Their current strength had been reduced to twenty-three pilots after the loss of around seventy Zero fighters the previous month. Onoda, a journalist attached to the navy and on hand to record the events, noted that when the call went out for volunteers, the reserve officers and officers promoted from the ranks all volunteered but none of the graduates of the elite naval academy did (Onoda 1971: 27). This presented the commanders with a problem, as they knew it would be bad for morale if an academy man did not also make this sacrifice. Onoda (1971: 28) suggests that Lieutenant Seki Yukio was chosen to go because he had recently been transferred to the 201st from Taiwan, where he had been flying carrier bombers and was not fully integrated into the bluff fighter-pilot canteen culture. He was also suffering from amoebic dysentery. He was not chosen because he was the best man for the job but because he was an outsider.

The unit was given the name *Shinpū* ('divine wind') Special Attack Corps. The characters for *Shinpū* can also be read Kamikaze, as did Japanese-American translators operating with the Allied fleet.

The first four sorties of the new *Shinpū* Special Attack Corps failed to locate the Allied fleet and the pilots returned to base. On the fifth (25 November 1944), they were lucky. Two flights, together totalling eleven planes, attacked, damaging five carriers and a destroyer. On the same day ninety-three fighters and fifty-seven bombers were deployed in conventional attacks, resulting in no damage to the enemy. This was taken as vindication of the superiority of Kamikaze attacks over conventional methods.

Despite the sacrifices of these pilots and their successors, the battle of Leyte Gulf, the largest naval engagement of the whole war, resulted in a mortal blow to the Japanese navy; four carriers, three battleships (including the super-battleship *Musashi*), nine cruisers, and ten destroyers, totalling 300,000 tons, were sunk. The only effective offensive resource left to Japan was, therefore, its land-based fighter force.

Although the battle of Leyte Gulf was the first occasion on which the official term Kamikaze/*Shinpū* was used, it was not actually the first organized deliberate attack of this sort. On 27 May 1944, army pilots in New Guinea conducted a premeditated 'body-crash' attack against a US landing fleet in which the two fighter bombers tasked for the mission narrowly missed their targets due to enemy fire (O'Neill 1981: 136).

Types of Suicide Missions

Plane Attacks

These were by far the most numerous of all attacks and used from the Battle of Leyte Gulf until the end of the war. Of the various types of suicide weapons used, they were also by far the most effective. Most of the evidence presented elsewhere in this chapter relates to aircraft Kamikaze attacks. They were first used systematically off the Philippines (October 1944–January 1945) and then, much more heavily, off Okinawa, Kyushu, and Iwo Jima (February–August 1945).

Although Zero fighters were the first planes used, eventually all sorts of planes were sent on Kamikaze missions, including dilapidated old trainers and obsolete light bombers. In the case of interviewee Hashiuchi, his plane was an old three-seater Nakajima-type 97 bomber. The two spare seats were replaced with explosives.

Ōka

The *Ōka* ('cherry blossom') was a rocket-powered piloted bomb developed
by Navy Sub Lieutenant Ōta who, when presenting his plans to his superiors,
volunteered to fly it himself. Due to the severe shortage of construction
materials, it was composed largely of wood. The *Ōka* had a fuselage of 6 m,
a wingspan of 5 m, a crew of one, and a 1,200 kg charge of TNT-type
explosive. It was powered by five rockets, though these generated thrust for
only nine seconds. The weapon was therefore carried to within range of
enemy ships beneath a specially adapted bomber. Once released from his
mother plane, the pilot would fly in a shallow glide until he had identified a
target, he would then go into a steep attack dive of fifty degrees and ignite his
rockets. This would give an attack speed of 648 kmph, making it very hard to
shoot down. The *Ōka* had one other advantage over using conventional
aircraft in Kamikaze attacks in that the explosives were positioned right in
the armoured nose of the craft and the fuses had a slight delay so that they
would explode after penetrating the deck of the target.

The decision to produce the *Ōka* was actually made in August 1944 and
therefore predates the formation of Ōnishi's *Shinpū* Special Attack Corps by
two months. In October 1944 the *Ōka* unit was set up under the name of
Jinrai ('thunder gods' or 'divine thunderbolt') Special Attack Corps. Training began in November.

The operational use of the *Ōka*s was not a great success. The bombers
carrying them were considerably slowed down by their burden and were
consequently very easy to shoot down. A second model of *Ōka*, with an
improved rocket engine (and therefore greater range), was in development in
the closing months of the war. It was proposed to launch these from catapults
hidden on the coastline of the Japanese mainland. Towards the end of the
war, other dedicated special attack aircraft were being developed. Like the
Ōka, the *Tsurugi* ('sword') was built as cheaply as possible. It had appalling
handling characteristics and was never used.

Airborne Saboteur Assault

On 24 May 1945, twelve 'Sally' heavy bombers, each carrying fourteen
heavily armed combat engineers from the *Giretsu Kūtei-tai* ('Heroism Airborne Unit'), set off to attack two US-held airfields in Okinawa. Four of the
planes suffered mechanical problems and landed in Japan, seven were shot
down, and just one reached Yontan Airfield in Okinawa. Once it had made
its forced landing, the soldiers on board rushed out with sub-machine guns,
grenades, and incendiary charges. Before they were killed the following

morning by US marines, these troops managed to blow up 70,000 gallons of fuel and seven planes as well as damage another twenty-six (Shiino 1998: 84–9). A much bigger operation of this type, involving 200 aircraft and 2,000 troops, was planned to attack the B29 airfields in the Marianas. Because Japanese codes had been broken, on 9 and 10 August 1945 US and British air strikes hit the assembled transport planes on the ground, thereby preventing the mission (O'Neill 1981: 267).

Suicide Submarine Attacks

By early 1943 manned torpedoes had been developed by two junior-ranking naval officers who petitioned the Naval General Staff for these to be deployed operationally. Initially these requests were ignored, and it was not until early 1944 that senior commanders in the Naval General Staff formally approved the development of this weapon. Recruitment began in August 1944 and the first mission took place in November. *Kaiten* ('turning heaven') torpedoes were basically two standard 'long-lance' torpedoes joined together and fitted with a small conning tower and periscope. The type-1 *kaiten* had a 1,550 kg charge and a range of 23–78 km depending on speed (maximum 30 knots). They had a crew of one. Larger two-man *kaiten* were also built but in small numbers and they were not deployed operationally. Although it was obvious that the use of *kaiten* necessarily involved the pilot's death, it was insisted that escape hatches be installed (O'Neill 1981: 226).

Advances in US anti-submarine warfare had made it difficult for Japanese submarines to get within attack range without themselves being detected and attacked. The supposed advantage of manned torpedoes over conventional ones was, therefore, that submarines could release their weapons at a safe distance and the torpedoes would still be able to hit their targets. In fact, it was extraordinarily difficult for the pilots to gauge their attack. Through their periscope they would estimate the speed, course, and distance of the target and then set a course to intercept it. During their attack they could see nothing and consequently could determine their proximity to the enemy only by stopwatch. If too much time elapsed they would resurface and reset their attack course.

Suicide Motorboats

Japanese conventional torpedo boats were too slow to be militarily effective. This problem could be overcome if speedboats were used as torpedoes. Both the army and navy constructed boats specially for SMs. Army boats were named *maru-re* (not *maru ni*, as much of the English-language literature

asserts) and naval ones *shinyō* ('ocean shaker'). They were generally built
of plywood on a wooden frame (though the biggest type was made of metal),
5–5.5 m long, had a top speed of 26 knots (30 for the metal boats), and were
armed with a 250 kg depth charge and two 12 cm rockets. The larger, command boats were also equipped with a 13 mm machine gun which would
provide covering fire for the rest of the attack group before themselves
seeking a target (Shiino 1998: 155; O'Neill 1981: 97). Although officially all
but command boats had a crew of one, some *maru-re* squadrons (which for
some reason were overmanned given their number of boats) went into action
with as many as four men, armed with grenades, side arms, and Molotov
cocktails in each boat (O'Neill 1981: 102). Not only was this not necessary for
the military effectiveness of the mission, but by slowing the boats down
it presumably impaired it.

Over 6,000 suicide motor boats had been constructed by the end of the
war. Most of these were never used as they were deployed along Japan's
coastline in anticipation of enemy landings. Estimating the total number of
suicide-boat attacks is very difficult as they were usually stationed close to
areas of land fighting and most of the records have not survived; Hattori
(1993: 25) cautiously suggests that between 319 and 849 boats set off on these
attacks.

Frogman Mines

With the invasion of the main islands of Japan becoming increasingly likely,
military planners proposed the use of underwater human mines. Men
equipped with breathing apparatus and mines attached to one end of poles
would be deployed by small boats close to enemy landing sites, walk along
the sea bed to their targets, and then detonate their mines against the hulls of
landing craft. This weapon was known as *fukuryū* ('crouching dragon').
When in October 1944 the 400 students at the torpedo boat school at
Kawatana were given the choice of training for conventional torpedo
boats, suicide boats, or *fukuryū* missions, they chose as follows: 200 for
conventional boats, 150 for suicide boats, and 50 for *fukuryū* (Millot 1971:
153–4). The *fukuryū* were never operationally deployed.

Effectiveness

Generally, with the exception of the aircraft-crashing attacks, these were not
effective weapons. In the case of the *kaiten*, the results were very poor. Out of
a total of 106 *kaiten* pilots who died on active service, only three are con-

sidered to have hit ships. Although some of the dead were killed in training (seventeen) or with their mother submarines (unknown), most were unsuccessfully deployed. Despite this, the Japanese navy consistently overestimated the effectiveness of this weapon (Torisu and Chihaya 1986: 447, 451).

The results of *shinyō* operations were similarly unimpressive. They were first used in January 1945 against a US landing force in the Philippines. Of the seventy boats that were dispatched, six actually hit enemy landing craft and landing ships, only one of which sank. The remaining *shinyō* were largely destroyed by US gunfire, though some returned to base or got lost.

In his analysis of the effectiveness of special attack methods, Hattori (1993: 26) puts the combined impact of the estimated 347–849 *shinyō/maru-re* boats dispatched on missions at two enemy ships sunk and fifteen damaged. Many of the attacking boats capsized due to the heavy weight of fire in the surrounding water and, given the inadequate (and highly inaccurate) weaponry of the motor boats, there was no way of suppressing this fire.

Even in the case of the air attacks, only a minority of Kamikaze planes hit enemy ships. Using both Allied and Japanese sources, Hattori (1993: 23) estimates that 11.6 per cent of special-attack-plane sorties achieved direct hits. A further 5.7 per cent had near misses and 27.5 per cent returned. The figures for the first Kamikaze attack are more impressive with 20.8 per cent direct hits, 16.7 per cent near misses, and 41.7 per cent returned.

Once they had recognized the threat of this type of attack, Allied fleets deployed a cordon of radar ships well out from their carriers. Once the Kamikaze planes were spotted, an immense weight of anti-aircraft fire was put out by all ships. The proximity fuses in the 5-inch shells of the US and British dual-purpose guns were enormously significant in limiting the effectiveness of plane-crashing attacks. The fleet-based Allied planes also enjoyed air superiority.

Tables 1.1 and 1.2 give a rough idea of the effectiveness (both perceived and actual) of the Kamikaze. These show that the Japanese overestimated both the size of the ships they hit and the extent of damage they caused to them. As Admiral Yokoi recalls, the Japanese High Command overestimated the impact of suicide weapons: there was a desperate hope that the superior will power of the Kamikaze would be the salvation of Japan; unit commanders over-reported the results of their pilots, perhaps unable to accept that their men had died for nothing (Yokoi 1986: 469). Note, however, that in both campaigns the Japanese actually *underestimated* the total number of ships sunk or damaged compared with the US records (96: 103 and 186: 201, respectively).

Figure 1.1 shows the number of Kamikaze sorties per month for the period October 1944 to August 1945. Figure 1.2 shows the results claimed over the same period. Although this is drawn from Japanese estimates rather than US

TABLE 1.1. Impact of Kamikaze attacks in the Philippines, October 1944–January 1945

Ships	Sunk		Damaged	
	Japanese estimates	US records	Japanese estimates	US records
Carriers	5	2	13	23
Battleships	1	0	3	5
Cruisers	5	0	8	9
Destroyers	3	3	1	28
Transports	23	5	34	12
Others	—	6	—	10
TOTAL	37	16	59	87

Source: Inoguchi et al. (1961: 107).

TABLE 1.2. Impact of Kamikaze attacks in the Okinawa campaign, March–August 1945

Ships	Sunk		Damaged	
	Japanese estimates	US records	Japanese estimates	US records
Carriers	8	0	11	7
Battleships	12	0	18	10
Cruisers	29	0	27	5
Destroyers	18	11	9	61
Minesweepers	3	1	2	22
Others	27	4	22	80
TOTAL	97	16	89	185

Source: Inoguchi et al. (1961: 145–6).

reports, the tables suggest that, *in aggregate*, they may slightly underestimate the real figure.

Although the Kamikaze planes achieved only limited success, they were considerably more effective than conventional attacks given the remaining military assets available to the Japanese. Those planes that did get through the protective cordon did considerable damage; Vice-Admiral Brown of the US navy makes the claim that the Kamikaze 'inflicted more casualties in the US fleet off Okinawa than the Japanese army did to the invading troops in the long battle ashore' (Inoguchi et al. 1961: 7). British aircraft carriers, with their armoured runways and hangars, fared considerably better than US ones; in cases where US carriers would require repairs in dock, British ships were able to use their runways within hours (Lamont-Brown 2000:

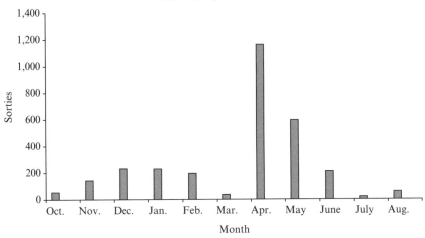

FIGURE 1.1.   Kamikaze sorties, October 1944–August 1945

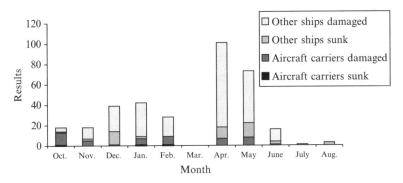

FIGURE 1.2.   Results claimed for Kamikaze missions, October 1944–August 1945
Source: Nagatsuka (1974: 205–12).

113; Hoyt 1985: 281). In addition to the physical effects of these attacks, there
was a noticeable impact on the morale of those subjected to it. So significant
was this that commanders stopped warning their crews when mass attacks
were due. War correspondent Hanson Baldwin observed that the 'strain of
waiting, the anticipated terror, made vivid from past experience sends some
men into hysteria, insanity, breakdown' (O'Neill 1981: 158)

Demographic Data on Participants

Certain problems arise in calculating the number of Japanese military personnel who died carrying out special attack missions. Frequently figures

include members of special attack squads who died in training, in accidents, or due to enemy bombing. Moreover, some may include those who were killed in battle but not on designated SMs (observers, those providing fighter cover, and so on) (Shirai 2002: 21).

It is commonly accepted that just under 4,000 pilots died in aircraft special attack missions. Morioka (1995: 11, 51) suggests 3,843 (1,329 from the navy, 2,514 from the army).[3] These pilots were predominantly between 18 and 24 years of age. According to the data provided in Shiino (2000: 122–93), none of the participants was born after 1928, so the youngest would have had their seventeenth birthday in 1945. All of the participants were male.

In both the navy and army, over half the pilots were non-commissioned officers (69 per cent and 53 per cent respectively). Comparatively few of the pilots were graduates from the elite military academies (5 per cent and 12 per cent) and most of the commissioned officers who died as air Kamikaze were university students who were drafted into the forces and hastily trained as the war situation deteriorated (Morioka 1995: 11, 51). Because these students left behind far more written material than the less educated career officers and enlisted men, they have attracted a disproportionately large degree of interest.

Many of the navy's non-commissioned officer Kamikaze pilots were drawn from the *Yokaren* ('Youth Training Corps'), a naval-aviation junior high school for boys in their mid-teens unlikely to succeed academically in a conventional academic environment. These youngsters possessed great natural ability and their youth made them fearless fliers (Hashiuchi interview, 16 January 2002). The army ran a similar programme for *rikugun shōnen hikōhei* ('army youth pilots').

What is clear is that, at the early stage of the use of SMs, the participants were fully trained combat pilots. Once the use of the Kamikaze became a large-scale operation, orders were given that less valuable personnel be used (Larteguy 1956: 130). There is therefore a perceptible shift in the composition of the Kamikaze. In the first wave of the navy's Kamikaze attacks in the Philippines, 87 per cent were enlisted men, 7 per cent were elite academy men, and 6 per cent reserve officers (drafted students). In the large-scale Kamikaze attacks launched from Kyūshū, Taiwan, Okinawa, and mainland Japan in the last five months of the war, this had changed to 64 per cent enlisted men, 4 per cent academy, 32 per cent students (Morioka 1995: 51). Although it is less pronounced, the proportion of students in army Kamikaze attacks also increases (while, proportionately, elite participation declines). This pattern may partially explain the higher rate of success of the first wave noted above.

In the case of the *kaiten*, the ages of the 1,375 men trained as *kaiten* pilots ranged from 17 to 28, though most were around 20. The figures given by the National Kaiten Association show that three-quarters of them were recruited from the *Yokaren*.

Cultural Factors

These events did not take place in a vacuum. In this section we shall explore various constituents of the cultural matrix in which these missions took place.

Religion

Religion in Japan is a confusing phenomenon in that nearly all Japanese are formally simultaneously Buddhist and Shintō. It should also be added that Confucian values such as filial piety, respect for authority, and education and diligence were, and still are, important cultural factors in Japan. There is no conception in Japan of exclusive adherence to one religious faith; tradition-ally there has been a basic division of labour in that Shintō has generally concentrated on rites associated with birth, marriage, and fertility, while Buddhism deals with the afterlife as well as the development of self-awareness and liberation from worldly concerns.

Shintō

Shintō, literally 'the way of the gods', is the oldest of Japan's religious traditions and is based on animist nature worship in which spirits are to be found not only in living animals and plants but also in mountains, streams, winds, and trees. According to Shintō's creation myths, the Japanese islands are of divine origin, as is the imperial line, which is descended from the sun goddess Amaterasu. In the words of Hirata Atsutane, an influential pre-Meiji thinker, Japan is therefore 'the land of the gods and ... their descendants. Japanese differ completely from and are superior to the peoples of China, India, Russia, Holland, Siam, Cambodia and all the other peoples of the world' (Beasley 1990: 24–5).

Following the Meiji restoration of 1868, the reformers exploited Shintō's message of Japanese uniqueness to bolster national cohesion at a time when foreign ideas and technologies were rapidly being introduced after over two centuries of national isolation. The Meiji Constitution of 1889 stated that the emperor was 'sacred and inviolable' and 'of a lineal succession unbroken for ages eternal'. One aspect of this nation-building was the development of State Shintō, the main purposes of which were emperor veneration and a celebration of patriotism. Other religions were tolerated (an early Meiji attempt to eradicate them had failed) provided they also observed the rites of State Shintō.

In pre-Buddhist Japan, the spirits of the dead were thought to eventually join the ranks of the *kami* ('divinities') and were worshipped as protective ancestral spirits. Following the introduction of Buddhism, conceptions of the afterlife become confused and modern Japanese religion contains logically contradictory views. However, the idea that the dead can become *kami* remains; those who died fighting for the emperor in the battles of the Meiji restoration and thereafter were formally enshrined at the Yasukuni shrine in Tokyo:

The Yasukuni shrine received respect exceeded only by that accorded the Ise Grand Shrines. The special status of this shrine derived from the fact that the emperor himself paid tribute there to the souls of the war dead. . . . In no other case did the emperor so honor the enshrined souls of commoners. For this reason it was believed to be a great honor to be enshrined there. Enshrinement was a privilege bestowed by the emperor; it was not a right. . . . The significance of enshrining the soul of a human being in Yasukuni is that the rite of enshrining is an apotheosis symbolically changing the soul's status to that of a national deity. Accordingly, it ceases to be a mere ancestor of some household and instead attaches to the nation. (Hardacre 1989: 90)

A parting remark supposedly made by soldiers going into battle was 'see you in Yasukuni shrine'. However, former navy pilot Yasunaga suggests that this is largely propaganda:

I never heard anyone saying that. It was the same thing for that song ... you know '*dōki no sakura*' ... they have scenes like that in movies but when you see them drinking sake and singing. You think 'bullshit!' It's a film, so if they don't have scenes like that you wouldn't be able to create the atmosphere. (Interview, June 2003)

In addition to the Yasukuni shrine, there were numerous local shrines for the war dead in Japan built up from the early Meiji period onwards. Like the Yasukuni shrine, these were generally supported financially by the state. War memorials, at which annual ceremonies took place, also started appearing after the 1905 Russo-Japanese war. Interestingly, these tended to be built next to schools rather than temples or shrines.

Buddhism

Japanese Buddhism is divided into numerous sects with a diversity of doctrines. There is considerable difficulty with the issue of the afterlife; there is reincarnation, nirvana, and the idea of the dead as ancestors. According to Reader, a noted scholar of Japanese religions, this is an area in which 'popular/folk ideas and pure Buddhist ideals conflict—and a murky compromise exists. . . . Basically the reality for Japanese Buddhists is the belief that the spirits become ancestors exist somewhere in the other realm but still with connections to, and capabilities to offer protection to, this realm' (private correspondence, December 2001).

Although Buddhism does not endorse suicide (the monks who burned themselves to death in protest at the Vietnam war did not find widespread support from their co-religionists), ascetic Japanese sects such as Zen place a high priority on liberation from excessive attachment to life and this-worldly concerns:

To acquire the knowledge of *mujō* (a sense of eternal change and the ephemeral quality of all things, including human beings) is the purpose of Japanese religions, and to develop the capacity for meeting death with complete equanimity is a *sine qua non* of Japanese maturity. (Iga 1986: 145)

It should be noted that enshrinement at Yasukuni shrine and a post-death existence in Buddhist heaven were not seen as mutually exclusive (Reader, private correspondence, December 2001).

Yasunaga (interview June 2003) assesses the impact of religion as minor:

For the young grunts [slang for infantrymen] on the battlefield, I don't think it [religion] had much. It had practically no influence at all. At the time of the Pacific war, the Buddhist view that if you have lived a good life, you will get a good reward by going to heaven when you die, had become hackneyed and outworn. And Shintō had an even lighter impact than Buddhism.

Education

From 1890 to 1945 the Imperial Rescript on Education was issued to all schools in the country. Because, as the Meiji Emperor told his education minister at the time, the people were 'easily led astray and confused by foreign doctrines, it was essential to define the moral basis of the nation for them' (quoted by Jansen 2000: 410). This document was a compulsory part of the curriculum and pupils learned it by heart:

Our Imperial Ancestors have founded Our Empire on a basis broad and everlasting, and have deeply and firmly implanted virtue; our subjects ever united in loyalty and filial piety have from generation to generation illustrated the beauty thereof. This is the glory of the fundamental character of Our Empire, and herein lies also the source of Our Education. Ye, Our subjects, be filial to your parents ... always respect the Constitution and observe the laws; should emergency arise, offer yourself courage-ously to the State; and thus guard and maintain the prosperity of Our Imperial Throne coeval with heaven and earth. So shall ye not only be Our good and faithful subjects but render illustrious the best traditions of your forefathers. The Way here set forth is indeed the teaching bequeathed by Our Imperial Ancestors, to be observed alike by Their Descendants and the subjects alike, infallible for all ages and in all places. It is Our wish to lay it to heart in all reverence, in common with you, Our subjects, that we may all attain to the same virtue. (Hozumi 1913: 111–12)

During its half century of use, this rescript was the foundation of all moral education in Japan. In his study of state textbooks on ethics, Fridell notes that, by the late Meiji period, there was a strong emphasis on the importance of national ethics stressing the superiority of state interests over those of the individual. Following are excerpts taken from a 1910 ninth-grade ethics textbook:

It is the first duty of the subjects to obey and protect the state.

The state exists independently forever, but the individual for only a time, and compared with the state, his life is very brief. It is only natural that the people must conform to the purposes of the eternal state and give no heed to personal interests. (Quoted in Fridell 1970: 830)

Emperor loyalty was predicated not only on his divine descent. Extending the concept of filial piety to the wider Japanese family was another strategy used to enhance the emperor's position:

It is only natural for children to love and respect their parents, and the great loyalty– filial piety principle springs from this natural feeling ... Our country is based on the family system. The whole country is one great family, and the Imperial House is the Head family. It is with feelings of filial love and respect for parents that we Japanese people express our reverence toward the Throne of unbroken Imperial line. (Quoted in Fridell 1970: 831)

In 1924, military training under regular army officers was made compulsory in all middle and senior schools. From 1939 universities and colleges were also made to conduct military training courses for all students (obligatory military lectures had existed since 1931). Military training was seen as useful not only because it was 'very efficient at adapting pupils to the good custom of obeying rules' (Terauchi cabinet 1917, quoted in Iritani 1991: 175) but because, in the words of one contemporary high school principal:

The quintessence of military education is to cultivate the attitude of patriotic martyr-dom and patriotism. It exists in bringing up the people who work in readiness to die for the Emperor at any time. We desire to convert the people into thinking that they should be ready to die, not scared of dying for the Emperor.... As for school education, it means total obedience only to the Emperor, and the attitude of absolute service. (Quoted in Iritani 1991: 178)

Yet military education was by no means popular; Kōzu (2000: 313) recalls the army officers at his school as 'swaggering bastards' and suggests that his dislike of them was one reason why he opted to join the navy. The same was true for university students. An English teacher at the elite Tokyo Imperial University recalled shortly after his repatriation to Britain in 1942 that:

There is among the present generation of university students fairly widespread dislike of the army, and I have little doubt that even today if it were left to individual choice, only a comparatively small number of them would enlist. Many of the students in my own classes seize every opportunity to absent themselves from military training. (Morris 1943: 202, quoted in Shillony 1986: 781)

Another teacher at Tokyo Imperial University, disgusted by the derisive reaction to one of his lectures in 1942 on the Japanese expansion in Asia, noted in his diary that the intellectual climate in university campuses was 'far behind the times' with the dangerous liberal views of the 1920s still prevalent (Shillony 1986: 781). The writings of students who served as Kamikaze pilots suggests they did not uncritically endorse the views imposed upon them by their ethics textbooks and military training. Many held highly progressive views. Perhaps in keeping with these ideals, there was general support among students for ridding Asia of European colonialism (which was the one area in which government rhetoric coincided with student sympathies). As Japan's military situation deteriorated, student idealism underwent a shift in favour of defending the homeland. This can be seen in the final writings of students (see Appendix at the end of this chapter).

Although there was a system of national military conscription for male 20-year-olds, students were given a deferral (five years for college students and seven for those at university). This period of deferral was progressively whittled away from 1939 onwards (except for medical students). In September 1943, the system of deferment was abolished for students with the exception of those in the strategically important disciplines of medicine, natural sciences, engineering, and agriculture.

Most drafted students opted for the navy rather than the army: the former was associated with smart white uniforms, technological advance, and the popular war against European and US colonialism; the latter with the unpopular China war and domestic repression (Shillony 1986: 782). Many of the later Kamikaze pilots were students drawn from the arts, humanities, and law faculties drafted into the navy following the abolition of deferral. Hashiuchi, one such pilot we interviewed, now explains his preference for the navy over the army more simply: 'Would you prefer to die slowly with a bullet in your guts or die quickly in the air?' That he was to die in combat was taken as given. This answer is puzzling as the army also had pilots but his wife added helpfully that naval uniforms were popular with the girls (interview, 16 January 2002). In addition, as former army pilot Naemura recalls, both food and promotion prospects were better in the navy (interview, 8 October 2002).

The question remains how strongly individuals subscribed to the ideals of State Shintō and pre-war education. In the mid-1930s, during the height of emperor worship, two US anthropologists spent a year in Suye Mura, an

agricultural community in southern Japan. During the course of this field-
work, one of the rural women was asked why the emperor was portrayed on a
scroll alongside a Japanese goddess. The following dialogue ensued:

I don't know, but they are both there because she is the greatest *kamisama* [god] and
he is the head of the country, the greatest person in Japan.

Then the emperor is not a *kamisama*?

No, he is just worshipped like a god, but he is not a real god. He is human, a very great
man. (Smith and Wiswell 1982: 12)

Even if his divinity was discounted, to what extent did the emperor feature as
a focus for loyalty? Yasunaga, for one, did not interpret his duty exclusively,
or even predominantly, in terms of emperor loyalty:

In the Japanese Navy, expressions like 'die for the emperor' weren't very popular. So,
in that song we sang most frequently 'Duty is heavier than a mountain'; obviously
duty towards the emperor was implicit but there was also the idea of faithfulness, and
that included trust and obedience, towards your superiors and loyalty towards your
comrades in this idea of 'Gi' [righteousness, loyalty, justice, duty]. This is how I think
we all interpreted this. (Interview, June 2003)

By contrast, Donald Keene, the literary translator and at the time working as
an interpreter involved in the interrogation of Japanese prisoners, recalls that
'although I was impressed by their knowledge and intelligence, it baffled me
that they remained convinced of the sacred nature of Japan's mission and the
rest of the wartime ideology' (quoted in Jansen 2000: 654–5). Both Hashiuchi
and his wife stressed that the moral education based on the 1890 rescript was
the most important factor in creating a popular preparedness to die for Japan.

   These two aspects need not be irreconcilable. The peasant woman and
Yasunaga here reflect their innermost personal views (which the woman
acknowledges would incur punishment if heard by the village policeman),
whilst Keene's interrogatees project the socially endorsed ideology. Given
Keene's position of authority, this is unsurprising.

Japanese Traditions of Voluntary Death

Although Japan is usually seen as a country with a high suicide rate, in the
decades prior to the Second World War Japan's annual suicide rate was
roughly about 20 per 100,000. This was similar to those in Western European
countries such as France at the same time and much lower than other Asian
countries such as China (which had a rate of fifty in the 1890s) (Pinguet 1993:
17). However, it is true that suicide in Japan does not carry the moral

opprobrium it does in Europe; it is seen as an acceptable, and indeed honourable, way out of an otherwise impossible situation:

Since the earliest recorded period of Japanese history a warrior's self destruction was accepted as a release from shame, an act of honour and courage, and an ultimate proof of integrity. (Morris 1975: 15)

The classical manner of self-immolation is the samurai ritual disembowelment known as *seppuku* (or more vulgarly as *hara-kiri*). The extraordinary level of self-inflicted pain concomitant with this act is indeed a powerful demonstration of the protagonist's courage and sincerity; for this reason many of Japan's tragic heroes who have met their deaths in this way are venerated.

Foremost among these are the forty-seven samurai. These paragons endured two years of extreme humiliation and privation while they plotted to avenge their lord who, in 1701, had been ordered to commit *seppuku* after violently reacting to public humiliation by a rival. Eventually they managed to kill their dead lord's nemesis and presented his severed head at their master's grave. Because they had broken the Shogunate's rules concerning vendettas, they were condemned to die: because their actions were considered so virtuous, they were allowed the honourable death of *seppuku*. This tale has been known to all Japanese schoolchildren ever since.

Perhaps even more famous, and for our purposes significant, is the story of Kusonoki Masashige. Kusonoki was a samurai of obscure origins who had risen in prominence due to his effectiveness as a guerrilla commander in the service of the fourteenth-century emperor Godaigo and his ill-fated attempt to wrest power from the military government and re-establish imperial rule. Despite significant deficiencies in Godaigo's judgement and the erosion of military support for the emperor, Kusonoki stayed loyal to a cause he knew was doomed. After meeting with defeat at the battle of Minatogawa in 1336, Kusonoki and his brother Masasue disembowelled themselves in a nearby farmhouse. Before they died Masashige asked his brother's last wish. Masasue laughingly replied 'I should like to be reborn seven times into this world of men that I might destroy the enemies of the court' (Morris 1975: 106–42). The popularity of Kusonoki reached new heights following the Meiji restoration of imperial rule in 1868 and his story was held up as an example in school textbooks. References to Kusonoki, his water chrysanthemum crest, and his brother's wish for 'seven lives' abound in the iconography of the wartime Kamikaze.

Among the traditional virtues of the samurai was a preparedness to die. This was stated most clearly in the *Hagakure*, a collection of thoughts passed on by Yamamoto (2000: 17), a samurai-turned-monk, to a young protégé in the early eighteenth century: 'The Way of the Samurai is found in Death.

When it comes to either/or, there is only the quick choice of death.... If by setting one's heart right every morning and evening one is able to live as though his body were already dead, he gains freedom in the Way. His whole life will be without blame, and he will succeed in his calling'. This book is generally held to be the definitive exposition of the way of the warrior (*bushidō*) and enjoyed a renaissance during the 1930s in Japan when its message resonated with the prevalent militaristic Zeitgeist.

Among the extreme rightists during the 1930s, a preparedness to die for their beliefs and public pronouncements of this preparedness were seen as proof of their superior moral integrity and sincerity vis-à-vis their supposedly weaker-willed liberal opponents.[4]

Military Training

Following the modernization of the army in the Meiji period, efforts were made to inculcate the traditional ideals of the samurai elite in the peasant conscripts. This is amply reflected in the *Senjin Kun* ('field service code'),[5] which was compulsory reading for all Japanese servicemen. This document left the reader in no doubt as to what was expected of him:

To transcend considerations of life and death is to have a spirit of sublime self-sacrifice. Stand aloof from thoughts of life and death and concentrate all your attention on pushing forward in the completion of your duty! Use up all your mental and physical strength and take joy in living in the principle of eternal righteousness! (*Senjin Kun*, section 1, part 7)

Don't suffer the shame of being captured alive! Die and avoid leaving behind a bad name due to dishonourable conduct! (*Senjin Kun*, section 1, part 8)

The ignominy of being taken prisoner was roughly equivalent to that of treason in European countries at the same time. Official exhortations to avoid capture at all costs were reinforced with warnings that captives would be subjected to torture by the enemy (women would be raped and then killed). As the tide of the Pacific War turned against Japan, surrender to the enemy became an offence punishable by death.

Military training in the Japanese armed forces was more brutal than that in comparable forces. Physical beating of recruits was commonplace and was carried out not merely as a punishment but because it was seen to be a good character builder. Former *kaiten* pilot Kōzu (2000: 318) recalls the navy's 'almost superstitious belief that brutality and physical punishment made better sailors'. During the course of his training as a *kaiten* pilot he was regularly beaten by the officers who had graduated from the elite naval academy at Etajima,[6] as they resented the university students drafted after

1943 (and commissioned after only three months training). This had the effect of increasing the bloody-mindedness of the students and their desire to show that they were as tough as the regular officers. Aviators were less likely to be beaten in the course of their training as it was believed that this would cause them to be too tense in the air (Nagatsuka 1974: 50).

Methods of Selection: Volunteering

The call for volunteers was initially very strong. In the case of the first *Shinpū Tokkōtai* attack, all of the non-commissioned officers and reserve officer pilots (though significantly none of the academy graduates) volunteered to participate in the mission. In Yokota's graduating class of navy pilots, 94 per cent marked their papers with a double circle (indicating a strong desire to volunteer), 5 per cent put a single circle (indicating indifference one way or the other), and fewer than 1 per cent threw the paper away (they did not want to go) (Yokota 2000: 307). The comments made by Yokota's classmates are revealing:

What a chance for glory! How proud your parents and friends would be!

I'm tearing up my paper! I have a sweetheart and I want to marry her when this war is over.
Should I make one circle, or two? I wouldn't want anyone to think I had no *Yamato damashii* [Japanese spirit]. My patriotism is as great as any man's.

I know I'm making two circles! Think what an adventure! One's name would appear in history books. (Yokota and Harrington 1962: 12)

Some volunteers, afraid that merely volunteering would not ensure their selection, wrote in blood or appended to their papers earnest requests for inclusion.

However, this should not be taken as proof that all pilots were whole-heartedly enthusiastic volunteers. Ichikawa, for example, had a strong urge to decline but realized that this was impossible; to do so would be considered unbefitting a naval pilot. Eventually he wrote 'yes' on his ID card in small letters (Naitō 1989: 31). Nagatsuka (1974: 157) records that, despite being prepared to accept their SM, he and his comrades felt a persistent and deep-rooted reluctance to do so. Both Ichikawa and Nagatusuka comment on how it was contrary to all their military training to be *requested* to do anything. In an environment which stressed unquestioning obedience to orders, and in which requests were unheard of, how was a request to be interpreted?

The criteria for the selection of volunteers changed as the course of the war proceeded. Initially, highly trained combat pilots who were already oper-ational were chosen. It was also considered important to show that the navy was not merely sacrificing wartime draftees but its own elite graduates of the naval academy. As the scale of the Kamikaze attacks was stepped up, using its best pilots in this way was seen as a colossal waste of Japan's most precious remaining military asset. There was therefore a switch in policy. 'Secret instructions from the general Staff recommended that the corps should take either bad pilots or quite young ones who had not yet undergone a serious training-course, as the others were essential for the defence of Japan and the archipelago still under her control' (Larteguy 1956: 129). Time after time, just before a unit was assigned to special attack duties, the old-timers would receive a transfer order; Yasunaga's mess-mates would observe 'Ah! Just that guy got out!' (interview, June 2003).

The best pilots were used to escort the Kamikaze to their targets. In doing so the escorts played a number of roles: they guided the navigationally untrained Kamikaze; they protected them from enemy fighters; they observed their attacks; and they provided an environment encouraging completion of the mission (the realization that someone was watching bolstered the resolution of pilots).

Some of the escort pilots resented their role and protested that they should be allowed to participate in SMs too. They were usually informed that they would get their chance but not yet.

Training

In the early plane-crash attacks, the pilots were already trained and needed no further training; nor had they the time. Inoguchi, who was responsible for training Kamikaze pilots in Formosa at the end of 1944, recalls that specialized Kamikaze training lasted for a week. Because the airfields from which Kamikaze attacks were launched were subject to frequent attack, it was very important to minimize the time between taking the planes out of hiding and getting them in the air. Rapid take-off practice was therefore an important part of the training.

The other key aspect of their training was the attack profile. Two basic styles of attack were found to be the most effective. The high-altitude attack consisted of an approach at 6,000–7,000 m followed by a shallow dive to an altitude of 1,000–2,000 m followed by a final steep dive at an angle of 45–55 degrees. Although this tactic had the disadvantage of early identification by enemy radar, it made the aircraft less vulnerable to enemy fighters. The alternative was the low altitude approach at 10–15 m followed by a rapid climb to 400–500 m and then a dive at 45–55 degrees onto the target. Low-level approaches made radar detection harder for the enemy. Dives steeper than 55 degrees made the plane very difficult to control (Inoguchi et al. 1961:

86–91). One reason was that, without hydraulically assisted controls, controlling a plane at high speeds is enormously difficult due to the force of the air over rudders and flaps and the increased lift that such speeds generate (Hattori 1993: 24). This problem would be exacerbated with inexperienced pilots.

The first rule of the Kamikaze was that they should not be too hasty to die. If they could not select an adequate target, they should return to try again later. Although some reports say that by the end of the war planes would only have enough fuel for a one-way trip, thereby precluding return, Naemura dismisses this as post-war propaganda to discredit the Kamikaze programme; the type of explosion on impact indicated that the planes had full tanks (interview, 8 October 2002).[7] However, whatever the official line, returning to base was not unproblematic. Nagatsuka was ordered to turn back by his flight commander due to thick fog. When he and his comrades returned, they were punched by his commanding officer, blamed for bringing disgrace on the squadron, and ordered to 'copy out the sacred words of the Emperor until further notice' (Nagatsuka 1974: 196–7).

Another aspect of Kamikaze attacks that was stressed was that pilots should keep their eyes open right up to the moment of impact so as to be sure that they hit their target. In fact, many of the pilots overshot their targets. Hashiuchi maintains that this last-minute overshoot was more likely to be due to an instinctive reaction on the part of the pilot that overwhelmed his conscious intention to crash the plane (interview, 16 January 2002), though problems of control at high speed must also have played a part.

Another mistake that pilots frequently made was to forget to arm their bombs as soon as they had identified their targets. Bombs were not armed prior to this to enable pilots who failed to identify a target to return to base and land safely. Inoguchi's training programme stressed the importance of remembering to arm bombs but, for whatever reason, a number of his students were still observed to successfully crash but without their bombs detonating (Inoguchi et al. 1961: 91). Hashiuchi says that, on his assignment to a special attack unit, neither he nor his colleagues received Kamikaze-specific training.

Rewards

As mentioned above, soldiers who died in battle were formally enshrined at Yasukuni Jinja. They thereby became national gods. In terms of other-worldly post-death benefits of gods, it does not appear that Kamikaze pilots achieved greater rewards than other dead warriors. They were, however, lionized in the press and official communiqués in which they were referred to as god-heroes. Their photos would appear in the newspapers. One young pilot writing to his parents prior to his departure writes that a film crew had just visited his unit ('I hope I looked photogenic today'). Kamikaze pilots would also receive fan mail and handmade dolls from schoolgirls to take on their mission. Civilians would approach them in the street and thank them.

Although there does not seem to have been a distinction between Kamikaze and other naval pilots in this respect, Hashiuchi recalls that naval pilots were extremely well fed at a time when the rest of the country was facing severe shortages of food. In addition to providing them with superior rations (including scarce sweets, alcohol, and cigarettes), the Army General Staff instructed units to billet pilots in the highest-quality inns available (Axell and Kase 2002: 72).

Members of the *Ōka* special attack group were given a distinctive uniform with buttons bearing a cherry blossom with three petals. *Kaiten* pilots had a water chrysanthemum badge on their sleeve. All Kamikaze pilots had white silk scarves.

On completing their missions, Kamikaze pilots were posthumously awarded a two-rank promotion. This entitled their families to increased pension rights. Families of dead Kamikaze pilots received other benefits including the title '*homare no ie*' (literally, a 'household of honour'), better rations (a very considerable reward by this stage of the war), and places of honour at official ceremonies (Larteguy 1956: 128).

Manifest Motivations

Despite whatever comforts these benefits might have afforded, they are rarely mentioned in the available literature as motivating factors. Nor, despite the importance of the rhetoric concerning the glory of dying for him, is the emperor. In this regard two other factors stand out: protecting family and protecting country. Lieutenant Seki, the man selected to lead the first officially named *Shinpū* (Kamikaze) attack, made the following remark to Onoda, a correspondent attached to the navy:

Japan is finished! Killing ace pilots like me, strewth! If it was up to me, I know I could get a direct hit on the flight deck of a carrier with a number 50 [500 kg bomb] without plane-ramming. I am not going out for the Emperor or the Japanese Empire. I am going for my beloved wife. If Japan were defeated, I reckon she would be raped by American GIs. I am dying to protect her. (Onoda 1971: 28–9)

Kaiten pilot Kōzu (2000: 319) said:

I didn't see myself throwing my life away for him [the emperor], nor for the government either, nor for the nation. I saw myself dying to defend my parents, my brothers and sisters. For them I must die, I thought.

Zero ace Sakai (2000: 142) remarked:

I called to Mutō, a close friend from our China Incident days and asked 'They say 'go'; what do we do?' 'What do we do, you say? It's decided,' he said. 'We go.' 'We can't live long anyway. You're right, let's go,' I chimed in. I never thought 'Long Live the Emperor!' To bring the nation to victory was our thought, and what was that nation? The land of my parents, younger brothers, and sister. Can we bear seeing our country being invaded by outside enemies? That was what was on my mind.

Sometimes when the emperor is mentioned it is with resentment rather than reverence:

I too would have thought my death worthwhile if it saved my family from being massacred by the Americans. My thoughts, never at any moment, turned to the Emperor, who, in any case had closed his eyes when this rash and inhuman tactic had been described to him. Did the Emperor have any idea of what went on in the mind and feelings of a suicide-pilot?... I would have liked to cry out to him ... 'To hell with it! Give me some fuel and good weather, not your words! I would set out this minute on a suicide-mission to defend my family and my country but I do not want to die for a man that calls himself Emperor!' (Nagatsuka 1974: 198)

Kōzu, the *kaiten* pilot who felt he had been deceived, had no desire to participate in a SM. He observed that it would be possible to escape this role if he proved himself to be incompetent to operate the weapon in training. He did not, however, adopt this strategy:

That would have only meant somebody else dying in my place. Even if the whole unit had been replaced, they'd have found others. It was that kind of system. I couldn't bear the idea of sacrificing someone else by quitting. I knew if I did, I'd regret it for the rest of my life, even if I never knew his name. I hated the thought that I'd fail and they'd say 'those reserve students are no good!' I couldn't do that to the others. I *wanted* to navigate well. Like they say in Chinese – 'Mei Fa' 'it can't be helped.' I was resigned to it. (Kōzu 2000: 316)

Kōzu's recognition of the guilt involved in non-participation when others were sacrificing themselves was undoubtedly a motivational factor for other protagonists. Naemura, who instructed Kamikaze pilots and then saw them die, repeatedly stresses the importance of solidarity in his own reflections on special attack missions (and, by implication, in his own decision to volunteer) (personal communication). In her analysis of the writings of Kamikaze pilots' writings, Ohnuki-Tierney (2002: 169) also observes the significance of this factor.

While the Kamikaze pilots have often been seen as fanatically devoted to their cause, this is not unambiguously supported by the available evidence. Those who psyched themselves up repeating the official propaganda on the radio were labelled by their comrades as *kichigai* ('nutters'). In fact, the

Kamikaze pilots held very diverse views. Among those pilots whose views have been made known in the available literature, we can see atheists, admirers of Marx and Lenin, liberals, Christians, and even an old boy from an English public school.

When one of his officers and fellow volunteers calmly tells him that Japan will lose the war, Yokota expresses amazement (Yokota and Harrington 1962: 174). Given the frequent references to tragic (and failed) figures in Japanese history throughout the various Kamikaze programmes, we might expect such an attitude to have been widespread among Kamikaze pilots, but this was not always the case; some, like Seki, recognized that Japan was finished and others expressed shock when they heard the emperor's announcement of surrender.

Other Attitudes

There was a sense of crisis. We had to save the country. Anyhow, there was the feeling that, if we were to die in battle, wasn't a special attack as good a way as any? Pilots all have pride, we are different from other people—the so-called chosen ones. Won't everybody praise us! (Naemura, interview, 8 October 2002)

Naval aviator Hashiuchi corroborates this elite consciousness of pilots, adding that 'when you get into that sort of atmosphere, there is not really anything like fear. When you turn on the engine—waaghh!'. With these words the octogenarian interviewee grabbed an imaginary joystick and momentarily relived the fierce joy of being a teenager at the controls of fighter plane.

Closely related to pride is vanity:

Because we were men we were vain. It would have been a disgrace to lose composure ... you didn't have much time but still you looked back down and forced yourself to smile ... you wanted to be praised after you died, just as much as you wanted it during your life. You wanted them to say, 'Yokota was young, but he went with incredible bravery. He was dignified to the end.' It would be terrible if they said, 'He went shaking. So unlike a *Kaiten* pilot. There was only one like that in our whole group. He was a disgrace to the *Kaiten* Corps.' (Yokota 2000: 310)

This is echoed by Nagatsuka (1974: 183), who observed of his comrades and himself that 'man's vanity is such that he will always act a part, right up till the end'. War correspondent Kawachi, who frequently went to cover the final days of Kamikaze pilots, noted that they 'wanted some kind of flashy legacy. They wanted to die a "good death". .... Almost all of them practically reeked of perfume. Some of them even wanted to have their teeth fixed so that they died in perfect shape' (Kawachi 2000: 119–20).

Sometimes the vanity cracked; on his way to his craft, Ōka pilot Shibata bragged about how he would attack his target dead in the centre after hugging along the surface of the sea—and then burst out 'Mother! The Navy is trying to kill me!'. Naitō (1989: 172) observes that this type of behaviour was not uncommon amongst the Ōka pilots.

Conflicts of this type could also be internal. After being ordered by his flight lieutenant to turn back due to thick fog, Nagatsuka finds himself divided into two distinct characters arguing as to the course of action. Once back at base he is racked by his inability to determine whether his relief to be alive is indicative of cowardice or of rationality. When given the chance to go again he is 'joyful' but can't work out whether this is due to 'patriotic zeal or the desire to wipe out (his) shame' (Nagatsuka 1974: 192, 199).

Whatever the emotions experienced by Yasunaga's comrades, there was a recognition that it would not be fitting for these to be openly acknowledged:

Those guys that were transferred [out of special attacks], they didn't let that show on their face as if to say 'Ah! That was lucky! I was the only one to have been excluded from special attacks!' Obviously it would have been a bit off to have shown relief. ... Many of the people I was with were designated on the [special attack] roster. They may well have thought in their hearts that 'tomorrow, it's all over for me' and thought about their loved ones at home but it would have been bad form to let that show on your face. Honestly, the guys that returned from having seen the roster they all had the same expression (those that were included on the list and those that weren't). (Interview, June 2003)

Yasunaga's comrades reflect not just a concern for appropriate image management but a grim acceptance of their role. As one of them said to him, 'looks like it's curtains for me' (interview, June 2003).

The attitude of Kamikaze pilots changed considerably as the special attack programme expanded. It is perhaps useful to consider the Kamikaze as two separate populations. The first group was composed of men who had already been in combat. The second were those who went straight from military training to special attack squads. Generally speaking, the first group exhibited greater enthusiasm for their mission. A number of possible factors are at work here.

Early Kamikaze already had a minimal life expectancy as normal combat pilots; they had seen many of their comrades die uselessly; they were graduates of full training programmes and were therefore more thoroughly imbued with the warrior ethos; at the end of 1944 Kamikaze pilots could feel that their deaths would make some difference to the course of the war.

Nakajima, while admitting that there was a problem of morale with the later Kamikaze, suggests that they came to terms with the nature of their mission:

Many of the new arrivals seemed at first not only to lack enthusiasm, but, indeed, to be disturbed with their situation. With some, this condition lasted only a few hours, with others for several days. It was a period of melancholy that passed with time and eventually gave way to a spiritual awakening. Then like an attainment of wisdom, care vanished and tranquillity of spirit appeared as life came to terms with death, mortality with immortality. (Inoguchi et al. 1961: 144)

There are, however, a number of problems with Inoguchi's and Nakajima's self-serving treatments of the Kamikaze.[8] Compare the above quotation with Admiral Yokoi's comments on the morale of drafted Kamikaze:

(T)he difficulties became especially apparent when men in aviation training were peremptorily ordered to the front and to death. When it came time for their take off, the pilot's attitudes ranged from the despair of sheep destined for the slaughter to open expressions of contempt for their superior officers. There were frequent and obvious cases of pilots returning from sorties claiming that they could not find any enemy ships and one pilot even strafed his commanding officer's quarters as he took off. (Yokoi 1986: 468)

At the end of May 1945, the Army Air Force Education Department sent Mochizuki Mamoru, a technical expert, to assess the psychological state of the Kamikaze pilots of the Sixth Air Army. Mochizuki found that about one-third of the pilots were vacillating, unable to forge a firm resolve and that 'the atmosphere immediately prior to departure is extremely delicate' (Ninagawa 1998: 130).

Even if this resolve had been made, waiting to go was not easy. One *Yokaren* pilot records that 'in order to escape as quickly as possible from the insurmountable suffering, the unbearable waiting, there was nothing to do but pray for the order to go' (Ninagawa 1998: 131).

Another problem highly motivated Kamikaze pilots like Yokota faced was the crushing effect on morale of repeatedly cancelled missions. Several times he departed by submarine on missions and in some of them he boarded his *kaiten* and heard his comrades depart for their deaths. Due to mechanical failure, lack of targets, and depth-charge damage to the flimsy *kaiten*, despite his best efforts he continues to return. To make matters worse, he and his fellow pilots are publicly berated by senior officers back at base due to their failure to deploy. On his third excursion, faced with a faulty weapon, he despairingly asks to double up with one of his squad-mates as returning again would be worse than death; he is refused (Yokota and Harrington 1962: 227–8).

Military discipline could also be negatively affected by the psychological pressures involved in being a 'living god'. This was especially so for those involved in lengthy training periods. The mutinous behaviour of the petty officers of the Ōka Thunder Gods Corps is a good example of this. They

started to question why they should continue to maintain customary standards of military discipline; their salutes were casual or non-existent; they grew
their hair long although this was a right reserved only for officers; they
complained about the food; they indulged in heavy drinking bouts. There
was also considerable resentment among the petty officers at the harsh
treatment they received from the reserve officers (students called up in the
1943 mobilization and graduates of an accelerated three-month course rather
than the Naval Academy at Etajima). After one drinking session the petty
officers raided the reserve officers' quarters to beat up a particular martinet,
resulting in an hour-long brawl between the two groups.

There were also arguments over who would be in the first group to use the
new weapon in combat:

They knew they were going to die and the waiting often seemed worse than death.
Besides, they were all anxious to be the first Thunder Gods heroes to die. 'The first
attack will make national headlines, but the second one will be buried somewhere on
the inside' they said. . . . Having been treated as live heroes, the men did not want to be
forgotten so quickly and easily when they died. (Naitō 1989: 85)[9]

They were also disgruntled when told that some of them would have to die in
an ordinary fighter plane rather than in the new *Ōkas*. When given a choice of
which weapon to use, the men became confused and bitter. After arguing
among themselves, most of the men agreed to accept this change of attack
but some resolutely refused to die in anything other than the new bomb
(Naitō 1989: 138–9).

Not only was the means of dying important, but so also the choice of
target. Yokota (2000: 309) recalls kissing the bow of his *kaiten* and asking it
to get an aircraft carrier for him. As he left port, he shouted out 'Nothing less
than thirty thousand tons! No suicide for a tiny ship!'. This preoccupation
with aircraft carriers and big ships is also seen among other Kamikaze pilots;
last letters frequently make such references. During the Okinawa campaign,
two *Ōka* pilots were ordered to crash into an airfield thereby preventing
US planes from intercepting a Kamikaze raid on the Allied fleet. They
complained.

Life in the Days Before Departure

In the morning of his departure from base, *kaiten* torpedo pilot Yokota and
his comrades paraded in their dress uniforms and were presented with a short
sword as if they were passing out from the elite Naval Academy. They were
also each given a white headband bearing the legend 'Given seven lives I'll
serve the nation with each of them', alluding to the Kusonoki brothers' final
wish. The significance of white headbands (worn by all Kamikaze) was that,

traditionally, a samurai would wear one to show that he was ready to fight to the death.[10] As the submarines left their bases, they would be surrounded by a flotilla of boats bearing flag-waving crowds shouting out the names of the pilots who stood astride their torpedoes waving their swords in acknowledgement. While on board the submarines, pilots would be made as comfortable as possible by the remainder of the crew and, despite the pilots' offers of help, were not expected to carry out duties. Before arriving in the expected hunting area, they received a feast and were toasted by the captain (Yokota 2000: 308–10; Millot 1971: 143–4).

In the early days of the air attacks, Kamikaze pilots would be given a funeral banquet on the eve of their mission. Larteguy (1956: 137) observes that 'soon the last night of the Kamikaze degenerated into a licensed orgy. The sake flowed like water. They were provided with women and even with very young girls who had been fetched from the villages around the air-bases.' However, this was neither the case at all bases nor universally condoned.

While the commanders of Kamikaze squads tended to see the sexual gratification of their young pilots as something to be encouraged, higher-level staff officers felt that this diminished the enthusiasm of pilots for a glorious death. Army research conducted at the time revealed that there was a correlation between wavering commitment (indicated by pilots failing to complete their missions) and the proximity of bases to centres of entertainment. In June 1945, the Army Air Force Education Department issued a circular to all army Kamikaze units concerning the morale of pilots:

In case there is a long waiting period between the formation of a Kamikaze unit and the final sortie, mental pressure increases and many instances results in a change of determination about being a Kamikaze pilot. Although there are some who seek to conclude their lives in pure and clean ways, there is a tendency among many Kamikaze pilots to seek earthly pleasures. This condition allows innocent men to try such pleasures, resulting in an increased tenacity for life. (Quoted in Axell and Kase 2002: 69–70)

Although he does not suggest it had this effect, navy pilot Hashiuchi recalls that, after being transferred to the Fifth Air Fleet (by then dedicated to special attack), most of his time was spent drinking and having fun:

Nearby Kanoya naval air-base there was a big, well to speak frankly, a big brothel— about five storeys high. In there everyone would have their favourite woman, wouldn't they. The night before they would go, they would go and tell her that they were off, you weren't supposed to but everyone did. . . . At twilight, about an hour before dawn when the planes would leave, they would turn up at the fence holding sheets . . . and they'd wave them like flags as the planes flew over. (Interview, 16 January 2002)

Because their families would not have a body to cremate in a funeral service, pilots would cut their hair and finger nails, which would be sent home. Occasionally the ashes of a pilot who had died in training would be taken on a mission by one of his comrades so that he too could participate. The Thunder Gods Corps pilots burned their old uniforms and changed into new ones, as did *kaiten* pilots. They then composed their parting words (see Appendix at the end of this chapter).

Immediately prior to departure, a ceremony would take place. In the case of the first Thunder Gods Corps attack, the pilots paraded in front of Vice-Admiral Ukagi. Okamura, their commanding officer, addressed them:

Today's mission will not be an easy one, but brave and resolute action will scatter even devils. With your passionate spirit of martyrdom, you will be able to overcome any kind of difficulty! You will succeed! Keep this conviction strong in your minds! Looking back, your serene state of mind and outstanding behaviour since last November has impressed me. I could not be more proud of you. Now you will go into the next world. And just as you have been in this world, I pray that you continue to be pure, beautiful, healthy and cheerful. Your colleagues and I will soon be following you. Please remember the ties we had in this world! (Naitō 1989: 115–16)

The pilots then exchanged sake with Ugaki and Okamura, saluted, and, when dismissed, sprinted towards their aircraft.

The End

With the announcement of Japan's surrender and the end of the war, the reactions of people involved in SMs varied. Admiral Ugaki, a keen proponent of special attack methods, insisted on leading a last attack against Allied shipping off Okinawa. When a subordinate tried to dissuade him, he replied: 'This is my chance to die like a samurai. I must be permitted my chance' (Millot 1971: 223). Although this last mission was planned to consist of only three dive-bombers, the whole unit of eleven planes along with their twenty-two crew was drawn up on the runway. Although they knew that the war was over, all of them volunteered to accompany Ugaki in death. Four planes actually returned with engine failure; the rest presumably crashed but US naval records do not show any Kamikaze activity against them on that day.

By contrast, Okamura, the commander of the Thunder Gods Corps, did not keep his promise to his departing subordinates that he would be 'following them soon'. He instructed his men to abide by the emperor's surrender. But in 1948 he jumped in front of a train and killed himself, leaving no suicide note (Naitō 1989: 205).

Ōnishi committed suicide by traditional *hara-kiri*; refusing either medical attention or assistance when discovered, he took twelve hours to die. In his suicide note he wrote:

To the spirits of the fallen heroes of the Special Attack Corps, I say this: My sincere gratitude for fighting so well. Believing in our ultimate victory, as living bombs you fell like scattered flowers. However, it so happened that this belief was not ultimately realised. With my death I apologise to the heroic spirits of my former subordinates and their bereaved families. (Akinaga 1999: 322)

Ōta, the man credited with inventing the *Ōka* flying bomb, climbed into a plane, claiming he was going to crash it into an enemy ship. In reality, he landed his plane in the sea and was rescued by fishermen; several months later he turned up at a village near his old airbase and was well looked after by the villagers who remembered his earlier kindnesses to them. After assuming a new identity and travelling around the country borrowing money from former comrades from the *Jinrai* Corps, Ōta disappeared in 1949. In 1994 he was discovered suffering from cancer in a Kyoto hospital after his son contacted a journalist. He died the same year (Shiino 1998: 28–30).

Dower (1999: 59) observes that members of Kamikaze corps were not above indulging in the looting of military property that was endemic in other units following the surrender announcement. One pilot crammed his plane with goods, flew it home, and then burned it after having offloaded his cargo.

Interviewees and Informants

Hashiuchi, Senichi: university draftee naval pilot. Assigned to Special Attack duties at the age of 19.

Naemura, Hichirō: university draftee army pilot. Instructed special attack pilots and, after volunteering three times, was given permission to participate in special attack duties himself.

Reader, Ian: internationally recognized authority on Japanese religions.

Yasunaga, Hiroshi: Yokaren graduate and naval reconnaissance pilot attached to the *Jinrai-tai* ('Divine Thunderbolt Corps').

Marktscheffel, Fritz: Volunteer pilot and later archivist of Sonderkommando ELBE.

APPENDIX

Poems and Songs

The Song of the Thunder God Corps

As we are born aloft as samurai of the skies,
Our eyes ever searching for signs of battle,
See how our outstretched arms carry us forward
Like divine wings.

Here we are—comrades of the sacred land of the rising sun!
Enemy ships are sighted—loud alerts are sounded.
Let us drive them beneath the waves!

Men of the cherry blossom squadrons—rally to the charge!
As we look down at our base spread below us,
Through the flow of tears that fills up our hearts,
We can see a fading glimpse of hands waving farewell!

Now is the time for our final, plunging blow.
We are ready to spill our blood, oh so red.
See how we dive towards the ships in the seas of the south!

The cool waves will console our departed spirits
And some day we will be reborn as cherry blossoms
In the garden of Yasukuni Jinja.

Dōki no Sakura—Flowers of the Same Season

You and I, we are flowers of the same season,
Blossoming in the garden of the same air squadron.
A flower that has blossomed is resolved to fall.
Let us fall splendidly for the sake of our country!

You and I, we are flowers of the same season,
Blossoming in the garden of the same air squadron.
Are we not flesh and blood comrades?
Our spirits are joined and cannot be separated.

Umi Yukaba—If I go away to sea

If I go away to sea,
A water-logged corpse:
If I go away to the mountains,
A grassy corpse;
I die close to the Emperor
And regret nothing.

Poem by Admiral Ōnishi

Blossoming today, tomorrow scattered;
Life is like a delicate flower;
Could one expect the fragrance to last forever?

Last Testimonies

Attempting to ascertain the true emotions of special attack pilots from their last writings is problematic. While pilots generally left behind final statements, frequently they had been told to do so by their superiors in order that these documents might be publicly displayed as evidence of their heroism (Ohnuki-Tierney 2002: 21). Yasunaga says this is why they are all such 'splendid, noble things'; [pilot's would think] 'Ah! People are going to see my last writings! I'll produce a magnificent statement' (interview, June 2003). In the light of this, such writings are perhaps useful indicators of what pilots wanted people to think they felt, or what they thought they were expected to feel, but may not tell us much about what they actually did feel. Letters were heavily censored and are, therefore, also an imperfect source. Diary material is most likely to provide an accurate reflection of the mental state of Kamikaze pilots. Such diaries were strictly forbidden and kept in secret.

The most widely read collection of last writings is the book Kike Wadatsumi no Koe ('Listen to the Voices of the Sea Gods'[a]). This is a collection of diary, letter, and testimony material left by university student war dead, compiled shortly after the war. There was a very conscious selection bias, and material that might be interpreted as supporting militaristic or ultra-nationalist views was deliberately excluded. A sensitive analysis of the writings of five such university student pilots is given by Ohnuki-Tierney (2002). While these highly educated and intellectually cosmopolitan students left behind a fascinating collection of writings, they cannot be considered representative of Kamikaze pilots as a whole.

Bearing these caveats in mind, we can detect certain themes recurring among the documents that have survived. These include apologies for filial inadequacies despite great parental benevolence:

---

[a] There are two English translations of this book, Larteguy (1956) and Yamanouchi and Quinn (2000). Translations used here are my own.

At this stage there is not much to say except that I cannot judge how I can apologise to you for not having had one scrap of filial piety though you, my honoured parents and grandparents, raised me indeed these twenty years. (Kiyomizu Masaharu*[b])

A concern for the future health of parents—often including an injunction to surviving siblings to fulfil the filial duties of the deceased:

I have nothing to write. Only that, honoured parents and Kumiko, I pray for your health. ... Kumiko, I'm relying on you to look after our parents. Do your best for them. (Itō Tsutomu[b])

The hope that the correspondent's parents will not be sad:

When you hear of my death don't cook red rice and or put on a black kimono. Yell 'Banzai' and greet my remains with joy. (Komatsu Takeshi[b])

When you get the photograph, please don't cry but praise me. (Itō Tsutomu[b])

In addition to these general themes, a broad range of emotions can be discerned in the last writings of pilots ranging from joy to despair, from pride to disgust.

Lieutenant Mitsuhashi, age 22 (Naitō 1989: 113–14):

When men did their best and left the rest to providence, they were rewarded with divine winds. Will there be other divine winds to protect our homeland now? Of course, I believe that there will be. But that only happens when men do their best.

Reserve Sub Lieutenant Ogata, age 23 (Naitō 1989: 114):

With my mission now at hand, my dear old town, my dear old people, I now abandon everything and leave to protect this country; to pursue our eternal and just cause, I now go forth. My body will collapse like a falling cherry blossom, but my soul will live and protect this land for ever. Farewell. I am a glorious wild cherry blossom. I shall return to my mother's place and bloom!

Flight Petty Officer Shimamura, age 20 (Naitō 1989: 114):

I shall fall smiling and singing songs. Please visit and worship at Yasukuni Shrine this spring. There I shall be a cherry blossom, smiling with many other colleagues. I died smiling so please smile. Please do not cry. Make my death meaningful.

Flight Petty Officer Kameda, age 19 (Naitō 1989: 114):

A man will die sooner or later. The value of being a man is given at the time of his death.

---

[b] Taken from Yokaren website www.st.rim.or.jp/~k-kawano/yokaren/isyo.html.

Flight Petty Officer Matsuo, age 20 (Naitō 1989: 114):

I am going but I am not feeling lonely because I have the haramaki [belly warmer] which mother made to protect me.

Ensign Okabe (diary extract):

My life will be rounded out in the next thirty days. My chance will come! Death and I are waiting. The training and practice have been rigorous, but it is worthwhile if we can die beautifully and for a cause.[c] (Inoguchi et al. 1961: 187)

Unknown *kaiten* pilot:

May my death be as clean and sudden as the shattering of crystal ... like cherry blossom in the spring, let us fall clean and radiant ... most important, do not weep for me. (Lamont-Brown 2000: 132)

The following diary and letter extracts are all from drafted university students who died as either Kamikaze or *kaiten* pilots (Nihon Senbotsu Gakusei Kinen-kai 1995: 279).

Otsuka Akio, age 23 (362, 366):

[To his siblings] To speak frankly, I am not dying voluntarily, I am not dying without regrets. The outlook for this country upsets me terribly. No! I'm even more worried about the outlook for Mother, Father and you lot. With worry piled on worry, I can't bear it.... [To his parents] Stay healthy. Believing in the victory of greater Asia, praying for the happiness of you all, and apologising for being such a poor son, I set out on my attack with a smile on my face. ... I will show you a committed and brave death.

Uebara Ryoji, age 22 (last writing: 375–6):

[Undated] I have long thought that if Japan is really going to continue for ever, liberalism is necessary. At present, with Japan enveloped in its totalitarian mood, this may sound crazy. But when you really open your eyes wide and think about human nature, Liberalism is the most rational ideology. It had been my dream to make Japan like the Great British Empire of Old. This ideal is shattered. Because of this, simply for the freedom and independence of Japan, I happily sacrifice my life. For a person, the rise or fall of a country is really a matter of great importance: when considered on a universal scale it really is an insignificant thing.

---

[c] An interesting echo can be found in the actions of the Japanese terrorists who blew themselves up after killing or injuring over 100 tourists at Lod Airport (Tel Aviv, Israel) in 1972. Okamoto, who failed to kill himself, later said that he 'wanted to die a beautiful death for a great cause, but since I am a human being, there are some things I cannot quite explain reasonably' (Iga 1986: 156).

Hasegawa Shin, age 23 (diary extract: 279, 84):

[24 November 1944] If only my suffering and death made even the slightest positive contribution to the wellbeing of those that I love! [18 January 1945] I am convinced that brutality is something that is deeply rooted in human nature. Since man first made this world, he has not progressed in the slightest. In this war there is no longer any question of righteousness, it is nothing more than an explosion of hate between races. These opposing races will not stop fighting until one or the other is exterminated. It is terrifying and shameful! Man? A species of ape!

Ichijima Yasuo, age 23 (diary extract: 361):

[24 April 1945] Next door they are drinking and kicking up a racket but that's OK too. As for me, I want to remain with a calm spirit until death. People should continue to work on self-control until they die. This is even more important for us members of the tokkōtai who represent the Spirit of Japan. Right up to the end I want to behave in a way that will not besmirch its name. I believe that the life I have lived has followed one of the most beautiful paths that a human life can take. I feel great joy and pride in being able to sacrifice my pure life to my ineffably beautiful fatherland.

Hayashi Ichizo, age 23 (344):

[Last letter to his mother] I am happy that I was chosen as a member of the tokkōtai and go forth into battle, but when I think of you it brings tears to my eyes. ... These days I read the Bible every day. That is because when I read it, I feel close to you. When I crash, I shall have the Bible and the Book of Psalms in my aircraft. I will also take along the mission badge which the college principal gave me, and your lucky charm.

Hayashi Norimasu, age 25 (diary extract: 391):

[23 April 1945] A bit drunk. I got furious with lieutenant K. We were discussing the status of us reserve officers in the navy. I made the following declaration! I will never fight for the navy. If I am to die I will do so for the country or, to put it in extreme terms, for my own personal pride. I feel nothing but hate towards the navy! I say this directly to my heart. I am able to die if it is for the sake of my pride. I will absolutely not die for the Imperial Navy. We ex-student pilots from the 13th year are continually persecuted. Right now, who is it who is doing the fighting! Over half of my class mates who were on carrier bombers are already dead. It is for my country, for my mates from the 13th year, even for the ex-university warriors who have gone before, and ultimately for my pride, that I live and die—whilst cursing the Imperial Navy. ... [30 June] I am unable to do anything. In the very near future I will have to depart this world. I would like to go to war soon. I would like to die soon.

Ugaki Matome (diary extract):

[15 August 1945] I am going to follow in the footsteps of those many loyal officers and men who devoted themselves to their country, and I want to live in the noble spirit of the Special Attack. (Ugaki 1991)

However, not all pilots left last testimonies. Yokota, leaving on his mission and wanting to know what is 'usually done by *kaiten* men at such times', asks one of his more experienced comrades if he has written one. The reply comes:

Wills are all nonsense! I am not going to write any will. I did write one, when we were out before. Then, when ... we had to turn back, I read that will. It was so pompous and presumptuous that I actually blushed when I read it. ... Men like us don't need to write a memorial of ourselves. (Yokota and Harrington 1962: 126).

Thankfully for us, Yokota provides a memorial to the silent Kamikaze.

Names of Special Attack Units

Certain themes recur in the names of special attack units. These names would be typically prefixed with the type of group and suffixed with -*tai* ('unit') as in Shinpū Tokubetsu Kōgeki-tai, Tanshin-tai. References to sincerity and loyalty are the most common.

Sincerity/Loyalty/Emperor

Tanshin	Sincerity
Issei	One sincerity
Shisei	Utmost sincerity
Kinnō	Loyalty to the emperor
Chūyū	Loyal bravery
Junchū	Pure loyalty
Seichū	Loyalty (literally sincere loyalty)
Jungi	Righteous martyrs (composed of the characters for *jun*—following someone into death/laying down one's life—and *gi*—justice, righteousness, loyalty).
Nōkon	Spirit of the emperor
Shichishō	Seven lives (alluding to Kusonoki's famous wish to be reborn seven times to smite the emperor's enemies)
Gyotate	Emperor's shield
Seika	Quintessence

Divine/Philosophical

Jinrai	Thunder gods/divine thunderbolt
Tenpei	Heaven's soldiers
Shinpei	Divine soldiers
Kōtoku	Eminent virtue
Hakkō	The whole world

Ichiu   Under one roof (*hakkō ichiu* is a Japanese four-character
                 compound used to express the idea of universal brother-
                 hood—under Japanese tutelage)

Nature/Japan

Kikusui   Water chrysanthemum (the crest of Kusonoki
                 was adopted by both *kaiten* and aeroplane Kamikaze)
Kyōfū   Strong wind
Shippū   Swift wind
Taifū   Typhoon
Hazakura   Cherry tree in leaf
Wakazakura   Young cherry
Yasukuni   Peaceful country (also the name of the national
                 shrine of the war dead)
Kyokkō   Rays of the rising sun
Shikishima*   Japan (classical)
Yamato*   Japan (classical)
Asahi*   Morning sun
Yamazakura*   Mountain cherry

The four asterisked names were given to the first four units of the *Shinpū*
Special Attack Corps. They are drawn from a famous tanka by the nationalist poet Motoori Norinaga (1730–1801).

Hard

Tesshin   Iron will
Sekichō   Stone guts
Gokoku   Defence of the country
Kongō   Adamantine/strong man
Giretsu   Heroism
Shingeki   Charge
Hakko   White tigers
Shinbu   Brandished weapon

Non-Japanese Suicide Missions
of the Second World War

As was the case with Japan, such measures were usually adopted by countries facing unusually desperate circumstances. As such, the instrumental aspect of the mission had a clear priority over the symbolic. Taken by surprise by Hitler's invasion, Russian commanders instructed fighter pilots to crash their planes into those of the enemy. Once the tide of the war had turned, Germany established squadrons of *Rammjäger* (battering-ram) aircraft which were to crash into enemy bombers. These had been hardened to better withstand aerial collisions and were not strict SMs; it was hoped that pilots would be able to bail out if their planes were downed. Goebbels's diary for 31 March 1945 records that 'the Rammjägers are now to make suicide attacks ... 90 per cent casualties are expected'. Initially these were composed of volunteers but later took those found guilty of military infractions (O'Neill 1981:196–7). A more unambiguously suicidal set of missions began in April 1945 and involved the use of planes to crash into bridges, thereby impeding the Soviet armies by then closing in on Berlin. The pilots were reported to have signed the statement 'I am above all else clear that the mission will end in my death' (Beevor 2002: 238).

In contrast to the purely instrumental SMs of Soviet and German forces is the more flamboyant behaviour of the Italian Navy's Tenth Light Flotilla. Most of its work, though highly risky, falls short of our definition of SMs. On one particularly dangerous mission, however, the naval Major Teseo Tesei, who knew that continued operational duty would prove personally fatal due to an existing heart condition, wrote a valedictory message in which he gave as his aim 'winning the highest of all honours, that of giving my life for the King and the honour of the Flag'. He had earlier argued that the mission, an attack on the harbour at Valletta in Malta, should be undertaken to show Italian valour and serve as a model 'to our sons and Italy's future generations'. Tesei's 'pig' (manned-torpedo) detonated against the harbour defensive netting with the aim of breaching it, thereby permitting explosive motor boats to attack enemy ships at anchor. Despite the fulfilment of Tesei's wish, the mission itself was, in military terms, a complete failure (O'Neill 1981: 81–2).

2

Tamil Tigers, 1987–2002

STEPHEN HOPGOOD

The Liberation Tigers of Tamil Eelam (LTTE) have been fighting a war for the national liberation of Tamils living in the north and east of Sri Lanka since the early 1970s.[1] The LTTE began as one of several armed insurgency groups that took the seemingly doomed political struggle for Tamil independence out of the electoral arena and into an armed struggle to set up a separate state to be called 'Tamil Eelam'. For nearly six decades, since the former British colony of Ceylon secured its independence in 1948, the Tamils have experienced systematic and unrelenting discrimination from the majority Sinhalese population in Sri Lanka.[2] The Sinhalese, closely allied to an influential and unusually militant Buddhist clergy, have dominated the political, economic, and cultural life of Sri Lanka throughout this period. Once the simmering armed confrontation became fully fledged open warfare in the 1980s, the LTTE gradually became the dominant force opposing the Sri Lankan state, militarily and politically, showing a remarkable tenacity in resisting a much larger and better equipped national army. Important in this armed resistance, although only a part of it, have been the actions and ensuing reputation of an elite unit, the so-called Black Tigers (including Black Sea Tigers), a band of specially selected and trained LTTE soldiers whose missions give them little chance of survival.[3] The Black Tigers' reputation is such that, under a current ceasefire, Sri Lankan President Chandrika Kumaratunga explicitly asked the LTTE to disband the Black Tigers as a sign of its commitment to the peace process (the LTTE refused) (Jayasinghe 2003).[4]

Said to date from 1987, the Black Tigers carried out numerous successful missions against the Sri Lankan Army (SLA), navy, and air force throughout the 1990s.[5] Although the exact size of the LTTE is a closely guarded secret, an estimate on the *tamilnet* website put the LTTE's strength at 3,000 in 1997.[6] Other estimates are higher, although all confirm that the LTTE is heavily outnumbered by the Sri Lankan armed forces. One news account from 2000 put the LTTE's strength at 5,000–10,000, and the SLA's at 120,000 (*AFP* 2000*a*). By the LTTE's own admission, since 1982 it has suffered nearly 18,000 combat deaths. Of these fatalities, 241 were Black Tigers, male and female, who have died in operations since 1987.[7]

The number of overall 'Black Tiger attacks' is lower than the number of Black Tigers fatalities because some of their missions take place with more than one Black Tiger in the context of land or sea battles and accompanied by regular soldiers, while others are solo missions. It is, however, impossible to estimate accurately. Of the various available estimates, Pape (2003), by running a search on LexisNexis, comes up with the smallest, an unfeasibly low seventy-five.[8] An oft-cited table compiled by *Jane's Intelligence Review* (2000) put the LTTE well ahead of any other armed group undertaking such 'suicide attacks' in terms of number of missions (168), while estimates from other authors are as high as 200. Well-known terrorism research centres—the Israeli Institute for Counter-Terrorism and the US-based National Memorial Institute for the Prevention of Terrorism—have produced data that are far from systematic. Ricolfi (Chapter 3, this volume), in aggregating some such sources, comes up with a plausible figure of 191. The actual figure is probably somewhere between 100 and 200. We simply cannot be more accurate than that. The Black Tigers appear to operate in three distinct ways: conventional combat (land and sea), guerrilla attacks, and targeted assassinations or bombings. The majority of these attacks have involved military objectives in the north and east of the country. Relatively speaking, there have been fewer operations in the south where most of the Sinhalese live, especially in the capital Colombo, although such attacks have often engaged high-profile targets and attracted much international publicity as a result.

Most controversially, the Black Tigers have been accused of several political assassinations, including successful attempts against ex-Indian Prime Minister Rajiv Gandhi (in India) and Sri Lankan President Ranasinghe Premadasa, and a less successful one against the current Sri Lankan President Chandrika Kumaratunga, who lost an eye in an alleged Black Tiger attack. High-casualty bombings of financial targets in Colombo like the Central Bank have also been attributed to the Black Tigers. But the lack of clear evidence, the widespread use of propaganda, the presence of other possible perpetrators, and the frequent refusal of the LTTE to comment, all make it difficult to reach definitive conclusions.[9]

The historical material is clear in broad outline, if not in detail; the pattern of Sinhalese-Buddhist chauvinism and extreme violence against the Tamil population is well documented in a variety of sources. But the difficulty of finding fully reliable empirical material and of gaining access to authoritative sources seriously impairs any work on this subject and inevitably affects this chapter as a whole.[10] Most reliable material on the LTTE is produced only in the Tamil language. Also, the Sri Lankan state is actively engaged in managing the state's public image as an ardent opponent of 'terrorism' through various academic and other sources, and one must presume the LTTE engages in propaganda as well.[11] The evidence, such as it is, is more plentiful on the reasons why the LTTE may have established the Black Tigers to undertake suicide missions (SMs); and it is possible to make some observations, as we will see, about the background factors in their emergence. But operational questions about how Black Tigers are selected and trained and how their targets are chosen and their missions carried out are much harder to answer, and reliable material about the personal motivations of the volunteers themselves is scarce.[12] On operational matters the best available English-language sources are pro-Tamil news websites with which the LTTE cooperates, especially *tamilnet* and *eelamweb*. As a result of these informational limitations, this chapter raises more issues than it resolves, asking questions that will have to await primary empirical research.

These limitations affect other work on the LTTE. In prominent recent accounts about SMs, the LTTE and the war with the Sri Lankan state, though mentioned, have featured to a surprisingly small degree. Pape (2003), for example, stresses the organized nature of the LTTE's 'suicide units' but greatly exaggerates when he describes the LTTE as a Marxist-Leninist group, a claim for which the evidence is scant indeed. Such questionable claims would not matter so much were this a marginal case rather than, arguably, the most sophisticated example of what Pape calls 'suicide terrorism' (inaccurately so, as the LTTE's primary targets have not been civilians). Iannaccone (2003) has only one footnote on the LTTE in his paper and even that is an attempt to suggest that the conflict has a religious dimension—for which, once again, there is virtually no evidence (but see Roberts forthcoming). Pirabakaran is said to be an atheist, for example.

In a different vein, Berman and Laitin (2003) try to link Fearon and Laitin's earlier work (2003) on insurgency to 'terrorist' attacks.[13] This earlier work contains important observations for understanding the origins of the LTTE, including its occupation of difficult terrain (enhancing survival), and a badly organized and 'low information' enemy (the SLA) which tends to 'rely heavily on indiscriminate bombing that has the unintended effect of enriching the pool of potential recruits' (Berman and Laitin 2003).[14] From a comparison of a typical insurgent with a typical suicide bomber, Berman and Laitin (2003: 5), propose the following conjecture:

When insurgency is favored, suicide terrorism decreases in value; on the other hand, where insurgency is not favored, leaders need means alternate from standard insurgency tactics to succeed, and without a guerrilla force as a real threat, insurgents seek through spectacular heroic events demonstrating their tactical prowess and their commitment to the cause to gain advantage over a ruling regime.

Where the Palestine Liberation Organization (PLO) has failed, Hamas has stepped in—that is the authors' implicit frame of reference. This conjecture is not supported by the case of the Black Tigers, which, as noted, is hardly a marginal example. For the LTTE, the Black Tigers have not been a weapon of last resort but an integral part of, even an intensification of, a strategy of insurgency. The LTTE has been dominant in terms of military and political opposition to the government, and the insurgency was well under way before Black Tiger operations began. All of this strongly suggests that all suicide attacks do not have the same organizational motivation. As we will see, the Black Tigers serve two main strategic purposes for the LTTE: first, to compensate for a lack of heavier weaponry; and second, to engage in commando-like actions to secure inaccessible or difficult targets, including assassinations. They are best understood, in other words, as elite soldiers selected for the most dangerous missions—ones with very little chance of survival, and none at all in many cases.

In the sections that follow I deal with a series of questions concerning both organizational and individual motivations. Why were the Black Tigers formed? How and why have they been deployed? Why did the intensity of their use fluctuate? Who becomes a Black Tiger? Why have they acquired such a powerful reputation? The first section gives a brief history of the conflict. The second section looks at the Black Tigers in the context of the LTTE, the third at the Black Tigers as a unit, and the fourth at what little can be said about personal motivations. The conclusion develops some conjectures about the Black Tigers at both the organizational and personal levels.

History of the Conflict

Demographic figures for Sri Lanka tend to rely on the 1981 census as the 2001 census could not be completed in the north (Danish Refugee Council 2000). The population was estimated to be nearly 19 million in 1997, although the conflict has created a large Tamil diaspora, and estimates of the number of internally displaced persons at the time of the 2002 ceasefire were as high as 730,000. Out of this figure of 19 million, approximately 74 per cent are Sinhalese (who speak Sinhala), 18 per cent ethnically Tamil, and 7 per cent Muslim (who also speak Tamil).[15] The Tamil figure is divided between indigenous Tamils and a smaller minority of Indian Tamils brought from Tamil Nadu in the nineteenth century as labourers on the tea plantations in Sri Lanka's central province. These Indian (or 'Estate') Tamils have been as much a target of Sinhalese domination as the indigenous Tamils and it was they who were first stripped of their citizenship immediately after independence in 1948.[16] Tamil populations are in the majority in the north and east of

Sri Lanka (despite efforts by the Sri Lankan government to promote Sinhalese migration into Tamil areas), and there is a sizeable minority population in Colombo, Sri Lanka's capital. In religious terms, the Sinhalese are overwhelmingly Buddhist (with a few Christians), while the Tamils are more than 90 per cent Hindu with a small minority of Christians.

From 1948 onwards the Sinhalese increased their control over Sri Lankan government.[17] This outcome had been feared by Tamil leaders like G.G. Ponnambalam (of the Tamil Congress), who tried until the last minute to persuade the British not to decolonize before adequate minority protections had been established (Wilson 2000: 76–7; also Roberts 2004). After the Indian Tamils were disenfranchised, Sinhala was made the official language of Ceylon in 1956 (after the election of Sinhalese Prime Minister S.W.R.D. Bandaranaike, who promised to make Sinhala the official language within twenty-four hours). The 'Sinhala Only Act' sparked off non-violent civil disobedience by Tamil politicians that immediately provoked the first violent anti-Tamil riots (Swamy 1994: 10–11).[18] These were followed by more serious anti-Tamil riots two years later, in 1958, after Bandaranaike reneged on an agreement in 1957 with Tamil Federal Party leader S. J. V. Chelvanayakam to set up regional councils for the Tamils. Then, in 1959, Bandaranaike was assassinated.[19] Bandaranaike's widow, Sirimavo, followed him as prime minister in 1960.[20] She took an even tougher line with the Tamils, vigorously implementing the Sinhala Only Act (Wilson 2000). With some respite for the Tamils after her election defeat in 1965, Mrs Bandaranaike's return in 1970 prefaced the next and fatal step in the intensification of Tamil resistance.

In 1972, discriminatory legislation was enacted under a new republican constitution.[21] It confirmed Sinhala as the national language, effectively made Buddhism the state religion, changed the country's name from Ceylon to Sri Lanka, eliminated protections for minorities contained in the post-independence constitution of 1947, and—perhaps most far-reaching of all—introduced quotas and unequal examination requirements to prevent Tamils from entering university and public and professional service (especially in medicine and engineering) on merit alone (Bose 1994: 69–71).[22] This 'standardization', as it was called, had the momentous effect of shutting Tamils out of higher education, thereby blighting the employment prospects of a strand of young Tamils from the Jaffna peninsula; Bose (1994: 71) describes them as the 'urban petty-bourgeoisie' who were important as a breeding ground for the LTTE.

Aware that passive resistance was failing, younger Tamils began to contemplate armed struggle. One of the more militant groups was founded in 1972 by Vellupillai Pirabakaran. Called at that time the Tamil New Tigers, in 1976 it was renamed the LTTE. Claims that the LTTE espouses a Marxist-Leninist ideology have little empirical support. Marxist categories were used in the early days of the struggle, and the LTTE's 'theoretician' and political adviser, Anton Balasingham, did bring a Marxist analysis with him when he became more heavily involved in the LTTE from 1979. Pirabakaran is reported to have asserted in 1986 that he espoused revolutionary socialism and defined socialism as 'the construction of an egalitarian society where there is no class contradiction and exploitation of man by man; a free, rational society where human freedom and rights are protected and progress enhanced. Che Guevara is the guerrilla leader who inspires me the most.'[23] But the formal language of the LTTE is overwhelmingly nationalist, not Marxist. It appears to have little more than a general sense of being socially progressive on issues like gender and caste—what Balasingham's wife, Adele, describes as 'social equalitarianism' (Balasingham 2003: 45). Swamy (1994: 51) claims that Pirabakaran has a 'near total disinterest in Marxist politics and ideology'. He describes him as 'quietly pious'; born to a middle-class family, as a young man he idolized the Indian nationalist Subash Chandra Bose. He asserts Pirabakaran would repeat Bose's slogan: 'I shall fight for the freedom of my land until I shed the last drop of blood' (Swamy 1994: 68–9).

Pirabakaran's first high-profile act of violence was the assassination of Alfred Duriappah, mayor of the Tamil capital, Jaffna.[24] As other groups also became more heavily engaged in violent acts against the state, the Tamil United Liberation Front (TULF) fought the 1977 election on the sole issue of obtaining a separate sovereign state, Tamil Eelam, and swept to victory in Tamil areas.[25] Anti-Tamil violence increased in intensity over the next two years, as did attacks by the LTTE and other Tamil groups on the police and other targets, including bank robberies to raise finance (Swamy 1994: 65). After declaring a state of emergency in 1979, President Jayawardene sent the army to occupy Jaffna (Senaratne 1997). Many Tamil militants, including Pirabakaran, fled to Tamil Nadu in India, from where they continued to direct operations. After the Jaffna library, with its 90,000 Tamil books and manuscripts, was torched in 1981, violence again escalated (Senaratne 1997: 65–8).[26] The LTTE dates the war proper to the death of its first combat 'martyr', Lieutenant Shankar, who died on 27 November 1982. This is the date of the LTTE's annual Heroes' Day. Shankar was shot in Jaffna by Sri Lankan soldiers hunting for LTTE cadres after an attack on a police station.

The war began in earnest in 1983. The initial catalyst was an LTTE attack on an army convoy on 23 July 1983 outside Jaffna, in which thirteen soldiers were killed. Pirabakaran himself took part in this attack, according to Swamy (2003: 1–7). Anti-Tamil riots began the following day in Colombo, after the army publicly displayed the soldiers' corpses, and spread throughout

Sri Lanka (Tambiah 1986: 15, 21–2). In the words of Sanmugathasan (1984: 65–6), General Secretary of the Ceylon Community Party:

Tamil shops, houses and business premises were systematically fired. In Colombo at least 500 cars—some with drivers and passengers inside—were burnt. Tamil-owned buses, running between Colombo and Jaffna, were burnt. Tamil patients in hospitals were attacked and killed—some had their throats cut as they lay in their beds. Tamil doctors had their dispensaries and houses burnt and destroyed. In Welikade jail, Tamil detainees were brutally and cold-bloodedly murdered, over two separate days. Thirty-five were killed on the 25th, another seventeen on the 27th in a 'prison riot'.

The riots left as many as 2,000 dead on Tamil estimates (350 according to the government), created up to 100,000 Tamil refugees, and destroyed thousands of Tamil-owned homes, shops, and businesses (Tambiah 1986: 22).[27] As Pfaffenberger (1994: 11) says, Tamils now came to believe that their very survival was possible only in a separate state.[28]

One of the main consequences of the outbreak of war was that the Indian government, and influential politicians in Tamil Nadu, began to train and equip the Tamils, many of them in camps in India. This Indian involvement exacerbated tensions between the rival Tamil groups out of which the LTTE eventually emerged victorious. It also led in 1987 to thousands of troops from an Indian Peacekeeping Force (IPKF) arriving in Sri Lanka under the terms of an India–Sri Lanka Accord signed on 29 July 1987.[29] By October, the LTTE and the IPKF were at war with each other in the north and east. The IPKF was as unwelcome among Sinhalese as it was among the Tamils, and it was forced to withdraw in 1990 after new Sri Lankan President Premadasa allied himself with the LTTE in order to drive IPKF out.

Once the IPKF had left, warfare soon resumed between the LTTE and the Sri Lankan state. It was interrupted only for approximately six months between November 1994 and April 1995, during which time the LTTE and the new government of President Chandrika Kumaratunga conducted peace talks. Their failure was notable because it led in October 1995 to the capture of Jaffna by the SLA, causing a flood of hundreds of thousands of Tamils into the surrounding countryside. The war continued with increasing ferocity until a ceasefire was agreed in February 2002, followed by peace negotiations.[30] During the twenty years of fighting, both sides have been accused of atrocities (see, for example, Amnesty International 1999). A frequent estimate of casualties during this period is 65,000–75,000, but the evidence for this claim is unclear. As mentioned above, the LTTE has admitted to losing nearly 18,000 soldiers since 1982, including Black Tigers. Figures for the Sri Lankan armed forces are not freely available. The figures for civilian deaths, especially of Tamils, are likely to be high given the ferocity of the campaigns the army has waged in the north and east of Sri Lanka, where Tamils are in the vast majority.

The Black Tigers and the LTTE

The First Attack: 1987

The first LTTE suicide attack took place on 5 July 1987.[31] A soldier known as Captain Miller—in a way reminiscent of the first deadly Hezbollah attacks in Lebanon in the early 1980s (see Chapter 3, this volume)—drove a truck packed with explosives into an SLA camp stationed in a former college at Nelliady, in the north of the Jaffna peninsula near Point Pedro.[32] Sources differ on the number of casualties, ranging from 39 to more than 100. Unlike in Lebanon, however, this attack was part of a larger military operation and, once the truck had exploded, regular LTTE cadres followed up, overwhelming the stunned SLA soldiers. This single attack was hugely effective, shocking the Sri Lankan government and stopping a major army offensive, Operation Liberation, in its tracks.

There is no absolute certainty about whether or not Captain Miller was supposed to die in the explosion. A sentence in a *tamilnet* story commemorating this first Black Tiger attack ten years on (in 1997) leaves a margin of doubt by suggesting that 'Miller was unable to get clear and was also killed in the blast'.[33] The LTTE certainly claims Miller as the first Black Tiger, holding Black Tigers' Day on the anniversary of his death each year (a practice that began only after 1990). But it is not clear whether a unit along the lines of the post-1990 Black Tigers, carefully selected and trained, existed at this stage, and furthermore whether the idea of launching 'suicide' attacks had already taken root. Did Miller ever hear the words 'Black Tiger' or was his example, whether intended or otherwise, an inspiration for setting up the Black Tigers to pursue this new tactic? It is impossible to say on the basis of what we know. In his book on the Tamil resistance, Bose (1994: 11) interviews 'Mama' (a *nom de guerre*) whom he describes as 'a member of the "Black Tigers", an elite suicide commando unit'. Mama's attack took place soon after Miller's in Mannar on 27 July 1987. After driving his truck into the camp (he had previously been supplying the camp with provisions), Mama broke into 'a furious run' for cover as the truck exploded, killing on Bose's account sixty-eight soldiers. Mama told Bose (1994: 11–13) his act was one of 'revolutionary violence' against 'state terrorists' and that he would be prepared to make such a 'sacrifice' again to bring the 'day of freedom' nearer. Bose (1994: 12) claims, '[Mama] is also one of only two "Black Tigers" to have ever survived their missions (he got away with an ugly gash on his arm, from the barbed wire, and punctured ear drums from the explosion)'. In other words, Mama tried successfully to escape. Whether or not the term 'Black Tiger' was current at the time, or the unit yet fully established, this account suggests that it is consistent with being a Black Tiger that one tries to evade death as long as the mission objective has been secured.

The exact reason for the use of Black Tigers as part of the LTTE's strategy is unclear. According to Indian journalist Swamy (1994: 97–101), Tamil militants had been abroad for training from the PLO in the 1970s, suggesting that when the first major suicide attacks occurred in 1983 in Lebanon the LTTE would have been aware of them.[34] There is a provoking sentence in Adele Balasingham's book (2003: 55–6) in which she reveals that in 1981 Pirabakaran had to be talked out of an operation to free two members of another Tamil group who were in prison: an operation, she says, which would have been a 'dangerous suicidal mission' for him and his cadres. By this time the wearing of cyanide capsules on a string around the neck by LTTE soldiers was being established. This suggests that the idea of some kind of suicide attack, or at least a unit dedicated to missions of that sort, might have been somewhere in Pirabakaran's mind. Still, there must have been some reluctance to adopt this tactic as it was four years after the war began in earnest in 1983 before Captain Miller's attack occurred. Perhaps the LTTE was unsure about the effectiveness of such a tactic or about how it would be received by the Tamil population.

The decision to begin Black Tiger attacks seems to have been related to an intensification of the Sri Lankan government's military and economic campaign against the LTTE. After 1983, the government established an economic blockade that not only cut off food supplies but also made it harder for the LTTE to obtain raw materials for the weapons it was making, like grenades, mines, and mortars. Then, in mid-1987, the SLA launched a major offensive, Operation Liberation, with increased troop numbers and air and naval power. This offensive involved the establishment of large SLA camps in the north, like that at Nelliady, to subdue the local population. These fixed concentrations of soldiers were simultaneously a significant threat and a tempting target. A large-scale assault without heavy weapons would have been extremely costly for the LTTE at a time when its numbers were relatively small. As it was, Captain Miller's truck bomb was the equivalent of a massive artillery shell delivered with such surprise that the devastated camp could then be (as it was) overwhelmed by LTTE regulars. The power of this blast contrasts with the weapons Swamy (1994: 212) attributes to the LTTE in 1986:

AK-47 rifles, self-loading rifles, light machine guns, heavy machine guns, Singapore assault rifles, M-16 rifles, Mausers...hand grenades, RPGs [rocket propelled grenades], Browning automatic pistols, 25-inch mortars and land and claymore mines.

An impressive enough list for a guerrilla army, but nothing with the firepower of heavy artillery or an air strike. In 1987, Pirabakaran even appealed to the Indian government for help with arms and ammunition (Swamy 2003:

150). Thus, as Operation Liberation continued, the LTTE did not have the heavy conventional weapons required to attack such a large camp. The problem was not explosives, which can be manufactured relatively easily and cheaply. The vast expense of artillery pieces, missiles, and fighter-bombers is all about delivering the explosive to the target. In this case it was difficult: it had to be delivered into the middle of a military camp (rather than being parked in a civilian street, for example). Thus, target and delivery system complemented each other. It is a brutal calculation to have to make, but what the LTTE had was committed volunteers, not the $1 million that each cruise missile costs to deliver its warhead.[35]

Operation Liberation, allied to the negative effects of the economic embargo, substantially increased the tactical value of a Black Tiger-style attack regardless of any enhancement of bargaining power such a demonstration of resolve might generate. The LTTE's use of this new 'weapon' raised the stakes for the government substantially by sending a powerful signal of commitment and capability. If this speculation is correct, the origins and continuation of Black Tiger-style attacks are contingent on their effectiveness. It is not the act itself—killing by suicide—that is the Black Tigers' original or even main aim, but the military impact of the act. That the deliberate sacrifice of a life is a tactical decision not taken lightly is also demonstrated by how relatively sparingly the Black Tigers have been used on SMs.

After 1987, the next SM did not come until 1990, which raises an intriguing question: why were there no Black Tiger attacks against the IPKF between 1987 and 1990?[36] One possible reason is that the selection, training, and operational processes were not yet developed. It is even possible that, had Captain Miller's attack been less successful, the attacks would never have evolved in the way they did. Perhaps Miller was supposed to try to escape, like Mama, and could not or did not for some reason. In other words, it may have been precisely the effectiveness of this first bombing that explains the establishment of what came to be known as the Black Tigers.[37] In this sense, the tactic was new and untested, making it unlikely that trained recruits were ready and willing as 'Black Tigers' to be deployed in conventional combat against the IPKF.

A second reason, if we follow the logic of the argument so far, is related to the likely effectiveness of Black Tigers. For example, IPKF camps were better protected against such attacks, and the Indian army's weaponry, when captured by the LTTE, was superior to that of the SLA and so made the use of Black Tigers less advantageous. The massive size of the IPKF (as many as 100,000 soldiers, according to Senaratne 1997: 93) may also have made large-scale attacks less feasible; the Indian army's occupation of large areas of the north drove the LTTE back into more guerrilla-style tactics, making it harder for members of the LTTE to assemble without detection in big enough numbers to take advantage of a Miller-style truck bomb. This speculation supports the suggestion made above about the lack of trained Black Tigers at this stage. As the IPKF was based in the north and east, and relations with the government of President Premadasa improved to the point where he and the LTTE cooperated in getting India to leave, attacks in the south or on Sinhalese political targets would also have been less likely at this time.

The Number and Type of Missions

Little certain can be said about the total number of Black Tiger attacks. Pape's tally of seventy-five covers naval engagements in which the LTTE has admitted that Black Tigers were used, as well as a large number of assassinations and bombings, although the LTTE rarely confirms or denies involvement in these attacks. The main element missing from his account is the use of Black Tigers under land-battle conditions (see below). The LTTE's acknowledged figure for Black Tiger deaths is also an unreliable guide to the number of attacks as often more than one operative is involved, and Black Tigers do sometimes return from their missions. This makes the lone 'suicide bomber' a misleading image of Black Tiger operations. Between the first Black Tiger death in 1987 and the 2002 ceasefire, there were an average of sixteen Black Tiger deaths each year. If we exclude the years 1987–90, this number increases to an average of twenty.

According to the LTTE's website in 2002, Black Tiger deaths between November 1982 and November 1996 amounted to 94 (out of 9,301 LTTE fighters killed). The updated figures on *eelamweb* (as of November 2003) run to September 2002 (seven months after the ceasefire). These list 17,648 total combat deaths and 241 Black Tiger deaths. From 1996 to 2002, Black Tigers have been killed at a rate approximately one-and-a-half times that before 1996 (147 against 94).[38] The LTTE also released cumulative total figures for Black Tiger deaths in 1997 (105), 1999 (147), 2000 (188), and 2001 (217).[39] These show that, in the five years up to the ceasefire in 2002, the LTTE lost 136 Black Tigers at an annual rate of more than 25. In the year 1999/2000, 41 Black Tigers died.

What explains this? The main strategic differences in this period were the intensification of the conflict along more conventional lines, with several huge set-piece battles between the armies of the SLA and the LTTE, and an increasing number of naval engagements as the LTTE struggled to keep its seaborne lines of supply open in the face of Sri Lankan navy patrols. These battles can be very costly. The 'Voice of Tigers' radio reported the

LTTE as losing nineteen Black Tigers in two simultaneous attacks on one day in February 1998 (out of a total of 150 cadres killed) (*AFP* 1998*a*). February 1998 was a high-casualty month, if the press reports are to be believed: on the 28th the LTTE lost eleven Black Tigers (specifically Black Sea Tigers, including seven women) in an operation to sink two navy ships by ramming them with boatloads of explosives (*AFP* 1998*b*).[40] Throughout these years the SLA was proving a more tenacious opponent, spurred on by improved resources, recruits, and the occupation of Jaffna after 1995, as well as benefiting from the post-cold war arms trade bonanza that included naval vessels, helicopter gunships, fighter-bombers, and heavy artillery from, among others, ex-Soviet Republics, China, and Israel. In other words, it was mainly strategic military necessity that explained the more extensive use of Black Tigers.

Information and propaganda problems are not the only sources of difficulty in accurately estimating the number of Black Tiger attacks. As we can see, these elite soldiers are used for three distinct kinds of missions: combat, guerrilla, and assassination. The LTTE rarely claims (or denies) guerrilla and assassination missions, but the results are almost always so publicized that extensive press coverage makes some attempt at counting feasible. Black Tiger deaths in naval encounters, whether on the surface or using divers, are usually admitted by the LTTE, which lists the names and ranks of the suicide cadres who died. The problems come with deaths in conventional combat, especially those on land. In land battles, the set-piece nature of naval engagements is absent. Various reports suggest the use of Black Tigers in combat, often in quite large numbers, but because the intense fighting may last weeks one ends up with an aggregate figure and little or no information about the way these Black Tigers died. For example, Colonel Balraj, a senior LTTE commander, in describing how the elite Charles Anthony Brigade had fought the SLA over many years in the 1990s for the strategic route to the north of Sri Lanka through Elephant Pass, claimed that 'fifteen Black Tigers of the Charles Anthony formation sacrificed their lives for its many victories and for this country'.[41]

These Black Tigers are used to try to secure difficult targets or to lead offensive operations. Some scholars allege that Black Tigers function in these battles as 'human waves' leading the assault so as to make an initial breach that the regular soldiers can then exploit.[42] One attack of this sort, reported by *Agence France Presse* (*AFP*), concerned an assault on the town of Paranthan in September 1996 in which LTTE regulars were said to have followed up the Black Tigers' initial strike (Jayasinghe 1996). The whole idea of a 'human wave' is somewhat misleading, especially as the relatively small number of Black Tiger deaths suggests they are used in anything but an indiscriminate way.[43] Other accounts of LTTE attacks suggest that a few

Black Tigers make the initial strike, followed by much larger numbers of regulars. The goal of the Black Tigers in these conventional operations appears to be to destroy army fortifications. Such tactical aims further support the argument for a military rationale: Black Tigers provide accuracy compared with imprecisely targeted artillery shells. If the success of a whole battle—and the lives of many hundreds of regular soldiers—depends on an accurate initial strike, the benefits of having the explosives delivered personally to the target are obvious.

This point about the majority of Black Tigers being used for conventional military objectives, and only then for guerrilla operations and assassinations, is further supported by the relative lack of Black Tiger operations in the south since November 2000. According to the Indian magazine *Frontline* (Subramanian 2001*a*), after meeting Norwegian peace negotiator Eric Solheim, Pirabakaran agreed to suspend attacks in the south in order to get talks going with the government, and possibly also in return for a relaxation of the economic blockade. These operations tended to be attacks on political and military figures, and on infrastructure and economic targets. After 2000, the only major Black Tiger attack in the south came at Katunayake air force base and Bandaranaike civilian airport, which are located next to each other near Colombo (see below). This attack was designed to stop an intensified aerial bombing campaign against the Tamils which was itself a result of LTTE successes. After making progress in 1998 and 1999, the SLA lost much of its territory very quickly when the LTTE launched a major offensive, Unceasing Waves 3, in November 1999.[44] By April 2000 the SLA had lost Elephant Pass, a key negotiating asset. The SLA was therefore cut off in the north and had to be supplied by sea. This inaugurated the intensified air campaign.

Target Selection

Black Tiger attacks aim primarily to win the war, not to spread terror. As a result, there are no clear examples of civilians being directly targeted by SMs (although there have been many civilian casualties).[45] If inflicting military and economic damage on the Sri Lankan state is the first objective, these attacks do have the inherent and (for the LTTE) welcome side effect of signalling resolve and strength to the enemy. We have noted, for example, that President Kumaratunga sought the disbandment of the Black Tigers as a signal of the LTTE's commitment to peace. It is also illuminating that, when the LTTE ended the peace talks of 1994–5, alleging that the government of Mrs Kumaratunga was preparing for a new military offensive, it did so with a Black Tiger attack (using underwater divers) against two warships in Trincomalee harbour, a key supply point for the Sri Lankan military.[46] This was a military target of importance, but the use of Black Tigers also sent a message to Kumaratunga.

The targets the Black Tigers have attacked obviously fit the roles for which they are trained. Conventional warfare goals include taking territory, strategic assets, and weapons, destroying enemy military resources, and maximizing enemy casualties: hence their goals of controlling Elephant Pass or sinking Sri Lankan gunboats. These targets have also included what we might call 'infrastructure'.[47] These are more likely to be the province of those trained in guerrilla operations. In 1995 it was claimed that eight Black Tigers died attacking Sri Lanka's main oil depot outside Colombo and destroying 25 per cent of the country's oil reserves (Spaeth and Pratap 1995).[48] Financial centres have also been targets. Perhaps the most notorious attack of this kind, blamed on the LTTE, was the bombing of Sri Lanka's Central Bank in Colombo in 1996, in which more than eighty people were killed (*The Times* 1996).

The third category of targets—assassinations—is the most controversial. The list of assassinations attributed to the LTTE is long. It includes many local officials, such as policemen, and also ministers and defence and senior military personnel. It also includes Tamils who have been associated in one way or another with making concessions to Sinhalese governments. It is alleged, for example, that the LTTE assassinated the vice-president of the TULF, Neelan Thiruchelvam, in a suicide attack on his car in 1999. The most high-profile failed attempt attributed to the LTTE was that on President Kumaratunga at an election rally for her People's Alliance party in 1999. Given the long history of antipathy between the president and the LTTE, and the president's singular zeal in continuing the war against the Tamils, her death might be considered as much a military as a political goal. In the explosion, she escaped with serious injuries to her right eye while more than twenty people were killed and many others injured. This trademark Black Tiger attack obviously sent a potent message to her and her electorate. As usual, the LTTE declined to comment. Spaeth and Pratap (1995) claim that, much earlier than this, in 1995, a 24-year-old Black Tiger named Sinnadurai Mukundan masqueraded as a journalist and spent ten weeks stalking Kumaratunga looking for a weakness in her personal security.

The LTTE has been accused of the assassination of another president, Premadasa, in 1993, although he was equally loathed by the political right wing in Sri Lanka, especially the People's Liberation Front (JVP), which rose up again during the IPKF occupation in the late 1980s.[49] The LTTE has also explicitly denied killing Premadasa, who was suspected by opposition politicians of having had their leader assassinated just days before his own death (*AFP* 1993). Of all these allegations of assassination, the most notorious is that of Rajiv Gandhi in Tamil Nadu in 1991. This was outside Sri Lanka, of course, and Pirabakaran has explicitly denied, according to the BBC, ordering the assassination.[50] Yet the notion persists that it was an LTTE operation, designed probably to prevent Gandhi being re-elected as prime minister, an office he lost after sending the IPKF into Sri Lanka, and considering reintervention. The story is that a young LTTE woman named Dhanu, presumably a Black Tiger, detonated an explosive jacket she was wearing as she bowed in front of Gandhi while he was making an election visit to the province (Swamy 1994: 332–4).[51] According to *The Times* (1992), there were other Tamil suicide bombers present to support this operation, of whom four died in the explosion while others committed suicide by taking cyanide. Eventually, four alleged members of the LTTE were sentenced to death in India.[52] Still, in one of the most informed books on the LTTE, Dagmar Hellmann-Rajanayagam (1994: 118–20) casts some doubt on its responsibility for Gandhi's assassination, describing its effect in terms of creating hostility inside Tamil Nadu as a 'disaster'.

In his book on the failure of the 1994–5 Jaffna peace talks, chief Tamil negotiator Balasingham (2000) offers an intriguing possible reason for one notorious assassination, suggesting the LTTE has a long memory. He refers to the assassination by suicide bombing of Gamini Dissanayake, a presidential candidate, at an election rally in 1994 (the election that Kumaratunga won). The LTTE, blamed by Dissanayake's United National Party (UNP), refused to comment and the government also refrained from blaming the Tigers. Balasingham (2000: 33) goes on:

It is widely speculated in the Tamil political circles that the assassination was carried out by the LTTE for the central role played by Gamini Dissanayake in burning down the Jaffna Public Library in 1981, reducing to ashes 90,000 volumes of invaluable and irreplaceable historical books and archives—a deed condemned as an act of cultural genocide against the Tamils.

One further assassination deserves brief mention. On 7 June 2000, the LTTE allegedly killed industry minister C.V. Gooneratne on the first occasion of a newly inaugurated War Heroes' Day. He was at a parade to collect contributions for Sri Lankan troops. Such timing suggests that signalling, as much as targeting a key representative of the enemy, may have been a consideration in this case (*AFP* 2000*b*).

The chances of Black Tiger survival depend crucially on the target. Assassinations in which the explosives are strapped to the operative give no chance unless the whole operation is called off. Conventional conflict gives slightly better odds, perhaps, although ramming ships with boats packed with explosives is presumably always fatal. Achieving the objective in these cases will require the death of the agent not because of any signalling considerations about resolve but because the target cannot be achieved without it. The one type of Black Tiger operation in which returning alive is feasible seems to be guerrilla attacks. These rely, of course, on surprise and this may be what gives the operatives their chance. They must remain hidden as long as possible in order to fully infiltrate the enemy's territory and secure the objective, which improves the chances of survival in the ensuing confusion.

One of the most ambitious of all Black Tiger guerrilla attacks, and also one of the last, was on both the Katunayake air force base and the adjacent Bandaranaike International Airport on 24 July 2001 (the airports are just outside Colombo; 24 July is the anniversary of the 1983 LTTE attack on the SLA that inaugurated the war proper). This appears to be the only major exception to an informal cessation of Black Tiger operations in the south after 2000. Indeed, the well-informed D.B.S Jeyaraj claims the LTTE had planned and trained for the attack in 2000, but after Pirabakaran agreed to the Norwegian request to suspend operations in the south it was called off, despite continued government bombing.[53] Its rationale, as already noted, was to hinder the intense bombing of the north by the Sri Lankan air force, using its Israeli-built Kfir fighter bombers, and to target the Sri Lankan tourist trade. It was also retaliation against a particularly heavy bombing raid in the north on 30 June. Some detail of this attack is provided by Jansz (2001), who claims the 'dreaded Tiger suicide squad and fighters' had arrived at the base dressed in air force lookalike boots and jackets. They cut through a fence and appeared to know where security mines were buried. She claims: 'Having studied easily accessible flight schedules, the Tigers were aware that early on Tuesday not a single international carrier was expected.'[54] The LTTE cadres watched a wheelchair passenger disembark from the last plane to land that night. Then, explosions at the adjacent air force base were followed by an attack on Sri Lankan Airlines aeroplanes on the ground. The fighting appeared to last for several hours. Jansz claims that two Airbus A330s and one A340 were destroyed at a cost of $330 million, with serious damage to three other Airbuses. Military aircraft destroyed included two Kfirs, two Mi-17 helicopter gunships, one MiG-27 fighter, and three Chinese K-8 trainer aircraft (Subramanian 2001*a*). Fatalities included either thirteen or fourteen Black Tigers and six security personnel.[55] No civilians were killed.

This hugely successful attack was also caught on video by Black Tigers who returned from the operation. Another newspaper, *The Island*, reported in September 2001 that footage of the attack, prefaced by scenes in which the Black Tigers share a meal before their mission with Pirabakaran, was shown in the north and east in an effort to increase recruitment. This same account stresses that Pirabakaran and the LTTE believed they could win the war against the Sri Lankan government, citing unidentified sources who claimed that Black Tigers would soon be used against further economic targets (the port of Colombo is mentioned). It claimed that the LTTE was under virtually no pressure on the battlefield in the north and east and could therefore concentrate on Colombo (*The Island* 2001).

These targets suggest careful planning and selection; with the Katunayake attack so well prepared it could be suspended for a while and then carried out later. They have also required different means. Delivery mechanisms for the explosives have included trucks, motorcycles, boats, and bicycles. One press report even claimed Thai security forces had discovered a 'midget submarine' the LTTE was having built in Thailand (*The Statesman* 2000). The most notorious delivery means are the explosive jackets that Black Tigers can detonate at will (Harris 2002). These jackets may be essential in the case of certain political assassinations, but their rationale in guerrilla and battle conditions is unclear. In attacks on fortified positions they may be essential for delivering the charge, while in guerrilla operations they may function as a more damaging form of cyanide capsule, to be detonated at the last minute to evade capture.

In none of these examples was damage to civilians, or the spreading of 'terror', a principal motivation. On the assumption that the LTTE was responsible for these attacks, the deaths of civilians seem to have been 'collateral damage', a side effect of assassinations since it is only in public places that the required access to high-profile politicians is available.[56] Given the evident success of the LTTE in using SMs militarily, a wave of civilian-targeted attacks in restaurants and shops in Colombo, for example, would be devastating. As we saw in the Katunayake case, however, avoiding civilian deaths is an important consideration. It is not that there is no danger to civilians in the south. Many died in bombings of the Central Bank in Colombo and in the attack on Kumaratunga. But civilians are neither the sole nor intended targets of such attacks.[57] This was recognized by the United States in late September 2001 when a US embassy spokesman in Colombo, Stephen Holgate, distinguished the LTTE from al-Qaeda because 'the LTTE is not involved in unbridled terror, has specific political demands and is not averse to negotiations' (Jeyaraj 2001).

In his 'Heroes' Day' message of 2001, made after September 11, Piraba-karan told Sri Lankans:

We are not enemies of the Sinhala people, nor is our struggle against them. It is because of the oppressive policy of the racist Sinhala politicians that contradictions arose between the Sinhala and Tamil nations, resulting in a war. We are fighting this war against a state and its armed forces determined to subjugate our people through the force of arms. We are well aware that this war has not only affected the Tamils but also affects the Sinhala people deeply. Thousands of innocent Sinhala youth have perished as a consequence of the repressive policies of the war mongering elites.[58]

In the same message, Pirabakaran also called on Western states to redefine terrorism to exclude groups like the LTTE, which had a 'concrete political objective' and was fighting 'for the love of a noble cause, that is, human freedom'. The Tigers were not terrorists he said:

Western democratic nations should provide a clear and comprehensive definition of the concept of terrorism that would distinguish between freedom struggles based on the right to self-determination and blind terrorist acts based on fanaticism. (Subramanian 2001*b*)

We now turn to the Black Tigers themselves.

The Black Tigers as a Unit

Recruitment

Black Tigers are drawn from the regular ranks of the LTTE and they write letters addressed to Pirabakaran requesting selection. In an interview said to be with a commander called Karikalan, described as the LTTE's 'political number three', the recruitment process was explained as follows:

To become Black Tigers, our cadre must apply in writing to our leader, Mr Velupillai Prabhakaran. He then goes through the applications, looking at the applicant's particular skills, the kinds of missions he or she has been involved in, their motivations and their family situation. Are they an only son or daughter? Do they have dependents? All these things are considered, after which the applicant is told whether he can become a Black Tiger. (Elliott 2003)

According to Thamilini, a senior female LTTE member, the reply to a letter requesting selection was sometimes 'an outright refusal'. More often, the answer was: 'There are many applicants. Do what duties are sent to you. If the necessity arises we'll call you' (Waldman 2003). Thamilini confirms that those selected undergo 'intense physical and psychological training' and that the motivations of highly disciplined Black Tigers are not to be compared with those of Palestinian suicide bombers. She is quoted as saying: 'People dejected in life won't be able to go as Black Tigers. . . . There must be a clear conception of why and for what we are fighting. A deep humanitarianism is very necessary—a love of others, for the people' (Waldman 2003).

There are suggestions of forced recruitment into both the LTTE and the Black Tigers, but this seems implausible. Hellmann-Rajanayagam (1994: 66) argues, for example, that the LTTE does not seek widespread entry into its ranks. It is much more exclusive than this, she says, seeking strong, committed fighters. She maintains:

Apart from its demands for moral—and financial—support LTTE sees comparatively little scope for the population at large in the armed fight. Active fight is not something to be taken up by everybody; on the contrary, the ritual acceptance into the movement is quite tough and elaborate, it is a society in itself.... Though the LTTE now presents itself as a conventional army, this is not considered to be a fight on a mass basis, which involves a major part of the people in armed conflict, and there is no general mobilisation or conscription. This would run counter to LTTE's philosophy and probably in its eyes weaken its fighting strength. Its soldiers have to be committed and they do not trust in the run-of-the-mill Jaffna man to be that. It is actually an honour to be a member of the LTTE, and this membership is not open to everybody. Given this structure of the movement one would not expect it to go in for forced recruitment, as has been alleged, since it would be extremely difficult to foster this commitment among forced recruits. New recruits have to undergo a fairly rigorous training and trial period before they are accepted.

This was written in 1994. In 1997 *tamilnet* claimed that:

Despite the need for more front-line troops, the LTTE instructors say that they would prefer to send fully trained fighters to the front. 'There is no point rushing them to the front to die for lack of preparation' said one. 'A handful of good fighters are more useful than a battalion of lambs.'[59]

It is possible that recruitment has at times been a higher priority than these accounts suggest. Heroes' Day began in 1989, for example, and may have come about in part as a way to try to recruit new members (especially under pressure from the IPKF intervention). In the same way, inaugurating Black Tigers' Day after 1990 may have been an attempt to 'advertise' the Black Tigers to aid recruitment. The extensive documentary and drama footage the LTTE produces obviously serves to maintain interest and support amongst the Tamil diaspora, but it may also have the added advantage of attracting new recruits. Suicide bombing is a high-profile way of signalling to one's recruitment constituency that one is serious. There is no evidence, however, that the choice for Tamils is, as it would have been twenty years ago, between joining rival Tamil resistance groups; it is now between civilian life and joining the LTTE.

Training

What little we know about the training of Black Tigers confirms the picture of them as thoroughly prepared professional soldiers.[60] The LTTE is a regular army, distinct and separate from the surrounding Tamils, with bases in the jungle, uniforms, selection processes, ranks, and so forth. According to *Jane's Intelligence Review* (2000), 'As the quality of targets chosen by the LTTE is high, it has a sophisticated training programme that lasts for about a year.' Joshi's account (2000) of a young Tamil considering becoming a Black Tiger suggests:

If Mahendran seeks to join the suicide squads, he will undergo six months of arduous training at a Tiger camp; at the end he will swear an oath of personal loyalty to the Tigers' leader, Velupillai Prabhakaran and place an amulet containing a cyanide capsule around his neck.

This sort of training, and the wearing of a suicide capsule, is a feature of joining the LTTE, not just the Black Tigers. The exact details of the training are difficult to discern. As Black Tiger volunteers are drawn from the ranks of the LTTE, all recruits will already have gone through the training process described for one 18-year-old LTTE volunteer as follows:

At an LTTE boot camp in the Vanni scrub, he and dozens of other recruits are going through basic training. Though he is eager to strike back at the Sinhalese troops, it will be several months before he will see combat. He has not been given a weapon yet. As in many armies the world over, the next few months will be spent learning basic infantry skills, developing fitness and assisting rear echelon LTTE units.[61]

It is likely, therefore, that the time spent undergoing the next phase of training if one is accepted into the Black Tigers is devoted to building up mental strength and honing the specific skills for particular kinds of operation. For seaborne missions, for example, Black Sea Tigers must presumably master various maritime skills, as divers must learn to use breathing apparatus.

A further issue arises here. If the gaps between civilian life and the LTTE, and between the LTTE and the Black Tigers, constitute two steps towards more or less certain death, then the 'posting' one gets is a third. As we have seen, assassinations and sea battles give no real hope of survival, while guerrilla attacks have slightly improved chances. It is presumably consistent with the ethos of the Black Tigers that, once one has been trained, and death is an expectation, the decision as to where one will be most effective is made by recruiters, most likely on the basis of aptitude and skills. If a Black Tiger spoke Sinhala, he or she might be more likely to be deployed in a unit in Colombo rather than in an infantry brigade, for example. Is there scope for volunteering or choosing here? Again, we know too little to say.

Much training presumably develops the same discipline of body and mind required by an elite professional soldier as in any unit of this sort anywhere in the world. This mental preparation is crucial if one is to wait to be called on for a mission perhaps quite some time in the future (see Chapter 7, this volume, on 'the difficulty of waiting'). The emphasis on personal discipline is very strong throughout the LTTE and lies at the heart of allegations that

Pirabakaran has somehow developed a personality cult. Many accounts talk of the stress Pirabakaran puts on disciplined personal habits, from sexual propriety and personal appearance to restrictions on smoking, drinking, and even card playing.[62] Balasingham (2003: 338) says:

Courage in human beings is, for Pirabakaran, an admirable trait. He admires and respects manifestations of bravery, not only in his cadres, but people in general. Courage is inextricably linked to a positive and certainly inspiring feature of his character, which is that of not being subdued or deterred by anything in life, no matter how formidable and powerful it may be. He has an indomitable will and confidence that anything can be achieved if the mind is applied and focused on the project.

One cannot read off the discipline instilled in individual Black Tigers from Pirabakaran's own, of course. Black Tigers are individuals who must volunteer, train, and often die through the force of their own will. Nevertheless, as a unit they seem to embody a spirit of ultimate sacrifice and it may well be this that the Black Tiger training is designed to instil (see Pratap 2001:102–4). According to Schalk (1997: 79):

Pirapaharan says: 'The death of a liberation hero is not a normal event of death. This death is an event of history, a lofty ideal, a miraculous event which bestows life. The truth is that a liberation fighter does not die. . . . Indeed, what is called "flame of his aim" which has shone for his life will not be extinguished. This aim is like a fire, like a force in history and it takes hold of others. The national soul of the people has been touched and awakened.'

It is said that every Black Tiger has a final meal and a photograph taken with Pirabakaran.[63] This may not be plausible for every Black Tiger given that Pirabakaran moves around, the Black Tiger camps are presumably dispersed, and it would require Pirabakaran to have oversight of operations at a very detailed level. Pirabakaran may, indeed, have a photograph taken with each Black Tiger, or with a Black Tiger unit, and even a meal with a group of them, but perhaps at some point in their training or when they graduate. With so few deaths in fifteen years, some personal attention is certainly feasible, and the aura of the Black Tigers that adds so much to their mythology is certainly enhanced by this sense of receiving special attention from the LTTE's revered leader. Yet the suggestion of this last, ritual meal plays again into enduring myths about the Black Tigers. First, the symbolism of the last meal signifies some kind of religious devotion, whether to Pirabakaran or to a more formal religious system. Second, it isolates the lone 'suicide bomber' rather than the missions in which several Black Tigers are involved in cooperation with regular cadres, often in battle situations where the use or otherwise of a Black Tiger may be a decision made in a relatively short time frame.

The Black Tigers' Symbolic Power

Nevertheless, the symbolic power of the Black Tigers is obviously not lost on the LTTE. Even if their rationale is a military one, the personal example set by individual Black Tigers has come to embody the notion of self-sacrifice for the cause of Tamil Eelam as captured in the LTTE's chanted refrain: 'The task (or thirst) of the Tigers (is to achieve) Motherland Tamililam' (Schalk 1997: 64). In a speech on the 1996 Black Tigers' Day, Pirabakaran described them as 'the men of flame', the 'self-protective armour of our race' (*AFP* 1996a). On the same day in 1993, he said:

I have groomed my weak brethren into a strong weapon called Black Tigers . . . They are the balls of fire smashing the military prowess of the enemy with sheer determination. The Black Tigers are different and are also unique human beings. They possess an iron will, yet their hearts are so very soft. They have deep human characteristics of perceiving the advancement of the interest of the people through their own annihilation. The Black Tigers have cast aside fear from its very roots. Death has surrendered to them. They keep eagerly waiting for the day they would die. They just don't bother about death. This is the era of Black Tigers. No force on earth today can suppress the fierce uprising of the Tamils who seek freedom. (Swamy 2003: 243–4)

The signs of this symbolic power are highly visible. The names of Black Tigers (including Black Sea Tigers) are publicized by the LTTE, often with their ranks, after their operations so they can be honoured in Tamil newspapers and on the various Tamil websites. It is part of the secrecy surrounding them that most regular LTTE cadres do not know whether their comrades are trained as Black Tigers. A *tamilnet* story on the 2003 Black Tigers' Day celebration in Vavuniya claimed:

Black Tigers' identities are closely guarded. Having completed their training, they serve in regular LTTE units, concealing their membership. When called up for a mission, they take routine leave and if they survive, return to regular service again. Membership is only revealed if they are killed in combat.[64]

This has a security dimension, of course, but it also adds to the Black Tigers' aura. In the casualty figures for the war since 1982 released by the LTTE, only the toll for Black Tigers is recorded separately (rather than for other elite units like the so-called Leopard Commandos). While there is one Heroes' Day for the movement as a whole (27 November), the Black Tigers are the only unit to have their own day—5 July—the anniversary of Captain Miller's attack. News coverage on *tamilnet* of each year's Black Tigers' Day celebrations shows them occurring throughout the north and east of Sri Lanka.

Particular districts construct memorials to Black Tigers who came from their areas. In Trincomalee in 2003, *tamilnet* reported a memorial being opened to sixteen Black Tigers as well as to Captain Miller and the first female Black Tiger, Angayarkanni, who were from the district.[65] Another report talks about Captain Miller's mother lighting a flame of remembrance in 2002 at Nelliady (close relatives seem to be involved in these celebrations).[66] These memorials consist of a photograph that is garlanded with flowers on Black Tigers' Day and a 'flame of sacrifice' lit in front of each one. In a similar vein, in Batticaloa an LTTE official from the region quoted Pirabakaran as saying that the Black Tigers 'use their mental strength to break the military strength of the enemy forces'.[67] Black Tiger tombstones are distinguished only by having the words 'Black Tiger' written on them. A report on the Canadian Tamil website about Black Tigers' Day in 2002 says that pictures of all 241 Black Tigers were prominently displayed so people could pay their respects.[68] Red and yellow Tamil Eelam flags are a common sight on these occasions, along with posters announcing Black Tigers' Day. The SLA, it is reported, tries to stop shops and offices from closing on that day and threatens forcibly to reopen them.[69]

In sum, Black Tigers embody the sacrifices required to win Tamil liberation, and thus they play a prominent role in boosting Tamil resolve and morale. It is important, therefore, that they are a disciplined and impressive military unit. They are an inspiration for Tamils. This, too, is a reason for the emphasis on high-quality training, personal discipline, and preparation: if they are to be a source of pride, they must be soldiers one can be proud of.

As well as embodying a sense of sacrifice, the Black Tigers' willingness to give their lives also communicates strong commitment to their Sri Lankan adversary. As *tamilnet* is happy to point out:

The Black Tigers constitute a successful military unit that has inflicted disproportionately severe physical and psychological damage on the Sri Lankan military, the latter with the help of the Sri Lankan government's own propaganda.[70]

Some authors see in this willingness to sacrifice life the signs of a cult. Schalk (1997) has written of a 'cult of martyrdom', as have Roberts (1996, forthcoming) and Reuter (2004). There is little doubt, as numerous sources attest, that Pirabakaran is uniquely dominant in the LTTE and that he exercises powerful and highly effective personal control over the functioning of the organization (see Pratap 2001; Swamy 2003). In no other case where SMs are used is there a leader who is both as revered *and* as much a part of the day-to-day struggle. But this is not enough to account for the organizational rationale behind the Black Tigers, unless they exist just to perpetuate a 'cult' of personal devotion at a collective level to Pirabakaran. The 'cult' has to be *for* something. It has to serve a purpose *at the organizational level*. Given the absence of any powerful transcending religious or political ideology, and the ubiquitous statements of attachment only to the cause of national liberation, the best explanation for the adoption of SMs at the collective level is as a tactic in a wider military strategy for victory in a war of uneven force. The psychological impact of Black Tiger operations is significant, and may well attract volunteers and undermine the enemy's resolve. It may even be deliberately used by the LTTE to achieve this double effect. But the driving rationale is military not symbolic, as that of the cyanide capsules is to prevent damaging revelations being made under torture.

A further question concerns the reaction of non-LTTE Tamils and the Tamil diaspora to the attacks. On the diaspora side, funding from Tamils, especially in Europe, Canada, and the United States, has been important in sustaining the LTTE, but there is no indication that this affects the decisions made by Pirabakaran and his commanders about military tactics. There is no evidence of any pressure, for example, on the LTTE not to undertake Black Tiger missions where civilians may get killed.[71]

Relations between the LTTE and the Tamils in Sri Lanka are complex, making it difficult to see clearly what kind of audience this background population might be. This is for at least three reasons: historical contests, social order, and war support. In terms of *historical contests*, details of the long-running and often very violent struggles among different Tamil militant groups can be found in various books (for example, Swamy 1994, 2003; Hellmann-Rajanayagam 1994). Even when confronted by an Indian government effort after 1987 to create various anti-LTTE coalitions during the time of the IPKF, the LTTE emerged victorious and has had no serious challengers for at least a decade and probably longer. Thus the Tamils have no serious alternative to the LTTE. The LTTE also provides discipline and *social order* in much of the north and east, running a shadow state system of courts, police, and so on. The LTTE raises taxes from local businesses (the rates have even been published in Jaffna newspapers), and these tariffs are enforced with sanctions against non-payers. Thus, the LTTE is not a detached guerrilla army; it is an integral part of Tamil society in the north and east. The LTTE also seeks other forms of aid from the local population to provide *war support*, but the details of this are sketchy—some claim the LTTE requires 'one child per family', money, or help with activities like digging trenches or logistics. The discipline evident in the LTTE's selection and training means that we should treat the 'one-child-per-family' claim, like allegations of enforced conscription,with caution until better information is available.[72]

As these accounts suggest, the LTTE is selective, with access to its ranks and promotion within them a scarcer good than may have been appreciated. Scarce goods (where demand outstrips supply) tend to attract status, and so entry to the LTTE may also be reflected in the even tougher competition to get into the Black Tigers. This is then nurtured through the camaraderie that is a feature of all successful military elites, a sense of collective endeavour fostered intensely within the LTTE through the award of one's cyanide capsule, the daily oath of commitment to Pirabakaran, and the struggle for Tamil Eelam. But this goes for the LTTE as a whole, not just the Black Tigers. Why take the extra step towards death? It is to this decision that we now turn.

Why do LTTE Cadres Volunteer to Become Black Tigers?

Members of the LTTE tend to be young, although we do not know very much about the ratios of men to women, the married to the unmarried, or how many may have children (see above on Pirabakaran's selection criteria). It is impossible to say whether those who volunteer for the Black Tigers share a quality of some significance that distinguishes them from their comrades. We do not know how many apply, how many are rejected, whether any change their minds, or how many fail the training and what happens to them then. There are alternatives to the Black Tigers, like the prestigious Charles Anthony infantry brigade in which many LTTE recruits may prefer to serve. We do not know if Black Tigers are 'tested' in some way to demonstrate their mental strength. The camaraderie of Black Tiger training may be very important in encouraging a sense of duty and obligation on missions, especially to one's comrades (rather than to the more abstract goal of Tamil Eelam). It may be that a great many LTTE cadres apply and it is therefore the selection criteria of the recruiters that explain the sociological characteristics of the Black Tigers. Knowing someone who has volunteered may also make one more likely to volunteer. There is no strong evidence that Black Tigers are forcibly recruited or that they are somehow drugged into joining. Everything we have seen militates against this account, including the strong discipline that Pirabakaran tries to instil in his soldiers. What we do have is circumstantial evidence about why people join the LTTE, about their willingness to embrace danger and contemplate death, and about how suicide of this non-despairing kind (non-suicidal suicide, as it were) is viewed among the Tamils more widely.

The LTTE provides very little detailed information about Black Tiger deaths. For example, unlike for total LTTE deaths, it does not break down Black Tiger deaths by gender (Table 2.1).

An earlier table, taken from the same website in 2001, did make this gender breakdown for the numbers up to 1996 (Table 2.2).

The participation of women fighters in the LTTE has increased dramatically in the 1990s, including their promotion to more senior roles, and there is no reason not to expect this to be true of the Black Tigers as well. The ratio of dead female LTTE fighters to men has (very approximately) doubled from 1:8 to 1:4. If the same were to be true of Black Tiger numbers, the 147 Black Tiger deaths since 1996 would include at least 30 women and may even have

TABLE 2.1. Breakdown of Tamil and Black Tigers killed, 27 November 1982–30 September 2002

	Female	Male	Total
Total Black Tigers	—	—	241
Total LTTE fighters killed	3,766	13,882	17,648

Source: www.eelamweb.com/maveerar/statistics.

TABLE 2.2. Breakdown of Tamil and Black Tigers killed, 27 November 1982–30 November 1996

	Female	Male	Total
Black Tigers	0	33	33
Black Sea Tigers	16	45	61
Total Black Tigers killed	16	78	94
Total LTTE fighters killed	1,079	8,222	9,301

Source: Official LTTE website statistics of LTTE fighters who died (1982–1996), found in 2001 at www.eelamweb.com/maveerar/statistics.

been higher if women were also involved in land attacks (the reasons for the gender distinction in terms of sea/land operations are noteworthy but again unanswerable at this stage).[73]

The first death by suicide, specifically by cyanide, linked to the armed Tamil struggle was that of Ponnudarai Sivakumaran in 1974 after a failed bank raid. Sivakumaran, one of many founders of armed Tamil resistance, was known to Pirabakaran, and Swamy (1994: 26) suggests he was linked to various assassination attempts in the early 1970s. During a bank robbery, Sivakumaran was surrounded by police and, fearing torture, he took a suicide pill he carried with him for the purpose of ending his own life in such a situation. Says Swamy (1994: 28–9): 'Thus was born Sri Lanka's cyanide culture.'[74] After a very well-attended public funeral, a statue was erected to Sivakumaran in Jaffna showing him with a clenched fist and dangling a broken chain (Swamy 1994: 29).

According to Schalk, other methods of suicide were considered at first. The decision to systematically use cyanide was not just Pirabakaran's alone. The first recorded case, he says, of death by cyanide in the LTTE occurred in 1984. The reasoning behind taking the cyanide is, Schalk (1997: 75–6) argues, twofold. First, it is to protect the LTTE from information that captured cadres may divulge under torture, and second, it is to show commitment by signalling that one has overcome the fear of death. This does not really deal with individual motivation as distinct from a group interest or dynamic, although, at an individual level, taking cyanide is a wise precaution against torture. And torture is to be expected as it seems to be endemic in the war, with each side making allegations against the other. The Medical Foundation for the Victims of Torture produced a report (2000), for example, on forty-nine Tamils seeking help in the United Kingdom as survivors of torture. Many claimed they had been harassed or ill-treated by the LTTE, and even that they had been coerced into various pro-LTTE activities, but that they had all suffered far more serious torture at the hands of the SLA, which arrested them in the north after 1995 when Jaffna was taken. The purpose both of the arrest and of the torture seems to have been to extract information about the LTTE.

The single most notorious episode of taking cyanide involved seventeen senior LTTE commanders who were intercepted by the Sri Lankan navy in October 1987 in contravention of the India–Sri Lanka Accord that granted an amnesty to all Tamil militants. According to Swamy (1994: 265), the cadres' cyanide capsules were removed upon capture. Fearing being taken to Colombo for torture and execution, the seventeen asked for more cyanide. Before visiting the prisoners, Anton Balasingham and an LTTE commander, Mahattaya, each put several capsules around their necks (Pirabakaran gave them his). During the visit the cyanide was transferred and the detainees later took the poison, twelve dying and five surviving (Balasingham 2003: 139). This incident is said by Swamy (2003: 176–8) to have been the catalyst for turning LTTE–IPKF confrontation into actual combat.

In addition to cyanide, there are examples in which the threat of death by fasting has been made and carried through by LTTE members (unlike in Tamil Nadu, there seems to be no well-documented case of Tamil self-immolation by fire in the Sri Lankan case; on self-immolation, see Chapter 5, this volume). Pirabakaran himself started a fast to death in Tamil Nadu in the early 1980s after the LTTE's priceless communications equipment was confiscated by the police (it was soon returned) (Swamy 1994: 217). The most influential fast to death was that of an LTTE commander in Jaffna, Thileepan, who very publicly took no fluids or food in September 1987 in protest at the IPKF intervention and colonization of Tamil areas by the Sinhalese. He died in twelve days. A statue was later erected to his memory and his death is still commemorated widely (Balasingham 2003: 131–5).

Suicide to evade torture can, in other words, be a heroic, not a desperate, act. In the Sri Lankan case, the high incidence of suicide more generally also makes it a pervasive feature of the background culture. This latter point means both that suicide is not necessarily culturally stigmatized and that it is a well-known and *legitimate* response to suffering. Although the argument in this chapter is that the pathology of heroic suicide—and thus of the Black Tigers—is totally different from that of depressive suicides, it is important to recognize that Sri Lanka has some of the highest per capita suicide rates in the world, according to the World Health Organization (WHO 2003). For women, Sri Lanka has the highest figure in the world (data from 1991) of 16.8 suicides per 100,000 of population. The highest rate for men is 75.6 per 100,000 of population in Lithuania. Sri Lanka's rate for men is 44.6, which puts it ninth according to the WHO (as above, the figures are from 1991).[75] Yet there is no obvious link between Black Tiger missions and suicide rates. Although one may join the LTTE because one knows someone who has been killed or suffered in an attack or been bombed, or has experienced such things oneself, there is no way for us to establish whether this increases the likelihood of joining the Black Tigers. In the same vein, although knowing someone who has committed suicide increases one's own chances of committing suicide, there is no way to establish such a link in this case.

The war has had a deep negative impact on the Tamil population in the north and east. A *Médecins sans Frontières* (MSF) mental health survey conducted among the 23,000, mostly Tamil, inhabitants of a government-run welfare centre in Vavuniya in November 2000 found high rates of traumatic stress among the 163 respondents. The scale of the suffering these camp inhabitants experienced is scarcely comprehensible: 65 per cent a direct attack on their village, 77 per cent aerial bombing, and 54 per cent a mortar attack by the SLA. As many as 30 per cent had actually witnessed the death of someone close to them. Added to this were the very poor conditions in which people within the camps were held, and a pass system which prevented them from leaving and made them feel like hostages. In Vavuniya, the numbers of suicides (62) and of attempted suicides (691) were very high, three times higher than the already high background rate in Sri Lanka, according to MSF, and possibly higher as these are the rates reported by the Vavuniya hospital. Indeed, nearly 24 per cent of the survey respondents were reported as having someone in the family who had attempted suicide (de Jong et al. 2001).

The existence of intense and sustained trauma is likely to play a role in recruiting volunteers for the LTTE and this is borne out by what little material exists on personal motivations. Death and suffering are ubiquitous among the Tamils. Joshi (2000), for example, records a Jesuit priest, Father Harry Miller, who headed a Peace Committee at Batticaloa, in eastern Sri Lanka, as saying: 'The abuse that ordinary people suffer at the hands of the army becomes the primary motivating factor to join the Tigers.' The areas in which the Tamils fight the SLA seem, unsurprisingly, to provide fertile ground for recruiting the Tigers (and so the Black Tigers).

Kokkurill, a village in the north of Batticaloa, is a typical example. Villagers say that during a crackdown on the Tigers in 1990, the SLA arbitrarily arrested 183 people from the village, including women and children. In the years since, say the Tigers, the village has sacrificed more lives for the cause than any other in Sri Lanka: 100 men from this village of 500 have already left to fight for the rebels, never to return (Joshi 2000). Furthermore:

Academics and prominent business people in the region insist the Tigers don't carry out forced recruitment; what pressure there is tends to be psychological. In areas run by the Tigers 'young students are shown LTTE war movies and are given speeches by members of the political wing of the Tigers. That is all,' says a schoolteacher. Every day, the teacher travels through checkpoints to get from his home in an army-administered district to his government-run school, which lies in an area controlled by the Tigers. (Joshi 2000)

tamilnet's story from 1997 of Ragu, an 18-year-old recruit, shows his dawning awareness of the war coming through personal experiences, including carrying those wounded by an SLA artillery strike on a market to a makeshift ambulance. *tamilnet* quotes an LTTE recruitment officer saying that 'times of massive Sri Lankan violence are the easiest time to sign youth up'.[76]

Schalk refers to a film produced by the LTTE television station in 1993, called *tayakkanavu* or 'the dream of the motherland (homeland)', about a Black Tiger (a *karuppulli* in Tamil according to Schalk). It is worth quoting at length because the film spends time establishing the main character's motivation. In Schalk's words (1997: 77–8):

It starts by showing a happy family consisting of parents, a daughter and a son, the *tiyaki* [martyr]-to-be. They are all happy sitting in the garden celebrating a birthday. They feed each other with hands as signs of intimacy. They also have good relations with their neighbours. The son takes the neighbour's young daughter to school on his motor-bike. One day the Lankan air force drops bombs on the school, and the boy can only take the body of his young friend to her parents. In his inner vision, he anticipates that this could have happened to his own younger sister [*tankacci*]. He decides he will enter the squad of Black Tigers. Having obtained his father's permission, the film shows the hard training given to a Black Tiger and spends much time in describing the comradeship that develops within the group, especially between our hero and a comrade.

After being selected for his mission, one very similar to Captain Miller's truck bomb, the Black Tiger divides his property between his comrades, giving his prized harmonium to his best friend, then he bids farewell to his family and finally to Pirabakaran. Schalk (1997: 77–8) goes on:

Then he went for his last task that he accomplished as calculated. The enemy camp was eliminated and he was killed by the explosion. The next day all read and talked about him. His picture was put up on a commemorative altar. Then the parents were informed by two officials from the LTTE that he had reached *viramaranam*, 'heroic death'. Above all his *tankacci* wailed. His comrade also wailed. His turn will come soon to make the next attack on a Sinhala army camp, incited by the heroic death of his comrade. The hero of the film is described as *tavan*, 'ascetic', in his behaviour. Although he is of marriageable age there is no sign of a girlfriend, not even among the mourners. He has a *tankacci*, 'younger sister', and not a *talaivi*, 'wife'.

Experiencing a war of unequal force clearly plays a major role in stimulating some to join the LTTE. When one's enemy engages in indiscriminate aerial bombing, the danger to one's own life and that of one's family is already heightened. There will also be positive feelings associated with being able to 'do something' active rather than passively waiting and hoping. Joining the LTTE is thus a shorter step away from civilian life when one lives in a war zone. The decision to become a Black Tiger is another step again.

Would the prospect of a meal and a photograph with Pirabakaran be enough to induce an application? Without knowing more about the individual Black Tigers' motivations for volunteering, it is impossible to say whether this makes *the* difference. The same can be said of other 'rewards'. Whether, for example, knowing one's family will be the family of a liberation hero, or knowing in advance that one will be revered after one's death, are strong enough incentives to induce some to self-sacrifice is unclear (we have already seen the high esteem in which Black Tigers are held by the movement at large). Whether Black Tiger families receive some compensation is also unknown.

The determination to do something to resist Sri Lankan military attacks may explain joining the LTTE but, given the huge risks involved in that in any case, we need more evidence on personal motivation because many evidently courageous LTTE fighters do not volunteer for the Black Tigers (if most LTTE cadres did volunteer, and selection by trainers rather than self-selection is at work, then there may be a much stronger link between the decisions to join the LTTE and to try to join the Black Tigers).

It is important to stress that the agent does not always die in Black Tiger attacks. In some attacks, once the objective has been achieved, escape is clearly a possibility. Mama's early mission suggests this, as does a short *tamilnet* story from January 1998 based on information it must have received from the LTTE itself:

An LTTE Black Tiger unit of Friday 4 January 1998 completely destroyed a landed Sri Lankan airforce MI 17 helicopter, after penetrating the army's perimeter defences in the vicinity of Karipattamurippu (Vanni). The helicopter was distributing supplies to the occupying Sinhalese forces when the attack took place, around 1.30 PM. All members of the Black Tiger unit returned to base safely after successful completion of the operation.[77]

Whatever else this story demonstrates, it shows at a minimum that for the LTTE there is no necessary contradiction between going on a Black Tiger mission (and the suggestion here is of a commando-style raid that did not include non-Black Tigers) and returning alive. The Black Tigers are not, therefore, a suicide unit in the sense that the agent must die for the operation to be a success. Given the amount of training Black Tigers seem to receive, it is obviously preferable if they do survive and return *as long as the mission is accomplished*. Thus, dying is a cost both for them and for the organization, and survival is, for both, preferable to death but not to failure.

In most kinds of Black Tiger operations, death is more or less certain if the objective is to be attained. It is only in guerrilla-style attacks that survival seems more feasible. This has a further dimension: going on an SM is not something that one does only once, as one's 'turn' in a collective struggle. The Black Tigers are a special unit trained to do the 'suicide' missions; they are a highly professional force and they may therefore go on more than one mission. Overall, Black Tigers are willing and trained to give their lives when called on, and this is what distinguishes them, in the end, from other elite units and from other commandos in the LTTE itself.

At the group level, the benefits of this are clear: rather than allowing the 'natural heroes' to emerge under battle conditions (for which we might see the award of bravery medals as an indicator, many Victoria Cross holders in Britain having received them posthumously for acts of 'suicidal' courage), why not pre-select them, train them, and position them with the kind of explosives or other weapons with which they can hope to fully realize their military goal? How many acts of impulsive bravery in war have taken place with a hand grenade rather than several pounds of high explosive, making such a sacrifice far less effective? Under battle conditions, military commanders faced, for example, with a machine gun nest or a communications centre have at hand precisely the troops trained and ready to deal with these dangers especially when the heavy weaponry that is an alternative is unavailable. What is remarkable is the fortitude of those trained to die, who have the mental strength to live with this knowledge and return more than once to a situation of such great peril. This is even more true of those Black Tigers who may be 'sleepers' in the south and thereby miss out on the day-to-day morale-boosting comradeship of friends serving in a frontline unit.[78]

Conclusion

For a small unit, the impact of Black Tiger attacks has been immense. The LTTE as a whole is a formidably led and organized military force, and the Black Tigers are a unit within that army for which missions with a high to certain likelihood of death are a special responsibility. This unit was developed to compensate for the absence of heavy weaponry. The special naming and marking out of Black Tigers attests to the fact that they are more than merely elite commandos, they are *the* elite commandos, those with the most difficult missions and the highest esteem. They embody Tamil resistance like no other units in the LTTE. Most of their missions are not achievable without their own deaths and they are trained and ready to accept this fact, presumably without question, when called. Such a request of another kind of commando, however elite, who had neither self-selected nor been trained for certain death would presumably elicit understandable resistance.

The men and women of the Black Tigers are carefully selected and highly trained. Some survive their missions and return to fight another day but most do not. The targeting of civilians through aerial bombing by the Sri Lankan military narrowed the risk gap between civilian and army life for Tamils. Once in the LTTE, dangers were such that the LTTE–Black Tiger gap was also narrower than we might imagine (although real enough). Also, defending one's own home rather than conquering a territory where one does not live ought, logically, to intensify commitment and make SMs more likely, other things being equal (this is true of the Kamikaze; see Chapter 1, this volume).

Unlike with other cases in this volume, a Black Tiger's sacrifice is also made in the knowledge that the LTTE is clearly capable of winning the war. The existence of a comprehensible and non-negotiable goal—sovereignty— means that Black Tigers, as all LTTE cadres, know what they are dying for, that it is achievable, and that the commitment of the LTTE, exemplified by Pirabakaran, has never wavered. It is also worth noting that the LTTE's trajectory, from guerrilla movement (prior to 1983) to a regular army, is unusual among armed resistance groups of this sort and is testament both to a degree of exclusive territorial control and to a supportive infrastructure within the wider Tamil community.

The word 'suicide' is much too limited to describe this complex socio-logical phenomenon. We should distinguish at least three kinds of self-inflicted death. First is what we commonly refer to as 'suicide', a desire to cease living for reasons to do with depression, unbearable sadness, grinding poverty, and so forth. This is usually a highly individualistic act in which one's intentions are carefully hidden even from one's closest relatives. In the most extreme cases, no note is left and no explanation given. In the grip of depression, this can be an impulsive decision, although preparations may well have been made in advance. There is simply no evidence that this characterizes the volunteers for Black Tiger units or the 241 Black Tigers listed as 'martyrs' by the LTTE. Indeed, Black Tiger recruiters seem to screen out such candidates as inappropriate to be elite soldiers.

Second, there is suicide by cyanide. There is clearly an organizational rationale here, preventing information being divulged under torture, and a strong personal rationale given that excruciating torture would most likely be followed by execution in any event. Schalk (1997: 74) suggests the LTTE sees this kind of suicide as 'an anticipation of death inflicted by the enemy . . . The cause of and responsibility for getting killed through cyanide is the enemy's'.

Third, there are the Black Tigers. According to the head of the LTTE's political wing, S. P. Thamilchelvam, while the Tamil word for 'suicide' is *thatkolai*, the Tigers prefer *thatkodai*, meaning 'to give yourself'. He says: 'It is a gift of the self . . . The Person gives him or herself in full' (quoted in Waldman 2003). If we obscure these differences under the common label 'suicide', we obscure the extent to which the motivating factors for behaviour in these three cases are all potentially different: despair, prudence, and what? Heroism? This is where we meet the insurmountable hurdle of lack of evidence. We can read the motives of Black Tigers from the motives for joining the LTTE, but we miss out the crucial step some LTTE cadres take to endanger themselves even more completely. It is this that has led to the various allegations of 'culthood', especially the idea of a cult of devotion to Pirabakaran, to whom the LTTE cadres swear an oath of allegiance as well as to the cause of Tamil Eelam. This sense of a 'cult' specifically centred on Pirabakaran is too redolent of explanations based on a kind of tribal allegiance or an insufficiently individuated society. The Black Tigers have been highly effective at the group level but they have, by any measure, been sparingly used. Other LTTE martyrs have received a substantial level of public recognition, and are accorded a similar but not identical status. The cyanide, as suggested, has a more prudential explanation and should not be regarded as a proxy for a kind of fanaticism.

Yet the LTTE does have a strong internal culture of personal and professional discipline, it appears, and, if Hellmann-Rajanayagam is right, access to LTTE ranks is a scarce resource increasing its allure. The training intensifies this as does the roll-call of LTTE heroes among whom the Black Tigers stand in a singular position at its apex. The fact is that some individuals out of a preselected group of already highly motivated individuals are prepared to make 'the ultimate sacrifice' for the good of others. What we have with the Black Tigers is 'heroic suicide', Durkheim's careful definition of suicide in terms of the act itself, not the end sought, including this category of motivations. He said:

The soldier facing certain death to save his regiment does not wish to die, and yet is he not as much the author of his own death as the manufacturer or merchant who kills himself to avoid bankruptcy? (Durkheim 1952: 43)[79]

One feature of Durkheim's definition of suicide is worth further comment. Suicide, for him, concerns:

all cases of death resulting directly or indirectly from a positive or negative act of the victim himself, which he knows will produce this result. (Durkheim 1952: 44; emphasis in original)

The first part of this sentence, apart from its gender specificity, describes the Black Tigers accurately enough; but the phrase 'which he knows will produce this result' is more of a problem. Durkheim (1952: 44) is clear that 'at the moment of acting the victim knows the certain result'. This is not invariably the case for all Black Tigers. For some, especially those on assassination missions or attacking navy ships with boats full of explosives, this holds true. But some Black Tigers do survive to go on subsequent missions. They know that, with their excellent training, good planning, and luck, they may return alive, especially after guerrilla operations. Not all of them will, but those who will not do not know that in advance. And the LTTE cares about getting them back: it values these lives even if it cannot build escape into the mission objectives. A 1 per cent chance of survival is half as good as a 2 per cent chance, but a 1 per cent chance is very different from no chance at all (see Chapter 7, this volume, on 'certainty effect'). The collective life within Black Tiger units also seems to be important: the training process concentrates on building psychological strength, but this comradely environment must also build a powerful bond between cadres who are viewed as the best of the best. While a heightened sense of personal responsibility may be essential for volunteering, its consolidation and testing under training conditions may increase the sense of being 'chosen', of being one of the elect with others, and therefore of having a special obligation to one's own comrades to uphold the honour of the unit. These questions cannot be answered with any certainty and may never be answered unless the LTTE has kept detailed records on dead Black Tigers.

Religion is not a feature which can explain the emergence of SMs in the Tamil case. This means that *no* religion, let alone a specific one like Islam, is a necessary part of explanations for SMs. To say that a desire for national liberation substitutes for this is to say nothing more than that a Black Tiger must be motivated by something meaningful, which is a truism. The 're-wards' that Black Tigers receive appear to have little or nothing to do with their decision and are entirely posthumous (although there may be pleasure in anticipating something like the pride of their families). They do not believe they are going to the afterlife; and although Hinduism is the religion of most LTTE cadres, and Hinduism does subscribe to the reincarnation of the soul, neither the language nor the symbolism of reincarnation figures in LTTE or Black Tiger culture.

Would such units be feasible in other societies? Elite commando units approximate this, with those dropped behind enemy lines responsible usually for their own escape. The history of missions by special forces is replete with examples of tremendous courage, of cyanide pills, capture and torture, and survival against the odds. There appears to be no shortage of volunteers for such units. We must not become overly concerned with what looks like a species of 'suicide' at the cost of ignoring cognate behaviour like heroism. We see acts of great courage and self-sacrifice around us all the time, in most societies; people who struggle against the odds for others or against great personal hardships. The Black Tigers are clearly not 'suicidal' and the puzzle they present may turn out to be less exotic than we think.

3

Palestinians, 1981–2003

LUCA RICOLFI

This chapter examines the suicide missions (SMs) related to the Arab–Israeli conflict that took place from 1981 to December 2003. SMs are a relatively recent phenomenon in the Middle East, with only sporadic cases before 1981. They are also relatively concentrated within certain territorial limits. In the two decades under examination, the great majority of the SMs related to the Arab–Israeli conflict took place in three geographic areas: Israel, the Occupied Territories (Gaza Strip and the West Bank), and Lebanon (primarily in the south). This concentration is largely due to the outcome of the 1967 war, the so-called Six Day War. Israel managed to sign effective peace agreements with its neighbours in the south (Egypt) and in the east (Jordan), but not in the north (Syria). Hence a shift in the conflict towards the Occupied Territories and Lebanon, the latter squeezed between the Israeli army in the south and Syrian influence in the north.

Furthermore, several experts (Karmon 2000; Morris 2002; Margalit 2001) believe that the war between the Lebanese Hezbollah and the Israeli army provided Palestinians with a crucial model. The link between the two conflicts (Israel against Lebanon and Israel against Palestine) became very direct in the winter of 1992–3, when Israel deported 415 Islamic activists to Lebanon, where SMs had already a long history. All this makes it difficult to separate the Israeli–Palestinian conflict from the wider conflict between Israel and the insurgent organizations operating in Lebanon. SMs began in Lebanon, and from there they spread.

There is no single geographic or geopolitical term for the area that embraces Israel, the Occupied Territories, and Lebanon. I will call it for convenience the 'Middle East area' (ME area), even though the territory under examination, while wider than historical Palestine, is far smaller than the Middle East as a whole.

Suicide Missions Defined

Before we can attempt an explanation of SMs, we need to know in detail exactly what it is that we want to explain. My first task is therefore to provide as accurate a measure as possible of the pattern of SMs in the ME area. This task has to contend with two difficulties: the distinction between SMs and other kinds of violent attacks, and—the more onerous of the two—the quality of the sources.

Empirically, the concept of SM is rather elusive since in various sources, and especially in the main databases recording them, no accurate distinction is made between missions that succeeded in that the target was hit and the attacker died (SM_3), missions that were foiled (primarily by counter-terrorism) prior to execution (SM_1), and missions that failed at the time of execution due to the perpetrator's errors or external intervention (SM_2). SMs_1 are not usually included in the statistics on 'attacks' but do sometimes appear in more general statistics comprising counter-terrorist actions. In addition, some databases, such as that of the Israeli Institute for Counter-Terrorism (ICT), do not include the category 'suicide mission'. They deal with only 'suicide bombing' (SB), a narrower category than SM because it excludes those cases in which the agent's death, though certain, is caused by others (attacks against military targets with no escape plan, infiltrations in protected settlements, and so forth). In addition, it should be noted that the ICT database classifies attacks by explosive-laden vehicles (trucks, cars, and so forth) at times as SBs and at other times as bombings or car bombings.[1]

The major problem in my empirical analysis, however, is not the omission of SMs_1 or the absence of the category 'suicide mission', but the incompleteness of the main available databases: those of the ICT, the American Memorial Institute for the Prevention of Terrorism (MIPT), and the Terrorism Research Center (TRC). Even the most complete—the ICT database and the MIPT database in the Palestinian area—do not record all known suicide attacks but only about 70 per cent of them.[2]

Here I focus on executed missions (SMs_2 and SMs_3) and, unless otherwise stated, I rely on a new integrated database that merges twelve different kinds of sources (see Appendix on 'Suicide Missions'). In other words, calculations are based on an SM definition located between the wider definition ($SM_1 + SM_2 + SM_3$) and the narrow one proposed by Yoram Schweitzer (SB_3).

The suicide bomber carries the explosives on his body or in a vehicle driven by himself and, by personal choice and with full self-awareness, he approaches a previously chosen target and blows himself up. The suicide bomber himself, in accordance with the prevailing circumstances, chooses the time and place to execute the explosion so that it will cause the maximum damage to the target. Defining a terror attack as a suicide bombing depends primarily on whether the perpetrator is killed. In the event that his mission is incomplete, it is not a suicide bombing. The death of the perpetrator is the key to the success of the attack; and he knows in advance that success depends entirely on this death. (Schweitzer 2001)

As far as can be inferred from the few existing estimates, failed missions (SM_2) amount to 5–10 per cent of total executed missions[3] ($SM_2 + SM_3$), while the incidence of foiled missions (SM_1) is extremely difficult to estimate and certainly liable to ample fluctuations.[4]

To summarize, the present definition of SMs—primarily conceived so as to perform the statistical calculations presented in the text—*excludes* the actions of those people who immolate themselves for a cause, killing themselves only, since they carry out no act of violence against others, as well as actions that are highly risky (because death is not certain[5]). At the same time, it not only *includes* actions in which the agent's death is directly caused by the agent himself; it also comprises those in which the agent's death, even though caused by others, is the *certain* consequence of his behaviour (such as actions against military or militarily protected targets with no escape plan).

In a narrower definition the agent himself would be the direct cause of his death, and in an even narrower one the agent's death would be part and parcel of the aim of the action in that the agent *prefers* the action to culminate in his death rather than in the enemy's death only. It seems to be what Palestinian ideologists have in mind when they reject the label 'terrorism' which the Israeli and Western press apply to 'martyr operations'. Recently, they have used 'sacred explosions', a term laden with meaning. In her excellent report on suicide bombers' motives, Nasra Hassan illustrates the meaning of this definition thus:

They were not inclined to argue, but they were happy to discuss, far into the night, the issues and the purpose of their activities. One condition of the interviews was that, in our discussion, I should not refer to their deeds as 'suicide', which is forbidden in Islam. (The preferred term is 'sacred explosions'.) One member of al-Qassam said: 'We do not have tanks or rockets, but we have something superior—our exploding Islamic human bombs. In place of a nuclear arsenal, we are proud of our arsenal of believers.' (Hassan 2001*a*)

Despite the appeal of this definition, I will not include *preference* for one's death in the SM concept. It would be difficult to distinguish empirically, since intentions cannot be easily observed and, furthermore, the history of suicide actions in Palestine suggests that instrumental and symbolic actions are intertwined, with symbolic actions possibly gaining ground. The problems relating to the definition are important not merely for conceptual and

statistical clarity. Motives, legitimacy, and terminology are part of the conflict itself and of its split rhetoric, and in this regard the latter definition is
quite relevant.

In this chapter I try to stick to three basic conventions. First of all,
following Ganor (2000), I distinguish between terror attacks (which have
civilian targets) and guerrilla attacks (which have military targets). Second,
the agents are called terrorists when involved in a terror attack, guerrillas
when involved in a guerrilla attack, and simply attackers when we refer to
both. Third, organizations are called terrorist only if they resort to terror
attacks at least sometimes, however infrequently. In the ME area, the majority of anti-Israeli organizations do attack civilian targets, and in this sense
can be considered terrorist organizations.[6] Only four secular (now dormant)
organizations hit only (or almost exclusively) military targets, and are better
viewed as guerrilla organizations: the Syrian Social Nationalist Party
(SSNP), the Baath Party of Syria, the Lebanese Communist Party (LCP),
and the Nasserite Socialist Party of Syria.[7]

The Palestinian Case

According to most experts, SMs in the Middle East began in Lebanon. On 23
October 1983, simultaneous attacks was carried out by Lebanese Hezbollah
(Party of God) militants against the US Marines' headquarters in Beirut and
against the French multinational peace force in Lebanon.[8] Altogether 241
Americans and 58 French nationals were killed in the attack, which prompted
the withdrawal of the multinational force from Lebanon at the end of September 1984. No less effective were the subsequent Hezbollah attacks against
the Israeli army and the posts of the Southern Lebanon Army (the Israeli-
allied militia in Lebanon). During the three-year Israeli invasion of Lebanon
(June 1982–June 1985), about eleven car-bomb suicide attacks were launched
against international targets in the Middle East.[9] In June 1985 the Israeli
army withdrew from central Lebanon, limiting its occupation to a small strip
(the so-called Security Zone) in southern Lebanon on the border with Israel.

As a matter of fact, at least three devastating suicide attacks had been
perpetrated well before the actions against US and French troops, all of them
in Lebanon. On 15 December 1981, a car bomb crashed into the Iraqi
embassy in Beirut causing sixty-one deaths; on 11 November 1982 an attack
against Israeli headquarters in Tyre killed seventy-five Israeli soldiers and
fifteen Palestinian or Lebanese prisoners. Finally, sixty-three people were
killed in an attack against the US embassy on 18 April 1983. The origin of
these attacks is not known exactly, but most of the sources[10] attribute
responsibility to Shiite organizations, such as Amal and Hezbollah. And

even before these actions, at least eleven missions, either suicide or quasi-suicide, had taken place in Israel in 1973 (one attack by al-Fatah[11]), in 1974 (six attacks, three by the Popular Front for the Liberation of Palestine General Command, PFLP-GC[12]), in 1978 (one attack, led by a nineteen-year-old woman of al-Fatah[13]), in 1979 (one attack, attributed to militants from the Palestine Liberation Organization, PLO), and in 1980 (one attack by the Arab Liberation Front, ALF).

After the Israeli withdrawal from most Lebanese territory in June 1985, the frequency of suicide attacks dropped dramatically (from nineteen attacks in 1985 to four in 1986) and then regained some, albeit limited, vigour only in the hot period (1988–90) of the first Intifada.[14] Only after the Oslo Agreement (1993–5) did SMs gain new impetus, this time both in Israel and in the Occupied Territories. From 1981 to December 2003, at least 224 SMs were launched in the ME area, reaching a peak in terms of number of attacks per month during the so-called al-Aqsa Intifada that began[15] on 28 September 2000, and gradually lost vigour after the truce signed on 29 June 2003.

If one excludes the Japanese Kamikaze, the Lebanon episodes are the beginning of the first massive wave of SMs in the twentieth century. Only later did they spread to other areas, in particular to Sri Lanka (1987), Turkish and Iraqi Kurdistan (1996), Kashmir (1999), Chechnya (2000), and recently to Iraq (2003). But to what extent do SMs in the ME area contribute to the worldwide total number of SMs?

No precise figures can be given, because of incomplete and sometimes contradictory sources[16] as well as the lack of a clear and shared definition of SMs. Nonetheless, there is enough empirical evidence to make possible a rough estimate.[17] All sources agree that over the last two decades over 80 per cent of suicide attacks have been concentrated in two tiny plots of land: the island of Sri Lanka (formerly Ceylon) and the areas of the Israeli–Palestinian conflict. Since the early 1980s there have been about 200 SMs in Sri Lanka, carried out by Tamil Tigers, the elite militia of Liberation Tigers of Tamil Eelam (LTTE; see Chapter 2, this volume). In the ME area, at least 224 SMs have been launched, mainly by eight organizations: the Shiite groups Hezbollah and Amal, the Sunni groups Hamas and Palestinian Islamic Jihad (PIJ), PFLP, SSNP, Lebanese Baath Party (Baath-Leb), and al-Aqsa Martyr Brigades (all secular, Marxist, nationalist, or pan-Arab organizations). Besides Sri Lanka and the ME area, only four other areas have been witness to at least ten suicide attacks: Kurdistan (since 1996), Kashmir (since 1999), Chechnya (since 2000), and Iraq (since 2003) (Figure 3.1).

The conflicts in all these areas absorb over 96 per cent of SM attacks, and involve over twenty organizations.[18] The remaining 4 per cent of SMs are divided among a dozen or so groups, of various political backgrounds, scattered around the world (Algeria, Morocco, Kenya, Tanzania, Saudi

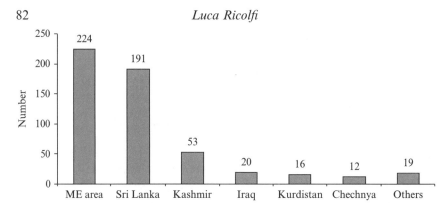

FIGURE 3.1. Suicide missions worldwide: rough estimates, 1 January 1981–31 December 2003
Source: See n. 17.

Arabia, Kuwait, Panama, Argentina, Pakistan, Croatia, Indonesia, India, and the United States). Al-Qaeda is the most important of these groups, and is also the only one among them to have reached the figure of ten suicide attacks.

On the whole, the toll exacted by these thirty or so groups is quite heavy. In fact, even if we omit September 11, suicide attacks have had ten to fifteen times the destructive power of ordinary terrorist attacks. If we rely, for instance, on the partial[19] reconstruction by Pape (2003), from 1980 to 2001 there were at least 2,500 victims of suicide attacks, equal to 48 per cent of the total terror toll, even though SMs have amounted to only 3 per cent of total terror attacks.

Overall, no fewer than 535 SMs have taken place around the world since 1980, one-third of which were in the ME area. Nevertheless, SMs have not been the main mode of dying for a cause. During the last three decades SMs have amounted to about one-third of self-immolation cases and to about half of those in the period after 1980 (Chapter 5, this volume).[20]

Historical Precedents

Historiographical research has identified several precedents[21] for this recent proliferation. In the West, the case of anarchists around 1900, briefly described by Kalyvas and Sánchez-Cuenca (Chapter 6, this volume), can be cited.[22] But there are some precedents also in the Islamic world. In a recent work prepared for the Federal Research Division, for example, Rex Hudson claims that Shiite self-destructive actions, such as public executions (and self-executions) by so-called Assassins, a sect operating between 1000 and 1200, are relevant to present-day suicide terrorism.

From the eleventh through the thirteenth century a sect of Shiite Muslims called the Assassins used assassination as a tool for purifying the Muslim religion. The Assassins' victims, who were generally officials, were killed in public to communicate the error of the targeted official. By carrying out the assassination in public, the Assassin would allow himself to be apprehended and killed in order to demonstrate the purity of his motives and to enter Heaven. (Hudson 1999)

In his recent international review on suicide terrorism, Schweitzer (2000) also mentions eleventh-century Assassins (Hashishiyun) and, earlier still, Jewish Sicaris in the first century. Atran (2003*a*) quotes the Zealots' and the Sicaris' struggle against Roman occupation in Judea, and the tragic Sicari uprising in the Masada fortress in AD 73. The insurrection ended in mass suicide by the Sicaris and the beginning of the Jewish Diaspora (an episode reminiscent of, and an apparent forerunner of, Husseini's defeat at Karbala in AD 680, which represents the Shiite supreme sacrifice).

The most important historical contribution to understanding SMs is a study by Stephen Dale, 'Religious Suicide in Islamic Asia', which was published in 1988, well before the phenomenon attracted the attention of the mass media and scholars. Dale argues that suicide attacks are not a recent invention but have deep roots in the historical relations between Islam and the West, even more than in Islamic culture itself. Reconstructing the history of three Islamic communities in Asia, one in India (Malabar), one in Sumatra (Atjeh), and one in Indonesia (Philippines), Dale (1988) shows that for centuries suicide terrorist attacks have been an Islamic way of resisting foreign occupation, especially European colonial powers. Suicidal jihads have been repeatedly launched against the British in Malabar, the Portuguese and Dutch in Atjeh, and Spaniards and Americans in the Philippines.

Outline of the Chapter

The remainder of the chapter deals first with the characteristics and motives of organizations, and then with the characteristics and motives of individuals. This arrangement is based on the fundamental fact that, in the ME area, SMs are hardly ever isolated actions by single individuals. Behind an SM there is usually an organization or one of its local cells, which, as we shall see, finely regulate SMs.[23] Thus, identifying their strategies is a key element in understanding the rationale and the dynamics of SMs. At the same time, however, if no individuals were willing to sacrifice their lives in these missions, terrorist and guerrilla organizations would lack the raw material to put their strategies into practice. In fact, this raw material appears to be so abundant in the ME area[24] that organizations face a serious problem in selecting and choosing the agents.

The Missions

Four Waves of Suicide Missions

Since 1981, resorting to suicide attacks has become recurrent in the Israeli–Palestinian conflict, and in the Middle Eastern conflict generally.

As Figure 3.2 shows, the absolute frequency of suicide attacks has varied considerably.[25] The three-year moving average shows the presence of four waves, two during the 1980s, and the other two after the beginning of the 1990s. The peaks reached during the 1980s coincide with the Lebanon war (1982–5, major peak) and with the beginning of the first Intifada (1988–90, minor peak). Of the two subsequent peaks, the first coincides with the implementation of the Oslo Agreements and the institution of the Palestinian Authority (1994–6) and the second with the central years of the second Intifada, or al-Aqsa Intifada (2001–2).

A key question is whether these four waves merely reflect the general course of the Israeli–Palestinian conflict or also reveal any changes in the propensity to resort to SMs in preference to more conventional actions. In order to give an extensive answer, we would have to calculate the ratio of suicide attacks to total attacks: in other words, we would require estimates not just of the numerator but also of the denominator. Unfortunately, it is at present impossible to construct a precise historical series of the total number of attacks.[26] It is, however, possible to create a *frequency index* of total attacks, which gives us some idea of the general trend (Figure 3.3).[27]

The index, which integrates ICT and MIPT databases, shows only *three* waves, since the wave associated to the first Intifada disappears.[28] There

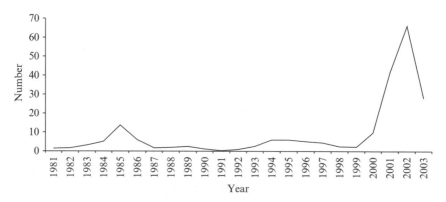

FIGURE 3.2.   Number of suicide missions in the Middle East area, 1981–2003 (three-year moving average, see n. 25)
Source: Integrated database.

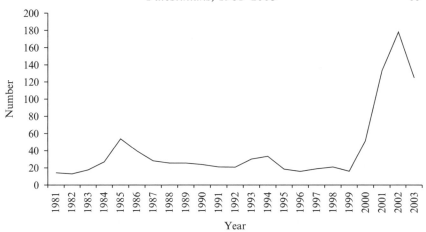

FIGURE 3.3. Frequency index of total attacks in Middle East area
Source: ICT and MIPT databases.

seems, however, to be a certain correspondence between SMs and total attacks. In part, it is an obvious correspondence, since SMs are a fraction of the number of total attacks (around 15 per cent in the period between 1980 and 2003, according to our denominator).

To get a clearer understanding we need to calculate the ratio between the number of SMs and the frequency index of total attacks. This ratio, which may be interpreted as a sort of 'preference' or 'propensity' for SMs over other violent actions,[29] shows once again four waves (Figure 3.4), located approximately in the same periods as those represented in the absolute number of SMs: Lebanon war, first Intifada, post-Oslo, al-Aqsa Intifada.

If we focus on the general trend of the propensity to SMs, the first thing we notice is the absence of a clear trend.[30] SMs appear suddenly in Palestinian history, just as Athena sprang fully armed from Jupiter's head, yet thereafter they do not show a clear increasing or decreasing trend. The impression that SMs have become a predominant option in recent years thus seems to be a mere effect of the selectivity of the media (and of our attention) following the outbreak of the al-Aqsa Intifada (28 September 2000). Only the number of total attacks has soared, but not the propensity for SMs in preference to conventional attacks.

However, the propensity for SMs does display a cyclical pattern with a five-year interval between one peak and the next. But it is important to observe that the course of the propensity does not always correspond to the number of attacks. Sometimes the two series move together, but at other times they move as the mirror image of each other: for example, during the first Intifada (1987–91) and after Oslo (1994–9). It is also interesting to note that in the last

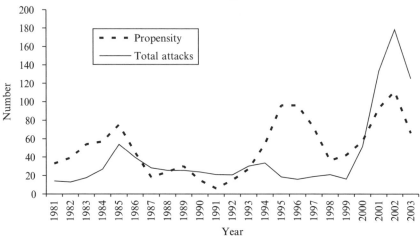

FIGURE 3.4. Total attacks and propensity to suicide missions
Source: Author's estimates (see Appendix, sections on 'Suicide Missions' and 'Attacks').

two waves the intensification of total attacks (suicide or not) *precedes* the increase in the propensity for SMs.

Such independence of the propensity for SMs is confirmed by a number of simple statistical assessments. The correlation between total number of attacks and propensity for SMs is quite low[31] and entirely due to the three years of the second Intifada. The joint distribution (not displayed here) neatly shows that the years 2001–3 are outliers. If we remove them, every connection between the total number of attacks and propensity for SMs disappears.

We now look at the four waves in detail. It is important to be clear from the outset, however, that the reasoning behind the total number of attacks is distinct from the reasoning behind the preference or propensity for SMs. The apparent independence between the two historical series suggests that SMs constitute a relatively autonomous phenomenon that is not merely an ancillary to other forms of violent action.

The Lebanon Wave

The first SM wave took place in Lebanon between the end of 1981 and 1985, in the context of the Lebanese civil war (1975–90), of the Iran–Iraq war (1980–8), and of the Israeli invasion of Lebanon (6 June 1982). As mentioned above, on 15 December 1981 a suicide agent drove a car, packed with explosives, against the Iraqi embassy in Beirut, razing the building to the ground and killing sixty-one people. The attack was attributed to Amal, the pro-Syrian Shiite organization. Around one year later, a few months after the Israeli invasion of Lebanon and after the attack (non-suicidal) that killed the Lebanese President Beshir Gemayel (14 September), another suicide attack destroyed the Israeli headquarters in Beirut, killing seventy-five soldiers and fifteen Palestinian prisoners. The following year, in 1983, there were five spectacular suicide attacks, among which was the devastating double attack against the multinational peace force. The attacks continued in 1984 and 1985, until the complete withdrawal of the multinational force (1984) and of the Israeli army (1985).

It is difficult to calculate fully the number of attacks in the Lebanese arena in these years (1981–5), since the sources tend to report only the most sensational episodes. We have managed to record, and accurately describe, twenty-eight attacks in our integrated database, including one with hundreds of victims and fourteen with almost ten victims each. However, if we took into account the opinions of journalists, historians, and secret-service specialists, the total number of suicide attacks performed during the 1981–5 period could be a little higher.[32] Among the latter there were the first two cases of female suicide attacks, both by the secular SSNP (these attacks are not always recorded in databases even if reported in newspaper articles). One was by Sana Mehaidli, a 16-year-old who blew herself up against an Israeli checkpoint in Lebanon;[33] the other was by Ibtissam Harb, a party activist who drove her car into a South Lebanon Army checkpoint (Fisk 1990: 610–11). During the same year (1985) at least six attacks were carried out by women, and responsibility was for the first time claimed on videotape (at least five videotapes were made, four by men and one by a woman).

The attacks carried out in this period are the work of at least five groups operating in Lebanon: the Baath-Leb, SSNP, LCP (all secular), Amal (pro-Syrian Shiites), and Hezbollah (pro-Iranian Shiites). The latter organization first saw the light in 1982, also thanks to the support of Iran, which sent a number of 'Iranian Revolutionary Guards' to assist with the establishment of a revolutionary Islamic movement in Lebanon whose members were to participate in the jihad against Israel. During the Iran–Iraq war at the beginning of the 1980s, Iran made widespread use of adolescent martyrs, known as 'human waves', in suicide attacks against Iraqi troops and in demining operations. We cannot rule out the possibility that the ideal of martyrdom, which has subsequently proven so important, was imported from or roused by this.[34]

The Hezbollah movement played a major role in the expulsion of foreign armed forces from Lebanon (a success that was repeated in 2000 with the withdrawal of Israeli forces ordered by the Barak administration), and its strategy—to drive the foreigners out 'inch by inch'—has become a kind of model for the Palestinians and a sort of nightmare for the Israelis. The expulsion of foreign armed forces from Lebanon that took place between

1984 and 1985 is one of the most prominent cases of a political–military victory by a network of terrorist and guerrilla organizations against an overwhelming military power (another is the expulsion of the Soviet army from Afghanistan).

It is reasonable to suppose that the strong support by Palestinian public opinion for violent operations against Israel, seen as complementary to the peace process rather than as an alternative to it, stems from here.[35] It is likely that Israel's constant reluctance to leave the Occupied Territories also originates here. It is commonly believed that the Israeli withdrawal from Lebanon in 1985 led to the consolidation of the Hezbollah,[36] from which the two Sunni terrorist organizations, Hamas and the PIJ, sprang in the 1980s.[37]

It should be stressed, however, that the 'copy' (Palestinian terrorism) and the 'model' (Shiite guerrilla) are of quite different natures. Shiite organizations such as Amal and Hezbollah resorted to suicide actions against civilians (terrorism), but the majority of their actions during the Lebanon[38] wave were directed against military targets (guerrilla). The opposite is true for Sunni organizations, such Hamas and the PIJ, which from the beginning (in the early 1990, just at the beginning of the Oslo process) preferred to attack civilian targets.

The First Intifada Wave

After two years of relative calm,[39] a slight resurgence of suicide attacks took place in the years 1988–90. Such attacks, responsibility for which was not always claimed, were concentrated in Lebanon, and directed against Israeli troops in the so-called security zone (a 5–10 km-wide strip to which the Israeli army withdrew in 1985). This wave began on 19 August 1988 with an unsuccessful suicide attack organized by the PFLP-GC and carried out by a young woman against an Israeli convoy in the security zone. The following October, a Hezbollah attack killed seven Israeli soldiers. In 1989 two Hezbollah and one PFLP attack injured eleven but caused no deaths. This series of attacks ended in 1990 with a female suicide attack carried out by the SSNP that wounded three people.

According to Morris (2002: 695), the attacks that took place in the fifteen years 1986–2000, following the Israeli withdrawal from Lebanon, can be explained by the territorial intransigence of the Hezbollah:

With the occasional assistance of Palestinian and Amal fighters, the Hezbollah allegedly continued the campaign against Israel and the SLA [Southern Lebanon Army] inside the security zone well after 1985, up to the end of the 90s. Shiite leaders demanded that the Israelis withdraw down to the last centimetre from the Lebanese territory; the Israelis were worried that if they had done so, the Hezbollah would have picked on settlements inside Israel itself.

Indeed, attacks (suicide and non-suicide) in Lebanese territory ceased only in 2000 with the complete Israeli withdrawal, promised by Barak during his election campaign (spring 1999) and carried out—as he promised—within a year of forming a government (spring 2000).[40]

Two circumstances remain to be explained. During 1988–9 non-suicide attacks decreased while suicide attacks increased, so raising the propensity for suicide attacks, and the SMs became much less efficient than those of the Oslo wave. The explanation may lie in the different aims of the attacks, which were mostly military during Israel's occupation of Lebanon and mostly political after the outbreak of the first Intifada on 8 December 1987. According to many analysts, the Intifada, which the PLO did not foresee or inspire, caused a radical change in PLO strategy, and dramatically upset relations between Palestinian factions.

Arafat, who was still confined to Tunis,[41] understood that renunciation of terrorism and a cautious management of the Intifada could have brought the Palestinian issue back to the attention of international public opinion. The resumption of talks with the United States, interrupted at Camp David in 1978 due to the Palestinian refusal to support the separate peace between Egypt and Israel, could restore the PLO's authority and further the founding of a Palestinian state. This line of thought prompted Arafat to shift his position somewhat and led in 1988 to the Declaration of Algiers, in which Arafat declared the existence of the state of Palestine and recognized Israel.[42]

A completely opposite standpoint was adopted by the most radical factions, both in Palestine, where Hamas was being forged in the flames of the Intifada, and in Lebanon, where the 'Damascus Cartel' (Hezbollah, PFLP, Amal, and SSNP) opposed every attempt to start the peace process. The Declaration of Algiers was considered treason, a cowardly waiver of Palestinian rights. The Intifada had to be harnessed and ridden against the Israeli occupier. It is from this point that a new military strategy appeared in the Palestinian camp. Conventional non-suicidal attacks were progressively carried out inside Israel with the aim of threatening its security and consequently jeopardizing the peace process. Attacks inside Lebanese territory triggered a new round of martyrdom operations which was consummated only during the second Intifada, when the radical factions grew stronger and suicide attacks moved to the Occupied Territories (West Bank and Gaza). With the withdrawal of Israeli troops from most of Lebanon, the key aim of the attacks was no longer their expulsion but the radicalization of the first Intifada, the development of a climate of opinion against compromise and for relentless struggle. To this end, one can surmise, one does not need to carry out devastating attacks, since small-scale but 'heroic' actions carried out by suicide attackers may convey the message even more effectively than large-scale ones. Devotion to the cause could be marked precisely by the *mediocritas* (golden mean) of the achieved result. If the damage inflicted on the enemy in terms of destruction and lives lost is insignificant, as with self-immolation, it seems ineffective in promoting the radicals' goal of the destruction of Israel. If the damage is too great, the display of military strength could obscure the fundamental message, namely, the activists' absolute devotion to the Palestinian cause. Medium levels of damage, neither insignificant nor very large, do promote both the radicals' goals: to inflict objective damage and to display complete subjective dedication to the cause.[43]

Of course, this interpretation is highly speculative. The answer to the question of why spectacular attacks ceased after 1985 may be in part technical–military: perhaps once the Israeli army left Lebanon there were simply fewer reachable targets with high concentrations of people, such as checkpoints or the military barracks targeted during the first attacks in Lebanon. In order to assess the plausibility of this interpretation, we would require a historical–geographical analysis of the concentration of Israeli military and diplomatic personnel in the three key territories (southern Lebanon, West Bank, Gaza), as well as detailed knowledge of the restrictions on the free movement of people and goods in the years following the Israeli withdrawal from Lebanon.

The Oslo Wave

After the first Iraqi war following Iraq's invasion of Kuwait, waged by the US-led coalition, President Bush invited the PLO, whose leaders were still exiled in Tunis, back into play even though Arafat had sided with Iraq. On 30 October 1991 the Madrid Conference opened, supported by the PLO and opposed by the radical Palestinian factions (Hamas, PIJ, and the Habash Popular Front).

In Palestine, a period of creeping civil war began, with Arafat's men supporting the peace process and the Islamic fundamentalists opposing it. Despite the violent opposition of Hamas and al-Qassam brigades (the armed wing of Hamas, founded in 1991), the peace process continued. In June 1992 Rabin's Labour Party was elected to office in Israel and on 13 September of the following year the Oslo Agreements (Oslo I) were signed in Washington. In 1994, a further agreement between Arafat and Rabin, signed at Cairo on 4 May ('Gaza and Jericho first'), inaugurated Israel's withdrawal from Gaza and allowed Arafat to return to Palestine and set up the first nucleus of the Palestinian Authority. At the end of the year, Arafat, Rabin, and Peres (Israel's foreign minister) were awarded the Nobel Prize for peace. In 1995 the Oslo Agreements were further advanced in Taba, Egypt, with the drafting of a peace agenda (Oslo II) extending to 1999, when the transfer of authority from Israel to the newly established Palestinian Authority should have been completed.

During all this time radical factions, both Israeli and Palestinian, were not just idly watching. On the Israeli side, two episodes in particular constituted a serious threat to peace. On 25 February 1994, a Jewish settler and activist in Kach (an extremist religious nationalist movement), armed with a machine gun, killed thirty worshippers during prayers in the Ibrahimi Mosque (Cave of the Patriarchs). The government disbanded Kach and a similar movement, Kahane Chai, but on 4 November 1995 Yigal Amir, an extreme right-wing activist from the disbanded Kach movement, gunned down Prime Minister Rabin.

On the Palestinian side Hamas, in particular, was trying to undermine the peace process. But its methods were different from those of the past: first, because its attacks were now taking place inside Israel's borders, and second because Hamas's main aim was no longer to drive out an occupying army (as in Lebanon in 1982–5), or moral support for a population in revolt (as in the first Intifada), but undermining the peace process which began when US President Bush opened a window of opportunity for the Palestinians (March 1991) and which not even the assassination of Israeli Prime Minister Rabin succeeded in closing.[44] To bring the peace process to a halt, it was necessary to spread terror among the Israeli population so as to undermine its support for the Labour government.

It is this change of objectives that explains the new terrorist profile. Hamas's campaign against peace began in 1992 with thirteen attacks (for the most part conventional), according to the ICT database. From this viewpoint, the claim by Kydd and Walter (2002: 280–2) that Hamas mobilized only *after* Oslo is not borne out by the evidence. The series of attacks that followed the signing of the Oslo Agreements on 13 September 1993 had been preceded by a greater number of attacks that began in May 1992, just before Rabin's election on 23 June 1992. According to the ICT database, Hamas carried out thirteen attacks in 1992 and ten in 1993, three before the signing of the agreements.

In the years following the signing of the Oslo Agreements, from 1994 to 1996, the attacks continued (especially in 1994), though their composition changed. There was an increase in both the proportion of civilian targets and in the recourse to SMs. It cannot be ruled out that this increase in the propensity for SMs was partly due to the direct contact with the Hezbollah, an unintended consequence of the Israeli decision to deport 415 Palestinian activists (for the most part Islamic) to Lebanon in winter 1992–3. The number of deaths per attack, which had fallen to one or two at the turn of the 1990s, soared to around ten, not much lower than the exceptional level recorded during the last years of the Lebanon wave. At the same time, female suicide attacks, which had been a distinctive trait of the second half of the 1980s—working on data collected by Merari (1990), Beyler (2003) counted at least seven of them between 1985 and 1987—were completely absent. Hamas and the PIJ now had as their primary objectives terrorizing Israeli public opinion and derailing the peace process, and ultimately they succeeded: on 29 May 1996, after a bloodstained election campaign, the Peres-led Labour Party lost and Benjamin Netanyahu, the Likud leader, took over.

The al-Aqsa wave

Netanyahu's election inaugurated a long deadlock in the peace process during which, despite the declarations made by both sides, there was very little progress in implementing the Oslo Agreements. According to Kydd and Walter (2002), Arafat's success in the Palestinian elections of 20 January 1996 contributed to the deadlock. In fact, Arafat's sweeping success revealed the Palestinian leader's strength, and therefore made the continuation of terrorist attacks less acceptable to the Israelis: the Palestinian Authority's failure to oppose terrorism could no longer be explained as weakness, but was perceived to reflect a lack of will. Here the Kydd and Walter approach appears especially appropriate.

After the 1994–6 wave, attacks became less frequent and fluctuated around an intermediate level that prevented the peace process from progressing but did not end it completely. Despite the Wye Plantation Agreement in October 1998,[45] Netanyahu's administration seemed unable or unwilling to push the peace process forward. Change came in the first months of 1999 when, following US President Clinton's historic visit to Gaza, Arafat made some significant gestures: abrogation of the clause in the Palestinian Charter regarding the destruction of Israel, substantial action against Hamas, renunciation of the unilateral proclamation of the state of Palestine before the elections in Israel, and support for Ehud Barak, leader of the Israeli Labour Party. With Barak's victory on 18 May 1999, the peace process resumed and, in the spring of 2000, following a number of diplomatic successes,[46] it appeared on the verge of reaching a positive conclusion. President Clinton staked all his authority on promoting an historic peace agreement, and chaired top-level negotiations at Camp David, where Begin and Sadat had ended the Egypt–Israel war twenty-two years before.

Then something went wrong. In mid-May, fierce battles between Israeli soldiers and Palestinian Authority police revealed that Arafat was no longer able to control his people. At the same time in Israel the National Religious

Party, the champion of the Israeli settlers, withdrew from the coalition government, further increasing the pressure on Prime Minister Barak.[47] At more or less the same time the recurrent survey carried out by the Palestinian Center for Policy and Survey Research (CPSR) revealed that Arafat's approval rating had fallen by eight points in only one month, down from 47 per cent at the end of February to 39 per cent at the end of March, its lowest level since 1994. On 17 May, Barak started to withdraw the Israeli army from Lebanon, thereby keeping an important election promise. As we have noted, some observers[48] believe that, instead of furthering the peace, this gesture may have strengthened the Palestinian opinion that terrorism pays.[49] At the end of July, after two weeks of negotiations at Camp David, Arafat decided to turn down Barak's territorial offer.[50] The peace process had failed once again, and in a short time the new Intifada, known as the al-Aqsa Intifada, would break out.

It is interesting to observe that throughout 2000, until the outbreak of the Intifada on 28 September, in Israel and in the Territories there was no sign of any terrorist attack, whether conventional or suicidal.[51] Hamas also remained inactive. If the peace process failed, it was not because of terrorism. Terrorism, and thus recourse to SMs, would resume only *after* the outbreak of the Intifada in the autumn of 2000.[52] Why then did Arafat and Barak fail to reach an agreement?

There are many possible answers to this question, often strongly influenced by the political beliefs of those who advance them (a review of such answers may be found, for example, in the extensive debate on Camp David published in *The New York Review of Books* between June and September 2001).

Among the possible interpretations is a simple one, suggested by the findings of a joint survey of Israeli and Palestinian public opinion[53] carried out immediately after the failure of Camp David.[54] The main result of the survey is concisely expressed in the heading of the press release: 'Israelis and Palestinians support the peace process and reconciliation but are less willing to pay the price than their leaders.' Responses revealed highly radicalized public opinion on both sides, which viewed their leaders as inclined to compromise. In July 2000, following his breach with Barak, Arafat's popularity, which in April 2000 had fallen to the historical low reached in 1994 when an agreement was looming, bounced back to the highest levels of the past. When Arafat returned from Camp David, he was hailed as a victor. The promise to declare the state of Palestine by a deadline of 13 September fired the Territories, where demonstrators called out to their leader, 'We're ready to give our blood and our souls for you, Abu Ammar' (Arafat's *nom de guerre*).

In this case, then, the failure of the peace process could apparently not be attributed to terrorism or to a lack of political will on the part of the Israeli and Palestinian leaders. Behind the failure of Camp David, there seemed to be also a radicalization of both Israeli and Palestinian public opinion that neither Barak nor Arafat seemed able to oppose with sufficient determination. The outbreak of the al-Aqsa Intifada is usually connected to the visit of Ariel Sharon, leader of the Likud Party and a future prime minister of Israel, to the Esplanade of the Mosques. Palestinians considered this gesture an affront, designed to assert Israeli sovereignty over an area administrated by the Islamic religious fund Watq. However, the situation was already tense. Only two weeks before, convinced that he could still keep the negotiation process alive, Arafat declined unilaterally to declare the state of Palestine, against the expectations of the majority of the Palestinians. The July survey did indeed highlight two important findings: that most Palestinians admired the methods adopted by the Hezbollah in Lebanon and thought that the Palestinians should emulate them (62.6 per cent in favour, 28.9 per cent against); and that most Palestinians believed that, in the event of failure to reach an agreement with Israel, Arafat should unilaterally declare the state of Palestine on 13 September (55.8 per cent in favour, 36.8 per cent against).

This cocktail, which combined frustration over the failed declaration of the state of Palestine and admiration for Hezbollah's successes in winning its twenty-year war against Israel in Lebanon, may well have contributed to the eruption of the Intifada. Once again, as in 1987, the outbreak of the Intifada took the political and military leaders of Palestinian organizations by surprise. The al-Aqsa Intifada produced the most impressive wave of terrorist attacks yet and an unprecedented increase in SMs. However, a disaggregated analysis of the historical series of total attacks yields quite a few surprises in view of the image spread by most mass media. As the Israelis themselves admit (Radlauer 2002), the first months of the Intifada were characterized by the harshness of the Israeli retaliation and by the weakness of the Palestinian response. While in the entire al-Aqsa Intifada the ratio of Palestinian victims to Israelis was around three to one, in the first three months (up to December 2000) it was ten to one. At the same time, contrary to what we may be led to believe, the second Intifada did not start with SMs and did not feature the radical Islamic organizations, like Hamas and the PIJ, among its protagonists. The first suicide attack—which was, moreover, only an attempt, without victims and unclaimed—is recorded on 6 November 2000, more than one month after the beginning of the Intifada. In the first five months, out of fifty-three violent attacks only three were SMs and none of them caused any injury. The first 'real' suicide attack did not occur until 4 March 2001, when a bus in Netanya inside Israel was attacked (three people were killed and fifty wounded).

The total historical series of attacks, suicidal and conventional,[55] reveals that the al-Aqsa Intifada comprised four distinct and successive waves

(Figure 3.5). The first strikes came from traditional secular organizations such as al-Fatah and the Tanzim (the al-Fatah's grass roots). During the first five months of the Intifada, at least twenty-five attacks out of fifty-three were claimed by the Tanzim and fourteen by al-Fatah and Force 17 (Arafat's security force). At the same time, there were only nine 'Islamic' attacks, four of which were claimed by Hamas and five by the PIJ. In fact, the centre of gravity of the struggle, which had moved from Lebanon to Israel after Oslo, now moved inside the Occupied Territories, where Bargouthi's generation grew up during the years of the first Intifada and where Bargouthi was very popular. Throughout those first five months, most attacks (over 80 per cent) were carried out by secular organizations, and recourse to SMs was quite rare (three missions out of fifty-three).

The other three waves of attacks, which took off in rapid succession between the first and the final months of 2001, made extensive use of SMs and were respectively attributed to the PIJ (or to its armed wing, the al-Quds brigades), to Hamas (or to its armed wing, the al-Qassam brigades), and to the so-called al-Aqsa martyr brigades (suicide wing[56] of al-Fatah). Female suicide attacks reappeared during these new waves, initially only among the secular factions, but subsequently—as of 2002—also among the Islamic factions.[57] The al-Aqsa Intifada lasted thirty-three months, almost 1,000 days, that is, from 28 September 2000 to 29 June 2003, the first day of the three-month truce signed by Israeli Prime Minister Sharon and Palestinian Prime Minister Abu Mazen, who managed to obtain the consent of the main secular and Islamic Palestinian factions.

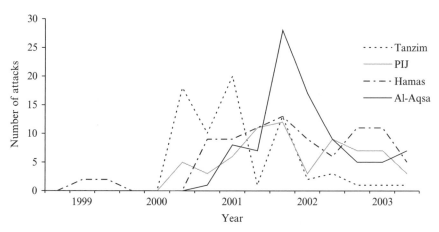

FIGURE 3.5.   The al-Aqsa wave
Source: ICT database.

The number of SMs during the Intifada reached enormous proportions, but this increase mostly reflected the increase in total attacks.[58] However, the propensity for SMs, which increased during the Intifada, never exceeded that reached during the preceding Oslo wave. Even the brutality of the attacks remained within the 'normal' range (four to five deaths per attack) between the first Intifada wave (one death per attack) and the Oslo wave (ten deaths per attack). The new features were the shifting of martyr operations into the Territories and the increase in the number of the groups involved to six:[59] Hamas (thirty-nine SMs), al-Aqsa (twenty-two), PIJ (twenty-one), al-Fatah (two), Tanzim (one), and PFLP (one).

This seems to contradict those interpretations that stress the role of Islamic extremists and their persistent opposition to the peace process (Kydd and Walter 2002), and supports the idea of a competition between secular and religious organizations to achieve political control over the Palestinian insurgency (Bloom 2004; De Giovannangeli 2003). The al-Aqsa Intifada was not aimed at undermining the peace negotiations for the simple reason that, by September 2000, those negotiations had already failed. Besides, the Intifada did not begin with a wave of suicide attacks but with *guerrilla* operations directed by al-Fatah and al-Fatah linked militias. After the failure of Camp David in the summer of 2000, the lack of territorial acquisitions combined with the renunciation of the plan to unilaterally declare the state of Palestine (expected for 13 September, just two weeks before the outbreak of the Intifada), seriously undermined the prestige of Arafat and the Palestinian Authority. At the same time the prestige and authority of the Islamic factions and of their leaders were rapidly growing *due to the mere failure of the peace process*,[60] with no need for 'martyr operations' to boost them. The first problem that Arafat and his men faced was how to regain authority over the Palestinians who, after 13 September 2000, were left without the perspective of peace and without the proclamation of the state of Palestine. The Intifada, which Arafat neither sought nor caused, provided him none the less with an opportunity to recover support. For this reason, the secular factions, not the Islamic ones, were the first to stoke the Intifada fire. By contrast, in the beginning, SMs could be counted on the fingers of one hand. SMs—or rather 'martyr operations'— began later as the Islamic reaction to the attempt by the secular factions to regain full supremacy over the Palestinians. It is this reaction that would compel the secular factions to join in the 'martyr operations' auction, launching the al-Aqsa brigades.

Schematically, we present the following sequence:

Failure of Camp David → Palestinian Authority crisis → Tanzim campaign → Islamic reaction (Hamas, PIJ) → al-Aqsa re-reaction → Palestinian Authority consolidation

The outcome apparently did little for Arafat's popularity, which remained around the minimum historical values (32.7 per cent) throughout the Intifada, and never went above 35–36 per cent. Yet, even though Arafat's star did not shine, the Palestinian Authority and the secular organizations regained strength. In particular, Marwan Bargouthi gained in popularity and, in the survey, attained the best position as Vice-President of the Palestinian Authority: his approval rating was 2.3 per cent in July 2001, 11.3 per cent in December of the same year, 18.9 per cent in May 2002, and continuously over 20 per cent as of August of the same year. Indeed, Bargouthi, imprisoned since April 2002 in an Israeli jail, persuaded—through a mobile telephone call—the most radical Palestinian factions to support the truce proposed by Abu Mazen, the essential condition for starting the Road Map.[61] After three years of struggle and around 100 martyr operations,[62] despite the consolidation of the Islamic factions, power remained steadily in secular hands and the peace process came back under the control of the Palestinian Authority.

The following six months, from July to December 2003, would see the progressive weakening of the Palestinian struggle, with both suicidal and non-suicidal attacks almost halved but not completely stopped. The Road Map would remain unimplemented for the remainder of 2003: on 6 September the Palestinian premier Abu Mazen was constrained to resign (soon replaced by Abu Ala, more loyal to Arafat), and on 18 December Israeli Prime Minister Ariel Sharon announced a 'plan of separation' from the Palestinians in the Occupied Territories.

General Explanations

A striking fact that we can infer from the analysis of the four suicide attack waves is that they seem to have little in common. They are all part of the same story, the Israeli–Palestinian conflict; they took place in a relatively short period of time and on a tiny piece of land, historical Palestine and southern Lebanon; yet the SMs carried out at different times each have markedly distinctive characteristics.

First of all, the territory: the centre of gravity of the SMs is Lebanon in the 1980s; it moves to Israel in the 1990s and then to the Occupied Territories in 2000. Then the type of organizations: Hezbollah and the SSNP in the 1980s, Hamas and PIJ in the 1990s, various martyr brigades, both Islamic and secular, during the second Intifada (al-Qassam, al-Quds, al-Aqsa). To say nothing of the recourse to women: several female attacks occur in the 1980s (mostly secular), they almost totally disappear in the 1990s, and yet they reappear in the new millennium, initially in a secular setting, then also—for the first time—in an Islamic one. Last, the targets: mostly military in the 1980s, civilian in the 1990s, and a mixture of both during the second Intifada.

TABLE 3.1.   Technology of suicide missions

Wave	Period	Frequency	Death toll
Lebanon	1982–5	Medium	Very high
Intifada	1988–90	Low	Low
Oslo	1994–6	Medium	High
Al-Aqsa	2000–3	Very high	Medium

Source: Integrated database.

Above all, it is the frequency and the lethality (the death toll per attack) that changes radically from one period to the other. Table 3.1 summarizes, in qualitative terms, the main characteristics of the four SM waves.

Even if we disregard all external differences—territory, organization, role of women, objectives—the fact remains that it is the very same *technology* (mix of frequency and lethality) of the SMs that changes in the four waves during the 1981–2003 period. This circumstance should make us think carefully before attempting to find an overarching explanation of the phenomenon. All of these cases may have something deep in common. Likewise, it is just as possible, and maybe even probable, that the logic behind SMs differs significantly from one period to the next, and that the search for a common function or denominator is bound to fail.

The first datum that an explanation of SMs has to contend with is that SMs and the overall series of violent episodes in the Middle East conflict, even if related, are distinct phenomena. SMs have existed in the Middle East for around a quarter of a century, yet the propensity of the various insurgent organizations to engage in SMs in the last twenty-five years has varied in a *cyclical* manner, which appears to be substantially independent of the intensity of other violent actions. This simple empirical fact makes the theories that try to explain SMs through generic interpretations of terrorist attack trends useless. Two such theories are particularly widespread among not only the scientific community but also the general public. The first sees terrorism as a tool for undermining the peace process (Kydd and Walter 2002). But this interpretation is incompatible with the evidence: the most spectacular wave of guerrilla operations and SMs—the al-Aqsa Intifada wave—started a few months *after* the failure of Camp David. The second theory, often found in the press,[63] and equally incompatible with the evidence, holds that SMs are part of a *vicious circle of violence* (De Figueiredo and Weingast 1998): every terrorist action would be followed by an Israeli retaliation and every Israeli retaliation would be followed by a terrorist attack. Yet an in-depth analysis of the sequence of terrorist attacks and of Israeli reactions shows that the relationship between Palestinian attacks and Israeli attacks is extremely asymmetrical: Israeli attacks are (in part) explained by Palestinian attacks, but most of the Palestinian attacks are *not* explained by Israeli attacks.[64] This asymmetry stands out in both the analysis Goldstein et al. (2000) pertaining to the 1991–5 period and in our analysis of the second Intifada (see Appendix at the end of this chapter). We cannot rule out the possibility that a more precise knowledge of the attacks (including foiled missions) or a different choice of time lag between actions and reactions[65] could change the empirical results shown here. But in the meantime the hypothesis of a vicious circle of violence does not seem easy to sustain. Rather than such generic explanations of terrorism, it seems more promising to concentrate on focused hypotheses that try to explain why terrorist and guerrilla organizations make ample use of SMs in certain periods but not in others.

The most interesting hypotheses—which are mutually compatible—are those that outline two possible generic purposes of the Palestinian organizations:

1. to boost the morale of its members (especially radical militants) and of the population the organization sets out to represent (Schweitzer 2000; Chandran 2001; Bloom 2004; Kramer 2003); and
2. to enhance the prestige of the organization in relation to that of rival organizations.

The first explanation has been put forward in connection with the cases of the Tamil Tigers in Sri Lanka (Chandran 2001), the Kashmir fedayeen (Wani 2002), and the short cycle of Kurdistan Workers' Party (Partiya Karkeran Kurdistan, PKK) SMs during the second half of the 1990s (Schweitzer 2000); it seems plausible for certain moments of Palestinian history,[66] in particular for the waves related to the first and second Intifadas. Especially with respect to the latter, we may surmise that many Palestinian radical leaders view the Palestinian fight against Israel as a *longue durée* affair, and thus view martyrdom mythology and operations as a means to keep the flame of the cause alive, not just as the sole effective weapon in face of an omnipotent enemy.

The second explanation was first put forward some years ago by Kramer (1991) in relation to the first wave of SMs in Lebanon (1981–5) and to the fierce rivalry between Hezbollah and Amal. Recently, it was put forward again in connection with the second Intifada (Bloom 2004; De Giovannangeli 2003). In fact, the latter period saw not only an intensification of the activism of all major Palestinian organizations, but also the creation of a new armed wing of the Palestinian Authority—the al-Aqsa martyrs brigade—whose main role was to organize martyr operations, just as the Islamic organizations (Hamas and the PIJ) had been doing for a long time.

The competition hypothesis seems quite compatible with the empirical evidence from the al-Aqsa Intifada. The Tanzim → PIJ → Hamas →

al-Aqsa brigades sequence develops in the absence of a peace process and follows a relatively autonomous time pattern that cannot be interpreted as a tit-for-tat reaction to Israeli military actions.[67] Nevertheless, we should stress that the competition hypothesis can be interpreted in two different ways. Some argue that there could be a sort of overbidding game going on between rival organizations that are truly competing with each other (this seems to be the interpretation suggested by, for example, Bloom 2004). Others argue that this competition could take on, at least at a local level, forms of cooperation, a little like in the industrial world when two companies share fundamental research even though they still compete on the market. This theory is supported in particular by ethnographic evidence: it is certain, for example, that meetings between cells of rival organizations are not infrequent at a local level (Bennet 2003a), especially in relation to defence and policing tasks. Furthermore, we may mention that the three 'martyrs' of one of the last suicide attacks carried out before and against the so-called *hudna* (truce) of June 2003 were members of the three main rival organizations (Hamas, PIJ, and al-Aqsa). Moreover, the three attackers left a common last will and testament, a single video recording containing pictures and declarations of the three martyrs.[68] Joint and multiple claims were uncommon in the first period of the al-Aqsa Intifada, but became relatively frequent in the second, especially after the 'Jenin battle' of April 2002 and the subsequent strengthening of the counter-terror operations by the Israel Defence Forces (IDF). Competitive cooperation could have arisen due to the need to join forces both against the Israeli army and against the moderate leaders in the Palestinian camp. Perhaps after the Jenin battle (or Operation Defensive Shield, as the Israelis called it) the main stake for the radical cells in the West Bank and in Gaza became the survival of the Intifada itself.

It is reasonable to believe that there is a degree of truth in both variants of the competition hypothesis. Ethnographic evidence in support of the competitive cooperation hypothesis is indisputable though limited, and thus does not allow us to understand whether cases of cooperation are the rule or the exception. On the other hand, a close examination of the several historical series of all kinds of al-Aqsa Intifada incidents (from suicide attacks to targeted killings, from street demonstrations to military operations) provides a result worth meditating on. We investigated fifteen series of different kinds of incidents, which fall into two main groups: street violence and army–insurgent battles. The second group includes both operations (suicidal or otherwise) against Israeli targets and intra-Palestinian violence, namely, punishment killings of 'collaborationists' and activists of rival organizations (internecine violence,[69] INV). Indeed, the historical series that is most related to SMs is intra-Palestinian violence, while there seems to be no connection between intra-Palestinian violence and other types of attacks (Table 3.2).

TABLE 3.2.   Correlations between internecine violence and attacks (weekly data)

| Correlations and significance ($N = 143$) | | Intra-Palestinian violence | |
		Number of attacks	Number of victims
Suicide missions	Number of attacks	**0.335**	0.341
		($p = 0.000$)	($p = 0.000$)
	Number of victims	**0.406**	0.425
		(0.000)	($p = 0.000$)
Non-suicide attacks	Number of attacks	−0.024	−0.019
		($p = 0.775$)	($p = 0.820$)
	Number of victims	0.081	0.098
		($p = 0.338$)	($p = 0.246$)

Source: ICT database.

Of course, the resulting correlation is just a clue; it cannot prove the over-bidding theory, though it certainly supports it. The simplest way to explain the positive correlation between the frequency of intra-Palestinian violence and that of SMs (a correlation that is not only statistically significant but is also much higher than that of the other fourteen historical series) is to imagine that in periods of maximum competition there is a surge of both SMs and INV, since both are means of strengthening one's position in the internecine competition for the leadership of the anti-Israeli struggle.

The Technology of Suicide Bombing: A Viewpoint on the Palestinian Case

The pattern of SMs raises two distinct questions. Why did several insurgent organizations decide in the early 1980s to resort to SMs? And, once this tactic had become part of an organization's toolkit, what explains temporal variations in the propensity to engage in SMs?

There is no easy answer to the first question. SMs make their way into the Palestinian armed struggle little by little, and it is hard to reconstruct the micro history of the events and causes involved and the sequences of decisions that led to their emergence and diffusion. Perhaps the onset of SMs during the Lebanon wave could be ascribed to contingent and strictly local causes: recourse to SMs was the only way to drive the foreign troops out of Lebanon and there were individuals willing to sacrifice their lives for this cause.

Nonetheless, there is a striking coincidence with the pattern of *international* terrorism: the years in which SMs 'take off' (the first half of the 1980s) are ones in which recourse to air hijacking falls (Figure 3.6).

From the 1950s to the late 1970s, air hijackings were frequent. Over 200 episodes have been counted in three decades, almost one a month, with peaks

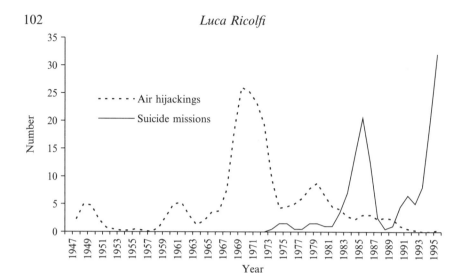

FIGURE 3.6.   The turn of the 1970s: from air hijackings to suicide missions (three-year moving averages with weights: 1/4, 2/4, 1/4)
Source: Nash (1999) for the series of air hijackings; Pape (2003) for the series of (worldwide) SMs from 1980 to 1997; and a mixture of sources (chronologies and databases) for the period 1946–79. These sources do not completely cover the phenomenon, but are probably sufficient to provide an idea of its general trend.

of almost one hijacking per week in 1968–72. Then, as of 1980, resort to this type of action started to fall, and almost completely ceased during the 1990s.

This could be just a coincidence, if nothing else because the onset of suicide attacks in the Middle East is ascribable to important historic and local factors, such as the victory of the Khomeinist revolution in Iran and the presence of foreign troops in Lebanon. Nevertheless, we can speculate that SMs and air hijackings are, in part at least, different means to the same end, that is, to provide visibility to a political cause by bringing it to the top of the international agenda.

Of course, there are also important differences between these two 'technologies'. Although they both put the perpetrators' lives in danger, SMs— when properly managed at the communicative level—seem more likely to enhance the image of the cause for which they are carried out, especially if— as at the beginning—the target is military. Hijacking an aeroplane is almost always seen as blackmail, directed to obtaining something such as the release of prisoners, an amount of money, or the diffusion of announcements. By contrast, SMs convey a greater purity of motives: the simple fact that a number of men and women voluntarily give up their lives for a cause can increase respect for the cause itself. In literary terms, the hijacker is like Ulysses, a fighter who values his life and thus makes an extensive use of *metis* (cunning), whereas the suicide bomber can be perceived to be like Achilles or Hector, a true tragic hero. This is probably one of the roots of the sympathy that causes like those of the Palestinians, the Chechens, or the Kurds evoke in some sections of the public, especially in Europe.[70]

In the Palestinian case, recourse to hijacking was fuelled, in the first place, by its success, that is, by the fact that for many years—between the end of the 1960s and the end of the 1970s—the international community (from the UN to the Pope) came to support the Palestinian cause, up to the point of complete recognition of the PLO (Dershowitz 2002). In the second half of the 1980s, however, air hijackings became less productive, both for the aims of the peace process and, more generally, as a tool for further promoting the Palestinian cause before an international audience which already recognized it. The decreasing efficiency of hijackings broadened the area for actions such as SMs, capable of generating a wider spectrum of desirable consequences for the organizations: to inflict ample military damage, sustain Palestinian morale, directly hit Israeli citizens,[71] and keep the Palestinian issue on the international agenda without disqualifying it.

Of course, SMs have been adopted as a means of struggle at different moments in time and for different reasons: by the Hezbollah and by Amal in the 1980s, by Hamas and the PIJ in the 1990s, and by the al-Aqsa martyr brigades after 2001. Yet it is not implausible to think that the reduced efficiency of air hijackings could be among the reasons that led to SMs becoming established among the *feasible set* of fighting means, especially once these started for specific reasons during the Lebanon wave. From this viewpoint, the 'invention' of SMs by several insurgent and terrorist organizations in the 1980s and 1990s could be seen as a sort of technological leap, which allowed those organizations to enhance the effectiveness of their actions and to pursue agenda-setting objectives without paying the same high price in international opprobrium that hijacking attracted.

As for the second question, on the explanation of temporal variations in the propensity to engage in SMs: as we have seen, recourse to SMs by terror and guerrilla organizations in Lebanon and Palestine follows a cyclic pattern, but at every cycle the 'technology' of the attacks seems to be different (see Table 3.1). The key variable that characterizes the technology of the attacks is their *efficiency*, that is, the count of deaths and wounded per attack. Analytically, it may be useful to single out at least three levels:

1. high-efficiency attacks, al-Qaeda style;
2. medium efficiency attacks, Hamas style; and
3. low-efficiency attacks, PKK style.

Palestinian organizations have successively used all three levels of attacks, with a different mix. In the 1982–5 period (Lebanon wave), there is a prevalence of the al-Qaeda style. In the 1988–90 period, there is a prevalence of the PKK style. In the 1994–6 period (Oslo wave), there is a prevalence of the Hamas style. During the second Intifada (al-Aqsa wave), there is a mix of Hamas and PKK styles.

The purposes of the three types of SM differ. The al-Qaeda style inevitably places martyrdom in the background, since its very high number of victims suggests that the death of the attacker is in the first place a *means*, because it is technically necessary (irreplaceable), rather than an intrinsic *aim* of the mission. The PKK style has an important disrupting purpose, and has always been the prevailing means during quiet times (1986–7, 1991–3, 1997–2000). It resembles a sort of background noise, sometimes broken off by more spectacular actions, carried out in Hamas or quasi-Hamas style. Only the latter, with an *intermediate* number of victims, is able to spark such a mix of terror (in the Israelis) and enthusiasm (in the Palestinians) that seems to be the distinctive trait of the second Intifada.

In conclusion, it is fruitless to ask oneself *in general* why SMs are carried out, whether in reply to Israeli violence (De Figueiredo and Weingast 1998), to block the peace process (Kydd and Walter 2002), or for intra-Palestinian reasons (Bloom 2004). It makes more sense to acknowledge the *versatility* of SMs in as much as an SM can serve purposes that are thoroughly different from each other depending on the context and on the 'technology' employed.

If we look at the four major waves of SMs it seems reasonable to suppose that the prevailing purpose during the Lebanon wave (1982–5) was a *military* one: only a means such as SMs could cause significant losses, and only significant losses could induce the 'foreigners' (multinational troops and the Israeli army) to leave Lebanon. The al-Qaeda style prevails. It is much more difficult to identify a predominating purpose during the first Intifada wave (1988–90), the less pronounced and less distinct of the four waves. SMs, carried out with limited frequency and effectiveness, probably were a means both to keep the Intifada alive and to stop the first faint 'peace attempts' announced through the Declaration of Algiers (the first acknowledgement of Israel by Arafat). The PKK style prevails.

During the Oslo wave (1994–6), SMs become frequent again and their efficiency becomes rather high. Now their main aim seems to be *strategic*: to disconcert the Palestinian Authority and disrupt the peace process. The Hamas style prevails.

Finally, during the al-Aqsa wave, the prevailing aims of SMs seem to be connected to Palestinian *internal policy* issues: to recover the support of most radical militants, sustain Palestinian morale, fuel the Intifada, and legitimize the leadership of one's organization. Frequent and fairly effective SMs are carried out with a mix of the Hamas and PKK styles.

To achieve a real understanding of SMs, perhaps we should abandon the concept of a unique phenomenon and correspondingly the idea of a unitary explanation. The expression 'suicide missions' actually covers many different types of means used by organizations to fight Israel. The variety of such means is in the first place a consequence of the changing and kaleidoscopic nature of the Middle Eastern theatre. If the means have changed so frequently, this is on account of the many changes in constraints and resources that organizations have had to face. There has not always been a strong presence of a foreign army in Lebanon. There has not always been a peace process to disrupt. The Palestinian Authority has not always been on the Occupied Territories, and the secular nationalist organizations have not always been seriously threatened by Islamic competition.

Above all, there has not always been an abundance of volunteers as in recent years,[72] and the will to sacrifice one's own life has not always taken on the guise of the desire for martyrdom. Whatever the goal of the organization, SMs require individuals ready to die. It is on the latter and their motivations that we now concentrate our attention.

The Agents

Profile of Suicide Bombers

Ever since terrorism became a major political issue, many attempts have been made to trace the sociological—and, at times, psychological—profile of the terrorist. The best-known among these attempts is a study by Russell and Miller first published in 1977. The study[73] contained interesting findings, perhaps the most distinct one of which is the high standard of education and prevalent urban origin of terrorists in most of the countries examined, yet *not* in the Arab countries or in the Palestinian context.

A small number of recent studies (Table 3.3), some strictly on SBs, others on militants or activists, allow us to establish a few facts.

These studies agree on a number of typical traits: the age is around twenty-five, the gender is predominantly male, and most subjects are unmarried and childless. Yet, less predictably, all of the studies also find that social background, income, and education are higher than in the general reference population, a fact that confirms the conclusion of Russell and Miller's classic study (1977). The novelty lies in the fact that the relationship between militancy and (high) social status survives most econometric assessments, whether one uses individual data or ecological data (Krueger and Maleckova 2003; Berrebi 2003), and that the same correlation can now be found also in the Palestinian context.[74] Two fundamental points can thus be derived from these studies.

TABLE 3.3.   Some recent studies of terrorists

Author	Sample	*N*
Krueger, Maleckova (2002)	Hezbollah militants	129
Berrebi (2003)	Palestinian suicide bombers	285
Tal (2002)	Palestinian suicide bombers	149
Saleh (2003*a*)	Palestinian militants killed (half were suicide attackers)	171
Barber (2003)	Muslim adolescents during Gaza's first Intifada	900

individual poverty does not influence individual propensity to terrorism; and the effect of education is a positive one. It is not clear, however, whether the effect also relates to the *type* of education imparted or if it is associated solely with the political radicalization induced by education—an association that is also extensively documented for public opinion in several Western countries.

Other findings are more uncertain, but interesting nonetheless. Militancy in insurgent organizations and involvement in suicide attacks seem to be connected to the economic cycle (negative relation: see Gambill 2003*a*), to downward social mobility processes (see Atran 2003*a*), and, most of all, to particularly traumatizing personal experiences, such as the killing of friends and relatives, imprisonment, and isolation due to emigration.[75] This suggests that the motivational drive to engage in SMs is likely to be found in a cocktail of feelings, which include desire for revenge, resentment, and a sense of obligation towards the victims,[76] as also revealed in the many video-recorded pronouncements.

From a psychological standpoint, the most important finding is that there is no apparent connection between violent militant activity and personality disorders—with the exception of a few rare cases, found for instance among some members of *Rote Armee Fraktion*, the German terrorist group also known as Baader Meinhof. In the great majority of cases, psychiatric evidence indicates that terrorists are perfectly normal individuals. Nor is there any apparent significant association between the inclination towards militancy (suicidal or otherwise) and particular types of personality.[77]

All of these results, whose political importance cannot be underestimated—just think of President Bush's and the Dalai Lama's idea of fighting terrorism by raising educational standards—are subject to a caveat. We do not know for sure how many SMs may be ascribed to veteran militants who at some point in their career decide to become martyrs, or to civilian volunteers who apply to enrol *directly* as the martyrs of an organization. Whatever the case, most of our data on the perpetrators of SMs relate to people who have been screened by the organizations. The selection process tends to be strict—indeed, eighteen months of training and preparation (Atran 2003*b*)—even though during the second Intifada the length of the training periods seems to have decreased significantly, especially for women.[78] This means that the traits of aspiring martyrs and of those who are chosen among them can be significantly different. The ethnographic evidence suggests the existence of a large surplus of candidates (Hassan 2001*a*), a circumstance which would increase the significance of the selection.

As Hudson (1999: 47) reports:

The highly selective terrorist recruitment process explains why most terrorist groups have only a few pathological members. Candidates who exhibit signs of psychopathy or other mental illness are deselected in the interest of group survival. Terrorist groups need members whose behaviour appears to be normal and who would not arouse suspicion. A member who exhibits traits of psychopathy or any noticeable degree of mental illness would only be a liability for the group, whatever his or her skills. That individual could not be depended on to carry out the assigned mission. On the contrary, such an individual would be more likely to sabotage the group by, for example, botching an operation or revealing group secrets if captured. Nor would a psychotic member be likely to enhance group solidarity. A former PKK spokesman has even stated publicly that the PKK policy was to exclude psychopaths.

In the Palestinian context, this exclusion of fragile or disturbed personalities is explicitly acknowledged by both secular organizations, such as al-Aqsa (Zoroya 2002), and religious ones, such as Hamas and the PIJ:

Islamic Jihad, which along with Hamas trains the suicide killers, explains 'We do not take depressed people. If there were a one-in-a-thousand chance that a person was suicidal, we would not allow him to martyr himself. In order to be a martyr bomber, you have to want to live'. The same strange logic applies for Hamas, which rejects anyone 'who commits suicide because he hates the world'. (Pipes 2001*b*)

Similar recruitment and sorting mechanisms are presumably adopted for training. Even if we leave out the extreme case of September 11, where some of the required skills were highly specialized, it is clear that, at equal conditions, a trained aspiring militant has a better chance of being selected than an untrained applicant. Once again, Hudson calls our attention to this point, reporting a study by Edgar O'Balance on the PKK.

[The author] suggests the following essential characteristics of the 'successful' terrorist: dedication, including absolute obedience to the leader of the movement; personal bravery; a lack of feelings of pity or remorse, even though victims are likely to include innocent men, women, and children; a fairly high standard of intelligence, for a terrorist must collect and analyze information, devise and implement complex plans, and evade police and security forces; a fairly high degree of sophistication, in order to be able to blend into the first class section on airlines, stay at first class hotels, and mix inconspicuously with the international executive set; and have a reasonably good educational background and possess a fair share of general knowledge (a university degree is almost mandatory), including being able to speak English as well as one other language. (Hudson 1999: 39).

If Hudson's considerations are correct, then both the lack of a connection with specific personality disorders and the positive association with education could be the outcome of the recruitment process. Until we have data on aspiring militants and martyrs *before* the selection process, a firm conclusion would be premature. There is, however, one element that leads us to believe that the association between SMs and education might survive a similar test. A survey of Palestinian public opinion reveals that in the general population more radical political views—including support of martyr operations—are associated with higher educational levels, while less educated people tend to endorse more moderate views—the latter pattern is not only Palestinian.[79] It is thus plausible to suggest that the gap between the educational standards of the population and those of the martyrs outlined by empirical research is only *amplified* rather than created by the sorting processes.

Attitudes Towards Suicide Bombers

The Palestinian public's attitude towards SMs, while revealing significant differences between social categories, has also changed considerably over time. According to the Jerusalem Media and Communication Centre (JMCC), one of the two institutes that has been conducting periodic surveys since 1993,[80] support for SMs remained decidedly low (around 25 per cent) until 1999 and soared abruptly to around 75 per cent during the first two years of the al-Aqsa Intifada, to then drop progressively during the last twelve months of the Intifada. In April 2003, eight weeks before the declaration of the truce on 29 June 2003, it fell to around 60 per cent. Support for SMs, and in general for a hard line against Israel (mistrust in negotiations, furtherance of the Intifada), seems to vary mostly on account of two parameters: social residence and centrality. More radical positions prevail in the Gaza Strip and in the refugee camps, and moderate ones in the West Bank and smaller villages. Furthermore, as is the case in Western societies, the more radical positions are adopted by 'strong' social categories (male, educated, young) while the more moderate ones are adopted by weaker or marginal social categories (female, poorly educated, elderly).

As such, support for SMs does not surprise us so much. It spread especially after the failure of Camp David in July 2000, and may thus be interpreted as a reaction to the failure of the peace negotiations. What might surprise us is the fact that, in the Palestinian surveys conducted between April and June 2003 (that is, immediately before the truce was declared), a majority of interviewees declared their support for *both* of the following positions:

1. continue the Intifada and suicide operations (JMCC poll of 5–9 April); and
2. support the Road Map (CPSR survey of 3–7 April).

The contradiction between these two positions may be ascribed to the diversity of sources, yet an internal review of each source reveals similar contradictions, which implies that at least some respondents must hold both views simultaneously. If we consider only the first source (CPSR), we notice that the majority of Palestinians (66 per cent) believe that 'armed confrontations so far helped achieve Palestinians' rights in a way that negotiations could not'. If we consider only the second source (JMCC), we notice that the prevailing position among the Palestinians is that of carrying on *concurrently* both negotiations and the Intifada. Where does this apparent schizophrenia in Palestinian public opinion come from?

A possible early source, as reported by Karmon (2000), might be found in the so-called phase strategy adopted by the PLO at its first national congress in 1974. It foresees 'the liberation of every inch of Palestinian territory which can be obtained through political negotiations with Israel and the continuation of the struggle from this territory for the liberation of all occupied Palestine'. This strategic goal of the PLO might be 'stored' in the minds of the public. Still, it cannot be the whole story. The majority support for attacking Israeli civilians is, after all, relatively recent, given that as late as in 1999 SMs were opposed by the majority of Palestinians.

In order to understand the recent Palestinian mindset, we should look at other elements stored in public opinion. The first is the growing distrust of the Palestinian Authority, that is, of the subject supposed to be conducting successful negotiations with Israel. For several years surveys carried out by CPSR have documented the poor reputation of the Palestinian Authority, which is accused of corruption, of lacking democracy, and of using strong-arm methods. Another element is objective lack of tangible results in the peace process, even, if not especially, in relatively peaceful times (such as during the Netanyahu administration of 1996–9). Palestinians may have become convinced that the only way to place their right to a state of their own at the top of the political agenda is through resounding violence.[81] Finally, there is the belief that negotiations on their own are insufficient to extract concessions from Israel, as well as the wild overestimation of the military power of the Arab world: a week before the fall of Baghdad in 2003 the majority of Palestinians prophesied Saddam Hussein's victory, and only 11.9 per cent expected a US victory.

Yet the element that might better help us understand the Palestinian position is the fear, often revealed by the polls, of a flare-up of the fratricidal strife that proved responsible for a considerable number of Palestinian deaths even during the al-Aqsa Intifada.[82] The Palestinians are aware that the peace process could come to a halt should the Palestinian Authority fail to take steps to prevent attacks against the Israelis. At the same time, they are aware of the strength of the radical factions, whose moral integrity they admire in contrast to the corruption of the Palestinian Authority. They believe that a new period of internal conflict would begin if the Palestinian Authority were to confront forcibly the thugs of the Intifada. This is the main concern of the majority of Palestinians (78.9 per cent), and this is the prospect—above the failure of the peace process—that must be avoided.

Therefore, what the opinion polls reveal is that the Palestinian public is in favour of peace negotiations but at the same time does not believe that negotiations alone are sufficient to free Palestine. Furthermore, it is not willing to pay the price set by Israel—disarmament of the more radical factions—for fear of a civil war. It is probably from this cluster of beliefs and preferences that the continuing support which, despite everything, SMs receive from the Palestinians stems.

The Motives of Suicide Bombers

Ethnographic evidence on 'martyrs' is scarcer than social-demographic evidence. The only extensive studies are by Andoni (1997), carried out at the end of the Oslo Wave in the al-Shati refugee camp in the Gaza strip, and the investigation by Hassan (2001a), a Pakistani researcher who interviewed around 250 recruiters, trainers, would-be suicide bombers, and relations of suicide bombers between 1996 and 1999.

These two studies, the second of which is still largely unpublished, give us a first-hand idea of the beliefs and motivations of aspiring martyrs. They have to be considered with some caution, since they could provide only a partial picture of the phenomenon. They cover a period when SMs were being monopolized by Islamic organizations. In order to obtain a complete picture, we would also need to have a number of equally extensive ethnographies of suicide bombers from secular organizations, which played an important role both before and after the period investigated by the two researchers (during the Lebanon and the al-Aqsa waves).

Hassan's study (2001a) of suicide bombers' traits confirms the central results of the profile analyses:

None of the suicide bombers—they ranged in age from eighteen to thirty eight—conformed to the typical profile of the suicidal personality. None of them were uneducated, desperately poor, simple-minded, or depressed. Many were middle class and, unless they were fugitive, held paying jobs. More than half of them were refugees from what is now Israel. Two were the sons of millionaires. They all seemed to be entirely normal members of their families. They were polite and serious, and in their communities they were considered to be model youth. Most were bearded. All were deeply religious.

The motivations that emerge most frequently from the subjects interviewed by Andoni and Hassan are of three types. First of all, they believe they have been 'chosen' by Allah ('it is Allah who selects the martyrs'), and that they will appear before him in Heaven—'it is very, very near, right in front of our eyes. It lies beneath the thumb. On the other side of the detonator'—with all the advantages that this entails: the immediate absolution of all their sins, the possibility to intercede for one's relatives, and to enjoy the company of seventy-two *houris*.

Second, they feel humiliation, anger, and indignation about Israeli violence and the desire for revenge ('The Israelis humiliate us. They occupy our land, and deny our history'). Objective confirmations of the association between suffered harassments and the wish to become a martyr also begin to emerge. Saleh, a young Palestinian economist, writes:

I have constructed a socioeconomic profile on 67 Palestinian suicide attackers. My preliminary findings suggest that almost all of them had a prior history of injury or arrest by the Israel Defence Force (IDF). Moreover several of the suicide bombers have had an immediate family member killed by IDF. (Saleh 2003a)

In this cluster of motivations, the desire for revenge is important, though it should not be separated from the other motives. As such, revenge could lead to the *sole* pursuit of the enemy's death rather than its pursuit through *one's own* death.[83] Revenge takes on the guise of martyrdom because it is mixed with other motives and states of mind. One can surmise, for example, that the losses experienced daily by the Palestinians through the deaths of family and friends can lead not only to humiliation, resentment, or desire for revenge, but also to a sense of obligation towards one's loved ones, to some kind of disintegration of one's own personal identity, and to indifference to death (Ceronetti 2003).

Finally, there is a third, very important set of motives: deep involvement in the Palestinian cause and an aversion to the moderate position of the PLO. This last motive emerges starkly from one of the two cases investigated by Andoni, regarding Alì. Alì was a youth during the years of the first Intifada, and he enlisted in al-Fatah after having personally witnessed a long string of killings of friends and relatives by Israeli soldiers. At first, Alì was a very involved member of al-Fatah, but as time went by he became increasingly sceptical and disenchanted. The lack of progress made by the peace negotiations, which did not bring any real change into the arena, had drawn him step by step away from al-Fatah and close to religion, up to the point of turning him into a martyr of PIJ.

Alì does not look upon religion as a primary force leading him to martyr-dom, but as a resource for his mind. More than a religious choice, Alì's conversion is a reaction to his *disappointment* with the moderate and com-promising positions adopted by the secular organizations. Religion, as Fes-tinger (1957) says, helps to reduce cognitive dissonance—in Alì's case the dissonance between his intentions, pure thus radical, and the reality of the organization he belongs to, corrupt and too defeatist. From this point of view nothing is more deceptive than the interpretation of 'martyrdom operations' as an effect of religious manipulation or brainwashing: if the story of Alì has anything to teach it is that an individual's role can be decidedly active in his decision to become a suicide bomber.[84] Religious beliefs do not mould individuals, forcing them to become martyrs; they are sets of ideas that 'are there', as on the shelves of a supermarket, waiting for someone to make them their own. The question we should ask ourselves, then, is under what condi-tions individuals involved in a political cause discover the symbolic resources that religion, or perhaps certain religions more than others,[85] has to offer. An answer to this question would require a lot of work. Yet it might be worth-while to note that, from this point of view, Palestine is not the exception, it is the rule. Indeed, ten years ago (1994) Casanova reported, in one of the most brilliant and profound studies on the secularization theory, that as of the end of the 1970s religions started their 'reconquest of the public sphere'. The Khomeinist revolution in Iran, the Catholic victory against the Communist regime in Poland, the Sandinista revolution and the theologies of liberation in Latin America, and the reawakening of Protestant fundamentalism in the United States, are all phenomena indicating the pressing, sudden, unexpected irruption of religion in political and social conflicts in the last years of the twentieth century. In most of the historical cases studied by Casanova, religions apparently were not the principal causes of the radicalization of the conflicts, but rather conflict radicalization found symbolic resources in religion to further certain social and political causes. Today, religion, which the illuminist revolution progressively confined to the private sphere, is tending to 'de-privatize' itself and make its way back to the heart of public debate and involvement. From this viewpoint, the case of Palestine and SMs appears altogether less special.

Other-worldly aspirations, desire for revenge, and frustrated political radicalism clearly emerge as key motivations from the interviews. There are others, however, that are not so easy to infer directly from the interviews, but that surely play a non-marginal role. One of these is external pressures, which in a context like the Palestinian one are extremely strong. Palestinian public opinion polls, for example, reveal that around half of the population believes the Palestinian Authority cannot be criticized without fear of retaliation.[86] One of the latest surveys also reveals that Palestinian public opinion has a distorted picture of itself, in as much as it overestimates the will to continue the armed struggle and underestimates the disposition to compromise.[87] This widespread radical ideology and feeling makes it very difficult for moderate Palestinians to express their opinions.

A stark sign of the presence of context effects—peer pressure, emulation—is evinced by the 'clustering' of the places of origin of suicide bombers. A tiny number of refugee camps around the West Bank towns of Hebron, Nablus, and Jenin supply the great majority of martyrs. On 17–18 May 2003, for example, three suicide attacks were carried out by three students of the Hebron Polytechnic University. The most striking case was a football team from Hebron (the 'Jihad Mosque') that provided Hamas with eight attackers out of its eleven players. Six of the eight attackers were next-door neighbours and members of the same clan, the El Kwassama (Olimpio 2003).

We should also mention certain individual and family factors. It is well known that martyr operations bring a number of benefits to the martyr's family: a boost in prestige within the local community, compensation in cash from the group that organized the operation, and—until he was overthrown in 2003—a 'bonus' from Saddam Hussein's emissaries that, relative to the income of Palestinians, is a very large sum. Economists Krueger and Maleckova (2003) wonder whether there may be a causal connection between the increase of said amount from \$10,000 to \$25,000 between February and March 2002 and the soaring increase of SMs in March 2002, an increase that led to the 'battle of Jenin' (also a media battle, with allegations and counter-allegations between Palestinians, IDF, and Amnesty International[88]). We might add that Saddam's financial rewards to martyrs began in 2000, straight after the first Intifada. The Israelis took this set of motivations seriously; they have been trying to lessen the incentive effects by inflicting heavy costs posthumously on the martyrs' families, and from July 2002 they began to systematically destroy houses of martyrs' families. Yet, without solid econometric evidence, we cannot be sure whether these connections are more than just coincidences.

Finally, there is a further source of potential motivations, which we might call the 'symbolic calculation'. Diego Gambetta drew the attention of the authors of this book to two circumstances: as far as we know, several suicide bombers are not militants but civilian *volunteers*;[89] and martyr operations are *signed*. A martyr is not an anonymous militant who carries out a mission decided by his organization, and whose name may remain unknown. A martyr is a volunteer who has been selected, who leaves a last will and testament (normally on a videotape[90]), and who will be remembered by his fellow countrymen through photographs, posters, murals, and plaques exhibited in public places. In other words, one of the rewards of a martyr is fame, the prestige that the operation will bring to his name and his family.

While a militant may die anonymously, and thus sacrifice himself twice, a martyr pays 'only' with his life but obtains fame and recognition in return. The symbolic calculation may explain why certain people may prefer to choose martyrdom directly over militancy of a more traditional kind.

This type of motivation reveals an individualistic aspect of martyr operations, and helps us understand why such operations manage to attract individuals lacking religious motivations (secular SMs). Furthermore, if it is true that, among the motivations of suicide operations, revenge occupies an important place, it might be reasonable to believe that SMs are preferred indeed because a signed operation is more effective in satisfying the thirst for revenge than an anonymous one.[91] And, in fact, the contents both of official announcements and of certain videotapes often explicitly refer to Palestinian victims that the suicide operation aims to avenge (Margalit 2003).

Why dying to kill?

So far, we have listed a series of reasons and causes that can induce individuals to carry out SMs: resentment of harassment, community or group pressures, radicalization of the conflict, as well as various other economic, symbolic, and religious factors. While these may be the ingredients of the cocktail, what is it that keeps them together, 'precipitating' them in a wish for martyrdom?

Given our presently limited knowledge, any answer to this question is unavoidably conjectural. We can, however, try to 'assemble' the pieces and workings of a hypothetical mechanism. This operation is not just optional, for once we consider the individual causes it emerges that none of them is sufficient by itself to explain the phenomenon and some of them are not even necessary.

Take revenge, for example. As strong a motive for action as it may be, as such the wish for revenge should lead to desiring the other's deaths rather than one's own. To survive the enemy is normally thought an essential part of revenge, unless dying is the only way to take revenge. Here the key concept does not seem to be hatred but indifference to death.[92]

Similarly with money. Regardless of how big Saddam Hussein's cheque may have been, especially in proportion to Palestinian living conditions, it is clear that the martyr will not enjoy even one dollar. And many missions have taken place with little or no financial reward for the martyr's family.

Religion too is not a necessary motive, if nothing else because—in Palestine as elsewere—a significant number of martyrs are secular. Even external pressures, while making a difference for some, may not be always a motive if it is true that in various cases (especially referred to by women) the wish to become a martyr seems to have developed in isolation, and *against* the wishes of the individual's family and friends.[93]

None of these elements seems decisive, and it is their combined presence that makes the cocktail explosive. Yet the problem remains: why is the cocktail explosive? Considering the cases of the Kurds, the Chechens, and the Tamils, one can see that these peoples, whose militants have engaged in SMs, have all suffered from severe repression which has involved civilians and which has imposed serious restrictions on the minimal conditions in which individuals can socialize and earn a living. This repression has assumed extreme forms in Palestine. Military occupation town by town and neighbourhood by neighbourhood, uninterrupted growth of settlers,[94] networks of checkpoints, curfews, travelling restrictions, control of water and energy sources, and confiscations of property and of bank accounts have not just humiliated the Palestinians but produced a drastic, extreme, and tragic contraction of an individual's set of options. In a country with an economy that depends heavily on exchanges with Israel, and in which society depends entirely on external aid from Arab countries and the international community, the so-called closure of the territories implies having literally nothing to do or to imagine.

Severe material deprivation—accompanied by the experience of having family members, friends, and acquaintances killed, injured, arrested, or forcibly stripped of their means of livelihood—can generate a progressive dismantling of a person's emotional world.[95] To say that all of this causes despair would not be sufficient. A farmer whose crops are destroyed by drought, or a woman who loses her child in an accident, is desperate. Yet a Palestinian experiences something different. A person who cannot live in a world made of real alternatives is naturally driven to create and live in a highly mental world, in which symbols and fantasies take the place of reality. If political ideologies and religious myths are so important in Palestine, this is mostly because, especially after the failure of the Oslo Agreement and the closure of Occupied Territories,[96] reality has shrunk to a minimum (Said 2000), a result not of an accident but of a conflict with a well-defined antagonist.

In a society in which social life is frozen and horizons and normal careers do not exist, war and the Intifada are not just the only world but the only real *social system*. In such a social system, solidarity spreads with exceptional speed, and the only real careers are those connected to the political factions: administrator, officer, policeman, political leader, militant, or volunteer. Among this handful of careers, the shortest route to the highest position, since it confers prestige and can bestow eternal glory, is indeed that of the martyr. As Biggs points out (Chapter 5, this volume) the appeal of martyrdom is that it combines the images of the victim and of the hero.[97]

On their own, external pressures are not sufficient even if, in such conditions, they can drive an individual towards one of the few possibilities of giving a meaning to his life. Money, as such, is not a sufficient motivation for an individual to give up his own life, but knowing that his family will be generously compensated can help remove an important impediment to his self-sacrifice. The thirst for revenge should lead to a desire for the death only of the enemy but, if decisions are driven by the desire for glory, then one's *own* death can become an objective that is just as important as the enemy's death. In a world where real alternatives are scarce, and symbols represent everything, the sense of obligation and the desire for glory can spark extreme individual reactions,[98] bestowing effectiveness on group pressures, financial rewards, resentment, and metaphysical beliefs—motives that on their own are unlikely to generate martyrdom.

An observer coming from a rich and secularized society might be perplexed by the idea that the quest for glory, albeit of a desperate kind, can become such a driving force. After all, economic theory holds that, in pursuing his own interests, man is averse to risk. Nevertheless, if we want to understand martyr operations, we cannot use as the point of reference the society we live in. Contemporary Western society is just *one* type of social system. There are also 'Durkheimian' types of social system, in which society gains moral primacy over the individual. Furthermore, the individualistic form assumed by Western social systems is relatively recent. As Berger (1974) reminds us, one of the crucial expressions of individualization is the 'obsolescence of the concept of honour'. One of the consequences of such obsolescence is that the quest for glory is supplanted by the quest for fame, which can be achieved without paying a high price or running an extreme risk. But glory is unachievable without a heroic deed and the sacrifice that goes with it.

For these reasons, wondering why Palestinians are willing to risk their lives to the point of the supreme sacrifice is misleading. If glory becomes a key aim of the action, risk ceases to be a cost and becomes a resource, an irreplaceable means of advancement in the most prestigious career. The real question to ask is: why has glory become so important in Palestine? The answer is as simple as it is disarming: because almost everything else is missing.

APPENDIX

Data Quality and Sources

Quality of the Sources

This appendix reports essential information on organizations, attacks, and public opinion. Readers should be aware that the quality of basic information is quite poor, and should therefore be very cautious about accepting as 'data' empirical evidence that is quite dubious and controversial (obviously, caution should also be used with our data, despite my efforts to avoid inaccuracies and mistakes).

The following six main issues should be borne in mind.

Internet style. A considerable amount of literature and information on the Arabic–Palestinian conflict can be found on the Internet. It suffers from the shabby and imprecise styles of many papers published on the Internet. The sources of information are often omitted or stated imprecisely. This often makes it impossible to know whether two coherent pieces of information are independent of each other. In fact, authors quite frequently reproduce parts of essays or articles published by others in an uncritical manner, thus propagating errors.

Conflicts between sources. Both data on SMs and data on public opinion are often inconsistent. The same episode is often described in totally different ways in the main databases: dates, death and injured counts, and organizations can differ according to source.[a] The same is true of surveys. The two principal sources of information on Palestinian public opinion are the Palestinian Center for Policy and Survey Research (PSR; CPSR up to 2001) and the Jerusalem Media and Communication Center (JMCC), which, however, often supply contradictory data: in the case of voting preferences, for example, Islamic organizations obtain greater support in the JMCC sample, while nationalist support is greater in the PSR sample.

---

[a] This is true, quite surprisingly, also for very famous episodes that were in the news at that time, and in some cases are already included in history texts. See, for example, the attack on Lod airport in 1972: date, number of casualties, and number of wounded vary considerably depending on the sources.

Incomplete databases. There is no truly complete and reliable database on terrorism. Even the two main databases (Israeli Institute for Counter-Terrorism, ICT, and Memorial Institute for the Prevention of Terrorism, MIPT) contain remarkable omissions. The ICT database on the Israeli–Palestinian conflict disregards most of the episodes that took place in Lebanon, while the ICT database on international terrorism provides only a sample of the episodes that took place after 1970.[b] The MIPT database, resulting from a combination of two different databases (1968–97 and 1998 to date), aspires to completeness, yet it ignores many SMs that took place in Israel and in the Occupied Territories, especially in recent years (during the 1998–2002 five-year period, for example, MIPT's underestimation verges on 50 per cent).

Quality of data in academic essays. In many cases, the reviewing of papers published in scientific journals is inadequate. Take, for example, two important essays like Kydd and Walter (2002) and Pape (2003). The fundamental series of attacks by Hamas reported by Kydd and Walter does not correspond to any known series (Bloom 2004). The 'universe' of SMs reported by Robert Pape is by no means a universe (it contains around 50 per cent of the events), and many episodes have been improperly classified (Kramer 2003).

Terminology. Some issues are trivial, others are not. Among the trivial issues is the wide variety of transliterations from Arabic, as a result of which the name of a person or of an organization may be spelled in completely different ways (making searches on the Internet complex). Among the less trivial issues is the fact that the main databases adopt similar categories that, however, rarely coincide exactly. The MIPT database concentrates on incidents, while the ICT database focuses on attacks. In the first section of the MIPT database (1968–97), there is no 'suicide mission' category, while there is in the second section (1998 to date) and in the ICT database. But in these two databases it is restrictively defined as 'suicide bombing'. In the ICT database, secular organizations connected to the Palestinian Authority are divided into 'mother' organizations (al-Fatah) and armed wings (al-Aqsa, Tanzim, Force 17), but in the case of Islamic organizations no equivalent distinction is drawn between political wings and armed wings (Hamas/Izz al-din al-Qassam; PIJ/al-Quds). On the other hand, in the MIPT database even the attributions of the secular groups are often generic, in as much as no distinction is made between al-Fatah and other groups or branches of them connected to the same (Force 17, Tanzim, al-Aqsa).

Ideology. Finally, the war of words should not be neglected. The territories conquered by Israel in 1967 are 'occupied' territories for the Palestinians but

---

[b] The ICT site declares willingness to provide the universe of attacks, but two separate official requests by members of our group to obtain such universe (international database) remain unanswered.

'disputed' territories for the Israelis. Suicide attacks are acts of terrorism for the Israelis, while they are 'martyrdom operations' for the Palestinians when they are not 'sacred explosions' (Hassan 2001*a*). In particular, it is essential for the Muslim to avoid the word 'suicide' (an act that is condemned by the Koran) and to replace it with the word 'jihad' (an act that is encouraged by the Koran, according to its prevailing interpretation). Furthermore, Palestinians, Lebanese, and Syrians believe that the martyr concept includes anyone whose death is caused by the Israelis, from the youth who throws stones to the baby killed accidentally by a missile.[c] Therefore, we should be alert when we use the Internet: the key words we have to use in a Western context are not the same for a Middle East one.

Organizations

At least twenty organizations,[d] of various backgrounds and origins, operate or have operated during 1981–2003 in the geographical area studied here. Two organizations are Israeli: Kach, founded by Meir Kahane at the beginning of the 1970s, and Kahane Chai, founded by Kahane's son following the assassination of his father in 1990. Both organizations were declared terrorist by the Israeli government in 1994 after the massacre committed by settler Baruch Goldstein, a member of Kach. Of the anti-Israeli terrorist and guerrilla organizations, at least five are Lebanese or Syrian, the rest are of Palestinian origin. To save space, we have preferred to use acronyms and short names in this section as in the text, adhering mostly to the transliterations adopted in the ICT database. The following list includes organizations or factions (armed wings) covered by our reconstruction of events:

al-Fatah	'Victory', acronym of 'Conquest by means of the Jihad'
Amal	'Hope', acronym of 'Lebanese resistance detachments'
al-Aqsa	al-Aqsa martyr brigades (suicide wing of al-Fatah)
Al-Qassam	Izz al-din al-Qassam brigades (battalions, forces)
Al-Quds	Al-Quds brigades (squads)
Baath-Leb	'Resurrection', Lebanese Baath Party
Force 17	Arafat's security force
Hamas	'Zeal', acronym of 'Islamic resistance movement'

---

[c] In January 2004 the Palestinian Authority asked the journalists working for Arab satellite TV stations to describe as 'martyred' instead of simply 'dead' the Palestinians killed by IDF soldiers (*Jerusalem Post*, 12 January 2004).

[d] I am referring here to the terror organizations (such as Hamas, PIJ, al-Aqsa), the guerrilla organizations (such as SSNP and LCP), and also the organizations that were basically guerrilla organizations in some periods and basically terror organizations in other periods (such as Hezbollah).

Hezbollah	Party of God
LCP	Lebanese Communist Party
SNO	Socialist Nasserite Organization
PFLP	Popular Front for the Liberation of Palestine
PFLP-GC	Popular Front for the Liberation of Palestine-General Command
PIJ	Palestinian Islamic Jihad
SSNP	Syrian Socialist Nationalist Party
Tanzim	'Organization', al-Fatah's grass roots

The following table lists only those organizations involved in the Israeli-Palestinian conflict that have resorted to SMs on at least four occasions. They total nine organizations, which could become twelve if we add at least another three considered responsible for between one and three SMs.[e] Table A3.1 provides some essential, and inevitably brief, information on each organization.

TABLE A3.1. Organizations in the Israeli–Palestinian conflict resorting to suicide missions

Name	Year founded	Founder	Leader	Ideology	Region of operation	Links
Hamas/ Al-Qassam	1987–91	Yassin/ Zaccaria Walid Akel	Rantisi	Islam (Sunni)	Territories, Israel	Iran, Syria
PIJ/al-Quds	1979	Fathi Shaqaqi	Abdallah Shalah	Islam (Sunni)	Gaza (West Bank)	Iran, Syria
al-Aqsa (22 + 0)	2001	Marwan Barghouti?	?	Nationalist	West Bank (Gaza)	al-Fatah
Hezbollah	1982	Hussein Fadlallah	Hassan Nasrallah	Shiite (Khom.)	Lebanon	Iran, Syria
Amal	1975	Musa Sadr	Nabih Berri	Shiite	Lebanon, International	Iran, Syria post-1985
Baath-Leb	1966	Michel Aflaq?	Assem Kanso	Pan-Arab	Lebanon	Syria
SSNP	1932	Anton Saadeh	?	Nationalist	Lebanon	Syria
al-Fatah/ Tanzim	1964	Arafat	Arafat	Nationalist	Israel, Territories	—
PFLP	1967	Habash	Abu Ali Mustafa	Marxist Pan-Arab	International, Israel	Syria

[e] The organizations credited with a low number (1–3) of executed SMs (with or without success) are: LCP, SNO, PFLP-GC (al-Fatah and the Tanzim, both credited with fewer than four SMs, have been considered together in Table A3.1). The list has to be viewed with extreme caution, given the uncertainty of several attributions and the poor reliability of several sources. Furthermore, it should be specified that the number of SMs of Amal (which we include in the table of the main organizations) is very uncertain, and could also be fewer than four.

To interpret correctly the last column of the table, we should bear in mind that some terrorist organizations make a sharp distinction between their political and military levels, while others make a weak one. For example, in secular and nationalist organizations connected to the Palestinian Authority it is quite common for the political level (al-Fatah) not to claim, or even to condemn, the actions committed by its suicide wing (al-Aqsa martyr brigades). In this case we considered the armed wing as a separate organization, and indicated the mother political organization in the last column (links).

In other organizations, the political and military levels are difficult to distinguish; at most, a useful distinction may be made between central leadership and local groups. Hamas and PIJ, for example, at times claim attacks in their own names, at other times in the names of their respective armed wings (al-Qassam and al-Quds), but in general the political level does not dissociate itself form the military level. In such cases we doubled the names of the organizations (Hamas/al-Qassam) and of the founders (Yassin/ Akel), indicating the nation or nations sponsoring the organizations in the last column (links).

For many organizations located in Lebanon and Syria (Hezbollah, Amal, SSNP, Baath-Leb), there are no acronyms identifying the military level. Also, in these cases we indicated only the sponsor nation in the last column.

Suicide Missions

A quantitative picture of SMs can be built from three main sources: aggregate evaluations by experts (at times based on personal or classified databases), large databases available to researchers (ICT, MIPT, TRC[f]), and chronologies of principal terrorist events. A recent addition to these three sources is the reconstruction of the universe of SMs (1980–2001) performed by Pape working on the online Lexis-Nexis database (Pape 2003).

The first source (expert evaluations) differs fundamentally from the others in that it allows only for large aggregate comparisons (between organizations, between nations, and at times between historical periods) and it does not produce any data-sets since there are no records of single events. This makes it impossible to make cross-tabulations and, more generally, to apply data analysis techniques. On the other hand, we can prepare useful data-sets relying on databases, chronologies, and press articles (as Pape did), but the number of 'cases' is usually fewer than those estimated by experts.

[f] Terrorism Research Center, founded in 1996 (www.terrorism.com).

In order to build up a picture of SMs in the ME area that is as complete as possible, I created a new database that integrates information from five types of sources:

1. three large databases (ICT, MIPT, TRC) plus the international ICT database (which contains a sample of attacks);
2. three chronologies (MIPT, CDISS[g], Nash[h]) plus Clara Beyler's chronology of female SMs (2003);
3. all of the SMs reconstructed by Pape (2003);
4. a number of very specific pieces of news provided by two experts on Lebanon (Robert Fisk and Martin Kramer); and
5. press articles published on the Internet, in particular by the *New York Times*, *Haaretz*, and the *Jerusalem Post*.

The database (which will be called the 'integrated database') contains all of the single episodes that meet at least five requirements:

1. to be mentioned in at least one of the above-mentioned sources;
2. to have taken place in a known place and at a known date;
3. to have taken place in the ME area in the thirty-four year period between 1 January 1970 and 31 December 2003;
4. to have an Israeli or Israeli-related target;[i] and
5. to fulfil the essential requirements of an SM (self-explosion or no-escape-plan mission), or at least of almost-suicide missions (very high-risk missions, VHRM).

In the database, missions are classified as foiled missions (SM_1), failed missions (SM_2), successful missions (SM_3), and almost-suicide missions (VHRM). Successful missions are further divided into 'certainly suicidal' and 'probably suicidal', depending on the accuracy of the available description of the event.

From this database, whose characteristics have been described in detail elsewhere (Ricolfi and Campana 2005), we have selected a set of suicide attacks that took place between 1981 and 2003. An attack is defined as a mission that has been executed (with or without success), and that can be considered certainly suicidal. Thus, the database on which we relied completely ignores three kinds of records: foiled missions (SM_1), inadequately documented successful SMs (uncertain SM_1), and VHRMs. Overall, there are 224 cases, of which sixteen failed (SM_2) and 208 were carried out successfully (SM_3).

[g] Centre for Defense and International Security Studies (Lancaster, www.cdiss.org).
[h] See Nash (1999).
[i] Our analyses exclude the (very few) episodes of anti-Palestinian or anti-Arab actions carried out by individuals or terror organizations connected with Israel.

This mixture of sources allows us to increase considerably the total number of SMs. To provide an idea of the information gained by our database, we performed a comparison, restricted to the total attacks ($SM_2 + SM_3$) in the 1981–2003 period,[j] with the three main chronologies, the three principal databases, and Pape's 'universe' (Figure A3.1).

As we can see, none of the individual sources covers all the SMs, while an aggregate recourse to all twelve sources selected by us provides estimates that are quite close to the aggregate estimates calculated by the experts[k] (around 250 SMs between 1981 and 2003).

The totality of the SMs can be divided into four main types, according to their outcome (success or failure) and to the adopted technology (self-explosion or no-escape mission) (Table A3.2).

As a rule, our calculations consider only the entirety of certain and actually performed SMs regardless of their more or less complete success. In our detailed analysis of the incidents that took place during the al-Aqsa Intifada, entirely and exclusively based on ICT data, we used the attacks that ICT itself classified as suicide bombing (see section on 'Incidents during the Intifada') as the proxy for the number of SMs.

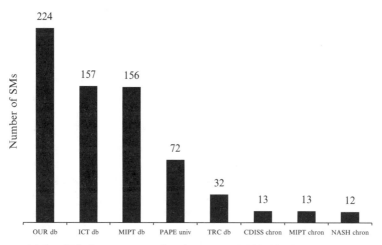

FIGURE A3.1.   Relative coverage of main sources (1981–2003)

[j] The comparison gives an idea of the amount of data actually contained in different sources (1981-2003). To obtain an idea of the differential selectivity of the sources, we should restrict our attention to a period covered by all seven sources (1988–97). In this case, the relative coverage (our database: 100) shows 71.9% for the MIPT database, 68.7% for the ICT database, 53.1% for Pape's 'universe', 28.1% for the TRC database, 25.%, 21.9%, and 18.7% for the CDISS, MIPT, and Nash's chronologies respectively.

[k] The only important discrepancy concerns the period of the Lebanon wave, for which the estimates by Schweitzer exceed the number of records in our database by 15–20 units (see n. 32).

TABLE A3.2. Suicide missions by result and technology

	Successful	Failed	Total
Self-explosion	162	6	168
No-escape mission	46	10	56
Total	208	16	224

Attacks

In order to calculate the 'preference' or 'propensity' for SMs, which is the key variable of our historical analysis of the attacks, it is not sufficient to know the absolute number of SMs (numerator) since this number has to be related to the number of total attacks (denominator). The problem is that, while the number of SMs does not vary much from one source to the other (since they are intrinsically striking events), the total number of attacks is critically dependent on the conventions and stipulations of the various sources.

Chronologies, for example, relate lists of events, which often also include political and judicial decisions. Some sources (MIPT database and Israel Defence Forces, IDF) prefer to record incidents, which may in turn be defined in a very restrictive manner (as in the case of the MIPT database) or in an ultra-extensive way (as in the case of the Israeli army statistics). Some databases (ICT and TRC) record only attacks, but with levels of coverage that differ considerably according to geographical areas and historical periods.

Usually, chronologies of global terrorism record only a few tens of events every year. Databases, on the other hand, can record even several hundreds of attacks or incidents. In 2001, for example, the US State Department database recorded 348 attacks, the MIPT database recorded as many as 1,531 incidents, and the TRC database recorded 128 attacks (the number of international terrorism attacks recorded in the ICT database is unknown because only a sample of ICT data is available online).

If we look at the Israeli–Palestinian conflict, matters become even more complex. In 2001, 132 attacks were recorded in the ICT database, 259 incidents were recorded in the MIPT database, and nine attacks were recorded in the TRC database. MIPT coverage is almost thirty times that of TRC. The picture gets even more complicated when we consider the Israeli databases that record incidents. For the period of the Intifada both the IDF, or rather the Israeli army, and the ICT provide statistics on incidents and not only on attacks. These numbers are much greater than the number of attacks reported by ICT itself. On average, for each 'attack' recorded in the ICT database there are four 'incidents and casualties' (same source) and forty-two 'terrorist attacks' (according to the IDF database).

In conclusion, we may state that between a chronology on main 'terrorist events' and an accurate database on 'terrorist incidents' there can be a 1:1,000 ratio. In practice, this means that any estimation of the propensity to engage in SMs should be considered extremely conventional, and should thus be used with extreme caution.

In our case, we thought that a reasonable choice could be represented by the exclusion of both extremes (chronologies and IDF incidents) and the adoption as denominator of the number of attacks recorded by the more specialized database, the ICT 'terror attacks' database (which in actual fact contains both the terrorist attacks, in the strict sense of the word, and those which ICT itself defines as guerrilla attacks). The only, serious, flaws of this database are that it does not adequately cover Lebanon, which has been the theatre of countless terrorist attacks, mostly during the 1980s, and that it seems quite incomplete before 1988. To remedy these drawbacks, we integrated the ICT historical series of attacks in the Palestinian area (Israel + West Bank + Gaza) with the MIPT historical series of incidents in the Lebanese area (both databases: 1968–97 and 1998 to date). Of course, the various historical series are not directly comparable, because the average number of MIPT incidents is considerably greater than the number of ICT attacks, and the selectivity of the two MIPT databases looks different.[1] Furthermore, the 'attention' to Lebanon is completely different in the three most complete sources available: maximal in the first MIPT database (1968–97), minimal in the ICT database,[m] and moderate in the second MIPT database (1998 to date).

To integrate the different sources and build a summary index of the number of attacks, we used the following formula:

$$\text{Total attacks} = tot_{sm} + [wx_{mipt} + (1 - w)x_{ict}](1 + \lambda)$$

Where:

tot_{sm} = total number of executed SMs in ME area (our integrated database)

x_{mipt} = estimated number of non-suicidal attacks in Great Israel[n] (first MIPT database)

x_{ict} = number of non-suicidal attacks in Great Israel (ICT database)

w = 0.50

λ = MIPT ratio of Lebanon (non-suicidal) attacks to Great Israel (non-suicidal) attacks.

[1] A comparison between the ICT and the MIPT databases clearly shows that the latter is more selective in 1968–97 than in 1998–2003. This difference in selectivity grew wider following the last updating of the MIPT database (in November 2003) in which several incidents were dropped from the 1968–97 period and several incidents were added to the 1998–2003 period.

[m] The ICT database includes terror and guerrilla episodes from 1970 up to the present, but it is not clear from what date the database can be regarded as relatively complete (until 2003 the database was presented as complete from 1970, now it is presented as complete from 1988).

[n] By Great Israel we mean Israel plus Occupied Territories (West Bank and Gaza).

The expression within square brackets indicates an estimate of the number of non-suicidal attacks in Israel. It is defined as the arithmetic average of the observed ICT series and the MIPT series transformed into an ICT-like scale. In the 1992–2003 period x_{mipt} is given as equal to x_{ict}, while in the 1981–91 period it is given as equal to the series of MIPT incidents multiplied by an appropriate chaining coefficient (1.3286, which is the ratio between ICT attacks and MIPT incidents in the years 1992–7 during which the two databases behave in the most consistent manner).

The value of λ is taken from the second MIPT database (1998 to date) for the most recent period, while for the period prior to 1998 it is taken from the first MIPT database (1968–97). To make the two series comparable the λ values prior to 1998 were compressed in order to eliminate the gap which divides the two series (to this end we assumed: $\lambda_{96-97} = \lambda_{97-98}$).

Incidents during the Intifada

As we have already seen, besides the 'terror attacks' database, ICT also has a database on 'incidents and casualties' that allows us to add another thirteen historical series to the two historical series of SMs and non-suicide attacks, for a total of fifteen historical series:

- attacks (terror and guerrilla) classified as suicide bombing
- attacks not classified as suicide bombing
- counter-terror operation/interception
- riot/violent demonstration
- crossfire
- roadblock confrontation
- internecine violence
- violent clash
- initiated military operation
- work accident
- unrelated accident
- targeted killing
- infiltration
- unclaimed killing
- unknown

Starting with the records of single incidents, each historical series can be aggregated on a daily, weekly, monthly, and annual basis and can also be split into three levels: incidents, deaths, and injured. This opens up to a wide range of analyses, starting with the simpler ones. We can, for example, try to identify series that are not correlated with SMs, or try to understand which sets of historical series tend to covariate together, or check whether SMs behave essentially as dependent variables or rather as a response to Israeli violence and in particular to targeted assassinations. This is not the place to report the whole of our investigations on this data-set, which include various factorial analyses and multiple regressions (on both levels and increments). We can, however, report some general results.

First, when we subjected the fifteen historical weekly series to factor analyses, three main factors, corresponding to three levels of the conflict, emerged:

1. extremist Palestinian militancy (suicide and fratricidal missions);
2. military combat (conventional terrorist attacks and Israeli military operations); and
3. street violence (the so-called popular Intifada°).

This pattern turns up when we work on the number of attacks as well as when we consider the number of people killed.

Second, using the markers of one factor as dependent variables and the markers of the other two, lagged by one week, as independent variables, we usually see causal relationships from terrorism to anti-terrorism but not vice versa (targeted killings, in particular, do not seem to constitute typical causal precedents for SMs). Table A3.3 briefly represents, by way of example, the matrix containing all of the principal correlations between markers of the three main factors.

The above table shows the main possible influence relations between variables. Only three correlations (in boldface) are statistically significant, and only two of them survive when the lagged dependent variable is introduced as a second regressor (the square brackets indicate that the relationship does not survive this last check). As we can see, SMs seem to have two main effects: to spark off Israeli military reaction (r = 0.42) and to rouse the crowd (r = 0.33). However, they do not seem to be susceptible to Israeli military operations (no matter how we look at them) or mass demonstrations.

TABLE A3.3. Main correlations between variables

		Independent variables (lagged)		
$N = 142$		Suicide missions	Military operations	Violent clash
Dependent variable	Suicide missions	—	0.04	0.07
	Military operations	**0.42**	—	0.08
	Violent clash	**0.33**	[0.20]	—

° On the distinction between 'military Intifada' and 'popular Intifada', likewise on the split of Palestinian public opinion in followers of the two, see JMCC, poll 48 (April 2003).

The conclusion to this analysis, which is of course tentative due to the simplicity of our checks, is that the historical series of the al-Aqsa Intifada shows a marked asymmetry between SMs and Israeli reaction. SMs appear as some kind of *primum mobile*, which explains a lot of things but does not seem to be so easily ascribable to the changes in the main variables of the conflict. In this sense, the theory of the spiral of violence, which sees the conflict as a vicious circle of actions and reactions by both parties, is hardly compatible with available empirical evidence.

Opinion Polls

The two main sources of information on Palestinian public opinion are the Palestinian Center for Policy and Survey Research (PSR; CPSR up to 2001) and the Jerusalem Media and Communication Center (JMCC).

Data published by both sources cover the 1993–2003 decade. The first JMCC survey dates back to February 1993; the first CPSR survey dates back to September 1993. In one decade the two centres carried out around 110 surveys, or one survey a month.

Even if the questions in the surveys of the two centres are quite similar, the results often diverge considerably. On the whole, it seems that the answers provided by the PSR sample are relatively moderate and secular, while those provided by the JMCC sample are more radical and pro-Islamist.

To obtain an idea of the differences, it could be interesting to compare the answers given to two surveys carried out during the last days of the war in Iraq, just after the appointment of Abu Mazen and the presentation of the Road Map. Opposition to the Intifada swings between 15.2 per cent and 21.4 per cent according to the wording of the question[p] in the 'radical' sample (JMCC), but it grows to 30.8 per cent in the 'moderate' sample (PSR). Attacks against Israeli civilians are supported by 47.3 per cent of the 'moderate' sample[q] and by 59.9 per cent of the 'radical' sample.[r]

Yet probably the most direct and clear way to evaluate the divergence between the two samples is to compare the relative weights of the nationalists and of the Islamists within them. This can be achieved through two questions, one about the leaders and one about the parties.[s]

---

[p] Questions 6 and 7, JMCC poll 48.
[q] Question 23, PSR poll 7.
[r] Question 11, JMCC poll 48.
[s] For the sake of precision we should note that the PSR question is open-ended, while the JMCC one is closed. Furthermore, the JMCC questions are about trust, while the PSR questions are about voting intentions. Nevertheless, we feel that the differences detected are so wide that they can hardly be ascribed to such methodological technicalities.

TABLE A3.4.   Relative weight of nationalists and Islamists in two samples: leaders

Leader	JMCC	PSR
Arafat + Shafi (Palestinian Authority)	25.4	45.8
Yasin (Hamas)	10.5	15.4
Others	25.0	1.1
No one/no vote	39.1	37.7
Total	100.0	100.0
Nationalist–Islamist difference	14.9	30.4

TABLE A3.5.   Relative weight of nationalists and Islamists in two samples: parties

Party	JMCC	PSR
al-Fatah	25.0	25.8
Hamas + PIJ	31.3	22.7
Others	5.7	18.1
No one	38.0	33.4
Total	100.0	100.0
Nationalist–Islamist difference	−6.3	+3.1

With regard to the leaders, assuming 100 as the number of expressed opinions, we obtain the following picture (Table A3.4).

On JMCC data, Arafat and Shafi, the two most prominent figures of the Palestinian Authority, collect more than twice the votes collected by Sheik Yasin, spiritual leader of Hamas (25.4% against 10.5%). Yet the difference between nationalists and Islamists, which is already considerable in JMCC data (14.9%), becomes much greater if we use PSR data (30.4%).

A similar variation may be observed when we look at the support to various Palestinian parties (Table A3.5).

Arafat's party obtains fewer votes than the two Islamist parties together if we use JMCC data (−6.3 per cent), but it obtains more votes if we use PSR data (+3.1 per cent).

4

Al-Qaeda, September 11, 2001

STEPHEN HOLMES

On 11 September, 2001, nineteen young men—fifteen from Saudi Arabia, two from the United Arab Emirates, and one each from Egypt and Lebanon—seized control of four large commercial airliners departing from Boston, Newark, and Washington, DC. At 8.47 a.m., mission leader Mohamed Atta piloted American Airlines flight No. 11 into the North Tower of Manhattan's World Trade Center (WTC), and at 9.05 a.m., with the world's television cameras now trained on the site, a second group barrelled United Airlines flight No. 175 into the South Tower. Finally, after a third suicide squad had crashed American Airlines flight No. 77 into the Pentagon at 9.39 a.m., the fourth team, under assault by a group of passengers, ditched United Airlines flight No. 93 into the Pennsylvania countryside at 10.03 a.m. These transcontinental flights were apparently selected because of the negligible number of passengers likely to be on board at the time and the 10,000 gallons of aviation fuel that, upon impact, transformed the planes into immense incendiary bombs. At the WTC, the hydrocarbon fires caused by the burning fuel overcame flimsy fireproofing and, after a very short time, brought the massive skyscrapers crashing down, killing close to 2,750 people; 198 more were killed in the Pentagon attack. Although suicide terrorists had been loading vehicles with explosives and ramming them into buildings for decades, this was the first time that hijacked airplanes had been successfully deployed for such an assault. The political after-effects have been so massive that we can, without much exaggeration, describe 9/11 as the suicide mission (SM) that shook the world.

We know that passengers on some of the flights were lulled into passivity by being informed that the aircraft were returning to the airports. We also know that the hijackers murdered some pilots and members of the crew before impact, probably by slitting their throats. But except for a few cellphone conversations, mostly from United Airlines flight No. 93, little direct evidence informs us about what actually happened on board. Common sense, however, supplemented by the massive inquiries made after the fact, supports one elementary proposition, namely, that this was a carefully

planned and organized operation conducted efficiently by trained and disciplined operatives. Not only did the hijackers or their dispatchers choose
these specific flights to minimize passenger resistance and maximize the fuel
load; they also carried on board lethal weapons that were inconspicuous
enough to pass undetected through lax baggage screening. In the weeks
leading up to the attacks, some of the hijackers had made dummy runs on
these same transcontinental flights to study flight procedures and crew
behaviour. This detail, too, suggests that the hijackers were cool professionals. They were not simply zealots but disciplined zealots, capable of
patience, able to execute a dangerous plan without attracting attention.

To succeed in such an audacious operation, the perpetrators also needed,
besides instruction in terrorist tradecraft, logistical support from a variety of
co-conspirators positioned around the world, especially in Europe and the
Middle East. Money funnelled through Dubai, among other places, allowed
the future suicide pilots to take flying lessons on single-engine aircraft and
flight simulator practice for commercial jets. The final decision to undertake
the 9/11 attack was probably made when Khalid Shaikh Mohammed and a
handful of men around Osama bin Laden met Atta and other members of the
Hamburg cell in Afghanistan sometime around November or December
1999. As the plot unfolded and members of the Hamburg cell moved to the
United States, supervisors abroad kept track of their doings, and eventually
coordinated the just-in-time arrival of the rest of the squad. But not even a
highly detailed chart of the 9/11 chain of command would answer the most
important questions, namely: why did the operational chief behind 9/11,
Khalid Shaikh Mohammed (arrested in Pakistan in March 2003), decide to
deploy a suicide team to attack these specific US targets? Why did he not
instead send hit-and-run commando teams, as he apparently did in 1993?[1]
And why did the hijackers, especially the fully informed pilots, agree to
follow his instructions in this case, even though it involved participation in
a predictably terminal mission?[2]

The role of religious beliefs, sentiments, and codes of conduct in the 9/11
plot remains a subject of intense dispute. Many well-informed commentators
insist that 'what bin Laden has said and done has everything to do with
religion' (Anon. 2002: 16). Religious convictions can no doubt lead young
men to grow beards, avoid supposedly unclean foods, and embark on pil-
grimages. But can we plausibly assert that the religious beliefs of the 9/11
terrorists *caused* them to plan and carry out the attack? This question arises
because many of those involved in the plot have let the world know that they
did it to express devotion to God or to curry favour with God.

Such professions of piety deserve a respectful hearing, no doubt. But they
obviously do not decide the issue. Sometimes people do what they do for the
reasons they profess. But private motivations cannot always be inferred from

public justifications. The problem is not so much that individuals with secretly secular purposes may feign religious goals to burnish their reputations for purity. The problem, instead, is that one and the same decision could have been taken for either religious or secular reasons. In that case, it is often impossible to tell which motive played the dominant role. For instance, emotions with a religious tinge, such as dread of contamination, might induce some individuals to face death without blinking; but so can non-religious emotions, such as the craving for blood revenge. An Islamic husband, living in Germany, may lock his wife inside the house because he wants to be pious and thinks that female sequestration is what piety demands; but he may also do it to exercise arbitrary power and thereby compensate psychologically for feelings of impotence and passivity that afflict the rest of his miserable life. According to one account, Islamic beliefs govern his behaviour but, according to the other and no less plausible account, Islamic beliefs merely provide an acceptable pretext. So how can we decide which account is more persuasive in any particular case?

Does Osama bin Laden want to eject the United States from Saudi Arabia because its troops were desecrating sacred soil, or is he aggrieved, like any anti-colonialist or nationalist insurgent, that the United States is plundering his country's natural resources? Does Ayman al-Zawahiri, the physician who founded Egyptian Islamic Jihad and who is usually considered bin Laden's closest associate, want to overthrow Egyptian President Hosni Mubarak because the latter is an apostate or because he is a tyrant? When secular and religious rationales are equally credible and would each, independently, trigger the action to be explained, we simply cannot know with any certainty that the decisive factor was religion.

Underestimating these methodological difficulties, some commentators have argued, without qualifications or disclaimers, that 9/11 was a faith-based initiative. When confronted by doubters, they even complain, like Benjamin and Simon (2002: 159), that 'So much of what was heard from al Qaeda after the attacks sounded to Americans like gibberish that many chords of the apocalypse were missed'. Americans are simply too secular to appreciate the grip of religion on the minds of militants and fanatics, they maintain. But is this correct? Not necessarily. In fact, the opposite may be true. Some Americans, at least, think more easily in Biblical than in secular terms. They certainly know much more about 'the end of days' than about political intrigue in Saudi Arabia. Shared by the terrorists and their targets, Biblical phraseology may therefore have attracted too much, not too little, attention, obscuring secular motivations less apparent to unsophisticated observers.

Why, for example, did the attackers target the WTC? According to Kobrin (2002), the targeting decision can be explained only by the planners' religious beliefs. Her analysis assumes, correctly, that knocking down great towers in lascivious cities is a Biblical theme. Radical Islamists, she goes on to say, viewed the Twin Towers as idols worshipped by the pagans. Assuming (falsely, it now appears) that an earlier al-Qaeda operation had targeted the Seattle Space Needle, she speculates that *the organizers of the 9/11 attack saw the Twin Towers as deliberately mocking Islamic minarets.* From the minaret, five times a day, all Muslims are called to prayer, that is, to total submission to God. Operating inside the Islamic belief system, Kobrin claims, the terrorists interpreted the United States' great skyscrapers as an affront to God, as a refusal to submit to God, and even as a supremely blasphemous attempt to become God.

This fanciful analysis cannot be falsified. But it cannot be demonstrated either. Moreover, the targeting of the WTC can be quite comprehensively explained without any reference to Islam. Haughty pride may be a sin before God, but it also and independently arouses outrage and resentment in ordinary mortals. Moreover, the 2001 attack on the towers was a return visit, a mopping up of unfinished business. The desire to redeem a botched attack of 1993, and therefore to communicate in blood the dogged persistence of the terrorist conspirators, must have played at least some role in the choice to strike the WTC a second time.

True, the attack took place in a symbolic space against meaningful targets where the high density of human life may even have been secondary to the perceived sentimental value of the buildings themselves. But the symbolism was not necessarily Biblical or messianic. The Twin Towers could have been targeted simply as symbols of the United States. To attack them was to attack the United States *in effigy.* Bin Laden himself referred to the towers as 'icons' not of the United States' blasphemy but of its arrogant power.[3] Depicting himself and his co-conspirators as rods of the Lord, he reported that 'God Almighty hit the United States at its most vulnerable spot. He destroyed its greatest buildings. Praise be to God.'[4] These expressions of US haughtiness were located in the country's greatest urban centre and were militarily impossible to defend. When explicating the symbolic meaning of the towers, bin Laden seldom mentions the United States' presumptive 'war against God' but stresses instead its hypocrisy: 'Those awesome symbolic towers that speak of liberty, human rights, and humanity have been destroyed. They have gone up in smoke.'[5] The symbol under attack was the illusory façade of liberty that the United States shows to the world even while colluding with non-democratic regimes around the world to oppress and despoil Muslims and indeed the majority of mankind.

Many of the key actors in the 9/11 drama, admittedly, articulate their grievances using archaic religious language. But the very fact that the code involved is ancient while the behaviour we want to explain is recent suggests the inadequacy of causal theories that overemphasize the religious element. If SMs are a consequence of Islamic fundamentalism, why did previous waves of Islamic fundamentalism not give rise to SMs? If the Kamikaze and the Black Tigers undertook SMs for secular reasons, how can we be confident that the 9/11 terrorists could have undertaken their suicide mission only if the religious reasons they allege were their deepest reasons? This sceptical line of thought suggests that non-religious motives may well have been predominant in the 9/11 mission as well. To pursue this suggestion, it will be helpful to divide our inquiry into two parts, discussing first the perpetrators and then the instigators and supervisors of the plot.

The Hijackers

According to Hume (1985: 577), 'such is our natural horror of death, that small motives will never be able to reconcile ourselves to it'. So what were the big motives that reconciled the hijackers to their impending deaths? Many commentators offhandedly assert that the hijackers were simply programmed for death, having been socialized inside a cultural system that normalizes suicide terrorism. Suicide terrorism, we are told, has become a social norm. Some interpreters are even willing to say of al-Qaeda that 'the culture of martyrdom is firmly embedded in its collective psyche' (Gunaratna 2002: 10).

Such appeals to social norms or a culture of martyrdom are not very helpful, however. They are tantamount to saying that suicide terrorism is caused by a proclivity to suicide terrorism. A less tautological approach starts elsewhere, with the observation that, at some level, Atta and the others did what they did because they were recruited, trained, and instructed to do so by their commanders in a quasi-military hierarchical organization that had 'declared war' on the United States. That is to say, their murderous act must be explained *organizationally* and not merely ideologically or psychologically or even sociologically. They were told what to do and behaved like soldiers, obeying superiors and dying for their (imaginary) country. They were no doubt recruited, in part, because of their observed zeal for the cause and their evident willingness to follow orders, especially after publicly sworn pledges made obedience a matter of personal honour.

But a willingness to follow orders, even when sealed by vows, needs a special explanation when it entails a willingness to face death. The most commonly fielded elucidation for this staggering readiness is also the most straightforwardly religious. The nineteen hijackers 'loved death', it is repeatedly alleged, not because they were nihilists but because they believed that, in their case, death did not exist. Each pilot interpreted the crash site as a doorway through which he would slip to another and happier life. They thought that the impact would vaporize them instantly into the presence of the Prophet, and that death in jihad was a pathway to redemption, a ticket to everlasting life. They did not have to overcome their fear of death, accordingly, because *they had no idea* that they were about to die.

Under some circumstances, presumably, young men with an exclusively technical education could genuinely believe something of the sort. Recruiters for the plot were no doubt looking for candidates who could at least entertain on occasion the hope of a rewarding afterlife. And a naive belief in paradise, as Voltaire waggishly remarks, can induce young 'imbeciles' to risk their lives:

Ce sont d'ordinaire les fripons qui conduisent les fanatiques, et qui mettent le poignard entre leurs mains; ils ressemblent à ce Vieux de la Montagne qui faisait, dit-on, gouter les joies du paradis à des imbéciles, et qui leur promettait une éternité de ces plaisirs dont il leur avait donné un avant-gout, à condition qu'ils iraient assassiner tous ceux qu'il leur nommerait. (Voltaire 1964: 190)

Let us call this 'the Voltaire thesis'. In religious conflicts, cunning priests exploit the blind folly of foot soldiers, especially their castle-in-the-sky fantasy of a never-ending afterlife. This irreverent claim assumes, in typical Enlightenment style, that charlatans and swindlers can easily 'run' young men who are gullible and easy to hoodwink.

No doubt, the distinction between dupers and duped has a lot to be said in its favour. And it may even help us understand something about the 9/11 plot. Perhaps the hijackers died with their eyes shut, without realizing that death was on the horizon. But we cannot be satisfied, at the outset, with the conclusion that the 9/11 hijackers were 'imbeciles' in this sense. Their belief that they were taking a plane ride to paradise cannot end all inquiry into the multiple causes of their extraordinary behaviour. So what other factors could account for their willingness to die? Another very simple answer comes immediately to mind. Perhaps some of them were willing to die because, for highly personal reasons, they wanted to die.

Professional terrorist organizations presumably aim to recruit effective and reliable killers, not maladjusted misfits. On the other hand, the need to find volunteers for self-destruction may occasionally force them to compromise the highest standards of mental health. Here is one account (of uncertain reliability) of Wail Alshehri and Waleed Alshehri, two brothers in Atta's crew, described as unmotivated and not very smart, devout to some degree but also willing to indulge in smoking and pop music.

A turning point came late in 1999 when Wael, 25, fell into a deep depression, Abdel Rahman said. His friends say it was not just depression, but perhaps even a suicidal tendency, and he was forced to take a leave of absence from his work as a gym teacher. He went to see a faith healer in Mecca accompanied by Walid, 21, who was 'just drifting in life,' his brother said. It was at this point that the two apparently fell under the sway of a militant Islamic cleric who counseled both to read the Koran, to fast, and to take up jihad. (Sennott 2002)

Although they prove nothing, such anecdotes are suggestive. Personalities prone to self-destruction may be impeded from acting as they wish by a powerful social norm that declares suicide dishonourable. In the Islamic tradition, as in Christian and Jewish traditions, suicide is also understood as 'a sin because only God has a right to take the life he has granted'.[6] Since man is God's property, self-murder is a form of theft. So how might individuals inclined to kill themselves get around such powerful prohibitions?

One way would be to enlist in a cause that redescribes suicide as honourable, pious, and heroic, as self-sacrifice for a 'higher' cause. The social stigma of suicide probably deters some clinically depressed youths in Muslim societies from taking their lives. But the ideal of militant jihad gives them a way to circumvent this taboo. By enlisting in an SM, a suicidally depressed individual can kill himself with social approval. All he has to do is agree to kill an enemy of Islam in the process. Needless to say, if Wail Alshehri or another one of the 9/11 hijackers was suicidally depressed, he would have had overpowering reasons to *conceal* his depression. Suicide terrorism patently undertaken to escape from personal despair would not only violate Islamic norms, it would also destroy the 'social meaning' of the act, which must *appear* to involve painful self-sacrifice for a higher cause. The incentives in this case for deceptive signalling are so great, in fact, that no public pronouncements by a suicide terrorist can provide decisive evidence about his private motivations. Religion may explain the hijackers' willingness to die or it may have simply made their non-religious desires more socially acceptable. It is hard to imagine discovering proof that demonstrates conclusively which explanation holds true.

Mohamed Atta

The most exhaustively studied member of the hijacking squad is the 33-year-old Egyptian team leader Mohamed Atta. He has been the focus of so much attention not only because he played a central role in the plot but also because his home bases of Cairo and Hamburg are accessible cities, where foreign policemen and journalists have considerably less difficulty in conducting probes than they would, say, in Saudi Arabia's Asir province. Nothing we have learned suggests that *he* was suicidally depressed. But this does not settle the question of his motive for joining a plot that would end his life. He may have been motivated by religious belief, as many commentators contend, or by non-religious desires wrapped in religious rhetoric, or by some combination of religious and non-religious commitments and convictions. How can we decide?

Atta's family was *not* exceptionally pious, and the women in the family did not wear the veil. His father was a relatively prosperous lawyer, without any apparent affiliation to the Muslim Brotherhood. His childhood was punctured in 1981 (Atta was 13), when Anwar Sadat, President of Egypt, was assassinated by Islamic militants. Whatever he felt about them at the time, as the years ticked by he may have gradually come to see Sadat's assassins as role models who laid down their lives to 'slay the Pharaoh'. In the manual consulted by the pilots before the attack (discussed below), the terrorists are told to imagine that they are re-enacting the heroic exploits of famous Islamic heroes and martyrs. But, for an Egyptian like Atta, Sadat's assassins may have provided more easily understandable models than the early caliphs and imams.

Atta eventually graduated in architecture from Cairo University but seems to have had no sustained contacts at the time with militant Islamic organizations. He began his studies in city planning in Germany in 1992, at the Hamburg-Harburg Technical University, working part-time with a German company for the next five years. His path to radicalization is uncertain. Some observers have tried, but it is probably impossible, to pinpoint the moment when he started 'marching to a different drummer'.[7] We know a little more about his turn toward religious observance. Soon after arriving in Hamburg, for instance, a homesick Atta quickly became more devout than he had seemed to be back home in Egypt. He displayed his devoutness by establishing cultural distance, isolating himself from his surroundings, 'refusing to touch food prepared in pots used to cook anything that was not *halal,* and avoiding contact with dogs and women' (Burke 2003: 214–15).

In August 1995, Atta arrived back in Cairo for a three-month study visit just as the Egyptian government was unleashing a violent crackdown on the Muslim Brotherhood in response to that summer's attempt to assassinate President Mubarak in Addis Ababa. Atta now sported a full beard, having recently undertaken a pilgrimage to Mecca. When he returned to Hamburg in November 1995, he was even more outwardly devout. His mastery of Islamic texts was apparently rudimentary but, in April 1996, he swore before acquaintances to die as a martyr. The 'last will and testament' that he authored at the time at a radical mosque near Hamburg railway station is an almost hallucinatory document.[8] It has attracted attention mostly because of the anxiety it expresses about posthumous pollution by females ('I don't want any women to go to my grave at all during my funeral') and because it asks the men who would be washing his dead body to avoid unshielded contact with his genitals.

By late 1998, together with his fellow conspirators, Atta had rented an apartment at 54 Marienstrasse in the Harburg district of Hamburg. This flat served as the headquarters where three of the 9/11 pilots ironed out details of the attack.[9] Sometime around November 1999, Atta visited Afghanistan in the company of Ramzi bin al-Shibh, Marwan al-Shehhi, and Ziad Jarrah. Plans for 9/11 were apparently finalized during this trip, which included meetings with Khalid Shaikh Mohammed and Osama bin Laden. Upon returning to Germany, Atta reported his passport stolen evidently to expunge all traces of his travels to Afghanistan and elsewhere. Continuing to follow instructions, he moved to the United States in early June 2000, joining Marwan al-Shehhi, one of his companions and room-mates in Germany. With the money wired to them from Germany and the United Arab Emirates, the pair began flying lessons in Florida in November 2000, receiving their pilots' licences in December. Immediately afterwards, they spent some hours on a Boeing flight simulator.[10]

It would be possible, but not necessarily helpful, to flesh out this thumbnail sketch of Atta's career. The important question for us is: why did such a man choose to enlist in such a deadly mission? His sexually tormented will has convinced many commentators that his motivations must have been deeply religious, rooted in a dread of sin, impurity, and contamination; and we should not dismiss this hypothesis out of hand. But before we accept it, we should consider some alternatives.

The numerous reporters who, after the attack, attempted to piece together psychological portraits of Atta during the 1990s agree on one striking point, namely, that the grievances he loudly and frequently articulated against the United States and the Muslim autocracies that the United States supports were *almost entirely secular*. Most of those who knew him before 1996 stress not Atta's religious piety, that is to say, but his implacable fury at the plight of the poor and the indifference of the rich: 'Atta could get exercised by the world's shortcomings, big and small. He spoke out impulsively against injustice' (Cloud 2001; Burke 2003: 216). He was bitterly angry at the visible juxtaposition, in Cairo, of extravagant and frivolous luxury with mass squalor and hopelessness. Egypt's elite, in particular, was hypocritical, he believed. They showed a 'democratic face' to the West, while displaying complete indifference to the misery of ordinary people at home. They had sold their country to the West for trinkets.

Interviews with German fellow students at Harburg reveal that, around 1995 (that is, only a short time before he composed his 'last will'), Atta was still expressing fury at the way the homes of poor people in Cairo were being torn down to make way for tourist parking. Egypt's city planners were refashioning a few choice neighbourhoods in overcrowded Cairo into a kind of Disneyland for Americans and Europeans. The inequalities that caught Atta's attention were also global, of course. Here is one very interesting report, relayed by a German friend: 'Egypt, he said, had opened up to Western influence and market capitalism regardless of the real needs of the people. "He told me it was grotesque that strawberries were being grown in the Nile delta for the European market, luxury goods, while the poor could not afford to buy wheat imported from America," remembers Ralph Bodenstein' (Corbin 2002: 121).

There is obviously nothing distinctively Islamic about such laments. A generation earlier, the same burning indignation would have been expressed in Marxist or nationalist idioms. In the mid-1990s, it is also worth noting, Atta repeatedly promised to return to 'Arabia' to build better communities. Like his anger, in other words, his ambition was perfectly secular at this time. His frequently expressed hope was to help fellow Arabs improve their *worldly* condition. This sounds like a perfectly secular cause with a nationalist tinge. It also sits awkwardly with his later rhetorical turn to an intensely religious ideology that doubts the worth of anything that occurs during our sin-stained life on earth.

Another point also merits mention. During his brief stay in Cairo in 1995, Atta experienced personally the sting of religious discrimination. His technical credentials had been unfairly devalued, he thought, simply because of his religious appearance and behaviour. But he was also defiant: 'Atta informed two German traveling companions that he would not be cowed by the country's "fat cats," who he believed were criminalizing religious traditionalists while bowing shamefully to the West in foreign and economic policies' (Finn 2001). This personal slant on social injustice arises in a different context as well: 'Adding to Atta's distress was his realization that Cairo's planning administration was a nest of nepotism. Jobs were handed down from generation to generation, and none was about to be handed to an upstart who sympathized with the fundamentalists' (Miller and Stone 2002: 252). He was being treated unjustly by an 'apostate' Muslim regime.

It is impossible to know if he was bothered more by the injustice or the apostasy of Egypt's public power. The two issues seem to have been inextricably intertwined in his thinking. The problem here is probably a general one, in fact. Personal motivations are often experienced subjectively as murky, jumbled, and unstable. The human psyche is a tangled skein, and what is true for the rest of us was presumably true in Atta's case as well. Resentment at unfair personal treatment and indignation at elite selfishness were no doubt mixed promiscuously together, in his mind, with religious distress at disobedience to God's will. Such a blurring of personal frustration, political protest, and religious convictions makes it very difficult, if not impossible, to demonstrate the specifically *religious* roots of Atta's commitment to jihadist violence. When the rich and powerful are accused simultan eously of impiety and injustice (or of apostasy and tyranny), we cannot be certain how much relative weight to ascribe to each charge. But it is at least possible that Atta hated Cairo's 'fat cats' more for their selfish greed and indifference to the poor than for their disbelief. It may even be true that the repression of Islamic radicals *represented*, in Atta's mind, the suffering of all Egyptians, religious or not, at the hands of Egypt's selfish elite.

Another minor story bears retelling in this context. This is Atta's apparent belief that traditional Muslim cities had been desecrated by modern high-rise buildings: 'In his view skyscrapers were symbols of a Western civilization that had relegated his own culture to the sidelines' (Aust and Schnibben 2002: 186). He repeatedly 'bemoaned Western influence—specifically, the rise of skyscrapers—in Arab cities' (Cloud 2001). Did Atta's personal aversion to skyscrapers motivate him to enlist in the attack on the WTC? Did he want to desecrate New York City's landscape the way 'Americanization' had desecrated Cairo's? Such speculations seem a bit far-fetched, or at least unverifiable. But his palpable anger at the destruction of ancient cities nevertheless provides an important clue to his thinking.

Atta's 1999 German dissertation focused lovingly on the 5,000-year-old *souk*, or marketplace, of Aleppo (now Halab, Syria), with its miles of laby-rinthine covered streets, that had grown organically, without the deadening influence of modern rationalism.[11] Much has been made of the last-minute inscription to the dissertation, reading: 'my prayer and my sacrifice and my life and my death are all for God, the Lord of the World' (cited in Gunaratna 2002: 140). Less attention has been given to the contents of the dissertation. The important point to notice here is that ancient Aleppo was a pre-Islamic or *jahili* city. Nostalgia for a bronze-age pagan society is not piously Islamic. Radical Islamists, in particular, has never felt squeamish about attacking pre-Islamic traditions, however venerable. (Think of Afghanistan's Bud-dhas.) Militant Islam does not honour local customs and traditions, but smashes them zealously to bring them into conformity with God's will.[12] Thus, Atta's intense concern to preserve *non-Islamic* traditions that were being destroyed by modernization is, at best, only tenuously connected to his Islamic radicalism. Perhaps the 'authentic' values that Atta perceived to have been traduced in the modernization of Aleppo may even have had more to do with the lachrymose German romanticism of some of his Harburg professors than with the root-and-branch fundamentalism of Sayyid Qutb.

What originally attracted Atta towards Islamic militancy may have been less its doctrinal stringency, in fact, than the uncompromising bellicosity toward Egypt's rich and powerful and their US supporters that he encoun-tered in radical mosques. In such incubators of animosity and insurrection, his bitter class resentments resonated powerfully with the fury of a large group of similarly angry young men. But if Atta became a jihadist because

Islamic militancy was the only feasible way to express his hatred of Egypt's elite and their foreign backers, then we cannot say that his religious beliefs in any way *caused* him to join the 9/11 attack. It would be more plausible to say that the same secular fury against the privileged that led to his joining the plot had propelled him earlier to affiliate with radical Islamic groups.

This pattern may not be limited to Atta. Throughout the nominally Islamic world and beyond, individuals who are spoiling to fight against the established powers are turning to extreme versions of Islam because radical Islamic sects appear to be the only organizations that are sending out a call to arms. Such individuals are naturally attracted to the aggressive passages in the Koran. But the *source* of their aggressive feelings cannot be found in scripture. Rather than Islamic traditions producing militancy, currents of militancy are finding their way towards previously marginal streams of Islam, boosting their membership and driving them into increasing bellicosity and violence. This is not to deny, of course, that religious teachings can sometimes intensify and coordinate pre-existent anger, channelling it, for instance, against specific enemies. Least of all is it meant to question the 'sincerity' of Atta's religious beliefs. But it should make us doubt the *causal efficacy* of religious beliefs, however sincere, in a context where secular anger and frustration could explain, on their own, why young men would embrace violent militancy. To pursue this line of inquiry, it will help to look briefly at some of the others who voluntarily died in the attack.

Social Background

The two other suicide pilots in the Hamburg cell, Marwan al-Shehhi (from the United Arab Emirates) and Ziad Jarrah (from Lebanon), first arrived in Germany in 1996. Their backgrounds and characters cannot be described here in any detail. But we should probably mention that their personalities were quite unlike Atta's. They were, at least reportedly, as convivial as he was sombre. Jarrah in particular lacked Atta's puritanism and burning sense of social injustice.[13] Such differences even within the Hamburg cell suggest the futility of trying to draw a composite portrait of 'the 9/11 suicide pilot'. These young men had different psychological make-ups; and it is quite unlikely that any single motive explains why all three proved willing to die.

Despite their clashing personalities, the Hamburg three did have a few traits in common.[14] First and foremost, they all seem to have been radicalized while living as expatriates in Germany. One prominent journalist has therefore aired the extravagant claim that 'The personal encounter between these young men and Europe is the key to the story' (Friedman 2002: 163). That they were drawn to the al-Quds mosque as a welcoming oasis in an unwelcoming society is easy enough to imagine; and that European Islamophobia might fuel an upsurge of political Islam among Muslims living in Europe cannot be excluded. But discrimination and cultural exclusivity were not the only potential sources of personal hurt. Atta, for instance, seems to have experienced acute culture shock when he first moved from puritanical Egypt to anything-goes Germany.

But whether or not he or his companions were disoriented by Western licence, young Muslims who came to Europe in the 1990s probably proved easy pickings for radical imams simply because they were cut loose from family monitoring and control. Unlike other suicide terrorists discussed in this volume (such as members of the Black Tigers or the al-Aqsa brigade), these three young men operated in the lengthy run-up to the attacks as a criminal conspiracy, isolated from older relatives and with minimal solidarity from a wider national community. When the smoke cleared, moreover, their families did not boast about their deeds. Many of the parents even denied their sons' participation. Their mothers certainly did not celebrate their deaths, as have some mothers of Palestinian suicide bombers.

All the members of the Hamburg cell also came from middle-class backgrounds. This is why they are so often said to defy 'the stereotypical profile' of the young terrorist as poor, uneducated, and desperate. Their fairly prosperous families presumably had no need for the 'martyrdom allowance' that still seems to play a role in encouraging Palestinian suicide bombing. But their relatively privileged upbringing also makes their willingness to commit suicide somewhat more mysterious. These young men did not have their backs to the wall, as did the 'jumpers' from the WTC on 11 September. They were not suffering from survivor's guilt. Nor did they face a cruel choice between dying passively and dying actively, exiting from the world pointlessly or taking some enemies with them. They were in a very different situation, in short, than the suicide bombers of Palestine. Their life prospects were not hopeless, and therefore the opportunity costs of suicide, especially in a mission with such an uncertain outcome, seem quite high. So what led them to overcome their instinctive fear of death?

In recent decades, it may be pertinent to recall, the middle classes in many Middle Eastern countries have been living under a constant threat of downward mobility. According to his acquaintances at the time, 'by the early '90s, Atta felt the intense pressures on middle-class Egyptians not to slip social rank. His friend Khalifa says Atta grew frustrated because he was unable to fulfill his academic ambitions in his homeland. He believed that political favoritism at Egyptian universities would keep him from the top spots' (Cloud 2001). That similar anxieties may have afflicted the Saudi members of the team is suggested by the dramatic drop in per capita Saudi GDP during the 1980s and 1990s.[15] The expatriate children of middle-class Lebanese,

Egyptian, and Emirate families were certainly not as desperate as some Palestinian suicide bombers. But they may still have been fearful of tumbling down the social ladder. Carrying their families' class anxieties inside them, they may also have been psychologically traumatized by their move to Europe, where they conceivably experienced, overnight, a bruising loss of status and prestige.

That middle-class apprehensions, reflecting precarious economic conditions in the Middle East, played some role in the inner lives of the 9/11 pilots is quite probable. But we obviously have no way of gauging the influence of such anxieties on their eventual decision to join an unforgiving jihad against the United States. We simply cannot know if the endangered privileges of their class made them especially concerned to redeem what they considered the lost dignity of the world Islamic community, as they imagined it.

What we *can* say, on the other hand, is that their middle-class background recalls, to some extent, the social profile of members of the Red Brigades, the Baader-Meinhof gang, and other European terrorist groups who, while perfectly secular, were also indifferent to nationalist goals. The members of the Hamburg cell certainly lacked the kind of community support received by the Irish Republican Army (IRA), Euzkadi ta Askatasuna (ETA), or Hamas. They were a vanguard without a mass following. There was no global *intifada* to buoy them up. In that sense, they eerily resemble the European radicals of the 1970s and even the Russian anarchists of the 1880s. Such analogies, while playful, are also suggestive because they make us ask, once again, whether radical Islamic ideology was really a necessary condition for their decision to embrace terrorist violence in a transnational cause.

Psychological Background

None of these doubts is meant to deny the influence of religiously tinged indoctrination upon the hijackers' behaviour and thought. As mentioned, all nineteen hijackers seem to have spent some time in Afghanistan. In the training camps, among other skills, they learned to kill ritualistically by slitting throats. They were also, without doubt, taught another military technique with strong religious connotations, namely, martyrdom. The promise of paradise was certainly not the sole inducement offered to the future 9/11 terrorists. Their indoctrinators probably pitched martyrdom to them by stressing the brevity and vanity of life, the certainty of death, and the need, in the face of life's all-consuming flux, to attach oneself to something they could imagine to be imperishable. That something could have been God, of course, but it could just as well have been the 'Islamic nation'.[16]

As an empirical matter, incidentally, quite apart from the teachings of Islam, life *is* brief, and therefore the human impulse toward self-preservation invariably, in the end, proves futile. This may be the single most effective way in which training-camp indoctrination may have contributed to the willingness of these young men, already inclined in that direction, to scrap their dim lives for a radiant cause. While in Afghanistan, they were no doubt reminded of excruciating truths about mortality that the rest of humanity, clinging desperately to the fiction that life will always go on as before, prefers to ignore. No matter how long we manage to live, we will not shorten the time we will be dead. The future hijackers could have been reminded of other secular truths as well, for instance, that they could just as well die any day in a stupid accident. And they were surely encouraged to draw the logical conclusion that it would be better to make their deaths meaningful rather than meaningless, to exit life with flags flying, on a combat mission, for their community's honour, rather than as insignificant observers sitting on the sidelines. Since death is inevitable anyway, there is nothing of 'infinite value' to lose in dying for a cause. This is true whether the cause is secular (bloodying the enemy) or religious (serving God). In effect, mankind's natural horror of death may be overcome to some extent by a perfectly realistic focus on death's inevitability, without any religious certainty that a 'sacred explosion' will rocket a would-be martyr instantly to paradise.

The hijackers may also have blunted their natural fear of death with a strong dose of visceral hate for the people they were about to obliterate. One of the most effective painkillers known to man, in fact, is the imagined pain of one's enemies. Revenge is 'sweeter than honey' and the backward-looking desire to retaliate is famously strong enough to draw human beings into fatal situations. Single-minded focus on redressing past grievances may crowd out strategic consideration of unintended (even if predictable) future consequences. A strong personal need to slake the craving for vengeance is universally thought to have motivated some of the Palestinian suicide bombers. But most commentators downplay this possibility when discussing 9/11. They do so because of the seemingly attenuated nature of the revenge motif in their case. Unlike the Palestinian suicide bombers, none of the 9/11 pilots seem to have been trying to avenge the blood of a friend or a relative killed by the target society. Because of the 'long fuse' of the plot, it is also said, the 9/11 terrorists acted in cold blood, and could not have felt much visceral craving for revenge.

This analysis is reasonable, in a way, but it may also underestimate the power of artfully contrived 'narratives of blame' to capture the imagination of uprooted young men in search of meaning and purpose and to give focus to their otherwise diffuse impulse to punish someone, anyone, for their feelings of frustration and humiliation. An ideology can refashion subjective perceptions of self-interest. It can also, presumably, rechannel the hard-wired revenge impulse, retargeting it towards a hitherto unappreciated enemy, even one who is distant or merely imagined rather than personally known. That something of the sort may have happened is suggested by one of the hijackers, who left the following message behind: 'It is time to kill the Americans in their own backyards, among their sons, and near their forces and intelligence.'[17] It is time to kill Americans in their own backyard not because of their impiety but because they have been killing Muslims in the Muslims' own backyards. The archaic principle of an eye for an eye, far from gaining legitimacy from Allah's approval, is prior to and deeper than any religious doctrine, and indeed attracts revenge-minded supporters to any religious tradition that sanctifies vengeance as a holy duty. Islam enters the picture here, not as a religious creed, therefore, but as a political marker, identifying the imaginary community that has been wronged and that therefore has a *natural right*—that is, a non-religious or pre-religious right—to retaliate in kind.

But how could so much rage build up in these men's hearts against a country that was so far away? TV images of Palestinian children killed by US-backed Israelis provide a vicarious experience of 'pan-Arab victimhood' to a worldwide viewing audience.[18] The narrative built around these images demonizes the United States as a heartless oppressor and whitewashes 'the Arab nation' as innocent, humiliated, and despoiled. Intensified by envy of the United States' prosperity and power, such a widely repeated storyline is probably enough to inflame the desire for wreaking revenge on the United States, even in individuals who never personally experienced US violence. The five-year lag between Atta's vow to die a martyr and the 9/11 attacks does not demonstrate conclusively that he felt no desire for revenge. It only suggests that whatever hatred he brought with him from the Middle East had to be kept simmering for years as they were gradually redirected from the Cairo elite to those he eventually came to see as the insolent and heartless Americans.

Martyrs are Soldiers

But 'narratives of blame' that demonize the United States, even when supplemented by a heightened awareness of the brevity of life, do not seem to be wholly sufficient explanations for the decision by young men with no outward reasons for desperation to undertake a suicide mission. What other non-religious factors might have been involved? Another reason why they were willing to die, even though they were not psychologically desperate, is that *they thought of themselves as soldiers*. There is nothing unusual about young men stationed far from home and cut off from broad social support who are willing to sacrifice their lives in a violent conflict with personally unknown enemies. The idea of martyrdom itself, in Muslim culture, is closely associated with a soldier's death. Throughout the Middle East, 'whether in Arabic, Turkish, Persian or Pashto Muslim society, *shahid* is today used for any man who falls in battle' (Naby and Frye 2003: 11). This accent on the soldier's self-sacrifice for his country, significantly, associates Muslim suicide terrorists with secular terrorists such as the Japanese Kamikaze during the Second World War and the Black Tigers of Sri Lanka.

But is not martyrdom (*istishad*) also, or even primarily, a religious ideal? Is it not an important part of the cultural repertoire of the Islamic tradition? And were not the 9/11 hijackers simply enacting a venerable religious practice? Not exactly. In the Islamic tradition, it turns out, '*Shahid* is the warrior who was killed by the enemy in battle, not the one who killed himself' (Merari 1998: 197). Deliberately killing oneself in battle is not the same as being killed by an enemy in battle. When defenders of 9/11 assert that 'it is wrong to call such operations a "suicide"' (Abu Ruqaiyah 1996–7), therefore, their defensive tone may betray lingering doubts. They may be protesting too much. In reality, 'self-martyrdom' lies somewhere *between* martyrdom and suicide, and does not reflect any well-established Islamic practice. Self-martyrs are not re-enacting any traditional social role, certainly not that of the too frequently cited medieval 'assassins'. Mass casualty attacks in which the attackers kill their victims by killing themselves are, more or less, a twentieth-century innovation: 'This form of jihad, in which the body is used as a weapon, is a recent development in the annals of Islamic warfare, even if the concept of holy war and martyrdom is as old as the religion itself' (Davis 2003: 94). The influence of religious traditions on the choice of SMs as a technique for conducting terrorism, therefore, remains unproven.

Not suicide alone, but also the killing of thousands of innocent civilians is difficult to reconcile with traditional Islamic morality. One neglected piece of evidence for this claim is the rumour, apparently common throughout the Islamic world, that the attacks were orchestrated by the CIA or Mossad. Flatly incompatible with Islamic pride in the attacks, this fantasy suggests latent qualms about mass-casualty terrorism. How might such qualms be managed or stilled? One paradoxical, but interesting, line of thought on this matter is that suicide itself provides a way to overcome the norms that prohibit the killing of innocents. In *Les justes*, Albert Camus describes such a strategy for assuaging the guilty conscience of killers. His idea, put succinctly, is that dying justifies killing. At one point, the Russian anarchist hero of the play, Ivan Kaliayev, says: 'Si je ne mourais pas, c'est alors que je serais un meurtrier.'[19] In other words, doubts about the morality of murder can be answered by the willingness of the killer to die. Readiness for self-sacrifice established the Christ-like purity of the assassin. It shows that he is not a common criminal, that he is, above all, not a murderer. Willingness to die demonstrates publicly that a cause larger than any personal interest or wish is at stake: 'The truth of the cause is established by the individual's willingness to sacrifice everything in its behalf' (Crenshaw 2001: 28). On this account, suicide attacks are, psychologically speaking, self-justifying. That is to say, in a hit-and-run terrorist attack, the 'moral cause' that overrides the ordinary prohibition against the killing of innocent civilians must be extraordinarily compelling, even to the point of admitting no doubts. In suicide attacks, at least according to Camus, the cause need not be so obviously compelling, for the willingness of the killers to die by itself demonstrates their subjective belief in the righteousness of their cause. Third-party observers may disapprove of the cause, but no one can plausibly deny that the terrorists themselves were convinced that the ends justified the means. For those with a moral conscience, if Camus is right, suicide terrorism is psychologically easier than hit-and-run terrorism.

Did such thinking play any role in the 9/11 attacks? Did self-sacrifice help assuage the hijackers' guilt at killing innocent civilians? Something of the sort might be possible, I suppose. But the conspirators had available to them a much less roundabout way to justify mass murder. If the hijackers felt a twinge of guilt at the thought of murdering innocent civilians, this guilt could be most easily assuaged by the thought that they were 'at war'.[20] A soldier can kill without being labelled a murderer. This is the real banality of evil. Soldiering is a high-risk profession. There is nothing especially rare about young soldiers imagining that they are dying for their country.[21] It is not hard to imagine, in fact, that the martial distinction between the courageous and the cowardly was more important to the 9/11 terrorists than the religious distinction between the saved and the damned. Willingness to face death unflinchingly, and scorn for materialists who cling pathetically to life, have more to do with martial ethics than with religious ethics, even though the two moral codes can sometimes overlap. There is nothing uniquely Islamic about bravado and fealty, in any case, nor about the desire to uphold manly honour or display courage in battle.

In al-Qaeda statements, the suicide hijackers are referred to not only by the term 'martyr' (*shahid*) but also by the term 'holy warrior' (*mujaheed*). The 'holiness' in question may no doubt have something to do with an ancient religion. But the proximate reference is to the pan-Arab fighters in the Afghan war. All soldiers, in any case, whether holy or not, have a right to kill. They are authorized to kill aggressors and other enemies of the community, just as executioners have a right to put to death criminals convicted of capital crimes. Rather than dying justifying killing, therefore, we have the more traditional pattern (well-known to all revenge cultures) of killing justifying dying. The foreseeable but unintended death of fellow Muslims in the course of an attack on infidels, too, can be explained away, in banally secular terms, as friendly fire, without reference to their expected welcome into paradise.

The warrior ideal, in sum, goes a long way towards explaining how the hijackers managed to armour themselves psychologically against the fear of death. They surely felt the warrior's pride at having been selected to participate in an important mission. They expected to win glory and be celebrated for their valour. They hoped to become role models whom only a few young Muslims would have the courage to emulate. There is nothing especially religious about desiring to make a splash, to be involved in large affairs, or to be celebrated all over the world.[22] Even if they were not certain that they had starring roles in the Last Judgment, they were embarked on a remarkable rite of passage, putting themselves to the test and demonstrating their worthiness of adult respect.

For various psychologically complex reasons, the honour and dishonour of their group became bound up with their own personal honour and dishonour. They may have been willing to die simply because they identified strongly with an enduring community that would benefit from their deaths, a community that might eventually sing their praises. This was a perfectly secular way to overcome the fear of death. It required them to imagine death away, not by focusing on paradise, but by focusing on the honour to be enjoyed by their dishonoured community after the enemy who dishonoured them was humiliatingly drenched in its own blood.

Sustaining Determination

It is one thing to explain why the 9/11 hijackers agreed to enlist in an SM. A somewhat different question is how they managed to stay on course, without flinching, even when their fiery end drew near. According to one expert on suicide terrorism, 'it is reasonable to assume that volunteers for such missions have to be used rapidly lest they change their mind, an eventuality that becomes more likely the greater the distance in time and place from their launching point' (Merari 1998: 207, 206). On the spur of the moment, many people may feel committed enough to a cause to volunteer to die for it, but not so many will wake up the next morning with the same fierce determination. This observation raises a vital question for students of 9/11. Behind-the-scenes handlers could not keep watch on the hit team, punish would-be defectors, give periodic pep talks, stiffen the future hijackers' resolve, or escort them to the site. So how did al-Qaeda, by remote control, make its volunteer commandos stick to their extravagant promises, even as the moment of death drew near? What we need to explain, in other words, is how the attackers were kept on track, far behind enemy lines, without the usual forms of external monitoring and opportunistic intervention, cali-brated to prevent a predictable last-minute recoiling in the face of death.

The simplest answer to this question is team spirit or small-group loyalty. The sheer excitement of a cloak-and-dagger life behind enemy lines had presumably helped keep the Hamburg cell together in the run-up to the attacks. The pleasure of partaking in a secret combat mission is itself a motivation. The same can be said about the chance to be, for once, the member of a highly select group, a killer elite.

Team spirit can be instilled particularly effectively in isolated circumstan-ces. The life of the Hamburg cell was built around concealing and masking. The conspirators looked like hapless students, but only because no one around them knew that they had studied the black arts in Afghanistan. This contrast between their banal appearance in their neighbours' eyes and the shocking reality of their 'true lives' presumably allowed the cell's mem-bers to experience a sense of elation and deep purposefulness. As Simmel (1950: 330) remarks, 'the secret produces an immense enlargement of life'. And he continues: 'The secret offers, so to speak, the possibility of a second world alongside the manifest world.' Loyalty to their small counter-society was reinforced by pleasures of cloaked intrigue. While members of the enemy society around them viewed them as marginal men, *they* knew better. They knew that they were really central characters in what would soon be con-sidered the greatest spectacle on earth.

The group loyalty developed before the attack presumably influenced the hijackers' behaviour on 11 September itself. There is no reason why the same logic that applies to high-risk military attacks should not apply to a suicide mission: 'It probably takes more courage to stay behind when one's platoon rises for assault than to charge with the others' (Merari 1998: 198). Peer pressure and norms of solidarity would not affect a lone terrorist, of course. But the 9/11 hijackers could certainly draw upon the 'intragroup commit-ment' possible in 'chain or concurrent multiple suicidal attacks' (Merari 1998: 297). Fraternal bonds, even without supervision from above, helps explain the lunatic bravery of warriors in this case just as in conventional war. Mutual pledges and vows, sworn ahead of time, before instinctive fear at approaching death had a chance to upset it, may also have functioned as an independent reason for steadfastness. And the al-Qaeda trademark of *syn-chronized attacks* may, among its other rationales, have allowed group solidarity to function as a precommitment device to help thwart last-minute bail-outs. All these factors, together with the pilots' 'learned incompetence' at landing hijacked Boeings, could presumably have kept the team on mis-sion without close-up supervision by behind-the-scenes handlers. Their desire to please God, however authentically felt, would have been almost redundant in such a case.

Secrecy and surprise are the principal assets of the weaker party in an asymmetrical conflict. To ask how religion contributed to the plot, therefore, is also to ask how it contributed to secrecy and surprise. Formulated that way, it seems suddenly much easier to answer, for religious practices obviously helped maintain the veil of secrecy around the plot. Membership in a non-Christian religious sect enhanced the clandestine detachment, isolation, and relative impenetrability of the cell behind enemy lines. Both the al-Quds mosque in Hamburg and the Islamic 'study room' at the university in Harburg provided difficult-to-penetrate walls behind which the future hijackers could prepare their plot. At the al-Quds mosque in Hamburg and in the Marienstrasse apartment, the conspirators sometimes appeared to be wrapped in a mantle of devoutness. This may have been perfectly sincere for some future hijackers, Atta being a good example. But in his case, too, daily prayers performed a subsidiary function by cutting a militant off from his unsuspecting civilian surroundings. As one of his co-workers reported, Atta 'would get his prayer mat out five times a day. During that time he was utterly absorbed—he wouldn't hear you if you spoke to him' (Corbin 2002: 188). Similarly, after being welcomed into the home of a German couple, Mohamed Atta was eventually asked to leave, partly because 'Mohamed did not want to cook in pots that had ever cooked pork' (Aust and Schnibben 2002: 182).

On the other hand, some of the less puritanical members of the Hamburg cell are reported to have smoked and enjoyed pop music. Whether or not they took religious practices seriously as a matter of devotion, they certainly took them seriously as a matter of security. The conspirators probably protected themselves so effectively against infiltration because they had a ready-made religious excuse for walling out non-Islamic neighbours and observers. Sequestered from mainstream life in Hamburg and therefore insulated from any pressures to assimilate, they were able to incubate a violently aggressive project based on total rejection of reconciliation with the West.

That religious practices—as opposed to religious beliefs—played yet another role in the success of 9/11 is suggested by the manual outlining preparations for the attack, written by Abdul Aziz al-Omari and discovered in Atta's luggage that, by sheer chance, did not make it onto American Airlines flight No. 11. (This document was read by some but not necessarily all of the hijackers.) In the manual, several items stand out. The most important instruction is to keep reciting prayers and incantations and passages from the Koran—understood as an 'absolute text' that cannot be interpreted— during the entire operation: 'Keep busy with repeated invocation of God.' Prayer is behaviour, not thought. Indeed, prayer is ritual designed to block thought, to prevent the spontaneous upsurge of disobedient impulses and inclinations. Prayer is anaesthesia. Chanting supplications and religious poems and reciting scripture acts as a sedative. It can even induce a sort of trance. And, unlike daydreaming, it is a *regulated* behaviour. Reading the Koran into one's palms and then rubbing one's hands all over one's body, in a ritual self-blessing, takes time and crowds out other thoughts. Mantras, like counting sheep, are standard techniques, recommended by psychotherapists, for managing anxiety and keeping demons at bay. Unflappability, composure, and total focus on the job at hand can be achieved by mechanical repetition. The danger of last-minute faltering can be minimized by shutting down most cognitive functions.

An additional interesting detail in the manual is the instruction to stay awake all night. Even young and healthy men, presumably, would feel somewhat loopy after more than thirty hours without sleep. They might even have begun to hallucinate to some extent. The sleep-deprived may be especially susceptible to the numbing or sedating effects of religious rituals, perhaps even to the point of self-hypnosis. At the very least, the mental spontaneity of sleepwalkers is dimmed. Their grasp of context may easily be attenuated and they may lapse willy-nilly into default mode, performing mechanically practised operations by rote. Like the desire to injure one's imagined enemies, in other words, religious rituals may blunt the sting of death even when the promise of paradise seems uncertain. The capacity of religious ritual to deaden the senses or narrowly restrict the subjects of attention was probably important in the 9/11 case, because the pilots' fear of death did not have to be subdued for ever but only for a few hours.

Expiation by Suicide

The promise of paradise may not be the most effective instrument of control wielded by religious authorities. According to Hobbes, the power of priests has a much deeper source than the gullibility of 'imbeciles'. Preachers control their flocks, he argued, by first making people feel guilty for their own natural impulses and then offering to protect them from sin and damnation in exchange for obedience to spiritual authority (Hobbes 1990: 26). Once an individual is set at war with himself, he will be unable to make important life decisions autonomously, and will therefore naturally reach for an external crutch or authority figure, such as a psychotherapist or a guru, to lead him through life. The sicker people can be made to feel inwardly, the higher the price they will pay for religious supervision.

While speculative, this analysis is also suggestive, especially because of the peculiar life situations of the 9/11 suicide pilots. Because of their relatively privileged background, and especially their higher education, they were able to travel quite far on the road from the Middle East to Western Europe. They mastered foreign languages, for instance, and they were able to blend imperceptibly into a Western environment. This was undoubtedly an important consideration for those who recruited them into the plot. Having lived for some years in the West, however, they had also become, in some sense, limbo men. They were unable to arrive, we might say, yet also unable to return home. They were too westernized to feel completely comfortable back in the Middle East, but not westernized enough to be accepted in a bigoted Europe or North America.

Some commentators use the cliché of a 'love–hate relation' to explain the ambiguous attitude of such young men toward the Western societies that both attracted and rejected them. A further psychological key to our puzzle could conceivably lie here. The jihadist narrative of blame that channels anger towards the United States has a perverse codicil. The same radical worldview that reviles the United States simultaneously rebukes those Muslim youths who find the United States alluring. The ripest recruits for SMs, this analysis implies, would be half-way men, stuck in transit between the Middle East and the West, whose frustration is mingled with a feeling of being *tainted* by a society that seduces them. The hijackers' felt need to erase such a stain on their souls could conceivably have become so obsessive that it eclipsed all thought of future consequences.

One way to think about the political consequences of such a stressful psychological condition is to recall the classical Islamic distinction between the Greater Jihad and the Lesser Jihad. Embarked on the Lesser Jihad, holy warriors confront infidels on the field of battle, while on the Greater Jihad struggling Muslims fight a private battle against their own evil inclinations. Perhaps the 9/11 mission allowed the hijackers to perform both jihads at the same time. They could kill the enemy and, simultaneously, eliminate the sickening traces that their enemy had deposited in their own souls. If this fanciful analysis has any validity, the 9/11 hijackers may have actually preferred suicide terrorism to hit-and-run terrorism, since an SM, to speak crudely, allowed them to kill two birds with one stone. The potency of this connection between killing the enemy and purifying one's own soul by self-slaughter depends, as in the writings of Sayyid Qutb, on the association of personally experienced temptations with massive 'cultural aggression' by the West.

One advocate of this somewhat convoluted approach is Ruthven (2001: 21): 'The jihad (struggle) against *kufr* (disbelief) which the hijackers and other Islamists espouse is not so much a "war between civilizations" as a struggle waged over contested identities within the individual self'. Psychological conflicts within the minds of suicide terrorists are also stressed by Benjamin and Simon (2002: 165):

Atta was a man flagellating himself. At some point, how and when are not clear, he had a brush with temptation; perhaps he felt he had succumbed. Whatever touched him, he identified with the West. It might have been something as simple as a personal desire to be part of the West that caused him to feel contaminated. His repulsion was powerful, and he felt somehow humiliated. . . . All these jihadists react to the taint or seduction they felt by espousing a violent Islamism, as though that overcorrection would erase the sin of their earlier lives.

We are obviously treading on empirically unverifiable ground at this point. But the hypothesis entertained by these and other writers does have the ring of plausibility. The 9/11 pilots may have stayed on mission, despite the long incubation time of their plot and the remoteness of their masters, not only because they were devoted to redeeming collective honour (for which their deaths would have been a necessary evil), but also because they were devoted to self-mortification (for which their deaths would have been an intrinsic good).

It is at least conceivable that the hijackers were recruited into al-Qaeda because these young men, in particular, combined bitter anger at the West with psychologically stressful self-contempt and self-blame. Atta's sexually tormented 'will' is pertinent evidence in this regard. There is no reason to doubt that the idea of 'sin' can have a powerful effect on human behaviour. Whatever psychological processes lead a person to feel inwardly contaminated, such a feeling can be taken up, cultivated, and crystallized by religious indoctrination and training. Candidates for an SM might or might not believe that the first drop of their blood shed in martyrdom would wash away all their sins. But they will surely expect that suicide terrorism will permanently extinguish their burning sense of guilt. Attractive about this line of thought, needless to say, is that it allows us to imagine a connection between the *uprootedness* of the hijackers, their *envy* of the United States, their *blind obedience* to their superiors, and their *willingness* to die. But such a connection obviously remains unproven.

Nevertheless, if 9/11 'was a sacrifice made for the most common reason: expiation, the removal of a sin through and act of giving' (Benjamin and Simon 2002: 165), then religious belief had a direct effect on the behaviour of the suicide terrorists. Juergensmeyer (1992: 111) makes a similar point in another context:

It is one thing when the moral sanction of religion is brought to bear on such worldly and non-spiritual matters as political struggles. It is quite another when the struggles themselves are seen primarily as religious events. The crusades, for instance, are examples from Christian history when a military expedition was carried out with religious zeal. To engage in such a struggle was a salvific act.

If someone could conclusively show that the 9/11 hijackers performed the attacks as religious rituals to cleanse themselves of sin, we would have to admit that their religious faith functioned as a cause of the attacks.

While undemonstrated and probably indemonstrable, such speculations are consistent with Roy's basic line on Islamic fundamentalism: 'the literature of jihad places less emphasis on the objective (to create an Islamic state) than on the mystical dimension (to sacrifice one's life); it is the act of supreme devotion' (Roy 2001: 65). And that is also the perspective from which Makiya and Mneimneh analyse the instruction manual presumably consulted by the terrorists before the attack. Their principal and highly debatable point is that the hijackers no longer saw martyrdom as a weapon in a wider war or an instrument serving an ulterior purpose but as an end in itself. They did not see themselves as defending their community against aggression by infidels, but were instead caught up in a personal act of worship meant to please God: 'There is no mention of any communal purpose behind his behavior' (Makiya and Mneimneh 2002: 317).[23] Or perhaps the hijackers were offering themselves, along with their victims, as burnt offerings to God. If so, archaic myths impinged upon their belief systems to the point of delirium. There is no way to verify this speculation either, even though it is made plausible to some extent by a striking supplication, uttered by one of the hijackers in his pre-attack video-recorded message: 'Oh Allah, take from our blood today until you are satisfied.'[24] The idea that divinities need to be fed human blood is archaic indeed.[25]

This weird archaism leads us to another way in which religious sentiments might have helped neutralize the pilots' fear of death. In the manual, the hijackers are reminded that *fear is a form of worship* and that fearing anyone or anything besides God is a mortal sin that will damn them to everlasting hell. This suggests that the best way to 'manage fear' is to focus one's mind on a greater fear. That is exactly the diagnosis of Makiya and Mneimneh (2002: 308–9):

[F]or the author of this manual an overpowering fear of God must rule in the mind of the True Believer, a fear that so focuses the mind as to rid it of all mundane considerations arising from experience and observation, thus enabling the Believer to remain utterly concentrated on his mission. In support of this the manual cites the Koranic verse, 'Fear them not, but fear Me, if you are Believers.'

While this hypothesis is interesting, it is no more demonstrable than any of the others canvassed in this chapter. A hint of something more going on comes from many stories about the behaviour of various members of the team in the months leading up to the attacks. Many commentators have been titillated by the paradox of fundamentalists who occasionally lapsed into mundane forms of fun. But another paradox is even more eye-catching. These young men, who ostensibly believed that fear should be reserved for God, were, at the same time, intoxicated by the thought of making other people fear *them*. To cite one example among many, when Atta first arrived in the United States he visited a federal Farm Services agency in Florida to request a loan to buy an airplane. Hanging on the wall was an aerial photo of Washington, DC, where the agent remarked that she had many friends. After his request for a loan was politely refused, Atta looked at the photo and asked the agent: 'How would you like it if somebody flew an airplane into your friends' building?' (Miller and Stone 2002: 269).

If Makiya and Mneimneh are right, then anyone operating within a radical Islamist worldview must identify the desire to instil fear with the blasphemous desire to be godlike or perhaps to be God. The hijackers may have sought refuge from the all-corrosive flux of time by identifying themselves mentally with a God who was 'the vanquisher of the arrogant'.[26] On a mission to punish the United States, they probably thought of themselves, at the very least, as taking a ride on His Terrible Swift Sword. This myth, indeed, may have induced them to embrace two mutually clashing self-images. It could have made them see themselves simultaneously as memorable heroes and as expendable assets. They were omnipotent and impotent. They were liberating their people in the name of total personal enslavement. They were both thunder gods and despicable sinners. *They were conquering and surrendering at the same time.* Perhaps the psychological strain of maintaining simultaneously two mutually exclusive self-images was still another anaesthetic, adding to the other emotions, beliefs, and rituals that numbed them to their impending deaths. This conjecture, too, can neither be demonstrated nor ruled out.

The Masterminds

While Osama bin Laden, Ayman al-Zawahiri, and others instigated, encouraged, and blessed the 9/11 attacks, the organizational commander behind the plot appears to have been Khalid Shaikh Mohammad. [27] We must therefore turn to the question of why he and his confederates chose to send suicide commandos on this particular mission. What considerations influenced their decision to mount a 'martyrdom operation'? Was the death of the hijackers merely a matter of expediency for the mission's planners, or did it have a deeper, perhaps religious, meaning and purpose?

The Voltaire thesis, discussed above, implies that the 9/11 masterminds had totally different motivations from the 9/11 hijackers. A contemporary exponent of this thesis reformulates it as follows: 'Even if many suicide attackers are irrational or fanatical, the leadership groups that recruit and direct them are not' (Pape 2003: 344). The latter, according to this approach, are shrewd calculators of costs and benefits even if the former are robotic fanatics in the grip of myth. But such a contrast seems too sharp to capture the ambiguous undercurrents of the 9/11 plot. For one thing, the hallucinatory statements of al-Qaeda's leaders suggest that, whatever their skills as organizers of terror, they too have been living somewhat disconnected from reality. After all, they have been hiding like hunted animals for years, surrounded exclusively by people who think like themselves, isolated from the kind of heterogeneous community that can provide reality checks. It would not be surprising, therefore, if their worldview contained some genuinely strange beliefs, such as the idea that most of the world is poor *because* the West is rich.

Nonetheless, the Voltaire thesis probably applies to 9/11 some extent. It is only reasonable to assume that al-Qaeda masterminds, who apparently had no inclination to throw themselves into the flames, carried into the conspiracy a somewhat different set of beliefs, emotions, and dispositions from those of the suicide hijackers themselves. The masterminds, arguably, were neither so personally overwrought, nor so eager to escape into an afterlife purified of temptation. Their basic rationality can be inferred from their decision to mobilize fast-moving light forces acting in secrecy. This is a highly efficient way to deploy the modest resources at their disposal. Their targeting decisions, too, seem highly rational. By organizing the 1998 US embassy bombings in East Africa, for instance, Khalid Shaikh Mohammed managed to degrade the United States' intelligence-gathering capacities, to al-Qaeda's advantage, by compelling the Americans to shutter their embassies around the world. In all this they seem to be more the children of Lenin than the children of Mohammed. One commentators even describes al-Qaeda in such terms: 'Using techniques drawn from Leninism and operating on the Marxist militant model, it uses *noms de guerre*, adheres strictly to a cell structure, follows the idea of a cadre party, maintains tight discipline, promotes self-sacrifice and reverence for the leadership and is guided by a program of action' (Gunaratna 2002: 296).

Their basic strategy was probably to draw the United States into imperial overstretch, luring US sitting ducks into remote shooting galleries, engaging the country's security establishment in a global guerrilla war with so many distant battlefronts in foreign lands that the United States' cognitive capacities—not its military capacities alone—would be overtaxed. Whatever consequences it would unleash, a direct attack on the United States would predictably shake up the world order and open opportunities for the fleet of foot. At the very least, the 9/11 masterminds were anticipating their own next moves. Their subsequent plans may or may not have gone up in smoke. But the fact that they bothered to make them provides a good measure of the distance between the scheming minds of the behind-the-scenes planners and the mission-fixated minds of those who personally carried out the attack.

Why Did the Planners Send a Suicide Squad?

In 1993, Khalid Shaikh Mohammad's nephew, Ramzi Yousef, led a hit-and-run team in a failed attempt to topple the WTC.[28] In that 'prequel' to 9/11, the commandos themselves showed no inclination to die in the attacks. By contrast, the teams sent to carry out both the East African embassy bombings and the 2000 seaborne attack on the USS Cole were suicide terrorists.[29] From the standpoint of the designers and organizers of such attacks, however, the distinction between hit-and-run terrorists and suicide terrorists may not have been especially salient. Like the high command in wartime, they may view men and *matériel* indifferently, as resources to be consumed in pursuit of urgent military aims. If high-level commanders consider their foot soldiers to be expendable surplus youth, then (for them) an SM is just another form of remote-control terrorism.

But conspirators inside al-Qaeda and its affiliated organizations are increasingly recruiting suicide operatives to carry out their missions. They do so, presumably, because they have come to believe that this is an effective way to achieve their strategic goals. But does expediency alone provide an adequate and exhaustive explanation for why Khalid Shaikh Mohammad sent suicide squads to conduct the 9/11 attacks?

Gambetta and other contributors to this volume draw a distinction between suicide terrorism as a military strategy and suicide terrorism as a way to communicate a message. A good example of the former, attributable to al-Qaeda, would be the suicide assassination on 9 September 2001 of Ahmad Shah Massoud, the Northern Alliance commander who posed a serious threat to the Taliban regime hosting Osama bin Laden in Afghanistan. A suicide squad had a better chance than a hit-and-run squad to overcome Massoud's security precautions and was therefore presumably chosen for tactical reasons alone. The killing itself may have demoralized the enemy and lifted the spirits of the jihadists around Osama; but, in this case, employing suicide as an assassination technique probably provided no added value.

It seems highly likely that SMs are often chosen on purely military grounds since 'suicide attacks on average kill four times as many people as other terrorist acts' (Hoffman 2003: 42). A high-ranking member of al-Qaeda provides important evidence that this sort of rationale influenced the decision-making of the 9/11 plotters: 'the method of martyrdom operations [is] the most successful way of inflicting damage against the opponent and the least costly to the mujaheedin in terms of casualties.'[30] SMs also simplify planning because the suicide commandos who penetrate heavily defended security perimeters do not have to find an escape route. They are also well within the resources of modestly financed terrorist groups. Another consideration that may weigh heavily with the dispatchers of such missions is that, when suicide terrorists are used, no captured operatives will fall into enemy hands to squeal under torture, and thereby put the organization's higher-ups in personal danger.

For these and other tactical reasons, terrorist planners may opt for suicide terrorism over hit-and-run terrorism. But when is suicide terrorism *intrinsically* superior to hit-and-run terrorism? One plausible answer, to follow Gambetta, is when self-sacrifice has added value as propaganda, conveying important information about the cause that could not be delivered, or delivered so memorably, by a non-suicidal attack.

But the distinction between suicide terrorism as a military strategy and suicide terrorism as a way to communicate a message should not lead us to neglect the strategic and military value of communication itself. After all, sending a message is itself an action that can have serious and, to some extent, predictable psychological consequences. The 'war' between al-Qaeda and the United States, in which 9/11 was only an episode, is one of those asymmetrical confrontations in which the superpower's challenger has few weapons besides publicity. Murdering almost 3,000 people did not have any direct effect on the military power of the United States. But communicating a message can itself be, *sensu lato*, a military manoeuvre if it changes the equation, weakening the strong and strengthening the weak. From their own statements it seems clear that the al-Qaeda leadership mounted the mission hoping that it would have this effect.

Whether suicidal or not, terrorism is usually aimed at an audience rather than at its direct victims (Guttman 1979). Whatever else it accomplishes, it usually seeks to publicize a cause. Explaining 'the centrality of the urban setting in the history of early martyrdom', one historian says that 'martyrdom in a city provided the greatest possible visibility for the cause of the nascent Church' (Bowersock 1995: 42–3). The events of 9/11 did the same, providing unprecedented visibility for the cause of anti-US Islamic militancy, because it occurred not only in a great city but in the capital of the world's media. Islamic insurgencies throughout the world have struggled for decades to break through the wall of censorship that prevents them from attracting public attention to their causes. The events of 9/11 solved this problem in one fell swoop.

To attract public attention, *suicidal* terrorism carries the potential added value that 'martyrdom' confers upon it. Etymologically, a 'martyr' is a witness giving testimony before listeners on a jury or tribunal. Their desire to *bear witness* before a world audience seems to be an essential reason why 9/11's planners decided to mount an exploit of such staggering magnitude. Referring to the attacks as 'speeches', bin Laden himself boasted that 'The speeches are understood by both Arabs and non-Arabs—even by Chinese.'[31]

In a pre-attack videotape, one of the nineteen hijackers, Ahmad al-Haznawi al-Ghamidi, declared: 'We left our families to send a message, which has the color of blood, to reach the whole world.'[32]

Suicide Terrorism as a Communicative Act

But what was this bloody message? And what was its intended effect? The communicative strategy adopted by the 9/11 plotters can be inferred from various features of the attack itself as well as from pronouncements by bin Laden and others. Telling in this regard was the plotters' decision to mount four simultaneous hijackings. Al-Qaeda did not invent this method of synchronized attacks but borrowed it from others, such as Hezbollah. (One of the very first acts of suicide terrorism in modern times, the October 1983 operation by Lebanese Shiites, involved synchronized strikes, one against the US marines and the other against the French.) But it has now become an al-Qaeda trademark. One of its functions, presumably, is to *communicate* the skill and determination of the attackers. But the basic communicative strategy behind 9/11 was probably more subtle.

Various published pronouncements suggest that the attack's instigators and organizers began with the assumption that power can be destroyed non-militarily because power is ultimately based on myth. Al-Qaeda spokesmen have explicitly claimed that the dominance of a military superpower, such as the Soviet Union, depends on its reputation for invincibility. This reputation lulls oppressed and abused groups into passivity, fatalism, and acquiescence. For the ambitious organizers of insurgencies, therefore, the strategic question is how to dispel this fatalism and thereby to rouse a sleeping army against a dominant and oppressive power. Belief systems are military assets because beliefs can either inflame or sedate the emotional sources of violent behaviour. To dispel the paralysing illusions that keep the oppressed in a state of passive resignation, a vanguard must crack the superpower's protective shield and, by so doing, excite the desire of freelance warriors around the world to jump on the bandwagon. The effectiveness of this strategy remains uncertain; but the organizers of the 9/11 attack seemed to have sincerely believed that they could politicize and radicalize the Islamic masses by utilizing the instruments of mass communication to shatter the myth of superpower invincibility (Burke 2003: 211).

On the same pre-attack video just cited, Ahmad al-Haznawi al-Ghamidi says that 'The United States is nothing but propaganda and a huge mass of false statements and exaggeration. The purpose of this propaganda was to make the United States big in the eyes of the world.' [33] By implication, 9/11 was intended to be an act of counter-propaganda. Its explicit purpose was to cut the United States down to size, to demoralize the Americans, and encourage the Islamists by revealing how a lightly armed David can inflict a grave wound on a heavily armoured Goliath. David can defeat Goliath, not by delivering a knockout blow, but only indirectly, by throwing a stone that looses an avalanche to crush the giant. The organizers of 9/11 also seem to have had this indirect strategy in mind. The stone they threw was an audacious terrorist attack. The avalanche they anticipated was a worldwide Islamic insurgency against the United States and its client regimes in the Muslim world. The former would effect the latter by provoking the United States into lashing out indiscriminately against Muslims around the world, thereby politicizing and radicalizing groups that had hitherto remained passive. In other words, the 9/11 masterminds may have thought just like a character in the favourite novel of Timothy McVeigh, the executed Oklahoma City bomber: 'one of the major purposes of political terror, always and everywhere, is to force the authorities to take reprisals and to become more repressive, thus alienating a portion of the population and generating sympathy for the terrorists' (Macdonald 1996: 51).

The murder of 3,000 people from over 100 countries was not likely to unleash a great wave of sympathy for bin Laden and al-Qaeda. But US military retaliation on a massive scale, with the inevitable collateral damage to civilian bystanders, could probably be counted on to stir such sympathy and to make bin Laden into even more of a cult figure and global celebrity. Perhaps the organizers of the 9/11 attacks hedged their bets, calculating that the Americans could react to their audacious provocation *either* by weak retreat *or* by unfocused (and therefore self-defeating) retaliation. This is again speculation. But the planners might have allowed that the exact response to their 'message' was unpredictable, while welcoming either possible outcome: ignominious capitulation or panicky escalation.

The strength of the US government, including its ability to project force abroad, depends not only on its reputation for invincibility abroad. It also depends upon its legitimacy domestically. Here is a further context in which to situate the communicative strategy behind 9/11. The plotters aimed to kill US civilians, according to bin Laden's own account, because the United States is a democracy, that is, a system in which ordinary citizens have some influence over government policy.[34] They are legitimate targets not because they refuse to acknowledge the truth of Islam, but because they pay taxes and vote for a regime that conducts an unjust foreign policy.[35] One way to undermine the United States' capacity to project force abroad, therefore, is to attack the civilians who must finance and vote for deployment of US troops abroad. No government is legitimate unless it can effectively protect its citizens from violence. Various al-Qaeda pronouncements also suggest that the 9/11 conspirators explicitly aimed to unravel the US social contract, the elemental exchange of protection for obedience. They wanted to show Americans that their government could not protect them. But the question remains: how did the *suicide* of the attackers contribute to this aims? Would not a hit-and-run attack that successfully toppled the WTC have provided all the publicity that Osama bin Laden and Khalid Shaikh Mohammad craved? Was the suicide of the attackers really indispensable for disheartening the Americans and rallying Islamic youth to al-Qaeda's cause?

Of course, once they took up the audacious idea of using civilian airliners in the attack, the suicide of the operatives was dictated as a means to an end. Only the willingness of the hijackers to die allowed a certain kind of psychological victory. How else could they have forced Americans to watch endless reruns of their fellow citizens being transported like so many helpless sheep to the slaughter? In this sense, the willingness of airborne terrorists to sacrifice their lives in the attack allowed the organizers of the 9/11 attacks to maximize the audience for their call to arms by mounting a spectacular urban operation destined for worldwide television coverage.

But more needs to be said. The death of the perpetrators may have been meaningful as well as instrumental. It may have conveyed a message that would have been lost on the watching world if delivered in any other way. Most obviously, the suicide of the perpetrators *displayed* the futility of normal tactics for fending off enemy attackers. If disheartening the enemy was a strategic objective, then the suicide of the hijackers on 11 September was probably chosen for its value as an intensifier of enemy despair. Suicide terrorism also makes visible the contrast between the attackers who braved death and the victims scurrying from death in base fear. Arguing that cultural stereotypes may play a role in the decision to mount SMs, one theorist defines the message of such attacks as follows: 'the enemy is also a coward. Why is he perceived as a coward? Because Western society [is] primarily made up of pleasure seekers who fear death and suicide. These fears, combined with the quest for "the good life," are viewed as the basic tenets of Western culture' (Paz 2001: 97).

Osama bin Laden's ability to induce young men to die for him is also striking *testimony* to his 'Pied Piper' mystique and, by inference, to the persuasiveness of his cause. In his December videotape, bin Laden noted: 'When people see a strong horse and a weak horse, by nature they will like the strong horse.'[36] In this case, al-Qaeda's horse not only appeared strong but also looked virtuous. The purity of motives implied by self-sacrifice may have helped to recruit future terrorists and to inspire imitators as well. It was a form of proselytizing by deed. The astonishing willingness of nineteen young men to give up everything could conceivably trigger a bandwagon effect. The unidentified Sheikh from Saudi Arabia who appears with bin Laden in the 13 December videotape boasts: 'Hundreds of people used to doubt you and few would follow you until this huge event happened. Now hundreds of people are coming out to join you.'[37] True or not, this was evidently what some of the plotters had in mind.

The suicide of the terrorists, according to 'communicative' interpretations of 9/11, not only enhanced the recruitment effect of the attack. It also added to the attack's demoralizing effect. The plotters may have chosen an SM rather than a hit-and-run mission because it was a more effective form of psychological warfare. It was arguably a better way to break the United States' heart. The futility of deterrence in such cases makes target groups feel additionally helpless, forced to sit defencelessly awaiting future attacks.[38] But another psychological mechanism, while less frequently discussed, may be equally important. A terrorist who lobs a grenade into a café and runs away is just as frightening as a terrorist who explodes himself among his victims. Carnage produces nightmares however delivered. What makes suicide terrorism more disheartening than hit-and-run terrorism is that the former denies the victim group its ordinary after-the-fact consolation of inflicting pain upon those who have inflicted pain on it. There is no concrete evidence that this consideration influenced the 9/11 plotters, but the logic behind it is too compelling to be ignored. The chance for psychologically satisfying revenge is thwarted by SMs because the perpetrators have carefully placed themselves beyond the reach of human justice.[39] Punishment of a murderer is cathartic, providing the victim's kin with some measure of psychological relief. The elimination at the outset of all possibility for exacting vengeance upon the immediate perpetrators arguably makes suicide terrorism more dismaying—harder to recover from psychologically—than hit-and-run terrorism.

The use of suicide, finally, delivers the unnerving message that the terrorists have torn up the rule book and will stop at nothing. The 9/11 plotters certainly wanted this message to get across. It takes on especially ominous overtones when coupled with bin Laden's sabre-rattling about weapons of mass destruction. 'It would be a sin for Muslims not to try to possess the weapons that would prevent the infidels from inflicting harm on Muslims' (*Time* 2001). If this message was crafted to unbalance US foreign policy and alienate the United States from its allies, it seems to have succeeded, producing, for example, the Bush administration's universally reviled doctrine of preventive war against potential future threats for which only murky and unreliable evidence exists.

Retaliation and Self-Defence

To deepen our understanding of why Khalid Shaikh Mohammed chose to mount an SM on 11 September, we need to inspect the 'war aims' publicly announced by al-Qaeda. Osama bin Laden, Ayman al-Zawahiri, and others had been fairly articulate about the purposes of their decade-long struggle against the United States, a campaign that has included hit-and-run attacks as well as SMs, and has aimed at military as well as civilian targets. The war aims they have announced are ambiguous, contradictory, and constantly evolving, but not much more so than, say, the war aims announced by the United States in Iraq.

In the public statement of 1998, heralding the creation of the World Islamic Front for Jihad against Jews and Crusaders, bin Laden joined others in declaring:

The ruling to kill the Americans and their allies—civilians and military—is an individual duty for every Muslim who can do it in any country in which it is possible to do it, in order to liberate the al-Aqsa mosque and the holy mosque [Mecca] from their grip, and in order for their armies to move out of all the lands of Islam, defeated and unable to threaten any Muslim.[40]

Summarizing this and other pronouncements, we can say that al-Qaeda's principal aims in its 'war' with the United States are to drive US forces out of the Gulf, to end US support for Mubarak, and to end US support for Israel. All three aims are perfectly secular and, indeed, could easily be supported by Arab nationalists engaged in a struggle to end Western 'colonization' of the Middle East.

Admittedly, bin Laden has also described the conflict in overtly religious terms. He has said, for example: 'Under no circumstance should we forget this enmity between us and the infidels. For the enmity is based on creed.'[41] To assert that the enmity between Islam and the West is based on creed is to deny that it is based on deeds. To fight non-Muslims 'until they say there is no God but Allah' [42] is different from fighting Americans until they stop supporting Israel. So how can we explain this back and forth between national-liberation terrorism and all-consuming religious war? And does the very mention of religious war prove that the 9/11 masterminds were irrational 'fanatics'?

The first thing to say is that *the vast majority* of bin Laden's public statements provide secular not religious rationales for 9/11. The principal purpose of the attack, he repeatedly says, was to punish the 'unjust and tyrannical America'.[43] The *casus belli* he invokes over and over again is injustice not impiety. True, he occasionally remarks that the United States has declared war on God, but such statements would carry little conviction if not seconded by claims that the United States is tyrannizing and exploiting Muslim people. Under the Western boot, Islam is being persecuted and oppressed: 'Its sons are being killed, its blood is being shed, its holy places are being attacked.' To these secular accusations, bin Laden often adds a religious charge that Islamic nations are 'not being ruled according to what God has decreed'. The charge of apostasy is rhetorically prominent here, but its real importance is somewhat undermined by what comes next: 'Despite this, nobody cares.'[44] It sometimes seems as if *indifference* to Islamic suffering is the most hurtful form of *aggression* against the Islamic world. Passages of this sort even seem to signal an unacknowledged need for recognition by the West, a need that would be superfluous, or even blasphemous, for anyone who genuinely believed that the West was an enemy of all things sacred.

Be this as it may, bin Laden almost never justifies terrorism against the West as a means for subordinating Western unbelievers to the true faith. Instead, he almost always justifies terrorism against the West as a form of legitimate self-defence. The events of 9/11 were part of a 'defensive jihad'.[45] It embodied the perfectly secular need to punish the United States for its arrogance toward Muslims and to retaliate for US enmity and aggression. In the Islamic tradition, wars of self-defence are easier to justify than wars of aggression.[46] But there is nothing specifically or uniquely Islamic about this norm. Indeed, the superior legitimacy of wars of self-defence is virtually universal. If a community suffers 'a wholesale attack' (Paz 2001: 96), it can justly counteract in a way that its leaders judge proportionate.

In his 7 October 2001 videotape, bin Laden savoured the impact of 9/11 on Americans: 'What the United States tastes today is a very small thing compared to what we have tasted for tens of years. Our nation has been tasting this humiliation and contempt for almost eighty years.'[47] Following this pungent rationale, the 9/11 attack on the United States was an act of retaliation, a returning of the favour. Americans were forced to swallow some of their own medicine, compelled to witness the mass murder of fellow citizens on home soil. Indeed, the backward-looking principle of retaliatory justice—*do unto others as they have done unto you*—recurs obsessively in al-Qaeda statements. The 9/11 plotters adapted this basic norm to the age of mass communications: *Show the world that you can harm others the way they have shown that they can harm you.* For years, CNN had beamed vivid footage throughout the Muslim world, picturing Arabs humiliated and killed by the United States and its allies. In reply, the plotters decided to hand-deliver a colossal snuff flick to the United States' doorstep.

Of all the motivations driving the 9/11 conspirators, the intense craving for retaliation and the (real or imagined) imperatives of self-defence may turn out to have had the greatest impact. A month after the attack, an al-Qaeda spokesman ironized that 'when the victim tries to seek justice, he is described as a terrorist'.[48] The 9/11 suicide operatives were not terrorists, from his perspective, but seekers of justice, righters of wrongs, punishers of crime. The United States deserved the attack because it has committed a 'huge criminality'.[49] What crime do bin Laden and his companions have in mind? 'The

United States is the leader of the criminals in the crime of the establishment of Israel', Ayman al-Zawahiri explained, adding: 'It is a crime that continues to take place and that has been repeating itself for the past fifty years. The Muslim nation cannot accept the continuation of this crime.'[50] Like other criminals, the United States must be punished by the legitimate authorities. From this perspective, the hijackers were simply executing a death sentence passed by an al-Qaeda 'high court'. Although the crime being punished was sometimes hyped as a crime against God, it was also more mundanely interpreted as a crime against the Arab nation. The executioners who carried out the sentence needed no authority beyond the primordial right of every community to punish criminal injuries to itself.

Like Jesus Christ and George Orwell, bin Laden often speaks in animal fables to make his ideas accessible and memorable. The following characteristic passage about the US crime of supporting Israel is worth citing in its entirety. The need to punish criminal acts, here again, suggests a wholly secular rationale for retaliation against US acts of injustice.

What is taking place cannot be tolerated by any nation. I do not say from the nations of the human race, but from other creatures, from the animals. They would not tolerate what is taking place. A confidant of mine told me that he saw a butcher slaughtering a camel in front of another camel. The other camel got agitated while seeing the blood coming out of the other camel. Thus, it burst out with rage and bit the hand of the man and broke it. How can the weak mothers in Palestine endure the killing of their children in front of their eyes by the unjust Jewish executioners with US support and with US aircraft and tanks?[51]

Islamic law certainly justifies punishing the unjust. But the avenging camel of bin Laden's fable has no need to consult a religious principle to justify his instinctive—and therefore natural—retaliation. For the same reason, Islamic militants do not need the *sharia* to give them permission to shed American blood if the United States is (in their minds) committing atrocities against Muslims.

Identifying the Enemy

Those who look to religion to discover the source of al-Qaeda's hostility to the United States like to stress bin Laden's Manichaean worldview. One way to reply to this tack is to cite George W. Bush's idea that the United States today is at war with 'evil'. Without doubting the influence of religion on Bush's rhetoric, we can confidently state that his enmity has been aroused by al-Qaeda's actions not by its beliefs. Why cannot the same be true of bin Laden?

But the more important point here is that a Manichaean religious framework, while dividing the world into good and evil, does not specify a religious community's military enemy of the moment. Bin Laden's decision to declare war on the United States was promoted by historical circumstances. It was not foreordained by religious doctrine. To understand the circumstances in question, the best place to begin is probably the Afghan war. Although it failed miserably in the Middle East, pan-Arabism was spectacularly success-ful, at least in popular perception, in the effort to drive the Soviet Union out of Afghanistan. An international brigade drawn from diverse Arab countries helped to defeat a superpower (Engel 2001). After the Soviet retreat in 1989, however, this 'homeless phalanx' (Reuter 2002: 29) of Arab warriors was left in the lurch. Its members became mujahidin in search of a jihad. Many of the Arabs gathered around bin Laden in Afghanistan, during the 1990s, had nowhere else to go because they faced death sentences or imprisonment back home. (Some of them chose to join guerrilla campaigns in Bosnia, Chechnya, and Kashmir.) Although it provided a short-term remedy locally, in other words, the exile of radical Islamic insurgents from the Middle East produced a long-term problem globally, creating a pool of angry *déracinés* willing to enlist in violent causes around the world.

But self-selected 'warriors' are not the only dangerous political exiles from the Arab world. They have been joined abroad by self-selected 'priests' as well. As part of their governments' counter-insurgency strategy, the security appar-atuses of Egypt, Jordan, Syria, Algeria, and so forth exiled many home-grown radical imams not to Afghanistan but to Western Europe. The resulting Eur-ope-based diaspora of angry preachers was able to prey upon deracinated Arab youth, cut off from their families, feeling the sting of discrimination, and looking for some colourful purpose to orient their drifting lives. Searching for a cause that could appeal simultaneously to Algerians, Egyptians, Yemenis, Jordanians, Libyans, Syrians, and Saudis living in Europe, these preachers naturally idealized the jihad in Afghanistan in the 1980s, when a pan-Arab force had, as they recounted the story, brought a superpower to ruin.

If political Islam almost died in the Arab Middle East, it revived in the Arab diasporas of Western Europe, thanks precisely to this lethal syndicate of self-anointed preachers and would-be warriors, both under the sway of a mythic idea of the Afghan jihad. For both groups, the most attractive candidate for the role of a new unifying enemy was the United States. In the imagination of Islamic militants, it seems, the United States reoccupied the space vacated by the Soviet Union.[52] A jihad against the United States could allow radicalized Muslim youth to re-enact the celebrated victory of the Afghan war, but this time on a global scale.

These historical circumstances, not religious Manichaeism, explain why the 9/11 plotters directed their fury against the United States. Bin Laden was originally interested in overthrowing the Saudi regime, just as Zawahiri was focused initially on overthrowing the Egyptian regime. Unable to make any headway at home, they jointly evolved an *indirect strategy* of attacking their local autocrats' foreign backers. By attacking US interests, they hoped to force the United States to withdraw its troops from the Gulf and its support for Mubarak, just as attacks in Lebanon in 1983 and Somalia in 1993 had driven the Americans to pull out their troops. To overthrow both Mubarak and the House of Saud, the Americans must be induced to abandon their clients. The most effective way to undermine the near enemy was to attack the distant enemy.

But this instrumental logic does not wholly explain why the 9/11 plotters turned their fury against the United States. To pursue their indirect strategy for attacking 'apostate' regimes back home, bin Laden and Zawahiri also decided that they had to increase the size of their mujaheedin army. To rally more troops, in turn, they had to adjust their 'war aims'. Instead of looking for a means to achieve their ends, they deliberately set out to modify their ends to attain more plentiful and lethal means. They had to redefine their objectives to lend them the widest possible appeal, especially to Arab youths living in Europe, insulated to some extent from abuses by the powerful and wealthy back in the Middle East. Only a battle against the West in general and against the United States in particular could successfully rally this 'homeless phalanx' of potential jihadists.

What hit the United States on 11 September was not religion, therefore. Instead, the 9/11 terrorists represented the *pooled insurgencies* of the Arab Middle East. The fusing of these local insurgencies took place largely among diaspora Arabs outside the Middle East itself, in Afghanistan and Europe. The multinational or pan-Arab Hamburg cell exemplifies how uprooting can effect a blending of local insurgencies. It also shows how the internal logic of this merger can compel a redefining of the enemy in view: 'Though Atta loathed Mubarak's government in Egypt, there is little evidence that others in the Hamburg cell harboured any great ill will towards the political leaders of their own respective homelands. Their hatred was primarily directed at the West' (Burke 2003: 227).

When local insurrections are melded into a global jihad, they are transformed. When national-liberation terrorists redirect their hostility from the local enemy to the global enemy, they do not merely switch tactics. They undergo a deeper transformation, including, to some extent, the consolidation of a new identity. This explains why the conflict between al-Qaeda and the United States, far from being another rehashing of 'ancient hatreds', seems historically unprecedented.

From Decolonization to 'Religious' War

Far from being commanded by Islam, suicide terrorism has become increasingly common, despite the initial hostility of important religious authorities, because it proved so devastatingly effective. The mobilizing ideology behind 9/11 was not Islam, or even Islamic fundamentalism, but rather a specific narrative of blame. Even despair must be interpreted to become politically effective. To dispel fatalistic illusions and stimulate feelings of aggression, it is necessary to focus the mind on an ostensibly guilty party. Those who downplay the United States' crimes 'anesthetize the nation'.[53] Those who call attention to these crimes, by contrast, arouse the nation. An interpretation of suffering stirs the will to violence if it focuses attention on a culprit who can suffer pain in turn. According to the classic study of resentment, 'every sufferer instinctively seeks a cause for his suffering; more specifically, an agent, a "guilty" agent who is susceptible of pain—in short, some living being or other on whom he can vent his feelings directly or in effigy, under some pretext or other' (Nietzsche 1956: 263). If suffering is interpreted as natural or uncaused it will be considered misfortune instead of injustice, and it will produce resignation rather than rebellion. The most efficient way to incite, therefore, is to indict.

To rally Muslim youth to their cause, bin Laden and Zawahiri indulged in a veritable orgy of blame. They interpreted US actions as crimes by inserting them into an overarching narrative about the West's monstrous plot to dominate Muslims and plunder their wealth. They embroidered and myth-ically heightened observed facts to make them support a vast conspiracy theory. They implausibly but persistently interpreted 'Operation Restore Hope' in Somalia in 1992–3 as another case of a Western power coming to occupy Muslim lands. They wholly ignored the role of the United States in opposing Milosevic's malign ambitions against Muslims in Kosovo. But the ultimate charge that bin Laden levels against the United States is the charge of genocide. Evidence that the United States is engaged in 'a war of annihi-lation'[54] against Islam is its 'occupation' of Saudi Arabia. Bin Laden con-sistently says that the presence of US troops in 'the land of the two holy mosques' is a much graver offence than the Soviet invasion of Afghanistan, a conflict that, we should remember, killed one million Afghanis and exiled five million more (Bergen 2001: 26).

Demonizing the United States and all its inhabitants not only helps neu-tralize qualms about killing civilians. It also, presumably, helps intensify the otherwise lukewarm craving for blood revenge felt by jihadists who have had little personal contact with the United States. This is probably why Islamist entrepreneurs spend so much energy mythically magnifying the all-too-real injustices committed by the United States, interpreting them as parts of a vast sinister plot. But the essential point to make here is that there is nothing specifically Islamic in the charge of genocide. Unlike impiety, genocide is a crime against humanity. To accuse the United States of plotting to wipe out the Islamic nation is to accuse it of violating a Western norm accepted by atheists and non-Muslims alike.

The language of national liberation proved awkward as a means for rallying a *multinational* army of jihadists. To mobilize its *guérillas sans frontières*, al-Qaeda had to develop a different idiom. It also had to focus attention on a common enemy and specify its positive goal in a new way. Finding the new enemy, of course, was the easiest task. The United States was impossible to overlook. When articulating a positive goal, al-Qaeda spokesmen often mention a world Caliphate. But such a Caliphate, with the entire West (as well as India, China, and Russia) reduced to tribute status before Islamic powers, is the religious equivalent of Marx's Communist utopia. No one can object to it because no one can imagine it. This is one reason why it is so attractive. To make a world Caliphate into a primary aim of jihad posed no serious threat to the unity of a shaky coalition.

Neither the negative goal of destroying the United States nor the positive goal of achieving Islamic domination of the world is particularly reasonable or realistic. But the 9/11 masterminds had to speak this way to their multi-national army of mujaheedin. They could not plausibly say that their *ultimate* goal in attacking the United States was to topple Mubarak or the House of Saud. The masterminds could communicate with the hijackers only by repackaging micro-politics as macro-politics. For radicalized Arabs living in Europe, the purpose of attacking the United States could not have been to push it out of their various homelands, because they had loosened their ties to their homelands—or, rather, they had, in some sense, replaced their birth countries, where nationalism had failed, with an imaginary community of faith. The redefinition of al-Qaeda's war aims from decolonization to religious war can best be understood, therefore, as a by-product of the organization's all-points recruitment drive.

This logic is impeccable so far as it goes, but it is also unsatisfying, for several reasons. The idea that the 9/11 masterminds *really* declared war on the United States for its odious foreign policy, which it could easily abandon, rather than for deeper reasons does not mesh well with bin Laden's call to murder all Americans everywhere. The path to diplomacy does not run through the apocalypse. Pressuring US citizens is quite different from wiping them out. Extreme talk about visiting hellfire on US urban centres and annihilating the US way of life makes nonsense of a merely instrumental interpretation of the strategy behind 9/11, whereby a pinprick attack on the United States would serve the cause of local Islamic insurgencies by persuading it to withdraw its support for local autocracies.

Before al-Qaeda, it is sometimes said, terrorist groups wanted a lot of people watching, not a lot of people dead, on the grounds that mass casualties would alienate potential supporters. When Osama bin Laden promises to deliver to the United States 'its Hiroshima', as a result, he is commonly taken to have turned a corner, unleashing a kind of zero-compunction terrorism that had never been seen before. Only a religious mind that sincerely believed in 'cosmic war' could have done this, it is inferred.

But bin Laden and his associates may have very good non-religious reasons for sounding apocalyptic. For one thing, such talk is frightening. The more crazed and irrational al-Qaeda sounds, the more likely it becomes that the US government will lose its cool and react in panic. During the cold war, the United States' one source of psychological comfort was that its enemy, too, feared the apocalypse. This common fear of nuclear disaster provided the basis for negotiation and compromise between Washington and Moscow, even when relations grew turbulent. To take this solace away, as bin Laden has done, is a shrewd form of psychological warfare.

The problem is that threatening to deliver the apocalypse to a military superpower may not be a very good long-term strategy. It is bound to provoke a serious backlash.[55] In the ensuing maelstrom there is very little likelihood that Muslim states will be susceptible to a consolidated takeover by radical Islamic groups. Such considerations might lead us back to the hypothesis that the 9/11 plotters were basically irrational 'fanatics'. But there is another way of looking at the matter. The organizers of the attack are men who have spent years in an underground revolutionary organization. Honed in conflict, their skills are no doubt wholly inappropriate to the mundane tasks of a post-conflict situation. If apostate regimes fell down and were replaced, what roles in ordinary governance would they assume? For men such as these, terrorism has become a profession that can be exercised only under certain conditions. Not only do they have a strong incentive to keep these conditions in place; they also have the means to do so. For instance, they can raise unreasonable demands that their enemy cannot possibly accept. The 9/11 masterminds surely want to keep up the value of their investment in terrorism. This desire alone, even in the absence of irrational fanaticism, could explain why their demands seem hallucinatory and unrealistic. That might simply be the way they want them to seem.

By way of conclusion, we should probably mention that the 9/11 plotters, too, may have fallen victim to 'the fallacy of the instrument'. This fallacy, as is well known, causes people with a hammer to see every problem as a nail. The best-known contemporary example of this fallacy is the US decision to combat non-state terrorist groups using military force, not because military force is appropriate (it is not), but because military force is the 'best' instrument at the United States' disposal. When a group of weak and angry men, with poor technology at their disposal, face a military superpower, suicide terrorism may be the only method available for inflicting noticeable harm. Suicide terrorism may have been al-Qaeda's only effective 'hammer'. If so, the 9/11 masterminds may have easily overestimated its utility. They did not necessarily resort to it because it was so effective. They may, instead, have imagined that it was useful because it was the only weapon in their arsenal and, like all political leaders, they 'had to do something'. So even if the 9/11 plotters were irrational in some sense, their deviations from reason were not necessarily the result of their religious beliefs.

5

Dying Without Killing: Self-Immolations, 1963–2002

MICHAEL BIGGS

Flames were coming from a human being; his body was slowly withering and shriveling up, his head blackening and charring. In the air was the smell of burning flesh... Behind me I could hear the sobbing of the Vietnamese who were now gathering. I was too shocked to cry, too confused to take notes or ask questions, too bewildered to even think. (Halberstam 1965: 211)

David Halberstam, an American journalist, witnessed the self-immolation of Thich Quang Duc on 11 June 1963 (see also Browne 1965, 1993). It began when a Buddhist procession stopped at a major intersection in Saigon. The elderly monk assumed the lotus position; other monks doused him with petrol. He set himself alight. A student, Chân Không (1993: 38), watched him 'sitting bravely and peacefully, enveloped in flames. He was completely still, while those of us around him were crying and prostrating ourselves on the sidewalk.' This act was a dramatic escalation of conflict with the dictatorship of President Ngo Dinh Diem, which had persistently favoured the country's Catholic minority. A month earlier, police killed several Buddhist demonstrators. 'Before closing my eyes to go to Buddha', wrote Quang Duc, 'I have the honour to present my words to President Diem, asking him to be kind and tolerant towards his people and enforce a policy of religious equality' (quoted in Joiner 1964: 918).

This is my type specimen of 'self-immolation'. Like a suicidal attack, an act of self-immolation involves an individual intentionally killing himself or herself (or at least gambling with death) on behalf of a collective cause. Unlike a suicidal attack, an act of self-immolation is *not* intended to cause physical harm to anyone else or to inflict material damage.[1] The suicidal attack is an extraordinary weapon of war whereas self-immolation is an extreme form of protest. As an act of protest, it is intended to be public in at least one of two senses: performed in a public place in view of other people, or accompanied by a written letter addressed to political figures or to the general public. One point of terminology should be clarified at the outset.

Although the word 'immolation' strictly means 'sacrifice', since the 1960s it has become synonymous with fiery death.[2] My definition of self-immolation encompasses other methods of self-inflicted death. In addition, this is not always a solitary act; two or more individuals may coordinate their sacrifice.

Self-immolation, as an ideal type, can be clarified by distinguishing it from other actions. Personal suicides pertain to individual grievances (including conflict with other family members) rather than a collective cause. (The parallel distinction is between murder-suicides and suicidal attacks.) Suicides by members of a cult may be collective, but the believer seeks to attain a more exalted existence after death (what Baechler 1975 calls 'transfiguration'). The Hindu practice of a wife (*sati*) joining her husband on his funeral pyre defies precise characterization, but the intent is not to advance a collective cause (Hawley 1994).[3] Martyrdom can resemble self-immolation. Consider the archbishop of El Salvador, killed in 1980 after denouncing military repression. He had anticipated his own death as a sacrifice, and even made it more likely by refusing to employ security guards (Nepstad 2002). But he did not actually kill himself. Even more closely related to self-immolation is the hunger strike. Hunger strikes involve self-inflicted suffering, but few are undertaken as a fast until death. Even when a hunger striker seriously 'threatens' to starve to death, death can be averted by concessions.[4] 'No hunger striker aims at death', observed a Jesuit theologian in 1920, after an Irish Republican starved himself to death in a British prison. 'He aims at escaping from unjust detention, and, to do this is willing to run the risk of death, of which he has no desire, not even as a means' (quoted in Sweeney 1993*b*: 428). With self-immolation, by contrast, death is not conditional on the opponent's (in)action.

These criteria and distinctions serve to define self-immolation as an ideal type. Needless to say, some actions are ambiguous enough to complicate this classification, as will emerge in the course of our investigation. In my estimate, there have been between 800 and 3,000 individual acts of self-immolation (including non-fatal attempts) in the four decades since 1963. Apparently, Quang Duc was the progenitor of the great majority of these acts, including almost every case in which fire was used. They were modelled either directly on his action or indirectly on another's action that can in turn be traced back to him. Thus, self-immolation describes an historical lineage as well as a conceptual abstraction. We may apply the concept to cases before 1963 (some of these are discussed below). Significantly, however, Durkheim's (1952) discussion in 1897 of 'altruistic' suicide excludes anything resembling self-immolation as defined here.

Self-immolation became a subject of academic study at the end of the 1960s. Initial studies by psychologists and psychiatrists defined their subject as self-inflicted death by fire, thus including personal suicide (Bostic 1973;

Bourgeois 1969; Crosby et al. 1977). Medical professionals contribute to a specialized literature on suicide, which includes two diagnostic studies of Indians who attempted self-immolation in 1990 and survived (Mahla et al. 1992; Singh et al. 1998). Pacifists have evaluated self-immolation from a normative standpoint (King 2000; Ryan 1994). Film-makers have documented and dramatized individual acts (Puhovski 1997; Park 1995). Yet, with two important recent exceptions (Kim 2002; Uehling 2000), self-immolation has not attracted the attention of social scientists—which is surprising given the vast literature on collective protest and the classical importance of suicide for sociologists.[5]

This chapter is wider in scope than the others. It provides an overview of self-immolation in the last four decades, from an original database of over 500 individual acts. After introducing the sources used to compile this database, the chapter is divided into five main sections. The first sketches the history of self-immolation. The modern lineage originated with Quang Duc in 1963 and subsequently diffused to dozens of countries. The second section examines the prevalence of self-immolation among causes, across countries, and over time. The collective causes show great variation, but they are not associated with suicide attacks or other acts of violence. Vietnam, South Korea, and India are countries with the highest rates of self-immolation. Analysis reveals that self-immolation is most frequent in countries with Buddhist or Hindu religious traditions and with relatively democratic political systems. The clustering of self-immolation in waves reveals how one individual's action tends to inspire others to imitate it. The third section focuses on the orchestration of the individual action. Self-immolation is not generally preceded by threats, and it does not usually involve organization. By far the most common method is burning, which maximizes physical suffering but need not ensure death. The fourth section tackles the central question—why?—by elucidating the various motivations for self-immolation. Two are prominent: appealing to bystanders and inciting sympathizers. The promise of supernatural rewards is not a significant motive, nor are suicidal tendencies or psychopathology. The final section considers the effects of the action. While most acts of self-immolation have no discernible impact, a small minority evoke a tremendous response, especially from sympathizers. Some episodes of self-immolation have shifted the balance of power between protesters and their opponents, albeit sometimes in an unexpected direction.

Sources

This chapter rests on a database of 533 individual acts of self-immolation—including attempts which did not prove fatal—from 1963 to 2002. The aim was to include every act for which minimal information (in English) is available. The database began with a systematic search of news reports. For the period from 1963 to 1976, the *New York Times* (*NYT*) and *The Times* are used because they are comprehensively indexed.[6] The superior search capability of the Nexis database becomes available from 1977 onwards. This provides access to global news-wires: the *Associated Press* (*AP*) and *United Press International* (*UPI*) from 1981, and *Agence France Presse* (*AFP*) from 1991.[7] These news reports are used to compile a 'sample' of acts meeting my criteria for self-immolation. An act is counted whether or not the person actually died; that is often not reported when hospitalization is the immediate outcome. Thwarted attempts are included, but threats are not.[8] In many cases, only the most basic information was reported. This is an inevitable consequence of choosing *not* to select only the most notable or successful acts. A minimal amount of specific information is required for inclusion, namely, at least two of the following: name, date, and location. For this reason, it proves necessary to exclude self-killing by prison inmates. Whether a prisoner's 'suicide' is actually murder is often impossible to judge. Even where we are confident that the inmate did kill himself or herself, whether this counts as an act of protest is usually difficult to ascertain. Even outside prison the distinction between personal suicide and self-immolation is sometimes ambiguous. Refugees who kill themselves after being refused asylum, for example, usually act on an individual—albeit political—grievance, without any declared intent to advance a collective cause. Therefore these cases are excluded.[9]

The more serious concern is the extent of coverage. Needless to say, these media sources did not report every act which could be classified as self-immolation. Lack of information, lack of interest, and self-censorship all act as barriers. Totalitarian states can effectively suppress information on protest, including self-immolation. In 1980 tourists in Moscow saw someone on fire in Red Square. One was knocked down as he attempted to take a photograph; others had their film exposed by State Security Committee (KGB) agents. The authorities insisted that it was merely a burning cigarette or a 'garbage fire' (*AP*, 2 August 1980, 17 June 1981). How many others killed themselves in more remote locations, out of sight of Western visitors?[10] There is an important offsetting factor, however. Self-immolation is intended as a public act, and so individuals have good reason to orchestrate publicity—by travelling to a public place where there will be witnesses or by alerting journalists to be on hand. In 2001, for instance, several Falun Gong followers travelled 350 miles from Kaifeng to Tiananmen Square to set fire to themselves—before cameras from the Cable News Network (CNN).[11]

A second barrier is lack of interest. Self-immolation is rare and spectacular, and so it is exceptionally newsworthy—far more than conventional protests like strikes or demonstrations (McCarthy et al. 1996). Nevertheless, the space for news is limited.[12] Journalists and their audiences have different levels of interest in different parts of the world. During the mid-1960s, because Americans were focused on Vietnam, the *New York Times* reported every self-immolation there (ascertained by checking against more detailed accounts). But it never mentioned some incidents in South Asia—which we know about from reports in *The Times*. As this suggests, the bias can be partially offset by including news media from different countries. The sample also includes an additional forty-three individuals identified in historical accounts and other sources.[13] A rather different problem is posed by the massive wave of self-immolation in India in 1990 in protest against the plan to reserve more places for students and employees from lower castes. Western news-wires certainly reported this in some detail, but were overwhelmed by its magnitude. They provided specific information—sufficient to warrant inclusion in the sample—on only twenty individuals. Therefore, the sample was supplemented by a systematic search of the *Times of India* and *The Hindu*, from mid-September to the end of 1990. This yielded information on an additional 200 individuals.

A third barrier to news coverage is less obvious: self-censorship. Following studies by social scientists of the impact of publicized suicides, the World Health Organization in 1993 recommended 'toning down press reports' (Schmidtke and Schaller 2000: 691). Whether this has affected coverage of self-immolation—especially acts that could be construed as suicidal, committed locally—is not clear. One possible candidate is Graham Bamford, who set himself on fire in 1993 to protest at British inaction over atrocities in the Balkans (Puhovski 1997). Although this occurred outside the Houses of Parliament, *The Times* did not report it. Because of these barriers, the sample of 533 obviously underestimates the extent of the phenomenon. We can estimate the extent of the bias by comparing more comprehensive totals for particular times and places. The sample excludes slightly over half of the fatal immolations in South Korea from 1970 to 1997 (Kim 2002). More surprisingly, perhaps, the sources omit over two-thirds of the immolations in Europe that were committed by Kurdish refugees (Olivier Grojean, personal communication). For India, it is possible to tabulate reports in two major national newspapers (*Times of India* and *The Statesman*) for 2000. They reported eighteen instances of self-immolation—but only two filtered through to the Western news-wires. In sum, we may hazard a guess that the real total could be anywhere from two times to nine times larger than the sample (excluding the wave in India in 1990, which is not likely to be underestimated). The lower bound could hardly be less than 800; it is difficult to imagine that the upper bound could exceed 3,000.

History

Origins

We can certainly find examples of self-immolation before 1963, but these were isolated incidents or episodes; they did not inspire people elsewhere. At the height of the campaign for women's suffrage in Britain, Emily Wilding Davison ran on to the horse-race track during the Derby of 1913. With suffrage flags in hand, she fell under the King's racehorse and received fatal injuries. Apparently, she did not plan her own death. She was nonetheless willing to die: she had attempted to kill herself in prison as a protest against force-feeding during a hunger strike. Indeed, she intimated that 'a life would have to be given before the vote was won' (quoted in Colmore 1913: 49). Although the suffrage movement embraced her as a martyr, her death did not inspire others to sacrifice themselves.

Two episodes from the end of the Second World War are worth recounting. After Japan surrendered, many military leaders died by *seppuku* (ritual disembowelling) to atone for their failure. Closer to self-immolation as defined here, two groups of civilian nationalists—numbering twenty-six in total—and several members of the Imperial Guards Division committed *seppuku* before the Imperial Palace, in separate incidents (Morris 1960: 25–9). In Europe, when American and British troops repatriated former Soviet citizens who had been living under Nazi rule, hundreds killed themselves and some even killed their children (Bethell 1987). Knowing that their fate would be execution or life in the gulag, suicide represented a preferable option. To some extent, however, death was a protest against the actions of their captors. Although many soldiers were disturbed by the deaths, they continued to obey orders. Indeed, the military eventually designed procedures and modified trains to prevent people from taking their own lives. As the operation was carried out in secrecy, these deaths had no wider impact.

Quang Duc's death by fire in 1963 was different because it inspired many others. As a result of his act, within a few years self-immolation entered the global 'repertoire' of protest (Tilly 1986). His act was an unexpected combination of modern technology and religious tradition. The availability of flammable liquids like petrol and kerosene made it feasible to burn oneself in a public place; without instant ignition, police could thwart any attempt. The advent of photography—and technologies for the rapid transmission and cheap reproduction of images—made it possible for a single sacrifice to have a dramatic impact on a huge audience. These potentialities, however, were discovered only in 1963. Therefore, we must closely examine the context of Quang Duc's innovation.

It arose out of conflict between Buddhists and the Diem regime in South Vietnam.[14] Since coming to power, the Catholic ruling family had advanced the interests of the country's Catholic minority and discriminated against Buddhists. Open conflict erupted suddenly on 8 May 1963, Buddha's birthday (Oka 1966: TO-25, 5–6; Wulff 1963). The regime banned the display of religious flags in Hué, the centre of Vietnamese Buddhism. The Archbishop of Hué, Diem's older brother, was especially militant in his propagation of Catholicism; he had just flown Vatican flags to celebrate the anniversary of his reign, making the refusal to allow Buddhist flags especially galling. There was a mass demonstration; the police killed eight or nine protesters, including children. The government then ludicrously blamed the deaths on the Viet Cong and refused all compromise. Buddhist monks mobilized quickly and effectively, much to the surprise of the regime and its American patrons. There were mass demonstrations and hunger strikes in many cities, including Saigon.

According to Thich Giac Duc, an activist in Saigon, the initiative came from Quang Duc himself. He asked to burn himself 'as a donation to the struggle' (quoted in Thich Giac Duc 1986: 141). Like any cultural innovation, this was a creative mutation of pre-existing elements.[15] Burning the body was an established part of Mahayana Buddhism, predominant in Vietnam (Benn 1998). The ordination ceremony for monks and nuns involved burning part of the forehead. As the ultimate ascetic technique, burning oneself to death was first recorded in Buddhist texts from the fifth century. (It can be traced back as far as China in the first century, when an official supposedly use this technique to induce rain during a drought.) The practice was always doctrinally suspect because it clashed with a central precept of Buddhism—the injunction against killing. The last case of a Vietnamese monk cremating himself to honour the Buddha-dharma occurred in the late eighteenth century (Thich Thien-An 1975*a*: 172–3). Remarkably, in China a handful of monks had chosen such a death in Quang Duc's lifetime, albeit no longer in public (Welch 1967: 327). In 1948 a monk was supposed to have died by fire in protest at the suppression of Buddhism under Mao's regime, according to a report published in Hong Kong.[16] Perhaps Quang Duc had heard of this precursor. What is certain is that burning evoked reverence within the Buddhist tradition.

When Quang Duc offered his life for the cause, the movement's leaders initially spurned the idea. Giac Duc (1986: 141) viewed it as 'exotic and horrible'. But one monk was in favour: Thich Duc Nghiep, fluent in English, who was in charge of relations with foreign journalists. Did he grasp the potential impact on the American audience? After several days of prayer and fast, Quang Duc eventually won approval. The activist monks thoroughly planned the self-immolation. They conducted experiments with different fuels (Browne 1993: 9). They dropped hints, which could have reached

President Diem.[17] On the day, the spectacle was orchestrated with precision. A detachment of monks and nuns prevented fire engines from reaching the scene by lying under their wheels. The performance was designed for maximum publicity, with journalists being alerted beforehand. Thus Browne, working for the Associated Press, captured the scene on film. A monk with loudspeaker intoned, 'A Buddhist priest burns himself for five requests', while others distributed the text of Quang Duc's final declaration, all in English, for the benefit of American journalists.

The impact of Quang Duc's fiery death was immense and immediate. Within South Vietnam, it galvanized popular discontent in the cities. In July 1963 there was another self-immolation, though in a rather different context. Nguyen Tuong Tam was a celebrated poet, who had led the struggle against French colonialism. Facing trial for involvement in an earlier coup plot, he took poison. His testament referred to Quang Duc and explained his act 'as a warning to those people who are trampling on all freedoms' (*NYT*, 9 July 1963). As the upward spiral of repression and protest continued, Quang Duc's example was followed by other Buddhists. Four monks and a nun burned themselves to death before Diem was toppled by a coup at the beginning of November. It did not end there. Death by fire was now part of the repertoire of protest in South Vietnam. There was another wave of self-immolations in 1966 in protest against the American-backed military regime and its prosecution of the war; thirteen set themselves on fire within one week.

Diffusion

If Buddhists were 'using their bodies like a lamp for help' (Thich Thien-An 1975*b*: 138), the illumination carried far beyond Vietnam. Browne's photographs of Quang Duc's flaming body were immediately reproduced in countless newspapers and magazines (though the *New York Times* refused to print them). He won the World Press Photograph Award for 1963 (Browne 1993). China used the image as anti-American propaganda throughout South-east Asia. Buddhists in countries like Sri Lanka (then Ceylon), Cambodia, and Thailand were deeply concerned for their co-religionists, and they spurred the United Nations to dispatch a fact-finding mission to Vietnam. In fact, the very first imitation of Quang Duc occurred not in Vietnam but in Sri Lanka. Nurse aides were on hunger strike, refusing to clean the hospital wards. Vidanage Vinitha jumped to her death from the building which housed the Ministry of Health. Although she did not adopt the signature method of burning, her inspiration was clear. 'Thousands weep over the fate of a Buddhist monk in South Vietnam', she wrote, 'but nobody cares about 400 Singhalese girls in our own land' (*The Times*, 16 July 1963).

In subsequent years, the model was taken up elsewhere. In 1964 in India, a Tamil labourer called Chinnaswami set himself alight to protest against the encroachment of the Hindi language. A year later, when Hindi was supposed to replace English as the official language of India, five Tamils died by fire and three swallowed poison (Ramaswamy 1997: 231–3). Tamils had a tradition of self-sacrifice (Krishnan 1983: 94; Subrahmanian 1983: 43). Less than a decade earlier, someone fasted to death in an attempt to have Madras state renamed 'Tamil Nadu'. The method of burning, however, had no indigenous precedent, and was surely inspired by Quang Duc's act. In 1965, a politician in South Korea burned to death in protest against the country's first post-war treaty with Japan. This was not unprecedented. In 1905, a high official took his life with a dagger to protest against a treaty subordinating the country to Japan (Schmid 2002: 343). Once again, the method of burning was novel.

More remarkable was the diffusion of the practice to the United States, where there was no precedent either for politically motivated sacrifice or for death by fire. 'The self-burning of Vietnamese Buddhist monks in 1963 is somehow difficult for the Western Christian conscience to understand', acknowledged Thich Nhat Hanh (1967: 119), a monk who studied in the United States. He wrote an open letter to Martin Luther King, Jr., justifying their actions by drawing a distinction between self-destruction and self-sacrifice for the sake of others. Nevertheless, Christians began burning themselves in 1965, just as confrontation was flaring again in Vietnam. Alice Herz, an elderly Quaker, set fire to herself as a protest against American foreign policy. 'I wanted to burn myself like the monks in Vietnam did', she told police (*NYT*, 18 March 1965). Several months later, another Quaker, Norman Morrison, set fire to himself outside the Pentagon. He was deeply disturbed by the war, and had frequently discussed the Buddhist self-immolations (Hendrickson 1996: 223–4; Morrison Welsh 2000: 4). Only days later, Roger LaPorte, a Catholic who had once trained for monastic life, assumed the lotus position and set himself alight outside the United Nations.[18] These acts were celebrated in North Vietnam; a stamp was issued in Morrison's honour.

By the end of 1965, then, self-immolation had entered the global repertoire of protest. Over the next few years, there were examples in the Soviet Union, Malaysia, and Japan, as well as further cases in the United States and Vietnam. Nhat Chi Mai, who sacrificed herself in Saigon in 1967, even referred to Morrison along with Quang Duc—thus completing the circle of inspiration (Hassler 1970: 201). Most of these people, with the major exception of Tamils in India, were protesting against the foreign policy of the United States, and especially its war in Vietnam.[19] In 1969 came another wave of self-immolations by fire for a completely unrelated cause. On 16 January, Jan Palach set himself alight to protest against the Soviet occupation of Czechoslovakia. 'My act has fulfilled its purpose', he announced from hospital, 'but let nobody else do it.' Nevertheless, over the next four months, at least six others followed in sympathy, in Hungary, Great Britain, and the Soviet Union as well as in Czechoslovakia. By the end of 1969, Quang Duc's act had been repeated over eighty times, and in places far removed from Saigon. The model of sacrificial protest—especially by burning—was now truly available for any cause.

Just as it was possible to choose another method of death—like jumping or poison—for self-immolation, so burning could be used for purely personal suicide. This had been very rare in the West.[20] The *New York Times* and *The Times* reported only twenty cases in the half century before 1963 (Crosby et al. 1977); French newspapers reported a case about once every two years (Bourgeois 1969). This changed following Quang Duc's fiery death. The rate in France leapt to six a year. Examples became familiar in Britain and in the United States. Subsequently, famous acts of self-immolation by fire continued to inspire personal suicides. Within two weeks of Jan Palach's death, there were seven in Czechoslovakia—none apparently with any political motivation.[21] In 1970, after two French boys immolated themselves, the country experienced eight suicides by fire in the following two weeks (*NYT*, 31 January 1970). Besides spectacular short-term waves, there is evidence of a longer-term effect. In 1978, Lynette Phillips burned herself to death in Geneva as a protest against corruption in the United Nations; her death was widely publicized in England, where she had been arrested after threatening to do it in Parliament Square. In the following twelve months, eighty-two people committed suicide by burning—compared with a median of twenty-three (and maximum of thirty-three) a year, during the preceding decade (Ashton and Donnan 1981).[22]

The frequency of self-immolation has fluctuated in the four decades since 1963. Figure 5.1 depicts the distribution of the sample by year. Recall that the figure is based on different sources before and after 1977; the latter should be more comprehensive.[23] Note also that the world's urban population increased by about two-and-a-half times over these four decades. There was a relatively high frequency of self-immolation in the ten years following 1963. In 1975, moreover, at least fourteen Buddhists sacrificed themselves, this time in protest against the Communist government of newly unified Vietnam. There was a noticeable lull in the late 1970s and early 1980s. In 1990 came the unprecedented outbreak of self-immolation in India. This occurred after V. P. Singh's government proposed to set aside 27 per cent of places in universities and government employment for Other Backward Castes in addition to the existing 22.5 per cent for Scheduled Castes and Scheduled Tribes. Within six weeks, about 200 people—predominantly students from privileged castes—sacrificed (or attempted to sacrifice) themselves in protest.

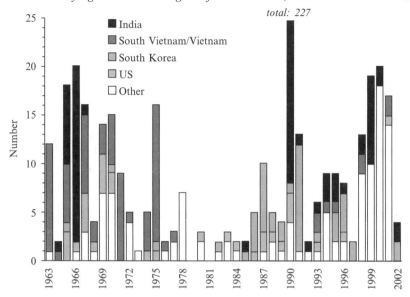

FIGURE 5.1.   Self-immolation, 1963–2002

In 1991, there followed another wave in South Korea, as leftist students and trade unionists campaigned against President Roh Tae-woo's government. The immediate provocation was the killing of a student by the police. In recent years, the tactic has been embraced for varied causes: Kurds protesting against Turkey's capture of Abdullah Ocalan in 1999; unemployed coal miners demanding government assistance in Romania in 1999; and Falun Gong followers protesting against persecution in China in 2001. Clearly, this model of protest remains viable at the turn of the twenty-first century. As this chapter was being written, in May 2003, eleven Iranians set themselves on fire in Western Europe after the French authorities arrested the leader of the National Council of Resistance of Iran, which aims to overthrow the current Iranian regime.

Prevalence

Characteristics of Collective Causes

As we have seen, individuals have committed self-immolation for a bewildering variety of collective causes. Although these defy systematic classification, two generalizations are possible. First, movements or causes that attract self-immolation do not incline towards suicidal terrorism, or indeed any actions intended to kill their opponents. There are two marginal exceptions, both from Turkey. The Kurdistan Workers' Party (PKK) was a typical violent organization, involved in a protracted and bloody insurgency in Turkey. It also carried out attacks on Turkish targets in Germany. In 1996, after it was banned there, Ocalan threatened retaliation: 'Each and every Kurd can become a suicide bomber' (quoted in Lyon and Uçarer 2001: 941). His statement was soon followed by the first suicide attack by a Kurdish separatist. This attack—by a woman—was an inspiration for Nejla Coskun, a 14-year-old girl, who set fire to herself in London in 1999 to protest against the capture of Ocalan. By that date, however, the PKK had ended violence in Europe, and it was even making overtures to the Turkish government— offering a ceasefire and retreating from its demand for a separate state. Within Turkey, inmates who burned themselves to death during prison protests in the late 1990s included members of the People's Revolutionary Liberation Party Front as well as the PKK. This non-Kurdish organization launched a suicide bombing in Istanbul to avenge the brutal suppression of the protest. These exceptions aside, self-immolation is clearly distinct from terrorism. It belongs with demonstrations, strikes, and sit-ins rather than with bombing or assassination.

The second generalization is negative. Hypothetically, one would expect an individual to be willing to die—whether by an act of self-immolation or a suicidal attack—only where the collective cause is especially 'grave' or 'momentous'. One objective indication is whether the opponent has previously killed proponents or beneficiaries of the cause. The cases of suicidal attacks in the other chapters apparently meet this criterion. So do many cases of self-immolation, like Buddhists in Vietnam and leftists in South Korea; state repression had killed some of their number. Similarly, Americans protesting against the Vietnam war had in view the killing of civilians by their armed forces. Yet there are also many cases of self-immolation where the cause seems to fall short of a matter of life or death.[24] Vidanage Vinitha in Sri Lanka is an example. Most significant is the wave of immolations in India in 1990. The government had not killed any of the students who had protested against the new policy of reservations for lower castes, though demonstrations had been quelled with force. Moreover, Singh had declared only his intention to adopt the policy; it was not actually being implemented. That could have been thwarted by the fall of his government (in fact, his government collapsed before the year's end) or by local non-compliance. All this is not to trivialize an issue which students perceived as an attack on their economic prospects as well as an affront to meritocratic justice. Yet one is still surprised by the number of people who were willing to die for this cause. It seems impossible for an outside observer to guess whether a collective cause will be considered by one or more individuals to warrant the ultimate sacrifice.

Variation Across Countries

Compared with suicidal terrorism, self-immolation has diffused widely around the world. The sample includes instances from three dozen countries. Table 5.1 shows the distribution by country. What is striking is the clustering of self-immolation in space. There are no reported cases from Africa or from the Middle East. Conversely, three-quarters of the total are concentrated in just three countries: India, Vietnam (South Vietnam until 1975), and South Korea. The figures for countries in Western Europe and North America are increased by refugees and immigrants. Kurdish refugees living in Europe are counted separately, as their acts were part of a struggle against the Turkish state. The figure for Turkey also excludes (for reasons explained above) at least two dozen prison inmates—most of whom were Kurdish—who have set themselves on fire since 1996.[25] To really compare countries, of course, it is necessary to adjust for population size. The denominator should be urban

TABLE 5.1.   Self-immolation by country, 1963–2002

Country	Number	Percentage of total	Rate per million
India	255	47.8	1.4
South Vietnam/Vietnam	92	17.3	8.0
South Korea	43	8.1	1.6
United States	29	5.4	0.2
Kurds outside Turkey	14	2.6	14.0
Romania	14	2.6	1.2
Soviet Union/ex-Soviet Union (except Lithuania)	12	2.3	0.1
China	9	1.7	0.0
Pakistan	9	1.7	0.3
France	5	0.9	0.5
Japan	5	0.9	0.1
Lithuanians	5	0.9	2.2
Czechoslovakia	4	0.8	0.5
East/West Germany	4	0.8	0.1
Turkey	4	0.8	0.2
Bulgaria	3	0.6	0.5
Chile	3	0.6	0.0
Taiwan	3	0.6	0.2
United Kingdom	3	0.6	0.1
Malaysia	2	0.4	0.3
Thailand	2	0.4	0.2
Elsewhere	13	2.4	0.0
Total	533	100.0	0.3

Source: see text.

rather than total population because virtually all the cases occurred in cities. Indeed, there are only five farmers (only 1 per cent of recorded occupations) in the sample. Estimates of urban population refer to 1985, approximately the mean year in the sample (United Nations Population Division 2001: Table A.3).[26] The resulting rates tell a slightly different story. The Kurdish diaspora has by far the highest rate. Vietnam, South Korea, and India remain prominent, ranked second, fourth, and fifth respectively. Lithuanians are treated separately, even though their nation was subsumed by the Soviet Union, because that reveals an unexpectedly high ranking of third. Four Lithuanians killed themselves in 1972 for the cause of national independence; in 1990, as the Soviet Union strove to maintain its rule, a fifth travelled to Moscow to die in protest. Another country in Eastern Europe, Romania, ranks sixth.

This variation invites a Durkheimian investigation of rates of self-immolation. Self-immolation fits into Durkheim's category of 'altruistic suicide' (Durkheim 1952)—the 'optional' sub-type. For Durkheim, altruistic suicide is characteristic of highly integrated primitive societies, though it survives in modern societies within the armed forces. He argued that modern types of suicide were symptomatic of a lack of social integration and regulation. Therefore, we would not expect self-immolation to be correlated with the general rate of suicide. In 1990, suicide rates were highest in China and in the ex-socialist countries of Eastern Europe; they were lowest in Sub-Saharan Africa and in Latin America (Reza et al. 2001). At first sight the inordinately high suicide rate in Lithuania might seem suggestive. The suicide rate in over thirty countries is not correlated, however, with the rate of self-immolation (Schmidtke et al. 1999; Cheng and Lee 2000).[27] Attitudes towards suicide can be measured with greater confidence than suicide rates. The World Values Survey for 1995–97 asked respondents whether suicide was justifiable (Inglehart et al. 2000). Once again, this is not correlated with self-immolation.

The World Values Survey allows us to investigate social correlates in thirty-seven countries, though this kind of analysis is inevitably crude. Durkheim's conception of social integration is notoriously difficult to operationalize. More tangible measures, such as the importance of inculcating obedience in children and the degree of tolerance for divorce, are not correlated with self-immolation. In so far as self-immolation is a form of protest, we would expect a positive correlation with the proportion of people who have participated in protest. This expectation is confounded. The only significant factor to emerge is religion. Durkheim emphasized the intensity of religious belief rather than the content of religious doctrine. For self-immolation, however, the extent of religiosity—measured for instance by belief in life after death—does not matter. What matters is the proportion of Hindus and Buddhists. Both of these are positively correlated with the rate of self-immolation, whereas the proportion of Christians and Muslims is not.[28]

Needless to say, this is an 'ecological' correlation, pertaining to society as a whole rather than the particular individuals who sacrifice themselves. The leftists in South Korea were guided by Marxism rather than Buddhism. Therefore, religious traditions are significant in shaping tacit preconceptions—the cultural background of action—rather than avowed doctrine. We could seek guidance from Weber (1958), who emphasized the distinction between the transcendent God of Semitic religions (Jewish, Christian, and Islamic) and the immanent divinity of Indic religions (Hindu, Jain, and Buddhist). The latter, he asserted, tend towards world-rejecting mysticism. As we will see below, however, nothing of this sort is apparent in the intentions of monks and nuns who sacrificed their lives. If anything, self-immolation seems more like a manifestation of this-worldly asceticism, which Weber identified with Protestantism.

Real differences emerge when we look for the religious valuation of *self-*inflicted death in sacred literatures (Harran 1987). There are no prominent exemplars in Semitic religions; Jesus and Husayn were martyred by their enemies. Hindu Puranas extol the karmic benefits that may be derived by killing oneself in a place of pilgrimage—above all in Allahabad (Dubey 1987; Lochtefeld 1987; Thakur 1963: 77–111). Mythical tales of the Buddha's past lives include instances of self-sacrifice; a Mahayana sutra describes him killing himself to feed a hungry tigress. Within both traditions, the legitimacy of religious suicide was hotly disputed; nevertheless, such acts were recorded in historical times.[29] A more mundane factor is the method of disposing of corpses. Cremation is deeply rooted in Indic religions. By extension, death by fire seems sacred—in a way that is still utterly repugnant in the West, despite the recent importation of cremation. (This serves to illustrate the enduring significance of religious tradition, for this repugnance is shared by non-believers.) 'It might be hard for Westerners to understand', explained a young monk who considered self-immolation, 'but going by fire is more clean—more pure' (quoted in Hope 1967: 159). Whatever the precise effect of religious traditions, the difference between the Semitic West and the Indic East remains inescapable. Contrast how Browne and Chân Không recalled the sight of Quang Duc's death.

Finally, we should not overlook the character of the political system. This requires analysis by year as well as by country. The Polity data series provides a score which summarizes the extent of democracy versus autocracy for each country in every year (Marshall and Jaggers 2003). Using negative binomial regression, and controlling for religious composition, we find self-immolation to be positively associated with the degree of democracy. (This result holds even excluding India in 1990.) In part, this finding must reflect the way totalitarian states suppress information about such acts, as noted above. But it seems more than a measure of our ignorance. Because self-immolation is less likely to have an impact, individuals in totalitarian states are less likely to commit such an act. There are some exceptions, of course, including Lithuanians in 1972 and Vietnamese Buddhists under Communist rule from 1975 onwards. On balance, however, self-immolation has occurred under less repressive political systems. The largest wave of immolation of all occurred in democratic India.

Clustering in Time

Just as self-immolation is concentrated in a small number of countries, it is also clustered in time: it occurs in waves. To a limited extent, this reflects deliberate coordination. For one-fifth of the individuals in the sample, the act of self-immolation occurred with one or more other acts of immolation. Most of these coordinated group actions involved two people. The largest occurred in a Vietnamese monastery in 1975: twelve monks and nuns, led by Thich Hue Hien, sacrificed themselves together in protest against persecution by the Communist government. Even aside from such intentional coordination, separate acts of self-immolation are clustered together. We can examine how much time elapses between one act and the next within the same country (classifying Kurds outside Turkey and Lithuanians separately, as above). In the sample, 47 per cent occurred on the same day; 16 per cent occurred from one to ten days later; and a further 4 per cent up to a month later. We can use the time between acts to demarcate waves of self-immolation. A parsimonious definition of 'wave' would aggregate all acts within the same country separated by intervals of ten days or less.[30] Thus defined, twenty-eight waves consist of two acts, and twenty-one consist of three or more. The latter are listed in Table 5.2, which shows the country and the collective cause associated with each.

To some extent, waves can be explained by particular exogenous events, which suddenly create or exacerbate a collective grievance. An endogenous process of inspiration is also clearly important. In other words, an individual is more likely to choose this sacrifice when someone else has done so; self-immolation is subject to positive feedback (Biggs 2003*a*). An Indian student, Monica Chadha, provides an illustration. After reading about self-immolation in the morning newspaper, she casually announced to her family that she would kill herself. 'If all these other boys and girls can sacrifice themselves like this to shout down the policies of this prime minister, then I will sacrifice my life as well' (*Los Angeles Times*, 20 October 1990). She then left the room and set herself alight. There are several instances of tangible connections between one action and another. A Vietnamese monk burned himself to death in 1963 to protest against the confiscation of a previous victim's body by the police. An Indian student set fire to herself outside the hospital where Rajeev Goswami—who initiated the huge wave of 1990—was

TABLE 5.2.   Waves involving more than three acts of self-immolation, 1963–2002

Country	Date begun	Collective cause	Number
China	23 Jan 2001	Falun Gong v government	7
India	11 Feb 1965	Tamil v Hindi	5
	19 Sep 1990	Protest against reservations for lower castes[*]	208
	19 Nov 1990	Protest against reservations for lower castes	15
	19 May 1999	Request for Sonia Gandhi to retract resignation	7
Pakistan	30 Sep 1978	Bhutto supporters v government	4
Romania	24 Mar 2000	Miners v government	10
South Korea	18 Dec 1987	Protest against electoral fraud	3
	29 Apr 1991	Protest against government	9
	16 Apr 1996	Protest against government	3
South Vietnam/Vietnam	13 Aug 1963	Buddhists v government	3
	21 Apr 1965	Buddhists v government	3
	29 May 1966	Buddhists v government	13
	3 Oct 1967	Buddhists v government	3
	22 Oct 1967	Buddhists v government	4
	4 Jun 1970	Buddhists v government	3
	9 May 1971	Buddhists v government	4
	16 Aug 1971	Protest against electoral fraud	4
	2 Nov 1975	Buddhists v government	12
Soviet Union	29 May 1972	Lithuanians v government	3
Western Europe	15 Feb 1999	Kurds v Turkey	7
Total			330

Note: 'wave' refers to all acts within a country separated by intervals of ten days or less.
[*] Includes two acts of protest against the protest against reservations, and one for the cause of Hindus v Muslims.
Source: see text.

recovering. Likewise, a Korean student jumped off the morgue containing the body of Park Sung Hee, who initiated the wave in 1991. Inspiration was not always confined to supporters of the collective cause. The largest wave in 1990 included a clothes washer and an autorickshaw driver who killed themselves in protest against the protests against reservations.

The positive feedback created by inspiration is, in one respect, not surprising. After all, this is also found in other forms of protest, like strikes (Biggs 2003*a*; Conell and Cohn 1995). The same is true for suicide: news reports and dramatic enactments alike increase the suicide rate (Bollen and Phillips 1982; Phillips and Carstensen 1986; Schmidtke and Schaller 2000). Yet the repetition of self-immolation for one specific collective cause raises a puzzle, for it surely is subject to diminishing marginal returns. At some point, even this most awe-inspiring of actions begins to lose its impact. This was recognized by Nhat Chi Mai in Vietnam. After the wave of immolations in 1966, she suggested that ten students should disembowel themselves for peace. 'Fasting and even self-immolation [by fire] no longer wake people up. We have to be imaginative!' (quoted in Chân Không 1993: 97).[31] The campaign against reservations in 1990 poses the puzzle of diminishing marginal returns with particular force. When Goswami set himself alight, his act revived the flagging protest movement. But after it was repeated the first dozen—or one hundred—times, was there any additional benefit to be gained? As we will see below, some of those who join a wave in its later phase may be moved by despair and therefore not concerned with the instrumental effect of their death. Nevertheless, this huge wave of immolation provides a chilling illustration of the power of imitation.

Orchestration

Threats

Now we can focus more closely on the act of self-immolation, examining how it is orchestrated. Rarely is self-immolation preceded by any public threat, to allow the opponent an opportunity to make concessions and thus avert the sacrifice. This absence is intriguing. To be sure, in some cases the decision to act is taken on the spur of the moment; moreover, in authoritarian political systems such a threat would simply invite detention. Most importantly, however, any threat of immolation would lack credibility. According to signalling theory, 'for a threat to be reliable, the signal must increase the danger to the threatener—and an escalation of the threat must increase that danger even further' (Zahavi and Zahavi 1997: 16). A hunger strike meets this condition because it gradually escalates physical suffering. If someone threatens to fast until death, then that threat becomes increasingly credible as the fast continues.

This does not imply that threats of immolation are rare. Indeed, threats are surely more numerous than actions.[32] Nevertheless, one is left with an overwhelming impression that individuals who make threats are not actually prepared to carry them out. Consider, as a prime example, South Vietnam in the mid-1960s, when so many Buddhists killed themselves. In July 1963, monks at one pagoda staged a press conference to announce that a nun— from a prestigious family—had requested to be allowed to burn herself. Foreign journalists found this spectacle repugnant (Schecter 1967: 191–2). And the nun never did kill herself. In May 1966, monks in Danang declared that three of their number would kill themselves if government troops attacked the city (*NYT*, 17 May 1966). Dozens were killed in the attack, but the pagoda surrendered a week later without a single self-immolation (Schecter 1967: 230–1). Similar examples abound in the wave of immolations by Kurds in 1999: those who made threats were not the same individuals as those who set themselves on fire.

There is one important example of a credible threat. Like Tamils in the south of India, Punjabi-speaking Sikhs in the north fought bitterly against the imposition of Hindi language (Grewal 1990: chs. 9–10). After a previous fast, Sant Fateh Singh threatened in 1965 to fast and then burn himself unless a new Punjabi state was created.[33] The outbreak of war with Pakistan led him to postpone the event. Within a year, a new state of Punjab was created. In 1967 Singh repeated the threat, demanding the accession of the city of Chandigarh, which was shared with the neighbouring state of Haryana. After he had fasted for nine days, and with a huge audience gathered at the Amritsar Temple to watch his impending death, Indira Gandhi suddenly offered to arbitrate (*NYT*, 27 December 1967). In 1970, after he repeated the threat yet again, she promised to transfer the city in five years' time—despite a countervailing threat from a politician in Haryana (*NYT*, 30 January 1970). Gandhi apparently believed that Singh was in earnest, and that his death would incite serious rioting by Sikhs. As a leader, if he had not made good his threat he would have been discredited among his followers.[34] His victory, however, was to prove hollow; Chandigarh was not subsequently transferred to Punjab. The campaign in Punjab had an unexpected echo in England. In 1969, a Sikh leader threatened to burn himself to death in protest against Wolverhampton's ban on bus drivers and conductors wearing beards or turbans; his demand was conceded (*The Times*, 7 January and 10 April 1969). These cases of successful threats are exceptional.[35]

Organization

Self-immolation does not require organization to be effective, unlike suicidal attacks. In some cases, the action is inherently individualistic, even idiosyncratic. Kathy Change set fire to herself on the campus of the University of Pennsylvania 'to spark a discussion of how we can peacefully transform our world' (*AP*, 23 October 1996). Although she was a familiar presence around campus and at protest demonstrations, no one else knew her well, or fully comprehended her public declaration. Over a third of the individuals in the sample performed the act in front of a crowd gathered to further the cause—an audience of potential sympathizers. But this audience was not necessarily complicit in the act. To take an extreme example, someone in Taiwan set himself alight in the midst of a packed memorial for a dissident, causing severe injuries to those standing beside him (*AP*, 19 May 1989). In most situations, protesters intervened to help the individual, such as dousing the flames. It is less common to find evidence that protesters deliberately assisted the sacrifice by preventing police from intervening, as they did during Quang Duc's highly organized immolation. Such cases are confined to South Vietnam and India.

Even if organization is not necessary in order to orchestrate immolation, it would still be possible for an organization to endorse or 'sign' an individual sacrifice performed on its behalf. This, however, is also rare. The clearest examples come from Vietnam. In 1963 Buddhist leaders explicitly sanctioned two deaths: those of Quang Duc and Thich Tieu Dieu. Both were elderly (as was the nun at the press conference), while there is evidence that younger novices were refused permission. This is understandable: the elderly had less life to sacrifice and had presumably attained sufficient wisdom to make a responsible choice. In 1966, the militant wing of the Unified Buddhist Church apparently staged at least one self-immolation—that of Thich Nu Thanh Quang (55 years old)—though officially it was announced that she had not received permission. 'Burning oneself to death is the noblest form of struggle', declared the militant leader, Thich Tri Quang, 'which symbolizes the spirit of nonviolence of Buddhism' (quoted in Schecter 1967: 233). After five deaths over the next few days, however, Tri Quang called on followers to halt (*NYT*, 31 May 1966). After the Communist invasion, when Buddhism was facing renewed persecution, the Unified Buddhist Church's Central Executive Council in 1977 asked monks and nuns in Ho Chi Minh City 'to be ready to act, to sacrifice ourselves if necessary' (quoted in Forest 1978: 41). By the late 1990s, however, the Church was apparently dissuading members from killing themselves.

Even in Vietnam, then, organizational endorsement was ambivalent. There are two clear examples of disavowal. One is the leadership of Falun Gong, discussed below. Another is the PKK. On the arrest of Ocalan, it orchestrated simultaneous protests across Western Europe, during which seven Kurds set themselves alight on a single day. Yet this did not accord with the wishes of Ocalan himself. Only months before, after PKK prisoners in Turkey had set themselves alight, he broadcast the following message: 'I categorically reject self-immolation. I strongly suggest that they should refrain from setting themselves on fire' (quoted in Ergil 2001: 115). Following Ocalan's capture, his brother Osman repeated the same message: he called on Kurds to end self-immolation and 'burn the enemy' instead (*AP*, 19 February 1999). By contrast, organizations that sponsor suicidal attacks invariably boast of their readiness to dispatch members to their death.

Degrees of Suffering

By far the most common method of self-immolation was Quang Duc's: four out of five individuals in the sample chose fire. Poison was the next most common method. As we have seen, burning has quite different cultural connotations in West and East. The common denominator is conspicuous suffering. 'To burn oneself by fire is to prove that what one is saying is of the utmost importance', as Thich Nhat Hanh (1967: 118) observed. 'There is nothing more painful than burning oneself.' In this respect, it is akin to *seppuku*. Yukio Mishima, a celebrated Japanese writer who eventually chose this method, explained: 'everybody knew that this was the most painful way to die...it proved the courage of the Samurai' (quoted in Scott-Stokes 1975: 16–17). In actuality, the agony was quickly terminated by beheading. Similarly, individuals could combine burning with a less painful means of death. Many in South Korea set themselves alight and then jumped from the top of a building.

Methods such as burning and poisoning do not always lead to death. Therefore I have deliberately included attempts that did not prove fatal. Thwarted attempts, when someone douses himself or herself with flammable liquid but is prevented from setting it aflame by the physical intervention of protesters or police, account for one in eight of the sample. Even when these thwarted attempts are included, the chance of surviving was only about 30 per cent. This, it should be emphasized, is comparatively low. Compare suicide attempts, in which the survival rate can be as high as 90 per cent (Stengel 1969). There is also a marked contrast with hunger strikes. Although systematic figures are not available, one has the impression that hunger strikers rarely starve to death. In 1923, for example, about 8,000 Republican prisoners in Ireland went on hunger strike to demand release; two died (Sweeney 1993*b*).

Although self-immolation most often results in death, we cannot assume that death is always intended. In many cases, the action could more appropriately be conceived as a gamble with death (cf. Firth 1961; Stengel 1969). This is not to trivialize it: survivors of burning will probably suffer permanent disfigurement. The gamble was explicit for Neusha Farrahi, an Iranian exile in Los Angeles. 'If I die in this little bout with fire...', he wrote (quoted in Kelley 1987: 24). Before setting himself alight at a demonstration against the visiting President of Iran, he placed a fire extinguisher on the ground; another protester found it in time to douse the fire. Yet his injuries proved fatal. More generally, it is telling that survivors do not consider themselves to have failed, nor do they try again. Disaggregated figures reveal significant variations in the severity of the gamble. In Vietnam, virtually everyone died. In India, about one-third survived. Among Kurdish refugees, over half survived. In Romania there seem to have been no deaths at all. These differences cannot be explained away by variations in the quality of medical care, because the United States also has a high death rate.

In some cases, then, self-immolation shades into self-mutilation. Explicit acts of self-mutilation—where there is obviously no risk of death—are exceedingly rare. This is surprising given that deliberate self-harm among the general population is far more prevalent than suicide (Hawton et al. 2002). Three notable examples come from South Vietnam in the 1960s. A student tried to chop off her left hand with an axe; in a letter to the President, she offered the hand as a gift, requesting him to understand his people's wishes to end the persecution (Chân Không 1993: 41–2). Immediately after a nun burned herself to death, a monk cut off part of his finger before a cheering crowd (*NYT*, 30 May 1966). A monk slowly roasted his finger in a candle flame before an audience of thousands (Hassler 1970: 142). Hypothetically, self-mutilation could be used to lend credibility to a threat of self-immolation, but I know of no case in which immolation has been preceded by mutilation.[36]

If self-immolation is often a gamble with death, can it be rigged to ensure survival? This would require assistance from others, of course. A handful of cases arouse suspicion. Seven women in the Congress Party of India tried to burn themselves outside the home of Sonia Gandhi in order to persuade her to retract her resignation as party president. The other protesters reacted swiftly, and the only casualty was one sari (*AP*, 19 May 1999). This seems more like a dramatic gesture. It cannot be dismissed as a fake, however, because the women did not—so far as we know—explicitly claim that they were attempting to kill themselves. Admissions or accusations of outright deception are scarce. The wave of immolations in India in 1990 was initiated by Goswami. According to his own account, students decided on 'staging a drama' to revive their protest against reservations (*India Today*, 15 October 1990). It was carefully planned, with photographers to witness the event and crowds of students to prevent the police from intervening. He soaked only his legs in kerosene, and his friends were detailed to quickly extinguish the fire. As the police charged, however, Goswami suddenly doused his body with kerosene and—with his confederates lost in the crowd—ignited himself.[37] He suffered severe burns and spent months in hospital. In a strange twist, Goswami again attempted self-immolation three years later. (He is the only individual entered in the sample twice.) This time his effort was thwarted by the police, thus incurring the ridicule of fellow students. 'It was all stage-managed', said one (*AFP*, 21 September 1993). In a horrific inversion of Goswami's account of what happened in 1990, a Pakistani journalist recalls a self-immolation in protest against Zulfikar Ali Bhutto's death sentence (*UPI*, 25 March 2002). According to the man's relatives, others in Bhutto's party assured him that it would be rigged—they would immediately extinguish the fire. But as he ran around in flames, screaming for help, the assembled crowd watched impassively.[38]

This discussion has complicated the category of self-immolation. It should be understood as traversing a continuum. At one extreme is a risky gesture of self-inflicted suffering, orchestrated with others, which is akin to self-mutilation. At the other is a determined attempt to kill oneself. Far more actions occur towards the latter extreme than the former. By comparison, hunger strikes traverse a similar continuum but make possible the precise calibration of suffering. Self-immolation by fire always involves some risk of death—that is the source of its power. Even including thwarted attempts, at least two-thirds of the actions proved fatal. This figure is surely comparable to the death rate among those volunteering for suicidal attacks.

Motivations

Having considered how the act was orchestrated, we can pose the central question: why did these individuals choose to sacrifice themselves—or at the very least gamble with their lives—in preference to other forms of protest? The evidence encompasses written declarations of intent and comments from survivors, as well as from those who entertained the act but did not carry it out. The task of dissecting, from the comfort of one's office, motivations for the ultimate sacrifice must be approached with trepidation. My ambition is simply to disentangle and explicate the various rational motivations for self-immolation (as Baechler 1975 and Douglas 1967 have done for suicide). Psychological explanations will be treated as a residual category.

My emphasis on teasing out the rationality—in the broadest sense of the term—of self-immolation reflects more than just a theoretical predisposition (cf. Weber 1978: ch. 1). For the most part, where sufficient evidence is available, one can discern adequate reason(s) for self-immolation. In many cases, the decision was the product of lengthy consideration, as with Quang Duc, Mishima, and Nhat Chi Mai (Chân Không 1993: ch. 10). A Crimean Tatar, Musa Mamut, declared his resolve a year before he acted. Admittedly, many others took the decision on the spur of the moment. (This follows from the fact that self-immolation requires no organization, as pointed out above.) 'We need more dedicated fighters, not more *yolsa* [martyrs]', said Chun Se Yong, a South Korean student, only two days before his immolation (*Time Magazine*, 3 June 1991). For Morrison too, the impulse to act came after reading a gruesome account of an American air raid in Vietnam. 'For weeks, even months, I have been praying only that I be shown what I must do. This morning with no warning I was shown' (quoted in Morrison Welsh 2000: 4). Goswami (in 1990) and Chadha apparently made a decision only minutes before they acted. Still, what is remarkable is the lack of expressions of regret. 'I am proud of what I have done', announced Chadha as she lay dying in hospital (*Los Angeles Times*, 20 October 1990). This sentiment was typical.

The typology begins, logically enough, with 'selfless' motivations that stem from commitment to the collective cause. Such a commitment may be manifested in instrumental rationality—treating one's own sacrifice as a means to advance the cause. Two significant motivations can be discerned: *appealing* to others by means of a costly signal, and *inciting* potential sympathizers by provoking an emotional response. A subsidiary mechanism involves supernatural *exchange*. Commitment to the cause may also be manifested in the non-instrumental motivation of *despair*. By contrast, 'egocentric' motivations lack the selflessness of commitment to a collective cause. One is *cheating* the adversary. Another is *transfiguration* (after Baechler 1975), attaining an exalted existence after death. Other personal motivations are unlikely to be publicly declared or even consciously acknowledged: *vanity*, gaining attention from others, and *redemption* from personal failings.

Selfless Motivations

In so far as individuals treat self-immolation as a means to advance their cause, it can be an appeal to others to change their behaviour. The appeal may be addressed directly to the adversary. Thus Quang Duc politely requested Diem to show religious tolerance. This was echoed over a decade later: in 1975 twelve monks and nuns offered their lives in an 'appeal to the Revolutionary Government . . . to respect the right to freedom of worship of all religions' (quoted in Forest 1978: 14). Whether or not they genuinely expected to convert their adversary, this sentiment is not frequent. More commonly, the appeal is addressed to a third party in the conflict, particularly to public opinion. Thich Nu Thanh Quang intended 'to raise the tragic voice of my people'. Her letter appealed to the arbiters of South Vietnam's future. 'Before dying, I hope and believe that the President of the United States of America, the Congress and the people of the United States will prove their clearsightedness and understanding and be our ally forever' (quoted in Schecter 1967: 233). She was under no illusions about the role of American power, which she denounced for 'approving the massacre of our monks, nuns, and Buddhist followers'. Nevertheless, it was a plausible attempt to appeal to American public opinion. Likewise, Coskun recalled, 'I wanted someone to stop and think about us' (*Guardian*, 8 June 1999). Implicitly, of course, the appeal derives its potency from sacrifice; self-immolation amplifies the individual's 'voice'. This is explicated by Chân Không: 'If you want to buy something, you should pay something. And now you want to buy something very, very precious—the understanding of people. You have nothing more precious than your life' (quoted in Forest 1978: 8; see also Chân Không 1993: 39, 105). Self-immolation, in other words, is a costly signal which conveys information: the depth of the individual's sense of injustice on behalf of the collective cause (see Biggs 2003*b*).

A slightly different—though compatible—motivation is to incite others who already share the collective cause. This is not a matter of altering their beliefs; it is a matter of galvanizing them to engage in protest. This motivated a student monk in Hué, who wanted to kill himself 'to rouse the people to defend themselves' (quoted in Hope 1967: 157). Though refused permission by his superior, he resolved to burn himself if all else failed. Then Thich Tieu Dieu's immolation led to mass defiance and increased repression. The student superior clearly treated his own death instrumentally: as it was now unnecessary, he went into hiding and published resistance pamphlets instead. This motivation of inciting others is common. A Korean student expressed the hope that his death would produce 'many warriors' against the government. On the day that he died, he wondered aloud to a friend: 'Don't you think we would have more fighting activists if someone else killed himself by immolation?' (*Time Magazine*, 3 June 1991: 34) 'Because our nations are on the brink of despair', wrote Jan Palach, 'we have decided to express our protest and wake up the people of this land' (quoted in Treptow 1992: 126). He concocted an elaborate threat, based on the fiction that he was the first in a group of volunteers. 'If our demands are not fulfilled within five days by January 21, 1969, and if the people do not support us sufficiently through a strike of indefinite duration, more torches will burn.' Implicitly, this was calculated to induce guilt among potential supporters: if they remained passive, then they would be responsible for further deaths.

Another instrumental motivation is very different, for it depends on belief in a supernatural agency. Self-immolation is an exchange: in return for the sacrifice, a supernatural agency will intervene on behalf of the cause. This motivation is exceedingly rare in the last four decades. Tran Bach Nga killed herself just *after* the overthrow of Diem (*NYT*, 31 November 1963). Having made a vow to Buddha to burn herself if the imprisoned monks and nuns were released, she kept her side of the bargain. A similar case occurred two months later.[39] For the sake of completeness, it is worth noting that supernatural beliefs may provide an alternative motivation: one kills oneself in order to become a ghost, with more formidable powers.[40]

All the above motivations are instrumental: death serves to advance the cause. Commitment to the cause can also produce a completely different motivation, namely, despair. Chân Không did not sacrifice herself (though she contemplated a fast until death), but she explains the impulse: 'Learning of the arrest of so many monks, nuns, and Buddhist friends, I wanted to scream and go to jail, or burn myself in despair' (Chân Không 1993: 41). This fits the psychological model of suicide proposed by Mark Williams: 'the "cry of pain" from a person who feels completely defeated, with no escape routes, and no possibility of rescue at all' (Williams and Pollock 2000: 89; also M. Williams 1997). Here, however, this defeat is collective and not personal:

it occurs only because the individual is devoted to the cause. Despair was the motivation for Jan Zajic, who killed himself after it was clear that Palach's sacrifice had not sparked mass defiance of the Soviet occupation. 'I hear your cowardice' was one line in his final poem (quoted in Treptow 1992: 130). 'Bells toll from the spires of churches for the nation, for the country.' This motivation is not merely to die, to escape the distress that stems from identification with the cause, but to make a final—albeit instrumentally useless—statement to the world.

Egocentric Motivations and Psychological Explanations

Closely related to despair is the motivation of cheating the enemy out of the satisfaction of one's capture, in an ultimate act of defiance. In so far as killing oneself is less bad than the alternative—imprisonment, torture, or execution—then the act is more compatible with self-interest; it may be unnecessary to invoke commitment to the collective cause. Cheating the enemy apparently motivated Nguyen Tuong Tam. Although he was about to be tried, a death sentence was not inevitable. Salvador Allende, by contrast, would have had no illusions about his fate if captured. He made a final defiant broadcast from the besieged presidential palace: 'I am ready to resist with whatever means, even at the cost of my life in that this serves as a lesson in the ignominious history of those who have strength but not reason' (*NYT*, 12 September 1973).[41] Both men were famous and both died in private. A contrast is an anonymous South Vietnamese official who killed himself on the fall of Saigon. He may have had sufficient reason to avoid capture. What is significant is that he chose a public death: on the steps of a monument to the war dead, watched by journalists. 'It is finished', he exclaimed, and shot himself (*NYT*, 21 May 1975).

The motivation of transfiguration—attaining a more exalted existence—depends on supernatural beliefs. It may seem paradoxical to call this the most nakedly 'self-interested' motivation, but surely one's death is a small price to pay for eternal heavenly life or karmic advancement. One would expect this motivation to be prevalent, given that so many individuals in the sample had religious vocations. After students, they formed the most common occupational group, comprising one-sixth of the total where occupation was recorded. Many more were deeply religious. Yet evidence of such a motivation is almost entirely absent. It may have helped to motivate the followers of Falun Gong. 'Let me go to heaven', cried Liu Hongjun—according to the state news agency—as police prevented her from igniting herself (*AP*, 30 January 2001). Another of the group, Hao Huijun, gave a perfectly mundane explanation of their act: after the failure of more conventional methods of protest, 'we decided to make a big event to tell the world' (*AP*, 4 April 2002).

In Vietnam, where one would expect transfiguration to loom large, many of the politically engaged monks embraced Buddhism as a means of attaining national liberation and social justice—an alternative to Marxism—rather than as a quest for spiritual perfection. Remarkably, the student monk in Hué did not even believe in reincarnation. Furthermore, certain beliefs raised rather than lowered the 'cost' of self-immolation. Contemplating a fast until death, Chân Không (1993: 97) understood that she would have 'to pay for the sin of impiety [towards her mother] in another life'. Similarly, Coskun believed that she would go to hell for defiling the body that God gave her (interview, 8 August 2003). In sum, although religious belief and discipline undoubtedly prepare an individual for self-sacrifice, the promise of supernatural rewards was not a significant motivation. This also holds for suicide attacks by the Japanese Kamikaze and the Tamil Tigers, of course.

All the motivations discussed thus far operate at the level of conscious intentions, and they would be openly declared. Now we survey a more ambiguous territory, which shades gradually into psychological explanation.

Although it would be absurdly cynical to reduce self-sacrifice to attention-seeking, vanity should not be overlooked as a potential motivation. This cannot be publicly declared. It would be an instance of the mental alchemy investigated by Elster (1999). If the individual was consciously aware that the act was motivated by vanity, then he or she would misrepresent the motivation. More insidiously, it could be unconsciously 'transmuted' into another motivation, beneath the individual's awareness. By its very nature, then, vanity will be exceedingly difficult to trace. One candidate is the host of a television talk show in Florida who shot herself on air, ostensibly protesting against violence on television. In reality, it seems to have been a purely personal suicide, staged as self-immolation in order to maximize publicity. The most plausible case of vanity is the death of Yukio Mishima (Nathan 1974; Scott-Stokes 1975). With four confederates, he kidnapped a general and demanded to address the troops. He exhorted them to overthrow the constitution and restore Japanese honour. He then committed *seppuku* and was beheaded by a confederate; another died in the same fashion, while the others surrendered. There is considerable evidence that Mishima misrepresented his real motivation. In making plans he had acknowledged that the troops would not revolt (Nathan 1974: 266). In the event they greeted his speech with derision. His death was the culmination of a lifelong erotic fascination with Japanese martial traditions. In the previous months, he had posed for a series of photographs entitled 'Death of a Man'. 'If I decided to commit *seppuku*, could you televise it live?', he had asked a friend in broadcasting (quoted by Nathan 1974: 265). He would surely have been pleased that gory pictures of his severed head appeared in the Japanese press and in *Life* magazine.

Vanity may be distinguished from a more worthy motivation, namely, redemption from personal failings. By choosing to die for a cause, an individual may compensate for an unsatisfactory life. 'Maybe because things hadn't all worked out for him professionally', wondered Morrison's wife, 'it was easier somehow (a little bit) to give away his life' (quoted in Hendrickson 1996: 235). But she certainly did not consider it suicide. A more ambiguous case is Tran Bach Nga, who apparently promised her life in return for Diem's overthrow. Yet she also wrote a final letter to a male acquaintance, apologizing for being unworthy of him. For the Buddhist authorities, at least, this hint of romantic disappointment posed the question of whether her act was suicide masquerading as self-sacrifice, which would not deserve a memorial ceremony. Occasionally, redemption is publicly acknowledged—though only as a subsidiary motivation, of course. 'I have never been a good son to you, mother and father', admitted Kim Ki Sol, a Korean student. 'But I am no longer your son but the son of the whole nation. I now want to be a good son' (*Independent*, 21 May 1991). A Lithuanian man likewise acknowledged marital problems in his final declaration (*AP*, 27 April 1990).

As motivations, even redemption and vanity 'make sense', though they are far removed from selfless motivations based on commitment to the cause. Psychopathology provides a quite different kind of explanation, which makes no reference to an individual's reasons. It is all too easy to attribute self-immolation to psychological disturbances. This stratagem is adopted by totalitarian states. When a German pastor lay dying after setting fire to himself to protest against Communist atheism, the government barred his wife from hospital; they would let her visit only when she 'admitted' he was mentally deranged (*The Times*, 23 August 1976). In the Soviet Union, any survivor of an immolation attempt was consigned to a psychiatric institution. Less obvious, and therefore more insidious, is the temptation to search for such explanations when the act fails to resonate with the public. When a woman set fire to herself in a Minneapolis sex shop, the media portrayed her as a rape victim with a history of mental instability (*AP*, 12 July 1984). But the context of the act was eminently reasonable: the city council was about to vote on a pioneering anti-pornography ordinance, which many American feminists viewed as a legal breakthrough.

Nevertheless, in some cases the expressed motivation does seem inadequate to account for the action. At the limit, the individual may not have a reason. Someone who set himself alight outside the United Nations apologized for the inconvenience to his rescuers, but was literally unable to explain his act (*NYT*, 6 December 1967). This is excluded from the sample, as are cases in which the 'cause' makes no sense whatsoever. There are still cases in which the avowed intention does not seem to match the situation. Charles Hook III shot himself in the gardens of the United Nations in 1975. He had been involved in the Student Peace Union several years before. 'I have always attempted to act in the interest of peace and the general defense of the planet', he declared (*NYT*, 8 May 1975). But there was no reference to contemporaneous political events which justified such a sacrifice. Moreover, the note implies paranoia: 'I have never knowingly and deliberately been a part of any secret political conspiracy . . .'. The only systematic psychological evidence comes from an investigation of twenty-two survivors (some of whom later died) of self-immolation in India in 1990 (Singh et al. 1998). Despite the propensity of psychiatrists to find disorders in everyone, only one of the subjects fitted the criteria for 'manifest psychopathology'. The battery of tests indicated that the subjects had a greater than average internal locus of control, and scored high on 'intropunitiveness'—self-criticism and guilt as contrasted with hostility to others.

In sum, psychopathology is not necessary to explain most cases of self-immolation. With sufficient evidence, it is not difficult to understand the act in terms of a combination of the motivations explicated above. Which of these are most common? Answering this question is especially difficult for egocentric motivations such as vanity or redemption, which one would expect to be misrepresented as or transmuted into more 'noble' motivations. There must be cases of personal suicide masquerading as self-immolation. A very large number of people commit suicide: in the order of three-quarters of a million each year (Reza et al. 2001). Organizations involved in suicidal terrorism claim to screen out individuals who just want to die, and they plausibly have an incentive to do so. By contrast, self-immolation (as we have seen) requires no organization; anyone who wants to put an end to his or her life anyway can easily choose self-immolation. What is remarkable, then, is that self-immolation is so rare. If we estimate at the most an average of seventy-five cases per year, then that equates to about one per 10,000 suicides! At the very least, we must conclude that suicidal tendencies almost never lead to self-immolation. I would go further and suggest that self-immolation is rarely explained by suicidal tendencies. For the most part, then, we should take avowed motivations seriously. Transfiguration and cheating are uncommon. Among the selfless motivations, supernatural exchange is rare; despair seems somewhat more common. The most frequently declared motivations are appealing to others and inciting potential sympathizers.

Effects

Responses

This leads us to the response that self-immolation invokes in other people. Following the distinction between the motivations of appeal and incitement, we can differentiate between the response of opponents or bystanders and of sympathizers. Because it is such a drastic act, self-immolation can convert people to a cause, altering their beliefs. 'I have always believed in President Diem', remarked an old servant of an American family in Saigon, after Quang Duc's death. 'But now this has happened. This proves that the President is bad' (quoted in Mecklin 1965: 167). That event led many people elsewhere—especially in Buddhist countries and in the United States—to embrace the cause of Vietnamese Buddhists, simply by bringing it to their attention. Morrison died within sight of the office of Robert McNamara, Secretary of Defense. 'I was horrified', McNamara recalls (quoted in Steinbach 1995). 'And I was also quite aware that my family was deeply disturbed by the event, and many other members of the public were.' Within months, he became convinced that the war in Vietnam was futile; a journalist speculates that Morrison's death was the 'emotional catalyst' for his conversion (Hendrickson 1996: 198). Self-immolation can also have the opposite effect: discrediting the cause in the eyes of others. This was the case for Falun Gong, discussed below.

Self-immolation can enhance the commitment of others who believe in the cause. As Chân Không (1993: 38) watched Quang Duc's fiery death, 'a deep vow sprang forth from me: I too would do something for the respect of human rights in as beautiful and gentle way.' A student monk in Huế helped Thich Tieu Dieu kill himself. The ceremony made him feel 'the emptiness of human life in comparison with the struggle for a higher idea' (quoted in Hope 1967: 155). Out of 400 people who wrote testimonials for Park Sung Hee after her death, over two-thirds explicitly resolved to intensify their efforts: 'I will fight a thousand, ten thousand times more steadfastly, fiercely, than I have until now' (quoted in Kim 2002: 163).

More systematically, we can count how many acts in the sample generated some kind of collective response: people taking to the streets on hearing of the death, attending a mass funeral, and so on. Such a response is reported in about one-sixth of cases. This proportion is inevitably biased downwards because news reports often do not cover subsequent events. If we confine our attention to cases in which there is more substantial information, the proportion is about a third. Note that the significance of this measure varies with the degree of repression exercised by the political system; in totalitarian states, where the cost of protest is exceedingly high, an act of self-immolation may have a significant impact on people's opinions without any public manifestation. At one extreme, a handful of individuals had a tremendous impact. They include Quang Duc, Nu Thanh Quang, Nhat Chi Mai, Jan Palach, Romas Kalanta in Soviet Lithuania, Rajeev Goswami (in 1990), and Park Sung Hee. These deaths brought thousands or tens of thousands or even hundreds of thousands[42] of people together—to express their rage, grief, and commitment. As we have seen, all these individuals became exemplars for others to sacrifice their own lives in turn. Still, we should not lose sight of the fact that most acts of self-immolation fail to generate any collective response.

This should not obscure a theoretical puzzle: why should a self-inflicted death ever have any influence? Self-immolation provides two stirring images: the victim who is innocent and the hero who braves death. A protester killed by police is a victim, but has not willed the ultimate sacrifice.[43] A suicide bomber may be seen as a hero, but hardly as a victim. Self-immolation carries such emotional power because it inspires sacrifice and also provokes outrage. The latter may seem paradoxical, because the victim actually killed himself or herself—why blame anyone else for the death? This becomes somewhat less surprising when we turn to examples in tribal societies. In some communities, anyone who committed suicide after publicly blaming someone else was treated as the victim of murder, requiring relatives to receive the same compensation or exact the same revenge (Jeffreys 1971). A familiar example is Kima'i in the Trobriand Islands. After being publicly insulted for an incestuous relationship with his maternal cousin, he climbed a tree, denounced his tormentor, and jumped to his death. His clansmen took revenge, severely injuring the culprit (Malinowski 1926).

Kim (2002) provides unique insight into the emotional response to self-immolation, examining the testimonials left at Park Sung Hee's grave. Renewed commitment was strongly and significantly associated with expressions of shame. (It was also strongly associated with expressions of anger and of patriotic love, though these are not statistically significant.) Besides the self-sacrifice of a martyr, these individuals felt guilty about their own relative lack of commitment. 'While looking at your face, fourteen years younger than mine, I feel ashamed through and through' (quoted by Kim 2002: 167). This motivated a pledge of enhanced commitment. 'I resolve that I will become a fighter who will not be ashamed to stand before you' (quoted by Kim 2002: 163). At the funeral of another Korean student, a dissident leader tried to instil this same emotion: 'We will never disappoint the martyr who devoted his dear life to the nation' (*AP*, 12 May 1991).

The most significant acts of self-immolation continue to evoke a response, long afterwards. The site of the event or burial can become a place of pilgrimage. On the intersection where Quang Duc died, there is a large memorial; it is still festooned with flowers to this day (Topmiller 1998: 272). Palach was first buried in Olsany Cemetery in Prague. To hinder people from laying flowers, the police removed the bronze tablet from his grave; eventually, in 1973 they translated the remains to his native village, which would be less accessible. Similarly, the date of the event can become a time of renewed attention. On the twentieth anniversary of Palach's death, in 1989, police resorted to tear gas and water cannons to break up a demonstration in Wenceslas Square. The Dravidian Progress Association celebrates the anniversary of Chinnaswamy's death as 'Language Martyrs' Day' (Ramaswamy 1997: 229).

Consequences

Self-immolation can spur sympathizers to greater effort on behalf of the cause, and it can even convert people to the cause. And it often inspires others to repeat the sacrifice. The effect of self-immolation is potentially far greater than any other individual contribution to a social movement. After all, the marginal effect of an individual participating in a demonstration or some other conventional protest is vanishingly small (Olson 1971). The ultimate consequences of self-immolation depend on the particular context because this sacrifice is usually only one element in a sustained interaction between protesters and their opponents. It is therefore worthwhile to explore two episodes in greater detail: Buddhists in South Vietnam in 1963 and 1966, and followers of Falun Gong in China in 2001. These serve to delineate the range of possible consequences, from beneficial to detrimental.

The overthrow of President Diem in 1963 provides a clear illustration of success. The coup occurred five months after Quang Duc's immolation, during which time five monks and nuns had followed his example. One can surmise that their deaths were a necessary—albeit not sufficient—cause of Diem's downfall, though the causal pathway is complex. The immolation of Quang Duc dramatically altered the climate of popular opinion in the cities. For the first time, ordinary citizens took to the streets of Saigon, alongside monks and nuns. Even the regime sensed the change. Diem hurriedly negotiated a compromise with the Buddhist movement in order to avoid a public funeral. In the event, thousands of women rioted as police tried to prevent them from attending. Quang Duc's ashes were distributed to pagodas across the country, along with photographs 'touched up to show the skeleton through the fire' (Hope 1967: 151). Widespread popular opposition—regularly inflamed by further immolations—stimulated more severe repression. All this was reported by American journalists, who were skilfully cultivated by the Buddhists.

The regime's repression alienated the United States. President John F. Kennedy supposedly exclaimed 'Jesus Christ' when he saw the image of the burning monk. It was not a good advertisement for the anti-Communist struggle, especially as the Buddhist crisis immediately became an international issue. As the crisis worsened, the ruling family became more irrational, joking about 'barbecues'. Even their stalwart supporters in the American mission realized that the regime was focused more on suppressing the Buddhists than on fighting the Viet Cong. Kennedy appointed a new ambassador to force compromise. At his initial briefing, there was the photograph of Quang Duc's death on the President's desk (Browne 1965: 182).[44] Then, in August, the government's special forces launched a concerted assault on pagodas across the country, injuring hundreds of monks and killing an unknown number. Thousands were arrested. The police even cut the telephones of American officials, to prevent them from intervening. This was Diem's fatal mistake, to openly defy the United States (cf. Kahin 1987: 431). Only when American officials intimated their need for a more pliable regime did army leaders launch a coup.

The success of self-immolation in 1963 should be contrasted with the failure in 1966. (Topmiller (1998) is the definitive monograph; Schecter (1967) provides a first-hand account.) By the spring of that year, South Vietnam was in turmoil. The military junta, headed by Premier Nguyen Cao Ky, had lost control of swathes of the country. Danang and Hué were held by dissident army units and popular forces, led by Buddhists. Ky announced his intention to limit the scope of forthcoming elections, and launched a military assault on the 'rebel' cities. In the course of a month, fourteen Buddhists burned themselves to death. By the end of June, however, the regime had successfully repressed all opposition, raiding the Buddhist headquarters in Saigon and placing Tri Quang under house arrest. The outcome may be partly explained by domestic factors. Ky was a wily operator compared with Diem; he made the most of factional conflict between Tri Quang and the conservative leader, Thich Tam Chau. The militant Buddhists were not merely fighting for religious freedom, they were attempting to dictate the country's political future; as a result, perhaps, they might not have enjoyed the breadth of popular support they had in 1963 (Schecter 1967: 235, 243; Oka 1966: TO-27, 11). But once again the decisive factor was the attitude of the United States (Kahin 1987: 431–2). By 1966, it was clear that the Buddhists were committed to ending the war through negotiations. Indeed, two monks had burned themselves to death during the previous year to plead for a ceasefire on Buddha's birthday. As the Americans came to realize that only a dictatorial regime would prosecute the war against the Viet Cong, so the Buddhists came to identify the United States as their foe. Though Nu Thanh Quang appealed to the United States for help, Buddhist students torched the United States Information Service and consulate in Hué. It is not surprising, then, that President Lyndon Johnson never wavered in his support for Ky.

The self-immolation of Chinese followers of Falun Gong provides an exceptional example of unintended—and detrimental—consequences (for a detailed chronology, see Human Rights Watch 2002*b*). The Chinese government banned Falun Gong, a spiritual movement based on the *qigong* healing tradition, in the middle of 1999. Because the movement had a huge following, including many in the Communist Party, and because local officials did not view it as a threat, the campaign of repression had little success. The movement was still able to orchestrate protests in Tiananmen Square, which was acutely embarrassing for the government. In January 2001, on the eve of Chinese New Year, five followers set themselves alight in the Square and two more were thwarted. The government initially tried to suppress news of the event, even though Western journalists had witnessed the scene. Then it was realized how this could be turned against the movement. A week later, state television broadcast a gruesome film of the incident, including images of a 12-year-old girl (daughter of one of the practitioners) writhing in agony (*NYT*, 31 January 2001). The official leadership of Falun Gong, exiled in the United States, immediately denied any connection with the movement; it released its own video, which accused the government of concocting the incident (Falun Dafa 2001). While there is no reason to believe that the leadership sanctioned these acts, it seems unnecessary to resort to any conspiracy theory. Some of the adults had taken part in previous protests (*Washington Post*, 4 February 2001). In addition, two more individuals set fire to themselves in the following months; another was arrested for planning to emulate their actions.

Self-immolation became the centrepiece of the government's continuing propaganda campaign. This framed the deaths as cultic suicide rather than political protest. 'Nirvana means slaughter' was one headline in the *People's Daily* (*AFP*, 17 February 2001). By all accounts this had a major impact on people's opinions. 'Previously, most Chinese thought the crackdown was stupid, like a dog catching a mouse', admitted an anonymous official (*Washington Post*, 5 August 2001). 'After those people burned themselves and the party broadcast that little girl's face on TV for almost a month straight, people's views here changed.'[45] Within weeks, the government ordered a massive increase in repression, including systematic torture. Not only was there a favourable climate of opinion; deaths in custody could now be used as evidence of the cult's deleterious effects. The official news agency boasts that a total of 1,700 have committed suicide.[46] The combination of torture, 're-education', and propaganda apparently yielded results. Within six months, Falun Gong was effectively eliminated as a movement within China. The maimed survivors were still being paraded before a press conference in the following year. 'Falun Gong is indeed an evil cult and it led me to this', said Chen Guo (*Xinhua News Agency*, 7 April 2002).[47] Presumably the state could not have scored such a propaganda triumph without the involvement of children in the immolation. The attempt by Falun Gong to disassociate itself from the act was probably also counterproductive.

Conclusion

In conclusion, we can revisit the comparison with suicide attacks. Quang Duc's self-immolation in Saigon in 1963 resembles the suicide bombing of the Iraqi embassy in Beirut in 1981: each initiated a continuing lineage of actions, directly or indirectly descending from the original event. There were earlier instances of self-immolation and of suicide attacks, of course, but they did not have the same inspirational effect on others. The lineage beginning with Quang Duc proliferated more widely in its first two decades: self-immolation has been adopted in more countries than has suicide bombing and for a greater range of collective causes. Overall, it is more prevalent within cultures shaped by Hindu and Buddhist traditions, whereas suicide bombing has an affinity with Islam.

In a fundamental sense, the two phenomena are disconnected: actors do not treat them as alternatives. It is not as if an individual resolves to die for the cause, and then chooses whether or not to kill. It is the reverse: the basic parameter is whether or not the enemy is to be killed—whether the situation is war (in the broadest sense) or protest. Within the confines of each situation, the decision is then whether to make the supreme sacrifice instead of engaging in a less costly form of action. Self-immolation is an alternative to participating in a demonstration or going on hunger strike, for example, just as a suicide attack is an alternative to an attack from which escape is possible. This disjunction helps explain the difference in orchestration: self-immolation is inherently individualistic, while a suicide attack is invariably organized. In part, this reflects practical constraints. Gasoline and a match suffice for self-immolation, whereas a suicide attack requires considerable planning and expertise. Yet the difference runs deeper, because organizations are unwilling to claim credit for self-immolation by their supporters. Outside of war, directing someone to make the ultimate sacrifice is unacceptable; that sacrifice is legitimate only as an individual choice.

Given the disjunction between self-immolation and suicide attacks, we would expect to find different sets of motivations. On the one hand, some motivations pertain especially or exclusively to suicide attacks. Such attacks provide greater scope for what I identify as vanity, due to the lengthy interval between volunteering and dying, during which the volunteer enjoys the approbation of others. Self-immolation, by contrast, is rarely announced beforehand, and so approbation is only posthumous. (Like threats, promises of self-immolation are apparently not credible.) A potential motivation for suicide attacks is the calculation that death in combat is highly probable anyway, and so little is lost by volunteering for a suicide attack. This resembles what I identify as cheating the enemy, but that applies to only a small fraction of cases of self-immolation. Another prominent motivation is the emotional 'reward' of anticipated harm to the enemy. While self-immolation may be spurred by anger, it cannot be motivated directly by revenge or retaliation. On the other hand, some motivations pertain especially or exclusively to self-immolation. Conceivably, suicide attacks could be intended to incite sympathizers, as I identify it, but this must be a minor theme.[48] Suicide attacks cannot be intended to appeal to bystanders or opponents. As an example, Vietnamese Buddhists killed themselves (in part) to appeal to American public opinion, and thus change the foreign policy of the United States; that motivation can hardly be shared by Palestinian suicide bombers.

This leads to the central puzzle posed by self-immolation: how is it effective? A suicide attack maximizes the costs imposed on the enemy, while self-immolation inflicts cost only on the perpetrator. Dying without killing is potentially effective in two ways. First, it can incite sympathizers to contribute more to the cause by evoking emotions like guilt or shame. Second, it can convert bystanders to the cause by signalling the depth of the collectivity's grievances. Only once has self-immolation proved detrimental, in allowing the Chinese state to frame Falun Gong as a suicidal cult. Although self-immolation is exceedingly rare, it provides a significant theoretical lesson: suffering can serve to advance a collective cause. We can discern the same logic—protest by 'communicative suffering' (Biggs 2003*b*)—in less costly forms, as when leaders seek arrest or when protesters provoke police violence. Alternatively, protesters can use the threat of their own suffering in order to constrain the actions of opponents, for example by ascending trees to prevent them from being felled. Self-immolation is unique in that it does not depend on the reaction of authorities or opponents; the individual chooses unconditionally to inflict extreme suffering on himself or herself. The efficacy of suffering is an unexplored dimension of protest, and deserves further research.

6

Killing Without Dying: the Absence of Suicide Missions

STATHIS N. KALYVAS AND IGNACIO SÁNCHEZ-CUENCA

Sean O'Callaghan was a member of the Irish Republican Army (IRA) who later became an informer for the Irish police. Having spent most of his life fighting against terrorism, O'Callaghan (1999: 308) concludes that 'the IRA is an organization that produces people prepared to starve themselves to death, people prepared to spend large part of their lives in prison. In short, it produces people who are prepared to inflict death, pain and suffering on themselves as well as on others in pursuit of a cause.' Yet, in spite of this, the IRA never launched a suicide mission (SM). The same holds for many other insurgent and terrorist organizations all over the world, no matter how violent their tactics, how virulent their ideology, or how extreme their members' preferences and commitment.[1] *Euzkadi ta Azkatasuna* (ETA) in Spain, the Red Brigades in Italy, the Baader Meinhof in Germany, the Shining Path in Peru, and the Kosovo Liberation Army, to name but a few, never engaged in SMs. Even the Algerian *Groupe Islamique Armé* (GIA), an extremely violent and militant Islamist organization that engaged in tens of massacres of civilians, resorted to SMs only once. In fact, according to a recent estimate only 113 out of 7,053 terrorist incidents (1.6 per cent) were suicide bombings and the great majority were attributed to a handful of organizations.[2] Here, we turn the central question of this volume on its head and ask why so many organizations do *not* resort to SMs.

Any explanation of why some organizations do engage in such missions must also account for the fact that the great majority of insurgent and terrorist organizations refrain from using this method. In particular, if we assume that SMs are instrumentally planned to achieve a set of specific goals, we must also be able to say whether the absence of SMs results from altogether different goals or, rather, from differences in the costs associated with the parameters of the production of violence. In Becker's terminology (1996), the variation on SMs can be attributed either to variations in preferences or to variations in the relative costs of the inputs that are necessary to produce the final commodity—in this case, violence. In general, we tend to favour the latter type of explanation.

The chapter is in two parts. In the first part we ask why organizations may be unwilling to resort to SMs. We examine five possible reasons: cognitive accessibility, normative preferences, counterproductive effects, constituency costs, and technological costs. However, we cannot rule out the possibility that organizations which are willing to resort to SMs are unable to do so because of the lack of individual volunteers. Thus, in the second part we explore the factors that affect individual members' willingness to participate in SMs. Because evidence on the reasons or causes for the absence of SMs is particularly hard to come by, this chapter is more analytical than empirical. It formulates hypotheses and illustrates them by examples rather than testing them.

Organizational Incentives

Both the long tradition of SMs and their spectacular success in at least some of the instances where they were used (for example, Lebanon in 1983 and the World Trade Center (WTC) in 2001) make their overall infrequent incidence puzzling.

Cognitive Accessibility

One answer to the puzzle is simple: some organizations may have never contemplated relying on SMs because they did not know about them. In other words, SMs are *inconceivable* for these organizations for reasons that are unrelated to any normative or rational rejection. SMs would just not appear on their radar screens.

There are at least two possible objections to this explanation, a strong one and a weak one. According to the strong objection, any strategy that is potentially beneficial for its users should belong to their choice set, particularly if that strategy is not conditional on some previous technological innovation. As Elster (Chapter 7, this volume) points out, it was obviously not easy to think of suicide bombings before the invention of dynamite. But once this became technologically feasible, what could have restrained organizations from considering this possibility? Indeed, high-risk operations that entailed almost certain death have been common in the history of warfare—and the leap from high-risk missions to SMs is rather small. As we show below, the idea of suicide bombing came naturally to Russian anarchists at the end of the nineteenth century.

The weak objection applies only to the last twenty years. During this period, SMs have been a highly visible strategy and hence it is difficult to make the case for a gap in knowledge. In fact, there is an evident contagion effect. In Lebanon, Hezbollah's initial use of SMs was first imitated by many other non-Islamic groups: Kramer (1994: 35) has calculated that, of all SMs in Lebanon between 1983 and 1986, only a quarter were carried out by Hezbollah. Later, Hezbollah was imitated by Hamas and Palestinian Islamic Jihad (PIJ) in Israel, where even groups linked to secular organizations, such as al-Fatah and the Popular Front for the Liberation of Palestine (PFLP), eventually adopted this weapon; more recently, Chechen insurgents have used spectacular SMs against Russian targets—though this strategy was first used during the battle of Grozny in 1994 to destroy Russian tanks (Knezys and Sedlickas 1999: 50, 65).[3] Most recently, SMs have been extensively used by groups fighting the presence of the US-led coalition in Iraq.

The fascination produced by the 9/11 attacks is illustrated by an operation designed by the *Fuerzas Armadas Revolucionarias de Colombia* (FARC), a Marxist guerrilla organization that has never been involved in SMs, to sabotage a ceremony in which newly appointed President Alvaro Uribe was to take office. The police foiled the FARC's plan to hire a pilot who would crash a plane into the presidential palace. The FARC had no volunteers for the mission and was offering to compensate the family of the pilot willing to crash the plane with $2 million. According to the BBC, the FARC was looking for pilots among former members of the Medellin cartel (note that this is clearly a case of an organization willing to undertake an SM but unwilling to do so unaided). The organization had to content itself with exploding several bombs around the presidential palace, killing seventeen people and injuring sixty-five others on the day Uribe took office.[4]

What could be called 'delegated' or 'forced' SMs indicate that rebel organizations that do not launch SMs are nevertheless well aware of their potential benefits. This kind of operation has some of the technical advantages of an SM and none of its drawbacks in terms of personnel costs. On 24 October 1990 the IRA took the family of Patsy Gillespie hostage; he worked in the canteen of an army base (which made him a 'legitimate target'). In order to release his family, Gillespie had to drive a car full of explosives that the IRA exploded by remote control when he arrived at a checkpoint. He was used as a human bomb.[5] That same day, the IRA tried the same tactic with James McEvoy, who was warned that, if he did not comply, two of his sons would be shot. He did comply and was wounded during the operation, but survived. A similar operation took place in Colombia on 28 May 2002, apparently organized by the FARC. A driver was given a box of vegetables concealing a bomb inside. The organization exploded the bomb when the van was very close to a populated square near Bogotá.[6] This has not been the only such case in Colombia.[7]

These episodes show that some organizations understand the benefits of potential SMs but, for reasons unrelated to cognitive accessibility, refrain from launching them. Those same episodes reveal also that some organizations lack volunteers or at least the will to use them (we discuss this case in greater detail in the last part of this chapter). However, we also found evidence that at least two organizations considered and then decided to reject SMs despite the availability of volunteers.

In its fight for independence for the Basque Country, ETA has unsuccessfully tried to kill the king of Spain at least five times (Zavala 1998). The latest attempt and the one that came closest to succeeding took place in 1995, when a member of the organization was ready to shoot the king during his vacation in Mallorca but at the last minute the police foiled the operation. Killing the king would have obviously attracted massive international attention to the Basque conflict, and would have humiliated the Spanish security services and demoralized the Spanish public. In 1995, ETA also tried to kill José María Aznar, leader of the Popular Party, who became prime minister the following year. Despite the importance of these targets, ETA rejected the option of an SM against the king even though there was a volunteer inside the organization willing to execute the attack. The police intercepted some letters written in the late 1990s by one of the leaders of the organization, José Javier Arizcuren ('*Kantauri*'); these letters addressed questions and demands by ETA's most important commando, *Donosti*. In one of them, *Kantauri* refers to the letter of the volunteer for the Kamikaze action against the king in these terms:

With regard to the militant's letter in which he offers himself for more extreme actions (kamikaze-like), we must say that in principle we do not agree with the idea of a militant blowing himself up in a car. Yet, if the militant is willing to run a high risk, there could be a chance to carry out an action following a funeral. Let me explain: after a powerful attack, we find out where the funeral will take place. We can, then, kidnap the people who live in a house close to the cemetery or church and from there gun down one of the politicians attending the funeral (the King, the Prince, the Minister of Interior, Aznar, etc.). If the police do not have a file about the militant and he abandons his shotgun there, he may be able to escape in the ensuing confusion. (Quoted in Díaz Herrera and Durán 2002: 729).

Unfortunately, *Kantauri* does not elaborate on the reasons why the organization rejects SMs. He just expresses disagreement with this method and offers instead a very hazardous operation, implicitly drawing a line between sending a militant to certain death and sending him on a high-risk mission.

The GIA in Algeria similarly rejected SMs after resorting to an SM only once. In January 1995, GIA suicide bombers killed at least 42 people in an attack near the central police headquarters in Algiers as part of a strategy designed to bring the civil war into the cities. However, all the other attacks that were part of the same strategy involved 'traditional' bombings and fell short of SMs. What makes this case interesting is that a key figure of the Front Islamique du Salut (FIS), Ali Belhadj, suggested around the same time that SMs were indeed on the agenda: 'From January 1995, suicide attacks will be carried out against French diplomatic missions and interests in the Arab world.' However, this opinion was apparently not shared by other leaders of the FIS, such as Anwar Haddam, who explicitly condemned SMs (Freeman 1994). The Algerian case also suggests that, while volunteers were available and an SM was tried out, internal debates about which we have no information led to their swift abandonment.[8]

Normative Preferences

These examples suggest that, at least in some cases, SMs are explicitly contemplated but rejected by insurgent organizations. Why? A first answer suggests that they have moral or ideological objections to this method.

First, moral constraints: insurgents tend to see themselves as engaged in some sort of just war in which some practices are outside acceptable bounds (Gilbert 1995: ch. 2). In both the Christian version of the just war and the Islamic one (jihad), killing others may be licit if certain external conditions are met (for instance, repression and denial of basic rights) and if the killing is not indiscriminate or does not affect innocent civilians. Thus, the expression 'legitimate target' is not uncommon in the discourse of many insurgent organizations: not every killing is acceptable, implying that some are. The fact that they feel the need to justify their actions, no matter how objectionable such justifications may seem for those who do not share their views, shows the importance organizations often attach to acting under just war constraints.[9] The story that inspired Camus to write *Les Justes* (1947) is relevant here: in 1905 Ivan Kaliayev refused to throw a bomb at Grand Duke Sergei Alexandrovich because of the unexpected presence of his children in the carriage. Yet he was to kill the Grand Duke a couple of days later (Pomper 1995: 91). It seems that purely self-imposed moral constraints restrained Kaliayev.

When civilians unconnected to the state apparatus are killed, insurgent groups resort to a wide range of exculpatory justifications: the killing was a mistake, it was an accident, the police did not take the warning seriously, in every war there are collateral victims, and so on. These defences are regularly cited even if the number of innocent victims is extremely high (curiously enough, civilians represent the same percentage of total victims, around 40 per cent, both in the IRA case (McKittrick et al. 1999: 1504) and in the ETA one (Sánchez-Cuenca 2001: 256)). When the IRA exploded twenty-one bombs in Belfast on Friday 21 July 1972 ('Bloody Friday'), killing nine people and injuring 130 others, the organization refused to accept responsibility for the consequences because it had issued warnings in every case. In his autobiography, Adams (1996: 210) admits that 'Bloody Friday' was a sort of technical mistake, but adds that 'the IRA had set out to cause economic damage and had sought to avoid civilian casualties by providing at least thirty minutes' warning in relation to each of the twenty-one bombs.'

This discourse, even if it sounds cynical or ad hoc from the outside, is still compatible with some just war doctrine. Members of the organization exonerate themselves for the killing of innocent civilians because it was a mistake or an accident. However, SMs cannot be so easily reconciled with just war, if only because excuses such as those just mentioned would not be available. SMs convey a clear intention. Hence, civilian victims or illegitimate fatalities are the intended outcome of the action. Imagine an SM in which a suicide bomber decides to blow himself up, fully realizing that his gesture is going to cause a massacre; even though his nervousness may induce a premature detonation, as is sometimes the case, it usually entails no mistakes or accidents, and warnings make no sense.[10] Therefore, the usual disclaimers are not available and the action cannot be justified in just war terms.

Of course, the argument that organizations renounce SMs because they are incompatible with the ideological or normative preferences of just war is subject to several caveats. SMs can be selective, as when used for selective assassinations of specific people; and it can be argued that under some circumstances SMs may deliver more precise ('surgical') attacks than unmanned car bombs.

There may also be moral or religious rejections of suicide itself regardless of its victims. For instance, Freeman (1994) argues that Sunni Muslims are traditionally less susceptible to violent extremism than Shia Muslims because, unlike the latter, they do not relish martyrdom. In fact, Islam forbids suicide and an SM has to be presented as an act of martyrdom which becomes licit only under certain circumstances. Yet such a rejection is at odds with the willingness of insurgent groups to kill people in order to achieve desired results. A doctrine that allows killing others but forbids suicide is not logically contradictory, but, to say the least, it seems strange.

Second, ideological constraints: Marxist theorists have traditionally rejected individualistic actions detached from the class struggle and its associated revolutionary activity. As Trotsky (1974: 8) put it in 1911: 'Social Democracy rejects all methods and means that have as their goal to artificially force the development of society and to substitute chemical preparations for the insufficient revolutionary strength of the proletariat.' He then went on to compare a strike with the murder of a factory owner: in the strike, workers develop and strengthen their self-consciousness and reinforce work-ing-class organizations, whereas the assassination of the factory owner quickly leads to his replacement and has no social implications. Writing in 1906 about guerrilla war, Lenin (1968: 85) insisted that Marxism did not reject any form of struggle as long as it did not lose its connection with the masses; and, when Mao (1961) justified guerrilla warfare as a necessary phase in the revolutionary war, he argued that it could succeed only if it was firmly based on society.

Clearly, SMs exacerbate the individualistic dimension of certain forms of terrorism disconnected from the masses. Unless martyrdom is seen as a natural and proper action by the population, isolated cases of suicide will only deepen the gap between the insurgents and the masses. In this sense, SMs are alien to the ideological inclinations of Marxism. Hence, it is not surprising that Marxist organizations have never endorsed SMs.[11] Given that many insurgent organizations, particularly those of the national liberation variety, have more or less remote Marxist origins, the absence of SMs could be partially explained by reference to ideologies. This conjecture is reinforced by the massive use of SMs in Sri Lanka by the Black Tigers of the Liberation Tigers of Tamil Eelam (LTTE), a national liberation organization that has no Marxist roots (Chapter 2, this volume).

Nevertheless, there are reasons to remain sceptical about the role of moral or ideological preferences. For instance, Hamas committed itself at the start of the 1990s not to kill civilians: when the organization reneged on this commitment in 1994, it found plenty of reasons for justifying the shift (Hroub 2000: 245–9). Likewise, Islamic doctrines either prohibit or constrain women from carrying out SMs—for instance, by forbidding disguises that involve removing their veils or moving around without a chaperone; yet as soon as Palestinian women began participating in SMs, influential Muslim clerics issued religious proclamations exempting women in Palestine from these rules and assuring them that they could reach paradise though suicide bombings (Bennet 2003*b*: A14). In Russia, Marxist groups, such as the Social Revolutionaries, that nominally rejected terrorist tactics because of their individualism ended up participating in individual acts of political violence (Geifman 1993: ch. 3).

Clearly, normative preferences are at best soft constraints on insurgent groups (ideologies and moral beliefs offer ample room for *ex post* rational-ization) and at worst little more than rhetorical devices used to prevent the loss of supporters. Furthermore, preference-based arguments have similar observational implications to other arguments (in terms of counterproduc-tive effects, constituency costs, and technological costs) which can be more easily tested since they entail public, measurable, and concrete indicators, whereas the operation of normative preferences has to be inferred from actions and words. Lastly, moral and ideological arguments are equally ad hoc in explaining either the use or the absence of SMs. It has now become commonplace in the media and elsewhere to account for SMs by reference to ideologies such as Islamism. However, there are two problems with this view. From an empirical point of view, Islamism is obviously neither a necessary nor a sufficient condition for SMs. From a methodological point of view, even if it were possible to define a particular strain of Islamism as conducive to SMs, it would be difficult to produce a truly falsifiable claim as ideologies are always open to multiple interpretations. Indeed, most arguments that point to particular ideologies (or theologies, for that matter) are circular if not tautological (Kalyvas 1998).

Counterproductive Effects

A third type of explanation points to the counterproductive effects of the subset of SMs that indiscriminately target civilians. Although civil wars differ from terrorist campaigns, interesting parallels may be drawn between them. In civil wars, the reliance on indiscriminate violence is generally counter-productive (Kalyvas forthcoming). SMs may be absent from the great ma-jority of insurgencies for the same reasons that indiscriminate violence by insurgents is relatively absent from civil wars.

Unlike selective or indiscriminate SMs that are directed at military targets, SMs that target civilians tend to be almost always indiscriminate in the sense that they do not aim at specific individuals. We identify two versions of this argument. The first stresses the negative effects of indiscriminate violence on potential recruits and supporters; the second points to the detrimental inter-national repercussions of such actions.

When aimed against civilian targets, SMs are a weapon particularly (though not exclusively) suited for random, massive, and indiscriminate violence: according to data from the Rand Corporation, 'suicide attacks on average kill four times as many people as other terrorist acts' (Hoffman 2003: 42). Yet, far from turning SMs into a popular enterprise, as Hoffman hastens to deduce, such violence may well be counterproductive for its users (Kalyvas forthcoming).[12] The underlying logic is as follows: although random violence may be useful to a dictator because of its ability to paralyse and atomize the population, it is less so under the conditions of fragmented sovereignty that characterize civil wars, in which the presence of a rival makes defection and resistance possible. In so far as one side's use of violence is intended to deter civilians from collaborating with its opponent and to compel them to collab-orate exclusively with itself, it usually fails when it forecloses the possibility of avoiding violence. That is, unless civilians are given options (such as that, if they act in certain ways, they will be safe), their behaviour will not be shaped by the violence aimed at them. The sheer unpredictability of indiscriminate violence makes populations fear lethal sanctions by the political actor who relies on such violence regardless of their behaviour: compliance with that actor is utterly impossible. Gross (1979: 212) elaborates on this point writing about German occupation of Poland during the Second World War:

One would expect that noncompliance with German demands carried such drastic penalties that scarcely anyone would dare to defy them. But full compliance was impossible; terror continued and even intensified with time. The population quickly recognized the new logic of the situation: whether one tried to meet German demands or not, one was equally exposed to violence.... It makes no sense, in the context of random punishment, to style one's life according to the possibility of being victimized, any more than it makes sense to orient all of one's everyday acts to the possibility of an accident.

Arendt (1970: 56) must have had indiscriminate violence in mind when she remarked that 'violence can destroy power; it is utterly incapable of creating it'. Indeed, even particularly vicious insurgents, like the Algerian Islamists of the GIA, curtailed their use of indiscriminate bombings in the cities, most likely because they were unwilling to countenance their counterproductive effects.[13]

Insurgent leaders have often argued on strategic grounds for selective violence and against indiscriminate violence. For example, Che Guevara (1998: 91) recommended that 'assaults and terrorism in indiscriminate form should not be employed'. Indeed, insurgents have often actually welcomed, or even provoked, indiscriminate army reprisals by ambushing an isolated enemy soldier close to a village so as to win recruits (for example, Aussaresses 2001: 62; Senaratne 1997: 95). Conversely, there is evidence suggesting that incumbent armies also gradually shy away from indiscriminate violence for the same reason (Kalyvas forthcoming).

This logic applies clearly to cases in which incumbents and insurgents compete for the same population: faced with selective and indiscriminate threats, civilians are better off collaborating with the actor that is selective. But what about ethnic or secessionist insurgencies? Presumably, no counter-productive effects can result from targeting a population that can never provide potential supporters, let alone recruits. But this is not quite so. For one, even ethnic insurgents may want to drive a wedge between a government and its popular basis by directing its struggle against the government rather than the population at large. Furthermore, intra-ethnic violence is almost always a feature of ethnic insurgencies as ethnic rebels use violence to induce collaboration (Kalyvas 2002). However, the indiscriminate character of SMs is likely to alienate the population base of ethnic insurgents and turn at least some people against them, particularly in societies with strong norms of revenge.[14] For example, Palestinian SMs have repeatedly killed Israeli Arabs, Chechen SMs have killed innocent Chechen civilians, and the WTC attack killed several Muslims;[15] most recently, the apparent al-Qaeda SMs in Riyadh, the capital of Saudi Arabia, and Casablanca, Morocco, in May 2003 killed mostly Muslims.[16]

Perhaps an indirect piece of evidence of the counterproductive aspect of SMs may be the timing of its use by the Chechen separatist insurgents. Although they have targeted for the most part military and political object-ives, they have also killed many Chechen civilians, including women. This, according to observers, may be an indicator of their desperation, a sign that they are losing the war. Myers (2003: A5) points out that 'unable to control territory or fight Russian forces head-on, [Chechen rebels] have increasingly resorted to suicide attacks'. Wines (2003:A3) concurs: 'as Russian forces have largely neutralized the guerrillas' ability to wage organized battles, the bombings have become more deadly and spectacular.' If these assessments are correct, they suggest that, for the Chechen guerrillas, the demonstration effect of spectacular suicide bombings outweighs their counterproductive effects, but this is certainly not a sustainable strategy.

A second counterproductive effect of SMs may be related to its inter-national repercussions. International repercussions are not always necessar-ily negative. Attracting international attention to a long-forgotten conflict may be so beneficial as to offset potential costs. However, in so far as suicide bombing is perceived as a particularly repugnant strategy and as long as the 'international community' under the influence of public opinion in hege-monic countries may be swayed by moral considerations (an expectation that violates prevailing realist assumptions in international relations), the expectation of such reactions may outweigh the benefits of advertising a cause and hence prevent SMs from being planned and implemented. Even if states are willing to close their eyes, the growth of transnational interest groups and non-governmental organizations may produce similar effects. An implication of this argument is that the domestic benefits of an SM must exceed its negative international effects. Perhaps this is rarely the case.

Constituency Costs

Most terrorists and insurgent organizations depend on the more or less active support of a pool of supporters. As Hamas admitted in a 1992 internal document, 'our real power is our popularity' (reproduced in Mishal and Sela 2000: 128). Because these supporters assist the organization and are usually necessary for its very existence, they may prevent some actions that otherwise the organization would be willing to carry out. Obviously, not all supporters are the same. It is possible to distinguish a hard core of those who explicitly help the organization from a more diffuse community of supporters who simply approve of the actions undertaken by the organization (Petersen 2001). Given that many organizations act for the sake of the people they claim to represent, it is possible to hypothesize that they need the support not only of the hard core but also of the wider community that they purport to defend.

Constituency costs have two components. First, they flow from the preferences and moral sentiments of the supporters. Second, however, those preferences have a greater or lesser constraining effect depending on the nature of the relations between organizations and their supporters. In either case, a trade-off exists between the intensity of killing or the selectivity of violence on the one hand and popular support on the other. Supporters may share the ends sought by the insurgent group but not support all the means it uses to achieve those ends. This disagreement over means can be normative or strategic. With regard to normative considerations, supporters could reject SMs simply because they object to suicide or do not see themselves, and thus do not want to be seen, as fanatics or extremists. Put otherwise, their preferences are not as intense as those of the terrorists and consequently the range of acceptable forms of struggle shrinks. In strategic terms, supporters may expect reprisals if the organization resorts to SMs (which are often disproportionally likely to affect them rather than the organization's hard-core members). Again, they may have different beliefs from those of the organization about the negative consequences of launching SMs: for instance, supporters could be more concerned than the terrorists about the image of the movement abroad, or they could believe that SMs are counterproductive.

A complete test of this hypothesis about constituency costs would require detailed data on the preferences of supporters and cadres. However, there is much indirect evidence about these constraints. Supporters of the IRA and ETA are more moderate than the terrorist organizations themselves, and reject indiscriminate attacks that provoke civilian victims. Were ETA or the IRA to carry out systematic indiscriminate bombings, support among important sectors of the nationalist communities would wane and the pool of volunteers would probably shrink. It is plausible to surmise, for instance, that, in the case of the IRA, SMs would have stopped some of the financial support it received from the Irish community in the United States. In fact, these organizations are well aware of the feelings of revulsion that some particularly bloody, brutal attacks would provoke among supporters— which is why ETA or the IRA have denied responsibility for some of their worst attacks.

The IRA did so several times: when a bomb exploded with no warning in a restaurant on 4 March 1972, killing two women and injuring over 100 people;[17] when three car bombs exploded on 31 July 1972 with no prior warning, killing nine people (Clarke and Johnston 2001: 78);[18] when bombs exploded in two pubs in Birmingham on 21 November 1974, killing nineteen people and injuring 182 (Taylor 1997:173); when an IRA gunman shot Joanne Mathers on 7 April 1981 (Clarke and Johnston 2001: 126); when a bomb exploded outside Harrods, the London department store, on 18 December 1983, killing six people (since the denial was not particularly credible, the IRA issued an statement trying to justify its deed: 'While the Army Council did not authorise this specific operation at Harrods, we do not believe that the Volunteers involved set out to deliberately kill civilians' (quoted in Clarke and Johnston 2001:143-4)); and when the IRA detonated a bomb that killed eleven Protestants on 8 November 1987 in Enniskillen, arguing (falsely, as it was later proved) that the British had triggered the bomb with a radio device (Moloney 2002: 341).

The sensitivity of the IRA to reactions in the Catholic community is well documented. Delegated SMs were quickly ruled out given the indignation of the community of support. As Taylor (1997: 317) writes, 'the vast majority of Catholics in Derry were sickened by the attack and no doubt let the IRA know what they thought.'[19] Likewise, Moloney (2002: 348-9) argues that the IRA stopped this practice because it was counterproductive in terms of public support.[20] In a speech delivered in 1977, Gerry Adams stated very clearly the dependence of the IRA on the community of support: 'In a war zone it is a necessity, if nothing else, to force the republican movement into a complete and utter reliance on the people's support' (quoted in Sharrock and Devenport 1997: 159). More tellingly, Sean MacStiofain (1975: 214), Chief of Staff of the IRA between 1970 and 1972, wrote in his autobiography that 'No resistance movement in history has ever succeeded in fighting a struggle for national freedom without some accidental casualties, but the Republican interest in retaining popular support clearly lay in causing as few as possible.' If the IRA has not resorted to more extreme tactics, this most likely reflects its dependence on popular support. Eamon Collins, a former member of the IRA who was killed by the organization in 1999, said clearly that the IRA had been acting under constraints: 'the IRA fought with one hand behind its back: in general it did not carry out the indiscriminate campaign of all-out war which it would have been capable of fighting.' He added that the IRA 'sought to avoid any operations which had obviously sectarian overtones: a policeman could be justified as a legitimate target, his non-combatant Protestant family could not' (Collins 1997: 8, 295).[21]

Likewise, ETA denied responsibility for the explosion of a bomb in a restaurant on 13 September 1974 that killed thirteen people and injured over seventy. The organization mistakenly thought that most of the customers were policemen, since the restaurant was close to the police headquarters in Madrid (Gurruchaga 2001: 91–3). The internal quarrelling about this bombing was one of the factors that led to the more important split in the history of ETA. Even a radical organization like Hezbollah denied responsibility for the indiscriminate bombings in Paris in 1986 (Kramer 1994:38–9).

ETA's bloodiest attack was the detonation of a bomb in a department store in Barcelona on 19 June 1987 that killed twenty-one people and injured forty. This action was rejected not only by the more diffuse support community but also by the hard core and even by members of the organization. As a former member of ETA put it in an interview: 'We really fucked it up. I think there is a wide feeling among a lot of people that can be described as "These guys [the terrorists] don't care at all". Fuck, we messed up!' (quoted in Alcedo 1996: 173).

Of course, this trade-off between violence and support vanishes when supporters are already (or have become) as radical as the organization itself. This appears to be case for organizations that launch SMs, like Hamas or Hezbollah, and raises the question of what determines the preferences of supporters in the first place. Their preferences may be largely determined by the behaviour of their opponents: harsh and indiscriminate reprisals by incumbents may produce support for SMs. We return to this issue in the second section.

An implication of this hypothesis is that organizations that launch SMs would refrain from doing so if SMs were to reduce substantially the degree of support they enjoyed. An expert on Hamas points out that 'Although Hamas has been unresponsive to all international requests to stop its military operations, the erosion of popular backing for such action is sufficient to twist its arm to do just that' (Hroub 2000: 250).

A second hypothesis revolves around the relations between organizations and their supporters rather than supporters' preferences. The less constrained an organization is by its supporters in terms of victim selection and forms of killing, the more likely it is to adopt SMs.

The relation between support and strategy may be U-shaped, with organizations enjoying very limited or very strong support better able to adopt very radical strategies. At one extreme we would then observe organizations like Hamas, Hezbollah, or LTTE with a strong degree of support among their underlying community; in the other extreme we would observe organizations such as al-Qaeda, PIJ, and the anarchist terrorists and Russian revolutionaries of the late nineteenth and early twentieth centuries: highly decentralized movements in which small and isolated cells commit 'magnicides' and indiscriminate killings with no popular backing (or direct support) whatsoever.

The U-shaped relationship is confirmed by the occasional presence of SMs in the old form of anarchist and nihilistic terrorism. After several failed attempts to kill Tsar Alexander II in 1880, on 1 March 1881 the People's

Will (*Narodnaya Volya*) finally did it. The tsar was travelling in a carriage. The first two bombs missed their target, wounding some Cossacks who were escorting him. The tsar stopped to see what had happened, and then Ignatei Grinevitski threw his bomb, killing Alexander II and himself (Hingley 1967: 13–14). SMs were frequent in Russia among Socialist Revolutionaries and anarchists in the first years of the twentieth century. On 23 April 1906 Boris Vnorovskii threw a bomb at the Governor General of Moscow, Dubasov, killing him and himself (Geifman 1993: 57). It could be argued that these were not SMs, since the terrorists were killed by their own devices unintentionally. Yet on 12 August 1906 three revolutionaries blew themselves up in St Petersburg, failing to kill their target, Prime Minister Petr Stolypin, along with thirty-three other people (Geifman 1993:74). On 7 February 1908 Vavolod Lebedintsev was arrested, also in St Petersburg, while wrapped with dynamite and prepared to act as a human bomb (Geifman 1993: 64). The anarchist Nisan Farber blew himself up in a police headquarters in October 1904 (Geifman 1993: 132). And the list goes on.

If there were not more SMs like the ones we observe today, it was not because of a lack of motivation (see below) but rather because it was not necessary from a technological point of view: at that time it was relatively easy to approach ministers or kings.

Anarchists and nihilists acted on their own, without relying on popular support. Their individualism was extreme. There was no organizational structure between the cells and within each cell an individual could act entirely alone. The Russian anarchist Sergei G. Nechaev, in his *Catechism of the Revolutionist* (1869), explicitly endorsed the isolation of the revolutionary. The second chapter, about the attitude of the revolutionary, proclaims several principles whereby the revolutionary is asked to cut all his links with society. According to one principle:

In the very depths of his being, not only in words but also in deeds, he has broken every tie with the civil order and the entire cultured world, with all its laws, proprieties, social conventions and its ethical rules. He is an implacable enemy of this world, and if he continues to live in it, that is only to destroy it more effectively. (Confino 1973: 100)

Likewise, according to another principle, the revolutionary 'despises public opinion'. It is not only that anarchists rejected, from a doctrinal point of view, a society that was seen as morally flawed and corrupt; anarchist terrorism increased after the masses failed to mobilize. In fact, terrorism was a desperate response to this failure (Pomper 1995: 76; Núñez 1983: 189–90; Linse 1982). Anarchist propaganda by the deed was both an attempt to shatter the mistaken convictions of the masses and an individualistic expression of rejection of an unjust society.

Between these two extremes at which we find evidence of SMs—organizations with strong support in society on the one hand and organizations that act on their own in complete isolation from the masses on the other—lie the intermediate cases, like those of ETA or IRA, in which the degree of popular support is crucial but generally weak, at least compared with the support that organizations like Hamas or Hezbollah enjoy: in 2001, 92 per cent of Palestinians defended armed struggle against Israeli troops and 58 per cent approved of attacks against civilians (Human Rights Watch 2002*b*: 13–14). The lack of stronger popular support in the intermediate cases may explain their unwillingness to resort to SMs.[22]

Technological Costs

Arguments stressing the technological cost of a terrorist action would explain the absence of SMs by pointing to non-suicide actions that can produce the same result at a lower cost or a better result at the same cost. On this view, the act of suicide adds no intrinsic value to the mission beyond advantages in terms of technical efficiency that implementation may offer. In other words, this is a cost-related 'technological' explanation of SMs as a weapon of last resort. This would help us understand the Kamikaze episode from 1944 onwards, or maybe Hamas and PIJ given their difficulties in penetrating Israel—though this would hold only after 1991, when the Palestinians' freedom of movement was more restricted.

If this argument is correct, most organizations reject SMs because they can achieve their desired results without them. Note that this argument assumes that suicide is perceived to be a cost, which seems to be the case most of the time. It follows that organizations that rely on SMs cannot achieve similar results without suicides. The attack on the WTC is clearly an example of a mission that could not have been accomplished in the absence of suicide (in fact, terrorists had already tried and failed to blow the buildings up using a traditional method). Likewise, the Pentagon could have been attacked using non-suicide car or truck bombs only with great difficulty—and the same is true of the attacks against the US embassy and French and US marines in Beirut. As the former US Under-Secretary of State Lawrence Eagleburger pointed out in a congressional investigating committee about the 18 April 1983 bomb attack against the embassy, it 'was virtually impossible to defend against if the driver was prepared to commit suicide' (quoted in Jaber 1997: 76). The advantages of a human bomb were clear: 'not only would it bring large-scale destruction, but it would incur minimum losses and ensure that no clues were left behind' (Jaber 1997: 82).

It is also probably the case that some targets can be destroyed only with difficulty, if at all, by non-state actors in the absence of SMs. SMs could also be seen as the weapon of organizations that lack access to even basic weapons, which would be consistent with a number of Palestinian actions. The argument that is sometimes made by wagers of jihad—that SMs constitute an 'intelligent weapon' that can match Israel's superior arsenal—is of such a kind. Hezbollah explicitly says that SMs are justified because it does not possess Israel's weaponry (Saad-Ghorayeb 2002: 132–3). A Hezbollah volunteer for an SM remarked in an interview that the only difference between US and Hezbollah combatants is that Americans 'had at their disposal state-of-the-art and top-of-the-range means and weaponry to achieve their aims. We have the minimum basics, but that does not bother us because we know that if and when required we also have ourselves to sacrifice' (quoted in Jaber 1997: 92). A similar argument has been advanced about Palestinian SMs: 'A person wearing a bomb is far more dangerous and far more difficult to defend against than a timed device left to explode in the marketplace. This human weapons system can effect last-minute changes based on the ease of approach, the paucity or density of people, and the security measures in evidence' (Hoffman 2003: 42).[23] Such an argument would be consistent with the non-use of SMs by Palestinian factions against each other (even when they are willing to resort to violence in such factional struggles). At the same time, it is difficult to make the case that many SMs in Israel could not have achieved the same (or even a better) result with no suicides.

Besides the advantages of resorting to SMs in terms of efficiency, the added value of suicide flows from its psychological effects on friends and foes. Many forms of terrorism can be conceptualized as a war of attrition between the terrorist organization and the state (Sánchez-Cuenca 2001: ch. 3). In the absence of terrorism or other forms of insurgency, the state has a monopoly of violence. When a group challenges the state with violent means, this monopoly is broken and the situation becomes one of duopoly. In a war of attrition, two firms become involved in a price war that makes the extension of the conflict costly for both firms. The firm with the greater resistance wins the war and becomes the new monopolist. In the context of terrorism, each party tries to inflict as much pain as possible on its rival in order to expel it from the market for violence. In many cases (ETA, IRA, LTTE, Hamas, Hezbollah) the war of attrition focuses on control over a territory.[24] ETA wants Spain to withdraw from the Basque Country; IRA wants the British out of Northern Ireland; Hamas wants Israel out of the Occupied Territories, at least; and so on and so forth.

In a war of attrition it is important to signal resistance capacity. Apart from their efficacy, SMs could also have a somewhat more elusive signalling value. On the one hand, when an organization resorts to SMs it shows that it has large pool of potential volunteers. The organization will be willing to sacrifice the life of its members only if it is certain that it can reproduce itself despite wasting its own human capital. On the other hand, if members of the organization are ready to die, the organization's resolve is augmented. This may help to terrorize and weaken the resistance capacity of the population that suffers from SMs. Both effects—resolve and terror—stem from the same feature of SMs: people understand that suicide bombers cannot be deterred, that their willingness to die frees them from the constraints that the love of life imposes on the rest of humanity. Willingness to die, therefore, implies that the suicide bomber will do anything to pursue the organization's goal and this provokes fear or terror among the targets of the SMs. This may demoralize the enemy and ultimately it may lead the state to make substantive concessions to rebel organizations.

Obviously, not all forms of terrorism involve wars of attrition. Anarchist terrorism or al-Qaeda's attacks are not aimed at any obvious person or persons. They are rather aimed at raising consciousness, attracting attention, mobilizing supporters, or simply destroying the social order. Given that terrorism that does advance any cause involving national liberation has less clear goals, it is hard to identify the psychological impact of SMs, since terrorists are not offering to make the cessation of their activities conditional on certain state action, such as withdrawal from a territory. Probably, by launching SMs an organization is seeking the greatest possible publicity or to make itself attractive to potential extremist recruits. In this sense, SMs are compatible with several scenarios: an insurgent organization that is losing ground and wants to signal that it is not (for example, Chechen rebels); an international organization that cannot rely on a compact population base and needs different ways to market itself, so to speak, and attract recruits (for example, al-Qaeda); or an insurgent organization that cannot launch an insurgency or even rely on standard bombing techniques because of constraining factors such as population density or its opponent's enormous military superiority (for example, Hamas).

Individual Incentives

The cost of SMs is relative not only to the cost of other methods, but also to the availability of willing 'disposable' individuals. One could hypothesize that the smaller the organization, the lower is the likelihood that SMs would be adopted, either because the pool of possible members is small or the cost of recruitment is high. That would certainly explain cases such as the Red Brigades in Italy or Baader Meinhof in Germany,[25] whose membership was small and whose members' lives were accordingly highly valuable—though not the case of PIJ in the Palestinian occupied territories, a small organization that has resorted consistently to SMs.[26] However, these examples raise the broader issue of individual incentives, to which we now turn.

Certain organizations may be willing to resort to SMs but are unable to do so because of a lack of individual volunteers. In other words, organizational ability hinges on individual willingness to participate in SMs. Individuals may be willing or unwilling to participate in SMs. Figure 6.1 maps four possible outcomes.

An instance of outcome 3, the one that concerns us in this section, might be the FARC episode: the organization could not find a volunteer to crash the plane into the new president of Colombia. Individuals may decline to sacrifice themselves for the same reasons that organizations reject SMs (outcome 4): for instance, it may be possible to achieve the same results with a car bomb as with an SM. But what if the organization has decided that it should resort to SMs? Why would individuals refuse to commit suicide if such an action would further their cause?

From the evidence presented in this book, it seems clear that a belief in the afterlife is neither a necessary nor a sufficient motive to commit suicide: not necessary, because there have been cases of SMs in which such a belief was absent (Chapters 1 and 2, this volume), and not sufficient because Catholics in the IRA or in ETA have not participated in SMs. Yet this does not mean that religious beliefs and values are irrelevant to motivating individuals to commit suicide for a collective cause. They can contribute to persuading individuals that they must fulfil some obligation, that sacrifice for the cause is a worthy deed. However, such religious beliefs or values do not have to refer to the afterlife. Indeed, the whole idea of martyrdom can be expressed in secular terms, as attested by the anarchist movement. As Hobsbawm (1959: 163) argued, 'anarchists are chiefly interesting in that they show millenarianism wholly divorced from traditional religious forms, and indeed in a militantly atheist and anti-Christian shape.'

The motivations of anarchist terrorists were not so different from those of contemporary participants in SMs. It is true that cases of SMs were rare among anarchists (except in Russia), but quite often, after provoking a massacre or participating in a 'magnicide', the perpetrators did not try to

FIGURE 6.1.   Organizational choices given individual choices

		Individuals	
		Willing	Unwilling
Organizations	Willing	1	3
	Unwilling	2	4

escape, but waited to be arrested by police, knowing beforehand that they would certainly be executed. This is the case of Paulino Pallás, a Catalan anarchist tried in 1893 for the failed attempt to assassinate a general by throwing two bombs during a military parade (Núñez 1983: 52, 132). Pallás caused only injuries. Although he survived, he did not try to run away: he let the police arrest him and was executed that same year. Before his execution he sent a letter to the press in which he made clear his suicidal intention (the letter is reproduced in Núñez 1983: 200–4): 'There cannot be any doubt that I acted with the intention of dying, either being killed by the pieces of shrapnel that injured the general, or, in case of surviving, by the people who were around the general.' One of the reasons he did not escape was that he did not want to be mistaken for a criminal. Angiolillo, the Italian anarchist who travelled to Spain solely to kill Prime Minister Canovas del Castillo, in 1897, did not try to escape either; he was executed only twelve days after his action (Núñez 1983: 60). Carl Nobiling, a German anarchist, committed suicide after failing to kill Bismarck (Miller 1995: 40). Russian anarchists 'often chose to end their own lives with their last bullets rather than fall into the hands of the authorities' (Geifman 1993: 130). As Camus showed in *L'Homme révolté* (1951), anarchists and Russian revolutionaries embraced suicide because of its supposed redeeming effect. In fact, people who wanted to become members of the People's Will had to answer the following question: 'Are you prepared this instant to offer your life, your personal freedom and all you possess for the liberation of your country?' (von Borcke 1982: 57).

The language of martyrdom was strangely similar to that of Hezbollah or Hamas today. An anarchist article referred to the failed attempt to kill the Emperor of Germany in the following terms (quoted in Joll 1980: 107):

Humanity will preserve the memory of the tinsmith Hoedel, who was prepared to sacrifice his life to make a superb act of defiance against society, and, as his blood spurted beneath the executioner's axe, was able to inscribe his name on the long list of martyrs who have shown the people the way to a better future, towards the abolition of all economic and political slavery.

It seems, then, that the motivations for participation in SMs need not include a belief in afterlife. For instance, by substituting in the above quotation 'Allah' for 'Humanity' and 'the destruction of Western imperialism' for 'the abolition of all economic and political slavery', we have a proclamation that looks very much like those produced by Islamic fundamentalists after an SM. As Goldman (1911:86) remarked, 'it is among the Anarchists that we must look for the modern martyrs who pay for their faith with their blood, and who welcome death with a smile, because they believe, as truly as Christ did, that their martyrdom will redeem humanity.'

Yet, apart from the motivating force of these beliefs and attitudes, additional factors must be adduced in any convincing explanation of SMs. After all, why are such beliefs ascribed to in the first place? Why are they not present in all cases of rebellion or insurgency? Opportunity costs and objective conditions may help here. The following conditional hypothesis can be advanced: the worse the level of political repression and economic misery, the more likely it is that an organization will find volunteers for an SM. This hypothesis provides a necessary but not a sufficient condition. Obviously, it does not imply that individuals who participate in SMs must themselves be poor or miserable. The variation in the socio-demographic traits (except, perhaps, age) of the suicide bombers shows this very clearly (Jaber 1997: 90; Chapter 3, this volume).[27] What matters is not that the individual personally experiences political repression or economic deprivation but, rather, that the living conditions of the community are so grim and hopeless as to move people to extreme acts.

This hypothesis is consistent with the absence of SMs among rebel organizations operating in affluent societies. ETA is probably the terrorist organization that operates under the 'best' conditions, from both economic and political points of view (here we leave aside the extreme-left terrorism of the 1970s in Western Europe). The Basque Country is a wealthy region of Spain, with per capita income over the Spanish mean. Basque families have dominated the banking system in Spain for decades and the Basque economy is completely integrated with the rest of the country. The decentralization process, from which the Basque Country has benefited more than any other region, began in 1978 when the democratic constitution was approved; it has its own parliament, police, fiscal resources, education system (run in the Basque language), health system, public TV channels, and so forth. Except for defence, foreign relations, social security, and some secondary issues (like a Basque football team for European competitions), the Basque Country is almost a sovereign entity. There is no political oppression whatsoever, but ETA claims that only full national independence will bring about peace. Under these circumstances, it is no wonder that members of ETA have shown little inclination for heroic acts of self-sacrifice. Although they have tried to imitate Irish hunger strikes, they have systematically failed (Domínguez 1998a: 176–85). And it is possible to detect many attempts on their part to minimize the risks of being caught or killed by security forces, even if this means that the terrorists had to resort to tactics that were highly unpopular among their community of support.

It is well documented that ETA decided to use car bombs from 1985 onwards because the conditions under which terrorists operated had worsened considerably (Letamendía 1994: iii, 27, 100; Domínguez 1998b: 56). First, France started to cooperate with the Spanish government in the fight against ETA. Until 1984, members of ETA circulated without hindrance in the south of France, which was referred to as the terrorists' 'sanctuary'. Second, in those years the Spanish government was involved in 'dirty war' against ETA, making the lives of the terrorists much less secure, while the greater part of the leadership was arrested. ETA decided that car bombs carried fewer risks for the terrorists than shooting at the security forces.

In 1991 ETA placed a booby trap in the car of a policeman. The explosion killed his 2-year-old son. The outcry in society was universal. Even some imprisoned members of ETA complained about the killing of children. The authors of the attack provided the following explanation: 'We shouldn't unnecessarily risk the lives of our fighters which are a hundred times more valuable than the life of a *txakurra*'s son' (quoted in Domínguez 2002: 295) (*txakurra* means 'dog' in Basque and is the word commonly used by terrorists and their followers to refer to the Spanish police). Domínguez (2002: 299), an expert on ETA, concludes that 'members of ETA have never shown suicidal behaviour when preparing their attacks. The rule has been to act under maximum personal security and, when in doubt, not to act.'

The degree of repression and deprivation was higher in Northern Ireland than in the Basque Country. The Catholic community lived under worse economic conditions than the Protestants—a consequence, to some extent, of discriminatory practices (in the housing system, in access to civil service careers, and so on). Moreover, Catholics could not effectively voice their grievances in a political system that was clearly designed from the beginning to favour Protestants. This contrasts sharply with the Basque Country, where nationalists have been in the regional government since the first regional elections in 1981. Though we do not find SMs in the IRA case either, self-sacrifice and martyrdom are clearly evidenced in the hunger strike of 1981, when ten people, most of them members of the IRA along with a few members of the Irish National Liberation Army (INLA, an organization whose members had defected from the IRA), died of self-imposed starvation (Beresford 1987; Sands 1997). Hunger striking has a long tradition in Ireland (Sweeney 1993*b*), yet its effects are unclear. Some think that hunger strikes, like SMs, signal resolve and therefore induce fear in the enemy. Father Denis Faul, a priest involved in the campaign against the bad conditions under which republican prisoners lived, said that the Protestants 'couldn't understand it, it terrified them that these men were prepared to go so far' (quoted in Sharrock and Devenport 1997: 180). For others, the effects of hunger striking to death are different: it mobilizes supporters because it shows that terrorists' motivations are "pure" in the sense that "the cause" is more valuable than life itself (Beresford 1987: 38–9). Indeed, electoral support for Sinn Fein increased extraordinarily as a consequence of the 1981 hunger strike.

Whereas SMs are a kind of instrumental self-sacrifice, hunger striking is a more expressive form of self-sacrifice (see Chapter 5, this volume).

The life conditions of Shia Muslims in Lebanon, Palestinians in Israel, or Tamils in Sri Lanka are scarcely comparable to those of Basques in Spain or Catholics in Northern Ireland. Hezbollah was born among Shiites living in the slums of Beirut, reflecting not only the Iranian revolution in 1979 but also the Israeli occupation of south Lebanon in 1978, the presence of international troops, and the massacres of Palestinians and Shiites in the camps of Sabra and Chatila (Kramer 1994; Jaber 1997; on the conditions for Palestinians in Israel or for Tamils in Sri Lanka, see Chapters 2 and 3, this volume). Economic deprivation and political repression are not sufficient conditions for the formation of motives leading to SMs, as the Algerian case shows, but they may well be necessary ones. Individuals may well be ready to sacrifice their lives only if they consider that the cause is sufficiently urgent and important. This insight is consistent with recent cross-national research by Krueger (2003) which suggests that the extent of civil liberties, along with country size, are the only variables that predict whether a given country's population is more or less likely to take part in international terrorism.

A complementary (or potentially alternative) explanation to structural conditions revolves around revenge as an individual motive to participate in SMs. The act of vengeance may be aimed at the general repressive conditions—for instance, Israel's occupation of Palestinian territories. But revenge is more often specific than generic in the sense that some particular act by the enemy triggers emotions of anger that move the agent to seek vengeance. When a person acts from this motivation, political or religious interest is transmuted into passion (Elster 1999: 355). For example, the first Hamas SM in 1994 was a response to the killing of twenty-nine Palestinians by the Israeli settler Baruch Goldstein. Many other Hamas SMs have been acts of retaliation, provoked by the killing of the organization's leaders or Palestinian civilians. A hypothesis here would be that the more radicalized the conflict becomes, the stronger are the emotions that may lead to suicide as a form of vengeance. An empirical implication is that SMs should be absent from the initial stages of terrorist campaigns or from countries where the conflict causes few casualties among civilians and does not affect most people. The empirical record is mixed in this respect. In any case, revenge as an individual motivation has to be coupled with SMs as an organizational strategy to explain its translation into SMs.

The discussion has so far focused on the decision to undertake SMs. A distinct, but possibly related, discussion could focus on the factors that sustain the practice once a campaign of SMs has begun. A key mechanism in this respect, operating at both individual and organizational levels, is emulation. In so far as participation in SMs is advertised and celebrated, it may spawn a process of emulation among individuals. As a friend of a British volunteer who joined the Taliban in Afghanistan (and is now held in Guantánamo Bay) pointed out: 'He was fascinated by Arab suicide bombers. He talked about how brave they were and said he thought he had the guts to be one' (quoted in Lyall 2002: 14). There is an obvious possibility of SMs turning into some sort of fashion. However, this fact alone should not lead to a multiplication of SMs, for outcome 2 in Figure 6.1 (individuals willing and organizations unwilling) is likely to obtain. While it is possible that individuals may undertake SMs on their own, without organizational backing and planning, such actions are likely to remain marginal.

Another mechanism that would also make SMs self-sustaining at the individual level is the sense of posthumous obligation that the deaths of members of a group engenders among surviving members, who feel compelled to act in such a way as to make the demise of their companions meaningful. This simplifies the explanandum, which is reduced to encompass only the initial outbreak of SMs. The same effect emerges from situations of organizational fragmentation, in which the use of SMs may generate organizational competition and outbidding as long as it is perceived to signal boldness and is thought to attract recruits. All these mechanisms can be observed in the Palestinian case (Bloom 2004).

Conclusion

Hoffman (2003: 40) argues that 'the fundamental characteristics of suicide bombing, and its strong attraction for the terrorist organizations behind it, are universal: Suicide bombings are inexpensive and effective. They are less complicated and compromising than other kinds of terrorist operations. They guarantee media coverage. The suicide terrorist is the ultimate smart bomb.' If this is true, why do we not observe many more instances of SMs? For, even if SMs have multiplied recently, they remain a marginal phenomenon overall. This chapter suggests a number of reasons why insurgent organizations do not launch SMs.

On the one hand, SMs will not be carried out if members of the insurgent organization do not volunteer for such actions. In our view, understanding the willingness to participate in SMs requires an analysis of the level of political repression and economic misery rather than belief in the afterlife. Unless repression is great and/or the surrounding (rather than individual) economic deprivation severe, the proper motivations leading to participation in SMs are unlikely to emerge.

On the other hand, organizations may refrain from SMs, even if there are volunteers willing to die, because SMs lead to indiscriminate violence which is counterproductive, its potential supporters reject such methods and are likely to be alienated by their use, or organizations can achieve the same (or more desirable) results by other methods that are less costly than SMs. In addition, we have identified the set of organizations that appear most likely to resort to SMs, using a hypothesis positing a U-shaped relationship between strategy and support. Organizations that act independently of the community in whose name they act, such as nineteenth-century anarchists, and organizations that are firmly grounded in their community like Hamas or LTTE, may resort to extreme tactics, including SMs. In contrast, organizations that depend crucially on the support of some community but whose actual degree of support is weak, like ETA or IRA, face higher costs from launching SMs: they know that such extreme tactics will provoke a decrease in support and are, therefore, likely to refrain from them. The empirical implication of this argument is that most insurgent organizations enjoy intermediate levels of support.

Conversely, we are sceptical, mainly on methodological grounds, about arguments stressing the normative rejection of SMs, though we can see their merits; we have also rejected the hypothesis that organizations do not resort to SMs because they do not know about them. This last point suggests that we are unlikely to see a broad and sustained adoption of this method. Even if SMs were to become attractive or fashionable among dispossessed youth across the world, they are unlikely to be adopted by the great majority of organizations that use violence to further their political aims. If we are correct, the trend in suicide bombing that has been observed in the early years of the twenty-first century may be more of a temporary aberration than a sign of things to come.

7

Motivations and Beliefs in Suicide Missions

JON ELSTER

Why do people kill themselves for other reasons than that they do not want to live? The special case of why they engage in suicide bombings or (as on 11 September 2001) other modes of suicide missions (SMs) is the main topic of the present chapter. I shall also, however, consider some broader issues of politically motivated suicides.

To address the special case, we need a distinction between two levels of actors. At the first level are those who sacrifice their lives (the suicide attackers). At the second level are those who incite and enable them to do so (the organizers).[1] Unlike self-immolations, which are largely individual acts, SMs are rarely undertaken spontaneously but instigated or coordinated by religious or political leaders. The bus driver Abu Olbeh who on 14 February 2001 drove his bus into a crowd of soldiers in Azur (near Tel-Aviv), killing eight, was apparently not affiliated with or sponsored by any political faction, but nor was his act suicidal.

To make sense of these missions, we can adopt the usual explanatory machinery of the social sciences, the key elements being the *motivations* and *beliefs* of the actors, attackers, and organizers, and the *constraints* they face. We may also want to consider *skills* as an explanatory element. The reason skills are not usually cited in standard analyses of actions is that their presence or absence can be accounted for in terms of motivations and constraints. For some individuals, some skills may be out of reach even with the strongest motivation to acquire them and with unlimited resources (the blind cannot become trapeze artists). They are *directly* skill-constrained. Those who lack the resources that would enable them to acquire the skills are *indirectly* skill-constrained (poor families cannot afford pianos or piano lessons for their children). Those who fail to acquire the skills because they are insufficiently motivated are subject to short-run constraints (I cannot speak Russian) but not to long-term constraints (I could learn it).

Making a reliable bomb is difficult. Flying a large plane into the towers of the World Trade Center (WTC) is probably even more difficult. The latter task, however, has to be carried out by the suicide attackers themselves, a fact that provides the necessary motivation. The former task can be delegated more efficiently to an organization. Suicide bombers are subject to a short-run skill constraint that they have no motivation to overcome, just as I have no motivation to learn Russian in order to read books that I can read in translation. In the absence of an organizational provider, would-be suicide bombers could nevertheless learn how to make their own bombs. It is a somewhat puzzling or at least interesting fact that so far, and as far as we know, this behaviour ('outcome 2' in Chapter 6, this volume) has not been observed. One might think that the 'mental model' provided by other suicide attacks would have inspired some individuals to emulate them by acting on their own. A possible explanation, further pursued below, might lie in the unstable and ephemeral nature of the motivations.

In a broad historical perspective, both attackers and organizers were constrained by the lack of technology before Nobel's invention of dynamite in 1866 and the invention in the twentieth century of aircraft that could be used as flying bombs. Although this technical constraint no longer operates, financial constraints may have some importance. While the costs of making a bomb, about $150 (Atran 2003*c*: 1537), are affordable for individuals as well as organizations, even an organization might not be able to buy a jumbo jet. Following 9/11, new constraints on hijacking planes were created by intensified security measures. Security forces in countries subject to suicide bombings also try to reduce the number of opportunities for attacks, thus constraining organizers as well. As Kalyvas and Sánchez-Cuenca (Chapter 6, this volume) argue, citing the *Fuerzas Armadas Revolucionarias de Colombia* (FARC) as an example, the lack of individuals willing to carry out SMs can also be a constraint on organizers ('outcome 3' in Chapter 6, this volume). To summarize, organizers need opportunities (vulnerable targets), funds, skill (to make bombs), and volunteers, while attackers need opportunities and either destructive technology (bombs) or skill (to fly a plane).

In the rest of the chapter I focus exclusively on motivations (or desires) and beliefs, assuming that the skill and constraint requirements are satisfied. The best-known scheme for explaining action in terms of desires and beliefs is that of rational-choice theory. According to the standard version of that theory, agents choose the best means to realize stable desires, acting on beliefs that are well-grounded in information that is the outcome of an optimal search process.[2] The relevant beliefs are those that, for a given motivation, can make a difference for action: for example, beliefs about the feasible options and, for each of them, their likely consequences. The importance of this restriction will be seen shortly.

In itself, there is nothing irrational in the willingness to sacrifice one's life for a cause, and even less in the willingness to send others to their death for it.

Also, for reasons discussed below, suicide attackers are rarely subject to pathological or suicidal motivations. I shall argue, nevertheless, that in some cases suicide attacks fall short of being fully rational due to the instability of the underlying motivations. I shall also argue that some attackers are subject to irrational belief formation and that, moreover, these irrational beliefs contribute to the explanation of their actions. It does *not* follow, however, that these actions are irrational. The reason is that the causal effect of these irrational beliefs is to shape or reinforce motivations, not to influence the choice of means to implement a given motivation. Hitler's hatred of the Jews was based on his irrational belief that they were evil, but that belief did not prevent him from carrying out the Holocaust in a methodical and rational way. Intuitively, we might want to say that his motivations and hence his actions were irrational, but standard rational-choice theory does not allow such statements.

I shall draw heavily on other chapters in this volume as well as on some other sources. Let me briefly indicate the *ten cases* of suicide attacks to which I shall refer, together with some of the main sources. They are listed in descending order of centrality, as a function not of their intrinsic importance but of how much we (or I) know about them.

1. Palestine (Chapter 3, this volume).
2. The attacks on 11 September 2001 (Chapter 4, this volume).
3. Lebanon (Reuter 2002: ch. 4).
4. Japanese SMs (Chapter 1, this volume).
5. The Tamil Tigers (Chapter 2, this volume).
6. The Kurdistan Workers' Party (PKK) in Turkey (Ergil 2002).
7. Teenage martyrs in the Iraq–Iran war (Reuter 2002: ch. 5).
8. Chechnya (Reuter 2002: ch. 9).
9. Kashmir (Reuter 2002: ch. 9).
10. Iraq (current news reports, 2004).

Inevitably, the intensively studied SMs originating in the Middle East will dominate the discussion. While drawing on Ricolfi (Chapter 3, this volume), I have tried to avoid repeating his analyses, but some overlap remains. The other cases serve mainly as background and as support for various generalizations. In addition, I shall discuss some cases of politically motivated suicide behaviours that are not intended to cause the death of other individuals: self-immolation (Chapter 5, this volume) and hunger strikes (Reyes 1998). The discussion will be organized as follows. First, I offer a general discussion of politically motivated suicide. Second, I focus on the beliefs and motivations of the suicide attackers. Then I turn to the beliefs and goals of the organizers of these attacks. The final section is an attempt to summarize what we know and, especially, what we do not.

Politically Motivated Suicide

'In a true suicide attack, the terrorist knows full well that the attack *will not be executed* if he is not killed in the process' (Ganor 2002: 141). It is one and the same act that causes his death and the accomplishment of his goal. This is a narrow and clear definition, which is useful for many purposes. In some contexts, however, it would be pointless to exclude cases in which an act by the actor causes the accomplishment of the goal, which in turn triggers the act that kills him. For a Muslim militant in Kashmir it may simply be a question of efficiency considerations whether to run into an Indian military installation with a gun to shoot as many enemy soldiers as he can before he is killed or to drive into it with a truck loaded with explosives (Reuter 2002: 326).[3] When three Japanese killed twenty-four persons at Ben Gurion Airport in Tel Aviv on 30 May 1972, they not only expected but wanted to die, as shown by the fact that the one survivor tried to strike a deal with the authorities to give him a gun and a bullet in exchange for a full confession (Reuter 2002: 311–12).

Yet we might not want to include acts that will bring about the actor's death with a very high probability that falls short of absolute certainty. Because of the 'certainty effect' (Kahneman and Tversky 1979), certainty is *not* merely a limiting case of high probability.[4] The fact that the Japanese Kamikaze pilots could not 'realistically expect to survive the war' even under conditions of normal fighting, as Hill (Chapter 1, this volume) notes, does not imply that the decision to volunteer for Kamikaze missions was a matter of near indifference. On the contrary, Hill shows that it was clearly a momentous one. Thus one might question Biggs's statement (Chapter 5, this volume) that 'A potential motivation for suicide attacks is the calculation that death in combat is highly probable anyway, and so little is lost by volunteering for a suicide attack'.[5]

Suicidal acts for political purposes, including matters of public policy towards religion, form a much wider category than suicide attacks thus narrowly defined. Biggs (Chapter 5, this volume) surveys cases of *self-immolation by burning* for purposes that range from the instrumental to the reactive. As he shows, the self-immolations of Buddhist monks in the 1960s had the clear instrumental purpose of affecting the discrimination against Buddhism practised by the Catholic Vietnamese government at the time.[6] The self-immolation of Jan Palach in Czechoslovakia, too, was intended to mobilize opinion against the Soviet regime. Whereas such instrumental acts are forward-looking, reactive acts of self-immolation are backward-looking. They express the sorrow, disappointment, or frustration caused by some meaningful event. When Russian and West European sympathizers of the

PKK set themselves ablaze after their leader Ocalan's capture, it was because they felt 'indignant and defeated. He represented all they stood and hoped for' (Ergil 2002: 119). After Prime Minister Indira Gandhi was assassinated in 1984, several people either committed suicide or attempted suicide by self-immolation. Since acts of self-immolation are invariably committed in public, these expressive acts, too, seem to have an instrumental component, that is, the desire to make an impression on the audience.

Another widely used strategy is that of *hunger strikes*, mainly but not exclusively in prison populations. In the classification of Reyes (1998), one may distinguish between food refusers and hunger strikers proper. Within the former, there is a further distinction between those who refuse to eat in order to gain some advantage (such as a better cell) but have no intention of putting their health at risk, and quasi-suicidal individuals who essentially stop eating because they are depressed. Within hunger strikers proper, Reyes distinguishes between the determined and the not-so-determined. Whereas the former make a voluntary and autonomous decision to refuse food until their demands are met, the latter are often 'volunteered' by their fellow prisoners. The determined hunger striker is not suicidal, but he is willing to die for the cause. In the face of this motivation, prison authorities have two decisions to make: whether to accede to the demands and whether to force-feed the strikers.

In Ireland, a country with a long history of hunger strikes (Sweeney 1993), the British government's practice has varied in this respect. In 1909, political hunger strikers were force-fed by court order. In 1919, prisoners were re-leased when they announced a hunger strike. In 1981, the authorities refused to give in to the demands of republican prisoners in Northern Ireland while respecting the autonomy of their decision; as a result ten prisoners died. In the case of PKK, we observe suicide attacks, self-immolation, *and* hunger strikes. During Ocalan's leadership, the PKK carried out fifteen suicide bombings. After his capture, his followers reacted with hunger strikes as well as self-immolation. Prior to his capture, there had already been several waves of hunger strikes in Turkish prisons, leaving at least twelve prisoners dead. Outside the prison walls, the most famous instances were the fastings in India of Gandhi and his followers. Gandhi made it clear, however, that fastings were not to be used as threats. As Biggs (Chapter 5, this volume) notes, unlike self-immolations hunger strikes can in fact be brandished as threats.

In suicide attacks narrowly defined, as well as in self-immolation and determined hunger strikes, there is an *intention to die* since only actual death will produce the desired end. (In hunger strikes, the truth of this statement depends on the intransigence of the authorities.) When individuals in wartime volunteer for highly dangerous missions, what we observe is rather a *willingness to die*, which is obviously consistent with taking precautions against dying. The teenagers that Ayatollah Khomeini, the Iranian leader, sent to die in the Iraqi mine fields in the 1980s seem to have displayed an *eagerness to die*. For them, death was seen as benefit or bonus rather than as a cost to be accepted or a risk to be minimized. Below, I discuss whether this might also be the case of other suicide attackers. I also consider at some length the robustness or stability of this motivation.

The Suicide Attackers

Two issues need to be addressed. First, we need to identify the *reasons*—motivations and beliefs—of suicide attackers. Second, we have to look at the *causes* of these reasons. Resentment, for instance, is a cause rather than a reason. The desire for national liberation is a reason rather than a cause. I am not denying that in a general philosophical sense reasons also are causes. I am simply here using 'reasons' and 'causes' as terms of art for proximate and ultimate causes of action. Better, perhaps, we may view the causes as determinants of the *strength* of the reasons. I shall begin with the reasons and then move on to the causes.

Reasons

Consider first the motivations of suicide attackers. The immediate goal is usually easy to identify: to kill as many enemy civilians or soldiers as possible. (As noted in the next section, the organizers may have a different aim.) The hard question is how this goal can motivate the agent when it can be realized only at the expense of his or her own life.

Before I address this issue, let me note the importance of target selection. Hill (Chapter 1, this volume) mentions that a Kamikaze pilot wanted to cause the damage *himself* rather than merely stop the enemy from preventing another pilot from doing so. This rings true, for reasons related to the urgency of the motivation (see below). I also conjecture that for the same reason (and probably for other reasons too) it would be difficult to recruit volunteers for killing moderates in one's own camp or leaders of rival oppositional groups. The Tamil Tigers are an exception to this statement. Motivations related to target selection may also explain why the goal of most SMs has been to kill people rather than to create material damage. To give up one's own life must be psychologically easier when one knows that enemy lives will be destroyed at the same time than when the goal is to blow up an oil depot. Again there are exceptions: the Iranian teenage martyrs, the Tamil

Tigers, and possibly the attack on the WTC. Although the last proved to be unique in terms of human fatalities, material destruction, and symbolic damage, we do not know whether all these effects were equally firmly expected or which was the more motivating.

I want to begin with what I take to be a very robust claim: 'Most suicide bombers are normal, fearless people with strong convictions' (Ariel Merari, cited in Reuter 2002: 204). Although made about Palestinian suicide attackers, the claim probably has quite general validity. The willingness to lay down one's life for a cause depends on the strength of one's conviction. Nobody will or should think it a serious puzzle why people sometimes volunteer for war service, or lie about their age and disabilities to get into a situation that is quite likely to get them killed. To obtain or defend a national homeland is a cause that may seem as compelling as was the defence of democracy in the struggle against Hitler. Although there is, as I said, a gap between engaging in an operation with high probability of death and accepting one in which death is certain, the voluntary acceptance of either may have, as a necessary condition, a strong attachment to a cause larger than oneself.

I am not saying this is all there is to the matter, just as patriotism is hardly the dominant motivation for regular soldiers. To pursue the comparison, we may note Aristotle's observation that in battle most soldiers refrain from cowardly behaviour because of the fear of being punished by their superiors, whereas others are held in check by the shame they would feel before their peers. The good man, Aristotle suggests, is motivated neither by fear nor by shame but by the intrinsic goodness of the action (for references and discussion see Elster 1999: 70–2). The case of suicide attackers presents a partial analogue. Since they are drawn from a pool of volunteers, coercion and fear play a much smaller role in their motivation than in that of drafted soldiers. To be sure, Hill (Chapter 1, this volume) makes it clear that the Japanese Kamikaze pilots were to some extent 'volunteered by' their superiors. Also, there are claims that the Liberation Tigers of Tamil Eelam (LTTE) relies on forced recruitments to the Tamil Tigers. As Hopgood (Chapter 2, this volume) argues (citing Dagmar Hellmann-Rajanayagam), however, this idea is implausible. Forced recruitment is not compatible with the degree of commitment and self-discipline required by suicide attackers. Another matter is that, once a volunteer has been accepted by an organization that uses the method of SMs, he or she may he the subject of extreme pressure. Thus one PKK member who refused to carry out an SM was allegedly 'executed in front of another who was offered the "honor"' (Ergil 2002: 118). The sources for this statement may, however, be biased.

By all accounts, peer pressure is an important factor in generating and especially in sustaining the motivation of suicide attackers.[7] Hopgood

(Chapter 2, this volume) cites reports about 'psychological pressure' to join the LTTE, and Hill (Chapter 1, this volume) argues that a feeling of guilt (or shame?) towards other pilots was among the motivations for volunteering. Hill also notes that, to sustain the motivation, the presence of other pilots who escorted the Kamikaze pilots to the target may have prevented them from backsliding. Ricolfi (Chapter 3, this volume) observes that the clustering of Palestine suicide volunteers in a few towns suggests the importance of peer pressure or emulation. Descriptions of the rituals surrounding Palestinian SMs also emphasize the goal of building up a pressure that will make it unbearably shameful to change one's mind. A widely respected expert on this topic, Ariel Merari, testified before the US Congress that a

[C]ritical element in this training process is the creation of a point of no return.... In order to make sure that the person does not change his mind, the organization makes points of no return. These are achieved by making the candidate to write last letters to his family, to his friends. The person, the candidate, is being videotaped saying farewell, and from that point on the person in the case of Hamas and Islamic Jihad, Palestinian Islamic Jihad, the person is actually referred to in Arabic as al-shahid al-hai, which means the living martyr. The living martyr, meaning that he is already dead. He is only temporarily here with us.[8]

Palestinian suicide attackers are thus kept on a short leash by their handlers, who are ready to provide more or less subtle additional pressures in case the primary motivation should falter.[9] As Merari also states (*CBS News*, 25 May 2003), 'There is no return for [the suicide bomber] without really losing any self-respect, the respect of others.' Judging from a recent report from Iraq (*New York Times*, 25 February 2004), the suicide attackers operating there are also carefully monitored. One man, who was captured and disarmed because of his visible nervousness, said that 'for three days before his mission, he had been locked in a room with an Ansar mullah who had talked about Paradise and fed him a special soup that made him strong'. The mental state that actually triggers the act of detonating the bomb may therefore be ephemeral and something of an artefact rather than a stable feature of the person. When asked how well he thought he understood the state of mind of suicide attackers in the minutes before they died, Merari answered: 'Some of them were elated, apparently. Ecstatic, in the last moments' (*CBS News*, 25 May 2003.). Such trance-like states most likely do not spring from a stable motivational system.[10]

In this respect as in others (see below), the participants in the missions on 11 September 2001 are in a different category. They seem to have been on a very long leash, except if we view the leaders such as Mohamed Atta as *handlers* rather than mere executants (Darius Rejali, personal communication). As Holmes (Chapter 4, this volume) asserts, the mechanical rituals of the 9/11 attackers were indeed suited to 'induce a sort of trance'. The category of the handler, who mediates between the attackers and the organization, is somewhat elusive. If Atta was a handler, he was also willing to die together with his foot soldiers. Hill (Chapter 1, this volume) notes that some of the escort pilots for the Kamikazes resented their passive role and wanted to be allowed to participate in SMs too. Nothing seems to be known about the handlers in the Middle East.

The desire to contribute to the creation or defence of a homeland or to drive infidels out of the holy lands are *other-related motivations*. The suicide attacker will not be able to benefit from the mission, but the hope is that his kin or compatriots will. On a smaller scale, the material benefits that will accrue to the family of the suicide attacker may provide an other-related motivation.[11] The desire to avoid shame is also an other-related motivation. The suicide attacker is sustained by the fearful anticipation of what others will think of him if he fails. A further other-related motivation is the desire to be well thought of by others if he succeeds. In other chapters in the present volume, varieties of this motivation are referred to as 'vanity' (Biggs, Hill), desire for 'fame' (Ricolfi, Biggs), or the search for 'glory' (Hill, Biggs, Holmes, Ricolfi). The common denominator of these motivations is a desire to transcend death by living on in the grateful or admiring memory of others, a memory that constitutes, as it were, a *secular hereafter*. We know from other contexts that this desire can be a powerful motive indeed (Adair 1998), and one that may well be an important ingredient in the motivational mix of suicide attackers and of politically motivated suicide behaviours more generally. These are all other-related motivations that involve members of the suicide attacker's own group. He acts to benefit them, to avoid their blame, and to gather their praise, albeit posthumously.

A quite different other-related motivation, *revenge*, involves members of the enemy group. Many reports suggest that revenge for an Israeli killing of a friend or relative has been an important motive in many Palestinian SMs. Margalit (2003), for instance, writes that his 'distinct impression is that the main motive of many of the suicide bombers is revenge for acts committed by Israelis, a revenge that will be known and celebrated in the Islamic world'. Specific evidence about this motivation is provided by Ricolfi (Chapter 3, this volume). Similarly, many reports indicate the importance of personal revenge as a motivation for suicide attacks in Chechnya, where 'the rules of *Adat*, the traditional code of honor, is more important than religion. . . . Although suicide is seen as shameful, the shame can be turned into honor if it is a question of avenging family members who have been killed and lost their honor' (Reuter 2002: 337). A survivor of the Dubrovka theatre hostage-taking in Moscow reports that a 'Chechen women said that they came to die, to take revenge for their husbands and children who were killed in the

Chechen war. They said that they had nothing to lose in their lives. However, it seemed that male terrorists intended to leave' (*Pravda*, 1 November 2002).

Acts motivated by hatred of the enemy are not acts of revenge. Revenge, typically, is tit for tat.[12] Once revenge has been taken and the thirst of the gods has been slaked, there may be no further violence.[13] Hatred of the enemy can never be stilled, however, until he has been completely exterminated. If the attack on the WTC had been part of a private vendetta of Saddam Hussein against the Bush family, as was sometimes suggested at the time, one might have hoped that no further attacks would be forthcoming. If by contrast the attacks were motivated by abiding hatred, only an 'Endlösung'—the destruction of the West—could satisfy it. A third possibility is that the motivation was purely instrumental: to drive the Americans out of Saudi Arabia just as earlier suicide attacks had driven them out of Lebanon.

One motivation of the suicide attacker which would not seem to be other-related is the desire to reach the *religious hereafter*.[14] Are religious suicide bombers in fact motivated by the desire to attain paradise? Within the Christian tradition, this would essentially be a form of simony. According to the *Catholic Encyclopedia*,[15] 'Simony is usually defined as "a deliberate intention of buying or selling for a temporal price such things as are spiritual or annexed unto spirituals". While this definition only speaks of purchase and sale, any exchange of spiritual for temporal things is simoniacal.' Even doing good works for the sole purpose of achieving salvation would be simony, notwithstanding that doing good works (for the love and fear of God) may be a condition for salvation. Salvation, that is, is essentially a by-product of actions undertaken for other ends (Elster 1983: ch. 2). A parallel in Islam is that, although Sunni theologians 'perpetuated the veneration [of] the early martyrs of Islam . . . they nonetheless rigorously opposed the culti-vation of a contemporary cult of martyrdom in their respective societies by emphasizing the illegality of suicide and equating the seeking of a martyr's death with this' (Lawson 1995: 57). The Shiite tradition, though, is more favourable to such instrumentalization of martyrdom.

The Koran itself prescribes no unambiguous ban on suicide (Clarke 1995: 133; Reuter 2002: 246). The prophetic canon, by contrast, 'frequently, clearly, and absolutely prohibits suicide' (Clarke 1995: 133). As an oper-ational criterion, the tradition ruled that a necessary condition for martyr-dom was that of not having brought one's affairs in order before dying (Reuter 2002: 248). To have done so would show premeditation and thus suicidal or simoniacal intent. This criterion would obviously rule out those suicide attackers in the Muslim world who go through elaborate departure rituals before setting out on their mission. By and large, however, contem-porary Islamic theologians seem to emulate the Jesuits by showing how 'you can get around a given norm in perfectly legal ways' (Reuter 2002: 54). It is all a matter of 'directing one's intention' to one aspect of the behaviour rather than to another.[16] As a result of their teaching, the religious legitimacy of selfless suicide now seems to be quite widely accepted, although not uncontroversial.[17]

The religious legitimacy of suicidal intentions does not, however, imply that suicide attackers are *motivated* by the desire for (a privileged position in) the afterlife, in the sense that they would have abstained from SMs had they not believed that these would assure them salvation. But this standard might be too rigorous. I might do X because I believe it will bring about A and B, but not do X if I thought it would bring about only A or only B. A would-be suicide bomber might abstain from a mission if he thought it would bring about salvation without political gains or vice versa, but commit himself if both goals can be achieved. Here, we are obviously approaching or crossing the borders of what can be empirically verified. Let me only say that to me, at least, Reuter (2002: 26, 263) rings true when he asserts that religion is a form of consolation or a bonus rather than a motivation.[18] Like the knowledge that one's relatives will be financially taken care of after one is dead, the belief in some kind of afterlife may attenuate the psychological costs of commitment. As suggested by Diego Gambetta (personal communication), rather than offering a positive motivation the religious and financial expectations might have the disinhibitory effect of lifting some of the normative constraints against SMs.

Let me elaborate. If those who claim to be religious believers were as sure of the afterlife as they are that the sun will rise tomorrow, *and* if they thought they could get there by performing good actions, we would observe a vastly greater number of martyrs than we actually do. Before the fall of Communism, Christians from the West would have overrun the borders to the Soviet Union to spread the gospel, knowing that the worst that could happen was that eternal bliss would begin sooner rather than later. I conjecture that the small number of contemporary martyrs has less to do with the fear of committing simony than with the somewhat shadowy nature of most people's belief in the existence of an afterlife. That belief may serve, in fact, as a kind of consumption good rather than as a premise for action.[19] This is not to exclude the possibility that in some cases it may tip the balance by preventing backsliding, or that it may acquire an ephemeral reality in the last moments before the action.

The previous discussion has already raised the issue of the *beliefs* of the suicide attackers with regard to the existence of an afterlife and the means for reaching it. As for their secular beliefs, I assume these rely heavily on the statements of the sponsoring organizations. I shall say more about that issue in the next section. Here I only briefly note that a prominent feature of these statements seems to be a curiously dual assumption about the enemy.

On the one hand, Israel and Zionism more generally is seen as an overwhelmingly powerful and evil force in history. On the other hand, the maximalist rhetoric of several organizations presupposes that the Palestinian people can drive this omnipotent enemy from its land and into the Mediterranean Sea. For those two beliefs to be consistent, the Palestinians would have to be even more omnipotent, if that were not a contradiction in terms.

Causes

From reasons, let me turn to causes. What are the features of individuals and of the societies in which they live that could generate motivations of the required kind and, especially, of the required strength? Among the causal factors commonly cited are gender, youth, lack of family attachments, resentment, inferiority feelings, poverty, frustrated expectations, downward mobility, and illiteracy. To assess these claims, two questions must be addressed. First, are these factors actually present? Second, is there a plausible causal link from the factors to the motivations (and ultimately the behaviour) we want to understand?

Prior to 9/11, there was a widespread belief that the typical suicide bomber in the Middle East was a single young unemployed man, perhaps sexually starved (see n. 19), for whom a religious movement could fill a vacuum that would otherwise be occupied by family and work (Moghadam 2003: 76). Then overnight, following the attack on the WTC, experts on terrorism decided that they had to 'rewrite the book' (Ehud Sprinzak, cited in *New York Times*, 15 September 2001, Section A, p. 2). Even before then, however, the frequent if oscillating deployment of female suicide bombers (Chapter 3, this volume) should have led scholars to question this stereotype. In the recent Palestinian Intifada, the use of female suicide bombers, some of them mothers or highly educated, is even more striking. Even if teenage hormones may partially explain the suicidal activists in Khomeini's war on Iraq, arguably the greatest self-sacrifice in history (Reuter 2002: 61), this cliché seems otherwise to have little explanatory power. Moreover, to the extent that there is a preponderance of unattached males it may be due to a selection effect. One Palestinian leader said, for instance, that the recruit should 'not be an only child, or the head of a family' (Moghadam 2003: 83).[20] Also, 'If two brothers ask to join in, one is turned away' (Hassan 2001*b*). Recently, though, the head-of-family constraint seems to have become weaker.

The factors of poverty and illiteracy also seem to have limited causal efficacy, at least as features of the individual suicide attackers. Among Palestinian suicide bombers, income and education tend in fact to be higher than in the general population (Chapter 3, this volume). Yet this finding does not exclude the causal efficacy of poverty and illiteracy at the population level. To see why, we may note that the founders of Marxism, coming themselves from the upper bourgeoisie, were directly motivated by the poverty they could see around them. Some writers on the topic seem to confuse the two levels, either using the well-off status of suicide bombers as evidence for the irrelevance of poverty[21] or citing the prevalence of poverty in the affected region to refute the claim that terrorists come from an affluent background.[22] It seems quite plausible, however, that *ceteris paribus* suicide attacks are both more likely to occur in poor and illiterate societies and more likely to be carried out by the better-off and most educated members of those societies. In addition, there could be a selection effect: leaders may prefer educated individuals who can more easily fit into a foreign environment and not, for instance, be given away by their local dialect (Krueger and Maleckova 2002).

Explanations in terms of poverty are also unsatisfying because it is not clear how poverty would generate the required motivation. In one common view, the gains from blowing oneself up have to be weighed against the cost of blowing oneself up—one's life. If life is not highly valued, the cost is less. According to this approach, a life in misery and poverty is worth so little to the individual that the costs of suicide become negligible. I am sceptical about this argument, since I think that poor people find their lives as worth living as anyone else. That people adjust their aspirations to their circumstances so that they maintain a more or less constant level of satisfaction is a pretty well-established psychological finding (Frederick and Loewenstein 1999). A more plausible factor than absolute deprivation is the gap between expectations and reality experienced by the many educated Palestinians who are now without any prospect of decent employment. Downward social mobility, an element stressed by Holmes (Chapter 4, this volume), could have the same effect.

The most relevant feature of the populations from which suicide bombers are drawn, at least in the Middle East and in Sri Lanka, seems to be permanent feelings of *inferiority* and *resentment*, the former emotion being based on comparison and the latter on interaction (Elster 1999: ch. III). On the participants in the 9/11 mission, Holmes (Chapter 4, this volume) conjectures that they were motivated in part by the 'bruising loss of status and prestige' they experienced when transplanted to the west European context. Their destructive urge, he also suggests, was 'intensified by envy of America's prosperity and power'. Most writers on the Palestinian suicide bombers emphasize the intense resentment caused by the daily humiliations that occur in interaction with the Israeli forces. Beyond the degrading checks and controls to which the Palestinians are subject, there is also their awareness that many Israelis think all Arabs 'lazy, cowardly, and cruel', as a Jerusalem taxi driver said to me almost twenty years ago. This deep-seated and widespread stereotype has ancient roots (Morris 2001: 42–5). For the

Palestinians, the perception that the Israelis view them as inferior must be doubly unsettling since under Ottoman rule the Jews were at the bottom of the social hierarchy (Morris 2001: 47). As Petersen (2002) has brought out, with special reference to the Jews of Central and Eastern Europe, reversal of status hierarchies is a very potent source of resentment.

Interaction-based emotions tend to be stronger than comparison-based ones (Elster 1999: 143). Envy of the United States' power will not provide the same multiplicator of the willingness to die as does the resentment of humiliation at the hands of the Israelis. The motivation of the participants in the attack on the WTC is in fact harder to fathom than that of the Intifada suicide attackers. The multiplicandum may have been larger, but what was it? Holmes (Chapter 4, this volume) explores, with an appropriate mix of boldness and caution, some of the complex psychic mechanisms that may have been at work in the 9/11 attackers. He makes a good argument that in their case religious motives may have been decisive, while also noting that for the time being we do not have the evidence that would enable us to reach any definite conclusions. In a later section I suggest that the difficulty may lie even deeper.

The Organizers

I shall now consider the motivations and beliefs we can impute to those who organize SMs. A prior question, however, is whether the imputation of motivations and beliefs to supra-individual actors such as organizations is at all meaningful, an issue that is especially acute when (as in the case of al-Qaeda) we are uncertain whether we are really dealing with an organization at all or with something more like a franchise. Aggregation issues and free-rider problems make it very problematic to apply individual-level categories to collective actors. In the case of organizations run on dictatorial lines such as the PKK or the LTTE this difficulty does not arise, but in organizations with internal factional struggles such as the Palestinian al-Fatah it can be quite intractable. Thus, when we consider the multiplicity of goals imputed to the organizers we may simply be dealing with the goals of different factions. Specific events may be explained by the motives of the faction or the individuals momentarily in ascendancy rather than by the (perhaps non-existent) goals of 'the organization'.

Motivations

Most of the organizations are defined by a stated official goal, which can be territorial, religious, or both. As we shall see shortly, their behaviour may also be due to other goals that bear a rather indirect relation to the official goal. Let me begin, nevertheless, by surveying the official goals and how SMs might be a means to their realization. Although these goals are often stated as being non-negotiable, this assertion may be merely a standard negotiating ploy. The LTTE is fighting for an independent state, and the Turkish PKK for a larger Kurdistan that would include all Kurds in the Middle East. Yet it is hard to know whether these maximalist claims are as non-negotiable as the organizations routinely claim them to be or whether they might accept a federalist solution. Although the official goal of the Palestinian Hamas and of Palestinian Islamic Jihad (PIJ) is to eliminate the state of Israel, the organizations might still come to accept a compromise (Mishal and Sela 2000: ch. 6).

Organizations making only territorial demands focus on the recovery of a homeland from the enemy (the PKK, the LTTE, al-Fatah), the defence of the homeland (the rationale of the Japanese Kamikaze missions), and the expulsion of occupying forces from the national territory (Iraq, Lebanon). Note the difference between the demand for *part* of the national territory that is made by the PKK, the LTTE, and al-Fatah, and the demand for *all* of it that is made by other Palestinian organizations.

Organizations making only religious demands focus on the defence of the holy sites of Islam, notably in Saudi Arabia and in Palestine, and more conjecturally on the destruction of the infidels. As far as we can understand, al-Qaeda seems to have purely or mainly religious motives. In Iraq, it is unclear whether the suicide attacks on 2 March 2004 against Shiite worshippers were carried out by Sunni extremists acting from religious motives or by groups trying to undermine the US occupation by triggering a civil war.

Organizations making both territorial and religious demands now include all organizations that sponsor suicide bombings in the Middle East (except al-Fatah), in Kashmir, and in Chechnya. Even the traditionally secular Popular Front for the Liberation of Palestine (PFLP) has begun to use religious language. The exact nature of the marriage between religion and nationalism remains unclear, at least to me. Israeli nationalism can be justified in religious terms, but there is no book holding out the promised land to the Palestinians. Although the al-Aqsa mosque is one of the holy sites of Islam, no Palestinian organization limits its goals to the recuperation of this place. There may simply be a tendency for any civil war in which Muslims are involved on one side to be transformed into a holy war (Reuter 2002: 369).

The officially stated connection between the official goal and the SMs is simple: they are intended to put intolerable pressure on the enemy until territorial or religious demands are granted or hostile intentions defeated. To create this pressure, the missions may use either focused attacks on military targets and civilian elites or random attacks on the population at large.

The Kamikaze attacks had a narrow military focus, as had the use of youngsters to trigger land mines in the Iraq–Iran war, the SMs of the LTTE, the Iran- and Syria-sponsored attacks on French, US, and Israeli military targets in Lebanon, and the suicide attacks in Kashmir and Chechnya. The targets have been enemy military forces, except for the LTTE, which has also sought to inflict material damage.

The purpose of targeting civilian elites could be twofold. On the one hand, the intention could be to weaken the regime by deterring individuals from taking up positions of responsibility. The PKK mainly used 'selective violence against official targets', although after the arrest of its leader it briefly engaged in 'indiscriminate terrorism for the sake of vengeance' (Ergil 2002: 123). At the time of writing (March 2004), we also observe SMs targeting Iraqis who collaborate with the US occupying forces. On the other hand, the purpose could be to persuade top officials that they or their families are personally at risk unless they change their policies.[23] This conjecture might explain an otherwise puzzling feature of al-Qaeda behaviour or, as I shall argue, non-behaviour. It is a striking fact that there has not been a single 'ordinary' SM on American soil, in spite of the ease with which it could have been organized. If the main goal of the leadership of al-Qaeda had been to strike terror in the US public, it could easily (I assume) have organized ten simultaneous suicide bombings in US shopping centres or subway stations. Instead, its preferred mode of action in the United States has been to strike at highly visible symbols of US wealth and power. The 9/11 attacks did, to be sure, instil terror, but the lack of follow-up actions suggests that this may not have been their main purpose.[24] Other possible intentions include humiliating the United States, mobilizing and recruiting al-Qaeda supporters, and deterring US leaders who might be concerned about their personal security.

The use of random or indiscriminate violence against enemy civilian populations is unique to the Palestine organizations and al-Qaeda. If my conjecture about the motives of the latter is correct, we can focus on the former. It is far from clear how the indiscriminate suicide killings are supposed to serve the official goal, harboured by some of them, of the destruction of the state of Israel. Pape (2003: 353) argues that 'Although Hamas objected to surrendering claims to all of historic Palestine, it did value the West Bank and Gaza as intermediate objectives, and certainly had no objection to obtaining this goal sooner rather than later'. Yet whereas there is a conceivable account (Pape offers one) of how suicide attacks could lead to the realization of these limited territorial goals, I cannot imagine any mechanism by which they could lead to the ultimate capitulation or destruction of the Israeli state.

Let me refer to the use of SMs to impose so much material and psychological damage on the enemy that it prefers making limited concessions rather than sustaining more damage as *deterrence*.[25] This strategy worked against the United States, France, and Israel in Lebanon, and seems to have had substantial success in Sri Lanka. Pape (2003) argues that the Hamas suicide attacks in 1994 and 1995 made the Israelis speed up their withdrawal from the Occupied Territories. Although I am not persuaded by his argument, which rests exclusively on ambiguous statements by the then Prime Minister Rabin and self-serving statements by Hamas spokesmen, the mechanism is not intrinsically implausible. In any case, it seems very doubtful that deterrence is the full explanation of the bulk of the many SMs that have taken place in Palestine since 1993. In the light of the available evidence, at least *four other mechanisms* seem to have been at work: sabotage, overbidding, provocation, and retaliation. Their relative importance at any given moment and over time depends on Israeli policies and on power struggles in and among the Palestinian organizations.

Sabotage occurs when an extremist organization with maximalist goals launches a wave of SMs to break up ongoing negotiations between the Israeli government and a moderate grouping. Kydd and Walter (2002) make a good case for the importance of this 'spoiler strategy'. I believe they go too far, however, when they argue that their game-theoretical model of 'sabotaging peace' is consistent with the entire pattern of events from October 1993 to October 1998. They do not mention that two of the four spikes in suicide attacks, in 1994 and in 1996, were probably direct retaliations for, respectively, the massacre committed by Baruch Goldstein and the killing of a master Palestinian bomb-maker. Also, as Ricolfi (Chapter 3, this volume) points out, the 1993 cut-off point leaves unexplained the fact that Hamas already organized intensive suicide attacks in 1992, before the Oslo agreement.

Overbidding occurs when an organization initiates or escalates suicide bombings to gain an ascendancy over other organizations (Bloom 2004). Here the target audience is not the Israeli government but the Palestinian population. The emergence of al-Fatah's al-Aqsa martyr brigades, for instance, was a direct response to the perceived success of Hamas. Rivalry among Palestinian organizations is also shown by the many cases in which several organizations lay competing claims of responsibility for the same attack (Human Rights Watch 2002a).[26]

Retaliation (not to be confused with revenge) seems to be a common motive for suicide bombings. When the Israelis kill a leading figure in a Palestinian movement, the latter is often compelled to retaliate to maintain internal loyalty and cohesion (Crenshaw 2002: 25). Not to retaliate against a 'targeted killing' of a leader or a bomb-maker would be perceived as tantamount to capitulation (Reuter 2002: 234, 367) and might trigger member defection to another organization. The Israeli side, too, tends to retaliate against increases in the level of Palestinian terrorism, but there is an asymmetry between the two parties. Massive retaliation by the Israelis is regularly perceived by world opinion as overreacting, and often triggers statements of condemnation even by actors normally friendly towards Israel.

Provocation relies precisely on the predictable tendency of Israel to respond in ways that will be perceived as overreaction. Here the target audience is not the Israeli government but world opinion. By contrast, I have not seen it credibly suggested that Israeli crackdowns could be motivated by the intention to provoke the Palestinians into overreacting. Whereas Israel does care about world (especially US) opinion, the Palestinian organizations care more about the opinions of their own constituencies, which have been largely supportive of random killings of Israeli civilians (Krueger and Maleckova 2002; Ricolfi, Chapter 3, this volume).

Beliefs

Consider now questions of organizational beliefs, to the extent they can be inferred from statements and behaviour. I shall limit myself to the two sets of beliefs I identified earlier, concerning (a) the evil omnipotence of Zionism and the Israeli state and (b) the Palestinian capacity to defeat the same state. In addition, I shall discuss the importance of mental models in the adoption of the SM strategy.

There is evidence that both the ordinary citizens from whom the suicide bombers are recruited and the political leaders of the factions that organize them share a conspiratorial and paranoid theory of history that makes dialogue and argument very difficult. In the classic statement by Hofstadter (1964: 36), 'the paranoid mentality is far more coherent than the real world, since it leaves no room for mistakes, failures, or ambiguities. It is, if not wholly rational, at least intensely rationalistic; it believes it is up against an enemy who is as infallibly rational as he is totally evil'. Reuter (2002: ch. 7) provides extensive evidence for such beliefs among citizens and leaders in the Muslim world. He cites, for instance, the leader of one of the largest Koran schools in Pakistan, referring to the claim that bin Laden was behind the 9/11 attacks as an 'American-Jewish-Indian conspiracy' (Reuter 2002: 273). Equally hallucinatory, and probably more consequential, is Article 22 from the Charter of Hamas:

For a long time, the enemies have been planning, skillfully and with precision, for the achievement of what they have attained. They took into consideration the causes affecting the current of events. They strived to amass great and substantive material wealth which they devoted to the realisation of their dream. With their money, they took control of the world media, news agencies, the press, publishing houses, broadcasting stations, and others. With their money they stirred revolutions in various parts of the world with the purpose of achieving their interests and reaping the fruit therein.

They were behind the French Revolution, the Communist revolution and most of the revolutions we heard and hear about, here and there. With their money they formed secret societies, such as Freemasons, Rotary Clubs, the Lions and others in different parts of the world for the purpose of sabotaging societies and achieving Zionist interests. With their money they were able to control imperialistic countries and instigate them to colonize many countries in order to enable them to exploit their resources and spread corruption there.

You may speak as much as you want about regional and world wars. They were behind World War I, when they were able to destroy the Islamic Caliphate, making financial gains and controlling resources. They obtained the Balfour Declaration, formed the League of Nations through which they could rule the world. They were behind World War II, through which they made huge financial gains by trading in armaments, and paved the way for the establishment of their state. It was they who instigated the replacement of the League of Nations with the United Nations and the Security Council to enable them to rule the world through them. There is no war going on anywhere, without having their finger in it.

It is easy to imagine how such beliefs can interact with the daily experience of humiliation to intensify emotional reactions. We may pause to note, however, that this idea of the Jews as long-standing oppressors is hard to square with the idea of Jews as a formerly oppressed people, with resentment being sparked when the status hierarchy is reversed. I do not know which idea is the dominant one. It seems plausible, however, that the general public in the Middle East sincerely believes in the existence of a Zionist conspiracy (Pipes 1998: 225). Whether the political elites share this view, or merely propagate it for manipulative purposes, is harder to tell (Pipes 1998: ch. 11). The manipulation theory would be consistent with the hypothesis that, unlike the population at large, the leadership is quite aware that a status reversal has taken place.

The conspiratorial frame of mind is irreducibly irrational. It is resistant to contrary evidence, which it can always twist around to make it appear as supporting the conspiracy theory, and it cares little about internal contradictions. If the theory serves as a cognitive premise for actions that would not have been undertaken had the actor not believed it to be true, these actions themselves are equally irrational. As far as I can see, however, the conspiracy theory does *not* serve as a cognitive premise for SMs. It does not include beliefs about options, constraints, or means–ends relationships that would make a rational difference for behaviour. Yet the theory, assuming it to be sincerely held, could affect behaviour by another causal pathway. If, as I suggested, the conspiracy theory interacts with the daily experience of humiliation, it might strengthen feelings of resentment to the point of bringing about a willingness to sacrifice one's life that would not have been produced by the belief that one is dealing with a more ordinary enemy. In standard rational-choice theory, this would not make the suicidal *actions* irrational. Yet it would still be true (a) that suicide *attackers* are irrational and (b) that they would not have opted for SMs had they been rational.

The other key element in the belief systems of Palestinian leaders and activists concerns the efficacy of SMs. Judging from behaviour, one might be tempted to infer that the more extremist groups actually believe that these missions, combined with other forms of attack, will ultimately bring about the maximalist goal, the elimination of the state of Israel. This belief could explain both the refusal—assuming it to be to genuine rather than a bargaining ploy—to engage in negotiations for a limited territorial solution and the persistence of suicide bombings. It is also, of course, utterly unrealistic and hardly consistent with the delusions about Israeli omnipotence. It is hard to believe that anyone would hold it, but easier to believe that the rank and file could entertain it more than that the leaders could. For the suicide attacker, the belief that the sacrifice might help bring about a Palestinian state 'from the river to the sea' would clearly be very attractive. Like belief in the afterlife, it might serve to bolster and support his resolve rather than serve as a causally efficacious premise.

I need not dwell on the speculative nature of the preceding remarks. Even if they are accepted, it remains to explain the behaviour of the leaders, on the assumption that they have a more realistic view of the situation. One interpretation is that they use strategies of deterrence, sabotage, overbidding, retaliation, and provocation for the purpose of obtaining the best feasible settlement, while using paranoid and maximalist language to motivate the rank and file. Another is that they are motivated mainly by the desire to stay in power, at the expense of their rivals, while again using inflammatory rhetoric in which they do not believe. These are two versions of what Holmes (Chapter 4, this volume) calls 'the Voltaire thesis'. Referring to the al-Qaeda leaders, he notes that their isolation and lack of reality checks makes it somewhat credible that they are as deluded as those whom they send to their deaths. As the fierce in-fighting of the Palestinian struggle may have made even the fundamentalist religious leaders in the region somewhat more subject to reality checks, the Voltaire thesis may apply better to them.

In explaining the adoption of the SM strategy by the organizations discussed in the present volume, we may appeal to another cognitive factor that I shall refer to as *mental models*.[27] To deploy the SM strategy in its modern form, which aims at large numbers of enemy deaths in exchange for the life of the suicide attacker, somebody first had to *think* of it. The inventions of explosives and of aircraft that could be used as guided bombs were a necessary condition for the idea to enter anyone's mind. If they had been a sufficient condition, we would have expected SMs to appear earlier and more widely than they in fact did. Somebody had to *do* it first, to provide a mental model that others could imitate. As far as I can see, the early use of this strategy by the Kamikaze pilots did not find any direct imitators.[28] The idea was reinvented independently by Iran during the war with Iraq, and spread from Iran to Lebanon (Reuter 2002: 94). From Lebanon it diffused possibly to the LTTE (Swamy 2001: 102) and later to Palestine, Kashmir, al-Qaeda, Chechnya, and now Iraq. The PKK seems to have been influenced by the LTTE (Reuter 2002: 356), which it also resembles in many other respects (secular ideology, selective targeting, dictatorial leader, widespread use of female suicide attackers).

The transfer from Iran to Lebanon and from Lebanon to Sri Lanka and Palestine involved more than just a mental model. More than a thousand Iranian revolutionary guards were operating in Lebanon in the early 1980s (Reuter 2002: 94), whereas Tamil Tigers were actually trained in Lebanon (Swamy 2001: 97–102). The Hamas operatives who introduced suicide bombing to Israel were among the 415 Palestinians deported to Lebanon in 1992, where they established fruitful contacts with Hezbollah.

The importance of mental models in ordinary suicide behaviour has often been noted (Wasserman 1984; Jamison 1999: 277–80). Biggs (Chapter 5, this volume) provides a specific set of examples. In his cases, no technical break-through was needed. Nor was training required: self-immolation is easy. Nor is there any learning effect: one does not need to see others burning them-selves to understand that it is likely to have an impact. What seems to happen is that, following one person's self-immolation, other people begin to see it as a realistic option rather than merely a conceivable alternative. That this happens seems clear. How it happens, I do not understand. The diffusion of the suicide bombing strategy is certainly more complex, but the basic mechanism (whatever it is) could be similar. At the level of the leaders the mental model may have caused them to take seriously the idea of recruiting suicide attackers, and for the recruits the model could have made the idea seem acceptable.

I conclude with some additional remarks on the relationship between the organization and the suicide attackers. The actual composition of the group of suicide attackers probably owes something to selection effects. Those who actually carry out the missions may differ in a number of respects from those who volunteer to do so. In addition to screening for family status and education, we may expect the organizers to try to eliminate those who have suicidal tendencies. As Hopgood (Chapter 2, this volume) and Ricolfi (Chapter 3, this volume) note, this is indeed what we observe. The main reason, I conjecture, is that suicidal types are less efficient, notably because they are incapable of *waiting* for the optimal target to come into sight. The decision to take one's life is, under any circumstances, a momentous one which is likely to trigger extremely strong emotions. One characteristic feature of the emotions is the *urgency* they lend to the corresponding action tendencies (Elster 2004*a*), thus inducing a preference for earlier action over later action (not to be confused with the phenomenon of time-discounting, which involves a preference for earlier reward over later reward). To resist this tendency, a stable and strong personality is needed.[29]

The importance as well as the difficulty of waiting is emphasized in much of the literature on SMs. Hill (Chapter 1, this volume) notes that 'the first rule of the Kamikaze was that they should not be too hasty to die'. He cites one pilot to the effect that the stress of waiting was 'unbearable'. Hopgood (Chapter 2, this volume) writes that, in the training of the Tamil Tigers, 'mental preparation [is] essential if one is to return to a regular unit . . . and wait to be called for a mission perhaps some time ahead'. Holmes (Chapter 4, this volume) observes that the 9/11 attackers 'were not simply zealots, but disciplined zealots, capable of patience'. Hassan (2001*b*) cites the praise for a suicide bomber offered by the father of his co-attacker: 'Even after Salah saw my son ripped to shreds, he did not flinch. He waited before exploding himself, in order to cause additional deaths.'

One can draw a parallel between suicide bombing and the use of torture. Whereas suicide bombing is the ultimate insurgency technique, torture is the ultimate counter-insurgency method. Although some insurgency groups practise torture, it is more frequently practised by governments. In both cases, individuals are being asked to perform extraordinary acts: killing themselves and deliberately inflicting pain on another human being. I conjecture that for this reason torture, no less than suicide bombing, requires volunteers. In both cases, an organization must take the decision to engage in the practice before asking for volunteers. In both cases, the set of agents who engage in these acts are the joint result of selection and self-selection. In both cases, the organization tries to weed out types who would spontaneously perform the acts in question: suicidal individuals (see above) and sadistic ones (Arendt 1994: 105), respectively. In both cases, a plausible reason for rejecting such individuals is that they are typically less efficient than others (a problem of adverse selection). Suicidal types might blow themselves up prematurely, and sadistic types might kill the tortured individual before he or she talks. In both cases, the organization would prefer individuals who are indifferent to respectively their own deaths and the pain of others. If they have a positive preference for these outcomes, they may be inefficient, as just noted. If they have a negative attitude, they might be reluctant to volunteer.

As I argued earlier, suicide attackers are likely to have a very focused motivation: to take as many enemy lives as possible. For them, this is the main benefit that justifies the high cost of their action, namely, their death. The organizers may have a different perspective. For one thing, if the supply of volunteers is limitless, as was the case in the Iran–Iraq war and in the second Palestinian Intifada, it is less important to ensure that each of them performs with maximal efficiency. By contrast, the Hezbollah attacks were constrained by limited supply and hence put greater weight on efficiency (Reuter 2002: 104), thus making the aims of attackers and of organizers converge.

For another thing, efficiency may be redefined to include symbolic values as well as the number of enemies killed. For the organizers, the death of the attackers may represent a benefit rather than a cost by symbolizing the strength of commitment to the movement. Martyrdom is crucial for the legitimacy of the movement (Crenshaw 2002: 26). Attacks are valued as a symbol of resistance and as a signal that 'we will rather die than accept a compromise'. For Khomeini, the Iranian teenagers' willingness to die was more important than their military significance (Reuter 2002: 76). Ricolfi (Chapter 3, this volume) draws the conclusion that, from the point of view of the organizers, the *maximal* number of enemy deaths may not be the *optimal* one. The more spectacular operations may be less effective overall, since they focus attention on the victims rather than on the martyrs.

The symbolic or intrinsic value of the death of a person who takes his or her life for political ends can be measured by the strength of commitment it requires, as revealed for instance by the size of the sacrifice involved. Thus, the political suicide of a healthy person, who has more to lose by dying than a sick one, has greater symbolic value. The instrumental value of the death is measured in most cases by the number of enemies that are killed. The relevant first- and second-order actors can order or weigh intrinsic and instrumental values in three ways: by giving absolute priority to the former, by giving absolute priority to the latter, and by allowing trade-offs between them.

The Buddhist self-immolations have only intrinsic value.[30] For the Buddhist, the optimal number of deaths in addition to his or her own is zero. For an efficiency-oriented organization such as the LTTE or Hezbollah, a suicide attack can be justified only by its instrumental value. For a given number of victims, the optimal number of martyrs is the minimal one; for a given number of martyrs, the optimal number of victims is the maximal one. If martyrdom has an intrinsic value, it is essentially a by-product of its instrumental value (see Reuter 2002: 111).[31] Ricolfi's argument (Chapter 3, this volume) is that, in the second Intifada, the organizers trade-off intrinsic and instrumental values—the number of martyrs and the number of victims— against one another. My suggestion is that the suicide attackers themselves, for intelligible psychological reasons, place a greater and perhaps exclusive weight on the instrumental efficacy of their action. Although the phenomenon of self-immolation shows that intrinsic value can be strongly motivating, I believe that the Palestinian suicide attacks are so strongly motivated by negative emotions against the Israelis that their destruction becomes the principal aim.

Conclusion: An Enigma Wrapped in a Puzzle

The innermost layer in the suicide attacks consists of the beliefs and motivations of the attackers. Many suggestions have been made concerning the objects of these attitudes. Some of them are discussed in the present chapter and elsewhere in this volume. Although some are more plausible than others, we may not ever know the exact motivational and cognitive states of the suicide attackers for the simple reason that (to some extent at least) *there is no fact of the matter*. Hill (Chapter 1, this volume) describes the inability of one Kamikaze pilot to decide 'whether his relief [at being ordered to abort a mission was] indicative of cowardice or of rationality' and similarly whether his joy at being given a new chance was due to 'patriotic zeal or the desire to wipe out [his] shame'. Referring to the motivations of Mohamed Atta, Holmes (Chapter 4, this volume) writes that 'It is impossible to know if he was bothered more by the injustice or the apostasy of Egypt's public power. The two issues must have seemed inextricably intertwined in his thinking.' I argued above that some of the motivational and cognitive states may be ephemeral, artefacts of the situation rather than stable features of the individual. Religious beliefs and the motivations stemming from them may be held for their consumption and consolation value ('opium of the masses') rather than as premises for action. Perhaps 'quasi-beliefs' 'and quasi-motivations' are better terms for these attitudes. A trivial example is the quasi-grief expressed by many people after the death in 1997 of Diana, Princess of Wales.

The complexity of beliefs about the afterlife is well brought out by Paul Veyne (1976: 428) in his comments on attitudes to death in classical antiquity.

At one and the same time an octogenarian can plant a tree for his great-nephew, believe in the immortality of the soul, wish to go to Paradise as late as possible, die with the resignation of a poor man, hope to live in the memory of posterity, order a beloved object to accompany him to his last resting-place, make sure that his funeral will be marked by all the splendour due to his rank, show in his will an unselfishness that was unknown when he himself had enjoyment of his possessions, never mention the dead without an abundance of *litotes*, and yet talk to those around him, with no embarrassments on either side, about his latest testamentary dispositions and the richness of his tomb, be afraid or unafraid of death (he may or may not spend the night after the death of a relative without a lighted lamp in his room) depending on whether or not he is deeply imbued with the feeling that death means a passage to a better state.

From this perspective, beliefs or quasi-beliefs are highly context-dependent. In different situations the same individual may express different or even contradictory beliefs about the same topic. The Jews are omnipotent, but can be defeated. In fact, two independent sources told me that they overheard Islamic militants charging that the Jews were behind the attack on the WTC while also expressing pride in this successful attack on the US enemy. Conspiratorial theories, with their enormous flexibility, do not reflect a stable cognitive attitude.

Even when the suicide attackers do act from stable motivations and independently held beliefs, we may not be able to identify them. The actors themselves are dead, while their families and the organizations that sent them on their way tend to put up a smokescreen of rhetoric that may have little to do with the actual mental states of the martyrs. Interviews with would-be suicide attackers who failed or were foiled are an intrinsically unreliable source. Even if they failed because they were detected, we do not know if they were careless because they wanted to be caught, nor if they would actually have gone through with the act had they not been stopped.[32] Thus, the aims and beliefs of the Palestinian suicide attackers are likely to remain an enigma. We may be able to identify some components, as I have tried to do, but their status and causal efficacy are elusive. It is possible that other SMs, notably in Sri Lanka, would lend themselves better to analysis if we knew more about them. The religious and conspiratorial elements that render the Palestinian missions so opaque do not seem to operate here. For the time being, however, individual-level evidence about the LTTE is lacking.

If we move to the level of the organizers, we confront a puzzle rather than an enigma. External observers do not know whether the maximalist rhetoric is sincere or strategic, but the actors themselves probably do. From the outside, a given attack may look overdetermined by goals of deterrence, sabotage, overbidding, retaliation, and provocation, but there is no reason to doubt that there is a fact of the matter if we could only get at it. The decision processes take place, however, under conditions of secrecy and dissimulation that make them virtually impenetrable.

Attempts to identify motivations by some combination of game-theoretic analysis and econometrics are, in my opinion, doomed to fail. For one thing, game theory has very little to say about the equilibrium outcome of strategic interaction among more than two actors. In Palestine, eight different groups have been involved in SMs (Chapter 3, this volume). Some of them are (or appear to be) divided into hardliners and moderates, or into a political and a military branch.[33] Their common opponent, the Israeli state, is also subject to multiple internal divisions.

For another thing, I do not think it makes sense to impute to the organizers (even if suitably disaggregated) the level of rationality presupposed by game theory. Although I have argued that irrational conspiracy theories may not by themselves affect the rationality of behaviour,[34] it would be surprising if those who believe in them were not also vulnerable to other and more significant mechanisms of irrational belief formation. To talk about rational actors with irrational beliefs would be an oxymoron. Also, in the emotionally charged atmosphere of the Middle East it would be surprising if second-order actors were moved exclusively by considerations of instrumental rationality. Retaliation may be induced by the need to satisfy a constituency, but also by spontaneous, self-destructive vindictiveness. Sometimes the parable of the scorpion and the frog seems to have more explanatory power than might be claimed by any model.

8

Can We Make Sense of Suicide Missions?

DIEGO GAMBETTA

On the evidence presented in this book, suicide missions (SMs) show such a diversity of traits as to make the search for an overarching explanation of their occurrence and patterns seem futile. The wealth of facts and arguments may even leave the reader wondering whether SMs should be treated as a single phenomenon rather than several.

There is no simple way to understand SMs without first identifying the different aspects of the whole phenomenon. In order to do this we need to shift our attention from the fine details of the individual cases, and adopt a comparative view of the evidence. To start with, I will review the variety and uniformity of features found in the missions and among their organizers. This exercise reveals that SMs display many uniformities in their conditions and features, but also that the types of SMs and their purposes vary significantly; and whereas the motivation of some is clearly rational in an instrumental sense, that of others is obscure. Next, I will review what we know about the perpetrators, arguing that the persons who die in SMs and the conditions that promote their self-sacrifice are fairly uniform, and although they are rare they are not historically or psychologically abnormal. This raises the further question of how different suicide attackers really are from other people who sacrifice their lives for a cause. To answer it, I will explore the similarities and differences between modern SMs on the one hand and both heroism and some cases of proto-SMs on the other. I will then describe how, despite the diversity of their purposes, the modern progeny of SMs shares the same roots, which emerged during an extraordinarily violent period in Lebanon. Finally, despite the rapid spread of SMs across the world since 1981, I discuss some of the limits to their further spread, showing among other things that religious beliefs can both encourage and discourage SMs.

Missions and Organizations

A number of generalizations suggest themselves. First, unlike self-immolations, which have been typically individual acts, *all SMs have been decided by and executed with the support of an organization*. This rule has virtually no exception in the modern history of SMs. The authors in this volume agree that understanding the organizations' rationale, while not more interesting, is more important than understanding individuals' motivations in explaining SMs.

Second, SMs are compatible with very *different* types of armed organizations. These include not only regular armies, such as the Japanese and more recently the Iranian, but insurgent armies such as the Liberation Tigers of Tamil Eelam (LTTE), militias of nationalist and separatist organizations (for example, Hezbollah, Hamas, al-Aqsa brigades, Kurdistan Workers' Party (PKK), and, finally, the al-Qaeda constellation of groups, which form a loose supranational entity.

Third, none of the organizations involved is monogamously wedded to SMs. SMs have been only a minuscule part of the arsenal deployed by the regular or insurgent armies that have used them. And all other organizations that have used them have resorted, to varying extent, to other options—a sign that the organizers adopt some kind of calculation in deciding whether to use SMs. Focusing obsessively on SMs as a signature trait of certain organizations hypostatizes a means, and risks diverting the attention away from the reasons why they choose SMs from an arsenal that includes other weapons.[1]

A fourth generalization is that organizations which have used SMs have been either those whose constituencies support the adoption of radical tactics, or those which are not rooted in any community, like the anarchists and al-Qaeda. We do not find any case in the middle: there is no radical organization linked to a moderate community that has used SMs (Chapter 6, this volume). Again, this is a sign that even such radical organizations as those that adopt SMs observe some constraints.

Fifth, *all SMs are carried out by the weaker side* in conflicts characterized by a marked asymmetry in the balance of military force (Atran 2003a; Pape 2003). The organizations that resort to SMs, as Merari (2005) points out, often decide to do so when they have their back to the wall and fear for their survival. This is again a sign that such organizations apply some measure of adaptive rationality before embarking on SMs—which appear extreme even for extremists. The vast majority of Palestinian SMs have taken place in Israel, which, as Berman and Laitin (2004) point out, is a well-protected target, while in the Occupied Territories other tactics have been used. Were the Palestinians better armed it is unlikely that they would use SMs.[2] At most, they would use them, not against civilians, but in combat operations, as the LTTE did.

Relative weakness is not, however, either a sufficient or a necessary condition for the use of SMs. This obtains in three ways. First, as Kalyvas and Sanchez-Cuenca (Chapter 6, this volume) elucidate, many organizations that might be expected to use SMs have not done so. Second, two organizations that have used them, though obviously weaker than their opponents, have not had their backs to the wall: the Hezbollah, who famously launched the first attacks of recent times in the early 1980s in Lebanon, was growing rather than waning, and became a significant political and military force after it launched the missions. Al-Qaeda resorted to SMs even without having been seriously engaged by any repressive force (Merari 2005); if anything, it picked the quarrel. While between two-thirds and three-quarters of al-Qaeda's core 4,000 members have now been either killed or arrested,[3] they succeeded in spawning a host of emulators around the world. Third, the Iranian 'human waves' of young martyrs employed in the war with Iraq in the 1980s, and which are the grand example of mass suicidal attacks knowingly and intentionally carried out, emerged out of radical religious fervour that the ayatollahs promoted to test and strengthen revolutionary zeal rather than for any discernible military reason.[4] Although this tragic episode still lacks a detailed historical account, we know that thousands of young lives were wasted for next to nothing (Brown 1990).

SMs are thus a weapon of last resort for some, but for others they seem a means of aggressively building up and establishing an organization by killing *and* by dying.

The religious and ideological affiliations of the SM groups are also far from uniform. While no religion apart from Islam is directly involved in SM groups, Islam-inspired missions account for only 34.6 per cent (Table 8.1). But SMs are not only clad with clerical robes, but don flags, uniforms, and revolutionary beards too. In fact, more than half of total world missions, even if one excludes the anarchists and the Kamikaze and counts only from 1981 to September 2003, were carried out by *secular* groups. However, although radical ideologies have often exacted a very high level of self-sacrifice from their adherents, they have not invariably done so: the anarchists carried out the very first dozen or so SMs of the modern era, but the Marxists eschewed SMs, despite the many revolutions they inspired (see Chapter 6, this volume).[5]

Likewise, the search for the typical SM target does not yield homogeneous results. The countries targeted by SMs, such as Israel, Russia, and the United States, have cast them wholesale as 'terrorism', thus endorsing a strict connection between SMs and the indiscriminate killing of non-combatants.[6] But matters are not so simple. Just as as *non-suicidal* terrorism targets civilians, as

TABLE 8.1.   Suicide missions by main Islamic and secular organisations, 1981–September 2003

Organization	Number of missions	Percentage
Hezbollah-e-Amal	25	5.1
Hamas	55	11.3
PIJ	27	5.5
Al-Qaeda	11	2.6
Lashkar-e-Toiba	47	9.7
Total Islamic	*165*	*34.6*
SSNP* and other Lebanese groups	25	5.1
LTTE	191	39.2
PKK	16	3.3
Al-Aqsa	25	5.1
Total Secular	*257*	*52.8*
Others of unclear attribution	*65*	*13.4*
Total	487	100.0

* SSNP = Syrian Social Nationalist Party
Source: Ricolfi (2003).

it did on 11 March 2004 in Madrid, SMs have not been invariably aimed at killing non-combatants; all the organizations that use SMs have also targeted enemy soldiers and equipment as well as political or symbolic objectives. In the LTTE, as Hopgood (Chapter 2, this volume) shows, they have been closely integrated with guerrilla-style attacks. Even with respect to 9/11, the most murderous SM attack in history, were one to offer al-Qaeda the counterfactual choice of hitting an empty World Trade Center (WTC) or of killing 3,000 US citizens in a nondescript middle-American mall, one can guess which it would choose. Although al-Qaeda's frequently stated aim is to kill Americans and their allies, on 11 September 2001 it was seeking above all to hit a symbol of the United States' success as well as the heart of its military might.

The amount of destruction SMs cause also differs significantly. Dryly depicted as a fighting tactic, they are a means which, by guiding explosive devices to a target, increases the range of targets that can be hit and the accuracy of the attack, and facilitates the timing of the explosion so as to achieve maximum effect. They are the high-precision artillery of the militarily challenged. If volunteers are plentiful, SMs can be rationally chosen over other options for their tactical advantages under given constraints: either different means would make the destruction smaller or impossible, or achieving the same amount of destruction would impose a higher number of casualties on one's ranks. Colonel Claus von Stauffenberg, who planted a bomb by Hitler's desk in July 1944, would have succeeded in assassinating the dictator had he stayed with the bomb to control the moment of the explosion. Two drivers of an explosive-filled truck launched against the US barracks in Lebanon killed 241 US servicemen—any combatant's dream ratio and more casualties than the United States suffered in the first stage of the 2003 war in Iraq.[7] As others have argued (Pape 2003; Merari 2005), SMs are an effective fighting means which have yielded clear, positive, and intended results for the organizations that have launched them, notably in Lebanon and in Sri Lanka, which could not have been as easily achieved otherwise. Yet most SMs seem of limited military significance in terms of their direct destructive effects.

Types of Suicide Mission

While the features described above overall strongly suggest that SMs are rationally decided upon by their organizers, the variety of types of SM organizations, targets chosen, and amount of destruction caused suggest different types of SMs responding to different rationales. Two questions can help us identify these rationales and impose some order on the diversity. Is the destruction of a target the organization's main goal or just an intermediate one? And is the death of the agents necessary for the success of the mission?

To answer the first question, one can try to discern whether the mission inflicts a significant cost on the military resources of the enemy per se *even if* the destruction does not become publicly known—in other words, whether its main consequences are independent of their propaganda effect. Such missions succeed if they achieve their direct destructive aims; they have nothing to do with terrorism or with psychological warfare generally, and resemble high-risk commando actions. Some political assassinations too are military operations in this sense because what matters is whom they remove rather than the 'lesson' they teach others or the emulation they inspire. Military missions may, of course, be exploited for, their 'communicative' effects—psychological warfare *is* warfare—so we have mixed cases. But the crucial point is that those SMs which have predominantly military aims— suicide military mission (SMM) in Figure 8.1—could have been carried out regardless of other considerations.

In missions of this type,[8] the death of the agent is usually a pure cost for the organization as well as for the individual perpetrators: a sadly necessary means to achieve the destructive results, which if possible would have been avoided. Kamikaze sorties, especially in the first period, and many of the LTTE attacks were of this type. However, many if not most SMs do not have a clear or direct military impact. There must be a selection effect which squeezes them out: when armies are in a position to use SMM, they are also in a position to do without them and can afford to stick to conventional

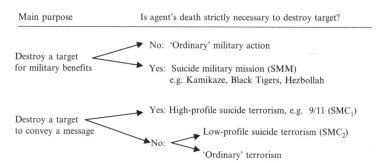

FIGURE 8.1.   Types of suicide mission by organizational goals and relevance of agents' death

military tactics. Only in extreme and rare cases do they deviate, and never do they resort to SMs as their predominant fighting option.

It is when organizations are very poorly armed or the enemy very well protected that SMs are, as we have seen, more likely to emerge, but in an altogether different form. The ultimate goal is not the direct destruction they inflict but something else. In such cases the perpetrators aim to modify the behaviour of their enemy to their advantage, but indirectly, by first modifying the opponents' beliefs and emotions about the situation they are confronting—instilling fear, weakening the enemy's resolve, making them believe that one's resolve cannot be broken, and forcing them to revise upward the likely cost of the conflict and to retaliate irrationally in a way that might increase one's own support. At the same time, SMs can also aim to modify the behaviour of their organizers' supporters, by signalling commitment and determination, setting an example of self-sacrifice and spurring more of them to join the fight. Whether aimed at friend or foe or both, in such cases the destruction of the target is an intermediate goal. The target destruction has a 'communicative' purpose aimed at an audience which is wider than the direct victims of the attack.

The following conversation between Osama bin Laden and an unidentified 'Shaykh', whom bin Laden visited in the late autumn of 2001 in Afghanistan, does not prove that 9/11 was carried out for these effects alone, but it reinforces the idea that SM organizers believe in the signalling efficacy of SM: martyrdom fortifies wavering followers and proves the authenticity of the perpetrators' determination and goals.[9] Bin Laden says:

Those young men said in deeds, in New York and Washington, speeches that overshadowed all other speeches made everywhere else in the world. The speeches are understood by both Arabs and non-Arabs, even by Chinese. It is above all [what] the media said. Some of them said that in Holland, at one of the centers, the number of people who accepted Islam during the days that followed the operations, were more

TABLE 8.2. Varying and uniform features of suicide missions

Varying features
Type of organization (armies, guerrillas, militias)
Type of target (military, political, civilian, symbolic)
Lethality (from 1 to 3,000)
Religious/ideological affiliation (see Table 8.1)
Purpose (see Figure 8.1)

Uniform features
Organized by groups, not by individuals
By groups with either a radical or no constituency
By weaker groups in high-asymmetry conflicts
All SM groups use also other tactics
Used only against democracies
Used mostly in conflicts among non-co-religionists
If a religion is involved at all, it is Islam
All modern SMs grew out of Lebanon, 1973–90
No overlap between SMs and self-immolation

than the people who accepted Islam in the last eleven years. I heard someone on Islamic radio who owns a school in America say: 'We don't have time to keep up with the demands of those who are asking about Islamic books to learn about Islam.' This event made people think (about true Islam) which benefited Islam greatly.

And the Shaykh replies:

Hundreds of people used to doubt you and few only would follow you until this huge event happened. Now hundreds of people are coming out to join you . . . the only ones who stay behind will be the mentally impotent and the liars (hypocrites). . . . This event [9/11] discriminated between the different types of followers.

A further major regularity of SMs indirectly points to the crucial importance of signalling: *SMs have been used to attack only democracies.*[10] 'There are plenty of national groups living under authoritarian regimes with grievances that could possibly inspire suicide terrorism, but none have' (Pape 2003: 350). Pape suggests three explanations for this regularity. One is that democracies are more sensitive to costs and thus more likely to change their policies even if 'only' marginal targets or civilians (voters) are attacked. Other regimes can afford not to care, and in fact most terror attacks historically have not been indiscriminate but have targeted people in authority. The second is that democracies are more restrained in their response, less likely to take full advantage of their military superiority and to annihilate the community which spawns the attackers. Third, and for our purposes most importantly, as Berman and Laitin (2004) put it:

It may therefore be the case that suicide bombings, because they generally cause little macro damage (the September 11th attacks being an exception), are only powerful where there is open media such that the target population is scared well beyond what would be justified by the probability of being killed by a suicide attack. Therefore it is a weapon most used when its (limited) damage is given (unlimited) publicity. This is not likely to occur in countries that have [a] restricted press. Therefore, suicide attacks are most efficient when aimed at democratic populations.

The recent attacks in Iraq are not in this sense an exception for, while the US-led occupation may not have brought instantaneous democracy, it has none-theless descended on the country with the world media on its tail.

Communicative benefits of SMs

What exactly does the signalling? Is it the dying, the killing, or both? 'Propa-ganda by deed' has traditionally been achieved by killing, so is the killer's death in a SM aimed at conveying a message just a cost incurred to carry out more efficient killing, as in SMM, or does it add something to the commu-nicative efficacy of the mission? Would 9/11 have had the same impact had it been a non-suicidal mission?

If the destructive effects are exceptionally high, in the eye of the victims the manner in which they are achieved is insignificant. Once they 'nuke' you, whether they died in order to do so does not matter very much. Still, in less extreme operations the willingness to sacrifice one's life sends a powerful signal of determination: it displays fighting intent that cannot be deterred. The applications of signalling theory show that the most feared opponents are those who can credibly signal fearlessness in combat. SMs go one step further: what can be scarier than knowing there are people who value their lives *less* than your death? And, from the point of view of potential friends, if one contemplates joining a violent struggle one will want to join the strongest group, as with the mafia. Violent games do not allow fine-tuning; one cannot be a little more or a little less tough but can only strive to be maximally so.

As Biggs (Chapter 5, this volume) shows, the incidence of self-immolation too is positively correlated with democracies. Even more so than SMs, the only conceivable effect of self-immolation is of a communicative kind. When no one else is killed, however, the message of dying for a cause is different. It testifies of the seriousness of one's belief in the cause, it attracts attention to it, and, if one is lucky, it shames the audience who either hinder or do not help the cause enough to mending its ways. Provided the audience is not repelled by the belief that self-immolation amounts to a suicide or to a crazy act, self-inflicted martyrdom, like the other-inflicted variety, has the effect of making people believe that, whatever the martyr believes in, it is intensely believed by him or her, and thus worthy of attention. Martyrdom is as strong a signal of the strength of a belief as one can get: only those who hold their beliefs very dear can contemplate making the ultimate sacrifice of dying for them.

While SMs signal strength of belief in the cause, self-immolation alone does not cause terror. To produce terror, dying must be coupled with killing. Much anecdotal evidence, even only the prominence given to SMs by the media, suggests that greater terror is indeed instilled by *suicide* bombing than by non-suicidal bombing. One of the first moves of Sri Lankan President Chandrika Kumaratunga was to ask the LTTE to disband the Black Tigers as a sign of its commitment to the peace process (Chapter 2, this volume).

And not only must the dying come with the killing, it has to be clearly perceived as an unavoidable component of it. When the dying in an SM is not strictly necessary to the mission's destructive aims, either because the victims are so few or, though several, they could have been killed while still escaping, the message that it sends becomes fuzzier, less legitimate (see below), and its effects less predictable. This problem is irrelevant to 9/11 or other high-profile attacks (SMC_1 in Figure 8.1) such as the seventeen missions carried out by Hezbollah since 1983, which killed an average of thirty-one people. The lethality and destruction these SMs caused could not have been achieved otherwise. It is not irrelevant at all, however, for the disturbingly long tail of SMs, especially in Israel, which do not fit the military model or even the communicative one very clearly (SMC_2 in Figure 8.1). These have been smaller in scale, at times chillingly desolate affairs with no obvious *intended* positive effect for the organizers. In the 2000–3 Intifada, about 120 SMs were foiled by the Israeli security services after having been launched, and yet more were prevented beforehand.[11] The 139 missions which succeeded in that period killed an average of 3.7 people.[12] Taken together they caused hundreds of casualties and affected the political and military choices of Israel, but whether the effects were the ones intended and whether they were beneficial for the organizations that launched them is doubtful. It is even doubtful that they caused enduring terror rather than mere revulsion. When asked how likely they think it is that they will die in a terrorist attack, Israelis overestimate the odds; but after each SM the Israelis do not really change their daily habits and after a few days they are back riding buses, strolling in malls, and patronizing bars.[13] It is thus hard to fathom what the marginal returns to each additional SM are.

Both Margalit (2003) and Merari (2005) believe that the Palestinian SMs did achieve some strategic effects. Margalit, for instance, thinks that a far-reaching success of the SMs is that:

Israel's leaders, in retaliating, have behaved so harshly, putting three million people under siege, with recurring curfews for unlimited periods of time, all in front of the world press and television, with the result that Israel may now be the most hated country in the world. This is hugely damaging to Israel, since the difference between being hated and losing legitimacy is dangerously narrow.

This may be so. However, I have seen no evidence that this is what they set out to achieve—rationally banking on what Margalit believes was 'not only cruel but also irrational response'.

This reflects, more intensely, a general problem with the rationality of terrorists' use of indiscriminate bombing—which, on reflection, seems a rather odd affair. Apart from the effects on their direct victims, whatever else terrorists cause by bombing, suicidal or otherwise, so much depends on the response chosen by the group or country they target that it is often impossible to say whether they struck *because* they wanted to achieve that particular response that happens to be chosen. After experiencing varying amounts of fear, anger, and shock after an attack, the victims can respond by *behaving* in any number of ways, which may or may not play into the hands of the terrorists. When the Italians and Germans were confronted, respectively, by their Red Brigades and Red Army Faction (Baader Meinhof), they did not lose their nerve, or round up half of the working class, or imprison scores of intellectuals, or suspend civil liberties and democracy. They hit the terrorists hard with better policing and effective legal tools. If Spain's Aznar government had not tried to mislead the public, pointing its finger prematurely to *Euzkadi ta Azkatasuna* (ETA) as the culprit of the series of (non-suicidal) bombings in Madrid on 11 March 2004 that killed 191 commuters and wounded more than 1800, it may well have been re-elected, as the polls had predicted. So can one really say, as many did, that its defeat at the polls was what the terrorists intended? Could they really bank on Aznar's error of judgement?[14] Terrorism of the indiscriminate variety finds its rationale, the link between cause and its effect, largely *ex post*. In fact, its only *ex ante* rationale may lie in the assumption that following a serious terrorist attack there will be *some* consequence that *will* be interpreted as the one the attackers intended from the start, when in fact their 'reasoning' is: 'strike first, [let others] make sense later'. The difference between a criminal and a terrorist in this respect is revealing: the former wants his crime to seem an accident, while the terrorist wants even an accident to seem designed. 'The soldiers of God have darkened the lives of the Americans', a member of the Abu Hafs el-Masri Brigades (an alleged al-Qaeda satellite) proclaimed, claiming responsibility for the totally accidental blackout that hit the east coast of the United States in August 2003.[15]

As the destructive effects of each mission become smaller, and the victims patently innocent and randomly picked, it becomes even harder to attribute any precise intent to the organizers of SMs. What motivates Palestinian groups to carry out SMs is not always clear, and it varies over time and from group to group (Chapter 3, this volume). Perhaps they count on the cumulative effects and do not bother about the lethality of each mission because they have so many volunteers. Perhaps they have learnt that their opponents are rock-solidly irrational in their choice of response. Or perhaps they simply have no better options to make themselves heard. Still, one cannot refrain from wondering with considerable anguish how may of the SMs they organized they could in retrospect have done without and still be no worse off than they are.

Whatever the case, the more elusive the organizational goals are, the more puzzling the actual perpetrators' choice becomes. Either the dying or the killing begins to seem pointless. While a high-profile destructive mission encourages volunteers, as they see clearly the point of what they are about to do, a small operation puts a tremendous weight on the perpetrators, for they must wonder what the additional contribution of *their* mission is going to be, and to go ahead they have to summon motives and beliefs that are extraneous to the instrumental value of their mission. Instrumental rationality dictates, even to altruists ready to die, that a mission should succeed *on its own terms* and make a difference to the cause—the more people one kills the better, the bigger the ship one sinks the better: 'if I have to sacrifice my life I want to take as many as I can with me.' Suicide bombers should feel even worse about carrying out small-scale operations after 9/11; and yet small-scale, often botched, SMs have continued. There is a puzzling insensitivity to the amount of destruction among Palestinian suicide bombers. Not only do they seem content with causing few victims at a time but they do not seem to mind even when they fail.[16] Their intentions and beliefs become harder to fathom, as Elster (Chapter 7, this volume) says. The burden of the explanation shifts from the 'reasons' towards the 'causes', related to the severe conditions the conflict imposes and to the perpetrators' religious or cultural make-up. They seem to be more pushed by the intensity of their feelings and the shock of their experience than pulled by the haziness of the instrumental goals. Palestinian suicide bombers, like pacifist self-immolators who kill nobody else, so often seem intent on an ultimate form of protest, on showing the world how unjust their enemy is, how genuine their suffering. They seem more focused on the dying than on maximizing lethality. Why then couple dying with killing? I shall return to this question at the end of the chapter.

Perpetrators

All the evidence shows that, in contrast with those who commit suicide, 90 per cent of whom are depressed or have diagnosable mental disorders (for example, Moscicki 2001; Conwell and Brent 1995), suicide attackers—just like self-immolators—are not suicidal nor do they display any serious psychopathology, not even those who carry out small-scale missions (several authors, this volume; Atran 2003c; Merari 2005). Most bombers are young, unmarried males, but some are not so young, some are married with children, and several are female. They are on average more educated and from a higher social background than other members of the communities to which they belong (Chapter 3, this volume; Atran 2003c). In Palestine, they represent a socio-economic cross section of the population of the Occupied Territories (Merari 2005). Although twice as many as one would expect proportionally come from refugee camps in the Occupied Territories[17], personal socio-economic desperation does not seem what drives the volunteers. Atran (2003d: 11) claims plausibly that a relevant background condition (though of course very far from a sufficient cause) would be 'rising aspirations followed by dwindling expectations' not only economically but regarding civil liberties—which roughly corresponds to Tocqueville's famous account of the motives behind the French Revolution. Even so, perpetrators are found among a variety of fighters with different histories and experiences— soldiers, guerrillas, militant members of radical groups—and, in the Palestinian and Chechen cases, even among civilians, people who up to the day before went about their lives as students, housewives, or bus drivers. What do these people share?

All agents who intentionally die in an SM have a major trait in common: although their action can be based on wrong or irrational beliefs (Chapter 7, this volume), they see themselves, and are often seen by their group, as altruists. All SMs belong to a family of actions in which people go to the extremes of self-sacrifice in the belief that by doing so they will best further the interests of a group or the cause they care about and identify with. This family of self-sacrificial actions has several members, among them religious martyrdom, self-immolation, hunger strikes, and war heroism—actions that humans have carried out since biblical times. While all of these actions involve being prepared to give up one's life, some of them involve at the same time the killing of others. Even though we instinctively think of altruism as doing purely good deeds, altruism and aggression are not antithetical—in warfare you risk your life to help kin, comrades, and country also by killing enemies.

As Durkheim argued, there is a difference between people who kill themselves for individualistic motives, whether pathological or acquired in response to personal catastrophes, which lead them to consider their lives as not worth living, and those who attach low value to their lives *in relation to* the greater value they attach to some principle, allegiance, or collective interest that transcends them. This is also how they see themselves: 'As the

Arab press emphasizes, if martyrs had nothing to lose, sacrifice would be senseless: "He who commits suicide kills himself for his own benefit, he who commits martyrdom sacrifices himself for the sake of his religion and his nation.... The Mujaheed is full of hope"' (quoted in Atran 2003c). The cause which people can hold in greater value than their own lives can be as narrow as the honour of one's kin or as abstract as social justice, and as human as one's people's fate or as heavenly as one's faith in God. The key in Durkheim's view is that the community of reference, whether a family, an army corps, or a religious sect, be so tightly knit as to generate and enforce the readiness to self-sacrifice.

It is thus in keeping with Durkheim's conceptual map that we should find that the majority of SM agents are not unbalanced. SMs, and extreme self-sacrifice generally, are rare events—far rarer than murders and suicides carried out for 'egoistic' motives, which run into hundred of thousands every year on earth—but not abnormal. It may be puzzling and unsettling, yet the human willingness to die for a cause, whether or not killing others in the process, is neither historically nor anthropologically a surprise. Coupled with the variety of ideological conditions compatible with the emergence of SMs, the presence of various forms of extreme self-sacrifice in human affairs suggests a simple factual conclusion: the disposition of humans, at least of some of them, to die for (what they believe to be) the good of their group is a flexible behavioural feature, which can manifest itself under a range of material, cultural, and organizational settings.

If we accept that SMs deserve a place in this conceptual map, then, ultimately, a complete explanation of SMs must contain an explanation of the enduring ability of humans to sacrifice themselves for the benefit of others. How this disposition evolved is a subject of intense discussion in evolutionary biology and anthropology—altruism and its foundations are indeed one of the prominent debates in that field (for example, Sober and Wilson 1998; Nesse 2001)—but is beyond the scope of this book. Here we take the existence of that disposition as given, leaving aside the difficult issue of its adaptive rationality in an evolutionary perspective.

All we can observe is that the frequency of participation in SMs, as in risk-taking or aggressive acts generally, is far higher among males than among females. Furthermore, SMs are perpetrated overwhelmingly by younger males. This is true also of acts of aggression generally, but not of suicide, which are disproportionately more common in older men. We also observe the same age and gender predominance in self-immolations in which organizations are not prominent. This suggests that that distribution is not an effect of organizational selection alone. Still, the deliberate exclusion of women and of older men by SM organizers intensifies it. When no discrimination is present, young women seem as eager to participate as men are:

eleven out of sixteen missions by the left-leaning secular Kurdish PKK were carried out by women; women have been active suicide bombers among the Black Tigers (Chapter 2, this volume); they were also among the first agents in Lebanon in the late 1970s and early 1980s, and have been employed again in the al-Aqsa wave by both secular and, more recently, religious groups (Chapter 3, this volume). Among the Chechens about half of the suicide attacks were carried out by women (*Los Angeles Times*, 30 March 2004).

The links between evolved traits and behavioural manifestations are far too complex to indulge in the type of conjectures that have become evolutionary psychology's favourite sport.[18] We can more usefully investigate the social and historical variations, first of all by trying to understand how distinct SM agents are vis-à-vis their relatives and ancestors. Can we reduce what seems to be a new phenomenon to elements of older, more familiar ones?

Heroism

Even readers who feel revulsion against SMs may be untroubled by war heroism. Are they justified or simply more familiar with the latter? Apart from whether one shares the goals of the agents or finds them repugnant—a factor which may bias one's appreciation of valour—are there significant differences between the mindsets of heroes and of suicide bombers?

Many heroes' deeds are probabilistically close to being SMs. The chance of surviving a Victoria Cross act—an act that earns 'the highest and most prestigious award for gallantry in the face of the enemy that can be awarded to British and Commonwealth forces'—is said to be one in ten.[19] This estimate is based on the 1,354 Victoria Crosses awarded since 1854, when they were first introduced following the Crimean War.[20] Low odds of survival can also inhere in the type of tasks a military unit has to face—all members can face heroic odds of survival by simply belonging to it. 'In some theatres of the war, an airman's chances of completing a tour of operational duty was little better than 50 per cent. For a period in 1942, RAF (Royal Air Force) bomber crews had no more than 10 per cent chance of surviving a full tour of operations' (Rachman 1990: 36). Many armies have also made use of special commando units, often formed ad hoc for a very high-risk mission. 'Forlorn hope', a term that dates to the middle of the sixteenth century, consisted, according to the Webster dictionary definition, of 'a body of men (called in French *enfants perdus*, in German *verlornen posten*) selected, usually from volunteers, to attempt a breach, scale the wall of a fortress, or perform other extraordinarily perilous service'.

It is likely that the certainty of death makes different demands on agents' psyches than a high probability of it does, and has different effects on their willingness to volunteer and ability to perform lucidly. The leap from very high-risk missions to certain-death ones, while numerically puny, may be psychologically large (for example, Chapter 7, this volume; Merari 2005). Certainty, for instance, prevents denial, which, as Edgar Jones, who teaches History of Medicine and Psychiatry, says,

is also an important mechanism—'I won't get shot; I'll survive; it will be someone else who gets killed'—which permits soldiers to function when facing high-risk combat conditions. Therapists treating civilians often spend a lot of time attempting to reduce reliance on denial as a defence mechanism, but my impression is that it is vital in battle because it allows men to function, think clearly and take calculated risks when exposed to great personal danger. (Edgar Jones, personal communication)

But, while we know something about soldiers' responses in combat, we know too little about suicide bombers to be able to say with any certainty what the differences really are.[21] Consider, however, that there are several acts of heroism in which even that difference does not exist, as death can be a certain prospect for heroes too, and this may be known to them. Like most children who grew up in Turin, I had an engrossing admiration for Pietro Micca, a soldier in the artillery regiment of the Duke of Savoy, who did not plan to die, and whose act is an archetypal act of heroism. In 1706, as the French were besieging Turin, Micca, a soldier in the engineers, realized that a party of the besiegers had succeeded in penetrating the network of tunnels that were part of the city citadel, and would have no doubt been able to take it. Despite having too short a fuse to run away in time, Micca ordered his companion to go before blowing himself up with a few barrels of gunpowder so as to destroy and block the tunnels. Micca, whose memory is still alive today—a museum is dedicated to him—could be dubbed a proto-suicide bomber.[22]

Apart from the mechanics of his gesture, however, there are significant differences between modern SMs and acts such as Micca's. First, there was no wish for martyrdom in Micca. Losing his life was a pure cost to him, not a means to achieve anything pertaining to his own self, not even a heavenly reward. We shall never know whether the bitter-sweet thought of his future glory traversed his mind. Since classical antiquity, the hero of secular armies and martial cultures has not strived to bear witness to anything. His motive is altruism towards comrades and country, courage and abnegation are his manly virtues, and glory his reward. Martyrdom is not part of the rhetoric of war heroes. This difference is, of course, relevant only if the perpetrators of SMs are religiously inspired, and not if they belong to secular movements.

Next, he did not mean to make a statement. Micca's sacrifice stopped the French assailants regardless of his deed being known. It was not designed to impress an audience; its consequences were transparent and, as a result, so were his instrumental motives. In this regard, too, his act is close to the SMs which have a military value. In crucial moments, when the consequences are patently beneficial to one's group, the pressure to attack at the cost of one's life becomes both compelling and understandable simply by reflecting on the beneficial consequences. It is not widely known that, strikingly, even the US air force contemplated launching SMs on 11 September 2001. There were only four armed jetfighters on duty on the north-east coast of the United States on that fateful morning. Other pilots were in the air for an exercise, but they were unarmed, and it is to those that Colonel Robert Marr, Commander, North-east Defence Sector, was referring to when he said in a BBC interview[23]:

Some of them would have just gotten in the air possibly without any arms on board and these would be the ones that if you have to stop an aircraft sometimes the only way to stop an aircraft is with your own aircraft if you do not have any weapon. *It is very possible they would have been asked to give their lives themselves to prevent further attacks if needed.* (Emphasis added)

That *ex post* statement may reveal daydreaming regret rather than a real intention. Still, it is striking that it should be mentioned at all as a possibility, and suggests that even people 'like us' can think of SMs as an option provided that the dangers are great enough.

The organizations' purposes frame the perpetrator's motives. In a military operation, including an SMM, with clear effects linked to success, the motive of the organization and those of the agent may coincide. What makes the many SMCs, which lack a clear military value, harder to make sense of relative to heroism is that as the organization goals depart from clear objectives drifting towards the 'communicative' side, the demand on the agents beliefs and motives becomes harder for their gesture is not straightforwardly justifiable in instrumental terms. The heroic acts too may be fuzzy in terms of their distant consequences—many heroes do not know whether their deeds made a difference to the overall success of the war or even of the battle. Unlike many suicide bombers, however, at least they know why they did what they did in terms of the direct local effects of their action: they killed and died to save comrades, reach a new position, or destroy an enemy gun. The hero's action transparently reflects instrumental motives understandable to all, while that of the suicide attacker is often opaque since its direct effects appear to be mindlessly murderous and its distant ones elusive and harder to comprehend.

Nerve-sustaining Conditions

There is a third difference between SMs on the one hand and both Micca's and the hypothetical situation depicted by Colonel Marr on the other: the latter lack premeditation. Micca's action was a response to unexpected circumstances, as most heroic deeds are. There are differences in the opportunity to find oneself in a situation that demands heroic acts. Different units and tasks run different risks, and different combat situations demand different risk-taking. On the western front in 1918—the home troops decimated and conscripted at age 41 in Britain—the fresher units of Australians, Canadians, and New Zealanders were assigned the toughest tasks, and earned a more-than-proportionate share of Victoria Crosses. However, most of the acts of heroism which receive those kinds of awards for valour are not premeditated, but even in high-risk units they emerge as *spontaneous* responses to events which unfold in battle. In SMs, by contrast, the certainty of death does not emerge as the combat unfolds but is planned—if you succeed you die. SM agents need not only an interest in the outcomes of self-sacrifice and a motivation to bring them about themselves; heroes must have those too. They need something else, namely, a quite extraordinary 'nerve' to stay the course until detonation. Heroes need that unflinching courage too, but the point of interest is the different levels of urgency which bring that fearlessness about in the two cases.

People who commit acts of great courage are often described as doing so while 'forgetting the self'. They experience a 'dissociative' state of mind which enables them at once to remain lucid and to face the prospect of death. The unpremeditated hero has a resource which the suicide bomber does not have in this respect: we know that triggers for self-forgetting include highly dangerous situations and intense emotions such as hatred or anger, which naturally arise in the immediacy and heat of conflict; for instance, when one sees one's comrades killed by the enemy. There is clinical evidence that anger is an inhibitor of fear (Rachman 1990: 56–7). By contrast, suicide attackers work themselves up to reach and sustain that state of self-oblivion, 'cold turkey' as it were. If unsupported by negative emotions produced by ongoing events, one may have to put all one's mental energy into fighting fear, leaving little of it available to employ in performing the action effectively. There is much anecdotal evidence that prior to detonation some bombers look dazed and automaton-like; sometimes they give up or falter, such as when they ask for a glass of water at the very establishment they are supposed to destroy, or evince symptoms that give them away.[24] Yet many go through with it. How?

One answer lies in the 'organizational practices' (some of which are described in Chapter 7, this volume) which sustain the ephemeral state of mind one requires to detonate. Attackers, whether in secular or religious groups, are part not just of an organization but of tightly knit units, which seem capable of producing the appropriate social devices for reinforcing and maintaining, not the motivation as such, but rather the commitment to act once there is the motivation to do so: 'In Hamas and the PIJ the preparation for suicide attacks is often done in cells, consisting of 3–5 volunteers. These cells are characterised in the organisation as "martyrdom cells", to differentiate them from ordinary "military cells". Members of these cells are mutually committed to each other in this kind of unbreakable social contract' (Merari 2005). The 'cell-effect' can also be clearly detected in other groups, such as the Kamikaze and the Black Tigers, who receive six months of training segregated from the rest (Chapter 2, this volume).

But is this all that different from the practices that prompt soldiers to sustain allegiance to each other? Bonding in small 'bands of brothers' is a key feature of military combat training, as each soldier must know that he can count on the selflessness of his comrades to be able to fight effectively.

The primary motivating force which more than anything kept these men flying and fighting was that they were members of a group in which flying and fighting were the only accepted way of behaving. The aircrew combat personnel were closely knit together ... the individual identified himself very closely with the group and took great pride in his membership of the group. (Flanagan 1948, quoted in Rachman 1990: 37–8)

The type of reciprocal obligations required for SMs, however, differs for those who are not going to face death in combat but perform their deeds one by one. The bonds cannot exert their influence when the fighters are all together in the same situation as soldiers often are. Flanagan points out that a crucial feature of the tightly knit groups of airmen was that 'in combat operations they lived together and had little contact with people outside the groups' (quoted in Rachman 1990: 38). But the actions of SM agents are isolated and staggered, and their bonds thus require a remarkable strength not to be broken. Some SMs, especially those involving driving or piloting a vehicle, require small teams—a group of nineteen in the case of the 9/11 hijackers—which may sustain each other's commitment to the end (see Chapter 4, this volume). But given that 'most people are more susceptible to fear when they are alone' (Rachman 1990: 59), what about the solo bomber?

Other binding practices may help. The Black Tigers are subjected to a commitment pressure by having a ritual dinner with their leader, Pirabakaran, before the missions—a subsequent defection would imply a catastrophic loss of face. Also the widespread practice of making videotaped statements a few days before the mission—sometimes jointly by a small group of martyrs (Chapter 3, this volume)—could be meant not so much for the consumption of an audience, but as commitment acts which make reneging so much harder (Merari 2005). 'Before setting off, the volunteers watch their video again and again, as well as videos of previous *shuhada* [martyrs]. "These videos encourage him to confront death, not to fear it," one dispatcher told Nasra Hassan. "He becomes intimately familiar with what he is about to do. Then he can greet death like an old friend"' (Margalit 2003). More mundanely, the videos may work by prolonging the inhibiting effects of vanity and pride, the pressure of which abates when one is alone (Rachman 1990: 60).

In addition, the SM volunteers feed on reserves produced in the natural course of a bloody conflict that involves a whole people. One such resource is hatred for the enemy, an emotion that can last and is not just locally triggered—unlike anger but which, like anger, inhibits fear. At least it did that to the volunteers of the Spanish Civil War though not to ordinary soldiers in the Second World War (Rachman 1990: 54–5; for 'hatred' see Chapter 7, this volume). Another is the obligation which grows in the living to vindicate rather than simply avenge those killed by the enemy or in previous missions.[25] Unlike soldiers, who are trained to think as a team when they are strangers to each other to start with, SM volunteers already feel part of a group formed not only by their living peers but the dead ones too. The sacrifice of people with whom one identifies has a powerful binding effect and adds to one's determination. When identification is strong, one's life feels devalued by the death of group members. What in the end changed the course of the Italian state's fight against the Mafia in Sicily, for example, was the small cohort of judges and law enforcers who, from the early 1980s to this day, swore to make the assassination of their predecessor by the Mafia meaningful by continuing the fight at high personal cost.

Further nerve-sustaining resources are afforded by religious practices to those groups that have them. Drawing on the rhetoric of martyrdom may help indirectly by offering consolation (Chapter 7, this volume) and social legitimacy. But religious exercises can also bring about and sustain the self-forgetting state, keeping people in a focused 'trance' in high-risk situations. As Holmes (Chapter 4, this volume) vividly argues, praying, devotion, and religious fervour were transparently at work in the group of hijackers of 9/11, which of all SMs is the one in which the cell had complete independence for the longest period and thus greatest opportunities for defection. Focusing the mind on the sweet details of paradise is not in this sense a motivational device, but rather a visual mantra that, if captivating enough, permits the 'dissociative' state to be sustained until the fatal crash. Faraj Shalhoub, an expert on Palestinian affairs, interviewed in June 2004 by al-Majd TV, a United Arab Emirates religious channel, together with Hamas spokesman in Gaza, Sami Abu Zuhri, said: 'They volunteer for martyrdom and self-sacrifice for the cause, and the first to be selected are the most believing, whose conviction is the deepest, because *they have the greatest chance of persevering to the very last minute*' (emphasis added).[26] Still, once again, even among ordinary soldiers we find a striking parallel: 'Pay, promotion, hatred of the enemy, and ideological commitment played little or no part in controlling fear. Praying in combat was said by three-quarters of an infantry sample to help, especially when they were in greatest danger' (Rachman 1990: 49–50).

There is also a parallel with self-immolation. We know that self-immolations are carried out not by organizations but by individuals. Looked at from a distance, this may encourage two inferences. One is that organizations are not a necessary component of all self-sacrificial actions relating to a cause, not even of those that require the utmost nerve and if not always fatal are exceedingly painful to be carried out, as self-immolations. The other is that an organization is always present in SMs to deal with practical problems that only organizations can solve rather than to manipulate and drive people into SMs. These inferences are broadly correct. Still, if we look at self-immolations closely, we realize that the differences may be thinner: one-fifth of self-immolations in Biggs' sample (Chapter 5, this volume) happened in a coordinated fashion, simultaneously involving a group of people numbering from two to twelve, who know one another and are in the same frame of mind. Partially at least, the 'cell effects' found in SMs and soldiers could be reinforcing commitments in this case too. Next, many self-immolations are connected with religion, either because the agents are in a religious occupation or because they have strong religious convictions. The religions which nurture self-immolators more vigorously, Buddhism and Hinduism, are those which most of all focus on practices of self-forgetting. A 'dissociative' state is something they strive for; oblivion of the self is a milestone on the road to spiritual elevation. While some self-immolators writhe in horrifying pain, others, especially the Buddhists, sit perfectly still in the lotus position as the flames consume them.

In conclusion, it is hard to find watertight differences between all heroic acts and all SMs, since there is an area of overlap, especially with commando-type SMs. It is plausible, as Hopgood (Chapter 2, this volume) argues, to think of the Black Tigers as an extreme instance of forlorn hope. In their case, all the extreme features of heroic acts are almost always, rather than only sometimes, present: successful SMs involve certain death (or at least the belief that death is certain), not merely a high risk of it; they are always premeditated rather than spontaneous; and they are very often carried out elsewhere than in combat situations. These features make them striking deeds, and indicate that the psychological resources required for this level of self-sacrifice are greater than, rather than qualitatively different from, those required for heroic deeds. Perhaps, the main difference is that SM goals are often less of decisive transparent importance than those of war heroes. The hero is quintessentially an *instrumental* altruist, while the suicide bomber may not always know very well what he is dying for.

Still, the groups to which the suicide bombers belong are not swayed by these subtleties, and treat them just as warring nations treat their war heroes: they celebrate them, cherish their memory in stories and ballads, look after their widows and children, and teach about them in schools.

Ancestors

It is common in the burgeoning literature devoted to SMs to sift through the past in search of the progenitors of SMs. Findings include the biblical Samson (whose famous deed took place in the Gaza region) and real historical groups, such as the Jewish sect of the Zealots-Sicarii in Roman Palestine (Atran 2003c) [27] and the Assassins, an Ismaili sect, part of the Shia branch of Islam, active in Persia, Syria, and Lebanon from AD 1090 for over two centuries (Lewis 2003). Further ancestors of people who value their lives less than the death of their enemies have been discovered by Dale. He assembled wide-ranging historical evidence to show how members of three Muslim communities in South Asia—in Malabar, south-west India, in Atjeh, northern Sumatra, and in Sulu, southern Philippines—fought their colonial rulers by engaging in murderous suicidal acts in periods ranging from the eighteenth century to the early twentieth century.

In all three areas Muslims attacked and killed Europeans or native Christians, fully expecting to be killed, or, more accurately, desiring to be martyred. They had recourse to the most attenuated form of guerrilla warfare, murderous individual assaults that could have little military significance, but that defended the integrity of their community and intimidated colonial rulers and their native allies. (Dale 1988: 48)

There could be something artificial in searching for ancestors, as we may be projecting backward concepts inspired by the diffusion of modern SMs. The notion of SMs as a *sui generis* category of actions has not been in circulation for long. In the late 1880s, Durkheim classified all imaginable kinds of suicide except SMs (nor did he mention self-immolation in the sense used here), while referring to many instances of altruistic suicides including martyrs. Not even after the Russian anarchists carried out a few such deeds in the early part of the twentieth century did the notion emerge. It gained worldwide currency only after the Japanese Kamikaze strikes in the Second World War—'Kamikaze' is now used as a generic term to refer to SM agents. Still, investigating similarities and differences between modern and proto-SMs yields some interesting results.

Similarities

Both the Assassins and the three Asian groups of mujaheedin were part of the Shia tradition, whose founding mythology is tied to the heroic military defeat of Imam Hussein in Karbala, Iraq, in 680BC. Soon after the Prophet's death in 632BC, Ali, Mohammed's nephew and son-in-law, lost his monopoly over the faith to the advantage of the Sunnis—a faction of non-blood-related followers led by a succession of Caliphs—and went on to form a smaller faction known as the Shiites (the party of Ali). An early episode in the violent conflict between the two factions, which continues sporadically to this day— in Pakistan and Iraq, for instance—involved Hussein, the son of Ali and the Prophet's daughter Fatima, and seventy of his companions who fought to the death against the army of the Umayyad Caliphate (Lewis 2003: 21–3) Although the heroes of Karbala were annihilated, 'It was precisely the self-sacrifice and defeat of its followers that would allow the "Shia" to survive and flourish as a faith. In the Shiite Muslim tradition, allegiance is pledged not to the victors, but to the vanquished' (Reuter 2004: 38; also Lewis 2003: 23). The link between this tradition and modern SMs is not just found historically by comparing two sets of unrelated events; some significant contemporary groups which have used SMs belong to and have revived the precise Shiite tradition of martyrdom. Whatever our opinion, *they* acknowledge them as their precursors.

There is a further remarkable element of convergence between proto- and modern SMs. The colonial powers of the day portrayed these murderous martyrs as being driven by folly, an echo of today's visceral or self-interested responses to SMs. Yet Dale (1988: 57) argues that the mujaheedin of the past, just like their modern counterparts, were mostly non-pathological: that is, they were not individuals who chose to die because they were depressed, unbalanced, and did not wish to live.

Another aspect similar to today's SMs is that, just as we now wonder why some suicide bombers do not choose means that could allow them to escape, so Lewis, in his history of the sect, wonders why the Assassins never choose poison or missiles as their murder weapons, but always daggers, which brought them face to face with their victims. According to Lewis (2003: ix–x), the Assassins did not even make any attempt to escape, apparently craving martyrdom.

A further point of convergence lies in the double nature of SMs, both as means to fight an aggressive war when much weaker than the opponent and as a means of last resort. On the one hand, both the Zealots and the Assassins caused serious problems for the rulers of the day, and their 'terrorist' tactics were part of their effectiveness. Even if they ultimately failed in their purpose, the Assassins were a major problem for 'caliphs, sultans, emirs, vizirs, qadis [judges]', whom they liberally assassinated for over two centuries (Atran 2003c, supporting material). On the other hand, the three south and south-east Asian Islamic communities resorted to suicidal jihads only when they had exhausted all other resources and were engaged in a losing conflict. Their acts were encouraged by some imams and condemned by others, just like today (Atran 2003c: 48), but many were individually conducted, apparently without support from what we would now call insurgent organizations. Very young men, or sometimes old ones, often impoverished and humiliated by the colonial powers, rather than the poor, joined the jihad by going on a lone killing rampage, slicing their way through as many enemy soldiers as they could before being killed. These acts were undertaken in desperate situations, apparently last-ditch gestures to testify to one's honour rather than well-thought-out military deeds (Atran 2003*c*: 56).

Differences

The agent's death in the proto-SMs is not normally self-inflicted, but results from the enemy's response to the attack. Unlike in modern SMs which rely on explosives, death was not technically essential for the success of the attack, and was only near-certain because the response of the attending guards was near-certain. These were no-escape or no-surrender missions, which are still carried out today by the same groups which carry out SMs. But whereas in the past all attacks were of this kind, now they represent, for instance, only 22 per cent of successful Palestinian suicide attacks (see Appendix to Chapter 3). Does the type of mission one contemplates make an 'operational' difference?

Successful no-escape missions do not imply certain death and, as we mentioned, an infinitesimally small chance of making it back safely could make a psychological difference. Furthermore, in terms of individual motivations, some people could prefer to let others bear the onus of killing them while others would never want to give the enemy that honour but would rather kill themselves. Still, we found no evidence that SM volunteers are choosy about these options, although the choice is now available in those organizations that practise both types of mission. In an interview, a 22-year-old member of Hamas said: 'I do not know whether my operation will involve a settlement or a bus. The leadership takes care of that' (*Telegraph Magazine*, 15 November 2003). This suggests that volunteers do not mind which way they go, whether being gunned down while spraying settlers with machine-gun fire or blowing up buses. The Palestinians regard those who die either way indifferently as martyrs, just as the Tamils regard the Black Tigers, who have also died in both types of operation.[28] A more important difference might reside in their legitimacy. One could argue, as Durkheim did, that it does not really matter:

All these neophytes [Christians] who without killing themselves, voluntarily allowed their own slaughter, are really suicides. Though they did not kill themselves, they sought death with all their power and behaved so as to make it inevitable. To be suicide, the act from which death must necessarily result need only to have been performed by the victim with the full knowledge of the facts. (Durkheim 1952: 227)

Yet it is easier to adapt the no-escape mission to the idea of martyrdom, for it is still the case that someone else kills the agent. It is harder to argue that suicide bombers are not committing suicide. The looser the links between the murderous assault and the death of the perpetrator, the easier it is to claim the act was not a suicide. Imagine a variant of the no-escape mission in which the agent, rather than being killed on the spot, as in the standard no-escape mission, is arrested and executed some time later. If the perpetrator knew that his execution was certain before he carried out the mission, this no-escape mission is identical to the one in which the perpetrator is dealt with there and then, as the time lag should make no conceptual difference. And yet it makes it psychologically easier to cast the perpetrator as a martyr put to death by the enemy for the cause since his death is temporally removed from his murderous act.

Thus, cultures which proscribe suicide, such as the three Semitic religions, involve fewer justificatory acrobatics to condone and legitimize the no-escape variety than modern SMs, in which death is directly rather than vicariously self-inflicted. The controversy surrounding the legitimacy of modern SMs in the Islamic world, discussed below, is evidence that this is not a trivial matter.

Technology

An obvious difference is the simple fact that proto-SMs could not rely on the opportunities which modern technology affords, in particular explosives. From the late nineteenth century on, the world of warfare underwent a monumental change; and the menu of explosives now available is worth a brief description since it is useful to be familiar with the toolkit of the modern suicide bomber.

In 1846 Ascanio Sobrero, a chemistry professor from Turin, invented nitroglycerine, which remained unsafe to handle until, in 1866, Alfred Nobel found a way to reduce the danger of explosion by shock by mixing it with an absorbent substance which gives it solid form. This mixture was *dynamite*.[29] By 1904 another compound enriched the world of military explosives—TNT (trinitrotoluene)—which is still used by Palestinians. Further advances came after the Second World War. In 1955 ammonium nitrate–fuel oil mixtures were developed. From ammonium nitrate, found in some fertilizers, it is possible to manufacture not just sophisticated bombs but also home-made ones. (Ammonium nitrate was used in Northern Ireland, in the Bali discotheque suicide attack in October 2002, and by Timothy McVeigh for the bomb which destroyed the federal government building in Oklahoma City.)[30] Semtex, patented and produced by the Czechs, appeared in 1966.

A favourite of the IRA, it has an indefinite shelf-life and is far stronger than TNT. Two other explosives popular with terrorists are Goma 2 Eco—a nitroglycerin-based high explosive manufactured in Spain for industrial purposes, but used also by ETA and by the Islamic terrorists in the 11 March 2004 Madrid bombings—and TATP (triacetone triperoxide). TATP 'can be made from hydrogen peroxide, which you can buy from the local pharmacy; acetone—not the type for fingernails, but the paint-thinner variety available in any hardware store; and a small amount of hydrochloric acid (sulfuric acid will also do)' (Beauchamp 2002: 27). TATP must be handled with extreme care. An estimated forty Palestinians have been killed manufacturing it.[31] Failed suicide bomber Richard Reid's basketball shoes were packed with TATP, [32] which he claims to have learned to make on the Internet[33].

Alfred Nobel also invented detonators, an essential device to trigger explosives efficiently. In 1865 he devised 'a small metal cap containing a charge of mercury fulminate that can be exploded by either shock or moderate heat. The invention of the blasting cap inaugurated the modern use of high explosives.'[34] The indispensable qualities of detonators—namely, safety and, especially in the case of SMs, also instantaneousness and portability—were not, however, present from the start. Bulky electric detonators, available by the end of the nineteenth century, did not fit into one's pockets (Podoliak 2004).

In operational terms, an important difference that the new technology introduces between proto- and modern SMs is that the use of daggers (or, nowadays, of automatic firearms, the typical weapon of contemporary no-escape missions) requires more dexterity than pressing a detonator. While bombs are more complicated to organize because of their financial and technical requirements, they are simpler to use. This implies that no-escape missions require some combat training, while suicide bombing extends the pool of potential perpetrators to civilian volunteers and shortens the time period between volunteering and acting. This has enhanced the opportunities for women, traditionally less well-versed than men in combat skills. Palestinian women have participated only in suicide bombing, not in shooting missions, and so have the 'three dozens Chechen women [who] have launched or attempted attacks against Russian targets since the second Chechen war began in 1999' (*Los Angeles Times*, 30 March 3). Among the LTTE the exploding belt was 'originally developed specially for the female body' (Reuter 2004: 161). Among the Chechen fighters who stormed the Dubrovka theatre in 2003 in Moscow, only the women—often relatives of dead fighters—were wearing explosive belts, while the men were armed with automatic weapons.[35]

The problem with the quality of early detonators was, curiously, picked up in *The Secret Agent*, first published in 1907. Joseph Conrad—who was inspired by real events happening at that time in the murkily intersecting worlds of the anarchists and the secret police—invents a major character in the story, whom he calls the 'Professor',[36] who makes a living out of selling explosives to the anarchists and is known to the police who nonetheless do not arrest him. Speaking with Ossipon, a devious and posturing anarchist, the Professor explains how he protects himself from arrest and in so doing gives the first known description of a suicide bomber belt:

'I walk always with my right hand closed round the indiarubber ball which I have in my trouser pocket. The pressing of this ball actuates a detonator inside the flask I carry in my pocket. It's the principle of the pneumatic instantaneous shutter for a camera lens. The tube leads up—' With a swift, disclosing gesture he gave Ossipon a glimpse of an indiarubber tube, resembling a slender brown worm, issuing from the armhole of his waistcoat and plunging into the inner breast pocket of his jacket. . . . 'The detonator is partly mechanical, partly chemical,' he explained, with casual condescension. (Conrad 1986: 91)

The police in the story knew he had that device and believed the Professor was ready to detonate it, so refrained from approaching him. However, the system was not perfect.

'It is instantaneous, of course?' murmured Ossipon, with a slight shudder. 'Far from it,' confessed the other, with a reluctance which seemed to twist his mouth dolorously. 'A full twenty seconds must elapse from the moment I press the ball till the explosion takes place.'

'Phew!' whistled Ossipon, completely appalled. 'Twenty seconds! Horrors! You mean to say that you could face that? I should go crazy—'

'Wouldn't matter if you did. Of course, it's the weak point of this special system, which is only for my own use. The worst is that the manner of exploding is always the weak point with us. I am trying to invent a detonator that would adjust itself to all conditions of action, and even to unexpected changes of conditions. A variable and yet perfectly precise mechanism. A really intelligent detonator.' (Conrad 1986: 92)

The Professor's dream is now fulfilled. Among the wide range of detonators available, some are simple enough to suit poorly equipped artificers: 'you can now buy organic detonators that don't even have metal housings. They are made of paper' (Beauchamp 2002: 30). According to several websites, run by pyrotechnicians who nurse political agendas to be handled with care, you can even 'use a flashlight bulb (or something about the same size). Break the glass, but not the filament! Put it inside your explosive and wire it up to a 9 volt battery with a switch.'[37] Richard Reid must, however, have missed these websites or found it impossible to pack the detonator in the sole of his shoes, for he was caught as he tried to set off the explosive with matches (Beauchamp 2002: 27). Despite the range of raw material now available, it is still arduous to make good bombs. We would have a lot more SMs and terror attacks generally were it not for the difficulty of finding, buying, and assembling explosive devices.

The Modern Lineage

Low quality of detonators apart, in 1907, when *The Secret Agent* came out, the basic ideas and technology of the modern suicide bomber were in circulation, and not just in fiction. Less fussy than Ossipon, '[a]narchists made their way into police headquarters in various parts of [Russia] and blew themselves up with dynamite, along with everyone present. Nisan ('Nisel') Farber, one of the most active members of a Belostok anarchist group, was responsible for such an exploit in October 1904' (Geifman 1993: 132). The anarchists also perpetrated many assassinations, the style of which, were it not for the use of firearms or grenades rather than daggers, is reminiscent of the Assassins'. Unlike the Assassins, however, they did not always wait to be killed by others but blew themselves up with their targets. 'No less than a dozen' other suicide attacks followed Farber's in the next three years (Geifman, personal communication). Not only did the anarchists practise terrorism as propaganda by deed, they also invented propaganda by dying.

They innovated in other ways too, with attacks that were indiscriminate rather than directed just at the authorities, like those of proto-SMs. They bombed cafés, trains, and factories (Geifman 1993). If you think we are living in dangerous times of terror, consider that in Russia alone '[b]y the end of 1907 the total number of state officials killed or injured [from 1905] came to nearly 4,500. The picture becomes a particularly terrifying one in consideration of the fact that an additional 2,180 private individuals were killed and 2530 wounded in terrorist attacks, between 1905 and 1907' (Geifman 1993: 21).[38] The anarchists' enemy was the bourgeoisie, any member of it in fact. 'We will not spare the women and children of the bourgeois, for the women and children of those we love have not been spared', declared Emile Henry at the trial which was to send him to the guillotine.[39] At the antipodes of religion, the early SM perpetrators were militant atheists who believed they were fighting for social justice. Nisan Farber, who like other anarchists came from an impoverished Jewish family and did not know a word of Russian (Geifman 1993: 134), is the first known suicide bomber of modern times.[40]

The anarchists' tactic did not spread. Anarchist groups are tamer these days, and the secular groups which use SMs have never invoked the anarchists as their precursors. It did not help that the anarchists failed miserably and became the epitome of mindless fanaticism. Not only did the state combat them but so too did Marxist groups, often viciously, in various parts of the world before the Second World War, and the Marxists did not resort to SMs despite the huge sacrifices they made.

The next wave of SMs—also secular—came forty years later, with the Kamikaze, but they too did not leave direct offspring. After their last sortie, in August 1945, there was again a hiatus of thirty-five years. The first massive wave of SMs of the modern era started in Lebanon. As we know, in 1981 a car bomb crashed into the Iraqi embassy in Beirut. A year later, there was an attack against the Israeli headquarters in Tyre. In 1983 there was an attack against the US embassy (April), and later, on 23 October, two simultaneous attacks against the US marines and the French headquarters in Beirut. In total these five attacks killed 513 people. This time, the attackers were not secular but Shiite groups, notably the Hezbollah. The multinational force withdrew from Lebanon at the end of September 1984 (Chapter 3, this volume).

The broth that inspired the Lebanese SMs was as violent as that in which the Russian anarchists had swum eighty years earlier. The basic ingredient was the Lebanese civil war, which raged for fifteen years from 1975 and was fought along all possible cleavages: ethnic, religious, social, nationalist, and political fault lines bloodily criss-crossed each other with an estimated toll of 150,000 victims out of a population of about 2.6 million (Cook 1995). Beirut was swarming with insurgents from various parts of the world, including Tamils (Chapters 2 and 7, this volume) and members of extreme left-wing European groups. Half a million Palestinians filled the refugee camps. Foreign secret services and troops—Syrians, Americans, French, and Italians (who apparently escaped being bombed because, instead of residing in barracks, they slept scattered in tents)—were roaming over Lebanese soil. As if that were not enough, Israel invaded Lebanon twice, first in 1978, in the south, and then in 1982, when her troops reached Beirut. The temperature was so high as to spur even the dimmest of insurgents' imagination and test the meekest of pacifists' restraint.

Meanwhile, the other main SM ingredient—the ideology of the Iranian revolution and of martyrdom—reached Lebanon through more than a thousand Pasdarans (Iranian revolutionary guards), who moved there in the early 1980s 'in order to erect a beachhead for the Islamic Revolution' (Reuter 2004: 57). They were instrumental in inspiring the local Shiite community and in the founding of Hezbollah, the party of God. During the Iran–Iraq conflict which was also raging at the time (1980–8), the Iranian ayatollahs resuscitated the idea of martyrdom on a massive scale. 'Human waves', as they were called, of young Iranians were sent to certain death either attacking the enemy scantily armed or demining the border areas. The Shiite tradition of faith-driven aggressive martyrdom—which is linked not to passively succumbing to persecutors as in the Christian tradition, but to going into battle, the more hopeless the better—came back on a grand scale. 'Overnight, the Lebanese Shiites, the poorest and weakest faction of Lebanese society, had, in Iran, a powerful ally, which brought with it money, weapons, and men. Above all, the new ally came with a new explosive idea' (Reuter 2004: 57).

The primordial broth, however, was not entirely halal. Contrary to a widespread belief, not only did SMs spread subsequently to secular organizations, but left-wing or nationalist groups actually started to carry them out, somewhat timidly. As Ricolfi writes (Chapter 3, this volume), already in the 1970s in Lebanon there were several alleged SMs, none of them carried out by religious groups: in 1973 there was 'A suicide attack against a bus station in Safad (close to the Lebanese border), foiled by the Israeli army' (Chapter 3, this volume) attributed to al-Fatah. This was followed by about ten minor SMs up to 1980 in Lebanon. And, even before, in 1972, a no-escape mission was carried out, bizarrely, by three members of the Japanese Red Army in Lod Airport in Tel Aviv, apparently on behalf of the Popular Front for the Liberation of Palestine (PFLP). Kozo Okamoto, Tsuyoshi Okudaira, and Yasuyuki Yasuda fired indiscriminately, killing twenty-six people and injuring seventy-eight, most of them pilgrims from Puerto Rico. Yasuda died from Israeli fire and Okudaira committed suicide using a grenade. Okamoto was injured but survived to be tried and sentenced to life imprisonment.

The inspired fervour of the Hezbollah, which was officially formed in 1982, added the final spice to an already preternaturally violent concoction, bringing SMs to new pinnacles of devastation and hence of fame. The availability of a religious tradition of martyrdom, though not a necessary condition for the emergence of SMs, did help (Reuter 2004).

Virtually unheard of before, from that period onward SMs have grown in number and spread rapidly to other parts of the world: Sri Lanka (1987), Israel (1993), Turkey (1996), Africa (al-Qaeda, 1998), Kashmir (1999) Chechnya (2000), and now Iraq (2003) (Table 8.3). They spread, as Elster writes (Chapter 7, this volume), via both personal and organizational contacts, but also on the less palpable wings of this new 'mental model' whose early materializations were proving so successful (Pape 2003).[41]

The Hezbollah 'mutation' crossed over to the Sunni Muslims in Hamas and al-Qaeda. Although the latter groups do not share the Shia mythology of martyrdom, they came up with one drawing on the shared notion of jihad. Not only did the SM's new trait spread from one pious subspecies to another; it also revived and strengthened in some of the secular groups within Lebanon that had started half-heartedly to undertake SMs before 1981; and from 1983 to 1986 the majority of SMs were in fact carried out again by secular groups (Chapters 3 and 6 this volume; Merari 2005). One should remember that at that time many in the left-wing in Europe, including Michel Foucault[42] and other French intellectuals and the Italian group *Lotta Continua*,

TABLE 8.3. Year of first suicide mission by different organizations

Organizations	Year of first mission	Country
Amal-(Syrian?)	1981	Lebanon
Hezbollah	1983	Lebanon
SSNP*	1985	Lebanon
LCP†	1985	Lebanon
LTTE	1987	Sri Lanka
Hamas	1993	Israel
PKK	1996	Turkey
al-Qaeda	1998	Kenya, Tanzania
Lashkar-e-Toiba	1999	Kashmir, India
Chechens	2000	Chechnya, Russia
DHKP	2001	Turkey
Jama'ah Islamiyya	2002	Indonesia
Ansar al-Islam	2003	Iraq

* SSNP = Syrian Social Nationalist Party
† LCP = Lebanese Communist Party

were naive enough to be looking up to Khomeini as a true revolutionary. Strange as this may now seem, these two ideologies were for some time open to each other's influence. A religious-to-secular contagion, incidentally, is reported also in the case of the three south Asian Islamic ancestors studied by Dale (1988).[43]

Once implanted in different situations, the new SM trait yielded an array of variants, but the source is the same: Lebanon 1973–86. The most striking common trait of modern SMs is that, despite having branched out in various directions and been put to use in different ways by different organizations for a host of purposes—that is, despite their great diversity—they *are the fruits of the same tree.*

Limits to Diffusion

Are there limits to the diffusion of SMs? The question, addressed by Kalyvas and Sanchez-Cuenca (Chapter 6, this volume), deserves to be revisited in view of a striking regularity detected by Berman and Laitin (2004): 'overall, 89.9 per cent of the suicide attacks were aimed at victims whose religion was different from that of the attackers.' What is striking is that, by contrast, 'only 16.5 per cent of civil wars were fought between guerrillas made up predominantly from one religious group against armies of the state who were largely of a different religious group'.[44] This means that 83.5 per cent of civil wars set people with the same religious background against each other, while SMs are rarely used against co-religionists. Belonging to the same religion seems to prevent the warring factions from adopting SMs. This could explain why, for instance, the Algerian *Groupe Islamique Armée* (GIA), which has been fighting a civil war since 1991 and has been brutally murderous, used SM only once and then renounced them.

To reach their conclusion, Berman and Laitin (2004) also include the cases in which religion is in the background, not at the forefront, of the conflict, in that the people on each side of the conflict, while themselves secular, belong to different spheres of religious influence. For example, the Tamils are predominantly Hindus and the Sinhalese predominantly Buddhists; the Kamikaze were mostly Shintō fighting Christian Allied forces. Also, in both Lebanon and Israel there have been attacks from secular groups whose members are all Muslims; and, more generally, the conflict involves Muslim groups. We can, for good measure, add the anarchists, who were militant atheists (several of them Jewish) fighting against a predominantly Orthodox establishment. Since 2000, a series of Islamic SMs in Saudi Arabia, Morocco, Iraq, and Indonesia have targeted mostly foreigners, though often causing many victims among co-religionists. Attacks on co-religionists, however, have been strongly criticized from within the Muslim world itself even when they were not of a suicidal kind. On 29 May 2004, an al-Qaeda-inspired group took fifty hostages and killed twenty-two of them (nineteen foreigners) in Khobar, Saudi Arabia; they deliberately hunted for non-Muslims, letting co-religionists go free, as if responding to the virulent criticism they had attracted after a previous religiously indiscriminate attack.

There are plenty of exceptions, in both directions, several of which are mentioned by Berman and Laitin. In a number of civil wars fought across religious divides, no SM occurred. Conversely, the secular Kurdish PKK launched sixteen missions in Turkey against non-Kurds, but they were still co-religionists. Muslims have also apparently killed other Muslims in suicide attacks in Iraq.[45] (Hitting co-religionists was incidentally a trait of the Assassins, who attacked Sunni co-religionists rather than crusaders: Lewis 2003; Atran 2003c: supporting material.) Several SM assassinations were also at the expense of co-religionists (see n. 46). Still, the correlation seems strong (Table 8.4).

Killing co-religionists without dying has been widely and energetically pursued, and backed by the religious doctrines of 'just war'—so why not go all the way? Berman and Laitin (2004) suggest two explanations. First, 'an explanation grounded in theology or empathy, namely that it would be hard to convince an attacker that killing coreligionists was a worthy enough act to warrant suicide'. Is the death of an 'infidel' of greater value than one's own life while that of a co-religionist is not?

Next, and in their view more importantly, they claim that 'coreligionists are also soft targets' and one does not need to go to extremes to attack them.

TABLE 8.4. Main suicide mission waves by religious affiliation or religious background of the opponents

Russia 1904–7	Atheists (some Jews) v Orthodox Christians
Japan 1944–5	Shintō v largely Christian Allied Navy
Sri Lanka 1987–2001	Hindus v Buddhists
Lebanon 1981–6	Muslims v Israeli Jews and Christian peace forces
Turkey 1996	Muslim Kurds v Muslims Turks
Israel 1993–	Muslims v Israeli Jews
Kashmir 1999–	Muslims v largely Hindus
Chechnya 2000–	Muslims v Orthodox Christians
Indonesia, Tunisia, United States 2000–	Muslims v predominantly 'foreigners'
Iraq, Morocco, Saudi Arabia 2000–	Muslims v both other Muslims and foreigners

The typical problem in defending ('hardening') a crowded target is that it is unfeasible to screen all individuals with access to the target for every possible weapon. The solution is generally to predict which individuals are at the highest risk of harboring violent intentions (by 'profiling') and then screen those individuals carefully. That method raises the probability of apprehension, before the attack or at least after it. The key point is that among coreligionists profiling is extremely difficult, since they are typically similar in appearance. (Berman and Laitin 2004)[46]

It follows that it would be easier for an attacker to pass unnoticed among co-religionists and to strike with a lower probability of being caught. Profiling by appearances is difficult among Northern Irish Protestant and Catholic individuals since they look alike (Gambetta and Hamill forthcoming) and, compatibly with the hypothesis, no SMs were used there. (Even when the target was very well protected the IRA chose 'traditional' means, as in 1982 when it planted a huge bomb to assassinate Mrs Thatcher and several of her ministers at the Brighton conference of the Conservative Party. Had they used an SM they might have succeeded.)

Though interesting, this hypothesis is not fully convincing. First, non-co-religionists too can look alike. For a Tamil it is apparently easy enough to pass off as a Sinhalese, and yet the Tamils have used SMs—though, to be fair, not so much against civilians as against troops and authorities, which are better protected. Or they can work hard to look alike: witness the Palestinians suicide bombers who donned Orthodox Jewish apparel. So, one wonders, if they can pass off to carry out an SM, could they not pass off to carry out non-suicidal attacks? Next, co-religionists too can be well defended by profiling if they differ ethnically. For an African National Congress (ANC) black insurgent to hit a white crowd would have been harder than for a Palestinian to mingle anonymously in an Israeli mall. And yet the ANC did not carry out SMs. By contrast, the targets of the recent Iraqi SMs, which were often new police recruits queuing outside enrolment offices, do not seem to be particularly hard to hit.

Alternatively, one could hypothesize a selection effect as the source of that regularity, which is stylized in Figure 8.2. Suppose that, *ceteris paribus*, the frequency of civil wars declines as the asymmetry of both aggressive and defensive resources between the potential opponents grows. It is plausible, at the extreme of asymmetry especially, to assume that a minority faction whose chances of success in a military confrontation are abysmally low is unlikely to take up arms. We do not know the shape of this whole relation. For instance, when factions have near-equal force they may also be reluctant to start a high-cost war with an uncertain result. As the asymmetry grows, the stronger faction may be tempted to behave more oppressively and spark a reaction. But for the purpose of this hypothesis what matters is what happens when asymmetry grows very high.

Even though there are more civil wars among co-religionists (83.5 per cent), there could still be more civil wars among non-co-religionists at the high-asymmetry end. This is expressed by the two lines intersecting each other on the right-hand side of Figure 8.2. In other words, even when the odds are strongly against the weakest faction, the chances of a confrontation erupting could be, *ceteris paribus*, higher among non-co-religionists.

Just about anything one can think of in connection with the effects of having a homogenous religious allegiance suggests that it affords greater fighting resources. It carries no room for compromise as it vies for exclusive loyalties, engenders greater fear of assimilation or annihilation by the other side, and excludes the empathy induced by shared sensitivities and beliefs. In short, it is entirely plausible to expect religious allegiances to generate a

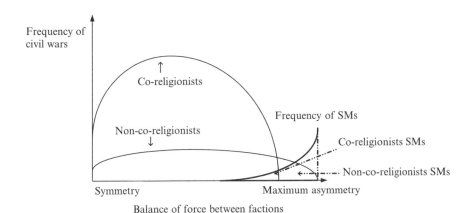

FIGURE 8.2.   Frequency of civil wars and of suicide missions by religion divide and balance of military force between factions

'bellicosity capital' which, other conditions being equal, leads religiously distinct factions in times of conflict to step more gingerly than factions of the same religion on to a war footing even if the odds are staked against them.

One of the few econometric models in which the effects of religious divisions on the incidence of civil wars has been measured shows that, in general, 'religious divided societies are more prone to intense conflict than countries where people have conflicting claims on resources based on interest groups or in language divisions' (Reynal-Querol 2002: 29). This effect is robust since 'religious polarization and animist diversity remains positive and significant no matter which polarization index we use' (Reynal-Querol 2002: 54).[47] Reynal-Querol's model does not control for factions' asymmetries of force. Still, it seems plausible to hypothesize further that the effect of religious divisions intensifies as the asymmetry between the forces grows. This could happen because religious minorities are both more likely to be targeted and more likely to fight back.

If civil wars are more likely to occur among factions with different religions when the balance of forces is heavily asymmetrical, this may explain why 89.9 per cent of SMs occur in such conflicts and only 10.1 per cent among co-religionists.[48] The reason is that the attraction—or, rather, the perceived necessity—of SMs too grows, both for individuals and organizations, the greater the asymmetry of forces in a conflict. Bermann and Laitin (2004) themselves, although they do not make the further link with religion, have both conjectured and discovered good evidence of this association: more precisely, they found that the vast majority of civil wars breaks out "in cases in which asymmetry is lower than in cases where asymmetry is at its peak (i.e. insurgents need to be relatively strong compared to the state)", while the nine civil wars in their database that produce SMs "are more likely to come in cases in which the asymmetry is at its peak (i.e. used when the state is too strong relative to insurgents)" (David Laitin, personal communication). As a consequence, the line in Figure 8.2 representing inter-religious conflicts would intersect the SM incidence curve at a higher point than the line of conflicts among co-religionists. The area of inter-religious SMs is thus greater than the area of co-religious SMs, simply because inter-religious conflicts are more likely to break out when the conditions are also more conducive to SMs.

Religious Accelerants and Retardants

It is, however, legitimate to wonder whether there is more than a selection effect, namely, that homogenous religious groups may be not only more prone to enter into conflicts with each other even when the odds are against success but also more prone to SMs. Furthermore, we can ask whether there are specific religions—notably Islam, which is directly or indirectly involved in the majority of conflicts which spawn SMs (see Table 8.4)—that foment more of both conflicts *and* SMs than others. Killing others and oneself are quite extreme acts and all religions have their own package of beliefs and controversies about them. As Biggs (Chapter 5, this volume) claims, they also forge sensitivities which guide responses to killing and dying, and to the manner of them, even among people who are not themselves religious.

As Elster (Chapter 7, this volume) argues, it is unclear how the idea of martyrdom has obtained a grip on the minds of believers and whether it motivates rather than simply consoles them. Yet a tradition of combative martyrdom, which is stronger in Islam than in any other main religion, seems to provide a rationalizing narrative for the perpetrators, their families, and constituencies without which an organization that banks on popular support could not run SMs. It can also lift social and normative constraints against abandoning one's family and wordly commitments by providing justification for high-cost, higher-order goals. To accept SMs as a legitimate means, people need to experience an intense level of political and economic oppression and possibly fear for the survival of their group. But if they do experience that, then a tradition which provides a repertoire of beliefs that acknowledges aggressive martyrdom as a self-sacrifice and links it to an array of worldly and heavenly rewards is suited to sustain unpromising conflicts *because* it is more suited to sustain self-sacrifice. While the real sources of the conflicts in which SMs emerge are ultimately social and political, and secular groups can resort to these attacks too, those organizations that can bank on the 'right' religious beliefs can more easily summon the energy to enter into or, as the story of Ali shows (Chapter 3, this volume), to continue, fighting against all odds.

In making this comparison we cannot be absolutely sure that everything else is the same but, in conflicts linked to other religions in which destructive martyrdom is not contemplated, such as Christianity or Buddhism, SMs have never emerged either among groups that find their explicit inspiration in these religions or in secular groups that simply inhabit a universe in which these religions are predominant. There is no sign of SMs in the IRA, or ETA, or among the many Central and Latin American insurgent groups. Even more striking is the absence of SMs in the various Christian groups and parties in the Middle East, like the Maronites who fought in the Lebanese civil war. There is a parallel with self-immolations, which as Biggs (Chapter 5, this volume) shows, are carried out mostly in India, Vietnam, and South Korea, countries in which Hinduism and Buddhism are predominant. Different sets of religious beliefs are enabling and disabling different forms of self-sacrifice.

One question is whether religions impose only soft constraints on SMs, acting as retardants rather than as suppressors, and whether, given the right conditions, all groups could eventually be driven to resort to SMs. A group of insurgents could simply bypass religious restrictions when popular feelings are strong enough to accept that, or religious authorities would labour harder to catch up with popular sentiments to construct new justifications of killing and dying.

The Jewish religious tradition of aggressive martyrdom, which goes back to the Zealots and the Sicarii, seems now completely defunct. There are no Jewish-related instances of SMs, though a no-escape mission was carried out by Baruch Goldstein, a Brooklyn-born Jewish extremist who killed twenty-nine Muslims and wounded scores of others on 25 February 1994 while they were praying in the Cave of the Patriarchs, a Hebron site holy to both Muslims and Jews. Goldstein was beaten to death by the crowd. His deed is akin to the no-escape missions carried out by the Palestinians against Jewish settlers. Goldstein may not have wanted to die, but he must have known what the likely cost of his act was going to be and had no plans to escape. His attack was condemned without hesitation by the Israelis, both government and people, and by Jewish organizations around the world. Still, Goldstein has retained a degree of popularity among Israel's right-wing extremists, who regard him as a martyr. On his tombstone one can read:

Here lies the saint, Dr. Baruch Kappel Goldstein, blessed be the memory of the righteous and holy man, may the Lord avenge his blood, who devoted his soul to the Jews, Jewish religion and Jewish land. His hands are innocent and his heart is pure. He was killed as a martyr of God on the 14th of Adar, Purim, in the year 5754.[49]

Goldstein's is an isolated gesture, yet one wonders whether, under completely different circumstances in which the Israeli people found themselves oppressed, humiliated, and militarily overwhelmed, this tradition could be revived, and how far it would be pushed. An interesting historical case, which might eventually shed light on the matter, is that of the Bund, the All-Jewish Workers' Union, which was formed in 1897 and was the first formal social democratic organization in the Russian Empire. In times in which terrorism was rife, the Bund officially rejected terrorism, but according to Geifman's evidence (1993: 101–22.) it supported and abetted it, as the modern phrase has it, and many of its members practised it. It was in this context that Nisan Farber struck in 1904 with the first SM in modern history.

Analogously, had the British army been more brutal and had the oppression of Catholics in Northern Ireland reached the same intensity it has reached for the Palestinians, we can wonder whether the IRA could have resorted to SMs. The Irish Catholic Church was ambivalent about the IRA hunger strikers in 1916–23: it did not condemn them against the British, but it condemned them as suicide against the Irish Free State in 1923, a sign that political considerations were more important than theological ones (Biggs 2004). In 1981 the Church hierarchy did not support the hunger strikers, and even tried to mediate behind the scenes, drawing the ire of the IRA. But it did not want to undermine them publicly either, since they had so much support from the Catholic community. Without fanfare the victims were buried with full religious rites, which would have been denied them had their demise been deemed a suicide (Beresford 1987; Sweeney 1993). Religious traditions have the plasticity to reconfigure themselves and accommodate just about anything. Still, one cannot easily see the Catholic Church justifying murderous suicidal martyrdom without taking monumental steps. The lack of a tradition of aggressive martyrdom would force one to create a new theology to justify SMs and make them acceptable to the flock. At present, we do not have even a single case of a non-Islamic faith justifying SMs, and this will have to remain a counterfactual question.

The SM Controversy within Islam

Even within Islam, SMs are far from being effortlessly justifiable, and they have sparked a heated and complex controversy.[50] The modern form of SMs poses a greater problem of legitimacy than the proto-SMs: 'The classical [Islamic] jurists distinguish clearly between facing certain death at the hands of the enemy and killing oneself by one's own hand. The one leads to heaven, the other to hell.'[51] The perpetrators need to overcome that distinction to persuade supporters who consider suicide a sin that they are martyrs and not suicides. After all, a paramount preoccupation shared by anyone who believes he is sacrificing his life for a cause, whatever that may be, is to make sure that the relevant others do not think of one as being either mentally ill or, if the audience is religiously inspired, sinful. Unless they are persuaded, one of the main purposes of SMs— to encourage others to fight and do the same—would be lost.

How much effort persuasion requires depends on the type of SM. In so far as the devastation planned is of clear military relevance, the sacrifice can make sense in purely consequential terms, such as those that apply to war heroes of secular armies. But as the links between SMs and their effects becomes tenuous the sacrifice gets murkier. Why should anyone sacrifice his life for killing a couple of retired Israelis? What exactly is the benefit in that? Why not just leave a parcel bomb and leave? Margalit (2003) has one explanation:

Vengeance through suicide bombing has, as I understand it, an additional value: that of making yourself the victim of your own act, and thereby putting your tormentors to moral shame. The idea of the suicide bombing, unlike that of an ordinary attack, is, perversely, a moral idea in which the killers, in acting out the drama of being the ultimate victim, claim for their cause the moral high ground.

This interpretation[52] is abstractly plausible, yet it is not easy to believe that the Palestinians feel they have to prove by dying that they hold the moral high ground.

Consider an alternative interpretation. Sheikh Yusuf al-Qaradawi, the 77-year-old Egypt-born cleric known as the spiritual leader of the Muslim

Brotherhood, and a moderate voice with a large following throughout the Muslim world, said:

It is not suicide, it is martyrdom in the name of God. Islamic theologians and jurisprudents have debated this issue, referring to it as a form of Jihad under the title of 'jeopardising the life of the mujaheed' (fighter). It is allowed to jeopardise your soul and cross the path of the enemy and be killed, if this act of jeopardy affects the enemy, even if it only generates fear in their hearts, shaking their morale, making them fear Muslims. *If it does not affect the enemy then it is not allowed....* If the Iraqis can confront the enemy, there's no need for these acts of martyrdom. If they don't have the means, acts of martyrdom are allowed. I didn't say that the Iraqis cannot—it depends on their need. (*Newsnight* 2004; emphasis added)

This view that extreme methods are justifiable if they are strictly necessary rules out patently unprovoked terrorist acts. (Al-Qaradawi has condemned the 9/11 attack as 'a grave sin', spoken out against the Madrid bombings, saying 'Islam does not permit aggression against innocent people', and called the Bali blast 'total barbarism'.[53]) It raises two problems, however. One is *how much* is enough: how much, that is, SMs need to affect the enemy to be allowable. If all one needs for an SM to be legitimate is that it strikes 'fear in the hearts of the enemy', this is not a very exacting criterion and tolerates the inclusion of intangible effects.

The other problem is an ambiguity between whether affecting the enemy is to be interpreted individually or collectively. Should we measure the relevant effect for each individual SM or for a series of them? The former is a more stringent criterion than the latter, for it implies that each mission rather than a series of them must make a difference.

Both interpretations are present in the Islamic world. 'The most highly regarded and influential Shiite cleric outside Iran, Sheikh Hussein Fadlallah had considerable difficulty finding a principled Islamic rationale for giving his blessing to Hezbollah's new weapon'. He eventually came round to the idea and 'issued a fatwa declaring suicide attacks... legitimate *provided that the greatest number of enemies would be killed by them*' (Reuter 2004: 121, emphasis added). This reasoning implies that the test must be stringently applied to each mission. One needs observable proof that the SM perpetrator is not simply masking a suicidal intention or striving for a self-centred martyrdom. In Fadlallah's view the only evidence one can offer that one is not throwing one's life away is the number of people one kills and the devastation one causes. This shows that dying is not itself the purpose but a true sacrifice by a genuine martyr. What is remarkable about this reasoning is that, in order to enforce a religious norm against suicide, an element of instrumental rationality must be brought back into martyrdom. This normative constraint also makes it less likely that untrained volunteers, essentially civilians, are used in SMs. It focuses the mind of the organizers, who cannot afford to waste the lives of militants, if only because that would reduce their legitimacy. Where this constraint rules we should find fewer missions larger in scale. Where it does not rule we should find more SMs, each of little effect.

Fadlallah's view is opposed to the Iranians' conception of martyrdom, which is unconcerned about the efficacy of the action.

[In the Iran–Iraq war] [w]henever Iranians fought in defence of their homes and towns, in effective isolation from the clerical leadership, by all accounts they did well against vastly superior odds. Nothing shook the Iraqi army more than the tenacious defence put up in Khorramshahr and Abadan. The character of such fighting is defensive and guerrilla-like with snipers and scattered pockets putting up a sustained resistance to armoured and infantry advance. The nature of the combat was such as to put life at a premium, and so tactics evolved that tended to guard it. When the clerics took over, the military conception changed dramatically. The idea became to *use the occasion of war to prove how good a Muslim one was*; winning versus losing took on an entirely new meaning. (Makiya 1998: 283, emphasis added)

One could become a martyr 'cheaply' just by getting oneself killed on a mine or shot while marching towards the Iraqi machine guns with abandon. For Khomeini and his followers, martyrdom was not a matter of accountancy. 'Using such "tactics" in the Basra region in the summer of 1982, the Iranians lost in two attempts a hundred thousand men and boys.' The same occurred in subsequent battles in which the level of casualties was 'unprecedented and militarily meaningless' (Makiya 1998: 285).

Even though the Iranian revolutionary guards contributed to the founding of the Hezbollah, and the Iranian clerics have maintained close contacts with them (Reuter 2004), the Hezbollah did not observe the same extreme form of martyrdom. Unlike the Iranian *enfants perdus*, the Hezbollah have been both highly lethal and parsimonious in their use of SMs. Perhaps this is because they could rely only on a scarce supply of volunteers. We do not know whether Fadlallah's argument had an effect, as it appeared in writing only in 1997 (Reuter 2004: ch. 5, n. 19), well after the Hezbollah's strategy had taken shape. There is a suspicion—as Reuter suggests—that fatwa are some-times ways to give retroactive support to practical decisions. Whatever the case, the less stringent view, widely shared in the Islamic world (Reuter 2004: 125), by contrast, accepts martyrdom even if the effects are harder to measure.

Still, even with that view, some destructive effect *must* be coupled with martyrdom to make it genuine. Self-immolation alone would not do. If justifying SMs is hard, justifying self-immolation is harder, from this per-spective. By killing others, no matter how few, one shows that one is having an effect, that one is not committing suicide but pursuing jihad. Killing proves that one did not want to die only because one did not want to live. So even though for many Palestinians dying in an SM seems to have a meaning closer to that of self-immolation—an act of extreme, indignant protest against oppressive humiliation carried out in a state of near-power-lessness—killing is necessary as a way to legitimize their choice of dying for the cause.

What Next?

Will SMs continue to spread or will they abate? Once in the repertoire, it is unlikely that a new tactic will disappear altogether. Plane hijacking waned (Chapter 3, this volume), but kidnapping (Elster 2004*b*) never has, and is back with a vengeance in Iraq and Saudi Arabia.

We know that the composition of SMs is changing. According to Merari (2005) '[o]f the 23 groups that used suicide terrorism before September 11, 2001, only 10 (43 per cent) were Islamic groups, whereas of the 17 groups which have used suicide attacks after 9/11, 13 (76 per cent) are Islamic'. But 9/11 simply accelerated a trend that began earlier: there has been an increase in the proportion of SMs carried out by Islamic groups since 1999 (Ricolfi 2003). This trend has been further reinforced by the attacks in Iraq since the 'end' of the war in 2003.

There are many signs, even predating the Iraqi war, that the clamouring for martyrdom is intensifying, and exerting its fascination on young minds. In Cairo, in April 2002, in a few hours 500 signatures in a martyrdom list were collected from students at the Islamic University al-Azhar (*La Repubblica*, 12 April 2002). At a recent 'peace' march in Paris:

Young French Arab teenagers from the poor suburbs chanted slogans pledging war and martyrdom in the name of both Palestinians and Iraqis and against Israel. 'We are all Palestinians, we are all Iraqis, we are all kamikazes!' chanted one group of teenagers, no older than 14 or 15, from the suburb of Garges-les-Gonesses. Others chanted: 'We are all martyrs! Allah-u Akbar! God is more powerful than the United States'. (*New York Times*, 30 March 2003)

In old British industrial towns like 'Crawley, Luton, Birmingham and Manchester, and in the Arab enclaves of Germany, France, Switzerland and other parts of Europe, intelligence officials say a fervor for militancy is intensifying', and that 'Iraq dramatically strengthened [radical groups'] recruitment efforts' (*New York Times*, 26 April 2004). And it is not all cheap talk. In late April 2003, two young British Muslims travelled together to Israel to carry out an SM targeting two pubs. The explosive belt of Omar Khan Sharif, age 27, failed to explode at a Jerusalem pub. He was later found dead in the sea. He had two young children, was the youngest of six children of Kashmiri immigrants, and attended a £12,000-a-year prep school. Asif Mohammed

Hanif, 21, from Hounslow, west London, died when his device detonated, killing three people and wounding six at a Tel Aviv club. Hanif was a former business studies student (*Guardian*, 2 May 2003). They were not acting on their own—Hamas and al-Aqsa Brigades claimed joint responsibility (*Jerusalem Post*, 9 May 2003).

There are divergent tendencies however. All seems quiet on the secular front. An outlier among SMs and terrorism generally, the nineteen hijackers' deed on 9/11 sealed the reputation of SMs as a signature trait of radical Islamic groups, with which secular groups now dread being confused. Gerry Adams, leader of Sinn Fein-IRA, quickly understood that 'Progressive struggles throughout the world have been set back by the attacks in the USA', and declared that 'Terrorism is ethically indefensible.... There is no excuse, no justification for those types of actions but neither should anyone who is truly concerned with world peace be deflected from the task or be carried away by the notion of a clash between civilisations' (*Sunday Times*, 30 September 2001). Pirabakaran, the leader of the LTTE, understood exactly the same point Adams made (Chapter 2, this volume), and in February 2002 the insurgents entered into a peace process with the Sri Lanka state that has not yet foundered. Any insurgent group that fights with a view to bargaining its way out of a civil war must now tread with care lest it is labelled as terrorist and bundled with a bad company that has become fair game worldwide.

Signs of hope come even from the Islamic world. Like Marx, who once declared he was not a Marxist, the Hezbollah, the founder of the modern SM wave, has become more rooted in political life as an ordinary party and is playing down the role of SMs (Atran 2003*c*, supporting material; Reuter 2004: ch. 9). It even condemned 9/11 as an act of terrorism (Shatz 2004). In Iran there seems to be embarrassment at the mention of the human waves of *enfants perdus*, as if they had been a passing cloud of rabid fervour to be rid of (Reuter 2004: ch. 9). The future of SMs will largely depend on whether, rather than a crude policy of war and intensifying the clangour of the clash of civilizations, opportunities for astute policing and genuine political processes will be taken up in earnest. Whatever our creed, most of us still want to succeed by living not by dying.

NOTES

Chapter 1

I would like to thank my fellow contributors, especially Diego Gambetta, for their enormously useful feedback. I have learned a great deal from all of them. I would also like to thank the British Academy for financially supporting this research.

1 Ramming of B-29 bombers did later become official policy.

2 Special attack, *tokubetsu kōgeki*, or in its abbreviated form *tokkō*, was the standard military euphemism for missions in which the death of the protagonist was a prerequisite for the mission's success.

3 These correspond closely to the figures in the General Dictionary of the Army and Navy (*Rikukaigun no sōgō Jiten*) and Asahi Chronicle (Shirai 2002: 22).

4 It should be noted that not all of these firebrands were able to make good on this commitment. On 26 February 1936, twenty-one extreme young officers took over central Tokyo, killing several leading politicians in the process, stating they would kill themselves if only their demands were met. Eventually, after the emperor had publicly dissociated himself from their aims, they surrendered (two of the twenty-one killed themselves). When the remaining mutineers were invited to kill themselves, they accepted this offer and were left with their weapons. They changed their minds, arguing that their cause would be better served by a public trial which would give a platform for their views (Pinguet 1993: 216–19).

5 Available in Japanese at http://archive.hp.infoseek.co.jp/senjinkun.html.

6 The prestige and exclusivity of this establishment was enormous. Yokota, for example, having passed the academic entrance exams, was failed because he had lost three teeth due to a sports-related injury. The families of applicants were also subjected to vetting by the secret police for signs of insanity or unsound political views. Training included a lengthy annual swim in open sea, in which it was expected that a couple of students would drown each year.

7 In fact, burning fuel frequently caused more damage than the impact itself.

8 Front-line pilot Yasunaga is particularly scornful of such records. 'The war memoirs of the staff officers are all the same . . . [pilots selected as Kamikaze] delightedly saying "Ah! I'm going too!" It wasn't like that . . . in various respects those brass hats don't disclose inconvenient facts in their memoirs' (interview, June 2003).

9 A similar obsession with being first can also be seen in Kanno, who, according to Inoguchi's account, would have taken Seki's place as the first leader of an official Kamikaze sortie had he not been in Japan picking up new planes. He complained to his superiors on returning to the Philippines (Inoguchi et al. 1961: 41).

Chapter 2

I would like to thank the other contributors to this volume, especially Diego Gambetta, two Tamil respondents, who must remain anonymous, and also Hélène Lavaix and Michael Roberts.

1   From 1972 to 1976 they were called the Tamil New Tigers, and then the LTTE from 1976 onwards.
2   Ceylon's name was changed to the more Sinhala-resonant Sri Lanka in 1972.
3   Although not a non-existent hope, as we will see.
4   By August 2004 the ceasefire was under strain, however, because of an intra-LTTE war, seemingly stoked by the Sri Lankan government, accompanied by a suicide attack in Colombo, in July, which killed four policemen. The LTTE denied this bombing, alleging it was a plot to destabilize the peace process.
5   From 1987 to 1990, the LTTE fought a large Indian peacekeeping force to a standstill.
6   www.tamilnet.com/art.html?artid=8&catid=13.
7   See www.eelamweb.com/maveerar/statistics.
8   In counting the LTTE's missions from 1990, Pape describes the first attack in 1987 as 'isolated'.
9   The LTTE's leader, Vellupillai Pirabakaran, did explicitly deny that the LTTE murdered Rajiv Gandhi in an interview with the BBC's Colombo Correspondent, Chris Morris, on 1 September 1991, as recorded in *Tamil Nation*, 15 October 1991, p. 9. *Tamil Nation* was a publication in English, in the United Kingdom, for the Tamil diaspora. The LTTE also denied killing Premadasa, according to United Press International (1 May 1993). Pirabakaran's name can also be spelled Prabhakaran and Pirapaharan.
10 My own limitations include the fact that by training I am a scholar neither of Sri Lanka nor of the sociology of extreme acts like SMs.
11 Compare, for example, the University Teachers of Human Rights (www.uthr.org), of whom president Kumaratunga speaks highly (see www.tamilnet.com/art.html?catid=13artd= 6431), with Sangam Research (www.sangam.org).
12 Some original material was gathered from the LTTE for these sections but unfortunately cannot now be used.
13 Berman and Laitin use Pape's data cross-referenced against that of the International Policy Institute for Counter-Terrorism (which, as of March 2004, listed only twenty-nine Black Tiger attacks). Berman and Laitin estimate the number of suicide attacks by the LTTE in Sri Lanka at seventy-five, the same as Pape.
14 Fearon and Laitin's suggestion (2003) that recruits to insurgencies tend not to grasp the ideological message of the leadership is not obviously borne out in the Tamil case.
15 The relationship between the LTTE and the Tamil-speaking Muslims is too complex to enter into in this chapter. There are deep-seated tensions between

the two communities but there have also been Muslim members of the LTTE. For the current situation in the east, see Jeyaraj (2002). This article is also enlightening about intra-LTTE politics.

16 On 'Estate Tamils' see Daniel (1996). See also Kurian (1984). There is little available evidence in English on the role of Indian Tamils in the LTTE, although of the Indian Tamils who migrate to the north and east some have joined the Tigers.

17 On this period in general see, for example, Wilson (1994) and Bose (1994).

18 Swamy is an Indian journalist who has done extensive interviews on the LTTE and Pirabakaran. In the wake of 11 September, he published *Inside An Elusive Mind: Pirabakaran* (New Delhi: Konark Publishers, 2003). See also Pratap (2001).

19 Various theories exist about his killer: either a Buddhist monk or a Sinhala nationalist disguised as a monk. There is no allegation that the Tamils were responsible.

20 Current President Chandrika Kumaratunga is their daughter.

21 1971 also saw the first JVP armed insurrection against the Sri Lankan state. The JVP was a revolutionary Marxist organization based among Sinhalese youths in the south. Swamy (1994: 18) claims 10,000 youths were killed in the suppression of this uprising.

22 According to Sharma (1988: 151), by 1978 not a single Tamil was recruited into the judiciary, with precipitate declines in other areas such as medicine and engineering; in 1969 Tamils made up 78.8 per cent of medical and engineering faculties.

23 The transcript of this interview is at www.eelamweb.com/leader/interview/in_1986.

24 Swamy (1994: 54) dates this to 1975 with a failed attempt on Duriappah's life in 1973 (Swamy 1994: 56); Wilson (2000: 107) dates Duriappah's murder to 1973.

25 It won eighteen of 168 seats. With the UNP under Prime Minister Junius Jayawardene (who soon became the country's first executive president under a second republican constitution) winning 140 seats, the TULF became the largest opposition party. Swamy (1994) gives many accounts of the violence undertaken by Tamil militants at this time.

26 Tambiah (1986: 20–1) says of this library burning that it 'has come to signify for many a living Tamil the apogean barbarity of Sinhalese vindictiveness that seeks physical as well as cultural obliteration'. But see Roberts (2004: 101, n. 54).

27 For more details on the killings, see Sharma (1988: 140–6) and Pratap (2001: 50–9).

28 The words 'holocaust' and 'genocide' are regularly used in the literature about these 1983 riots.

29 The politics of this Accord, like so much else in this story, are labyrinthine, right down to whether or not Pirabakaran and the LTTE accepted it (see Swamy 1994: 246, n. 9, but also Anton Balasingham's views as reported in Balasingham 2004: 101–2). What seems clear is that the LTTE, and Pirabakaran personally, felt betrayed by Indian Prime Minister Rajiv Gandhi, this sentiment being a possible reason for the assassination of Gandhi.

30 There have been several incidents during the current Norway-brokered ceasefire and peace process, including one in which three LTTE members, said to be in breach of ceasefire conditions, committed suicide after torching the trawler on which it is alleged they were smuggling an anti-aircraft gun.

31 Although this attack is well documented in hindsight, contemporaneous reports of it are hard to find.

32 A story in Sri Lanka's *Sunday Observer* has an interview with Miller's mother (Miller was his pseudonym, his real name being Wasanthan). She says the 20-year-old volunteered as a driver for the LTTE while studying for his advanced level in mathematics in Jaffna (Bulathsinghala 2003). Swamy (2003: 152) claims the planning for the operation took so long that a 'peeved' Miller told his handler to either 'carry out the suicide attack or let him off'.

33 www.tamilnet.com/art.html?artid=26&catid=13.

34 Swamy says the LTTE paid for sixteen fighters to travel to Lebanon, but problems ensued and it is unclear how many were actually trained. See also Balasingham (2004: 26).

35 Schalk (1997: 76) refers to Black Tigers as *tiyakis* or martyrs and their acts as *uyirayutam* or 'life as a weapon'.

36 Swamy (2003: 184) claims LTTE commander Mahattaya threatened to use suicide attacks against the IPKF.

37 This point about the 'creation' of the Black Tigers is developed in more detail below in discussion of the symbolic aspects of Black Tiger attacks.

38 Black Tiger deaths averaged fifteen a year from 1990 to 1996, and increased to just over twenty-four a year thereafter (at an overall average of twenty deaths a year for the twelve-year period).

39 These figures are contained in various press reports, by *AFP* and others, which attribute them to the Voice of Tigers radio. Exactly how these figures are calculated, whether they include those who died in unclaimed attacks, those who died accidentally, and so forth, are all open questions, of course.

40 A video produced by the LTTE for the Tamil diaspora, called *Oliveechu*, includes footage of battles in which Black Sea Tigers explode their boats into navy ships. Dramatizations are also made of successful LTTE operations, including those of the Black Tigers.

41 www.tamilnet.com/art.html?artid=10014&catid=13.

42 See Francis, 'LTTE's human wave tactics redefine guerrilla warfare', at www. ipcs.org. She fails here to distinguish between the different kinds of operations the Black Tigers engage in.

43 There is no reason to doubt this figure. Were it higher, it would show to the Sri Lankan government and army even more widespread commitment inside the LTTE. Were it lower, the great impact the Black Tigers have made would be even more impressive. Still, it is possible that the 241 does not include unclaimed attacks.

44 In this battle the LTTE appears to have deployed a few heavy artillery pieces it managed to acquire.

45 Swamy (2003: 149, for example) makes many claims about Sinhalese civilians being killed deliberately by the LTTE. If true, this makes the non-targeting of civilians by the Black Tigers even more intriguing.

46 On the reasons for LTTE withdrawal, see Balasingham (2000).

47 The LTTE is also said to have used Black Tigers to attack targets of symbolic importance to Buddhists. The most successful attack of this type was a truck bomb in January 1998 at the Temple of the Tooth in Kandy (which is said to hold the Buddha's left eye-tooth). This severely disrupted government plans for celebrating fifty years of Sri Lankan independence at the Temple, and the ceremony had to be moved to Colombo.

48 Although the target here consisted of infrastructure, the use of Black Tigers is presumably explained by the need to infiltrate the depot and overpower security. Here it is the elite skills of the Black Tigers as much as their preparedness to die that explains their role in the mission.

49 The JVP is a serious alternative candidate to the LTTE for some of these assassinations. It killed Kumaratunge's husband, for example. Nevertheless, Swamy (2003: 233–4) and Pratap (2001: 99–100) do have amazingly detailed information, if reliable, about the meticulously planned Black Tiger operation to kill Premadasa.

50 India still has an extradition warrant outstanding for his arrest. According to Pratap (2001: 126), Anton Balasingham admitted to her that the LTTE killed Gandhi, calling it an 'historical blunder'.

51 Again, Swamy's information (2003: 217–24) on the Black Tiger operation to kill Gandhi is very detailed. Its source is not made clear.

52 One had her sentence commuted to life imprisonment while, as far as one can tell from press material, none of the other three has yet been executed.

53 'In the aftermath of Katunayake', *TamilCanadian*, at www.tamilcanadian. com/pageview.php?ID=712&SID=129&pr_v=yes. Balasingham (2004: 351) calls the attackers commandos not Black Tigers.

54 Jeyaraj, in 'In the aftermath of Katunayake', says Pirabakaran oversaw the operation in minute detail to avoid civilian casualties. He stressed to his cadres that the air base was a military target and the airport an economic one. The base was attacked first to allow the civilian authorities to clear the airport. See also Balasingham (2004: 350–1).

55 Gunaratna (2001), a ubiquitous writer on terrorism and a relentless critic of the LTTE, makes a devastating indictment of the Sri Lankan defence and security services in the wake of this attack, pointing out how much more professional than the Sri Lankans the LTTE is in terms of training, intelligence, and commitment. Reading his account, especially given his dislike for the LTTE, one begins to see why the Tigers believe they can actually win the war rather than just fight it to a stalemate.

56 One difficult case (difficult because it is so unusual) was the bombing of a commuter train in Colombo in July 1996. This came on the thirteenth anniversary of the anti-Tamil riots that followed the LTTE attack on a convoy that

began the war proper. But it was also at a time when the LTTE was claiming to have killed 1,200 enemy soldiers in its biggest-ever conventional victory at a camp in Mullaitivu in the north-east; see *AFP* (1996*b*).

57 But see Roberts (forthcoming).

58 'LTTE leader makes special plea to the Sinhalese: reject racist forces: offer justice to the Tamils', 27 November 2001, at http://eelam.com/freedom_struggle/ltte_press_releases/2001/PR2001127.html.

59 www.tamilnet.com/art.html?artid=8&catid=13. The story adds that the cyanide capsule given to trained recruits is also a 'coveted recognition of graduation into the LTTE fighting ranks'. See also Balasingham (2004: 60–1).

60 A recurrent claim in some of the literature is that the LTTE uses young children for these attacks which, given their scale and effectiveness—attacking military bases and naval ships, or assassinating a president—seems improbable and should be treated with scepticism. On the role of children in the LTTE more generally, see Jeyaraj, 'Child soldiers, Amnesty International and the Tigers', *TamilCanadian*, at www.tamilcanadian.com/pageview.php?ID=103&SID=39, and an interview with Pratap in the *Daily News*, 29 October 2001, at http://origin.dailynews.lk/2001/10/29/fea01.html. See also Bloom (2005), who claims the LTTE has a distinct child soldier division called the 'Baby Tigers'. Since January 2004, the LTTE has handed over at least twenty-five members found to be younger than 18 years to UNICEF, arguing that these youths joined claiming to be older than 18, at www.tamilnet.com/art.html?catid=13&artid=11205.

61 6 November 2003, at www.tamilnet.com/art.html?artid=8&catid=13.

62 Pirabakaran is married to a Hindu and has three children.

63 Sabil Francis makes this claim in 'The uniqueness of LTTE's suicide bombers', at www.ipcs.org/issues/articles/321-sl-sabil.html.

64 www.tamilnet.com/art.html?artid=9362&catid=13.

65 www.tamilnet.com/print.html?artid=9365&catid=13.

66 www.tamilnet.com/art.html?artid=7148&catid=13.

67 www.tamilnet.com/print.html?artid=9365&catid=13. Pictures of these celebrations show the flame lighting, the garlanded photographs, a marching band, the raising of the Tamil Eelam flag, and LTTE officials standing to attention with their right hands held flat against their chests at right angles with the fingers pointing upwards. On *eelamweb* one can buy postcards carrying Black Tiger images, as well as songs and poems by and about them.

68 www.tamilcanadian.com/cgi-bin/pageview.php?ID=1889&SID=81.

69 www.tamilnet.com/print.html?artid=6124&catid=13.

70 www.tamilnet.com/art.html?artid=9353&catid=13.

71 On the Tamil diaspora in Norway, for example, see Fuglerud (1999).

72 UNICEF is adamant that children are kidnapped by the LTTE, which for its part continues to deny that there is any forced conscription. See www.unicef.org/Report_Nov_10_2003.pdf (and n. 60 above).

73 Schalk (1997) deals with women in the LTTE at length, including the role played by cyanide, but see also Balasingham (2003: 287), where she criticizes Schalk's

'armed virgins' view of women in the LTTE. By any comparison, the LTTE is an extremely gender-equal army.

74 Roberts (1996: 252) also claims Sivakumuran was 'the first martyr'. In O'Balance's oft-cited book *The Cyanide War* (1989) cyanide is barely mentioned. O'Balance does, however, make the claim (1989: 107) that, in defending Jaffna from the IPKF in 1987, suicide commandos were launched against them and that 500 such commandos had volunteered to make these assaults. No other source appears to mention this.

75 Many of these entries, like Sri Lanka's, are substantially out of date. Most eastern bloc entries, however, are more recent.

76 www.tamilnet.com/art.html?artid=8&catid=13.

77 www.tamilcanadian.com/pageview.php?ID496&SID82.

78 Although news accounts tend to claim that groups of Black Tigers, rather than individuals, infiltrate Colombo together in order to carry out assassination attacks.

79 Durkheim's chapter on 'altruistic' suicide bears only passing relevance to the case of the Black Tigers (even though Durkheim noted that in the West armies tend to have higher suicide rates than the general population and that within the army it was elite units that rated highest for suicide).

Chapter 3

For helpful comments and suggestions I am indebted to Michael Biggs, Diego Gambetta, Jon Elster, Peter Hill, Shany Mor, and Karma Nabulsi. I am also very grateful to Paolo Campana, who assisted me in preparing the integrated database.

1 In order to estimate the extent to which the number of SBs underestimates the number of SMs, we performed an extensive investigation on the ICT database on 'terror attacks' from 1981 to 2003, analysing in depth the descriptions of each attack. Out of a total of 638 attacks, 119 are classified as SBs and 155 as SMs. The difference (thirty-six cases) arises from forty SMs that are not classified as SBs and four SBs that we believed should not to be considered SMs ($36 = 40 - 4$). It, therefore, seems that the number of SMs in the ICT database exceeds the number of SBs by around 30 per cent.

2 For details see Appendix, section on 'Suicide Missions'.

3 In our integrated database, failed suicide missions (SM_2) amount to sixteen out of 224 executed missions ($SM_2 + SM_3$), or 7.1 per cent.

4 According to Schweitzer (2001), successful SMs by Hamas and PIJ (SM_3) from 1993 to mid-2001 amount to 50–55, yet the number grows to seventy ($SM_1 + SM_2 + SM_3$) if we also consider the failed or foiled ones. According to Margalit (2003), there were 198 SMs from the Oslo Agreements to the end of August 2002; 132 of these 'ended with the attackers blowing up others along with themselves'. According to IDF (www.idf.il), 'prevented' missions (SM_1) amount to thirty-nine out of 136 ($SM_1 + SM_2 + SM_3$) during the first twenty months the

Intifada, yet they rise to 271 out of 310 during the following nineteen months, from June 2002 to December 2003. From the little information we managed to gather, it appears that the percentage of foiled missions has grown considerably in the twenty-first century with a clear acceleration after the battle of Jenin (April 2002) and the end of the al-Aqsa Intifada (with the truce of 29 June 2003).

5 An example of this type is found in the attack by the Japanese Red Army terrorist group in 1972 against Tel Aviv's Lod airport, a civilian target. A group of three terrorists opened fire on passengers, killing and wounding tens of them. In this case one can surmise that the three terrorists did not undertake the attack thinking that the police would certainly kill them. Indeed, one of the three terrorists, Kozo Okamoto, survived and obtained asylum in Lebanon after a number of years of imprisonment. This example as well as others is reported by Schweitzer (2000) and Sprinzak (2000).

6 For a list of the main organizations see Appendix, section on 'Organizations'.

7 The distinction between terrorist and guerrilla organizations is based on the ICT database (on all attacks, suicidal and otherwise) and on our integrated database on suicide attacks.

8 According to Schweitzer (2002), for example, the SM era starts in 1983. Chandran (2001) agrees. According to Margalit (2003), it starts in November 1982.

9 According to Morris (2002: 695), who quotes Fisk (1990: 578–80), there would have been another ten SMs during the three months immediately after the Israeli withdrawal from Lebanon, which took place in June 1985 (the first on 9 July, and the other nine between July and September). These numbers are perfectly in line with the data contained in our integrated database, which records twenty-six SMs for the 1982–5 period (see Appendix, section on 'Suicide Missions').

10 These three attacks are completely ignored by the international ICT database (at least in the data available to the public), but are mentioned in the databases of MIPT (two events out of three) and TRC (three events out of three), as well as in a number of chronologies. Naturally, they have been included in our integrated database.

11 A suicide attack against a bus station in Safad (close to the Lebanese border), foiled by the Israeli army.

12 Of the other three attacks, one is ascribed to the PFLP-GC, one to al-Fatah, and one to the Democratic Front for the Liberation of Palestine (DFLP).

13 We are referring to Dalal al-Mughrabi, considered by some as a kind of originator of current female 'martyrdom operations'; others consider that Sana Mehaidli is the originator (see the subsection on the 'Lebanon Wave').

14 While the date and circumstances of the beginning of the first Intifada are well defined (on 8 December 1987 an Israeli truck hit a van packed with workers; the Palestinians celebrate the beginning of the Intifada on 9 December), the date of its end is controversial, since the Intifada faded away little by little; among the suggested dates (1991, 1992, 1993) we conventionally adopt the last, which coincides with the signing of the Oslo Agreement on 13 September 1993.

15 The date of the beginning of the al-Aqsa Intifada is controversial. According to the Israelis, it began on 27 September 2000 with the killing of an Israeli soldier at

the Netzarin Junction, while many Palestinian sources claim it starts the day after, with Sharon's controversial visit to the Temple Mount in Jerusalem (which the Palestinians call Haram al-Sherif). According to other sources the starting date is Friday 29 September, with the first casualties and wounded caused during the demonstrations that broke out after the Friday prayer in the al-Aqsa mosque. Conventionally we adopt 28 September.

16 See Appendix, especially sections on 'Quality of the Sources', 'Suicide Missions', and 'Attacks'.

17 The estimates of the number of SMs in the world provided in this paragraph have been obtained by combining four principal sources of information: estimates by the Institute of Peace and Conflict Studies, ICT database (for Israel and the Occupied Territories), articles by Schweitzer published on the ICT website (for Lebanon and for the Tamil), and an article by Wani for Kashmir (Wani 2002). For the number of SMs in Iraq, being recent, it was sufficient to undertake a search on the Internet.

18 The number of organizations operating in the six critical areas is in fact considerably more than twenty, since some organizations that resort to SMs are unknown or split into various cadres and factions; in our calculation, for example, we have considered as sole organizations all of the Chechen groups and all of the Iraqi groups.

19 We cite these assessments by Pape solely by way of example. The 'universe' (totality) of SMs reconstructed by Pape is in fact considerably underestimated (Ricolfi and Campana forthcoming), and the total number of events is critically dependent on the extent and content of the definition of a terrorist event (see Appendix, section on 'Suicide Missions').

20 According to Biggs (Chapter 5, this volume), the actual number of self-immolation cases in the 1963–2002 period could be in between 1,000 and 2,000. For our purposes we have adopted the median value of the interval, equal to 1,500, as our order of magnitude.

21 In this context we use the expression 'precedents' in an extended way to include objectively suicidal acts, such as many assassinations of celebrities and heads of state by anarchists and revolutionaries.

22 We are referring, in particular, to the great European cycle of assassinations of celebrities and heads of state carried out by anarchists and revolutionaries at the turn of the twentieth century, especially in Italy, France, Russia, and the Balkans (Elliott 1998). For further bibliographical references, see Chapter 6 in this volume by Kalyvas and Sánchez-Cuenca.

23 Readers who want a picture of the principal terrorist and guerrilla organizations operating in the Israeli–Palestinian conflict may refer to the Appendix, section on 'Organizations'.

24 The lack of data on the number of suicide candidates makes it impossible to undertake rigorous comparisons. Nevertheless, ethnographic evidence suggests that outside the Middle East such an abundance can be found only among the Tamil, and that within the Middle East the availability of volunteers is neither constant over time nor universal. According to some authors, the abundance of

aspiring martyrs found in the Palestinian area in recent years is a relatively new phenomenon: in 1994 Hamas still had to resort to persuasion (Kershner 1995), but a few years later, following an extensive field investigation, it discovered the existence of an 'arsenal of believers' (Hassan 2001).

25 Most of the data and figures we produce refer to the period in between 1 January 1981 and 31 December 2003. In some cases, however, we had to limit our analysis to more recent years, and in particular to the thirty-three months of the al-Aqsa Intifada, from 28 September 2000 to 29 June 2003, when the truce began. The weights chosen for the three-year moving average are 4/6 for the central year and 1/6 each for the two adjacent years. Moving average transformations have been used only to draw diagrams, avoiding fluctuations due to one or two episodes. Statistical computations are always performed on the raw series.

26 This impossibility arises mostly from two circumstances. In the first place the definitions of an attack (terrorist or guerrilla) used in the different databases and in the various chronologies differ greatly in their degree of inclusion (one source may report a number of incidents that is 10, 100, or even 1,000 times greater than another). In the second place, even when we keep one source constant, the relative degree of coverage can prove quite variable in time and in space (the ICT database, for example, is extensively documented on Israel and the Occupied Territories, but is decidedly deficient on Lebanon).

27 For a review on issues concerning the comparability of sources and the solutions adopted to build the index, see the Appendix, section on 'Attacks'.

28 In actual fact, stabilization of the total number of attacks during the 1987–92 period is given by the balance between the fading away of the conflict in the Lebanese area and its resurgence inside Israel and Occupied Territories.

29 Neither 'preference' nor 'propensity', which we use interchangeably, is entirely satisfactory. Both, in fact, recall agent intrinsic characteristics (likings or lean-ings), and do not take into account the eventual effect of limitations and resources. In our analysis, the 'preference for' or 'propensity to' SMs should thus be interpreted as mere descriptions of choice, which may derive both from preference in the strict sense of the term and from limitations (level of army security measures) and resources (supply of militants).

30 The correlation between preference for SMs and time is relatively low (0.463 over the raw series). If our database were complete, the correlation would quite probably be closer to zero, if not slightly negative. The Lebanon wave is, in fact, the only wave of SMs in which a significant number of cases is probably missing. Our database records thirty attacks in Lebanon in the 1983–2000 period, against a total of around fifty reported by Schweitzer (2000).

31 The correlation is 0.436 with raw data, but drops to 0.323 and becomes statis-tically insignificant once we remove the trend.

32 In this regard, see Schweitzer's assessments (2000, 2001, 2002) and the recon-structions by Fisk (1990: 610–11) and Morris (2002: 694–5).

33 Sana Mehaidli is considered the progenitor of all female martyrs for the Pales-tinian cause. Even though a member of the SSNP and her photograph still (2003) appears in the Gallery of Martyrs in the party's home page, it is quite common

for sources to talk about the 'Shiite girl' or the 'Muslim girl' or indeed to ascribe the attack to Amal, concealing in this way the secular matrix of this first female SM (the MIPT database also falls into this error). Israeli historian Benny Morris looks upon this first female SM as an attempt to emulate Islamic organizations (Hezbollah and Amal) by the secular organizations (SSNP in this case): 'Shiite suicide attackers started being imitated by agents of the Syrian Nationalist Party sent in the area by Damascus. Furthermore, the SNP started using female kamikazes, believing that at least in the beginning female attackers would arouse less suspicion. On April 9th a 16-year-old girl blew her car up next to an Israeli convoy close to Jezzine, causing two deaths and two wounded amongst Israeli soldiers, two deaths amongst Lebanese soldiers' (Morris 2002: 693).

34 On the ancient origins of martyrdom in Islamic culture, see Hudson (1999); on colonialism as the background of SMs, see Dale (1988); on the Iranian case, see Davis (2003) and Panella (2003).

35 See subsection on 'Attitudes Towards Suicide Bombers'.

36 See the *Hezbollah (Party of God)* file, published on the ICT website www.ict. org.il/organizations.

37 Morris (2002: 900) goes as far as to say that the (second) Israeli withdrawal from Lebanon, promised and carried out by Barak in the year 2000, was one of the triggering causes of the Intifada. This opinion is shared by ICT's Karmon (2000: 2).

38 Actually, Hezbollah's prevailing actions were guerrilla attacks by suicide bombers in the 1980s and conventional (non-suicidal) terror attacks in the 1990s (ICT database on terror attacks; our integrated database on SMs).

39 The incidence of SMs dropped significantly after January 1986 (three cases in the February–December period against nineteen in the previous year); only one SM in 1987.

40 To be precise, SMs ceased completely in 2000 until the outbreak of the al-Aqsa Intifada on 28 September 2000; the first SM took place four weeks after the outbreak of the new Intifada, on 26 October 2000.

41 Arafat and the PLO leadership were expelled from Lebanon in 1982 by the Israeli forces; they stayed in exile in Tunis from 1981 until 1994, when they returned to Palestine.

42 Nevertheless, in the following years Arafat did not keep his promise to remove from the PLO charter Article 15, which contemplates the destruction of the state of Israel ('elimination of Zionism in Palestine'); this shortcoming would be used by the Israelis as evidence of insincerity of Arafat's declared intentions.

43 On the importance of the number of SM victims, see also the interesting observations by Kramer (1991).

44 Prime Minister Rabin was immediately replaced by the other Nobel Prize winner, the Minister of Foreign Affairs, Shimon Peres.

45 Signed on 23 October by Arafat and Netanyahu in presence of the US President Clinton and King Hussein of Jordan.

46 On 5 October 1999 an agreement was reached on opening a Gaza–West Bank 'corridor'; on 4 January 2000 Israeli and Palestinian negotiators reached an agreement on withdrawal from the territories.

47 Reference is made to the reconstruction by Codovini (2002: 298–9).

48 See the quotation from Morris' book *Victims* (2002).

49 On this aspect of the functioning of Palestinian public opinion, see the data reported below on 'Attitudes Towards Suicide Bombers'.

50 On the content of the Barak's offer, see Margalit (2001) and, more generally, the debate on the Camp David negotiations published in *The New York Review of Books*, June–September 2001.

51 Before the breach between Arafat and Barak, the only significant incidents, carried out by Hezbollah guerrillas, occurred at the beginning of the year in Lebanon.

52 Strangely enough, Kydd and Walter (2002) do not take this anomaly seriously in their important essay and prefer to construct an ad hoc explanation (Hamas allegedly remained silent to hinder the election of the dove Barak in 1999 and favouring the re-election of the hawk Netanyahu; after Barak's election Hamas remained silent again 'since terrorist violence at this point was unlikely to change Barak's mind and halt negotiations').

53 The survey was carried out jointly by the Palestinian Center for Policy and Survey Research (PSR, Ramallah) and the Harry S. Truman Research Institute for the Advancement of Peace (Hebrew University, Jerusalem).

54 The survey took place during 27–31 July; the Camp David negotiations terminated on 26 July.

55 In this analysis, based on the comparison between suicidal and non-suicidal attacks, we are obliged to use the ICT database, which contains both types of actions. Consequently, the SMs that are taken into consideration are only those classified as suicide bombings in the ICT database.

56 In al-Fatah's case we made a distinction between al-Fatah's 'suicide wing' (al-Aqsa Martyr Brigades) and its grass roots (Tanzim), because the al-Aqsa Martyr Brigades make ample use of SMs (missions classified as SBs by ICT account for 27.2 per cent of the total), while the Tanzim rely almost exclusively on conventional actions (98.6 per cent according to the ICT database). It should be added that al-Aqsa militia is devoted not only to offensive actions but also to the defence of Palestinian camps.

57 In the Israeli–Palestinian conflict, if we exclude a number of uncertain cases in Lebanon in the second half of the 1980s, the first female suicide attack that may be ascribed to an Islamic organization is the one carried out by Hiba Daragmeh at Afula on 19 May 2003. In fact, the young woman's affiliation is controversial (the attack was also claimed by the al-Aqsa Martyr Brigades). If we exclude this case, the first Islamic female SM is the one that took place on 4 October 2003, claimed by the PIJ. In the period covered by our analysis (1981–2003), Hamas has carried out no female SMs even though on various occasions several Hamas officials (including Yassin and Rantisi) announced the possibility of involving women in SMs. See Daly (2001) and the anonymous article 'The Role of Palestinian Women in Suicide Terrorism' (www.mfa.gov.il, January 2003). The first female SM involving Hamas took place only at the beginning of 2004 (14 January), with 22-year-old Rim Salah Riyachi, who blew herself up at the Erez crossing. The attack was jointly claimed by the al-Qassam brigades (armed

wing of Hamas) and by the al-Aqsa Martyr Brigades (suicide wing of al-Fatah).

58 During the al-Aqsa Intifada, attacks against civilian targets accounted for 88 per cent of suicide bombing cases and for 75.4 per cent of conventional attacks (ICT database).

59 The total number of SMs during the al-Aqsa Intifada is ninety-six, according the ICT database (restricted definition, SB), but rises to 116 according to our integrated database (extended definition, SM).

60 The first survey following the one of 13 September, carried out at the beginning of July 2001, nine months after the beginning of the Intifada, reveals significant progress of the PIJ (from 3.7 per cent to 6.9 per cent), of Hamas (from 10.3 per cent to 16.7 per cent), and of Hamas's leader, Sheik Yassin (from 8.4 per cent to 12.9 per cent).

61 The Road Map is the peace plan, based on a permanent two-state solution, proposed by the so-called Quartet (USA, UN, EU, Russia). Support for the Road Map by Palestinian factions developed in a somewhat confused and ambiguous manner (Urquhart 2003).

62 During the thirty-three months of the al-Aqsa Intifada 143 SMs were carried out ($SM_2 + SM_3$), according to our database. Cases of self-explosion ($SB_2 + SB_3$) amounted to 103 according to our database, ninety-two according to the ICT database.

63 See, for example, the recent book by Italian-Israeli journalist Dviri (2003).

64 Even in the two cases most often cited as examples of Palestinian retaliation (response to the massacre carried out by settler Baruch Goldstein, 25 February 1994, and the killing of the bomb-maker, 'engineer' Ayash, 1 January 1996), the Palestinian response is apparently too belated to be interpreted with any certainty as an act of retaliation (of course, the reasons invoked to justify an attack are not necessarily the real reason for the attack).

65 In our empirical checks we mostly worked with a one-week delay (see Appendix, section on 'Incidents during the Intifada').

66 In the Middle East context there is at least one other important precedent suggesting a possible positive link between martyrdom and militant morale: the 'martyrdom' of the founder of the SSNP, betrayed by the Syrian government just after the proclamation of the state of Israel (see the 'History of the SSNP' section in the party's web site www.ssnp.com).

67 See Appendix , section on 'Incidents during the Intifada'.

68 The joint attack took place on 8 June at the Erez crossing. This SM is the first to be jointly claimed by the three principal Palestinian terrorist organizations (Hamas, PIJ, al-Aqsa). Previously, however, there had been many cases of joint claims by *two* organizations: for example, 27 January 2002 (al-Aqsa and PIJ), 24 April 2003 (Hamas and PFLP), and 30 April 2003 (al-Aqsa and Hamas).

69 Estimates of the death count during the al-Aqsa Intifada due to clashes and intra-Palestinian executions diverge significantly according to the adopted definitions and mostly to the sources. Nonetheless, the death toll is not insignificant (close to 100), even though certainly lower than that of the first Intifada (around 1,000).

70 Sympathy for SMs is presumably lower in Israel and the United States, though for different reasons. Unlike the Europeans, the Israelis are directly affected by Palestinian suicide terrorism. US citizens, unlike the Europeans, have a distant perception of the Chechen, Kurdish, and Palestinian struggles for independence (just as Europeans have for the Tamil).

71 In principle, even air hijackings are capable of directly harming Israeli citizens. They have, however, become more difficult to carry out because of strengthened security measures, which are not comparable in any air company with those adopted by El Al (La Guardia 2002).

72 According to some observers, not all SMs are carried out voluntarily. Especially during the war in Lebanon (1982–5) in some cases the attacker was apparently forced to carry out his action with threats and blackmail (Pipes 1986). Even ethnographic evidence suggests that the abundance of aspiring martyrs is a relatively recent phenomenon (see n. 24).

73 Based on rather heterogeneous material—350 individual cases from different countries—this pioneering study raises quite a few methodological reservations today (Hudson 1999).

74 Up to a few years ago, it seemed that the connection did not count for the Arab world (Hudson 1999).

75 For the role of individual and family tragedies, see especially Saleh (2003*b*).

76 See, in particular, the works by Brian Barber and Basel Saleh quoted in Atran (2003*a*), or the debate on suicide terrorism recently held at www.interdisciplines.org

77 Some authors point out that terrorism attracts certain types of personalities (action-oriented, aggressive, stimulus-hungry, excitement-seeking, narcissistic, with low self-esteem, and so forth), while others point out that the same personalities are over-represented in professions such as policeman or soldier, which entail high risks and a systematic recourse to violence (Laqueur 1987; Post 1990; Hudson 1999). For a critical review of available empirical evidence see Silke (1998, 2003).

78 See Margalit (2003) but also Tierney (2002) and Simon (2003).

79 A similar pattern emerges in Italian public opinion, in which the humbler classes prefer moderate and central parties.

80 The other centre is the Palestinian Center for Policy and Survey Research (PSR, PCSR until 2001). In this chapter we used data from both sources, but we should point out that there are apparent systematic differences between samples from JMCC and from PSR. This clearly emerges from a comparison of electoral preferences: Islamists obtain a higher consensus in the JMCC sample while the nationalist consensus is higher in the PSR sample (see Appendix, section on 'Opinion Polls').

81 A similar argument is advanced by Dershowitz in his recent book on terrorism, with particular regard to the air hijackings period (Dershowitz 2002).

82 According to ICT, by 2 July 2003 Palestinian victims of the Intifada killed by other Palestinians amounted to 293, equal to almost 15 per cent of total Palestinian victims.

83 According to Margalit (2003), vengeance was indeed the primary motivation of one of the first cases of 'almost-suicide' missions, carried out by Omar Abu Sirhan, who stabbed three people after the massacre at the al-Aqsa mosque on 8 October 1990. This is an interesting case because the mission was completely spontaneous, inspired by vengeance, but *not* intentionally suicidal: only afterwards would Hamas transform this potential vengeance harboured in the population into (organized and suicidal) martyrdom operations.

84 Of course, we cannot know to what extent Alī's story is representative. Interesting, however, is the fact that a similar pathway can be found in the biographies of military leaders once tied to secular organizations (PLO, al-Fatah, Force 17, and so on), who subsequently drew close to religion. See, for example, the story of Mounir al-Maqdah (*nom de guerre*: Abu Hassan), once commander of Force 17 (Gambill 2003*b*).

85 Of course, I do not have the competence to uphold one interpretation of the Koran over another, but as a common (and secular) reader I certainly got a clear impression: the letter of the Koran clearly is nimbly compatible with the extremist interpretation. I could quote the passages that call for the jihad or those that threaten atrocities against the unbelievers (see, for example, Sura 5. 33–4; Sura 9. 38–9, 41). But the most interesting passage is the one amply cited by the mass media after September 11. I am referring to verse 32 of Sura 5 (The Table), whose original text is, however, quite different from the quoted one. The text quoted by the mass media recites a categorical and unequivocal condemnation of homicide ('he who kills another human being is as if he had killed all mankind'). It is clearly an excellent source to prove that terrorism, and the killing of innocent civilians in particular, cannot be justified by the Koran. Yet the *complete* verse sounds very different: 'he who kills another human being *for other than manslaughter or corruption on earth* is as if he had killed all mankind.' The passage in italics has been censured and eliminated because of its incompatibility with the modern interpretation of the Koran. It admits both homicide for revenge and homicide against bearers of corruption (I should mention that corruption is exactly the charge that Islam is bringing against the Western world in general and against US society in particular). Worthy of note is the fact that the quoted verse is recited almost word for word in the Jewish Mishnah, the Rabbinic code of law written at the end of the second century AD. If, on top of all this, we add that revenge, which is essentially missing in the other main religions of the world (Christianity and Hinduism), is present as a law of retaliation (an eye for an eye, a tooth for a tooth) in very similar terms in both the Bible (Exod. 2: 21, 23–26) and the Koran (Sura 2. 178–9, 194; Sura 5. 45; Sura 17. 33; Sura 42. 39–41), all the elements are there in support of the idea that religion has been a fundamental matrix of the Israeli–Palestinian conflict.

86 We refer to PSR surveys; see Appendix, section on 'Opinion Polls'.

87 PSR, Poll 1 (27–31 July 2003).

88 Amnesty International's report (2002) made serious allegations against the IDF; shortly after, the IDF published a meticulous reconstruction of the 'Battle of Jenin', in which it responded item by item to the allegations contained in the report.

89 On this peculiarity of the Palestinian case, see also Margalit (2003) and Atran (2003*a*).

90 The adoption of audio–visual means to leave a trace after an SM, even though used especially in recent years and mostly by Islamic organizations, actually dates back almost twenty years, when, in the summer of 1985, it was introduced by activists of at least three secular organizations: the SSNP, the Baath-Leb, and the LCP. Recently, it has returned to the fore with the famous case of Jamal Sati, an activist of the LCP who died in an SM in southern Lebanon on 8 August 1985 (the videotape was broadcast on television after the suicide action). In 1999 the video-recorded testament of Jamal Sati was found by chance, and was exploited in theatrical performances.

91 We owe this last observation also to Diego Gambetta.

92 I am indebted to Jon Elster for this remark.

93 Despite political and religious pressures glorifying the so-called martyrdom operations, and despite the difficulty of resisting group pressure, there are numerous cases in which parents of martyrs or aspiring martyrs criticize their own sons and daughters, or challenge the opportunity to strike civilians, or take an active stand to prevent or stop SMs. For example, Musa Ziyada was recruited by the Islamists and saved by his father (Kershner 1995), and a girl from Gaza was discovered and reported by her father on 7 July 2003 just before she was about to carry out a suicide mission (Gonen 2003).

94 The number of settlers has grown continuously since 1980, regardless of the type of government in power in Israel. In 1982 settlers numbered around 22,000; at the beginning of the peace process (1991, Conference of Madrid) they numbered 100,000; nine years later, when the al-Aqsa Intifada broke out, they had grown to 200,000 (Israeli Interior Ministry and CBS; Consolidated Billing Services, www.paceinpalestina.it). Nevertheless, it should be remarked that the increment in the number of settlements, especially after 1986, was not very steep. From 1993 to 2000 the increment in the number of settlements ranges from zero to ten depending on sources and definitions (I am indebted to Shany Mor for this observation).

95 Here we do not refer to the general population but to people who directly suffered losses at the hands of the Israelis. Evidence collected by Saleh (2003*b*) suggests that suicide bombers have been distinctly hit harder by them.

96 The closure of Occupied Territories dates back to the 1992–3 period, during the Oslo peace process (I am indebted to Shany Mor for this observation).

97 Incidentally, we might note that this combination is imperfect both in the case of Palestinian suicide bombers, since the victim (the suicide bomber) is not innocent, and in the case of hunger strikers, since it is difficult to be a complete hero (in the classic, epic sense) without inflicting damage on the enemy. Different again is the concept of martyr in the Catholic tradition, in which the victim is such because he would rather die than renounce his faith: in this case there is neither political cause nor a real enemy. On the complex issue of the concept of martyr in the Israeli–Palestinian conflict, see the interesting reflections in Kramer (1991). On the logic of martyrdom, see Ferrero (2004).

98 On the role that obligation, pursuit of glory, and codes of honour can play in the decisions of Palestinian SBs, see Pipes (2001*a*).

Chapter 4

1 Evidence that Khalid Shaikh Mohammed was the chief organizer of both the failed 1993 attack and the successful 2001 attack on the WTC is circumstantial but impressive. See Fouda and Fielding (2003: 95).

2 Information to help us answer these questions comes from post-attack police investigations in many countries, leaked portions of detainee interrogations, unearthed documents, investigative journalism, court proceedings in the United States and Germany, wiretaps revealed in such proceedings, interviews with people who met the hijackers and the latter's close friends and relatives, filmed and written 'wills', a slew of al-Qaeda propaganda material (including training films, pamphlets, websites, proclamations, communiqués, fatwas, and amateur post-attack videotapes), published speculations by psychologists, dozens of 'the mind of a fanatic' newspaper and magazine articles, Internet searches, and a wave of recent books.

3 '*Dawn* Interview with Usama bin Ladin (November 10, 2001)', in Rubin and Rubin (2002: 261).

4 'Broadcast by Usama bin Ladin (October 7, 2001)', in Rubin and Rubin (2002: 249).

5 Osama bin Laden, interview with Tayseer Alouni (October 2001), cited in Benjamin and Simon (2002: 157).

6 'Suicide', in Esposito (1995: 134).

7 'A Mission to Die For', an interview with Jerrold M. Post, www.abc.net.au/4corners/atta/interviews/post.htm. Similar conversion stories are told about many of the other hijackers: in 1999, for instance, Ahmed Alnami 'began a rapid change, becoming obsessively pious after returning home from a Saudi-government sponsored religious summer camp' (Sennott 2002).

8 'Atta's Last Will', reprinted in Aust and Schnibben (2002: 304–7).

9 The only pilot not also a member of the Hamburg cell was Hani Hanjour, a Saudi who had been in the United States since 1996, revealing that Germany was not the sole forward operational base for 9/11 and demonstrating that the attack was coordinated at a higher level.

10 There is some question about whether or not Atta met with an Iraqi agent in Prague in late May 2001. If it occurred, this meeting would be pertinent to the current discussion, not because it would establish some ephemeral Iraqi influence on the 9/11 plot, but because it would suggest that a multifaceted rage against the United States was more important to the plotters than strict fidelity to Islamic fundamentalism. No reliable evidence seems to exist of this meeting, however.

11 His dissertation was titled 'Khareg Bab-en-Nasr: An Endangered Ancient Urban District of Aleppo: Urban District Development in an Islamic Oriental Town'.

12 Islamic fundamentalism fits modernity well in the sense that it allows young men to feel 'included' even as they walk away from their families.

13 About Jarrah, we learn: '"He was different," said Mzoudi. "A mixture of Westerner and real Muslim. Sometimes you couldn't tell him apart from the Europeans"' (Miller and Stone 2002: 264); he is consistently reported to have been 'Fun-loving' (Corbin 2002: 135) and, unlike Atta, gifted in human relations; although as 9/11 approached he did begin to pressure his girlfriend to wear the veil. It is also curious that his great uncle had served in the Stasi, the East German secret police (Fouda and Fielding 2003: 85).

14 The most important other member of the Hamburg cell was Ramzi bin al-Shibh, originally from Yemen and arrested in Karachi in September 2002.

15 Per capita GDP of Saudi Arabia went from $28,600 in 1981 to $6,800 in 2001 (Baer 2003: 55).

16 According to Mann (2003: 109), 'most suicide bombers have been nationalists, not fundamentalists. The immortality offered by sacrifice for the nation is much more real than any religious notion of heaven.'

17 Ahmad al-Haznawi al-Ghamidi's 'Pre-Attack Videotape' (Summer 2000), in Rubin and Rubin (2002: 276).

18 This stress on the Palestinian experience suggests another unverifiable hypothesis: to retaliate against Israelis, who regularly demolish the houses of the suicide bombers' families, might not al-Qaeda have chosen to demolish the 'houses' of Israel's tribal kin?

19 Camus 1977: 119; cf. 'Celui qui tue n'est coupable que s'il consent encore à vivre...Mourir, au contraire annule la culpabilité et le crime lui-même' (Camus 2002: 112).

20 US Attorney General, John Ashcroft, used the same argument to justify weakening civil liberties in the United States after 9/11.

21 Rather than being too secular to understand religious motives, as Benjamin and Simon (2002) contend, Americans may be too individualistic to understand strong corporate identity and the glorification of self-sacrifice it entails.

22 'Nous perdons encore la vie avec joie, pourvu qu'on en parle' (Pascal 1954: 1128).

23 This hyper-individualistic interpretation of the motives of the 9/11 hijackers, paradoxically, has a special appeal to modern American readers who have a highly attenuated sense of corporate identity and who cannot imagine dying for a group.

24 Ahmad al-Haznawi al-Ghamidi's 'Pre-Attack Videotape' (Summer 2000), in Rubin and Rubin (2002: 276).

25 Euripides, *The Bacchae*.

26 'Interview with Ayman al-Zawahiri (October 7, 2001), in Rubin and Rubin (2002: 288).

27 This is the principal theme of Fouda and Fielding (2003).

28 Although Khalid Shaikh Mohammad was probably the mastermind behind the first attack on the WTC, he was not closely affiliated with Osama bin Laden in 1993. The tight collaboration between them probably began sometime around 1996 (Fouda and Fielding 2003: 92).

29　As was the attack on the synagogue in Djerba, Tunisia, in April 2002. The suicide terrorist in that case telephoned Khalid Shaikh Mohammad three hours before completing his mission (Frantz and Butler 2002).

30　Ayman al-Zawahiri, 'Knights under the Prophet's Banner' (2001), cited in Gunaratna (2002: 299).

31　'Videotape of a Private Meeting (December 13, 2001)', in Rubin and Rubin (2002: 244).

32　Ahmad al-Haznawi al-Ghamidi's 'Pre-Attack Videotape' (Summer 2000), in Rubin and Rubin (2002: 276).

33　Ahmad al-Haznawi al-Ghamidi's 'Pre-Attack Videotape' (Summer 2000), in Rubin and Rubin (2002: 276).

34　See Pape's claim that 'the target state of every modern suicide campaign has been a democracy' (Pape 2003: 350).

35　'*Dawn* Interview with Usama bin Ladin (November 10, 2001)', in Rubin and Rubin (2002: 261).

36　'Videotape of a Private Meeting (December 13, 2001)', in Rubin and Rubin (2002: 244).

37　'Videotape of a Private Meeting (December 13, 2001)', in Rubin and Rubin (2002: 244).

38　'The element of suicide itself helps to increase the credibility of future attacks, because it suggests that attackers cannot be deterred' (Pape 2003: 347).

39　Retaliation against the family members of the attackers, whatever sense it makes tactically, is emotionally unsatisfying, especially in modern societies based on liberal-individualist norms.

40　'Statement: Jihad against Jews and Crusaders (February 23, 1998)', in Rubin and Rubin (2002: 150).

41　'Broadcast by Usama bin Laden (November 3, 2001)', in Rubin and Rubin (2002: 257).

42　'Videotape of a Private Meeting (December 13, 2001)', in Rubin and Rubin (2002: 244).

43　'Broadcast by Usama bin Laden (November 3, 2001)', in Rubin and Rubin (2002: 259); in the November 2002 audiotape attributed to bin Laden, Bush is referred to as 'the modern-day pharaoh' (Risen and MacFarquhar 2002: A18).

44　'Broadcast by Usama bin Ladin (October 7, 2001)', in Rubin and Rubin (2002: 249).

45　'Broadcast by Usama bin Ladin (October 7, 2001)', in Rubin and Rubin (2002: 262).

46　*Koran*, Sura 2: 190–1; Sura 22: 39–40.

47　'Broadcast by Usama bin Ladin (October 7, 2001)', in Rubin and Rubin (2002: 249); the Ottoman Caliphate was abolished in 1924.

48　'Al-Qa'ida Statement (October 10, 2001)', by Suleiman Abu Ghaith, in Rubin and Rubin (2002: 252).

49　'Al-Qa'ida Statement (October 10, 2001)', by Suleiman Abu Ghaith, in Rubin and Rubin (2002: 256). It is curious to observe the way that Osama bin Laden and George W. Bush both oscillate, in their descriptions of the ongoing conflict, between two mutually incompatible analogies: fighting a war and prosecuting a crime.

50 'Interview with Ayman al-Zawahiri (October 7, 2001)', in Rubin and Rubin (2002: 288).

51 'Broadcast by Usama bin Laden (November 3, 2001)', in Rubin and Rubin (2002: 260).

52 NATO suffered a similar identity crisis after the collapse of the Soviet Union but, unlike al-Qaeda, the Atlantic alliance has proved unable to regroup and reinvigorate itself by identifying a new common enemy.

53 'Broadcast by Usama bin Laden (November 3, 2001)', in Rubin and Rubin (2002: 260).

54 'Broadcast by Usama bin Laden (November 3, 2001)', in Rubin and Rubin (2002: 259).

55 Memories of Beirut in 1983 and Mogadishu in 1993 apparently played a major role in the thinking of the 9/11 plotters. These two earlier incidents suggested to Osama bin Laden, Khalid Shaikh Mohammad, and their co-conspirators that the United States would turn tail and run away when attacked. But the United States obviously had greater reasons to stay in the Gulf than it had to stay in Lebanon or Somalia. As a result, terrorism aimed at ousting the United States from the Gulf was much more likely to provoke retaliation than evacuation.

Chapter 5

This research was supported in part by a grant from the Economic and Social Research Council, no. 000-22-0033z. I am indebted to my fellow contributors and especially to Diego Gambetta, along with James Benn, Susanne Choi, Andreas Glaeser, Doug Grbic, Olivier Grojean, Heather Hamill, Keith Hawton, Nejla Coskun, Alistair McMillan, Christian List, Clark McPhail, Kate Meagher, Anna Maria Marshall, Sally Nhomi, Avner Offer, Nenad Puhovski, Alice de Sturler, Robert Topmiller, and Kamakshya Trivedi.

1 As with any social phenomena, there are boundary cases. Musa Mamut, a Crimean Tatar, set himself alight and ran towards a policeman; according to his father, he intended to harm or kill (Uehling 2000). More enigmatic is Norman Morrison's decision to bring his infant daughter: 'I shall not plan to go without my child, as Abraham did' (quoted in Morrison Welsh 2000: 4). He set himself alight, but she escaped unharmed.

2 This is not yet reflected in dictionary definitions, but it is apparent in news reports (for example, 'immolation' used to describe murder by fire in the *New York Times*, 22 January 1969). The shift in meaning indicates, yet again, the impact of Quang Duc's sacrifice.

3 The death of Roop Kanwar in 1987 was, however, used by the Hindu nationalist movement to symbolize its conflict with the secular state.

4   Hypothetically, an individual could fast to death without making any threat and without heeding any concessions, but this seems unlikely and I have found no examples.

5   After this chapter was written, Ben Park kindly sent me a paper on self-immolation in Vietnam and South Korea (Park 2004).

6   The index to the *New York Times* is searched under the heading 'suicide'; in addition, the electronic text (recently available through the ProQuest database) is searched by the keywords 'immolate', 'immolated', 'immolating', and 'immolation'. The index to *The Times* is searched electronically, under the heading 'suicide' until 1965 and 'self-immolation' thereafter.

7   Other news-wires, from different parts of the world, have recently been added to the Nexis database. These are not included because this would destroy comparability of coverage over time. The keywords utilized are 'immolate', 'immolated', 'immolating', and 'immolation'. Some reports, unfortunately, may not include these words, but this is the only feasible method of searching.

8   A thwarted attempt is included only if it was physically prevented at the last moment; this excludes arrests for apparently planning self-immolation.

9   I would tend to exclude suicides on the illness or death of a public figure—like that of Chief Minister M. G. Ramachandran in Tamil Nadu, India (Pandian 1992: 17–18)—though the point is moot because there is not sufficient information on individual cases, even in Indian newspapers.

10 One example is Musa Mamut (Uehling 2000).

11 CNN denied that it was tipped off beforehand; its producer just guessed that some sort of protest was likely (*AP*, 8 February 2001). The film was confiscated by the police.

12 This is indicated by *The Times* index, which includes articles dropped from later editions of the day's newspaper. Some tantalizing reports of self-immolation were driven off the page by late-breaking news. Because only the day's final edition is microfilmed and archived, these reports effectively vanish from the record. (Even *The Times* itself does not hold these early editions.)

13 Chân Không (1993: 206–8); Forest (1978: 31–41); Human Rights Watch (1995); Lee and Bishop (1998: 171); Puhovski (1997); Radio Praha (n.d.); Ramaswamy (1997: 233, 271–3); Uehling (1990). This includes a group of twelve which was actually reported in *The Times* (8 September 1976), though not indexed under 'immolation'; the newspaper report alone does not provide sufficient information to warrant inclusion in the sample.

14 Accounts by those in Vietnam at the time include Browne (1965, 1993); Chân Không (1993); Halberstam (1965); Hope (1967); Luce and Sommer (1969); Mecklin (1965); Schecter (1967); and Thich Giac Duc (1986). Joiner (1964) and Topmiller (1994) narrate the events.

15 This creative redeployment of religious tradition in political struggle has similarities with the contemporaneous American civil rights movement. Like Vietnamese Buddhists, Southern blacks practised militant non-violence, and were adept at using the media to discredit their opponents. Both took inspiration from Gandhi's similar synthesis of Hinduism and nationalism.

16   The report, which appeared two years afterwards, included some fanciful elem-
      ents; it mentions neither eyewitnesses nor any note (Tz'u-hsing Ch'an Ssu 1958).
      My thanks are due to Susanne Choi for translating this.

17   Schecter (1967: 178) claims that Diem was told three days in advance of the self-
      immolation, but did not take the warning seriously.

18   Curiously, Herz's sacrifice attracted far less attention in the United States than
      the subsequent two. Perhaps the neglect can be explained by gender (Ryan 1994).
      Note, however, that it occurred on a Detroit street corner, far from any place of
      national significance.

19   The case in the Soviet Union illustrates the difficulties of obtaining evidence in a
      totalitarian political system. 'Soviet sources' claimed that the man killed himself
      because officials would not let him fight in Vietnam, and this was reported
      without comment in the *New York Times* (12 April 1966). One wonders whether
      this was a conveniently patriotic cover story for an act of *anti*-Soviet protest.

20   Suicide by fire was not so rare in some non-Western cultures. Two Vietnamese
      men killed themselves in this manner in 1963, apparently because they were
      suffering serious illness (the *New York Times*, 12 December 1963). In India this
      method was 'very common', particularly among women (Thakur 1963: 112).
      More recent statistics show that suicide by fire is more frequent among Indians,
      including Indian immigrants to Britain and South Africa, than in the West
      (Adityanjee 1986; Soni and Balarajan 1992; Sukhai et al. 2002).

21   The figure is from *The Times* index (a report which was dropped before the final
      edition), 29 January 1969. Of course, it is impossible to be sure that these were
      not politically motivated, because the government would have suppressed infor-
      mation to that effect. I have been guided by two recent accounts (Radio Praha
      n.d; K. Williams 1997: 190) which name as protest suicides only Jan Zajic, Evzen
      Plocek, and Michal Leucik. (The latter is excluded from the sample only because
      I lack sufficient information.) Indeed, Zajic implied this when he signed himself
      as 'Torch number two'.

22   We should not necessarily conclude that this actually increased the *total* number
      of suicides. Because this is such a painful method, it is unlikely to have attracted
      people who were undecided whether to live or die.

23   The news-wires appear to be more comprehensive, at least to judge from 1977:
      the *Associated Press* reported two cases, but neither appeared in the *New York
      Times* or *The Times*.

24   I have concentrated on examples in which self-immolation was fatal. As we will
      see below, in a handful of cases the act falls short of a determined attempt to die,
      which implies that the relevant collective cause is not such a momentous one.

25   The news-wires reported twenty-one in total, but this is obviously an underesti-
      mate. For November 1998 alone, six appeared in news reports, but official
      Turkish figures counted twenty-two (Ergil 2001: 115).

26   Unfortunately, these estimates are not based on a uniform definition of 'urban';
      they reflect the different definitions adopted by each country's statistical office.
      The United Nations eliminates Taiwan from its statistics; the figure is estimated
      from Tsai (1996). The Kurdish population in Europe is estimated at a million

(following Oliver Grojean, personal communication). Obviously the rate of population growth varies greatly among countries, but this would not affect the comparison—though differential growth before and after 1985 would.

27 These suicide rates refer to a single year in the 1990s, whereas one ideally wants the average over the four decades. We know, however, that the ranking of European countries has proved quite stable over many decades.

28 This result holds even if Kurdish self-immolations are added to the figure for Turkey.

29 Self-sacrifice is especially prominent in the Jain tradition, but none in the sample of self-immolations is identified as Jain.

30 This interval is chosen because Bollen and Phillips (1982: 806–9) estimate that a television news story about a suicide has a discernible effect on the suicide rate over the subsequent ten days. Note that the term 'wave' is used with a less restrictive meaning elsewhere in this chapter.

31 There was no support for this gruesome plan, and she eventually died by fire. She orchestrated her death to appeal to Catholics—she died before a statue of the Virgin Mary as well as a Buddhist icon—which may be interpreted as further evidence of her strategic insight.

32 Because threats are far less newsworthy, it is not possible to compile comparable systematic evidence.

33 The shift from fasting in 1961 to (threatened) self-immolation by fire in 1965 is further evidence that the latter was ultimately derived from Quang Duc's act, possibly via the Tamil immolations.

34 There is a complicated history. In the early 1960s, Sant Fateh Singh and Master Tara Singh had each promised to fast until death; both gave up. The latter was blamed and subsequently discredited (Grewal 1990: 199–200).

35 I am aware of only one other successful threat, in Burma: in 1964, Buddhists threatened to burn themselves to protest against the regime's regulation of religious organizations (*NYT*, 6 May 1964).

36 This is suggested by the Charan caste in India, which specialized in the 'business of private protection' (cf. Gambetta 1993), like the mafia—but they enforced contracts and guaranteed security by threatening to harm *themselves*. This was known as *traga* (Gujarati spelling): graduated self-mutilation which would culminate in killing oneself (Weinberger-Thomas 1999: 58–63).

37 What really happened is not altogether clear. The police claimed, implausibly, that Goswami's rivals had set him alight. Although Goswami is not the most reliable witness, his story is consistent with contemporary reports. And surely he had no reason to emphasize momentary impulse rather than heroic resolve?

38 A recollection so many years after the event—in 1978—cannot be treated uncritically, but it obviously seared his memory. The event is in the sample, but *AP* did not report sufficient detail to verify his account (*AP*, 2 October 1978).

39 The same sort of sacrificial exchange can be found in tribal societies, as when a Tikopian chief tried to hang himself in order to compel the gods to cure his ailing son (Firth 1961).

40 This also undergirded the use of *traga* by the Charan caste, noted above. Defaulters feared that the ghosts of the dead would return to haunt them (Weinberger-Thomas 1999: 58–63; cf. Jeffreys 1971).

41 Conceivably Allende was captured and murdered, but his wife certainly believed that he killed himself (see also a bodyguard's testimony in the *Guardian*, 2 September 2003).

42 Jan Palach's funeral is supposed to have been attended by 'hundreds of thousands' (Treptow 1992: 129) or 'half a million' (Mastny 1972: 191). Whether these figures are exaggerated is unclear.

43 The distinction is illustrated by the wave of self-immolations in South Korea in 1991, after the police killed a student, Kang Kyung Dae. Although the movement already had an innocent victim, eight individuals killed themselves before Kang was buried, including one during the funeral procession.

44 The ambassador, Henry Cabot Lodge, wrote the preface to Browne's book, and must have relayed this to Browne.

45 It is not far-fetched to make a connection with report in May 2001 by Xinhua News Agency that a Tibetan monk had been sentenced (in January) for plotting to burn himself to death. The authorities apparently hoped to discredit the Dalai Lama as they had discredited Falun Gong.

46 There are sketchy reports that several adherents in a labour camp in Harbin killed themselves to protest against prison conditions, but the precise nature is impossible to confirm (*AFP*, 3 July 2001).

47 Curiously, another survivor, Liu Yunfang, declared his continued belief in the movement. This either testifies to the strength of his commitment or is a cunning ploy to enhance the credibility of state propaganda.

48 Another difference is relevant here: we do not find individuals who immolate themselves hoping for others to replicate their example, unlike those who volunteer for suicide attacks.

Chapter 6

We are grateful to the co-participants in this project for their helpful suggestions, particularly to Diego Gambetta for his extensive comments and Heather Hamill for her very valuable input.

1 In this chapter we use the terms 'terrorist' and 'insurgent' interchangeably to describe non-state actors who use violence to overthrow the existing political order.

2 According to the RAND-MIPT database on terrorism incidents for the period 1998–March 2003, http://db.mipt.org/rep_wprg_rep.cfm (accessed 30 June 2003), most terrorist incidents involved explosives (4,109: 58.3%) or firearms (1,946: 27.6%). Note that these figures are calculated in a period of a high number of SMs.

3 The fighters who composed this 'Kamikaze' group bear a striking resemblance to the Tamil Black Tigers: they were known as 'Gazavat' (Holy War) fighters and

wore black headbands. As many as eight of these fighters died in the first battle of Grozny by intentionally falling under the tracks of tanks and blowing them up. The latest Chechen SMs constitute a transition from this military use to a more conventional 'terrorist' version. These include the destruction by two trucks of Chechnya's main regional government offices in Grozny, killing about eighty people and wounding over 150 (on 27 December 2002); the truck bombing of a government compound in the town of Znamenskoye which killed fifty-nine and injured more than 200 (12 May 2003); the detonation of a bomb by a lone woman at an Islamic festival in the village of Ilishkan-Yurt in the region of Gudermes that killed eighteen people (14 May 2003); and another bomb detonated by a woman, which blew up a bus carrying military workers to a Russian air base in West Chechnya and killed at least eighteen people, many of them women (5 June 2003). In October 2002, Chechen militants seized a Moscow theatre, taking about 800 people hostage and threatening the blow themselves up with all of them.

4 Although still unclear, it seems that the FARC may have launched at least one SM in January 2003: see n. 7.

5 According to McKittrick et al. (1999: 1215), Gillespie had been forced to drive a car bomb four years earlier.

6 This kind of live human bomb is rather different from the body bomb, a technique used by the FARC since 1998. In that year, the terrorists placed two grenades in the body of a dead soldier. The corpse was moved by the army to Bogotá in a helicopter. When the body was taken out of the helicopter, the grenades exploded, killing several soldiers. Since then, the FARC has employed this technique several times, using occasionally the bodies of children. The IRA used dog bombs, but never dared to use human bodies. Unlike body bombs, delegated SMs can be more selective and can penetrate very easily into enemy zones.

7 In January 2003, several car bombs exploded in the department of Arauca, Colombia. In at least one case, there is some evidence pointing to an SM: on 8 January 2003, a car exploded as it was approaching a military base in Arauquita, killing one and wounding four. The driver died. According to the RAND-MIPT database, this counts as an SM, but it could have also been a delegated SM. On 9 January, a car drove into a military checkpoint in Fortul, killing four and injuring fifteen. It is unclear whether the two drivers, who died in the operation, were coerced by some terrorist organization (delegated SM) or were members of the organization willing to participate in an SM. Another military checkpoint in Tame was attacked two days later, resulting in four deaths and fourteen people wounded. Here the driver survived and alleged he was forced to drive the car. While some have held the FARC responsible for these attacks, the truth remains obscure.

8 There was some speculation that the hijacking of a French Airbus plane in Algiers, carried out on Christmas Eve in 1994 by four GIA Algerian terrorists, was intended as an SM, with the hijackers aiming to crash the plane in the centre of Paris. Indeed, the hijackers wanted to be flown to Paris, but because of insufficient fuel the captain landed at Marseilles, where French elite troops stormed the plane and killed all

four Algerian hijackers. The terrorists initially demanded the release of two leaders of the banned FIS, Abassi Madani and Ali Belhadj, but this demand was dropped after an ultimatum to Algerian authorities passed unheeded. Charles Pasqua, the French Interior Minister, claimed that the terrorists planned to fly the hijacked Air France passenger jet to Paris in a suicide operation, either exploding it over Paris or ramming it into the Eiffel Tower. What seemed far-fetched then is no longer so implausible in the light of 9/11; the date of the event too, prior to the post-1995 decision by GIA to renounce SMs, yields some credence to this interpretation which, however, is not universally held (Freeman 1994).

9 Obviously, a doctrine of just war in which almost every form of killing and almost every kind of target is legitimate does not impose too heavy constraints. This seems to be the case in the doctrines espoused by organizations like Hamas.

10 In fact, there are many examples of SMs in which the bomber adjusts his or her target to maximize the number of casualties (for example, Hoffman 2003:43).

11 The PFLP may be an exception to this: in spite of its Marxist origins in the 1960s, it has claimed responsibility for three SMs in 2002 (at least one of which has also been claimed by Hamas). This appears to be an interesting example of contagion.

12 Surprisingly, Hoffman (2003: 42) asserts that the lethality of SMs accounts for their popularity; yet the Rand data also show that SMs are, in fact, rather unpopular outside Israel (see n. 3).

13 Many of the village massacres for which they became notorious were in fact selective rather than indiscriminate (Kalyvas 1999).

14 Consider the following example from Palestine, which illustrates both the intra-ethnic violence of ethnic conflict and the power of the norm of revenge. In February 2002 a mob of Palestinians stormed the makeshift courtroom in Jenin and lynched three Palestinian men. These men had just been convicted of murdering Osama Kmail, a lieutenant of the Palestinian security forces, but were given what the mob thought were moderate sentences. Prior to joining the security forces, Osama Kmail was a member of a militant group called Black Panthers, which was affiliated to al-Fatah and specialized in killing collaborators of the Israelis. In this capacity, Osama Kmail had killed, in 1992, two Palestinian brothers from the neighbouring town of Qabatiya who were suspected of being Israeli collaborators. On 1 February 2002, Osama Kmail was found shot in a deserted area near Qabatiya. It turns out that he was assassinated by Jihad Kmail and Khaled Kmail, members of his own clan, who had been talked into committing the crime by Mahmoud Kmail, a brother of the two men killed in 1992. As the judge in charge of the case put it: 'The problem is revenge. It's kind of shame if you do not avenge the killing of a relative' (Bennet 2002: A8).

15 At least sixty Muslims were killed in the WTC attack; see http://islam.about.com/blvictims.htm (accessed 31 June 2003).

16 Although there is some overlap between this point and the argument about constituency costs that follows, the underlying mechanism is different: faced with a government that is selective in its violence and an insurgent organization that

kills blindly, many civilians will opt to collaborate with the former rather than the latter.

17 There is some controversy about this bomb. MacStiofain (1975: 237–8), then Chief of Staff, said the IRA had nothing to do with it. Actually, no organization claimed responsibility and nobody was ever charged for this action. Yet McKittrick et al. (1999:161) attribute responsibility to the IRA.

18 Again, MacStiofain (1975: 299–300) says the IRA had nothing to do with it.

19 Yet compare this with the reaction of a member of the IRA, Charlie Coogan: 'I was a bit horrified when I saw the pictures, it was a bit gruesome, but the feeling about Patsy Gillespie was he worked for the soldiers so fuck him' (quoted in Clarke and Johnston 2001: 187).

20 It is not only a matter of the cruelty of the attacks. In 1977 the IRA started a campaign against businessmen, but due to its unpopularity even within the republican movement it was soon abandoned (Clarke and Johnston 2001: 100).

21 Note that such restraint must be mutual; it requires an equilibrium whereby the rival also restrains from more extreme forms of actions. The conflict in Northern Ireland is characterized by such reciprocal restraint (Toolis 1997:21). Although the British authorities have committed human rights abuses including the systematic practice of torture, they 'have not ruthlessly and brutally suppressed the population which explicitly or tacitly supports insurrection in the manner experienced by Algerian Muslims, Afghan peasants, Iraqi Kurds, Kashmiri Muslims, Palestinian Muslims and Christians, South African blacks, Sri Lankan Tamils, and Vietnamese peasants' (O'Leary and McGarry 1993: 19). As an IRA member was told after his arrest by the security forces: 'If this was Beirut we would just take you out into that yard and shoot you' (Collins 1997:188).

22 Note that this distribution of organizations follows a 'necessary but not sufficient' logic. Organizations with very low or very high levels of support may not resort to SMs, but no organization with intermediate levels of support would. Note as well a possible endogeneity problem: an organization may resort to SMs, thus causing indiscriminate reprisals by its rivals against its social base, which may generate support for it.

23 Hoffman (2003: 42) also cites an example whereby the bomb strapped on the suicide bomber was detonated by remote control by someone else. In this case, the bomber simply provided a delivery device.

24 Interestingly, one of the first models of war of attrition was that of Maynard Smith (1984: ch. 3) about two animals fighting for a territory.

25 The in-prison suicide of the Baader Meinhof group leaders does not qualify as an SM.

26 While there is evidence suggesting that some organizations planning SMs recruit civilian volunteers rather than relying on their own seasoned activists (Gambetta, personal communication), it is also the case that SMs are complex operations requiring several handlers (Hoffman 2003: 43); in so far as these handlers are also put in danger, SMs lose their initial advantage in terms of their cost.

27 According to recent research, only 13 per cent of Palestinian suicide bombers are from impoverished families, while about a third of the Palestinian population

lives in poverty. Instead, a remarkable 57 per cent of suicide bombers have some education beyond high school, compared with just 15 per cent of the population of comparable age (Berrebi, quoted by Krueger 2003: C2).

Chapter 7

Many relevant studies published by International Policy Institute for Counterterrorism (ICT) at the Interdisciplinary Center, Herzliya can be found at www.ict.org.il

1   This chapter was written with the support of the Centre for the Study of Civil War at The International Peace Research Institute, Oslo. I am grateful to Richard Betts, Kristian Elster, Scott Gates, Shany Mor, Brigitte Nacos, Darius Rejali, Thomas Schelling, Martha Snodgrass, Stein Tønnesson, Elizabeth Wood, and the other contributors to this volume for helpful comments and suggestions. I am especially thankful for Diego Gambetta's many suggestions for improvement and clarification.

   The two-level analysis is in one sense a bit artificial. If we ask 'Who becomes a suicide attacker?' we are dealing with the level of actors. If instead we ask 'Who is selected to become a suicide attacker?', the emphasis shifts to the level of the organization. In reality, of course, the composition of the corps of suicide bombers results from the interaction between these two levels. The organization makes a choice among those who volunteer. The relative importance of selection and self-selection is discussed in several places in this chapter.

2   The requirement of stability is rarely explicitly stated by rational-choice theorists, but their work would make little sense without it. If we do not assume stability, an individual exhibiting cyclical choice behaviour (choosing A over B, B over C, and C over A) might be seen as rational.

3   If the militant believes that Islam tells him that suicide is unconditionally wrong, the former action would be preferable on religious grounds (Kristian Elster, personal communication). Although most Islamic theologians now condone suicide, some may still refuse to do so. See also n. 16.

4   As an example of this effect, most people prefer winning a one-week tour of England with certainty over a 50 per cent chance of winning a three-week tour of England, France, and Italy, but also prefer a 5 per cent chance of the second option over a 10 per cent chance of the first.

5   Even more questionable, of course, is a statement one occasionally comes across to the effect that Palestinians live under such miserable conditions that they have little to lose by blowing themselves up.

6   Whether Buddhist doctrine implies that suicide has a negative effect on the *individual,* by causing him or her to be reborn at a lower level in the next incarnation, seems to be a controversial issue.

7   An early example is found among the south-Asian Muslims on the Malabar coast, who carried out SMs against the dominant Hindus from the sixteenth to the twentieth centuries. Those 'who changed their mind at the last moment after having gone through the rituals were derided by other Muslims as . . . "half-

martyrs", and often this ridicule drove them to participate in later attacks' (Dale 1980: 122).

8   Testimony before the Special Oversight Panel on Terrorism of the Committee of Armed Services, House of Representatives, 13 July 2000.

9   Foreseeing a failure of will, individuals may voluntarily expose themselves to peer pressure. Thus many people who try to quit smoking tell their friends about their plans, so as to add fear of being shamed to their primary motivation. I have not seen it suggested, though, that would-be suicide bombers deliberately ask for will-sustaining rituals.

10   In his discussion of 'ecstatic suicide', Meltsberger (1997) mostly cites character features such as mania or 'malignant narcissism' as explanatory factors. As religiously motivated instances he mentions the Indian 'widows who threw themselves into the flames of their husband's funeral pyres . . . in the belief that they would be bettered in the afterlife' and (citing Gibbon 1776–88: ch. 16) the early Christians who sought martyrdom to enter 'into the immediate fruition of eternal bliss.' I am sceptical about the voluntary nature of suicide by Indian widows. As for the early Christians, the description of the Donatists and notably of the Circoncellions in the *Catholic Encyclopedia* suggests that their voluntary martyrdom had more in common with the collective madness of Jonestown than with instrumentally rational actions to get access to the afterlife.

11   The Israeli practice of destroying the homes of families of suicide attackers may to some extent counter (and be intended to counter) this motivation. A further step would be to kill the family members.

12   In fact, there is some evidence that revenge is often 'two tits for a tat', requiring two enemy deaths to compensate for one death on one's own side. Kalyvas (forthcomming: ch. 3) cites a Lebanese woman who in response to the killing of 365 Lebanese Muslims said that 'At this moment I want the [Moslem militia] . . . to go into offices and kill the first seven hundred and thirty defenseless Christians they can lay their hands on'. This corresponds remarkably well to the predictions of prospect theory (Kahneman and Tversky 1995).

13   If, however, both sides view revenge as 'two tits for a tat', the process may never reach an equilibrium.

14   Even this motivation might have an other-related component, however. According to Sheikh Raid Salad, an important leader of Israel's Arab population, the martyr 'receives from Allah six special things, including 70 virgins, no torment in the grave, *and the choice of 70 members of his family and his confidants to enter paradise with him*' (*Haaretz*, 26 October 2001, cited in http://ww.likud.nl/extrl47.html). The component of the package that I have italicized is never cited as a motivation of suicide bombers, and so I shall ignore it here.

15   This standard work is available on-line at www.newadvent.org/cathen.

16   A certain amount of casuistry is also needed to justify the killing of Israeli civilians and even of Muslims. One line of argument is that there are no Israeli civilians. Both men and women do military service, and children will grow up into men and women who will do the same. Another line is that the killing of innocents, however defined, is a form of collateral damage. A third claim is

that the settlers in Occupied Territories should be viewed as occupying forces rather than as civilians. These arguments are not only casuistic but disingenuous, since it is obvious to all that the main goal of the suicide attacks is to create fear in the population at large rather than to achieve military objectives. The killing of enemy civilians or soldiers is harnessed to that more general aim. Things were different in the early Hezbollah suicide missions in Lebanon, which had exclusively military aims. There it was argued that, if the enemy uses Muslims as human shields, it is legitimate to kill them as well, provided that the number of enemies killed exceeds that of Muslim victims (Reuter 2002: 107).

17 'The classical [Islamic] jurists distinguish clearly between facing certain death at the hands of the enemy and killing oneself by one's own hand. One leads to heaven, the other to hell. Some recent fundamentalist jurists and others have blurred or even dismissed this distinction, but their view is by no means unanimously accepted. The suicide bomber is thus taking a considerable risk on a theological nicety' (Lewis 2003: 30).

18 Note that this takes care of the by-product problem, but not of the ban on suicide. Theologically, you can go wrong in two ways: by choosing illegitimate means (suicide) to a valued end or by transforming the by-products of actions undertaken for the sake of that end into their principal aim.

19 In any case, claims that suicide bombers are motivated by the seventy or seventy-two virgins in paradise, or promises of a never-ending erection and orgasms lasting a hundred years (Reuter 2002: 262), strike me as absurd. Although one can see why Israeli propagandists might want to propagate a view of suicide bombers as sex-starved individuals who seek in the afterlife what they cannot find on earth, the image is hard to square with the descriptions offered by those who have talked to volunteers for SMs as well as to families of dead bombers (for example, Hassan 2001). The large and increasing number of female suicide bombers should also undermine this legend.

20 If we compare recruitment to SMs with conscription into military service, this double injunction is unusual. Whereas China has offered exemption from military service to young men without siblings (who have to take care of their parents) and the United States has exempted fathers (who have to take care of their children), no system known to me does both.

21 'Economic deprivation in and of itself...is an insufficient explanation for the emergence of a widespread willingness to die among large parts of the Palestinian population. Not only have these harsh economic conditions existed before the emergence of suicide attacks in Israel, but some of the suicide bombers have come from relatively well-off families' (Moghadam 2003: 76).

22 Referring to various earlier studies (omitted in the bibliography to the present volume), Khashan (2003: 1055) writes that 'Smith's viewpoint concurs with an earlier study by Dang (1988: 34), whose analysis of the profile of Punjabi terrorists determines that "they mainly come from landlord, rich peasant and upper middle class families". But many Arabs [sic] scholars would disagree. Haydar (1997:22) insists that the growth of Islamic militant terrorism in the

Middle East directly results from "poverty, backwardness, unemployment, weakness of academic curricula and decline of academic institutions"'.

23 Along somewhat similar lines it has been argued that among the causes of the US withdrawal from Vietnam was the introduction of the draft lottery that ended the student deferment that had protected children of elite decision-makers. I do not know of any evidence for this claim, but it might be true.

24 This conclusion is supported by the record of al-Qaeda's other activities. Besides the 9/11 attacks the main suicide attacks organized by al-Qaeda have taken place in Nairobi, Mombasa, Dar es Salaam, Karachi, and Riyadh (search under 'al-Qaeda' at http://db.mipt.org/mipt_rand.cfm). Except for the attack on the Israeli-owned and -frequented Paradise Hotel in Mombasa, all these targeted US installations. (The target in the Riyadh attack is ambiguous.)

25 For an analysis of why SMs were used instead of (or together with) other tactics, I refer the reader to Chapter 6, by Kalyvas and Sánchez-Cuenca.

26 Outperforming rivals is, of course, not the only way of achieving a dominant position. Eliminating them is another method. Thus, on the basis of the experience with competing opposition groups in Sri Lanka (Swamy 2001), one might ask whether the different Palestinian organizations have taken to assassinating each other's leaderships. Although there is considerable internecine Palestinian violence (see Chapter 3, this volume), it is not clear how it breaks down into punishment of collaborators with the Israeli forces, moderates within one's own organization, and leaders of rival organizations. As we know from other cases, the lines between the first category and the other two are easily blurred by the use of the idea of 'objective complicity'.

27 Other instances of diffusion of behaviour through mental models include the 1848 revolutions in Europe and the student movements of the 1960s. Mental models should be distinguished both from the domino effect (which explains the breakdown of Communism in Eastern Europe) and the common-cause effect (which explains the re-emergence of Communism in many of the same countries). Actual situations may have elements of all three.

28 For a possible link, see nevertheless Reuter (2002): 311–12.

29 One should not of course wait for too long. Reuter (2002: 12) cites the story of a would-be suicide attacker in Shiriat Motzkin, a suburb of Haifa, who showed the explosives strapped to his body so that everybody left, and then killed himself 'in the loneliness of the empty café'.

30 As Biggs (Chapter 6, this volume) writes, however, Buddhists do not measure the depth of commitment merely by the size of the sacrifice, since 'there is evidence that younger novices were refused permission' to kill themselves, the reason being that they might not have 'attained sufficient wisdom to make a responsible choice'.

31 This was, according to Reuter (2002: 110–11), the view at least of the main spiritual mentor of Hezbollah, Sheikh Fadlallah. A radical faction of Hezbollah claimed, however, that even a failed suicide bombing attempt should be counted as a success, since it showed the willingness to sacrifice oneself 'on the altar of resistance' (Reuter 2002: 111).

32 If the source of failure was a malfunctioning bomb, the testimony would be more
    reliable (Shany Mor, personal communication).
33 Although the al-Aqsa brigades (the military branch of al-Fatah) seem to be
    relatively independent of the political branch (Human Rights Watch 2002*a*),
    the opaqueness of the situation does not allow us to exclude the possibility that
    this could be mere appearance engineered for purposes of deniability. It is a
    standard tactic of 'moderate leaders' to claim that 'we cannot control our
    hardliners'.
34 This statement may be less valid for organizers than for attackers. If the organ-
    izers base their anticipation of enemy responses on conspiratorial theories rather
    than on strategic reasoning, their actions might violate the canons of rationality.
    To take a simple example, it would be pointless to try to drive in a wedge between
    Israel and the American Jewish community if these are seen as part of a single
    unified and coherent conspiracy.

Chapter 8

Several people—among them Bruce Bongar, Paolo Campana, John Darwin, Jim
Fearon, Anna Geifman, Heather Hamill, Edgar Jones, Ariel Merari, Valeria
Pizzini-Gambetta, Eleanor Robson, Anne Speckhard, Federico Varese, and Simon
Wessley—have offered me specific suggestions and leads, for which am I very
grateful. I am of course very much indebted for ideas, suggestions, and criticisms
to all the authors in this volume.

1 'It is a trademark of Al Qaeda to sacrifice its killers' (Wright 2004: 43). In fact,
   they have used non-suicidal attacks on various occasions, and when they have
   used SM the success of the attack was dependent on or greatly enhanced by the
   death of the attackers.
2 '[From May 2000 to September 2003] suicide attacks killed eight people in the
   West Bank and Gaza while killing 401 on the Israeli side of the green line. That is
   to say, 17,405 attacks in the West Bank and Gaza resulted in eight deaths due to
   suicide attacks while 730 attacks on the Israeli side of the green line resulted in
   401 deaths due to suicide attacks' (Berman and Laitin 2004).
3 Rohan Gunaratna, in an oral presentation at the conference on Suicide Terrorism: the Strategic Threat and Countermeasures, Lisbon, 11–14 June 2004.
4 To what extent other cases of the profligate use of troops—for example, by the
   Soviet Union in the Second World War or by the British and French in the First
   World War—are qualitatively different from the Iranian 'human waves' is an
   open question. One could argue that the slaughter of the Somme and Verdun
   were also 'unprecedented and militarily meaningless', as Makiya (1998: 283)
   describes the human waves. Of course, the former cases were due more to callous
   incompetence than to intention.
5 The Marxist contribution is close to non-existent. Two organizations carried out
   a small number of missions in Turkey, PKK and People's Revolutionary Liber-

ation Party (DHKP). Two or three missions have been attributed to the Lebanese Communist Party (LCP). Although some authors (for example, Pape 2003) consider the LTTE a Marxist organization, the evidence is that this ideology does not have much significance for them (Chapter 2, this volume).

6 In some of the scholarly literature too, all SM perpetrators are dubbed 'terrorists' (for example, Pape 2003).

7 From 20 March 2003 through 1 May 2003 (the end of major combat) there were 172 casualties among the coalition forces (http://icasualties.org/oif/).

8 I am grateful to Stathis Kalyvas for helping me think through these alternatives.

9 The episode was captured by a video that fell into the hands of the Pentagon during the Afghan war. The realistic quality of the dialogue is such that, if forged, it is also a masterpiece. The transcripts were published by many newspapers, for example, www.usatoday.com/news/attack/2001/12/13/transcript.htm.

10 'Democracy' is here understood in the broad sense of 'states [which] elect their chief executives and legislatures in multiparty elections and have seen at least one peaceful transfer of power, making them solidly democratic by standard criteria' (Pape 2003: 350). The dozen SMs of the Russian anarchists appear to be an exception to the rule. However, a key property of democracy existed in the Russian empire: freedom of the press, which was introduced by 1905. The news of the anarchists' violent deeds travelled all over the country as they occurred: 'Everyone was aware that the anarchists (and other extremists) were responsible for scores of political assassinations, expropriations, and other terrorist assaults' (Geifman, personal communication; also Geifman 1993: ch. 1). The suicide attacks in Saudi Arabia too would appear to be exceptions, but again the fact that they targeted mostly foreigners guaranteed wide publicity despite the fact that the country is not a democracy. The suicide assassination, on 9 September 2001 in Afghanistan, of Ahmad Shah Massoud, the Northern Alliance commander, is an exception, but that was, as Stephen Holmes argues (Chapter 4, this volume), a military operation and thus indifferent to the publicity effect.

11 Ariel Merari, oral presentation at the conference on Suicide Terrorism: the Strategic Threat and Countermeasures, Lisbon, 11–14 June 2004.

12 The data on lethality in this paragraph has been supplied by Luca Ricolfi and Paolo Campana, personal communication.

13 Ariel Merari, oral presentation at the conference on Suicide Terrorism: the Strategic Threat and Countermeasures, Lisbon, 11–14 June 2004.

14 The uncertainty over the intentions of the Madrid terrorists emerges from the detailed account provided by Wright (2004). For instance, on 2 April 2004, another large bomb—made with the same type of detonator and explosive as those used in Madrid a few weeks earlier—was found on the railway line of the high speed train that links the Spanish capital to Seville. It failed to detonate because it was wrongly wired. Given that it occurred over two weeks *after* the election, its purpose is obscure and at odds with the interpretation of the Madrid bombings as being aimed at causing Aznar's defeat.

15 By the Arab daily *Al-Hayat*, reported in *La Repubblica*, 19 August 2003.

16   Ariel Merari, oral presentation at the conference on Suicide Terrorism: the
     Strategic Threat and Countermeasures, Lisbon, 11–14 June 2004.

17   Ariel Merari, oral presentation at the conference on Suicide Terrorism: the
     Strategic Threat and Countermeasures, Lisbon, 11–14 June 2004.

18   An example of such conjectures: 'Such sentiments … may have emerged under
     natural selection's influence, to override rational calculations based on seemingly
     impossible or very long odds of achieving individual goals, such as lasting secur-
     ity. Although these sentiments seem to lack rationality in the short term (i.e., in
     the rational-choice sense of maximizing known or anticipated utility), they may be
     eminently rational as evolutionary strategies that refine the reward mechanism for
     pursuing individual self-interest by enhancing long-term benefits for members of a
     population *on average*. Provided that actual instances of self-sacrifice are rela-
     tively rare, yet frequent enough to convince people of their sincerity and efficacy,
     they may benefit many or most individuals in a population much of the time'
     (Atran 2003*a*, supporting material, p. 6, at www.sciencemag.org/cgi/data/299/
     5612/1534/DC1/1)

19   www.victoriacross.net/facts.asp. See also Arthur (2004).

20   The US equivalent is the Medal of Honor, which was created for the Civil War in
     1861 and made a permanent decoration by Congress in 1863. Since then, 3,459
     have been awarded. No woman has ever received the Victoria Cross while one
     received the Medal of Honor; www.cmohs.org/index.html.

21   While most people have stressed that certain death must make matters worse we
     cannot be altogether sure: there is evidence that knowing in advance 'about the
     duration of fear or about other aversive experiences, such as pain, may make
     the experience more tolerable' (Rachman 1990: 39). Whether this extends to the
     anticipation of self-inflicted death is an open question.

22   According to Count Giuseppe Solaro della Margherita, the commander of the
     Turin garrison at the time, it was through a miscalculation of the pace of the fuse,
     and not by deliberate intent, that he sacrificed his life. How he could say that is
     not known. But in all accounts Micca is universally believed as having acted
     intentionally.

23   On BBC2 (1 September 2002, 9 p.m.) a documentary was shown called 'Clear the
     Skies', which was the order given once the hijacking of the four planes on 9/11
     became clear. All planes were grounded or had to land.

24   Ariel Merari, at the conference on Suicide Terrorism: the Strategic Threat and
     Countermeasures, Lisbon, 11–14 June 2004.

25   See Chapters 3 and 7 (both this volume) for a discussion of revenge. Margalit
     (2003), who makes a strong claim that the predominant motivation of Palestinian
     suicide bombers is revenge, disregards the sense of obligation elicited by the
     death of other members of one's group in pursuit of a non-private cause.

26   This debate is translated by MEMRI Special Dispatch Series, 8 July 2004,
     No. 741; the transcript can be viewed at www.memri.org/bin/opener_latest.
     cgi?ID=SD74004

27   'The Zealots were an aggressive political party whose concern for the national
     and religious life of the Jewish people led them to despise even Jews who

sought peace and conciliation with the Roman authorities.... Extremists among the Zealots turned to terrorism and assassinations and became known as Sicarii (Greek *sikarioi*, "dagger men"). They frequented public places with hidden daggers to strike down persons friendly to Rome. In the first revolt against Rome (AD 66–70) the Zealots played a leading role, and at Masada in AD 73 they committed suicide rather than surrender the fortress' ('Zealot' 2004. Encyclopædia Britannica Online, http://search.eb.com/eb/article?eu=80388). Most of what we know about the Zealots and the Sicarii has reached us through the work of Josephus, a Jewish historian who was himself a leader of the anti-Roman rebellion which he then betrayed to go and live in Rome (see Rapoport 1984)

28 Ariel Merari (personal communication), who interviewed many failed bombers, says he never heard this choice mentioned.

29 Most of the information for this paragraph can be found at 'Explosive' 2004. Encyclopædia Britannica Online, http://search.eb.com/eb/ article?eu=114764.

30 http://news.bbc.co.uk/1/hi/uk/3582921.stm.

31 http://encyclopedia.thefreedictionary.com/Triacetonetriperoxide.

32 *Washington Post*, 30 December 2001.

33 *BBC Monitoring Europe—Political*, 9 January 2002.

34 'Alfred Bernhard Nobel.' 2004 Encyclopædia Britannica Online, http://search. eb.com/eb/article?eu=57414.

35 Anne Speckhard (personal communication).

36 The Professor, as described by Conrad (1986: 98): 'His parentage was obscure, and he was generally known only by his nickname of *Professor*. His title to that designation consisted in his having been once assistant demonstrator in chemistry at some technical institute. He quarrelled with the authorities upon a question of unfair treatment. Afterwards he obtained a post in the laboratory of a manufactory of dyes. There, too, he had been treated with revolting injustice. His struggles, his privations, his hard work to raise himself in the social scale, had filled him with such an exalted conviction of his merits that it was extremely difficult for the world to treat him with justice—the standard of that notion depending so much upon the patience of the individual. The Professor had genius, but lacked the great social virtue of resignation.'

37 www.textfiles.com/anarchy/gunpowder.

38 The total population of the Russian empire in 1900 was 132.9 million. www. tacitus.nu/historical-atlas/population/russia.htm.

39 recollectionbooks.com/bleed/Encyclopedia/HenryEmile.htm.

40 Geifman says: 'I am not entirely sure that this was the first recorded suicide mission in Russia. I assume it was because it happened so early in the revolutionary period. There might have been a less well-known case prior to Farber's, although this is highly unlikely' (personal communication).

41 There is evidence that imitators of hijacking emerged after successful hijacking, but not after unsuccessful ones (Holden 1986).

42 For a sympathetic account of Foucault's view of the Iranian revolution, see Eribon (1991: 281–91).

43 'Europeans who sought to deny the legitimacy of suicidal jihads by arguing that the individuals who undertook them were not engaging in a genuine religious protest were, in fact, sometimes correct when they assumed that certain muja-heeds were not particularly pious individuals. This belief was particularly well-founded in the last phase of the confrontation between Muslims and Europeans in all three areas' (Dale 1988: 54).

44 They calculate these frequencies on the basis of the Fearon–Laitin database (Fearon and Laitin 2003).

45 For the relationship to be maintained one would have to argue that Sunni and Shiites, if indeed victims and attackers were so divided, are to be considered as separate religious groups.

46 'In fact, in a few prominent cases in which we do see suicide attacks on coreli-gionists, they tend to be against very well defended targets, where the mechanism of defence went beyond profiling. That would be the case in the assassination of Egyptian President Anwar Sadat by the Egyptian Islamic Jihad, which was essentially suicidal, or in the assassination of Northern Alliance leader Ahmad Shah Masoud by Taliban suicide bombers disguised as journalists. In both those cases the attackers overcame any theological objections to killing Muslims, but may have chosen the suicide tactic as they faced targets for which the probability of apprehension in a conventional attack was close to one. Similarly with the LTTE murder of Rajiv Gandhi on 21 May 1991, which was Hindu on Hindu. He too, as Prime Minister of India, was an extraordinarily well defended target' (Berman and Laitin 2004).

47 This result applies only to 'ethnic civil wars' while 'revolutionary/ideological civil wars' were excluded from the model; it is also not confirmed by other models: for example, Fearon and Laitin (2003). And it is not confirmed by models that consider the duration rather than the incidence of civil wars (Collier et al. 2004; Fearon 2004.)

48 The data-set used by Berman and Laitin goes from 1980 through 2002, with the most recent suicide attack on November 22, 2002. The figure therefore does not include the SMs in Iraq, some of which have been intra-Islamic.

49 www.fact-index.com/b/ba/baruch_goldstein.html.

50 Well summarized by Reuter (2004: ch. 5).

51 Lewis, quoted in Elster (Chapter 7: n. 17, this volume).

52 Wright (2004: 43) suggests that sacrificing the attackers 'has provided [al-Qaeda with] a scanty moral cover for what would otherwise be seen simply as mass murder'.

53 www.theherald.co.uk/politics/19673.html.

REFERENCES

Abu Ruqaiyah (1996–7). 'The Islamic Legitimacy of the "Martyrdom Operations"',
Nida'ul Islam, December–January. http://islam.org.au/articles/16/martyrdom.htm.

Adair, D. (1998). *Fame and the Founding Fathers*. Indianapolis: Liberty Fund.

Adams, G. (1996). *Before the Dawn: An Autobiography*. Dingle: Brandon.

Adityanjee, D. (1986). 'Suicide Attempts and Suicides in India: Cross-Cultural Aspects', *International Journal of Social Psychiatry*, 32/2: 64–73.

AFP (*Agence France Presse*) (1993). 'Tamil Tigers Guerrillas Deny Involvement in Premadasa's Killing'. 1 May.

——(1996a). 'Suicide Bombers Lead Tigers' Main Armour: Rebel Chief'. 6 July.

——(1996b). 'Two Tamil Tiger Bombs Kill 70 in Colombo Commuter Train'. 25 July.

——(1998a). 'Sri Lanka Tigers Admit Losing 150 Cadres, Claim Killing 300 Troops'. 2 February.

——(1998b). 'Women Suicide Bombers in Attack on Sri Lanka Navy: Rebel Radio'. 24 February.

——(2000a). 'Ferocious Battle as Tamil Human Bombs Breach Sri Lanka Defences'. 10 May.

——(2000b). 'Suicide Bomber Assassinates Senior Sri Lankan Minister, Kills 19 Others'. 7 June.

Akinaga, Y. (1999). *Kaigun Chūjō Ōnishi Takijirō: 'Tokkō no Chichi' to Yobareta Teitoku no Shōgai*. Tokyo: Kōjinsha.

Alcedo, M. (1996). *Militar en ETA. Historias de Vida y Muerte*. San Sebastián: R & B Ediciones.

Amnesty International (1999). 'Torture in Custody'. June. AI Index ASA 37/10/99.

——(2002). *Israel and the Occupied Territories—Shielded from Scrutiny: IDF Violations in Jenin and Nablus*, Executive summary, 4 November.

Andoni, L. (1997). 'Searching for Answers: Gaza's Suicide Bombers', *Journal of Palestine Studies*, 24/4: 33–45.

Anon. (2002). *Through our Enemies' Eyes*. Washington, DC: Brassey's.

Arendt, H. (1970). *On Violence*. New York: Harcourt, Brace and World.

——(1994). *Eichmann in Jerusalem*. New York: Penguin.

Arthur, M. (2004). *Symbol of Courage: A Complete History of the Victoria Cross*. London: Sidgwick & Jackson.

Ashton, J. R. and Donnan, S. (1981). 'Suicide by Burning as an Epidemic Phenomenon: An Analysis of 82 Deaths and Inquests in England and Wales in 1978–9', *Psychological Medicine*, 11: 735–9.

Atran, S. (2003a). *Understanding Suicide Terrorism*. www.interdisciplines.org

——(2003b). 'Who Wants to be a Martyr?', *New York Times*, 5 May.

Atran, S. (2003c). 'Genesis of Suicide Terrorism', *Science*, 299: 1534–9.

Atran, S. (2003*d*). 'The Strategic Threat from Suicide Terror', Aei-Brookings Joint Center publication, December.

Aussaresses, P. (2001). *Services Spéciaux. Algérie 1955–1957*. Paris: Perrin.

Aust, S. and Schnibben, C. (eds.) (2002). *Inside 9/11: What Really Happened*. New York: St Martin's Press.

Axell, A. and Kase, H. (2002). *Kamikaze: Japan's Suicide Gods*. London: Pearson Education.

Baechler, J. (1975) *Suicides*. Oxford: Basil Blackwell.

Baer, R. (2003). 'The Fall of the House of Saud', *Atlantic Monthly*, May: 52–63.

Balasingham, A. (2000). *The Politics of Duplicity*. Mitcham: Fairmax.

—— (2004). *War and Peace: Armed Struggle and Peace Efforts of Liberation Tigers*. Mitcham: Fairmax.

—— Balasingham, A. (2003). *The Will to Freedom: An Inside View of Tamil Resistance*. Mitcham, Surrey: Fairmax Publishing.

Barber, B. (2003). *Heart and Stones*. New York: Palgrave Macmillan.

Beasley, W.G. (1990) *The Rise of Modern Japan*. London: Wiedenfeld and Nicolson.

Beauchamp, J.L. (2002). 'Countering Terrorism: The Role of Science and Technology. A Personal Perspective', *Engineering and Science*, 4: 26–35. http://pr.caltech.edu/periodicals/EandS/articles/LXV4/Beauchamp_Feature.pdf.

Becker, G. (1996). *Accounting for Tastes*. Cambridge, MA: Harvard University Press.

Beevor, A. (2002). *Berlin: The Downfall 1945*. London: Viking.

Benjamin, D. and Simon, S. (2002). *The Age of Sacred Terror*. New York: Random House.

Benn, J. A. (1998). 'Where Text Meets Flesh: Burning the Body as an Apocryphal Practice in Chinese Buddhism', *History of Religions*, 37: 295–322.

Bennet, J. (2002). 'Palestinian Justice Unravels as Mob Kills 3', *New York Times*, 6 February: A8.

—— (2003*a*). 'Armed Weapons and a Will, Palestinians Factions Plot Revenge', *New York Times*, 21 February.

—— (2003*b*). 'How 2 Took the Path of Suicide Bombers: A Scholar of English Who Clung to the Veil', *New York Times*, 30 May: A1, A14.

Beresford, D. (1987). *Ten Men Dead: The Story of the 1981 Hunger Strike*. London: HarperCollins.

Bergen, P. (2001). *Holy War, Inc.: Inside the Secret World of Osama bin Laden*. New York: Free Press.

Berger, P. (1974). 'On the Obsolescence of the Concept of Honour', in P. Berger, B. Berger, and H. Kellner, *The Homeless Mind*. Harmondsworth: Pelican Books.

—— (2003). 'Rational Martyrs: Evidence from Data on Suicide Attacks'. Unpublished manuscript.

Berman, E. and Laitin, D.D. (2004). 'Rational Martyrs: Evidence from Data on Suicide Attacks'. Paper presented at the conference on suicide bombing, Center for Democracy, Development and the Rule of Law, Stanford University, September 2003.

Berrebi, C. (2003). *Evidence about the Link between Education, Poverty and Terrorism among Palestinians*. www.irs.princeton.edu/pubs/pdfs/477.pdf.

Bethell, N. (1987). *The Last Secret: Forcible Repatriation to Russia (1944–7)*. London: Hodder and Stoughton.

Beyler, C. (2003). 'Chronology of Suicide Bombings Carried out by Women', www.ict.org.il/articles.

Biggs, M. (2003*a*). 'Positive Feedback in Collective Mobilization: The American Strike Wave of 1886', *Theory and Society*, 32: 217–54.

——(2003*b*). 'When Costs are Beneficial: Protest as Communicative Suffering'. Department of Sociology, University of Oxford, Working Paper, 2003–4.

——(2004). 'Hunger Strikes by Irish Republicans, 1916–1923'. Paper prepared for Workshop on Techniques of Violence in Civil War, Centre for the Study of Civil War, Oslo, August.

Bloom, M. (2004). 'Palestinian Suicide Bombing: Public Support, Market Share, and Outbidding, *Political Science Quarterly*, 119, no. 1, 39–59.'

——(2005). *Dying to Kill: The Global Phenomenon of Suicide Terror*. New York: Columbia University Press.

Bollen, K. A. and Phillips, D. P. (1982). 'Imitative Suicides: A National Study of the Effects of Television News Stories', *American Sociological Review*, 47: 802–9.

Bose, S. (1994). *States, Nations, Sovereignty: Sri Lanka, India and the Tamil Eelam Movement*. New Delhi: Sage.

Bostic, R. A. (1973). 'Self-Immolation: A Survey of the Last Decade', *Life-Threatening Behavior*, 3, no. 1: 66–74.

Bourgeois, M. (1969). 'Suicides par le feu à la manière des bonzes', *Société Medico-Psychologique*, May 19: 116–27

Bowersock, G. W. (1995). *Martyrdom and Rome*. Cambridge: Cambridge University Press.

Brown, I. (1990). *Khomeini's Forgotten Sons: The Story of Iran's Boy Soldiers*. London: Grey Seal Books.

Browne, M. W. (1965). *The New Face of War: A Report on a Communist Guerrilla Campaign*. London: Cassell.

——(1993). *Muddy Boots and Red Socks: A Reporter's Life*. New York: Random House.

Bulathsinghala, F. (2003). 'Interview with Black Tigers: Obsession with Death', *Sunday Observer*, 13 July, at http://origin.sundayobserver.lk/2003/07/13/fea27.html.

Burke, J. (2003). *Al-Qaeda: Casting a Shadow of Terror*. London: I.B. Tauris.

Camus, A. (1951). *L'Homme révolté*. Paris: Gallimard.

——(1977). *Les Justes*. Paris: Gallimard.

——(2002). *Réflexions sur le terrorisme*. Paris: Nicolas Philippe.

Casanova, J. (1994). *Public Religions in the Modern World*. Chicago: University of Chicago Press.

Ceronetti, G. (2003). 'Considerazioni sul valore del termine 'kamikaze', *La Stampa*, 16 November.

Chandran, S. (2001). 'Suicide Terrorism', *The Hindu*, 6 October, www.hinduonnet. com.

Che Guevara, E. (1998). *Guerrilla Warfare*. Lincoln: University of Nebraska Press.

Cheng, A. T. A. and Lee, C. (2000). 'Suicide in Asia and the Far East', in K. Hawton and K. van Heeringen (eds.), *The International Handbook of Suicide and Attempted Suicide*. Chichester: Wiley.

Chân Không (Cao Ngoc Phuong) (1993). *Learning True Love: How I Learned and Practiced Social Change in Vietnam*. Berkeley, CA: Parallax Press.

Clarke, L. (1995). 'Suicide', in J.L. Esposito (ed.), *Oxford Encyclopedia of the Modern Islamic World*, Vol. 4. Oxford: Oxford University Press.

——and Johnston, K. (2001). *Martin McGuinness: From Guns to Government*. Edinburgh: Mainstream.

Cloud, J. (2001). 'Atta's Odyssey', *Time*, 8 October.

Codovini, G. (2002). *Storia del conflitto arabo israeliano palestinese*. Milano: Mondadori.

Collier P., Hoeffler, A., and Söderbom, M. (2004). 'On the Duration of Civil War', *Journal of Peace Research*, 41: 253–74.

Collins, E. (1997). *Killing Rage*. London: Granta Books.

Colmore, G. (1913). *The Life of Emily Davison: An Outline*. London: The Woman's Press.

Conell, C. and Cohn, S. (1995). 'Learning from Other People's Actions: Environmental Variation and Diffusion in French Coal Mining Strikes, 1890–1935', *American Journal of Sociology*, 101: 366–403.

Confino, M. (1973). *Violence dans la violence. Le débat Bakounine-Nečaev*. Paris: Maspero.

Conrad, J. (1986 [1907]). *The Secret Agent*. London: Penguin Books.

Conwell, Y. and Brent, D. (1995). 'Suicide and Aging. I: Patterns of Psychiatric Diagnosis', *International Psychogeriatrics*, 7: 149–64.

Cook, C. (1995). *The Facts on File World Political Almanac: From 1945 to the Present*, 3rd edn. New York: Facts On File.

Corbin, J. (2002). *Al-Qaeda: In Search of the Terror Network that Threatens the World*. New York: Nation Books.

Crenshaw, M. (2001). ' "Suicide" Terrorism in Comparative Perspective', in *Countering Suicide Terrorism*, an international conference, Herzilya: International Policy Institute for Counter Terrorism.

—— (2002). ' "Suicide Terrorism" in Comparative Perspective', in International Policy Institute for Counterterrorism (ICT), *Countering Suicide Terrorism*. Herzliya: ICT.

Crosby, K., Rhee, J., and Holland, J. (1977). 'Suicide by Fire: A Contemporary Method of Political Protest', *International Journal of Social Psychiatry*, 23: 60–9.

Dale, S. (1980). *Islamic Society on the South-East Frontier*. Oxford: Oxford University Press.

—— (1988). 'Religious Suicide in Islamic Asia: Anticolonial Terrorism in India, Indonesia, and the Philippines', *Journal of Conflict Resolution*, 23: 37–59.

Daly, J. (2001). 'Suicide Bombing: No Warning, and No Total Solution', *Jane's Terrorism and Security Monitor*, 17 September. www.janes.com/security/ international_security/news/jtsm/jtsm010917_1_n.shtml.

Daniel, E. V. (1996). *Charred Lullabies: Chapters in an Anthropography of Violence.* Princeton: Princeton University Press.

Danish Refugee Council (2000). *DRC Sri Lanka 2000–2003*, at www.db.idpproject/ org.

Davis, J. M. (2003). *Martyrs: Innocence, Vengeance, and Despair in the Middle East.* New York: Palgrave.

Díaz Herrera, J. and Durán, I. (2002). *ETA. El saqueo de Euskadi.* Barcelona: Planeta.

De Figueiredo, R. and Weingast, B. (1998). 'Vicious Cycles: Endogenous Political Extremism and Political Violence'. Paper presented at the annual meeting of the American Political Science Association, University of California, Berkeley, CA, September.

De Giovannangeli, U. (2003). 'Palestinesi contro: la sanguinosa battaglia per il dopo-Arafat', *Limes*, 1: 259–70.

Dershowitz, A. (2002). *Why Terrorism Works: Understanding the Threat, Responding to the Challenge.* New Haven: Yale University Press.

Domínguez, F. (1998*a*). *ETA: Estrategia Organizativa y Actuaciones, 1978–1992.* Bilbao: Servicio Editorial de la Universidad del País Vasco.

—— (1998*b*). *De la Negociación a la Tregua. ¿ El Final de ETA?* Madrid: Taurus.

—— (2002). *Dentro de ETA. La Vida Diaria de los Terroristas.* Madrid: Aguilar.

Douglas, J. D. (1967). *The Social Meanings of Suicide.* Princeton: Princeton University Press.

Dower, J. (1999). *Embracing Defeat: Japan in the Aftermath of World War II.* London: Penguin.

Dubey, D. P. (1987). 'The Religious Practice of Suicides at Prayāga (Allahabad)', *Archív Orientální*, 55: 355–69.

Durkheim, E. (1952[1897]). *Suicide: A Study in Sociology*, trans. J. A. Spaulding and G. Simpson. London: Routledge & Kegan Paul.

Dviri, M. (2003). *La guerra negli occhi.* Cava de' Tirreni: Avagliano Editore.

Elliott. P. (1998). *Brotherhoods of Fear.* London: Blandford.

Elliott, T. (2003). 'Sri Lanka – a land in ruin', *New Zealand Herald*, 15 March.

Elster, J. (1983). *Sour Grapes.* Cambridge: Cambridge University Press

—— (1999). *Alchemies of the Mind.* Cambridge: Cambridge University Press

Elster, J. (2004*a*). 'Emotion and Action', in R. C. Solomon (ed.), *Thinking about Feeling: Contemporary Philosophers on Emotion.* Oxford: Oxford University Press.

—— (2004*b*). 'Kidnappings in Civil Wars'. Paper prepared for the Workshop on Techniques of Violence, Oslo, 20–1 August.

Engel, R. (2001). 'Inside Al-Qaeda: A Window into the World of Militant Islam and the Afghani Alumni', *Jane's Defense Weekly*, 28 September. www.janes.com/ security/international_security/news/misc/janes010928_1_n.shtml.

Ergil, D. (2001). 'Suicide Terrorism in Turkey: The Workers' Party of Kurdistan', in *Countering Suicide Terrorism: An International Conference*. Herzliya: International Policy Institute for Counter-Terrorism.

—— (2002). 'The Workers' Party of Kurdistan', in International Policy Institute for Counterterrorism (ICT), *Countering Suicide Terrorism*.: Herzliya ICT.

Eribon, D. (1991). *Michel Foucault*. London: Faber and Faber.

Esposito, J. (ed.) (1995). *The Oxford Encyclopedia of the Modern Islamic World*. New York: Oxford University Press.

Falun, D. (2001). 'Uncovering the Truth of the Self-Immolation' (video), http://minghui.cc/media/video/ immolation_doubts_broadband.ram.

Fearon, J. D. and Laitin, D. (2003). 'Ethnicity, Insurgency and Civil War', *American Political Science Review*, 97/1: 75–90.

—— (2004). 'Why Do Certain Civil Wars Last So Much Longer Than Others?', *Journal of Peace Research*, 41: 275–301.

Ferrero, M. (2004). 'Martyrdom Contracts'. www.pubchoicesoc.org/papers/ferrero. pdf.

Festinger L. (1957). *A Theory of Cognitive Dissonance*. Stanford: Stanford University Press.

Finn, P. (2001). 'A Fanatic's Quiet Path to Terror', *Washington Post*, 22 September.

Firth, R. (1961). 'Suicide and Risk-Taking in Tikopia Society', *Psychiatry*, 24: 1–17.

Fisk, R. (1990). *Pity the Nation: Lebanon at War*. London: André Deutsch.

Forest, J. H. (1978). *The Unified Buddhist Church of Vietnam: Fifteen Years for Reconciliation*. Alkmaar: International Fellowship for Reconciliation.

Fouda, Y. and Fielding, N. (2003). *Masterminds of Terror: The Truth Behind the Most Devastating Terrorist Attack the World Has Ever Seen*. New York: Arcade, 95.

Frantz, D. and Butler, D. (2002). 'Germans Lay Out Early Qaeda Ties to 9/11 Hijackers', *New York Times*, 24 August.

Frederick, S. and Loewenstein, G. (1999). 'Hedonic Adaptation', in D. Kahneman, E. Diener, and N. Schwartz (eds.), *Well-Being: The Foundations of Hedonic Psychology*. New York: Russell Sage Foundation.

Freeman, S. (1994). 'Learning the Fundamental Lessons of Religious Conviction', *The Scotsman*, 28 December: 14.

Fridell, W. (1970). 'Government Ethics Textbooks in Late Meiji Japan', *Journal of Asian Studies*, 29: 823–33.

Friedman, T. L. (2002). *Longitudes and Attitudes: Exploring the World After September 11*. New York: Farar Straus Giroux.

Fuglerud, O. (1999). *Life on the Outside: The Tamil Diaspora and Long Distance Nationalism*. London: Pluto Press.

Gambetta, D. (1993). *The Sicilian Mafia: The Business of Private Protection*. Cambridge, MA: Harvard University Press.

—— and Hamill, H. (forthcoming). *Streetwise: How Taxi Drivers Establish Customers' Trustworthiness*. New York: Russell Sage Foundation.

Gambill, G. C. (2003a). *The Economics of Palestinian Suicide Bombings*. www.economics.agnesscott.edu/esayre/research/bomb9.pdf.

—— (2003*b*). *Mounir al-Magdah former Fatah Commander*. www.meib.org/articles.

Ganor, B. (2000). 'Defining Terrorism: Is One Man's Terrorist Another Man's Freedom Fighter?' www.ict.org.il/articles.

—— (2002). 'Suicide Terrorism in Israel', in International Policy Institute for Counterterrorism (ICT), *Countering Suicide Terrorism*. Herzliya: ICT.

Geifman, A. (1993). *Thou Shalt Kill. Revolutionary Terrorism in Russia, 1894–1917*. Princeton: Princeton University Press.

Gibbon, E. (1776–88). *The Decline and Fall of the Roman Empire*.

Gilbert, P. (1995). *Terrorism, Security & Nationality*. London: Routledge.

Goldman, E. (1911). *Anarchism and Other Essays*. New York: Mother Earth.

Goldstein, J., Pevehouse, J., Gerner, D., and Telhamy, S. (2000). 'Reciprocity, Triangularity, and Cooperation in the Middle East, 1979–1997'. Unpublished manuscript. www.american.edu/academic.depts/sis/goldtext/me98papr.htm.

Gonen, Y. (2003). 'Ragazza kamikaze, a bloccarla sono i palestinesi', *La Stampa*, 8 July.

Grewal, J. S. (1990). *The New Cambridge History of India*, II. 3: *The Sikhs of the Punjab*, rev. edn. Cambridge: Cambridge University Press.

Gross, J. T. (1979). *Polish Society Under German Occupation: The Generalgouvernement, 1939–1944*. Princeton: Princeton University Press.

Gunaratna, R. (2001). 'A Wake-up Call'. *Frontline*, 18/17, 18–31 August.

—— (2002). *Inside Al Qaeda: Global Network of Terror*. New York: Berkley Books.

Gurruchaga, C. (2001). *Los Jefes de ETA*. Madrid: La Esfera.

Guttman, D. (1979). 'Killers and Consumers: The Terrorist and his Audience', *Social Research*, 46: 517–26.

Halberstam, D. (1965). *The Making of a Quagmire*. London: Bodley Head.

Hardacre, H. (1989) *Shintō and the State, 1868–1988*. Princeton: Princeton University Press.

Harran, M. J. (1987). 'Suicide', in M. Eliade (ed.), *The Encyclopedia of Religion*. New York: Macmillan.

Harris, P. (2002). 'The Terrorists Who Taught the World', *Daily Telegraph*, 26 January.

Hassan, N. (2001*a*). 'An Arsenal of Believers: Talking to the Human Bombs', *New Yorker*, 22 November.

—— (2001*b*). 'An Arsenal of Believers', *New Yorker*, 19 November.

Hassler, A. (1970). *Saigon, U.S.A*. New York: Richard W. Baron.

Hattori, S. (1993). 'Teikoku Rikukaigun Tokubetsu Kōgeki-tai no Jittai Bunseki' [An Analysis of the Facts of the Imperial Army and Navy Special Attack Units], in *Gunji Shigaku* [Studies in Military History], Vol. 29, No. 1.

Hawley, J. S. (ed.) (1994). *Sati: The Burning of Wives in India*. New York: Oxford University Press.

Hawton, K., Rodham, K., Evans, E., and Weatherall, R. (2002). 'Deliberate Self Harm in Adolescents: Self Report Survey in Schools in England', *British Medical Journal*, 325: 1207–11.

Hellmann-Rajanayagam, D. (1994). *The Tamil Tigers: Armed Struggle for Identity.* Stuttgart: Franz Steiner Verlag.

Hendrickson, P. (1996). *The Living and the Dead: Robert McNamara and Five Lives of a Lost War.* New York: Knopf.

Hingley, R. (1967). *Nihilists.* London: Weidenfeld and Nicolson.

Hobbes, T. (1990). *Behemoth or the Long Parliament* (1st edn. 1682). Chicago: University of Chicago Press.

Hobsbawm, E. J. (1959). *Primitive Rebels* (Manchester: Manchester University Press).

Hofstadter, R. (1964). *The Paranoid Style in American Politics.* Cambridge, MA: Harvard University Press.

Holden, R. T. (1986). 'The Contagiousness of Aircraft Hijacking', *American Journal of Sociology*, 91: 874–904.

Hoffman, B. (2003). 'The Logic of Suicide Terrorism', *Atlantic Monthly*, 291/5: 40–7.

Hope, M. (1967). 'The Reluctant Way: Self-Immolation in Vietnam', *Antioch Review*, 27/2: 149–63.

Hoyt, E. (1985). *The Kamikazes.* London: Panther Books.

Hozumi, N. (1913). *Ancestor-Worship and Japanese Law*, 3rd rev. edn. Tokyo: Maruzen.

Hroub, K. (2000). *Hamas: Political Thought and Practice.* Washington, DC: Institute for Palestine Studies.

Hudson, R. (1999). *The Sociology and Psychology of Terrorism: Who Becomes a Terrorist and Why?* Washington, DC: Federal Research Division, Library of Congress 20540–4840. www.loc.gov.

Human Rights Watch (1995). *Vietnam: The Suppression of the Unified Buddhist Church.* New York: Human Rights Watch.

—— (2002a). *Erased in a Moment: Suicide Bombing Attacks Against Israeli Civilians.* New York: Human Rights Watch.

—— (2002b). *Dangerous Meditation: China's Campaign Against Falungong.* New York: Human Rights Watch.

Hume, D. (1985). 'Of Suicide', *Essays: Moral, Political and Literary* (1st edn. 1741–2). Indianapolis: Liberty Classics.

Iannaccone, L. R. (2003). 'The Market for Martyrs'. Unpublished manuscript.

Iga, M. (1986). *The Thorn in the Chrysanthemum: Suicide and Economic Success in Modern Japan.* Berkeley, CA: University of California Press.

Jane's Intelligence Review (2000). 'Suicide Terrorism: A Global Threat'. 20 October.

Inglehart, R. et al. (2000). World Values Surveys (1995–97) (computer file), ICPSR. 2790. Ann Arbor: Inter-University Consortium for Political and Social Research.

Inoguchi, R. and Pineau, R. (1961). *The Divine Wind.* London: Hutchinson.

Iritani, T. (1991). *Group Psychology of the Japanese in Wartime.* London: Kegan Paul International.

Jaber, H. (1997). *Hezbollah: Born with a Vengeance.* New York: Columbia University Press.

Jamison, K. R. (1999). *Night Falls Fast: Understanding Suicide.* New York: Vintage Books.

Jansen, M. (2000). *The Making of Modern Japan*. Cambridge, MA: Harvard University Press.

Jansz, F. (2001). 'LTTE Attack: A Paradise Lost', *Sunday Leader*, 29 July, at http://xi.pair.com/isweb3/spot/sp0603/clip3.html.

Jayasinghe, A. (1996). 'Ferocious Battle Claims 532 Lives as Fighting Escalates', *AFP*, 27 September.

——(2003). 'Tamil Tigers Boost Peace Bargaining with Suicide Bombers', *AFP*, 3 July.

Jeffreys, M. D. (1971). 'Samsonic Suicides: Or Suicides of Revenge among Africans', in A. Giddens (ed.), *The Sociology of Suicide: A Selection of Readings*. London: Frank Cass.

Jeyaraj, D. B. S. (2001). 'USA Policy Towards the LTTE', *Sunday Leader*, 30 September, at http://xi.pair.com/isweb3/spot/sp0612/clip1.html.

——(2002). 'A Face-saving Manoeuvre', *Frontline*, 19/17, 17–30 August.

Joiner, C. A. (1964). 'South Vietnam's Buddhist Crisis: Organization for Charity, Dissidence, and Unity', *Asian Survey*, 4: 915–28.

Joll, J. (1980). *The Anarchists*. Cambridge, MA: Harvard University Press.

de Jong, K., Mulhern, M., Swan, A., and van der Kam, S. (2001). *Assessing Trauma in Sri Lanka: Psycho-Social Questionnaire, Vavuniya*. Amsterdam: MSF-Holland, May.

Joshi, C. L. (2000). 'Ultimate Sacrifice: Faced with Harassment and Economic Deprivation, Young Tamils Are Ready to Give up Their Lives', *Far Eastern Economic Review*, 1 June, at www.magportal.com/c/soc/reg/as/sl/old.php3/1.

Juergensmeyer, M. (1992). 'Sacrifice and Cosmic War', in M. Juergensmeyer (ed.), *Violence and the Sacred in the Modern World*. London: Frank Cass.

Kahin, G. M. (1987). *How America Became Involved in Vietnam*. New York: Knopf.

Kahneman, D. and Tversky, A. (1979). 'Prospect Theory', *Econometrica*, 47: 63–91.

————(1995). 'Conflict Resolution: A Cognitive Perspective', in K. Arrow et al. (eds.), *Barriers to Conflict Resolution*. New York: Norton.

Kalyvas, S. N. (1998). 'Democracy and Religious Politics: Evidence from Belgium', *Comparative Political Studies*, 31: 291–319.

——(1999). 'Wanton and Senseless? The Logic of Massacres in Algeria', *Rationality and Society*, 11: 243–85.

——(2002). 'The Logic of Violence in Civil War: Ethnic and Non-Ethnic Civil Wars'. Unpublished manuscript, University of Chicago.

——(forthcoming). 'The Logic of Violence in Civil War'. Cambridge: Cambridge University Press.

Karmon, E. (2000). 'Arafat's Strategy: Lebanization and Entanglement'. www.ict.org.il/articles.

Kawachi, U. (2000). 'Reporting from Imperial General Headquarters', in Haruko Cook and Theodore Cook (eds.), (2000). *Japan at War: An Oral History*. London: Phoenix Press.

Kelley, R. (1987). 'The Death of Neusha Farrahi: An Immolation in Westwood', *L.A. Weekly*, 23–7 October: 20–2, 24, 26–7.

Kershner, I. (1995). *Heaven Can Wait*. www.jrep.com.

Khashan, H. (2003). 'Collective Palestinian Frustration and Suicide Bombings'. *Third World Quarterly*, 24: 1049–67.

Kim, H. (2002). 'Shame, Anger, and Love in Collective Action: Emotional Consequences of Suicide Protest in South Korea 1991', *Mobilization*, 7/2: 159–76.

King, S. B. (2000). 'They Who Burned Themselves for Peace: Quaker and Buddhist Self-Immolators during the Vietnam War', *Buddhist-Christian Studies*, 20: 127–50.

Knezys, S. and Sedlickas, R. (1999). *The War in Chechnya*. College Station: Texas A&M University Press.

Kobrin, N. (2002). 'The Death Pilots of September 11th, 2001: The Ultimate Schizoid Dilemma', in J. Piven, C. Boyd, and H. Lawton (eds.), *Jihad and Genocide: Psychological Undercurrents of History*, vol. 3. New York: Universe/Bloomusalem.

Kramer, M. (1991). 'Sacrifice and "Self-Martyrdom" in Shi'ite Lebanon', *Terrorism and Political Violence*, 3/10: 30–47.

——(1994). 'Hizbullah: The Calculus of Jihad', *Bulletin of the American Academy of Arts and Sciences*, 47/8: 20–43.

——(2003). *Political Science Targets Suicide Terrorism. Bystanders: Take Cover!* www.geocities.com/martinkramerorg.

Krishnan, K. G. (1983). 'On Self-Immolation from Inscriptions', in N. Subrahmanian (ed.), *Self-Immolation in Tamil Society*. Madurai: International Institute of Tamil Historical Studies.

Krueger, A. and Maleckova, J. (2002). *Education, Poverty, Political Violence and Terrorism: Is There A Causal Connection?* Working Paper 9074. Cambridge, MA: National Bureau of Economic Research.

———(2003). 'Education, Poverty and Terrorism: Is there a Causal Connection?', May. www.econ.tau.ac.il/papers.

Krueger, A. B. (2003). 'Cash Rewards Alone do not Explain Terrorism', *New York Times*, 29 May: C2.

Kurian, R. (with J. Bourne and H. Waters) (1984). 'Plantation Politics in Sri Lanka: Racism and the Authoritarian State', *Race and Class*, special issue, 26/1: 83–95.

Kydd, A. and Waltes, B. (2002). 'Sabotaging the Peace: The Politics of Extremist Violence', *International Organization*, 56: 263–96.

Kōzu, N. (2000). 'Human Torpedo', in Haruko Cook and Theodore Cook (eds.), *Japan at War: An Oral History*. London: Phoenix Press.

La Guardia, A. (2002). *Holy Land, Unholy War: Israelis and Palestinians*. London: John Murray.

Lamont-Brown, R. (2000). *Kamikaze: Japan's Suicide Samurai*. London: Cassell.

Laqueur, W. (1987). *The Age of Terrorism*. Boston: Little, Brown.

Larteguy, J. (1956). *The Sun Goes Down: Last Letters from Japanese Suicide-Pilots and Soldiers*. London: W. Kimber.

Lawson, B. T. (1995). 'Martyrdom', in J. L. Esposito (ed.), *The Oxford Encyclopaedia of the Modern Islamic World*, Vol III. Oxford: Oxford University Press.

Lee, K. and Bishop, E. (1998). *The May 18 Kwangju Democratic Uprising*. Kwangju: May 18 History Compilation Committee of Kwangju City.

Lenin, V. I. (1968 [1906]). 'Guerrilla Warfare', in W. J. Pomeroy (ed.), *Guerrilla Warfare and Marxism*. New York: International.

Letamendía, F. (1994). *Historia del nacionalismo vasco y de ETA*, 3 vols. San Sebastián: R & B Ediciones.

Lewis, B. (2003 [1967]). *The Assassins: A Radical Sect in Islam*. London: Phoenix.

Linse, U. (1982). ' "Propaganda by Deed" and "Direct Action": Two Concepts of Anarchist Violence', in W. J. Mommsen and G. Hirschfeld (eds.), *Social Protest, Violence and Terror in Nineteenth- and Twentieth-century Europe*. London: Macmillan.

Lochtefeld, J. G. (1987). 'Suicide in the Hindu Tradition: Varieties, Propriety and Practice'. M.A. dissertation, University of Washington.

Luce, D. and Sommer, J. (1969). *Viet Nam: The Unheard Voices*. Ithaca: Cornell University Press.

Lyall, S. (2002). 'English Town Whispers of a Taliban Connection', *New York Times*, 3 February: 14.

Lyon, A. and Uçarer, E. (2001). 'Mobilizing Ethnic Conflict: Kurdish Separatism in Germany and the PKK', *Ethnic and Racial Studies*, 24: 925–48.

Macdonald, A. (pseudonym for William Pierce) (1996). *The Turner Diaries* (1st edn. 1978). Fort Lee, NJ: Barricade Books.

MacStiofain, S. (1975). *Revolutionary in Ireland*. Edinburgh: Gordon Cremonesi.

Mahla, V. P., Bharghava, S. C., Dogra, R., and Shome, S. (1992). 'The Psychology of Self-Immolation in India', *Indian Journal of Psychiatry*, 34/2: 108–13.

Makiya, K. (1998). *Republic of Fear: The Politics of Modern Iraq*. Berkeley, CA: University of California Press.

—— and Mneimneh, H. (2002). 'Manual for a "Raid" ', in R. Silvers and B. Epstein (eds.), *Striking Terror*. New York: New York Review of Books.

Malinowski, B. (1926). *Crime and Custom in Savage Society*. New York: Humanities Press.

Mann, M. (2003). *Incoherent Empire*. London: Verso.

Mao Tse-Tung (1968). *On Guerrilla Warfare*. New York: Praeger.

Margalit, A. (2001). 'Camp David: The Tragedy of Errors', *New York Review of Books*, 48/13, 9 August.

—— (2003). 'The Suicide Bombers'. *New York Review of Books*, 50/1, 16 January.

Marshall, M. G. and Jaggers, K. (2003). Polity IV: Political Regime Characteristics and Transitions, 1800–2002 (electronic data-set). Baltimore: Center for International Development and Conflict Management, University of Maryland.

Mastny, V. (ed.) (1972). *Czechoslovakia: Crisis in World Communism*. New York: Facts on File.

Maynard Smith, J. (1984). *Evolution and the Theory of Games*. Cambridge: Cambridge University Press.

McCarthy, J. D., McPhail, C., and Smith, J. (1996). 'Images of Protest: Dimensions of Selection Bias in Media Coverage of Washington Demonstrations 1982 and 1991', *American Sociological Review*, 61: 478–99.

McKittrick D., Kelters S., Feeney, B., and Thornton, C. (1999). *Lost Lives: The Stories of the Men, Women and Children who Died as a Result of the Northern Ireland Troubles.* Edinburgh: Mainstream.

Mecklin, J. (1965). *Mission in Torment: An Intimate Account of the U.S. Role in Vietnam.* New York: Doubleday.

Medical Foundation for the Victims of Torture (2000). *Caught in the Middle: A Study of Tamil Torture Survivors Coming to the UK from Sri Lanka.* London: Medical Foundation.

Meltsberger, J. (1997). 'Ecstatic Suicide', *Archives of Suicide Research*, 3: 283–301.

Merari, A. (1990). 'The Readiness to Kill and Die: Suicidal Terrorism in the Middle East', in W. Reich (ed.), *Origins of Terrorism.* New York: Cambridge University Press.

——(1998). 'The Readiness to Kill and Die: Suicidal Terrorism in the Middle East', in W. Reich (ed.), *Origins of Terrorism: Psychologies, Ideologies, Theologies, States of Mind.* Washington, DC: Woodrow Wilson Center Press.

——(2005). 'Social Organizational and Psychological Factors in Suicide Terrorism', in T. Bjorgo (ed.), *Root Causes of Terrorism.* London: Routledge.

Miller, J. and Stone, M. (2002). *The Cell: Inside the 9/11 Plot, and why the FBI and CIA Failed to Stop It.* New York: Hyperion.

Miller, M. A. (1995). 'The Intellectual Origins of Modern Terrorism in Europe', in M. Crenshaw (ed.), *Terrorism in Context.* University Park: Pennsylvania State University Press.

Millot, B. (1971). *Divine Thunder: The Life and Death of the Kamikaze.* London: Macdonald.

Mishal, S. and Sela, A. (2000). *The Palestinian Hamas: Vision, Violence, and Coexistence.* New York: Columbia University Press.

Mita, S. (1998). 'Tokkō-tai wa ika ni shite Umareta no ka?' [In What Way was the Special Attack Corps Born?], in Y. Shiino (ed.), *Gyokuseki-sen to Tokubetsu Kōgeki-tai* [The War of the Shattering Jewel and the Special Attack Corps]. Tokyo: Shinjinbutsu Shōrai-sha.

Moghadam, A. (2003). 'Palestinian Suicide Terrorism in the Second Intifada: Motivations and Organizational Aspects', *Studies in Conflict and Terrorism*, 26: 65–92.

Moloney, E. (2002). *A Secret History of the IRA.* New York: W. W. Norton.

Morioka, K. (1995). *Wakaki Tokkōtai-in to Taiheiyō Sensō* [Young Special Attack Unit Members and the Pacific War]. Tokyo: Yoshikawa Kōbunkan.

Morris, B. (2001). *Righteous Victims.* New York: Vintage Books.

——(2002). *Vittime. Storia del conflitto arabo-sionista 1881–2001.* Milan: Rizzoli.

Morris, I. (1975). *The Nobility of Failure.* London: Martin Secker and Warburg.

Morris, I. I. (1960). *Nationalism and the Right Wing in Japan.* London: Oxford University Press.

Morris, J. (1943). *Traveller from Japan.* London: Penguin.

Morrison Welsh, A. (2000). 'Norman Morrison, Deed of Life, Deed of Death' and 'A Healing Journey', *Winds of Change*, 2: 4–7.

Moscicki, E. K. (2001). 'Epidemiology of Completed and Attempted Suicide: Toward a Framework for Prevention', *Clinical Neuroscience Research*, 1: 310–23.

Myers, S. (2003). 'Putin Offers an Amnesty Plan Covering Most Chechen Rebels', *New York Times*, 16 May: A5.

Naby, E. and Frye, R. N. (2003). 'The Martyr Complex', *New York Times*, 14 September (section 4).

Nagatsuka, R. (1974). *I was a Kamikaze*. New York: Macmillan.

Naitō, H. (1989). *Thunder Gods: The Kamikaze Pilots Tell Their Story*. Tokyo: Kodansha International.

Nash, J. R. (1999). *Terrorism in the 20th Century*. New York: M. Evans & Co.

Nathan, J. (1974). *Mishima: A Biography*. London: Hamish Hamilton.

Nepstad, S. E. (2002). 'Creating Transnational Solidarity: The Use of Narrative in the U.S.–Central America Peace Movement', in J. Smith and H. Johnston (eds.), *Globalization and Resistance: Transnational Dimensions of Social Movements*. Lanham, MD: Rowman and Littlefield.

Nesse, R. M. (ed.) (2001). *Evolution and the Capacity for Commitment*. New York: Russell Sage Foundation.

Newsnight (2004). BBC2, 7 July

Nietzsche, F. (1956). *The Genealogy of Morals*, III, 15 (1st edn. 1887), in *The Birth of Tragedy and the Genealogy of Morals*. New York: Doubleday.

Nihon Senbotsu Gakusei Kinen-kai (1995). *Kike Wadatsumi no Koe* [Listen to the Voices of the Sea Gods]. Tokyo: Iwanami Shoten.

Ninagawa, J. (1998). *Gakuto Shutsujin: Sensō to Seishun* [Student Mobilization: War and Youth]. Tokyo: Yoshikawa Kōbunkan.

Núñez, R. (1983). *El Terrorismo Anarquista, 1888–1910*. Madrid: Siglo XXI.

O'Balance, E. (1989). *The Cyanide War*. London: Brassey's.

O'Callaghan, S. (1999). *The Informer*. London: Corgi.

Ohnuki-Tierney, E. (2002). *Kamikaze, Cherry Blossoms and Nationalisms: The Militarization of Aesthetics in Japanese History*. Chicago: University of Chicago Press.

Oka, T. (1966). 'Buddhism as a Political Force', Institute of Current World Affairs, *Newsletter*, TO-24–TO-27.

O'Leary, B. and McGarry, J. (1993). *The Politics of Antagonism: Understanding Northern Ireland*. London: Athlone Press.

Olimpio, G. (2003). 'I ragazzi della squadra della morte. Da terzini di calcio a bombe umane'. *Corriere della Sera*, 30 May.

Olson, M. (1971). *The Logic of Collective Action: Public Goods and the Theory of Groups*, 2nd edn. Cambridge, MA: Harvard University Press.

O'Neill, R. (1981). *Suicide Squads*. New York: Ballantine Books.

Onoda, M. (1971). 'Shinpū Tokkōtai Shutsugeki no Hi' [The Day the *Shinpū* Special Attack Squad Sortied], *Taiheiyō Sensō Dokyumentarī*, 23. Tokyo: Kyō no Wadaisha.

Pandian, M. S. S. (1992). *The Image Trap: M. G. Ramachandran in Film and Politics*. New Delhi: Sage.

Panella, C. (2003). *I piccoli martiri assassini di Dio*. Casale Monferrato: Piemme.

Pape, R. (2003). 'The Strategic Logic of Suicide Terrorism', *American Political Science Review*, 97: 343–61.

Park, B. C. Ben (2004). 'Sociopolitical Contexts of Self-Immolations in Vietnam and South Korea', *Archives of Suicide Research*, 8: 81–97.

Park, K. S. (1995). *A Single Spark* (film). Daewoo Cinema Network.

Pascal, B. (1954). *Pensées* (1st edn. 1669), in J. Chevalier (ed.), *Oeuvres complètes*. Paris: Bibliothèque de la Pléiade.

Paz, R. (2001). 'The Islamic Legitimacy of Suicide Terrorism', in *Countering Suicide Terrorism*, an international conference, Herzilya: an international conference, International Policy Institute for Counter Terrorism.

Petersen, R. (2001). *Resistance and Rebellion: Lessons from Eastern Europe*. Cambridge: Cambridge University Press.

——(2002). *Understanding Ethnic Violence : Fear, Hatred, and Resentment in Twentieth-Century Eastern Europe*. Cambridge: Cambridge University Press.

Pfaffenberger, B. (1994). 'Introduction: The Sri Lankan Tamils', in C. Manogaran and B. Pfaffenberger (eds.), *The Sri Lankan Tamils: Ethnicity and Identity*. Boulder, CO: Westview Press.

Phillips, D. P. and Carstensen, L. L. (1986). 'Clustering of Teenage Suicides after Television News Stories about Suicide', *New England Journal of Medicine*, 315/11: 685–89.

Pinguet, M. (1993). *Voluntary Death in Japan*. Cambridge: Polity Press.

Pipes, D. (1986). 'The Scourge of Suicide Terrorism', www.danielpipes.org/article/175.

——(1998). *The Hidden Hand: Middle East Fears of Conspiracy*. New York: St. Martin's Press.

——(2001*a*). 'A Father's Pride and Glory', www.danielpipes.org/article/390.

——(2001*b*). 'Arafat's Suicide Factory', *New York Post*, 9 December. www.danielpipes.org/article.

Podoliak, K. (2004). 'The Evolution of the Detonator', New Leaders' Conference, April. www.ausimm.com/presentations/podoliak.pdf.

Pomper, P. (1995). 'Russian Revolutionary Terrorism', in M. Crenshaw (ed.), *Terrorism in Context*. University Park: Pennsylvania State University Press.

Post, J. (1990). 'Terrorist Psycho-Logic: Terrorist Behavior as a product of Psychological Forces', in W. Reich (ed.), *Origins of Terrorism*. New York: Cambridge University Press.

Pratap, A. (2001). *Island of Blood*. New York: Penguin Books.

Puhovski, N. (1997). *I: A True Story* (film). Zagreb: Factum Productions.

Rachman, S. J. (1990). *Fear and Courage*. New York: W. H. Freeman and Company.

Radio Praha (n.d.). Jan Palach, 16.1.1969. http://archiv.radio.cz/palach99/eng.

Radlauer, D. (2002). 'An Engineered Tragedy', September, www.ict.org.il/articles.

Ramaswamy, S. (1997). *Passions of the Tongue: Language Devotion in Tamil India, 1891–1970*. Berkeley, CA: University of California Press.

Rapoport, D. C. (1984). 'Fear and Trembling: Terrorism in Three Religious Traditions', *American Political Science Review*, 78: 658–77.

Reuter, C. (2002). *Mein Leben is eine Waffe*. Munich: Bertelsmann.

——(2004). *My Life is a Weapon: A Modern History of Suicide Bombing*. Princeton: Princeton University Press.

Reyes, H. (1998). 'Medical and Ethical Aspects of Hunger Strikes in Custody and the Issue of Torture', in M. Oehmichen (ed.), *Research in Legal Medicine*, Vol XIX. Lübeck: Verlag Scmidt-Römhild.

Reynal-Querol, M. (2002). 'Ethnicity, Political Systems and Civil War', *Journal of Conflict Resolution*, 46: 29–54.

Reza, A., Mercy, J. A., and Krug, E. (2001). 'Epidemiology of Violent Deaths in the World', *Injury Prevention*, 7: 104–11.

Ricolfi, L. (2003). 'Terroristi, kamikaze o martiri? Le missioni suicide nel conflitto israelo-palestinese'. Unpublished paper, Turin, 9 November.

—— and Campana, P. (2005). 'Suicide Missions: A New Database on the Palestinian Area', *Polena*, 2, no. 1.

Risen, J. and MacFarquhar, N. (2002). 'New Recording May be from bin Laden', *New York Times*, 13 November: A18.

Roberts, M. (1996). 'Filial Devotion in Tamil Culture and the Tiger Cult of Martyrdom', *Contributions to Indian Sociology*, 30/2: 245–272.

—— (2004). 'Narrating Tamil Nationalism: Subjectivities and Issues', *South Asia: Journal of South Asian Studies*, 27/1: 87–108.

—— (forthcoming). 'Tamil Tigers "Martyrs": Regenerating Divine Potency'. *Studies in Conflict and Terrorism*.

Roy, O. (2001). *The Failure of Political Islam*. Cambridge, MA: Harvard University Press.

Rubin, B. and Rubin, J. C. (eds.) (2002). *Anti-American Terrorism and the Middle East*. Oxford: Oxford University Press.

Russell, C. A. and Miller, B. H. (1977). 'Profile of a Terrorist', *Terrorism: An International Journal*, 1/1: 17–34.

Ruthven, M. (2001). *A Fury for God: The Islamist Attack on America*. London: Granta Books.

Ryan, C. (1994). 'The One Who Burns Herself for Peace', in K. J. Warren and D. L. Cady (eds.), *Bringing Peace Home: Feminism, Violence, and Nature*. Bloomington: Indiana University Press.

Saad-Ghorayeb, A. (2002). *Hizbu'llah: Politics and Religion*. London: Pluto.

Said, E. W. (2000). *The End of the Peace Process: Oslo and After*. New York: Pantheon Books.

Sakai, S. (2000). 'Zero Ace', in H. Cook and T. Cook (eds.), *Japan at War: An Oral History*. London: Phoenix Press.

Saleh, B. (2003a). 'Socioeconomic Profile of Palestinian Militants from Hamas, Palestinian Islamic Jihad and Al-Aqsa Martyrs' Brigades'. Paper presented at the Graduate Research Forum, Kansas State University, 4 April.

—— (2003b). 'Deprivation Theory Offers an Answer'. www.interdisciplines.org/terrorism/papers.

Sands, B. (1997). *Writings from Prison*. Boulder, CO: Robert Rinehart.

Sanmugathasan, N. (1984). 'Sri Lanka: The Story of the Holocaust in Sri Lanka—Racism and the Authoritarian State, *Race and Class*, special issue, 26/1: 63–82.

Schalk, P. (1997). 'Resistance and Martyrdom in the Process of State Formation in Tamililam', in J. Pettigrew (ed.), *Martyrdom and Political Resistance, Essays from Asia and Europe*. Amsterdam: VU University Press.

Schecter, J. (1967). *The New Face of Buddha: Buddhism and Political Power in Southeast Asia*. London: Victor Gollancz.

Schmid, A. (2002). *Korea between Empires, 1895–1919*. New York: Columbia University Press.

Schmidtke, A. and Schaller, S. (2000). 'The Role of Mass Media in Suicide Prevention', in K. Hawton and K. van Heeringen (eds.), *The International Handbook of Suicide and Attempted Suicide*. Chichester: Wiley.

Schmidtke, A. et al. (1999). 'Suicide Rates in the World: Update', *Archives of Suicide Research*, 5: 81–9.

Schweitzer, Y. (2000). 'Suicide Terrorism: Development and Characteristics', 21 April, www.ict.org.il/articles.

——(2001). 'Suicide Bombings. The Ultimate Weapon?', 7 August, www.ict.org.il/articles.

——(2002). 'Suicide Terrorism and the September 11 Attacks', 20 October, www.ict.org.il/articles.

Scott-Stokes, H. (1975). *The Life and Death of Yukio Mishima*. London: Peter Owen.

Senaratne, J. P. (1997). *Political Violence in Sri Lanka, 1977–1990: Riots, Insurrections, Counterinsurgencies, Foreign Intervention*. Amsterdam: VU University Press.

Sennott, C. M. (2002). 'Before Oath to Jihad, Drifting and Boredom', *Boston Globe*, 3 March.

Sharma, K. L. (1988). *Society and Politics in Modern Sri Lanka*. New Delhi: South Asian Publications.

Sharrock, D. and Devenport, M. (1997). *Man of War, Man of Peace: The Unauthorized Biography of Gerry Adams*. London: Pan Books.

Shatz, A. (2004). 'In Search of Hezbollah', *New York Review of Books*, 51/7, 29 April.

Shiino, Y. (1998). *Gyokuseki-sen to Tokubetsu Kōgeki-tai* [The War of the Shattering Jewel and the Special Attack Corps]. Tokyo: Shinjinbutsu Shōrai-sha.

——(2000). *Kaigun Kōkū-tai to Kamikaze* [The Naval Air Force and the Kamikaze]. Tokyo: Shinjinbutsu Shōrai-sha.

Shillony, B. (1986). 'Universities and Students in Wartime Japan', *Journal of Asian Studies*, 45: 769–87.

Shirai, A. (2002) *Ima Tokkōtai no Shi o Kangaeru* [Considering the Deaths of the Tokkōtai Now], Iwanami Booklet No. 572. Tokyo: Iwanami Shoten.

Silke, A. (1998). 'Cheshire-Cat Logic: The Recurring Theme of Terrorist Abnormality in Psychological Research' *Psychology, Crime and Law*, 4: 51–69.

——(ed.) (2003). *Terrorists, Victims and Society: Psychological Perspectives on Terrorism and its Consequences*. Chichester: Wiley.

Simmel, G. (1950). 'Secrecy', in K. Wolff (trans. and ed.), *The Sociology of Georg Simmel*. New York: Free Press, 330.

Simon, B. (2003). 'The Bomber Next Door', *CBS News*, 28 May. www.cbsnews.com.

Singh, S., Santosh, J., Avasthi, A., and Kulhara, P. (1998). 'A Psychosocial Study of "Self-Immolation" in India', *Acta Psychiatrica Scandinavica*, 97: 71–5.

Smith, R. and Wiswell, E. (1982). *The Women of Suye Mura*. Chicago: University of Chicago Press.

Sánchez-Cuenca, I. (2001). *ETA contra el Estado. Las Estrategias del Terrorismo*. Barcelona: Tusquets.

Sober, E. and Wilson, D. S. (1998). *Unto Others. The Evolution and Psychology of Unselfish Behaviour*. Cambridge, MA: Harvard University Press.

Soni R. V. and Balarajan, R. (1992). 'Suicide and Self-Burning among Indians and West Indians in England and Wales', *British Journal of Psychiatry*, 161: 365–8.

Spaeth, A. and Pratap, A. (1995). 'Marked for Death', *Time.Com*, at www.time.com/time/international/1995/951211/srilanka.html.

Sprinzak, E. (2000). 'Rational Fanatics', *Foreign Policy*, September. www.foreignpolicy.com.

Steinbach, A. (1995). 'The Sacrifice of Norman Morrison', *Baltimore Sun*, 30 July: K1, K4–5.

Stengel, E. (1969). *Suicide and Attempted Suicide*, rev. edn. Harmondsworth: Penguin Books.

Subrahmanian, N. (1983). 'Self-Immolation in Tamil Society', in N. Subrahmanian (ed.), *Self-Immolation in Tamil Society*. Madurai: International Institute of Tamil Historical Studies.

Subramanian, N. (2001*a*). 'Terror at Katunayake', *Frontline*, 18/16, 4–17 August.

——(2001*b*). 'Prabhakaran Asks the West to Redefine Terrorism', *The Hindu*, 28 November, at www.hinduonnet.com/thehindu/2001/11/28/stories/03280003.htm.

Sukhai, A., Moorad, R. G. R., and Dada, M. A. (2002). 'Suicide by Self-Immolation in Durban, South Africa: A Five-Year Retrospective Review', *American Journal of Forensic Medicine and Pathology*, 23: 295–8.

Swamy, M. R. N. (1994). *Tigers of Lanka*. Delhi: Konark.

——(2001). *Tigers of Lanka*, 2nd edition. Delhi: Konark.

——(2003). *Inside An Elusive Mind: Prabhakaran*. Fremont, CA: Literate World.

Sweeney, G. (1993*a*). 'Self-Immolation in Ireland: Hunger Strikes and Political Confrontation', *Anthropology Today*, 9/5: 10–14.

——(1993*b*). 'Irish Hunger Strikes and the Cult of Self-Sacrifice', *Journal of Contemporary History*, 28: 421–37.

Tal, N. (2002). 'Suicide Attacks: Israel and Islamic Terrorism', *Strategic Assessment*, 5/1, June.

Tambiah, S. J. (1986). *Sri Lanka: Ethnic Fratricide and the Dismantling of Democracy*. Chicago: University of Chicago Press.

Taylor, P. (1997). *Provos: The IRA and Sinn Fein*. London: Bloomsbury.

Taylor, S. (1982). *Durkheim and the Study of Suicide*. London: Macmillan.

Thakur, U. (1963). *The History of Suicide in India: An Introduction*. Delhi: Munshi Ram Manohar Lal.

The Island (2001). 'Prabhakaran Calls for Final Phase of Eelam War'. 2 September, at www.island.lk2001/09/02/defenc01.html.

The Statesman (India) (2000). 'Tigers Sub Found in Thai Nook'. 1 June.

The Times (1992). 'Tiger chief named in Gandhi murder', 21 May: 11.

——(1996). 'Tamil lorry bomb rips apart Central Bank', 2 February: 15.

Time (2001). 'Conversations with Terror', 8 October.

Thich Giac Duc (1986). 'Buddhists and Catholics', in D. Chanoff and D. Van Toai (eds.), *Portrait of the Enemy*. New York: Random House.

Thich Nhat Hanh (1967). 'Letter to Martin Luther King, Jr. (1 June 1965)', in *Vietnam: The Lotus in the Sea of Fire*. London: SCM Press.

Thich Thien-An (1975*a*). *Buddhism and Zen in Vietnam in Relation to the Development of Buddhism in Asia* (Los Angeles: College of Oriental Studies, Graduate School; Rutland, VT: Charles E. Tuttle).

——(1975*b*). 'Interview', in R. Fields (ed.), *Loka: A Journal from Naropa Institute*. Garden City, NY: Anchor Books.

Tierney, M. (2002). 'All She Wants Is to Be a Suicide Bomber', August. www.theherald.co.uk.

Tilly, C. (1986). 'European Violence and Collective Action since 1700', *Social Research*, 53: 159–84.

Toolis, K. (1997). *Rebel Hearts: Journeys Within the IRA's Soul*. New York: St. Martin's Press.

Topmiller, R. (1994). 'The 1963 Buddhist Crisis in South Vietnam'. M.A. thesis, Central Washington University.

——(1998). 'The Lotus Unleashed: The Buddhist Struggle Movement in South Vietnam (1964–66)'. Ph.D. dissertation, University of Kentucky.

Torisu, K. and Chihaya M. (1986). 'Japanese Submarine Tactics and the Kaiten', in David Evans (ed.), *The Japanese Navy in World War II*. Annapolis, MD: Naval Institute Press.

Treptow, K. W. (1992 [1989]). 'The Winter of Despair: Jan Palach and the Collapse of the Prague Spring', in K. W. Treptow, *From Zalmoxis to Jan Palach: Studies in East European History*. New York: Columbia University Press.

Trotsky, L. (1974). *Against Individual Terrorism*. New York: Pathfinder.

Tsai, H. H. (1996). 'Globalization and the Urban System in Taiwan', in Fu-chen Lo and Yue-man Yeung (eds.), *Emerging World Cities in Pacific Asia*. Tokyo: United Nations University Press.

Tz'u-hsing Ch'an Ssu (1958). *Tu-lun ch'an shih shih chi* (Hong Kong: n.p.).

Uehling, G. (2000). 'Squatting, Self-Immolation, and the Repatriation of Crimean Tatars', *Nationalities Papers*. 28: 317–41.

Ugaki, M. (1991). *Fading Victory: The Diary of Admiral Matome Ugaki, 1941–1945* (trans. Chihaya, Masataka). Pittsburgh: University of Pittsburgh Press.

United Nations Population Division (2001). *World Urbanization Prospects: The 2001 Revision*. New York: United Nations.

Urquhart, C. (2003). 'Palestinians Militants Offer 3-Month Truce', *Guardian*, 26 June.

Veyne, P. (1976). *Le pain et le cirque*. Paris: Le Seuil.

Voltaire (1964). 'Fanatisme', *Dictionnaire philosophique* (1st edn. 1764). Paris: Flammarion.

von Borcke, A. (1982). 'Violence and Terror in Russian Revolutionary Populism: The Narodnaya Volya, 1879–83', in W. J. Mommsen and G. Hirschfeld (eds.), *Social Protest, Violence and Terror in Nineteenth- and Twentieth-century Europe*. London: Macmillan.

Waldman, A. (2003). 'Masters of Suicide Bombing: Tamil guerrillas of Sri Lanka', *New York Times*, 14 January.

Wani, I. (2002). 'Suicide Missions Introduced to Boost J&K Terrorists' Morale', *J & K News*, 1 December. www.jammu-kashmir.com.

Wasserman, I. (1984). 'Imitation and Suicide: A Reexamination of the Werther Effect', *American Sociological Review*, 49: 427–36.

Weber, M. (1958 [1916]). 'The Economic Ethic of World Religions: Introduction' and 'Intermediate Considerations' in H. H. Gerth and C. Wright Mills (eds.), *From Max Weber: Essays in Sociology*. New York : Oxford University Press.

——(1978). *Economy and Society: An Outline of Interpretive Sociology* (1st edn. 1922). Berkeley, CA: University of California Press.

Weinberger-Thomas, C. (1999). *Ashes of Immortality: Widow-Burning in India*. Chicago: University of Chicago Press.

Welch, H. (1967). *The Practice of Chinese Buddhism, 1900–1950*. Cambridge, MA: Harvard University Press.

WHO (World Health Organization) (2003) 'Suicide Rates', at www.who.int/mental_health/prevention/suicide/suiciderates/en.

Williams, J., Mark, G., and Pollock, L. R. (2000). 'The Psychology of Suicidal Behaviour', in K. Hawton and K. van Heeringen (eds.), *The International Handbook of Suicide and Attempted Suicide*. Chichester: Wiley.

Williams, K. (1997). *The Prague Spring and Its Aftermath: Czechoslovak Politics, 1968–1970*. Cambridge: Cambridge University Press.

Williams, M. (1997). *Cry of Pain: Understanding Suicide and Self-Harm*. Harmondsworth: Penguin Books.

Wilson, A. J. (1994). *SJV Chelvanayakam and the Crisis of Sri Lankan Tamil Nationalism, 1947–1977*. London: Hurst & Co.

——(2000). *Sri Lankan Tamil Nationalism*. London: Penguin.

Wines, M. (2003). '19 Die as Suicide Bomber Destroys Bus Near Chechnya', *New York Times*, 6 June: A3.

Wright, L. (2004). 'The Terror Web', *New Yorker*, 2 August.

Wulff, E. (1963). 'The Buddhist Revolt: Diem's New Opponents Deserve US Support', *New Republic*, 31 August: 11–14.

Yamamoto, T. (2000 [1716]). *Hagakure: The Book of the Samurai* (trans. William Wilson). Tokyo: Kodansha International.

Yamanouchi, M. and Quinn, J. (2000). *Listen to the Voices from the Sea*. Scranton, PA: University of Scranton Press.

Yokoi, T. (1986). 'Kamikaze in the Okinawa Campaign', in D. Evans (ed.), *The Japanese Navy in World War II*. Annapolis, MD: Naval Institute Press.

Yokota, Y. (2000) 'Volunteer', in H. Cook and T. Cook (eds.), *Japan at War: An Oral History*. London: Phoenix Press.

——and Harrington, J. (1962). *Kamikaze Submarine*. New York: Norden.

Zahavi, A. and Zahavi, A. (1997). *The Handicap Principle: A Missing Piece of Darwin's Puzzle*. New York: Oxford University Press.

Zavala, J. M. (1998). *Matar al Rey: La Casa Real en el Punto de Mira de ETA.* Madrid: Alianza.

Zoroya, G. (2002). 'Woman Describes The Mentality of a Suicide Bomber', *USA Today*, 22 April. www.usatoday.com.

INDEX

ability to wait 23, 28, 29, 253–4, 301 n.9, 50, 304 n.32
Abu Hafs el-Masri Brigades 268
Abu Hassan 315–6 n.84
Abu Mazen 95, 97, 128
Abu Olbeh 233
Abu Omar, Sirhan 314 n.83
Abu Ruqaiyah 147
Adair, D. 241
Adams, G. 214, 220, 299
adat, code of honour 241
Adityanjee, D. 322 n.20
Afghan war 148, 167
Afghanistan 88, 139, 169
Africa 287
African National Congress 290
Afula 312 n.57
airborne saboteur 6–7
Akinaga, Y. 32
al-Aqsa martyr brigades 81, 95, 97, 99, 143, 249, 257, 332 n.33
see also Palestinian Organizations
al-Aqsa Mosque 247
al-Azhar, Islamic University 298
al-Fatah 81, 95, 211, 246, 247, 308 n.12, 312 n.56
see also Palestinian Organizations
al-Haznawi, al-Ghamidi Ahmad 160, 318 n.17, 318 n.24
al-Mugrabi Dalal 81, 308 n.13
al-Omari, Abdul Aziz 151
al-Qaeda 59, 133, 148, 160, 170, 221, 225, 246, 247, 248, 253, 260, 287
leaders 157, 159, 252
and martyrdom 135, 158
al-Qaradawi, Sheikh Yusuf 296
al-Qassam brigades 90, 95, 97
al-Quds brigades 95, 97

al-Quds Mosque 142, 151
al-Shati, refugee camp 110
al-Shehhi, Marwan 139, 142
al-Zawahiri, Ayman 133, 156, 164, 166, 168, 169, 319 n.30
Alcedo, M. 221
ALF, *see* Arab Liberation Front
Algeria 81, 212–13
Aleppo 141
Allende, Salvador 198, 324 n.41
Alsheheri, Wail 136
Alsheheri, Waleed 136
altruism 269, 270
see also altruistic suicide; self-sacrifice
Amal 80, 81, 86–7
American Memorial Institute for the Prevention of Terrorism 78
Amir Yigal 91
Amnesty International 49, 113, 315 n.88
anarchists viii, 82, 210, 221, 222, 225, 226, 227, 260, 261, 279, 285, 289, 309 n.22, 333 n.10
see also *The Secret Agent*
ANC, *see* African National Congress
ancestors vii, 279, 288
see also precedents; proto-suicide missions
Andoni, L. 110, 111
anger 140, 141, 142, 153, 154, 268, 269, 275, 276, 277
Angiolillo 227
apocalypse 171
apostasy, apostates 133, 140, 141, 165, 168, 171
appealing to bystanders 175, 196, 201
see also inciting synpathizers; public opinion
Arab diaspora 167, 168

Arab Liberation Front 81
Arab-Israeli conflict 77, 84, 97, 312 n.57, 315 n.85, 316 n.97
Arafat, Yasser 89, 90, 92, 96, 129, 311 n.41, n.42, n.45
Arendt, H. 216, 254
Aristotle 239
Argentina 82
Arizcuren, José Javier ('*Kantauri*') 212
Ashcroft, J. 318 n.20
Ashton, J. R. 182
assassinations 44, 46, 52, 54, 56, 62, 91, 215, 221–2, 263, 285, 289, 309 n.22
    see also targets
Assassins, Islamic sect 82–3, 147, 279, 280, 289
Atheists 26
Atjeh, Northern Sumatra, 83, 279
Atran, S. 234, 260, 279, 281, 289, 299, 314 n.76, 316 n.89, 334 n.18
Atsutane, H. 13
Atta, Mohamed 137–42, 143, 151, 240
Aussaresses, P. 217
Aust, S. 151, 317 n.8
Ayash, Yahya (the "enginneer") 313 n.64
Axell, A. 24, 30
Aznar, José María 212

Baader Meinhof 106, 144, 209, 225, 268, 327 n.25
Baath Party of Lebanon 81, 87, 316 n.90
Baath Party of Syria 80
Baechler, J. 174, 195, 196
Balarajan, R. 322 n.20
Balasingham, Adele 48, 51, 306 n.73
Balasingham, Anton 48, 57, 69, 304 n.34, 305 n.46, n.50, n.53, n.54, 306 n.59
Balfour Declaration 251
Balraj, Colonel 54
Bamford, Graham 177
Bandaranaike Airport, attack on 55, 58
Bandaranaike Sirimavo, Prime Minister of Sri Lanka 47

Bandaranaike, S. W. R. D., Prime Minister of Sri Lanka 47, 303 n.19
Barak, Ehud 89, 92, 93, 311 n.37, 312 n.52
Barber, B. 314 n.76
Barcelona 221
Bargouthi, Marwan 95, 97
Basque Country 212, 228
Basques 230
Beasley, W. G. 13
Beauchamp, J. L. 283, 284
Becker, G. 209
Beevor, A. 42
Begin, Menachem 92
Beirut, attacks in 80, 86–7, 286, 320 n.55
Belhadj, Ali 213, 325 n.8
beliefs 110, 133, 134, 157, 160, 166, 197, 199, 228, 234–5, 244, 245, 250–6, 256–7, 264, 267, 269, 274, 291, 293
    in afterlife, *see* religious beliefs
    irrational 234, 235, 236, 252, 258, 270
    secular beliefs 93, 243
    see also conspiracy theory; convictions; myth
Benjamin, D. 133, 153, 154, 317 n.5, 318 n.21
Benn, J. A. 179
Bennet, J. 215, 326 n.14
Beresford, D. 229, 295
Bergen, P. 169
Berger, P. 116
Berman, E. viii n.1, 45, 260–1, 265, 288–9, 290, 292, 302 n.13, 332 n.2, 335 n.28
Berrebi, C. 105, 327 n.27
Bethell, N. 178
Beyler, C. 92
Bible 133–4, 315 n.85
Biggs, M. 188, 189, 196, 208, 294,
bin al-Shibh, Ramzi 139, 318 n.14
bin Laden, Osama 132, 139, 156, 159, 162, 164, 165, 166, 168, 169, 170–1, 250, 264, 318 n.28, 319 n.49, 320 n.55

Birmingham 220
Bishop, E. 321 n.13
Bismarck 227
Black Panthers 326 n.14
Black Sea Tigers 43, 54, 62
Black Tigers 43, 44, 73, 135, 143, 147, 278, 281
Black Tigers' Day 50, 61, 64, 65
blasphemy 134, 156
Bloody Friday 214
Bloom, M. 96, 99, 104, 231, 249
Bollen, K. A. 189, 323 n.30
bonding among soldiers 63, 66, 67, 73, 76, 150, 277, 276
   see also religious practice; cell effect
Bose, S. 50, 303 n.17
Bose, Subash Chandra 48
Bostic, R. A. 174
Bourgeois, M. 175, 182
Bowersock, G. W. 159
brainwashing 112
Brent, D. 270
brevity of life 144 , 146
Brown, Vice-Admiral 10
Brown, I. 261
Browne, M. 173, 179, 180, 205, 321 n.14
Buddhism 13, 14–15, 47, 199, 278, 293, 328 n.6
   see also Mahayana Buddhism; Zen
Buddhist tradition 175, 207
Buddhist clergy, *see* Buddhist monks
Buddhist monks 43, 179, 204, 205, 303 n.19, 331 n.30
Bulathsinghala, F. 304 n.32
Bund, Jewish Workers Union 294
Burke, J. 138, 139, 160, 168
Burma 323 n.35
Bush, family 242
Bush, G., President of the USA 90
Bush, G. W. President of the USA 106, 166, 319 n.43, n.49
Bushidō 20
Butler, D. 319 n.29

comradeship, *see* bonding among soldiers
Cambodia 180
Camp David 89, 92, 93, 108
Campana, P. 122, 309 n.19, 333 n.12
Camus, A. 147, 148, 213, 227, 318 n.19
Canovas del Castillo 227
convictions 239
career 106, 115, 116
Carstenen, L. L. 189
Casanova, J. 112
casualties 90, 305 n.56, 313 n.69, 326 n.10, 329 n.16, 332 n.2, 333 n.7
   see also suicide missions, efficiency
Catholic community 220
Catholic tradition, *see* Christian tradition
Catholics 226, 229, 230, 323 n.31
causal factors 244–6
Cave of the Patriarchs 91, 294
CDISS, *see* Centre for Defence and International Security Studies
celebration of the attacker 31, 278, 306 n.67
   see also Black Tigers' Day; Heroes' Day
cell effects 150, 278
   see also bonding among soldiers
Central Bank Colombo, attack on 44, 56, 59
Central Intelligence Agency 147
Center of Policy and Survey Research 93, 119, 128
Ceronetti, G. 111
certainty effect 236
Ceylon, *see* Sri Lanka
Chadha, Monica 188, 195
Chân Không 173, 194, 195, 196, 197, 199, 202, 321 n.13, n.14
Chandran, S. 99, 308 n.8
Change, Kathy 191
Charan caste (India) 323 n.36, 324 n.40
Charles Anthony Brigades 54, 67
   see also élite commando units
Che Guevara, Ernesto 48, 217

cheating the adversary 196, 198, 201
  see also motivations
Chechnya 81, 247, 248, 253, 287
Chechen people 115
Chechen rebels 211, 218, 225
Chechen war 241, 324 n.3
Chelvanayakam, S. J. V. 47
Chen Guo 206
Cheng, A. T. A. 186
Chihaya, M. 9
China 180, 183, 206
China war 17
Chinnaswami 181, 203–4
Christians 26, 186
Christian tradition 242, 293
Christianity, see Christian tradition
Chun Se Yong 195
CIA, *see* Central Intelligence Agency
civil wars 45, 90, 110, 216, 247, 288, 289,
  291, 292, 336 n.47
civilian targets of vi, 59, 80, 88, 91, 97,
  147, 161, 169, 216, 248, 261, 313
  n.58, 315 n.85, 329 n.16
  see also non-targeting civilians policy
Clarke, L. 220, 242, 327 n.19, n.20
Clinton, W. J., President of the USA 92,
  311 n.45
Cloud, J. 139, 141, 142
clustering, *see* emulation
coal miners 183
Codovini, G. 312 n.47
coercion 239
  see also motivations
cognitive dissonance 112
Cohn, S. 189
cold war 171
collateral damage 161
  see also civilian targets
collective causes 183–4
Collier, P. 336 n.47
Collins, Eamon 220, 327 n.21
Colombia 211–12
colonialism 17, 83, 164, 170, 279, 281
  see also social injustice
Colmore, G. 178

commando attacks 46
  see also élite commando units; high-
  risk missions
communicative purposes 55–6, 57, 61,
  68, 79, 102, 158, 159, 160–3, 255,
  263, 264, 266–9 274
  see also motivations; propaganda;
  psychological impact
Communist Revolution 251
community 165, 166, 170
competitive cooperation 100
  see also joint attacks
Conell, C. 189
Confino, M. 222
confucian values 13
Conrad, Joseph 283–4
conspiracy theory 169, 250–1, 257,
  332 n.34
  see also paranoia
constituency, *see* supporters
constituency costs 218–23
constraints 105, 213, 214, 215, 225, 234,
  297
contamination 133, 137, 139
contagion effect, *see* diffusion
conventional attacks 44, 52, 53, 54, 89,
  91, 94, 311 n.38, 312 n.56
  see also guerrilla attacks
Conwell, Y. 270
Coogan, Charlie 326 n.19
Cook, C. 286
Coral Sea, battle of 1
Corbin, J. 140, 151, 318 n.13
co-religionists 288–2, 336 n.46
corporate identity 318 n.21, n.23
Coskun, Nejla 184, 196, 199
cosmic war 171
  see also holy war
countermeasures to kamikaze attacks 9
counterproductive effects 216–8
CPSR, *see* Center for Policy and Survey
  Research
cremation 179
Crenshaw, M. 148, 249, 255
Croatia 82

Crosby, K. 175, 182
cyanide capsules 51, 62, 66, 68–9, 74, 306
   n.59, n.73
cyclic pattern 85
   see also waves of suicide missions
Czechoslovakia 182

Dalai Lama 106, 324 n.45
Dale, S. 83, 279, 280, 288, 311 n.34, 328
   n.7, 336 n.43
Daly, J. 312 n.57
Damascus Cartel 89
Daniel, E. V. 303 n.16
Dar es Salaam, attack 331 n.24
database 78, 118, 122, 124, 125, 175, 176
   Lexis-Nexis 44, 121, 176
Davis, J. M. 147, 311 n.34
Davison, Emily Wilding 178
death as a reward 116, 135–6, 154, 238
death as a goal vii, ix, 236, 295, 267, 332
   n.1, 336 n.52
death in combat 17, 207
Declaration of Algiers 89, 104
decolonization 168–72
   see also colonialism; imperialism;
   social injustice
De Figueiredo, R. 98, 104
De Giovannangeli, U. 96, 99
de Jong, K. 70
delivery mechanism vi, 59, 327 n.23
   see also technology
Democratic Front for the Liberation of
   Palestine 308 n.12
democratic political system 175
Dershowitz, A. 103, 314 n.81
despair 36, 115, 196, 197, 198, 201
deterrence 248–9, 252
Devenport, M. 220, 229
Dhanu, Gandhi 57
Díaz Herrera, J. 212
disappointment, *see* opposition to peace
   process
discipline 63, 65, 67
discriminatory practices 229
   see also religious discrimination

disgust 36
dishonour 20 , 23, 137, 149
Disputed Territories, *see* West Bank;
   Gaza Strip
Dissanayake, Gamini 57
Djerba, attack of 319 n.29
Dominguez, F. 228, 229
Donnan, S. 182
Donosti, ETA's commando 212
Douglas, J. D. 195
Dower, J. 32
downward mobility 106, 143–4, 244, 245
Dravidian Progress Association 204
Dubey, D. P. 187
Duran, I. 212
Duriappah, Alfred 303 n.24
Durkheim, E. 75, 174, 186, 270, 271,
   279, 281, 307 n.79
Dviri, M. 313 n.63

Eagleburger, Lawrence, US Under
   Secretary of State 223
economic deprivation 230, 330 n.21
Egyptian Islamic Jihad 133
Eiffel Tower 325 n.8
El Al 314 n.71
Elephant Pass, attack of 54, 55
élite commando unit 43, 73
elliott, P. 309 n.22
Elliott, T. 60
Elster, J. 199, 230, 239, 242, 245, 246,
   254, 298, 316 n.92
emotions 35, 36, 115, 133, 156, 157, 160,
   244, 246, 251, 254, 256, 258, 264,
   276, 277
emperor loyalty 16, 25
emperor worship 13, 17–18
emulation 113, 188–90, 230, 240, 310
   n.33, 324 n.48
Engel, R. 167
Enniskillen 220
envy 148, 154
Ergil, D. 192, 237, 239, 248, 322 n.25
Eribon, D. 335 n.42
Esplanade of the Mosques 94

Esposito, J. 317 n.6
Estate Tamils, *see* Indian Tamils
ETA, see *Euzkadi ta Azkatasuna*
ethnic conflicts 217, 326 n.14, 336
    n.47
ethnic discrimination 43, 44, 46, 47,
    303 n.22
  see also ethnic conflict; religious
    discrimination
Euripides 318 n.25
Euzkadi ta Azkatasuna 209, 213, 219,
    220–1, 223, 224, 228, 229, 293
evolutionary perspective ix, 271, 272,
    334 n.18
eye-for-an-eye principle 146, 315
    n.85
exchange 197, 201
  see also beliefs, religious beliefs,
    transfiguration
expiation 152–6
  see also sin

factional struggles, *see* internecine
    competition
Fadlallah, Sheikh Hussein 255 n.31,
    296, 297
Falun Gong 176, 183, 192, 198, 202, 204,
    205–6, 324 n.45
fame 113, 116, 241
  see also glory; vanity; honour
Farrahi, Neusha 193
Farber, Nisan 222, 285, 294, 335 n.40
  see also anarchists; ancestors
FARC, *see* Fuerza Armadas
    Revolucionarias de Colombia
fast until death, *see* hunger strike
fatwa 296, 297
fear 155, 239, 264, 267, 329 n.16
  see also motivations
fear inhibitors 151–2, 155, 273, 275,
    334 n.21
  see also incantations; religious
    practices
Fearon, J. D. 45, 302 n.14, 336 n.44,
    n.46, n.47

Ferrero, M. 316 n.97
Fielding, N. 317 n.1, 318 n.13, n.27,
    n.28
financial constraints 234
financial rewards, *see* rewards to
    family
Firth, R. 193, 323 n.39
FIS *see* Islamic Salvation Front
Fisk, R. 308 n.9, 310 n.32
Flanagan, 276
Force 17 95
Forest, J. H. 192, 196, 321 n.13
'Forlorn Hope' 272, 278
  see also heroism; high-risk missions
Foucault, M. 287
Fouda, Y. 317 n.1, 318 n.13, n.27,
    n.28
France 228
Frantz, D. 319 n.29
Fredereick, S. 245
Freeman, S. 325 n.8
Freemasons 251
free-rider problems 246
French Revolution 251
Fridell, W. 16
Friedman, T. L. 142
Frogman mines, see *Fukuryū*
Front Islamique du Salut 213
frustrated expectations 244, 245, 270,
    285
Frye, R. N. 147
Fuerza Armadas Revolucionarias de
    Colombia 211, 234, 326 n.4,
    n.6, n.7
Fuglerud, O. 306 n.71
Fukuryū (crouching dragon) 8
funeral 324 n.42
funeral banquet 30

Gambetta D., 113, 243, 290, 316 n.91,
    323 n.36, 327 n.26
Gambill, G. C. 315
Gandhi Indira, Prime Minister of
    India 191
Gandhi, Mahatma 237, 321 n.15

Gandhi, Rajiv., Prime Minister of
India 51, 56, 302 n.9, 303 n.29, 305
n.50, 336 n.46
Gandhi, Sonia 194
Ganor, B. 80, 236
Gaza Strip 92, 108, 248, 332 n.2
see also Palestinian Territories
'Gazavat' (Chechen kamikaze
group) 324 n.3
Geifman, A. 215, 222, 227, 285, 294, 333
n.10, 335 n.40
Gemayel Beshir 87
gender 244, 322 n.18
see also female suicide attackers
genocide 169, 303 n.28
German romanticism 141
GIA, see *Groupe Islamique Arméè*
Gibbon, E. 329 n.10
Gilbert, P. 213
Gillespie, Patsy 211, 325 n.5, 327 n.19
Giretsu Kutei-tai (Heroism Airborne
Units), *see* airborne saboteur
global jihad 168
glory ix, 21, 116, 149, 241, 273
see also fame; vanity; honour
goals viii, 89, 91, 158, 170, 225, 246–7,
248, 264, 268, 278
see also motivations; suicide missions,
rationality of
Goebbels 42
Goldman, Emma 227
Goldstein, Baruch 119, 230, 249, 294,
313 n.64
Goldstein, J. 99
Gooneratne, C. V. 57
Goswami, Rajeev188, 190, 194, 195, 202,
323 n.37
Great Britain 182
Grewal, J. S. 191, 323 n.34
Grinevitski, Ignatei 222
Grojean, Oliver 177, 322 n.26
Gross, J. T., 216, 217
Grozny, battle of 211
Groupe Islamique Arméè 209, 212–13,
216–17, 289, 325 n.8

Guadalcanal, battle of 1, 3
guerrilla attacks viii, 44, 52, 54, 58, 62,
73, 96, 157, 215, 262
guerrilla organizations 80, 119, 167
guerrilla war, *see* guerrilla attacks;
guerrilla organizations
guilt 25, 152, 154, 197, 240
see also shame
Gunaratna, R. 135, 141, 157, 305 n.55,
319 n.30, 332 n.3
Gurruchaga, C. 221
Guttman, D. 159
gyokusai (shattering jewels), *see*
kamikaze iconography

Habash Popular Front 90
Haddam, Anwar 213
Hagakure (Hidden Among the
Leaves) 19–20
Halberstam, D. 173, 321 n.14
Hamas 46, 81, 87, 89, 90, 91, 93, 95, 97,
211, 215, 221, 223, 225, 227, 240,
247, 248, 249, 287, 313 n.60
Charter of 250
see also Palestinian Organizations
Hamburg cell 132, 142, 143, 150, 168,
318 n.14
see also Mohamed Atta, Marwan al-
Shehhi, Ramzi bin al-Shibb, Ziad
Jarrah
Hamil, H. 290
handlers 149, 150, 240, 241, 327 n.26
see also suicide attackers
Hani, Hanjour 317 n.9
Hanif, Asif Mohammed 298–9
Hao Huijun 198
Harran, M.J. 187
Harrington, J. 21, 26
Harris, P. 59
Harrods 220
Hashiuchi, former kamikaze pilot 3, 5,
12, 17, 18, 23, 24, 30
Hassan, N. 79, 110, 244, 254, 276,
309 n.24, 330 n.19
Hassler, A. 181, 194

hatred for the enemy 242, 277
Hattori, S. 8, 9, 23
Hawley, J. S. 174
Hawton, K. 194
Haydar, 330 n.22
heavenly rewards ix, 273, 293
  see also religious beliefs
Hebron 113
Hellmann-Rajanayagam, D. 57, 60, 66,
  75, 239
Hendrickson, P. 181, 200, 202
Henry, Emile 285
Heroes' Day 48, 59, 61, 64
heroic suicide 69, 75
  see also cyanide capsules; torture
heroism 35, 73, 75, 149, 270, 272–4, 275,
  278
  spontaneity of 274, 275
  dissociative state in 275, 277, 278
  see also élite commando units; suicide
  attackers
Herz, Alice, 181, 322 n.18
Hezbollah 77, 80, 81, 87, 97, 160, 211,
  221, 223, 224, 227, 230, 261, 267,
  286, 287, 297, 299, 311 n.38,
  329 n.16
Hiba Daragmeh 312 n.57
high-risk missions vi, 7, 43, 150, 212,
  237–8, 263, 272, 273, 275
  see also heroism
hijacking 101–2, 103, 131, 298, 314 n.71,
  325 n.8
Hindi 181, 191
Hindu nationalist movement 320 n.3
Hindu Puranas 187
Hindu tradition 175, 207
Hinduism 76, 186, 278, 293, 321 n.14
hit-and-run terrorism 132, 148, 153, 158
  see also guerrilla attacks
Hitler, A. 235
Hobbes, T. 152
Hobsbawn, E. 226
Hoffman, B. 158, 216, 224, 231, 326
  n.10, n.12, 327 n.23, n.26
Hofstadter, R. 250

Holden, R. T. 335 n.40
Holgate, S. 59
Holocaust 235, 303 n.28
holy war 147, 148, 164, 168–72,
  213, 247
holy warrior 148, 149
honour 76, 116, 135, 145, 149, 154, 241,
  281
Hook III, Charles 200
Hope, M. 187, 197, 202, 204, 321 n.14
Hoyt, E. 11
Hozumi, N. 15–16
Hroub, K. 215, 221
hudna (truce) 95, 100
Hudson, R. 82, 83, 107–8, 311 n.34,
  314 n.73, n.74
Hué 179, 197
"human waves"
  in Iran 87, 261, 286, 297, 299; *see also*
  teenage martyrs
  by Japanese soldiers 1, 4
  in Sri Lanka 54
humiliation 166, 245, 246, 251
  see also resentment
Hungary 182
hunger strikes 174, 179, 181, 193, 195,
  199, 228, 229, 230, 237, 270, 295, 316
  n.97, 323 n.33
  as threats 69, 174, 190, 191, 237,
  321 n.4
  see also self-immolation; protest
Hussein, King of Jordan 311 n.45
Hussein (Husayn) son of Ali and the
  prophet's daughter Fatima 83, 187,
  279–80

Iannacone, L. R. 45
Ibrahimi Mosque 91
  see also Cave of the Patriarchs
Ibtissam Harb 87
ICT, *see* Institute or Peace and Conflict
  Studies
ideology, *see* narrative of blame
Iga, M. 15, 37
illiteracy 244, 245

imitation 175, 180, 190, 233–4, 252–3, 287, 331 n.27, 335 n.41
Imperial Rescript on Education 15, 16, 18
imperialism 134, 139–40, 141, 153, 169
impiety 141, 146,164, 165, 169, 170
incantations 151
inciting sympathizers 99, 163, 175, 196, 197, 201, 208, 295
India 82, 175, 181, 182, 184, 193, 293
India-Sri Lanka accord 69
India Tamil Nadu 48, 57, 69, 321 n.9
Indian Peacekeeping Force 43, 49, 52, 56, 302 n.5
Indian Tamils 46, 47
Indic religions 187
indiscriminate bombing 45, 71–2
indiscriminate violence 216–18, 219, 221, 229, 248, 250, 261, 285
individual incentives 225–31
Indonesia 82, 289
inferiority feelings 244, 245
   see also humiliation; resentment
Inglehart, R. 186
INLA, *see* Irish National Liberation Army
Inoguchi, R. 10, 22, 23, 28, 301 n.9
Institute of Peace and Conflict Studies 81 n.17
insurgency, *see* civil war
internecine competition 96, 99, 100, 101, 224, 231, 252, 326 n.14, 327 n.22
   see also overbidding
internecine violence 100, 109–10, 314 n.82, 331 n.26
international community 89, 218
   see also public opinion; supporters
Intifada 109, 244, 267, 311 n.37
   first 81, 85, 308 n.14
   second (al-Aqsa) 81, 85, 94, 110, 255, 308 n.15, 313 n.58, n.59
   see also waves of suicide missions
IPKF, *see* Indian Peacekeeping Force
IRA, *see* Irish Republican Army

Iran-Iraq war 247, 253, 254, 261, 286, 297
Iranian clerics 297; *see also* Khomeini
Iranian revolution 230, 286
Iranian Revolutionary Guard, *see* Pasdarans
Iranians 183
Iraq 81, 240, 247, 253, 266, 280, 287, 289
Ireland 193, 237
Irish Catholic Church 294–5
Irish National Liberation Army 229
Irish Republican Army 209, 213–14, 219, 220, 223, 224, 229, 293, 325 n.6, 327 n.17, n.20
Iritani, T. 16
Islam 146, 207, 242, 261, 264
Islamic Caliphate 170, 251
Islamic fundamentalism 90, 135, 141, 155, 169, 171, 227, 252, 318 n.12
Islamic jihad 240
Islamic Religious Fund Watq 94
Islamism 216
islamophobia 143
Ismailis, *see* Assassins
Israel 77, 81, 244, 257, 260, 261, 267, 268, 287, 289
   see also Middle East area
Israel Defence Forces 113, 315 n.88
Israeli Institute for Counter-Terrorism 44, 78, 91
Israeli people 329 n.16
   see also settlers
Israeli public opinion 90, 92, 93, 94, 251, 314 n.70, n.79
Italian judges and the mafia 277
Iwo Jima 5

Jaber, H. 223, 224, 228, 230
Jaffna library, destruction of 48, 303 n.26
Jaffna peace talks, *see* peace process
Jaggers, K. 187
Jain tradition 323 n.29
Jamal Sati 316 n.90

Jamison, K. R. 253
Jansen, M. 15, 18
Jansz, F. 58
Japan 181
Japanese Red Army 287, 308 n.5
Jarrah, Ziad 139, 142, 318 n.13
Jayasinghe, A. 43,
Jayawardene, President Junius 48
Jeffreys, M. D. 203, 324 n.40
Jenin 113
Jenin, battle of 100, 113
Jerusalem Media and Communication
    Centre 108, 117
Jesus 166, 187
Jesuits 174
Jewish diaspora 83
Jewish Mishnah, *see* Jewish tradition
Jewish people 246
Jewish tradition 294, 315 n.85
Jeyaraj, D. B. S. 58, 59
jihad 83, 119, 137, 153, 165, 213, 223,
    280, 281, 287, 296, 297–8, 315 n.85,
    336 n.43
Jinrai (thunder gods) Special Attack
    Corps, see *Oka*
Johnston, K. 220, 327 n.19, n.20
Johnson, Lyndon, President of the
    USA 205
Joiner, C. A. 321 n.14
joint attacks 100, 249, 299, 312 n.57,
    313 n.68
Joll, J. 227
Jones, E. 273
Joshi, C. L. 62, 70, 71
joy 36
Juergensmeyer, M. 154
just war 213, 214
JVP, *see* People's Liberation Front

Kach 91, 119
Kahane Chai 91, 119
Kahane, Meir 119
Kahin, G. M. 205
kaiten (turning heaven), torpedoes 7, 8,
    16, 20, 24, 25

Kalanta, Romas 202
Kaliayev, Ivan 147, 213
    see also Camus, A.
Kalyvas, S. 216, 217, 326 n.13, 329 n.12,
    333 n.8
kamikaze 81, 135, 147, 199, 223, 236,
    239, 241, 247, 261, 279, 289
    see also *Oka*; *Shinpu*; suicide attackers;
    suicide missions
kamikaze iconography 4, 19
kamikaze morale 27–8
kamikaze mutinous behaviour 28–9
Kandy, Temple of the Tooth
    305 n.47
Kang Kyung Dae 203 n.
Kahneman, D. 236, 329 n.12
Kanvar, Roop 320 n.3
Karachi, attack 331 n.24
Karbala 280
Karmon, E. 77, 109, 311 n.37
Kase, H. 24, 30
Kashmir 81, 247, 248, 253, 287
Kashmir fedayeen 99
Katunayake Air Force Base, attack
    on 55, 58, 59
Kawachi, U. 26
Keene, D. 18
Kelley, R. 193
Kennedy, John F., President of the
    USA 204–5
Kenya 81
kidnapping 298
Kim, H. 175, 177, 202
Kim Ki Sol 200, 203
King, S. B. 175
Khalid Shaikh Mohammed 132, 139,
    156, 157, 158, 163, 317 n.1, 318 n.28,
    320 n.55
Khashan, H. 330 n.22
Khomeini, Ayatollah 238, 255, 288
Khomeinist Revolution 102, 112
Knezys, S. 211
Kobrin, N. 133–4
Kokkurill 70
Koran 137, 142, 151, 242, 315 n.85

Korea, South 175, 177, 181, 183, 187, 193, 293
Kosovo 169
Kosovo Libertion Army 209
Kōzu, N. 16
Kramer, M. 99, 211, 221, 230, 311 n.43, 316 n.97
Krishnan, K. G. 181
Krueger, A. B. 105, 113, 245, 250, 327 n.27
Kumaratunga, President Chandrika 43, 44, 49, 55, 56, 59, 267, 303 n.20
Kurdish diaspora, *see* Kurdish refugees
Kurdish refugees 177, 193
Kurdistan 81
Kurdistan Workers Party 99, 107, 184, 192, 237, 239, 246, 247, 248, 253, 289, 332 n.5
Kurds 115, 183, 191
Kurian, R. 303 n.16
Kuroshima, Captain 2
Kusonoki Masashige 19, 29
Kusonoki, Masasue 19, 29
Kuwait 82
Kydd, A. 91, 92, 98, 104, 118, 249, 312 n.52
Kyushu 5

La Guardia, A. 314 n.71
Laitin, D. D. viii n.1, 45, 260–1, 265, 288–9, 290, 302, n.13, n.14, 332 n.2, 336 n.44, n.46, n.47
Lamont-Brown, R. 10
Language Martyrs' Day 204
LaPorte, Roger 181
Larteguy, J. 12, 22, 24, 35
Latin America 293
Lawson, B. T. 242
LCP, *see* Lebanese Communist Party
League of Nations 251
Lebanese Communist Party 80, 87, 316 n.90, 332 n.5
Lebanese Baath Party 81
Lebanese civil war 86, 286

Lebanon 51, 77, 97, 168, 210, 211, 247, 248, 253, 261, 263, 287, 288, 289
invasion of 80, 86
see also Middle East area
Lebedintsev, Vavolod 222
Lee, C. 186
Lee, K. 321 n.13
Lenin 26, 157, 215
Leninism 157
Letamendia, F. 228
Lewis, B. 279, 280, 289, 330 n.17, 336 n.51
Leyte Gulf, battle of 4, 5
Liberals 26
Liberation Tigers of Tamil Eelam 43, 221, 224, 239, 246, 247, 248, 253, 261, 262, 332 n.5
and child soldiers 66, 306 n.60, 306 n.72; *see also* forced recruitment
combat deaths 43–4
and Marxism 45, 48, 215
Muslims in 302 n.15
and Tamil supporters 66
and Tamil opposition groups 61, 66
weaponry, *see* military force, asymmetry
Lions 251
Linse, U. 222
Lithuanians 186, 188, 200
Liu Hongjun 198
Liu Yunfang 324 n.47
living martyrs 240
see also martyrdom; suicide attackers
Lochtefeld, J. G. 187
Lod Airport, Tel Aviv, attack on 37, 117, 236, 287, 307 n.5
Lodge, Henry Cabot 324 n.44
Loewenstein, G. 245
Lotta Continua 287–8
LTTE, *see* Liberation Tigers of Tamil Eelam
Luce, D. 321 n.14
Lyall, S. 231
Lyon, A. 182

Macdonald, A. 161
MacFarquhar, N. 319 n.43
MacStiofain, Sean 220, 327 n.17
Madani, Abassi 325 n.8
Madras 181
Madrid bombings (11 March
    2004) 262, 268, 333 n.14
Madrid Conference 90
Mahla, V. P. 175
Mahattaya 69
Mahayana Buddhism 179, 202
Makiya, K. 155, 156, 297, 332 n.4
Malabar, south-west India 83, 279,
    328 n.7
Malaysia 181
Maleckova, J. 105, 113, 245, 250
Malinovski, B. 203
Mama (*nom de guerre*) 50, 52, 72
Mamut, Musa 195, 320 n.1, 321 n.10,
Manichaeism 166, 167
Mann, M. 318 n.16
Mao Tze Dong 179, 215
Margalit, A. 77, 114, 267, 268, 276,
    295–6, 308 n.8, 312 n.50, 314 n.78,
    315 n.83, 316 n.89, 334 n.25
Mariana Islands 3
Maronites 293
    see also Lebanon civil war
Marr, Robert, Commander US Air Force
    Northeast Defence Sector, 274
Marshall Islands 3
Marshall, M. G. 187
martyrs 146–9, 159, 195, 203, 281, 316
    n.97
    see also suicide attackers
martyrdom 115, 119, 215, 226, 227, 229,
    255, 264, 273, 277, 286, 293, 294,
    298, 313 n.66
    allowance 143; *see also* rewards to
        family
    and Christian tradition 282, 286, 295,
        316 n.97, 329 n.10
    cult of 65, 242
    culture of 87, 135
    and Islam 214, 242, 270, 280, 282, 287,
        295, 297, 329 n.17
    as meaningful death 144–5, 162
    as rationalizing narrative 293
    see also anarchists; holy war; jihad
'martyrdom cells', *see* suicide attackers
'martyrdom operation', *see* suicide
    mission
Maru-re, see *shinyō*
Marx, K. 26
Marxism 140, 187, 199, 215, 245
Marxist terrorists 214, 261, 285, 326
    n.11, 332 n.5
Masada 83
mass suicide 83
Massoud, Ahmad Shah 158, 333 n.10,
    335 n.46
Mathers, Joanne 220
Maynard Smith, J. 327 n.24
McCarthy, J. D. 177
McEvoy, James 211
McGarry, J. 327 n.21
McKittrick, D. 325 n.5
McNamara, Robert, United States
    Secretary of Defence 202
McVeigh, T. 161
Mecklin, J. 202, 321 n.14
Medal of Honour 334 n.20
    see also heroism; Victoria Cross
Medellin cartel 211
Mehaidli, Sana 87, 308 n.13
Meiji Constitution 13
Meiji emperor 15
Meiji restoration 13, 16, 19, 20
Meltsberger, J. 329 n.10
"mental model", *see* imitation
Merari, A. 92, 147, 149, 150, 239, 240,
    260, 261, 263, 267, 270, 273, 276,
    298, 333 n.11, n.13, 334 n.16, n.17,
    n.24, 335 n.28
messianism 134
Micca, Pietro 273, 274, 334 n.22
Middle East 245, 247, 258
Middle East area 77

Midway, battle of 1, 4
militant non-violence 321 n.15
military force, asymmetry 46, 66, 71, 88,
    151, 159, 171, 260, 292
    see also suicide missions as weapons
military purposes 89, 104, 263
military targets vi, 44, 55, 80, 88, 97,
    247–8, 261, 262, 324 n.3, 329 n.16
military training in Japan 4, 6, 12,
    16–17, 20–1, 22, 301 n.6
Miller, Captain 50, 51, 52, 304 n.32
    see also Black Tigers
Miller, B. H. 105
Miller, J. 140, 156, 318 n.13
Miller, M. A. 227
Milosevic, S. 169
Millot, B. 8, 30, 31
MIPT, *see* American Memorial Institute
    for the Prevention of Terrorism
Mishal, S. 218, 247
Mishima, Yukio 193, 195, 199
Mita, S. 3
Mneimneh, H. 155, 156
Mochizuki, Mamoru 28
modernization 141
    see also decolonization; imperialism
Mogadishu, attack 320 n.55
Moghadam, A. 244, 330 n.21
Moloney, E. 220
Mombasa, attack 331 n.24
Mor, Shany 316 n.94, n.96, 331 n.32
moral education in Japan 15–16
Morioka, K. 12
Morocco 81, 289
Morris, B. 77, 88, 245, 246, 308 n.9, 310
    n.32, n.33, 311 n.37, 312 n.48
Morris, J. 17, 18
Morris, I. I. 178
Morrison, Norman 181, 195, 202, 320 n.1
Morrison Welsh, A. 181, 195, 320 n.1
Moscicki, E. K. 270
Moscow attack (Dubrovka
    Theatre) 241, 283, 325 n.3
Mossad 147
Mastny, V. 324 n.42

motivational system, *see* motivations
motivations ix, 24–6, 67–73, 74, 105,
    110–14, 116, 156, 195–6, 236–7,
    238, 246–50, 268–9, 274, 281, 329
    n.14
    egocentric 196, 198–201
    financial, *see* rewards to family
    instability of 140, 235
    instrumental 42, 79, 190, 196, 197,
        209, 230, 236, 242, 257–8, 269, 274
    other-related 241, 329 n.14
    selfless 195, 196–8, 201
    stable 234, 240, 257, 328 n.2,
    strategic 54, 164, 257, 332 n.34; *see*
        also suicide missions as weapons
Mounir al-Maqdah, *see* Abu Hassan
Mousa Ziyada 316 n.93
mujaheedin, *see* martyrdom
Mubarak, Hosni, President of
    Egypt 133, 138
Muslim Brotherhood 138, 296
Muslim world 250
    see also Islam
Muslims 186
Myers, S. 218
myth 156–7, 160
    see also conspiracy theory

Nablus 113
Naby, E. 147
Naemura, H. 17, 23, 25, 26
Nagatsuka, R. 21, 23, 25, 26, 27
Nairobi, attack 331 n.24
Naitō, H. 2, 21, 27, 29, 31
Nakajima, T. 27
Nakazawa, Rear Admiral 2–3
narrative of blame 145–6, 153, 169
    see also conspiracy theory; myth
Nash, J. R. 122
Nasserite Socialist Party of Syria 80
Nathan, J. 199
National Council of Resistance of
    Iran 183
National Memorial Institute for the
    Prevention of Terrorism 44

National Religious Party 92–3
nationalism 13, 48, 65, 140, 144, 164,
    166, 167, 170, 247, 318 n.16, 321
    n.14
NATO 320 n.52
Nechaev, Sergei G. 220
Nelliady 50
Nepstad, S. E. 174
Nesse, R. M. 271
Netanya, attack of 94
Netanyahu, Benjamin 92, 311 n.45, 312
    n.52
Netzarin Junction, attack of 308 n.15
Nietzsche, F. 169
Ninagawa, J. 28
Ngo Dinh Diem, President of
    Vietnam 173, 179, 196, 204
Nguyen Cao Ky 205
Nguyen Tuong Tam 198
Nhat Chi Mai 181, 190, 195, 202
9/11 attacks 211
    see also World Trade Centre, attacks
    on; Pentagon, attack on
Nobel, A. 282, 283
Nobiling, Carl 227
no-escape missions vii, 1, 280, 281, 282,
    283, 287, 294
    see also proto-suicide missions
non-negotiable goals 74, 247
non-targeting civilians policy 45, 55, 58,
    147–8, 213, 327 n.20
    see also guerrilla attacks; terrorism
Northern Ireland 229, 290
Núñez, R. 222, 227

O'Balance, E. 107, 307 n.74
obligation towards the dead 106, 111,
    231, 277, 334 n.25
    see also Italian judges and the Mafia;
    revenge
Ocalan, Abdullah 183, 184, 192, 237
O'Callaghan, Sean 209
O'leary, B. 327 n.21
Occupied Territories 77, 89, 95, 249,
    260, 316 n.96

    see also Gaza Strip; Middle East area;
    Palestine; West Bank
Ohnuki-Tierney, E. 25, 35
Oka, T. 179, 205
Ōka ('cherry blossom') 6, 24
Oka (Tunder Gods Corps) 28
Okamoto, Kozo 37, 287, 308 n.5
Okamura, Commander 31
Okinawa 5
Okudaira, Tsuyoshi 287
Olimpio, G. 113
Olson, M. 204
O'Neil, R. 5, 7, 8, 42, 121
Ōnishi, Admiral Takijirō 1, 4, 32
Onoda 4, 24
Operation Defensive Shield 100
Operation Liberation, in Sri Lanka 50,
    51, 52
Operation Restore Hope 169
opposition to peace process 96, 97, 111,
    312 n.52
    see also waves of suicide missions
Orwell, G. 166
Oslo agreements 81, 249
Oslo agreement I 90
Oslo Agreement II, 91
Ossipon, see *The Secret Agent*
Ota, Navy Sub Lieutenant 6, 32
overbidding 249, 331 n.26
overbidding game 100, 249
overbidding theory 101

Pacific war 3, 20
Pakistan 82, 194, 280
Palach, J. 181–2, 197, 198, 202, 203,
    236
Palestine 90, 97, 249, 253, 258, 270
Palestine Liberation Organization 46,
    51, 89, 103, 109
    see also Palestinian Organizations
Palestinian Authority 90, 91, 96, 97, 109,
    110, 112, 118, 119, 121
Palestinian Center for Policy and Survey
    Research (CPSR) 93, 117, 314
    n.80

Palestinian Charter 92

Palestinian Islamic Jihad 81, 87, 90, 95, 97, 211, 221, 223, 225, 240, 247, 313 n.60

see also Palestinian Organizations

Palestinian Organizations 119–20, 248, 249, 250, 261, 268–9

Palestinian people 230, 281

Palestinian public opinion 88, 93, 94, 108–10, 112–13, 117, 128–9, 251

see also constituencies; supporters

Palestinian state 89, 93, 252

Pallás, Paulino 227

Pan-Arabism, *see* nationalism

Panama 82

Panella, C. 311 n.34

Pape, R. viii n. 1, 44, 45, 53, 82, 118, 121, 123, 156, 248, 249, 260, 263, 265, 287, 302 n.13, 319 n.34, n.38, 332 n.5, 333 n.6, n.10

paranoia 252

see also conspiracy theory

Park, B. 175, 321 n.5

Park Sung Hee 189, 202, 203

Pascal, B. 318 n.22

Pasdarans 87, 253, 286, 297

Pasqua, Charles 325 n.8

patriotism 13, 18, 21, 27, 239, 256

Paz, R. 162, 165

peace process in Palestine 88, 89, 90–1, 92, 93, 97, 109, 110, 311 n.45, n.46, 312 n.50

see also Camp David; Oslo agreements; Road Map; Wye Plantation Agreement

peace process in Sri Lanka 49, 55, 57, 267, 299, 302 n.4, 303 n.29, 304 n.30

peace process negotiations, *see* peace process

peer pressure 113, 114, 116, 150, 239, 240, 329 n.9

see also emulation

Pentagon, attack on 131, 223

People's Liberation Front 56, 303 n.21, 305 n.49

People's Revolutionary Liberation Party Front (Turkish) 184, 332 n.5

People's Will (*Narodnaya Volya*) 221–2, 227

Peres, Simon 90

personal trauma 106

Petersen, R. 219, 246

Pfaffenberger, B. 49

PFLP, *see* Popular Front for the Liberation of Palestine

Philippines 83

Phillips, D. P. 189, 323 n.30

Phillips, Lynette 182

piety 132, 133, 139, 317 n.7

see also religious practices

PIJ, *see* Palestinian Islamic Jihad

Pinguet, M. 18, 301 n.4

Pipes, D. 107, 251, 314 n.72, 317 n.98

pledge 150

Pirabakaran Vellupilai 45, 47, 48, 55, 57, 59, 63, 69, 299, 302 n.9, 305 n.54

cult of 63, 65, 74

PKK, *see* Kurdistan Workers Party

PLO, *see* Palestine Liberation Organization

Podoliak, K. 283

political purposes 88, 161

political repression 115, 230

see also civil war

Pollock, L. R 197

pollution, *see* contamination; suicide attackers, sexual torments of

Pomper, P. 213, 222

Ponnambalam, G. G. 47

Popular Front for the Liberation of Palestine 81, 88, 211, 247, 287, 308 n.12, 326 n.11

see also Palestinian Organizations

poverty 228, 244, 245, 327 n.27, 328 n.5, 330 n.22

see also economic deprivation; social injustice

Pratap, A. 56, 65, 63, 303 n.27, 305 n.50

prayer, *see* religious practices

precedents 1–3, 82–3, 309 n.20

Premadasa, Ranasinghe 44, 49, 52, 56,
    302 n.9
preventive war, doctrine of 163
pride 36
Professor, the, see *The Secret Agent*
propaganda 14, 23, 25, 44, 54, 159, 160
protest 173, 178, 179, 181, 184, 189, 208,
    269, 298
protestant fundamentalism 112
proto-suicide missions 279–80, 281, 282,
    283, 285, 295
    see also ancestors; precedents
provocation 250, 252
psychological disturbances 200
psychological impact 66, 162–3, 224
public opinion 196, 206, 208, 222, 236,
    248, 250, 314 n.70
Puhovski, N. 175, 321 n.13

Quaker 181
Quinn, J. 35
Qutb, Sayid 141, 153

Rabin, Yitzhak, Israeli Prime
    Minister 90, 249
Rachman, S. J. 272, 275, 276, 277, 334
    n.21
Radlauer, D. 94
Ramachandran, M. G. 321 n.9
Rammjäger aircraft 42
random violence, *see* indiscriminate
    violence
Rantisi Abdel Aziz 96 n.59
Rapoport, D. C. 334 n.27
rational choice theory 234, 257–8
Rawaswamy, S. 180, 204, 321 n.13
Reader, I. 14–15
reasons, *see* motivations
recruitment (of suicide attackers) 60–1,
    107, 136, 168, 170, 225, 244, 248,
    299, 327 n.26, 302 n.14, 330 n.20
    adverse selection 254
    forced 60, 66, 67, 69, 71, 239, 314 n.72
    screening 106, 107, 201, 253
recruits 66

    see also recruitment; volunteers
Red Brigades 144, 209, 225, 268
redemption 196, 200
refugee camps 49, 113, 270, 286
    see also Sabra and Chatila, massacres
Reid, R. 283, 284
Rejali, D. 240
religion 13, 134–5, 152
    see also motivations; religious beliefs
religious beliefs 14, 132, 136, 154, 186,
    187, 197, 198, 226, 256, 293, 330
    n.19
    disinhibitory effect of 243
    lifting of social constraints 137, 293
    as motivations 76, 111–12, 114, 116,
        242, 243, 246, 247, 252, 293–4
    as obstacles 199
    as pretext 133, 137, 142
religious conflicts 136, 315 n.85, 336 n.43
religious discrimination 140, 143
    against Buddhism 179, 192, 236
religious fervour, *see* zeal
religious organizers 261
religious practices 133, 151, 152, 179,
    277
    see also incantations; trance-like state
    of mind
religious war, *see* holy war
Republican Constitution of Sri Lanka
    (1972) 47
resentment 106, 111, 140, 141–2, 145,
    169, 245–6, 251, 281
resistance 83
resolve 55, 225, 229, 264
retaliation 94, 163–6, 208, 230, 249, 252,
    258, 313 n.64, 318 n.18, 319 n.39,
    320 n.55, 329 n.11
retaliatory justice 165, 166
Reuter, C. 65, 167, 236, 239, 241, 242,
    244, 247, 249, 253, 255, 280, 283,
    286, 287, 296, 297, 299, 329 n.16,
    330 n.19, 331 n.28, n.29, n.31, 336
    n.50
revenge 106, 111, 112, 114, 116, 145,
    146, 207–8, 230, 241, 242, 248, 295–6

302 n.10, 315 n.83, n.85, 326 n.14, 329 n.12, n.13, 334 n.25
rewards 23–4
rewards to family 24, 76, 113, 114, 116, 277
Reyes, H. 235
Reynal-Querol, M. 292
Reza, A. 186, 201
Ricolfi, L. 122, 298, 309 n.19, 333 n.12
Rim Salah Riyachi 312 n.57
Risen, J. 319 n.43
ritual last meal 63, 276
ritual disembowelment, *see* "seppuku"
rituals 151–2, 154, 240–1, 242
   see also trance-like state of mind
Riyadh, attack 331 n.24
Road Map 97, 109, 128, 313 n.61
Roberts, M. 47, 65, 306 n.57, 307 n.74
role models 65, 138
Roh Tae-woo, President of Korea 183
Roy, O. 155
Romania 183, 193
Romero, Archbishop 174
Rotary Clubs 251
Rote Armee Fraction, *see* Baader Meinhof
Rubin, B. 317 n.3, 318 n.17, n.24, n.26, 319 n.31, n.32, n.35, n.36, n.40, n.45, n.50, 320 n.53
Rubin, J. C. 317 n.3, 318 n.17, n.24, n.26, 319 n.31, n.32, n.35, n.36, n.40, n.45, 320 n.50, n.53
Russell, C. A. 105
Russia 261
Russian pilots 42
Ruthven, M. 153
Ryan, C. 175

Saad-Ghorayeb, A. 224
sabotage 249, 252
   see also opposition to peace process
Sabra and Chatila, massacres 230
sacred explosion, *see* suicide missions
Sadat Anwar 92, 138, 336 n.46

Saddam Hussein 242
Saigon 173, 179, 181
Saipan 4
Sakai, S. 3, 24
Saleh, B. 111, 314 n.75, 76, 316 n.95
Samson 279
samurai 18–20, 30, 93
Sánchez-Cuenca, I. 214, 224
Sands, B. 229
Sanmugathasan, N. 49
sati 174, 329 n.10
   see also suicide
Saudi Arabia 81, 169, 289, 318 n.15, 333 n.10
Schalk, P. 64, 68, 71, 74, 304 n.35, 306 n.73
Schaller, S. 177, 189
Schecter, J. 190–1, 196, 205, 321 n.14, 322 n.17
Schmid, A. 181
Schmidtke, A. 177, 186, 189
Schnibben, C. 151, 317 n.8
Schweitzer, Y. 78–9, 83, 99, 123, 308 n.8, 309 n.17, 310 n.32
Scott-Stokes, H. 193, 199
secrecy 151, 171–2, 257
The Secret Agent 283–4, 285, 335 n.36
secular ideology 253
secular organizers viii, 261, 273, 275, 285, 287, 299
secularization theory 112
Security Zone 88
Sedlikas, R. 211
Seki, Lieutenant Yukio 4, 24, 26
Sela, A. 218, 247
selective violence 217, 219, 248, 253, 265, 326 n.13
   see also military targets
self-defence 163–6
self-explosion, *see* suicide missions
self-immolation 82, 237, 253
   audience for 173
   by burning 174, 175, 179, 182, 192, 193, 195, 236
   consequences of 204–6

self-immolation (*cont.*)
  as costly signal 196
  definition of 173, 174, 194–5, 208
  and democracy 187
  diffusion of 175, 180–2, 185–6, 207
  emotional power of 203; *see also* self-
      martyrdom
  as gamble with death 193, 194
  and media 176–7, 180, 204
  number of 174, 177
  orchestration of 179–80, 192, 194
  and organizations 183, 191–2, 193,
      233, 260
  by poison 192–3
  within prison 184, 192, 324 n.46
  progenitor of 174, 178, 179
  psychological explanations
      of 198–201
  and psychopathology 200, 201
  rationality of 195, 196
  and religions 186–7
  responses to 201–4
  and suffering 192–5
  suicide and 174, 182, 186, 193, 201,
      270
  and technologies 178
  as threat 190, 191, 194
  thwarted attempts 193, 194, 195
  and totalitarian political
      systems 187–8, 190, 200, 202, 322
      n.19
  variations of 185–8
  see also protest
self-martyrdom 147, 187, 203, 266–7
  see also suicide, legitimacy of
self-mutilation 193–4, 195
self-sacrifice 64, 147, 162, 270, 271, 280,
      318 n.21, 323 n.29
  see also martyrdom; self-immolation;
      suicide missions
selection effects 244, 245, 253, 263, 291
  see also recruitment
Semitic religions 187
Senaratne, J. P. 48, 52, 217
Senjin Kun (field service code) 20

Sennott, C. M. 137, 317 n.7
Seppuku (*hara-kiri*) 19, 178, 193, 199,
      301 n.4
settlers 316 n.94, 329 n.16
Shalhoub, Faraj 277
shame 27, 208, 239, 240, 241, 256, 295
Shankar, Lieutenant 48
sharia 166
Sharif, Omar Khan 298
Sharma, K. L. 303 n.22, n.27
Sharon Ariel 94, 95, 97
Sharrock, D. 220, 229
Shatz, A. 299
Shia tradition 242, 279, 286
Shiino, Y. 8
Shiite Muslims 214, 230, 247, 280, 287,
      336 n.45
Shillony, B. 17
Shining Path 209
Shintoism 13–14, 17
Shintō, *see* Shintoism
Shinpu (divine wind), Special Attack
      Corps 1, 5, 6
Shinpu Takkotai 21
Shinyō (suicide motorboats) 8, 9
Shirai, A. 12, 301 n.3
Sicarii, *see* Zealots
signalling, *see* signalling theory
signalling theory 190, 224, 225, 264, 265,
      266
Sikhs 191, 192
Silke, A. 314 n.77
Simmel, G. 150
Simon, D. 133, 153, 154, 314 n.78, 317
      n.5, 318 n.21
Simony 242
sin 139, 152, 153, 154
Singh, Sant Fateh 191, 323 n.34
Singh, S. 175, 201
Singh, V. P. 182, 184
Sinhala Only Act 47
Sinhalese people 43, 47, 289
Sinn Fein 229
Sinnadurai, Mukundan 56
Sivakumaran, Ponnudarai 68

Six Days War 77
Smith, R. 18
Sober, E. 271
Sobrero, A. 282
social injustice 140–2, 164, 166, 169
Socialist Revolutionaries 222
Solaro della Margherita, Count of 334 n.22
Solheim, E. 55
solidarity 143, 150
Somalia 168, 169
Sommer, J. 321 n.14
Soni R. V. 322 n.20
Southern New Guinea 3
Soviet Union 167, 181, 182, 332 n.4
Spaeth, A. 56
Speckhard, A. 335 n.35
Sprinzak, E. 244, 308 n.5
spiral of violence 98, 161
    see also terrorism
Sri Lanka 43, 81, 180, 245, 253, 263, 287, 302 n.2
Sri Lankan civil war 46–9
SSNP, *see* Syrian Social Nationalist Party
'standardization', *see* ethnic discrimination
State Shinto, *see* Shintoism
status loss, *see* downward mobility
Steinbach, A. 202
Stengel, E. 193
Stolypin, Petr 222
Stone, M. 140, 156, 318 n.13
strategy of insurgency 46, 160–1
    see also civil war; military targets
Subramanian, N. 55, 58, 60,
Subrahmanian, N. 181
suicide 18–19, 69, 119, 147, 174, 189, 194, 197, 322 n.20, n.22
    altruistic ix, 174, 186, 270, 271
    collective 174, 206
    depressive 69, 74, 253, 269
    legitimacy of 15, 69, 137, 214, 243 , 281, 282, 294–5, 296–7, 328 n.3,

330 n.18; *see also* martyrdom; religious beliefs
    opportunity costs of 143
    political 236–8, 241, 255, 322 n.21; *see also* self-immolation
    rates of 18, 69–70, 186, 193, 307 n.79, 323 n.27, n.30
suicide attackers 105–8, 244
    cells of 83, 221, 275–6; *see also* Hamburg cell; training
    psychologic traits of 144–6, 153, 314 n.77
    psychopathology of 106, 107, 270, 280
    sexual torments of 138, 154
    as soldiers 135, 146–9, 148
    socio-demographic traits of 11–12, 105–6, 110, 143, 228, 270, 271
    women 44, 54, 67–8, 81, 87, 88, 92, 95, 97, 107, 114–15, 184, 215, 241, 244, 253, 271–2, 283, 306 n.73, 312 n.57
suicide bombers, *see* suicide attackers
suicide missions 119, 121, 126–8, 184, 209
    definition of vi, 79
    "delegated" 211
    democracies as targets of 161, 265–6, 333 n.10
    differences among 281–2
    diffusion of 77, 81, 211, 253, 287, 288, 326 n.11
    early proponents of in Japan 2–3
    efficiency 89, 90, 103–4, 224, 236, 254–5
    effectiveness of 8–11, 51, 52, 82, 171, 252
    executed 12 ,209
    failed 78, 79, 269, 307 n.4, 331 n.31
    families' opposition to 316 n.93
    first cases of 5, 50, 230, 253, 285, 308 n.8
    foiled 78, 79, 267, 287, 307 n.4, 308 n.11
    free media and 159, 162, 266, 268, 333 n.10

suicide missions (*cont.*)
  Islamic 118, 298, 299; *see also*
    religious organizers
  Islamic debate on 295–8
  number of viii, 53, 81–2, 87, 95, 302
    n.13, 304 n.43, 307 n.1, n.4, 308 n.9,
    313 n.58, n.59, n.62
  objections to in Japan 2
  preference for 79, 85, 124, 310 n.29,
    n.30
  propensity for 85, 86, 89, 91, 96, 97,
    101, 103, 106, 124, 125, 310 n.29
  psychological explanations of 135,
    156
  rationality of viii–ix, 51, 66, 104,
    158–9, 167–8, 260, 263, 268
  and self-immolation vi–vii, 90, 173,
    183, 191, 192, 195, 199, 207, 233,
    260, 267, 271, 278, 293
  successful 12, 78, 267
  types of 5–8, 54, 103–5, 263–6
  and types of armed organizations 260
  uniformities of vi, ix, 231, 260, 279–81
  as weapons 51–2, 55, 103, 147, 155,
    158, 223, 224, 260, 261, 262, 263,
    266, 274, 304 n.35
suicide terrorism, *see* suicide missions
Sukhai, A. 322 n.20
Sulu, Southern Philippines 279
Sunni Muslims 214, 247, 280, 289, 336
    n.45
Sunni theologians 242
supporters (of insurgent organizations)
    61, 108, 144, 218, 219, 220, 221, 223,
    248, 250, 260, 327 n.22
  see also constituency costs; public
    opinion
surviving missions 9, 50, 58, 72
  see also guerrilla attacks; heroism;
    high-risk missions; no-escape
    missions
Swamy, M. R. N. 47, 48, 51, 57, 64, 65,
    66, 68, 69, 253, 303 n.18, n.21, n.24,
    304 n.32, n.35, n.36, 305 n.45, n.49,
    331 n.26

Sweeney, G. 174, 193, 237, 295
symbolic power 64
  see also martyrdom; self-sacrifice
symbolic targets vi, 133–4, 262, 305 n.47
symbolic values, *see* communicative
    purposes
syncronized attacks 160
Syrian Social Nationalist Party 80, 81,
    87, 97, 310 n.33, 316 n.90

Taliban 231
Tambiah, S. J. 49, 303 n.26
Tamil diaspora 46, 61, 66
Tamil Eelam 43, 48
Tamil New Tigers 47, 302 n.1
Tamils 46, 47, 115, 181, 230, 286, 289,
    309 n.24
  riots against 44, 47, 48–9
Tamil Tigers 99, 199, 238
Tamil United Liberation Front 303 n.25
Tanzania 81
Tanzim 95, 312 n.56
target selection 29, 238, 262
targets vi, 55–60, 262, 265, 305 n.48
team spirit, *see* cell effect
technology (for suicide missions) 101–5,
    234, 282–5
  ammonium nitrate 282
  availabity of, 285
  detonators 283, 284
  dynamite 234, 282
  explosives 282–3
  explosive belts 283
  explosive jackets 59
  innovation 210, 252
  see also *The Secret Agent*
technological costs 223–5
teenage martyrs 238, 244, 247, 255
terrorism 60, 79, 93, 101, 119, 170–1,
    209, 261, 324 n.3
  see also hit-and-run terrorism
Terrorism Research Centre 78
Tesei, Teseo 42
Thailand 180
Thakur, U. 187, 322 n.20

Thamilini 60
Thatcher, M. 290
Thich Duc Nghiep 179
Thich Giac Duc 179, 321 n.14
Thich Hue Hien 188
Thich Nhat Hanh 181, 193
Thich Nu Thanh Quang 192, 196, 202, 205
Thich Quang Duc 173, 174, 175, 178, 179, 181, 182, 192, 195, 196, 202, 203
Thich Tam Chau 205
Thich Thien-An 179, 180
Thich Tieu Dieu 192, 197, 202
Thich Tri Quang 192, 205
theologies of liberation 112
Thileepan 69
Thiruchelvam, Neelan 56
Tiananmen Square 176, 206
Tierney, M. 314 n.78
Tilly, C. 178
Tocqueville, Alexis de 270
Tojo, Japanese Prime Minister 4
Tokyo Imperial University 16, 17
Toolis, K. 327 n.21
Topmiller, R. 203, 205, 321 n.14
Torisu, K. 9
torture 68–9, 206, 254, 327 n.21
training 22–3, 27, 60, 61–7, 107, 144, 276, 283, 304 n.34
see also military training in Japan
Tran Bach Nga 197, 200
trance-like state of mind 152, 240, 275
transfiguration 174, 196, 198, 199, 201
traga, see Charan caste
Treptow, K. W. 197, 198, 324 n.42
Trobriand Islands 203
Trincomalee Memorial 64–5
Trincomalee Harbour, attack of 55
Trotsky 214
Tsai, H. H. 322 n.26
Tsurugi (sword) 6
TULF, *see* Tamil United Liberation Front
Turkey 287

Tversky, A. 236, 329 n.12
tyranny 133, 141
Tyre, attack 80, 286

Uçarer, E. 184
Uehling, G. 175, 320 n.1, 321 n.9, n.13
Ukagi, Vice-Admiral 31
UNICEF 306 n.72
Unified Buddhist Church 192
United Nations 180, 251
United States of America 82, 134, 181, 193, 261, 320 n.55
as unifying enemy 164–8, 169, 331 n.24
uprootedness due to emigration 106, 142–3, 146, 151, 153, 154, 168
Uribe, Alvaro 211
Ushiroku, General 2

valour, *see* heroism
vanguard 144
vanity 26–7, 196, 199, 200, 207, 241, 277
see also fame; glory; honour
vengeance *see* revenge
Veyne, P. 256
Victoria Cross 73, 272, 275
video-recording 58, 87, 100, 106, 113, 114, 155, 160, 240, 276, 304 n.40, 316 n.90, 333 n.9
Vietnam 175, 181, 199, 293
Vietnam, South 179, 193, 194, 204, 205
Vietnam War 15, 202
Vinitha, Vidanage 180, 184
visibility of a cause 102–3, 159
see also communicative porpouses
Vnorovskii, Boris 222
'Voice of Tigers' 53, 304 n.39
Voltaire 136, 156, 252
von Borcke, A. 227
von Stauffenberg, Colonel Claus 262
vows 135, 150
see also pledge
volunteers viii, 4, 21–2, 70, 83, 105, 113, 149, 211, 212, 224, 225, 226, 228, 234, 254, 309 n.24

Waldman, A. 60, 75
Walter, B. 91, 92, 98, 104, 118, 249, 312 n.52
Wani, I. 99, 309 n.17
war of attrition 224
war aims 163, 164, 168, 170
Wasserman, I. 253
wavering commitment 30
waves of self-immolation 175, 181, 182, 183, 188–9, 190, 237, 323 n.43
waves of suicide missions 84, 97, 249, 286
  Lebanon wave 81, 84, 86–7, 92, 97, 99, 101, 104, 123
  first Intifada wave 84, 85, 88–90, 96, 97, 99, 104
  Oslo Wave 84, 85–6, 90–2, 96, 97, 104
  al-Aqsa wave 84, 89, 93–97, 98, 99, 104, 313 n.62
Weber, M. 187, 195
Weinberger-Thomas, C. 323 n.36, n.40
Weingast, B. 98, 104
Welch, H. 179
West Bank 108, 248, 332 n.2
  see also Palestinian Territories
Wilson, D. S. 271
Wines, M. 218
Williams, J. 197
Williams, M. 198
Wilson, A. J. 47, 303 n.17, n.24
Wiswell, E. 18

Women, *see* suicide attackers, women
World Trade Center
  1993 attack on 134, 158
  2001 attack on 131, 134, 210, 223, 233, 239, 240, 242, 262, 264
  Iraqi connection 317 n.10
Wright, L. 332 n.1, 333 n.14, 336 n.52
Wulff, E. 179
Wye Plantation Agreement 92

Yamamoto Tsunemoto 19
Yamanuchi, M. 35
Yasin, Sheikh Ahmed 129, 312 n.57, 313 n.60
Yasuda, Yasuyuki 287
Yasukuni Shrine 14, 15, 23
Yasunaga, H. 14, 15, 18, 22, 301 n.8
Yokaren (Youth Training Corps) 12
Yokoi, Vice-Admiral 2, 9, 28
Yokota, Y. 21, 26, 29, 30
Yousef, Ramzi 158, 318 n.14
youth 244

Zahavi, A. 190
Zahavi, A. 190
Zajic, Jan 198, 322 n.21
zeal 56, 135, 154, 254, 261, 277
Zealots 83, 12, 279, 280, 294, 334 n.27
Zen 15
Zionism 244
Zionist conspiracy, *see* conspiracy theory